CW01335706

THE GREAT SEAL OF THE UNITED STATES OF AMERICA

Design Began 1776 – Design Completed 1782

OBVERSE

E Pluribus Unum – 'Out of Many, One': the union of the thirteen original states

Eagle – Symbol of strength and power and always turned to the olive branch as preferring peace; clutching our national symbol— 'E Pluribus Unum'

Olive Branch – Represents peace; Thirteen leaves and Thirteen olives

Blue – Signifies vigilance, perseverance and justice

White – Signifies purity and Innocence

Red – Signifies hardiness and valor

Constellation – Denotes a new State taking its place and rank among other sovereign powers (with thirteen stars)

Chief (upper part of shield) – Represents Congress unifying the original thirteen states

Pieces – In alternating colors representing the original thirteen states all joining in one solid compact supporting the Chief

Thirteen Arrows – Power of war prepared to defend Liberty which power is vested in Congress

Escutcheon (shield) – Protecting the American Eagle without any other support to hold the shield; America ought to rely on its own virtue for the preservation of the union through Congress

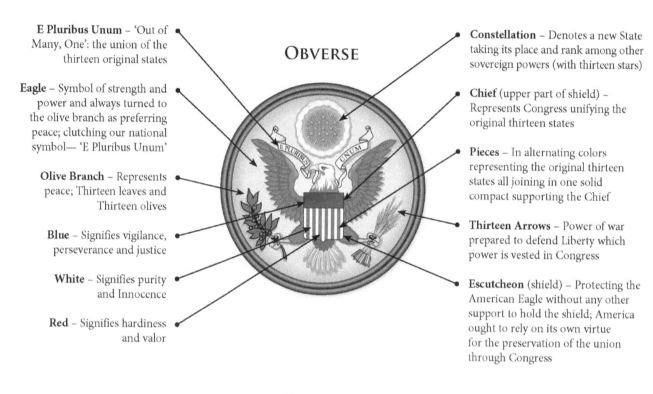

REVERSE
(Often referred to as the Spiritual side of the Shield)

The Eye of Providence – Alludes to the many signal interpositions of God in favor of the American cause

Annuit Coeptis – 'He' (God) has favored our undertakings

Thirteen layers of an unfinished pyramid representing the thirteen original colonies building a new nation based on new ideas and concepts of self-government never before attempted

Glory – The light of God, the Providence shining on a new nation based on God-given unalienable rights

Pyramid – Symbol of strength and duration

1776 – The year of America's birth

Novus Ordo Seclorum – 'New order of the Ages': symbol of a new nation built on the concept of permanent, unalienable (God-given) rights for all versus vested, man-made and non-permanent rights

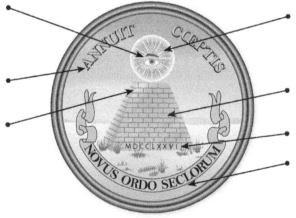

THE MEANING OF
THE GREAT SEAL OF THE UNITED STATES OF AMERICA

"Symbolically, the Seal reflects the beliefs and values that the Founding Fathers attached to the new nation and wished to pass on to their descendants."

- U.S. Department of State, Bureau of Public Affairs

CHARLES THOMSON'S "REMARKS AND EXPLANATION," ADOPTED BY THE CONTINENTAL CONGRESS, JUNE 20, 1782.

"The Escutcheon is composed of the chief [upper part of shield] & pale [perpendicular band], the two most honorable ordinaries [figures of heraldry]. The Pieces, paly [alternating pales], represent the several states all joined in one solid compact entire, supporting a Chief, which unites the whole & represents Congress. The Motto alludes to this union. The pales in the arms are kept closely united by the Chief and the Chief depends on that union & the strength resulting from it for its support, to denote the Confederacy of the United States of America & preservation of their union through Congress.

"The colours of the pales are those used in the flag of the United States of America; White signifies purity and innocence, Red, hardiness & valour, and Blue, the colour of the Chief, signifies vigilance, perseverance & justice. The Olive branch and arrows denote the power of peace & war which is exclusively vested in Congress. The Constellation denotes a new State taking its place and rank among other sovereign powers. The Escutcheon is born on the breast of an American Eagle without any other supporters [figures represented as holding up the shield] to denote that the United States of America ought to rely on their own Virtue.

"Reverse. The Pyramid signifies Strength and Duration: The Eye over it & the Motto allude to the many signal interpositions of providence in favour of the American cause. The date underneath is that of the Declaration of Independence and the words under it signify the beginning of the New American Era, which commences from that date."

USES OF THE GREAT SEAL

The Great Seal is used to guarantee the authenticity of a U. S. document. It is used to seal documents several thousand times a year. Custody of the Seal is assigned to the U. S. Department of State with the master die produced by the U. S. Bureau of Engraving. The Seal can only be affixed to a document by an office of the Secretary of State.

HISTORY OF THE GREAT SEAL

It is extremely significant that the responsibility of the design of the Great Seal was first given in 1776 to Thomas Jefferson, Benjamin Franklin and John Adams, the primary author and contributors of the writing of the Declaration of American Independence. Artist Pierre Eugene du Simitiere assisted with his knowledge of shields and coats of arms.

A second committee of James Lovell, John Morin Scott and William Churchill Houston worked on the design with consultant Francis Hopkinson.

A third committee of John Rutledge, Arthur Middleton, Elias Boudinot and William Barton worked on the design with Charles Thomson, Secretary of Congress, considering all previous recommendations. Congress adopted the design on June 20, 1782, six years after the design began.

We certainly stand at a critical moment now. It is a moment at which significant voices have called deeply into question principles, both political and moral, that have been foundational to our civilization: marriage and the family, sanctity of human life, Rule of Law, true democratic participation, the market economy, limited government. Those principles have been radically called into question as never before in our country. Now which way are we going to go? Are we going to abandon those principles? To my mind, that would be such a tragedy, such a loss to the dignity of the human being that is supported by those principles. Or will we defend those principles? Will we reaffirm those principles? If we do that, we make the right choice, and this country will be a greater country than it has ever been.

The American experiment in republican liberty is truly a miracle. In her informative and well-written book, Angela Kamrath helps to explain why. I warmly commend it, especially to younger readers who will inherit the noble responsibility for sustaining the miracle of America.

> Dr. Robert P. George
> McCormick Professor of Jurisprudence
> Director, James Madison Program in American Ideals and Institutions
> Princeton University

Until now, there has not been a systematic analysis of the relationship between core American political principles and religious principles. Angela Kamrath's clearly written work, *The Miracle of America*, links these two sets of principles in a non-denominational presentation. The many references to the Bible are apt, well-explicated, and thorough. References to the scholarly literature are sensible and unusually free of academic jargon. The result is a highly informative analysis that is a page-turner.

> Dr. Donald S. Lutz
> Professor Emeritus, Political Philosophy
> University of Houston

The Miracle of America is the most important book I have ever read, outside of the Bible. I have been in the Christian ministry since 1968, and I wish I had read this book back then. … It is the very best resource for the study of America's Christian Heritage I have read, and it is worth a college semester of studies.

> Pastor Billy Falling
> U. S. Army Veteran, Pastor, and Author

I have very much enjoyed delving into *The Miracle of America* and think Angela Kamrath has done a fantastic job on it. Well done.

> Jonathan Sandys
> Great-Grandson of Sir Winston Churchill
> Speaker & Author, *God & Churchill*

Well what can I say. I have just spent a few hours perusing *Miracle of America* and have been left fairly speechless. I cannot recall anything like this. Ever. If all young people in America could read this, I think we'd have a Second American Revolution and/or a Third Great Awakening.

The only real <u>solution</u> to the American crisis [of widespread ignorance and devaluing of America's founding and history] resides squarely in our ability to restore a Biblical worldview to our people. Now that is a daunting, exhaustive prospect, but it's where this book and others like it come to the fore. If we cannot restore that view, that heart, that vision, the republic may well fail.

> Dr. Cliff Kelly
> Online Professor of Communication
> Liberty University

The Miracle of America provides all the background on which Russell Kirk based his work. Super documentation. Very thorough research. All factual, historical. …A wonderful book which will not permit us to forget the essential Biblical roots underlying our American consensus. American Protestant Christian theology and belief inform all of the thinking that underlay the foundation of our Republic.

> Rev. Donald Nesti
> Director, Center for Faith and Culture
> University of St. Thomas

The Miracle of America is a ground-breaking, foundational work. Angela Kamrath's research and work is magnificent in helping to build the case that this was a Christian nation at birth and should remain so. It is important, IMPORTANT, to bringing a new understanding of why America's history and heritage are fundamentally relevant to our nation's continued success. The book shows not only history but evidence of God's Providence, and it should help awaken this nation to our need for God, Christianity, and the Bible as a nation.

> Mark K. Vogl
> U. S. Army Veteran, Educator, and Author
> Columnist, *America Today*, *The Nolan Chart*

Angela Kamrath has provided a well-researched contribution for the study of the foundations of American Government, especially detailing from primary source material the various philosophical and religious perspectives that helped promote revolution and shape those foundations. *The Miracle of America* provides much historic detail of argumentation that was adapted by our country's Founders from both Reformation and radical Reformation ideals and experiences. …An excellent history source book that includes helpful student learning exercises and research questions with each chapter.

> Dr. Brian H. Wagner
> Instructor of History, Theology, and Biblical Languages
> Virginia Baptist College

A counter to conventional teaching is Angela Kamrath's *Miracle of America*, which shows how biblical understanding influenced the founding of the United States. Homeschooling parents will find it a valuable reference.

> Dr. Marvin Olasky
> Editor, *World Magazine*
> Professor of Journalism
> The University of Texas at Austin

Very original is Angela Kamrath's linking of political and philosophical concepts to specific Biblical passages. She is to be congratulated on taking on such an ambitious project, reading the enormous body of literature, and coming up with a well-reasoned argument that historians, students, and citizens need to hear.

> Dr. Peter H. Gibbon
> Senior Research Fellow
> Boston University

In an age of historical amnesia, spiritual apathy, and political correctness, *The Miracle of America* is a sigh of relief and a breath of fresh air. It allows students and educators alike to appreciate and to understand America as an idea. It is a profound work, at once a model of intellectual, religious, and political history. The primary research is diligent. The activities at the end of each chapter reinforce major themes and should stimulate productive classroom discussions.

> Dr. Brian M. Jordan
> Professor of History
> Sam Houston State University

Angela Kamrath gets the main ideas right. Many prominent scholars think that notions such as the importance of consent, the right to revolt, natural rights, and limited government sprang from the head of a secularized John Locke, with seemingly no recognition that these ideas had long been a part of Christian (particularly Reformed) communities. I also like many of the exercises at the end of each chapter. A beautiful book.

> Dr. Mark David Hall
> Herbert Hoover Distinguished Professor of Politics
> George Fox University

Angela Kamrath provides a powerful demonstration of the strength of our republic's Judeo-Christian roots.

> Dr. Stephen H. Balch
> Director, Texas Tech Institute for the Study of Western Civilization
> Founder and Former President, National Association of Scholars

The idea that we are all created equal with inherent, God-given dignity was a radical idea and came primarily from our Judeo-Christian background, not from the Enlightenment. Angela Kamrath's incredible work documents basic American ideas and ideals in a way that has not been accomplished before. It is a must-read for people of all faiths or no faith.

> Dr. Robert C. Koons
> Professor of Philosophy
> Founding Director, Program in Western Civilization and American Institutions
> The University of Texas at Austin

I am impressed with the amount of work that Angela Kamrath has done in assembling this material and in documenting the importance of the Bible and the Christian tradition in the thinking of the Founders, from the Puritans to the Framers of the Constitution. I agree that today's students should be aware of this important history and, regrettably, that most are not. I am happy to have this impressive work.

> Dr. Bill Martin
> Senior Fellow for Religion and Public Policy
> Baker Institute for Public Policy, Rice Institute

The Miracle of America is excellently arranged for its argument. I've learned a lot unquestionably from reading this book. There was content new to me. … The work is neutral and balanced. It puts truth on the table. The truth will shine. … This book would be a great resource in an American political thought class.

> Dr. Michael Bordelon
> Professor of Government
> Houston Baptist University

Angela Kamrath's *The Miracle of America* is rich in documenting the importance of biblical ideals, not only on America's founding generation and the Great Awakening that occurred before the War of Independence, but at the very beginning of the European settlements in America at the time of the New England Puritans. It used to be that in courses on American history and American political philosophy, students would begin with the Puritans and their wider influence on American culture that Tocqueville and so many other foreign observers noted. Angela has done everyone a great service in trying to restore knowledge of these early beginnings.

> Dr. Russell Nieli
> Senior Preceptor and Lecturer
> James Madison Program in American Ideals and Institutions
> Princeton University

The Miracle of America is a book with a point, a point it makes no attempt to hide and for which it makes no apologies. That point is that the founding principles of the United States of America are strongly and unequivocally based on Biblical ideals. The ideals leading to those founding principles can be traced to their sources and identified through the actions and communications of the founding members of the culture. The task of this book is to provide evidence supporting this central point. The book accomplishes this task substantially enough to be persuasive to those who respect the power of original documents to establish such facts. The support is expansive enough to meet the test of validity.

This book traces the lineage of governmental institutions in the United States to Christian principles and specifically to Biblical underpinnings. The lineage is undeniable. The work basically creates a documentary family-tree that shows us clearly how many of these founding concepts were carried torch-like from generation to generation. Just about anyone can benefit from reading this book.

> Dr. Matthew Melton
> Dean, College of Arts and Sciences
> Lee University

The Miracle of America

The Influence of the Bible on the Founding History and Principles
of the United States of America for a People of Every Belief

Angela E. Kamrath

THIRD EDITION

American Heritage Education Foundation
Houston, TX

American Heritage Education Foundation, Inc.
3100 Weslayan Street, Suite 375
Houston, TX 77027 www.americanheritage.org

Cover Design by The Marion Group: www.marion.com

www.xulonpress.com

To my family,
my teachers and mentors,
past, present, and future generations,
and the glory of God

*"Can the liberties of a nation be thought secure when we have removed
their only firm basis, a conviction in the minds of the people that these liberties are
of the gift of God? That they are not to be violated but with His wrath?"[1]*

Thomas Jefferson (1743-1826)
Notes on the State of Virginia
1785

*"Almighty God hath created the mind free. All attempts to influence it by
temporal punishments or burdens, or by civil incapacitations...are a departure from
the plan of the Holy Author of our religion."[2]*

Thomas Jefferson
Virginia Statute for Religious Freedom
1786

Primary Author of and Signer of the Declaration of Independence
Third U. S. President
Statesman, Diplomat, and Congressman
Virginia State Legislator and Governor
Lawyer
Author, Statute of Virginia for Religious Freedom
Father of the University of Virginia

*"I do not believe that the Constitution was
the offspring of (divine) inspiration, but I am perfectly satisfied, that
the union of the states, in its form and adoption, is as much
the work of divine providence, as any of
the miracles recorded in the Old and New Testament were
the effects of a divine power. 'Tis done! We have become a nation."[3]*

Benjamin Rush (1745-1813)
Observations on the Federal Procession in Philadelphia
July 9, 1788

Signer of the Declaration of Independence
College of New Jersey (Princeton University) Graduate, Age 15
Medical Degree, University of Edinburg
Consultant to Thomas Paine and his writing of *Common Sense*
Physician, Surgeon General of the Continental Army
Professor of Chemistry, College of Philadelphia (Univ. of Pennsylvania)
Educator/Writer, Published first American textbook on Chemistry
Founder, Dickinson College
Founder, Bible Society of Philadelphia (Pennsylvania Bible Society)
"Father of Public Schools"
Abolitionist

*"Let us then search the Scriptures.... The Bible contains the revelation of
the will of God; it contains the history of
the creation, of the world and of mankind; and afterwards
the history of one peculiar nation, certainly
the most extraordinary nation that has ever appeared upon the earth."*[4]

John Quincy Adams (1767-1848)
Letter to his son, George Adams
September 1 and 8, 1811

Sixth U. S. President
U. S. Secretary of State, considered one of America's greatest Secretaries of State
Diplomat and Statesman
U. S. Senator and U. S. Representative
Harvard Professor
Abolitionist

*"But if we and our posterity reject religious instruction and authority, violate
the rules of eternal justice, trifle with
the injunctions of morality, and recklessly destroy
the political constitution which holds us together, no man can tell
how sudden a catastrophe may overwhelm us that shall bury
all our glory in profound obscurity."*[5]

Daniel Webster (1782-1852)
*The Dignity and Importance of History,
An Address Delivered Before the New York Historical Society*
February 23, 1852

Constitutional Scholar and Orator, "Great Expounder of the Constitution"
Dartmouth College Graduate, Phi Beta Kappa
Educator, Headmaster, Fryeburg Academy
Attorney at Law and Statesman
U. S. Representative, New Hampshire
U. S. Senator, Massachusetts
U. S. Secretary of State under 3 Presidents
Named 1 of the 5 greatest U. S. Senators by 1957 U. S. Senate

Tributes

The roots of the miracle of America stem firstly from the Pilgrims who came to this land with only the clothes on their backs, a few tools, and a belief in God. They believed that if they worked hard and led dignified and biblically inspired lives that they would somehow survive and perhaps even thrive. Their incredible courage, resolve, and sacrifice require that we understand what and how they were thinking when they migrated to this virtually unknown land.

Secondly, the philosophers and early Americans who inspired and contributed to new ideas uplifting the common individual and to the founding of a new nation must be recognized. Such a nation based on Judeo-Christian principles and the equality of all human beings had never before been attempted on a large scale. History tells us that without such philosophical understandings, just and moral nations cannot germinate, grow, and endure. All Americans have a duty to themselves, their families, their communities, their states, and their nation to learn and know America's founding ideas and ideals.

Thirdly, during and after the American founding, the men and women who have defended American ideas and self-government of, by, and for the people—sacrificing their lives and limbs—are due the highest honor. They bring to mind an inscription on a World War II Memorial: "When you go home, tell them of us and say, for your tomorrow we gave our today." Are the people of this nation today willing and able to make such sacrifices for their countrymen both physically and intellectually?

Fourthly, the teachers and professors who teach accurate, insightful American history and principles of Western Civilization to our nation's young students deserve a very special tribute. Amid growing ignorance, apathy, neglect, and misinformation regarding America's founding history and ideas, these patriot educators are priceless. Without their learned instruction in the true origins and history of our nation in the face of destructive criticisms and underminings against our country, America cannot survive as a bastion of Freedom, Unity, Progress, and Responsibility (FUPR™).

Finally, tribute is offered to the average American individual and family who take the time and effort to learn, understand, and promote the origins and meanings of our nation's great founding philosophy, principles, and values. In the face of ever-increasing demands on time and energy, the average American who understands the critical importance of the American idea for themselves, their friends, and their families is to be highly commended. Such citizens are the fiber of America, without whom the nation cannot endure as it was originally designed.

Acknowledgments

Richard J. Gonzalez
1912 - 1998
American Patriot

Eugenie S. K. Gonzalez
1912 - 2018
American Patriot

Special thanks go to my step-grandfather, Dr. Richard J. Gonzalez, and my grandmother, Eugenie S. K. Gonzalez, co-founders of the American Heritage Education Foundation, Inc. (AHEF), who stirred in me a love of country and an awareness of America's unique idea and ideals.

Dr. Gonzalez was the youngest son of a modest San Antonio, Texas, family of Rafael and Catarina Gonzalez. Rafael stressed the importance of education to his six children and took them to public libraries to read books. As a barber, he put all of his children through college. All graduated, some with advanced degrees. Five became teachers.

In 1931, at the age of 18, Dr. Gonzalez graduated with highest honors from The University of Texas at Austin with a B.A. in Mathematics. A year later, at 19, he received his M.A. in Economics. In 1934, at the age of 21, he completed his doctorate in Economics (Finance), Economic Theory, and Pure Mathematics. It is believed that he remains the youngest student to ever earn a Ph.D. at UT. He was recognized for outstanding achievement at his doctoral graduation ceremony by the graduate school dean, Dr. Henry W. Harper, who remarked as quoted in the Austin American-Statesman, "There is one among us (of 64 graduate students) whose record is most unusual. If the university were to name a graduate valedictorian, the honor would most likely have gone to Mr. Gonzalez."

In 1937, at the age of 25, Dr. Gonzalez was hired as chief economist by Humble Oil and Refining Company of Houston (now Exxon Mobil) to apply sound economic principles to the oil business and to plan future economic decisions for the company. During the Cold War following World War II, he wrote numerous articles and papers on the advantages of the American free-market, capitalist, incentive-based socio-economic system. He compared this system to other state-controlled, less incentivized economies and observed how the United States consistently out-produced countries like the USSR while having fewer natural resources. He defined the American system as Freedom, Unity, Progress, and Responsibility (FUPR™) and often referred to it as the "miracle of America" for its limited government and free-market principles that produce more socio-economic advances for more citizens than any other system ever designed.

Dr. Gonzalez believed that America's socio-economic advances were supported by the traditional American view that "with the help of God" an individual could achieve unlimited socio-economic advancement. He compared this incentive philosophy in America to other countries' governments and philosophies which, as he observed from his world-wide experience, often encouraged their citizens to accept their rung on life's ladder, no matter how low, as "the will of God."

Richard married my grandmother, Eugenie S. K. Gonzalez, in 1976. Richard and "Grandma Jean," a former member of the Houston School Board, became alarmed in the early 1980s at the lack of teaching of America's heritage and founding principles in Texas schools. They also noted the well-documented decline of patriotic, pro-American textbooks and the prevalence of anti-American perspectives in school texts. In response, the two of them and my father, Jack Kamrath, began the American Heritage Education Foundation, Inc. (AHEF) in 1994 to write, produce, and distribute free K-12 patriotic educational resources for teachers, students, and families nationwide and worldwide. AHEF has become one of the largest producers and distributors of free, K-12 patriotic social studies lesson plans in America, having distributed nearly 150,000 free lesson plan resources to teachers, schools, and families throughout America.

I have AHEF and its faithful supporters to thank for providing me with the opportunity to research and write about America's philosophical origins. In particular, I wish to thank my father, AHEF Co-Founder Jack Kamrath, who made this project possible. I thank all of my family for their support. Many thanks also to all of the reviewers who contributed time and knowledge to provide valuable feedback and intellectual support for this book. Finally, I offer thanks to God in Christ for the honor and privilege of studying America's Bible-based heritage and to you, dear reader, for endeavoring to preserve and strengthen America's incomparable heritage—history's first and greatest experiment in large-scale self-government among a diverse people that has endured for over 200 years.

Table of Contents

Table of Contents
with Subsections

Introduction

"Do not remove the ancient landmark which your fathers have set." –Proverbs 22:28

"Where there is no vision, the people perish." –Proverbs 29:18 KJV

"My people are destroyed for lack of knowledge." –Hosea 4:6

"If My people who are called by My name will humble themselves, and pray and seek My face, and turn from their wicked ways, then I will hear from heaven, and will forgive their sin and heal their land."
–2 Chronicles 7:14

"Blessed is the nation whose God is the Lord, the people He has chosen as His own inheritance."
–Psalm 33:12

"The advancement and diffusion of knowledge is the only guardian of true liberty." –James Madison[6]

"If a nation expects to be ignorant and free, in a state of civilization, it expects
what never was and never will be." –Thomas Jefferson[7]

America is a country founded on ideas. Yet research shows that, over the last thirty years, Americans have become increasingly uneducated and uninformed about our country's founding heritage and philosophical roots. Numerous studies indicate that the American idea is eroding in an environment of ignorance, apathy, neglect, divisiveness, lack of patriotism, opposition, and unbalanced and destructive negativity toward America. America's heritage and philosophical origins are at risk in our society, culture, institutions, and education today.

The Intercollegiate Studies Institute (ISI) recently found in its 2006 study, *The Coming Crisis of Citizenship*, and its 2007 study, *Failing Our Students, Failing America*, that most graduating college students failed a basic civic literacy exam on America's history and institutions. Most students were ignorant of America's founding documents. Less than half of college seniors knew that the phrase "We hold these truths to be self-evident, that all men are created equal" comes from the Declaration of Independence. The studies found that "America's colleges and universities failed to increase knowledge of America's history and institutions." This failure is due, in part, to "inadequate college curriculum." ISI found in its 2008 study, *Our Fading Heritage*, that 71% of Americans of all backgrounds, incomes, and education failed a basic civic literacy test. Many elected officials also performed poorly. Less than half of all Americans could name the three branches of government. This ignorance is due, in part, to growing social and cultural challenges.[8]

A 2008 report by the Bradley Foundation, *E Pluribus Unum*, found that while most Americans believe we share an important and unique national identity, more than half believe this identity is weakening. It states, "America is facing an identity crisis. The next generation of Americans will know less than their parents know about our history and our founding ideals. Many Americans are more aware of what divides us than of what unites us. We are in danger of becoming not 'from many, one'—E Pluribus Unum—but its opposite, 'from one, many.'"[9]

In 2011, the National Association of Scholars (NAS) conducted a study called *The Vanishing West: 1964-2010: The Disappearance of Western Civilization From the American Undergraduate Curriculum*. The study traces "the decline and near extinction of the Western Civilization history survey course in America's top colleges and universities from 1964 to 2010." The study found that Western Civilization and American history survey courses have "virtually disappeared" from general education requirements and are rarely required even for history majors. In 2012, NAS conducted a second study, *Recasting History: Are Race, Class, and Gender Dominating American History? A Study of U. S. History Courses at the University of Texas and Texas A&M University*, which examined assigned readings in lower-division American history courses at two universities in Texas where students are required to take two American history courses. The study found that college course readings gave such a strong emphasis to race, class, and gender social history that it "diminished the attention given to other subjects in American history (such as military, diplomatic, religious, intellectual history)." As a result, history departments excluded key concepts and documents of American history and "frequently offered students a less-than-comprehensive picture of U. S. history." These trends are shared by history departments around the United States.[10]

In 2012, the Educational Testing Service (ETS), conducted a study called *Fault Lines in our Democracy* that confirmed a lack of civic knowledge among K-12 students. This lack of knowledge, it states, "provides ample concern for our future because civic knowledge has effects on voting and civic participation" and because solutions to national problems require an educated, skilled citizenry. The study quotes Robert Maynard Hutchins: "The death of democracy is not likely to be an assassination from ambush. It will be a slow extinction from apathy, indifference, and undernourishment." It also quotes William Damon, "The most serious danger Americans now face—greater than terrorism—is that our country's future may not end up in the hands of a citizenry capable of sustaining the liberty that has been America's most precious legacy. If trends continue, many young Americans will grow up without an understanding of the benefits, privileges, and duties of citizens in a free society, and without acquiring the habits of character needed to live responsibly in one."[11]

Americans today are largely ignorant about the principles and ideas that have shaped our nation. As a result, we have become more fragmented as a nation and unclear and divided about what our nation stands for and where it is headed—or where it should be heading. Without citizens' learning of America's positive founding principles and values, the American idea is rapidly weakening.

Even fewer Americans understand or agree that the United States is founded on principles largely rooted in Bible-based or Judeo-Christian thought. Americans today lack awareness and understanding about the essential moral influence of the Bible and the Judeo-Christian ethic on America's foundational ethic, order, purpose, and freedoms. Yet history tells us that we are a nation and people distinctly shaped by the Bible's teachings. Our government, society, and values all reflect this influence. The American principles of self-government, equality, and unalienable rights are strongly influenced by Bible-based or Judeo-Christian ideas. At the same time, America is not a theocracy. It separates church and civil government and embraces free thought, free speech, debate, and religious freedom for all. Some call ours a Christian nation, yet we have no national religion. Others call it a secular society, yet we pledge "one nation under God." This seeming contradiction is often misunderstood and misrepresented.

What is the American ethic? Where does it come from? How does the Bible relate to this ethic, if at all? How would we describe or present America and its ideals to a foreigner? The author and the American Heritage Education Foundation, Inc. have endeavored to objectively and independently research and answer these questions to further the advancement of America's civilization. The findings allow every American free thought and choice to contemplate and decipher America's influences for themselves and to arrive at their own conclusions. Such critical evaluation is in the best historical tradition of America.

Two of the most important ideas of the American ethic are God-given freedom and equality. From the settlement of America to the founding of an independent nation to the present day, Americans of many different beliefs have held that freedom and equality are unalterable states of human existence granted to every human being—not just in America but in the entire world—by a higher source of Moral Truth or a Creator God. Without such a God-oriented worldview, human rights could be granted or taken away by whoever had the most power. Early Americans came to understand that they were not free because a king declared them so or because they held positions of high rank in society—most were commoners—but because a Creator God endowed all men with certain unremovable or unalienable rights. Freedom was a gift from God, not a privilege granted by a ruler or government. Armed with this belief, Americans ultimately made the controversial decision to fight for independence from Britain when their only seeming options were freedom or subjection. The idea of a Creator God can be found in America's public square—in the U. S. Pledge of Allegiance, in the display of the Ten Commandments in public buildings, in the motto "In God We Trust" on U. S. currency. Though Americans are free to believe or not believe in God, such public displays are reminders of America's God-oriented basis of American rights and freedoms.

To be sure, America is imperfect. It took 100-200 years after 1776, for example, for black Americans to achieve full equality and freedom. However, Thomas Jefferson and George Washington, two Founders who owned slaves because they were born into a pre-existing system of slave labor, helped to design and implement a new governing system that ultimately led to freedom for every American including all slaves. It is also important to remember that it took 1776 years from Jesus' birth (and thousands of years before that) for the common white man to achieve full freedom with America's first large-scale experiment in self-government.

The Miracle of America is a comprehensive study of America's philosophical origins or founding ethic and its relation to the Bible. Our research examines and presents documents, thinkers, and events in history, specific Bible references and scriptures as cited historically, and relevant scholarship. In doing so, it uncovers and articulates much of our nation's philosophy, values, and founding principles as they are rooted in Bible-based or Judeo-Christian thought. Ultimately, it shows how the Bible and Judeo-Christian thought are arguably the nation's most significant foundational root and its enduring source of strength.

The Miracle of America is recommended reading for all citizens, teachers, and students to whom the American Founders have entrusted our self-governing republic. It is vital that Americans learn, understand, discuss, share, teach, apply, and preserve the American idea—the great principles and values of our country—so that it may endure. This book is for people of all nations who would endeavor to preserve and promote Freedom, Unity, Progress, and Responsibility (FUPR™) in America and the world.

American Heritage Education Foundation, Inc.
Houston, TX

The Need and Legal Right to Teach Religious History in Public Schools

Liberty cannot be preserved without a general knowledge among the people, who have a right, from the frame of their nature, to knowledge, as their great Creator, who does nothing in vain, has given them understandings, and a desire to know....[12]

> John Adams
> Declaration signer and 2nd U. S. President

Knowing as we do that the moral foundations of national greatness can be laid only in the industry, the integrity, and the spiritual elevation of the people, are we equally sure that our schools are forming the character of the rising generation upon the everlasting principles of duty and humanity? ... Are they [children] so educated, that, when they grow up, they will make better philanthropists and Christians, or only grander savages? For, however loftily the intellect of man may have been gifted, however skilfully [sic] it may have been trained, if it be not guided by a sense of justice, a love of mankind and a devotion to duty, its possessor is only a more splendid, as he is a more dangerous, barbarian.[13]

> Horace Mann
> Massachusetts Secretary of Education (1837-1848) and "father of American public education"

Schools do more than train children's minds. They also help to nurture their souls by reinforcing the values they learn at home and in their communities. I believe that one of the best ways we can help out schools to do this is by supporting students' rights to voluntarily practice their religious beliefs, including prayer in schools.... For more than 200 years, the First Amendment has protected our religious freedom and allowed many faiths to flourish in our homes, in our work place and in our schools. Clearly understood and sensibly applied, it works.[14]

> William Clinton, 42nd U. S. President (1993-2001)
> Excerpt in Introductory Letter of U. S. Secretary of Education Richard Riley,
> U. S. Department of Education *Legal Guidelines on Religious Expression in Public Schools* (1995, 1998)

U. S. Department of Education:

Teaching about religion: Public schools may not provide religious instruction, but they may teach **about** religion, including the Bible or other scripture: the history of religion, comparative religion, the Bible (or other scripture)-as-literature, and the role of religion in the history of the United States and other countries all are permissible public school subjects. Similarly, it is permissible to consider religious influences on art, music, literature, and social studies.[15]

> U. S. Department of Education *Legal Guidelines on Religious Expression in Public Schools* (1995, 1998)

Teaching values: Though schools must be neutral with respect to religion, they may play an active role with respect to teaching civic values and virtue, and the moral code that holds us together as a community. The fact that some of these values are also held by religions does not make it unlawful to teach them in school.[16]

U. S. Department of Education *Legal Guidelines on Religious Expression in Public Schools* (1995, 1998)

Student Assignments: Students may express their beliefs about religion in the form of homework, artwork, and other written and oral assignments free of discrimination based on the religious content of their submissions. Such home and classroom work should be judged by ordinary academic standards of substance and relevance, and against other legitimate pedagogical concerns identified by the school.[17]

> U. S. Department of Education *Legal Guidelines on Religious Expression in Public Schools* (1995, 1998)

U. S. Supreme Court Decision:

It might well be said that one's education is not complete without a study of comparative religion or the history of religion and its relationship to the advancement of civilization. It certainly may be said that the Bible is worthy of study for its literary and historic qualities. Nothing we have said here indicates that such study of the Bible or of religion, when presented objectively as part of a secular program of education, may not be effected consistently with the First Amendment.[18]

> U. S. Supreme Court Justice Tom Clark, in *Abington v. Schempp*, 374 U.S. 203, 255 (1963), in the opinion of the court that public school education may include teaching about religion

The holding of the Court today plainly does not foreclose teaching about the Holy Scriptures or about the differences between religious sects in classes in literature or history. Indeed, whether or not the Bible is involved, it would be impossible to teach meaningfully many subjects in the social sciences or the humanities without some mention of religion.[19]

> U. S. Supreme Court Justice William Brennan, in *Abington v. Schempp*, 374 U.S. 203, 255 (1963), in a concurring opinion of the court that public school education may include teaching about religion

National Council for the Social Studies (NCSS):

Omitting study about religions gives students the impression that religions have not been, and are not now, part of the human experience. Religions have influenced the behavior of both individuals and nations, and have inspired some of the world's most beautiful art, architecture, literature, and music. History, our own nation's religious pluralism, and contemporary world events are testimony that religion has been and continues to be an important cultural influence.

The NCSS Curriculum Standards for Social Studies state that "Students in social studies programs must study the development of social phenomena and concepts over time; must have a sense of place and interrelationships…; must understand institutions and processes that define our democratic republic…." The study about religions, then, has "a rightful place in the public school curriculum because of the pervasive nature of religious beliefs, practices, institutions, and sensitivities."

Knowledge about religions is not only a characteristic of an educated person but is absolutely necessary for understanding and living in a world of diversity. Knowledge of religious differences and the role of religion in the contemporary world can help promote understanding and alleviate prejudice. Since the purpose of the social studies is to provide students with a knowledge of the world that has been, the world that is, and the world of the future, studying about religions should be an essential part of the social studies curriculum.[20]

> National Council for the Social Studies, *Study About Religions in the Social Studies Curriculum: A Position Statement of National Council for the Social Studies*

Religion in the Public School Curriculum Guidelines:

1. The school's approach to religion is *academic*, not *devotional*.
2. The school may strive for student *awareness* of religions, but should not press for student *acceptance* of any one religion.
3. The school may sponsor *study* about religion, but may not sponsor the *practice* of religion.
4. The school may *expose* students to a diversity of religious views, but may not *impose* any particular view.
5. The school may *educate* about all religions, but may not *promote* or *denigrate* any religion.
6. The school may *inform* the student about various beliefs, but should not seek to *conform* him or her to any particular belief.[21]

> Charles C. Haynes and Oliver Thomas, First Amendment Center, *Religion in the Public School Curriculum*, guide to how to teach about religion and religious history in public schools (2002)

The Bible and Public Schools: A First Amendment Guide Guidelines:

To adopt any particular Bible—or translation—is likely to suggest to students that it is normative, the best Bible. One solution is to use a biblical sourcebook that includes the key texts of each of the major Bibles or an anthology of various translations.

At the outset, and at crucial points in the course, teachers should remind students about the differences between the various Bibles and discuss some of the major views concerning authorship and compilation of the books of the Bible. Students should also understand the differences in translations, read from several translations, and reflect on the significance of these differences for various traditions.[22]

> Bible Literacy Project and First Amendment Center, *The Bible & Public Schools: A First Amendment Guide*, guide to teaching the Bible in public schools (1999)

Goals and Objectives
for Course or Group Study (if applicable)

General Goals and Objectives:

The student will…
- define and explain the inspired, noble, and virtuous ideals of our constitutional republic that is founded on certain unalienable rights and the equality and freedom of all persons.
- practice more patriotic, informed, responsible, active, enthusiastic, and united citizenship.
- associate ideas from the Bible with the principles we value as citizens in the United States of America.
- distinguish the role of the Bible and Bible-based philosophers in American political thought.
- detect and assess the relevance of the Bible to the founding documents in America including the Mayflower Compact, the Declaration of Independence, the Constitution, and the Bill of Rights.
- illustrate America's political, social, cultural, and economic advances resulting from freedom and unity among citizens of the nation.
- sketch a personal plan of action in his/her daily civic life to demonstrate basic principles from the Bible and to promote the American idea.

Chapter 1 Objectives: The Roots of Popular Sovereignty

The student will…
- recognize the main events, issues, and effects or outcomes of the Protestant Reformation.
- distinguish the main tenets of Protestants and Catholics.
- examine important writings that came out of the Reformation and Counter-Reformation that influenced Western and American political thought.
- define and explain the principle of popular sovereignty.
- identify the sources of and scriptures used to support popular sovereignty.
- compare/contrast the principle of popular sovereignty and the doctrine of the Divine Right of Kings.
- examine how the principle of popular sovereignty affected Western views of church and government.
- identify and explain the Bible-based or Judeo-Christian principles evident and important in this part of America's heritage.

Chapter 2 Objectives: The Pilgrims, the Mayflower Compact, and the First Thanksgiving of America

The student will…
- identify the purposes of the Pilgrims in coming to America—for religious freedom, to create a godly, Bible-centered society, to advance the Christian faith, and to glorify God.
- specify and analyze the Bible-based influences on the Pilgrims and in the Mayflower Compact.
- explain the significance of the creation of a self-governing contract and document, the first of its kind in the world.
- describe compacts or covenants and their significance, purpose, benefits, and commitments as found in the Mayflower Compact.
- discuss the historical, religious, and socio-cultural significance of the first Thanksgiving in America.
- identify and explain the Bible-based or Judeo-Christian principles evident and important in this part of America's heritage.

Chapter 3 Objectives: The Puritans Create Bible Commonwealths in Early America

The student will…

- examine the Judeo-Christian religious/spiritual and civic/political views of the Puritans.
- analyze the relation between the Puritans' Judeo-Christian beliefs and their civic state, society, and political ideas including consent of the governed, popular sovereignty, self-government, rule of law, covenants, constitutions, chosen representatives, limited government, literacy, and work ethic.
- express the Puritans' views on individual rights, with consideration for how individual rights are addressed in today's laws in the United States government.
- examine the Puritans' Bible-centered self-government and society.
- analyze the influence of the Puritans' Judeo-Christian beliefs and principles on the United States and modern American life.
- identify and explain the Bible-based or Judeo-Christian principles evident and important in this part of America's heritage.

Chapter 4 Objectives: Freedom of Conscience and Religious Tolerance in Early America

The student will…
- indicate the reasons why religious dissidents and non-conformists came to America.
- analyze the Bible-based arguments of Roger Williams, William Penn, and John Locke against religious intolerance and coercion and in support of freedom of conscience.
- summarize the views of Williams and Locke on the use of state power to enforce religious laws, the purpose and principle of separation of church and civil government, and the distinction between civil government and church roles and representatives.
- explain how the beliefs, ideas, arguments, and/or actions of Williams, Penn, and Cecil Calvert contributed to the development and support of individual rights, limited government, religious tolerance, and freedom of conscience and religion in America.
- analyze the influence of early Americans' Bible-based or Judeo-Christian beliefs and principles on the United States and modern American life.
- identify and explain the Bible-based or Judeo-Christian principles evident and important in this part of America's heritage.

Chapter 5 Objectives: The Great Awakening, An Evangelical Revival in the American Colonies

The student will…
- discuss the important ideas and beliefs of the Great Awakening.
- recognize important thinkers and leaders during the Great Awakening.
- review and evaluate the religious, social, and political effects and influences of the Great Awakening in America.
- detect and indicate the links between the Great Awakening and America's path to independence.
- assess how the Great Awakening helped develop America as a democratic nation influenced by Bible-based values.
- analyze the influence of early Americans' Bible-based or Judeo-Christian beliefs and principles on the United States, its founding as a nation, and modern American life.
- identify and explain the Bible-based or Judeo-Christian principles evident and important in this part of America's heritage.

Chapter 6 Objectives: The Bible-Centered Debate on Revolution

The student will…
- compare and contrast the arguments of the Bible-centered debate among Americans over the American Revolution.

- recognize and evaluate the influence of the Bible on American thought, politics, and culture during the Founding era.
- analyze the influence of the Bible and Bible-based principles—as referenced by America Founders, revolutionaries, clergy, and influential thinkers—on the American Revolution.
- distinguish and examine founding-era Americans' Bible-influenced views on the issues of submission to authority, freedom, resistance to tyranny, and revolution.
- identify and explain the Bible-based or Judeo-Christian principles evident and important in this part of America's heritage.

Chapter 7 Objectives: The Rationale of America's Revolution

The student will…
- describe the American rationale or philosophy for human rights and freedoms.
- determine the influence of the Bible, philosophers, and early Americans on the rationale of the American Revolution.
- explain the significance of the Declaration of Independence as a founding document of the United States of America.
- specify important phrases and principles expressed in the Declaration of Independence.
- define how the Bible and the Law of God and Nature are primary sources of American principles, freedoms, and natural, unalienable rights.
- identify and explain the Bible-based or Judeo-Christian principles evident and important in this part of America's heritage.

Chapter 8 Objectives: The Making of A Nation Under God

The student will…
- examine and explain the influence of state constitutions on the U. S. Constitution—specifically regarding the relationship between church and civil government and religious freedom as a natural right.
- analyze the influence of the Bible and Judeo-Christian principles on the American Founders and thinkers who developed and/or influenced the forming of the Constitution and nation.
- analyze the influence of the Bible and Judeo-Christian principles on the Constitution and nation as a constitutional republic—including the need for government to restrain sinful man, Law of Nature and Nature's God as the standard of civil law, Rule of Law, constitutional government, separation of powers, representative self-government, value of the individual, religious freedom as a natural right, consent of the governed, and civil covenants.
- relate and summarize the need for a virtuous citizenry in a republic and the Founders' view of religion as the best means to achieve this virtuous citizenry.
- recognize and explain the Founders' support for and encouragement of religion (specifically the Bible and Christianity) and education in society for a virtuous citizenry.
- analyze the meaning, purpose, and limits of the First Amendment's Religion Clause with regard to separation of church and civil government and the free exercise of religion.
- identify and analyze important, relevant laws and documents that address religious issues—including the Northwest Ordinance and Thomas Jefferson's "wall of separation" metaphor.
- review the effects of the 14th Amendment's application of the First Amendment to the states.
- distinguish the Declaration of Independence and the Constitution as a national covenant or compact.
- identify and explain the Bible-based or Judeo-Christian principles evident and important in this part of America's heritage.

Notes to the Reader and Group Facilitator (if applicable)

Resource Design

A reader or group facilitator (who wishes to guide study of this resource for educational purposes) has flexibility in the reading and/or delivery of the study. The resource may be read and studied in sequence order, but it may also be read and studied in segments or by principle/topic. Please note that the first chapter introduces important historical background and primary source information relevant to the other chapters. Readings in each chapter provide historical content and excerpts, analysis and synthesis of information, and important points. Review/study questions in each chapter provide for review and discussion of content. Activities in each chapter give readers an opportunity to analyze, synthesize, and understand information. The activities may be done during the group meeting or between meetings. Call to action questions in each chapter are designed to encourage reflection, application, and action from readers. Some chapters include handouts with additional information.

Group or Class Discussion Format

This resource may be used in a group and/or class discussion setting. All discussion questions and activities may be completed by participants during or outside group meetings and then discussed and shared in the group meetings. For the subgroup format, a facilitator divides a large group into smaller subgroups to discuss all or assigned questions and activities. These questions and activities may be prepared by participants outside or during subgroup meetings. One person in each subgroup is assigned to take notes and/or share the responses, findings, and insights with the large group. When the large group convenes, subgroup representatives share their subgroup's insights with the large group. The large group and facilitator may further discuss/respond to questions and responses.

Discussion

Facilitators may encourage participants to freely contribute to group discussions. Discussions benefit from the different backgrounds, experiences, knowledge, references, thoughts, feelings, and ideas of group participants. These differences can enrich discussions and insights. Participants should listen to and encourage one another, not be afraid to ask difficult questions, and/or feel free to share various authentic viewpoints. The facilitator may lead groups to synthesize or bring together participant contributions and form insights and conclusions to further understand a question/issue.

Facilitator Ideas

(Note: If two people co-facilitate, one might agree to do most of the facilitating on a regular basis. Or, the two might decide to alternate weeks to facilitate. Because of the in-depth material, the two might help one another fill in gaps of information or understanding when needed during each session.)

1. Take care of administrative tasks.

2. Introduce the topic, book, layout, length, reading schedule, etc. of the study. The study might occur weekly, for example, with the participants reading one or part of a chapter per session. Express the purpose, need, and importance of studying this book or topic, why citizens must learn and know it, and citizen and church responsibility. Maybe a current event or article comes to mind that arouses the interest and curiosity of participants. Indicate, when applicable, how this study may also serve as a training for other teachers/group facilitators who wish to lead/facilitate their own class or group reading of the book at church or elsewhere.

3. Review and explain chapter content at the beginning of or at intervals during each session (as needed). The questions in "Review: Checking Out the History" at the end of each chapter help participants review, discuss, and assess learning of chapter content.

4. Facilitate the discussion, posing questions from the book and some of your own questions if you wish.

5. Guide discussion and questions through the main points or sections of the chapter.

6. Let participants freely talk about the reading and their thoughts and associations from it. Let the discussion be dynamic, but draw the discussion back to a question or topic when needed.

7. Address questions from the reading with the input of others in the group.

8. Direct the group to focus on and analyze some selected excerpt(s) or quote(s) in the chapter, with the group reading and analyzing the excerpt(s) together. Let the group read, decipher, explain, question, answer, discuss, react, respond, make associations, etc. This analysis will help the group to grasp the meaning and force of the material.

9. Direct the group to complete in writing (perhaps before class) and discuss the "Activity" at the end of each chapter to stimulate more thinking about and interaction with the ideas in the reading.

10. Direct the group to complete in writing (perhaps before class) and discuss the "Call to Action" questions at the end of each chapter to have participants think about, reflect on, and apply chapter concepts in their own lives as citizens in society today.

11. For each chapter, consider having the group closely read and analyze one key primary source (a sermon, letter, charter, personal writing, or state constitution, for example). Historical documents in the public domain can be found in libraries or at online sources such as Google Books.

Chapter 1
The Roots of Popular Sovereignty

Various strands of thought in history play a role in America's political thought and founding. Early American political thought was affected to some degree by the ancient Greeks and Romans. Unlike most early Americans, the Greeks and Romans were polytheists—those who worshipped many Gods. Yet these pagan peoples developed intellectual, moral philosophies that endured for centuries. These peoples also implemented various forms of self-government in their empires. The American Founders admired the Romans' civil republic—an empire governed by representatives of the people. American political thought was also influenced to some degree by the European Enlightenment of the late 1600s and 1700s. The Enlightenment was a largely secular, intellectual movement that emphasized reason and science.

At the same time, a close examination of America's formative documents and ideas in history reveal that one of the most significant sources of ideas in America's political thought and founding was the Judeo-Christian worldview and ethic that comes from the Bible. This strand of thought includes the teachings and practices of the ancient Israelites who formed their own nation, the man Jesus Christ, and the early Christians of the Bible. It consists of Bible-based or Judeo-Christian thought as it developed through history and notably flourished during the Protestant Reformation of the 1500s in Europe. As will be seen, the Judeo-Christian worldview and ethic emerged in the philosophical ideas and writings most influential to American thought, in the deeply-held beliefs and values of early colonial Americans, among many American Founders, and in the founding of the new nation. Even the Enlightenment-era thinkers who most influenced early Americans were those who held a pro-God if not Bible-based worldview. Moreover, many Scottish Enlightenment thinkers who influenced American thought emphasized an innate "moral sense" in mankind that easily aligned with Judeo-Christian thought. **It is the thesis of this book that the Bible is one of the most influential sources of ideas and thought in the foundational history, philosophy, values, and principles of the United States of America.**

1.1 The Protestant Reformation and Counter-Reformation

When considering the influence of the Bible and Judeo-Christian thought on the founding principles of America, it is important to consider the religious and political backdrop of Europe in the 1500s and 1600s. A brief look at Europe during this time, from which the first Europeans would emigrate to America, reveals that one of the most significant events affecting European religious and political beliefs was the Protestant Reformation that occurred in the 1520s and 1530s. The Reformation greatly impacted the beliefs of many early settlers who came to the American colonies.

Prior to and during this time, the Roman Catholic Church was and had been, for centuries, the dominant organized form of the Christian church in the kingdoms of Europe. The model of power that existed in European kingdoms was based on the medieval Roman Catholic theory of "two powers" or "two swords" of church and civil government. The two-swords theory held that two separate powers ruled the world—pope and emperor. The pope, as the highest person in the hierarchical Catholic church, was considered the representative or vicar of Christ in the world. The emperor was the highest civil magistrate who ruled over the empire. In this model, the pope and other church officials wielded the spiritual sword of the church, and the emperor and kings wielded the earthly or temporal sword of the civil state. To govern the churches of Europe, the Catholic church instituted canon laws. Canon laws were basically church laws to govern Christians in church matters. The civil state, in turn, enforced civil laws in line with the canon law and defended Christendom. The civil magistrates' power was limited by the church, the law, and the lower nobles. Emperors and kings were often elected and/or subject to a public oath to rule justly. They could be dismissed for unjust rule.[23] Over time, the pope gained more political and legal power, and the official church became the highest political authority in the kingdoms. The emperor and kings were accountable to the church, but the pope was accountable only to God. Since the

1 pope was Christ's vicar, as it was asserted, anyone's attempt to judge the pope was acting contrary to God's
2 will.

3   The Protestant Reformation ignited in Europe in 1517 when German monk and professor Martin Luther
4 nailed his *95 Theses* to the Castle Church door in Wittenberg, Germany. Luther's *95 Theses* was a list of
5 grievances against the Catholic Church. Luther, who had read the Bible, sought Bible-based reform by means
6 of academic debate of what had become, in his view, a corrupt church.   He criticized the church for its
7 excessive clerical wealth and power, burdens on the poor, false teachings, and heretical sale of indulgences and
8 pardons to the people to take away God's judgment of their sins. He defended the authority of the Bible over
9 human institutions in matters of faith, salvation by faith alone, and peace with and access to God through Jesus
10 Christ.[24] Luther's *Theses* was copied, translated, and spread quickly throughout Europe. Since the Bible at that
11 time was only available in Latin, a language which only the clergy knew, the people, who spoke other regional
12 languages, had a limited understanding of the Bible's content apart from what the clergy taught. Upon reading
13 Luther's *Theses*, people were angered by what they saw as the church's exploitive, heretical practices and
14 doctrines and sought to do away with them. Religious civil wars broke out in Europe. Protesters or reformers
15 rose up all over Europe—including Luther of Germany who translated the Bible into German, John Calvin of
16 France, Ulrich Zwingli of Switzerland, John Knox of Scotland, and William Tyndale of England who translated
17 the Bible into English. Many reformers became martyrs. Due to the invention of the printing press in the 1440s
18 in Germany, affordable Bibles and books were able to be mass produced for the public. As a result of the
19 Protestant movement, some reforms occurred in the Catholic Church, and many new church groups emerged as
20 Protestant. The main Protestant groups were the Calvinists, Lutherans, Anabaptists who withdrew from civil
21 life, and moderate Anglicans.
22
23   In addition to his *95 Theses*, Luther wrote two additional pieces that further exposed corruptions in the
24 Catholic church and called for greater religious and political freedom. In his 1520 *Appeal to the Ruling Class of*
25 *German Nationality*, addressed to the German emperor and nobles, he criticizes the church for making itself
26 unaccountable by the church's claim that its spiritual authority came from heaven above and, therefore, that it
27 was exempt from civil authority and law. The church had also asserted that no one could interpret the Bible
28 except the Pope. Further, no one could call a council except the Pope, though councils were the means to
29 initiate church accountability and reform. Luther calls for reforms to these doctrines and practices. He asserts
30 the priesthood and equal standing of all Christians or believers. In his 1523 *Secular Authority: To What It*
31 *Extent It Should Be Obeyed*, Luther explores the proper purpose and role of civil government. Politically
32 radical for his time, Luther favored greater distinction between roles of church and civil government. His
33 political ideas would influence future, more radical European and American political thinkers.
34
35   One French pastor and theologian, John Calvin, joined in protest against church corruption and set up a
36 Reformed church in Geneva, Switzerland. In 1536, Calvin wrote his well-known set of volumes, *Institutes of*
37 *the Christian Religion*, that presents a reformed Christian doctrine recovering many truths in the Bible that had
38 been lost or distorted. This doctrine became known as Reformed Theology or "Calvinism."
39
40   In the new context of the Reformation, Protestants generally believed that the Bible is the inerrant Word
41 of God and the final source of authority for all religious doctrine and church matters. The church approves and
42 exalts the Bible because the Bible is believed to be inspired by the Holy Spirit. The church's authority is
43 secondary to the Bible. The church has authority *only* when it is consistent with the Bible. The Bible,
44 Protestants also believed, is plain enough for all to read, and able to be freely interpreted by Christians.
45 Protestants believed in salvation by grace or God's unmerited favor toward humans. They also believed in
46 justification, or the gift of God's grace, by faith alone. Further, they believed in the "priesthood of all
47 believers," with Christ as the High Priest. All Christians can go directly to God through Christ who, in the New
48 Testament, clears the way for all Christians. All Christians have ministerial responsibilities as priests who can
49 intercede and pray for and minister to others. Protestant clergymen were viewed as "ministers" or "pastors"

who minister to and shepherd God's people but who do not play the role of high priest or mediator for the church. The Protestants ultimately rejected the authority of the pope. Their Old Testament Bible included only the books originally found in the Hebrew language. While most Reformed groups generally shared these basic beliefs, some groups differed in their more specific interpretations of the Bible.

Calvinists, like other reformers, asserted the basic Protestant views. Specifically, Calvinists emphasized Covenant Theology or the idea that God relates with creation and mankind through covenants—an idea largely studied and presented by Calvinist thinkers. Calvinists believed in the total depravity or inability of sinful mankind to redeem themselves. They upheld the idea of "predestination," the view that God predestines some humans, not all, to be saved by His mercy and grace. A person does not choose salvation on his or her own. God elects who is saved. He grants the "elect" the gift of faith. Some Calvinists, however, believed that God elects those whom He knows ahead of time will love or choose Him. Calvinists believed a Christian's salvation is assured and, once gained, cannot be lost. In contrast, the Arminians, named after Dutch Reformed theologian Jacobus Arminius, believed God's salvation is available to all humans who choose faith in Christ by free will. A Christian can lose salvation by falling away from the faith. Arminianism later gained strength in America in the 1800s as people emphasized freedom and the ability to choose. Yet many later Arminians, like John Wesley, still emphasized that God's grace leads people to salvation and that a person needs to "cooperate" with grace. Salvation occurs when a person surrenders to God's grace. Arminians also made important contributions to Reformed Theology, namely in the area of salvation by free will.

Calvinism was widely studied and followed by many Christians in Europe and later America. Calvinism influenced many Protestants like the French Huguenots, the European and Scottish Presbyterians, and the English Pilgrims and Puritans. American Puritan minister John Cotton exemplified Calvin's great influence on the Puritans: *"I have read the fathers and the school-men, and* Calvin *too; but I find, that he that has* Calvin *has them all."*[25] Calvin was not a radical political reformer, but his Reformed Theology did, in fact, impact Western views of the church and civil state. Calvin's Reformed Theology, say some scholars, contributed greatly to the transformation of Western religious and political ideas. It helped to lay the foundation for the principles of natural law, religious freedom, individual rights, greater distinction between church and civil government, and civil republicanism. Over the next two centuries, European and American political reformers developed from Calvin's ideas a concept of civil republican government based on Rule of Law, democratic process, and individual liberty.[26] These principles will be discussed in this book. Calvinism affected a number of key European political thinkers who would, in turn, influence the early Americans. Some of these thinkers include Johannes Althusius, Samuel Rutherford, Samuel von Pufendorf, Algernon Sidney, and John Locke. Calvinism also affected, to some degree, the worldviews and religious beliefs of many American Founders such as John Witherspoon, John Hancock, Benjamin Rush, Samuel Adams, John Adams, Benjamin Franklin, Roger Sherman, John Trumbull, and Paul Revere.[27]

Not all reformers were as radical as Luther or Calvin. Some like Anglican clergyman Richard Hooker in England were more moderate in calling for church reform and re-organization. Hooker looked to reason and church tradition to interpret the Bible. He also took a moderated position on church organization between the hierarchical Roman Catholics and the radically non-hierarchical Puritans. His work *Of the Laws of Ecclesiastical Polity* of 1593 is one of the first major theological writings in English that examines church governance and law. It represented the Anglican thought of the reformed Church of England. It would later affect the social-political views of British philosopher John Locke who would be influential to the American Founders and American political thought.

In response to the Reformation, the Catholic "Counter-Reformation" also arose during the 1540s to 1650s. The Counter-Reformation was a Catholic revival that rejected the Protestant view but promoted institutional reform of the Catholic church. It was a return to the basic tenets of the early Roman Catholic faith. It prompted the founding of seminaries for proper education and training of priests, a return to the spiritual life of faith and a personal relationship with Christ, and a re-adherence to the Roman Catechism or Catholic

1 Christian teachings and the 300s Latin Vulgate or "commonly used" Bible. The Counter-Reformation upheld
2 the leadership of the pope but acknowledged that the pope is not infallible. The pope could err in some cases or
3 fall into heresy. A heretical pope could be deposed.
4
5   Counter-Reformation Catholics also believed that the Bible is the inerrant Word of God and their source
6 of authority in religious matters. However, Catholics believed the Bible has authority *because* the church has
7 said so. It is the church, empowered by the Holy Spirit, that declares the Bible to be authoritative. In other
8 words, the Bible is authoritative *because* the church is authoritative and filled with the Holy Spirit. Thus
9 Catholics believed the Bible as well as church tradition are authoritative in religious and church matters.
10 Further, the Bible needs to be interpreted correctly by the pope, deemed the highest person in the church.
11 Catholics, like Protestants, believed in salvation by grace. However, when it came to justification by faith,
12 Catholics believed there is no such thing as faith without works. Also, Catholics kept the Old Testament-
13 resembling practice of designated priests who mediate/intercede on behalf of God's people. The priests in the
14 Old Testament were a class of men who studied God's laws, devoted their lives to serving God, and interceded
15 and prayed for God's people. Catholics read the Vulgate Bible that contained in its Old Testament the Hebrew-
16 originated books but also included some non-Hebrew books of the intertestamental period, the period between
17 the Old and New Testaments, which Protestants did not recognize as part of the sacred text.
18
19   When many religious reformers rejected the authority of the pope and the Catholic Church during the
20 Reformation, the kings and queens of the monarchies of Europe gained power. Monarchical power increased as
21 reformers, counter-reformers, and the people sought the protection of their monarchies during the religious civil
22 wars. During this time, the doctrine of the "Divine Right of Kings" gained strength. The Divine Right of Kings
23 was the belief that the king or queen derived his or her authority to rule directly and only from God and so was
24 not accountable for his or her actions to any earthly authority or to the people. To be sure, the monarch or
25 hereditary ruler was expected to abide by God's moral law and civil laws, and he or she might also at times
26 answer to a church that held some power. For the most part, however, he or she could only be judged by God.
27 Any subject's attempt to judge the monarch was considered defiant of God's will. The monarchs, therefore,
28 tended to rule absolutely—without any real limit or restriction. Monarchs held the authority to determine and
29 enforce the religious doctrine of the official state church in his or her kingdom and to impose this doctrine on
30 the people. Religious oppression and persecution resulted for those who differed in their beliefs from the
31 official church.
32
33   **Subsequently, some Protestant thinkers rose up and challeged the Divine Right of Kings, calling**
34 **for not only religious but also political reform in the church and civil government. These reformers**
35 **included John Ponet, Theodore Beza, Philippe du Plessis-Mornay, and Samuel Rutherford among others.**
36 **Many of them advocated for greater religious and political freedom and the people's right to resist civil**
37 **tyranny. Notably, they defended their positions from the Bible. Thus a clear line of modern, Western**
38 **political ideas with explicit roots in the Bible can be traced through their unprecedented writings.**
39 **Because many of their writings impacted later European and American thinkers who influenced**
40 **American ideas, their writings reveal the Bible's significance to America's principles and founding.**
41
42   In 1556, British Anglican bishop John Ponet wrote one such political tract entitled *A Short Treatise of*
43 *Political Power, and the True Obedience Which Subjects Owe to Kings and Other Civil Governors, with An*
44 *Exhortation to All True and Natural Englishmen.* This treatise, published in Strasbourg, is one of the first
45 advocating resistance to civil tyranny based on the Bible.[28] According to American founder and second U. S.
46 President John Adams in his 1787 *A Defense of the Constitutions of Government of the United States of*
47 *America,* Ponet's treatise impacted important philosophers of America's Founding—John Locke and Algernon
48 Sidney—and American ideas of liberty. *Short Treatise,* Adams notes, "contains all the essential principles of
49 liberty, which were afterwards dilated on by Sidney and Locke."[29]

1   Then, in 1579, a radical political tract entitled *Vindiciae Contra Tyrannos* (Latin for *A Defense of*
2   *Liberty Against Tyrants*) was released in Europe by an anonymous French reformer under the pseudonym
3   "Stephen Junius Brutus" who also asserted resistance to civil tyranny based on the Bible. This tract became,
4   observe some historians, the most well-known and quoted writing of the French political thinkers in the 1600s.
5   British Calvinists like Samuel Rutherford—who affected philosopher John Locke—were influenced by
6   *Vindiciae*. The tract is attributed to a Huguenot political writer—thought most likely to be Philippe du Plessis-
7   Mornay but also possibly Theodore Beza or Hubert Languet, all of whom asserted a resistance theory. Beza,
8   Calvin's protégé and successor in Geneva, had argued in his 1574 *On the Rights of Magistrates* for the right of
9   civil resistance based on a political covenant that existed among the people, rulers, and God. Brutus's *Vindiciae*
10 expanded Beza's arguments.[30] Beza and Brutus's *Vindiciae* became some of the first of the modern era to
11 assert a Bible-inspired covenant theory, a principle that would later be taken up and secularized by Locke and
12 the American Founders. Many of the principles in *Vindiciae* are evident in the United States' Declaration of
13 Independence.[31] John Adams acknowledged Brutus's *Vindiciae* along with Ponet and English author John
14 Milton as influential to America's political thought and founding. He points out that between 1640 and 1660
15 "not only Ponnet and others were reprinted, but Harrington, Milton, the *Vindiciae contra Tyrannos*, and a
16 multitude of others came upon the stage."[32]
17

18   In 1644, Samuel Rutherford, a Scottish Presbyterian minister and member of the Westminster Assembly,
19 published his well-known tract *Lex Rex, or The Law and The Prince*. The title *Lex Rex* was interpreted by many
20 as a play on words, meaning *The Law Is King*. The idea that law is king, says Francis A. Schaeffer, was
21 "absolutely earthshaking." Before that, the order of the day was *Rex Lex* or the king is law. The king or state
22 was held as God's representative ruler, and so the king's word was law. *Lex Rex* argued, however, that rulers
23 are not the law but are rather subject to the law—the concept of Rule of Law. The civil law is based on God's
24 moral law.[33] *Lex Rex* applied the ideas in *Vindiciae* to the political situation in England.[34] *Lex Rex* significantly
25 impacted the English Civil War—the Puritan Revolution—of the mid 1600s. It drew on both Catholic and
26 Protestant sources.[35] Like *Vindiciae*, *Lex Rex* provided a Biblical basis for political covenants and resistance to
27 civil tyranny. *Lex Rex*, says Jon Roland, "systematized the Calvinistic political theories which had developed
28 over the previous century."[36] It "reflected the theological and political ideas of Calvin," affirm Gary Amos and
29 Richard Gardiner, "as they were transmitted through the French Huguenots to the Scottish Presbyterians and
30 English Puritans."[37] Though Rutherford was not a supporter of religious tolerance as other political reformers
31 were, his *Lex Rex* served as a source of ideas on Rule of Law and resistance to tyranny for European reformers
32 like John Knox and Locke and for American Founders like John Witherspoon. Locke drew heavily from and
33 secularized concepts found in *Lex Rex*.[38]
34

35   Additionally, the Westminster Confession of Faith of 1646, the doctrine of the Church of England and
36 Scotland, which Rutherford helped to write, would also affect early Americans' religious and political thought.
37 It was written by the Westminster Assembly, a group of reformed, largely Calvinist clergymen assembled by
38 British parliament at Westminster Abbey in England to restructure the church. The Confession affirmed the
39 Bible as highest authority, God's Biblical commandments and moral law, the Law of Nature, covenants,
40 freedom of conscience, and the right to resist tyranny. The Confession was, next to the Bible, the most widely
41 read document by early Americans in the pre-revolutionary colonies. It was required learning at all levels of
42 education in America and was known by nearly all colonists and American Founders. It became the core
43 statement of faith for many Protestants in America. The stated beliefs in the Confession undoubtedly
44 influenced early Americans' thinking and values.[39]
45

46   Religious reformers who were exiled in Geneva translated the Bible into English in 1560—producing
47 the Geneva Bible. Reformers John Calvin, Theodore Beza, and John Knox contributed to the translation.
48 Earlier English translations of the Bible by William Tyndale and Miles Coverdale also contributed to this
49 translation.[40] Easy to read and affordable, the Geneva Bible was accessible to the English-speaking public and
50 mass printed. It became the most popular edition of the Bible among English-speaking Protestants until the mid

1 1600s. This Bible was, in fact, studied by the Pilgrims and Puritans who brought it to America in 1620. The
2 unique feature of the Geneva Bible was its marginal notes and commentaries. The Puritans taught from these
3 notes. As such, this Bible is often known as the first study Bible. The marginal notes, however, presented the
4 radical Reformed Theology that challenged absolute power, including the powers of the king. As a result,
5 though the Bible was authorized in Scotland, it was rejected by King James I of England and the more moderate
6 Church of England. King James, instead, called for a new Bible to be translated without such marginal notes.
7 The King James Version (KJV) of the Bible came out in 1611 and became the authorized Bible of the Church of
8 England. Puritan leader John Winthrop brought the King James Bible to America in 1629. By the late 1600s
9 and 1700s, the King James Bible would become the most widely read Bible in the American colonies. Many
10 clergy later preferred it for its more moderate tone.[41]
11
12 **1.2 Popular Sovereignty**
13
14   While many political thinkers of the Reformation era supported the idea that civil authority came from
15 God, some argued that this political authority is given by God to the whole people of a community or state, not
16 to select individuals or groups as is typically practiced in a monarchy. A monarchy is a state ruled by a
17 sovereign monarch or head, like a king or queen, who often comes to power by hereditary succession. This
18 ruler often holds absolute or unlimited power. The political reformers argued that God makes all humans equal
19 and free. As such, God firstly and then the people are the source of earthly power. God holds supreme rule or
20 "sovereignty" over all humans and earthly spheres, and the people hold power—"popular sovereignty"—to rule
21 or govern in their state or nation. Importantly, this principle of popular sovereignty maintains God as the
22 highest sovereign in the world. The people do not replace or remove God. Rather, God's will is expressed
23 through the action of the people. In the principle of popular sovereignty, the people may select rulers to govern
24 for the people's good and protection. They may also limit the power of their rulers as well as resist or remove
25 rulers who are tyrannical. Popular sovereignty assumes that all who govern over the people do so by the
26 people's voluntary consent. Because if all humans are free and equal, no human has a right to rule over another
27 without the other's permission. Many thinkers asserted this principle based on the Bible.
28
29   A number of both Catholic and Protestant thinkers in Europe derived and recognized popular
30 sovereignty from the Bible. Two modern Catholic churchmen of the 1500s and 1600s—Italian Jesuit priest
31 Robert Bellarmine and Spanish Jesuit priest Francisco Suarez—notably presented and defended popular
32 sovereignty from scripture. They were influenced by Catholic theologian Thomas Aquinas. Bellarmine and
33 Suarez supported popular sovereignty based on the idea from the Bible that all humans are created free and
34 equal by God. For in the Bible, Adam and Eve, the first human beings created by God, are given authority by
35 God to multiply and to take dominion over the earth—according to Genesis 1, 2, and 9. Genesis 1:26-28 states,
36
37   Then God said, "Let Us make man in Our image, according to Our likeness; let them have dominion
38   over the fish of the sea, over the birds of the air, and over the cattle, over all the earth and over every
39   creeping thing that creeps on the earth." So God created man in His *own* image; in the image of God He
40   created him; male and female He created them. Then God blessed them, and God said to them, "Be
41   fruitful and multiply; fill the earth and subdue it; have dominion over the fish of the sea, over the birds
42   of the air, and over every living thing that moves on the earth."
43
44 During this period of mankind's creation and reproduction in Genesis, observes Bellarmine, God does not
45 appoint any particular individual, group, or lineage of humans to rule over other humans. Rather, all humans
46 have equal standing before God and equal right to dominion on earth. Civil power then, he concludes, resides
47 with the whole people or the multitude. However, the people may delegate political power to a person or group
48 by their consent. In his 1580s/1590s *De Laicis*, Latin for "Of the Laity," also known as his *Treatise on Civil
49 Government*, Bellarmine defends popular sovereignty from the Bible:
50

> Secular or civil power…is in the people, unless they bestow it on a prince. **This power is immediately in the whole multitude…for this power is in the divine law [the Bible], but the divine law hath given this power to no particular man**—if the positive law [man-made law] be taken away, there is left no reason why amongst a multitude (who are equal) one rather than another should bear rule over the rest. Power is given by the multitude to one man, or to more by the same law of nature…. It depends upon the consent of the multitude to ordain over themselves a king, or consul, or other magistrates….[42]

Interestingly, Bellarmine supported monarchy, the position and power of the pope, and the Counter-Reformation. Yet, as will later be seen, his view of popular sovereignty—including the consent of the governed, limited power, and accountability of rulers who were fallible—would be defended by thinkers important to the American Founding era like Locke and Sidney. As a result, this view would also be influential to the early Americans. Suarez, considered one of the greatest Catholic thinkers after Aquinas, similarly argues from Genesis that humans are created free and equal by nature, not slaves to one another.[43] In his 1612 *Tractatus de Legibus* or *Tract on Laws*, Suarez states,

> By right of creation…Adam had only economical power, but not political. He had a power over his wife, and a fatherly power over his sons…. … But political power did not begin until families began to be gathered together into one perfect community; …as the community did not begin by the creation of Adam, nor by his will alone, but of all them which did agree in this community, so we cannot say that Adam naturally had political primacy in that community; …because by the force of the law of Nature alone it is not due unto any progenitor to be also king of his posterity. And…we cannot say, God…gave him this power, for there is no revelation of this, nor testimony of Scripture.[44]

Suarez notes that God does not give to anyone political power over another, not even to Adam. Rather, political power begins when families, by agreement, gather together as a community. The whole people or multitude, therefore, not any particular person or family line, holds political authority in the community. Suarez's view of popular sovereignty, like Bellarmine's, would also influence Locke, Sidney, and the American Founders.

Popular sovereignty was also directly or indirectly supported by some of the Protestant reformers mentioned—Luther, Calvin, Ponet, Beza, Brutus, and Rutherford. The reformers also supported popular sovereignty from the Bible, though with different scriptures and strands of thought. Luther and Calvin indirectly supported popular sovereignty by defending the equal standing of believers in the Bible and church. Their views of the church undoubtedly influenced others' views of popular sovereignty among citizens in the civil state. Luther, in particular, challenged the nearly absolute, unlimited power of church leaders. In his *Appeal to the Ruling Class*, he argues that all believers, though exercising different functions in the church or occupations in the world, are priests or intercessors of God. All share the same Christian status, regardless of whether one's occupation is religious or secular. All are called to minister. This idea is often referred to as the "priesthood of all believers." Luther derives this idea from 1 Peter 2:9 and Revelation 5:9-10. In 1 Peter 2:9-10, the Apostle Peter says to believers in the church, "But you *are* a chosen generation, a royal priesthood, a holy nation, His [God's] own special people…; who once *were* not a people but *are* now the people of God…." In Revelation 5:9-10, believers sing of how Christ has made them "kings and priests to our God." Luther explains from these verses, "The fact is that our baptism consecrates us all without exception, and makes us all priests. As St. Peter says, I Pet. 2…, 'You are a royal priesthood and a realm of priests,' and Revelation, 'Thou hast made us priests and kings by Thy blood'…."[45] Luther also echoes 2 Corinthians 4:13 in saying that "we all have the one spirit of faith." As a result, he says, "each and all of us are priests because we all have the one faith, the one gospel, one and the same sacrament…."[46] Luther further refers to Romans 12:4 and 1 Corinthians 12 to emphasize the diverse but necessary capacities and trades of believers in the "one body" of the church. Romans 12:4-5 states, "For as we have many members in one body, but all the members do not have the same function, so we, being many, are one body in Christ, and individually members of one another." 1 Corinthians

12:12 states, "For as the body is one and has many members, but all the members of that body, being many, are one body, so also is Christ." All believers, Luther saw from these verses, may serve others through their varied capacities—whether as priest, bishop, pope, shoemaker, smith, farmer, etc. Every one, says Luther, ought to serve "in such a way that the various trades are all directed to the best advantage of the community, and promote the well-being of body and soul, just as all the organs of the body serve each other."[47]

A church leader or "office-bearer" differed from other church members only in his office or occupation, Luther argues, not in his Christian standing. Such a leader should be chosen by the consent and/or election of church members. Luther explains, "Just because we are all priests of equal standing, no one must push himself forward and, without the consent and choice of the rest, presume to do that for which we all have equal authority. Only by the consent and command of the community should any individual person claim for himself what belongs equally to all." Furthermore, such leaders should not have absolute, unlimited powers in the church but should be held accountable to the members. A leader can be removed from his office if he abuses his position.[48]

Calvin in his *Institutes* similarly addresses the equal standing among the believers in the early church of the Bible. Alluding to Acts, 1 Peter 5, and Galatians 1 and 2, he explains that in the early church the leading Apostles Peter and Paul practiced servant-leadership, not as absolute superiors but as equal church members. For example, in Acts 8:14-15, 11:2-4, and 15:6-29 and 1 Peter 5:1, Peter, a minister to the Jews, acts as a companion and colleague to the other believers, not as a master who has absolute authority over them. In 1 Peter 5:1, Peter reveals to the churches his equal position among the other elders, saying, "The elders who are among you I exhort, I who am a fellow elder and a witness of the sufferings of Christ, and also a partaker of the glory that will be revealed." Peter makes proposals and delivers opinions to the church and its pastors, but he also hears the observations of other members and lets them make decisions. He then honors and follows their decisions and commands. In Acts 8:14-15, when Peter is commanded by his colleagues to go with the disciple John to Samaria, he does not refuse. In Acts 8:14-15, the disciple Luke tells, "Now when the apostles who were at Jerusalem heard that Samaria had received the word of God, they sent Peter and John to them, who, when they had come down, prayed for them [the people] that they might receive the Holy Spirit." Calvin observes from this verse that "The apostles, by sending him [Peter], declared that they did not consider him as their superior. By his compliance and execution of the commission entrusted to him, he confessed that he was a colleague to them, but had no authority over them."[49] In addition, Peter is held accountable to others in the church for his actions. When he associates with Gentiles or non-Jews, he is questioned by some of the Jewish Christians in the church. Consequently, Peter explains and vindicates his actions when necessary, as he does on this occasion. Acts 11:2-4 states, "And when Peter came up to Jerusalem, those of the circumcision [Jewish believers] contended with him, saying, 'You went in to uncircumcised men and ate with them!' But Peter explained *it* to them in order from the beginning...." Further, in Galatians 1 and 2, Paul, a minister to the Gentiles, does not profess subjection to Peter but declares harmony with his teaching. Peter, on the other hand, does not ask for submission but only fellowship as a co-laborer of the Lord. In Galatians 2:9, Paul states that "when James, Cephas [Peter], and John, who seemed to be pillars, perceived the grace that had been given to me [Paul], they gave me and Barnabas the right hand of fellowship, that we *should go* to the Gentiles and they to the circumcised." Moreover, Paul corrects Peter when necessary, and Peter stands corrected by Pauls' reproval. In Galatians 2:11-16, Paul addresses Peter's hypocritical behavior. He explains,

Now when Peter had come to Antioch, I withstood him to his face, because he was to be blamed; for before certain men came from James [a Jewish Christian leader in the church], he would eat with the Gentiles; but when they came, he withdrew and separated himself, fearing those who were of the circumcision [Jewish believers]. And the rest of the Jews also played the hypocrite with him, so that even Barnabas was carried away with their hypocrisy. But when I saw that they were not straightforward about the truth of the gospel, I said to Peter before *them* all, "If you, being a Jew, live in the manner of Gentiles and not as the Jews, why do you compel Gentiles to live as Jews?"

"All these things fully prove," concludes Calvin, "either that there was an equality between Paul and Peter, or at least that Peter had no more power over the rest than they had over him."[50]

Luther's and Calvin's idea of the priesthood and equal standing of all believers had not only religious but also political implications for both church and civil state. This religious view led to more democratic ideas of church, society, and government in the world at large, though its application took time.[51] It undoubtedly contributed to many political reformers' favor of popular sovereignty over absolute rule in civil government.

The more radical political reformers of the Reformation era more directly supported popular sovereignty in the civil state, but also based on the Bible. Brutus in *Vindiciae* bases support for popular sovereignty on Deuteronomy 17:14-15 in which Moses prophesies that the Israelites will set over themselves a king when they entered the land of Canaan. In Deuteronomy 17:14-15 Moses says to the Israelites, "When you come to the land which the LORD your God is giving you, and possess it and dwell in it, and say, 'I will set a king over me like all the nations that *are* around me,' you shall surely set a king over you whom the LORD your God chooses; *one* from among your brethren you shall set as king over you…." In these verses, Brutus thought, God approves the people's sovereignty or rule in selecting their own king. Brutus observes,

> Several ages before the people of Israel petitioned God for a king, God had already sanctioned the law of the kingdom which is found in Deuteronomy ch. XVII: "When", says Moses, "you have come to that land which the Lord your God has given you in possession, and when you have dwelt there, you will say: 'Let me constitute a king over myself, like the other nations round about.' Then you will constitute that king, whom your Lord will have elected from the midst of your bretheren, etc." Here you see the king's election attributed to God, and his constitution to the people.[52]

Brutus also cites 1 Samuel 10 and 11 to support the people's authority from God in choosing a king or the view that kings are made by the people. In these verses, the people of Israel ask God for a king via the prophet Samuel. In response, Samuel anoints Saul following God's direction, but Saul does not become king until he is confirmed by the people. First, the king is nominated by the people, and then he is voted in by the people. Brutus explains,

> Partly because they [the people of Israel] were disgusted with Samuel's sons, who judged unjustly, and partly because they believed that their wars would be better conducted, they asked Samuel for a king [1 Samuel 8:4-5]. When consulted by Samuel, God revealed that He had elected Saul to rule the people [1 Samuel 9:16]. And so Samuel anointed Saul [1 Samuel 10:1]: for all these procedures pertained to the election of a king made at the request of the people.
> And perhaps it might have seemed sufficient, if Samuel had presented the king elected by God to the people and admonished it to obey him. Nevertheless, in order that the king should know himself to be constituted by the people, Samuel appointed an assembly [*comitia*] to meet at Mizpeh; there, as if the matter were still wholly unopened and unsettled—as if, I say the election of Saul had not yet been established—the lot was drawn. Out of the tribes, it fell on the tribe of Benjamin; out of the families, it fell on the family of Matri; and from that family, upon Saul, the same whom God had elected. Then finally, with the acclamation of the whole people, Saul was said to be nominated king [1 Samuel 10:17-24]. … Saul was confirmed as king in the presence of the Lord by all together [*universi*] at Gilgal, despite the dissent of a few of the people [1 Samuel 11:14-15, 1 Samuel 10:27]. **Here you see the one whom God Himself had elected, and who had been marked off from the rest by lot, constituted king by the votes of the people.**[53]

Brutus concludes that there is a scriptural basis for popular sovereignty, stating, "We have demonstrated… that God institutes kings, gives kingdoms to them, and elects them. We now say that the people constitute kings, confers kingdoms, and approves the election by its vote.... Indeed, God willed that it should be done this way...."[54]

    In *Lex Rex*, Rutherford similarly espouses the principle of popular sovereignty. He also bases his argument on the practice of the Israelites. In addition to citing 1 Samuel 10, 11, and 12 like *Vindiciae*, he also cites numerous other scriptures to show how the people of Israel held political authority. For instance, he cites Exodus 18:21 in which the Israelites are instructed to select their rulers, Judges 8:22 in which the men of Israel say to their military commander Gideon, "'Rule thou over us,'" Judges 9:6 in which the men of Shechem make Abimelech their king, Judges 11:8,11 in which the people make Jephthah commander over them, 1 Chronicles 12:38 in which the men of war "'came with a perfect heart to make David king of Hebron,'" 1 Kings 1 in which the people make Solomon king, 2 Chronicles 23:3 in which the people make a covenant with King Joash, 1 Kings 16 in which the people choose kings Omri and Achab, 2 Kings 10:5 in which the people say "'We will not make any king,'" and 2 Kings 14:21 in which "'The people made Azariah king.'"[55] From such scriptures, the Bible reveals the people's God-given authority, says Rutherford, by which they directly and God indirectly elect a ruler. Furthermore, since the people give political power to rulers to govern for the public good, the people have a right to resist that power when rulers become tyrannical. Rutherford argues this point based on 2 Chronicles 22 and 23. In these verses, Athaliah, mother of deceased King Ahaziah, tries to kill the royal line of Judah in the southern kingdom of Israel so no one else can take the throne after her son dies. She unlawfully usurps the throne and makes herself queen without the people's consent. But the godly high priest Johoiada intervenes. He hides the rightful successor, the infant Joash, who survives. When Joash turns seven, the people crown him king. Still, Athaliah refuses to recognize Joash as rightful king, and she is overthrown by the people. Rutherford responds to this occurrence,

> If the estates [ie. the people] of a kingdom give the power to a king, it is their own power in the fountain; and if they give it for their own good, they have power to judge when it is used against themselves, and for their evil, and so power to limit and resist the power that they gave. Now, that they may take away this power, is clear in Athaliah's case.[56]

Based on these observations from the Bible, Rutherford concludes that a ruler, though selected by God, must be elected and confirmed by the people. He asserts, "The power of creating a man a king is from the people" and "Expressly Scripture saith, that the people made the king, though under God."[57] He points out that many others including Calvin "do all hence conclude that the people, under God, make the king."[58]

    Popular sovereignty does not stem from some notion that the people replace God as the highest sovereign in the world or that God is absent from civil society. Rather, it is based on the idea that God as sovereign gives political power to the God-honoring people, and, ideally, that His sovereign purpose may be reflected in their actions. Rutherford explains,

> The Scripture saith plainly, as we heard before, the people made kings; and if they do, as other second causes produce their effects, it is all one that God, as the principal cause, maketh kings.... God, by that same action that the people createth a king, doth also, by them, as by his instruments, create a king.... ... The people can, and doth, limit and bind royal power in elected kings, therefore they have in them royal power to give to the king.[59]

Rutherford also says, "...[W]e cannot here find two actions, one of God, another of the people; but in one and the same action, God, by the people's free suffrages and voices, createth such a man king...." Alluding to 1 Kings 1:38-40, Rutherford affirms the principle of popular sovereignty in bringing up how the people of Israel make Solomon king after David. 1 Kings 1:38-40 states,

So Zadok the priest, Nathan the prophet, Benaiah the son of Jehoiada, the Cherethites, and the Pelethites went down and had Solomon ride on King David's mule, and took him to Gihon. Then Zadok the priest took a horn of oil from the tabernacle and anointed Solomon. And they blew the horn, and all the people said, *"Long* live King Solomon!" And all the people went up after him; and the people played the flutes and rejoiced with great joy, so that the earth *seemed to* split with their sound.

Rutherford reaffirms popular sovereignty from these scriptures, saying,

This is what we say, God by the people, by Nathan the prophet, and by the servants of David and the states crying "God save king Solomon!" made Solomon king; and here is a real action of the people. God is the first agent in all acts of the creature. Where a people maketh choice of a man to be their king, the states do no other thing, under God, but create this man rather than another; and we cannot here find two actions, one of God, another of the people; but in one and the same action, God, by the people's free suffrages and voices, createth such a man.[60]

Donald Lutz elaborates on the idea that government by the people is an expression of God's sovereignty. He explains,

Consent becomes the instrument for establishing authority in the community and for expressing the sovereignty of God. God transmits his sovereignty to the people through the broader covenants, and they in turn convey His sovereignty to the rulers on the basis of the specific covenant creating the civil community. The people's consent is the instrument for linking God with the rulers, whose authority then is viewed as sanctioned by Him, but because this authority comes through the people, the rulers are beholding to God through *them*.[61]

1.3 Conclusion: The Idea of Popular Sovereignty Emerges in Europe

The Reformation era prompted the spread of new religious and political ideas throughout Europe. Ideas such as the priesthood of all believers, equal standing before God, and a Bible for all to read became more widely accepted. In addition, the idea of popular sovereignty, or the people's God-given civil authority, found Biblical support among both Protestants and Catholics. Absolute power in both the church and civil state was challenged, and the consent of the governed was recognized. The corresponding view of the right to resist tyranny also emerged. Subsequently, the Bible-inspired principle of popular sovereignty impacted those who came to America and became an important principle in American political thought. As will be seen, popular sovereignty would first be demonstrated in America by the Pilgrims when they signed the Mayflower Compact. This principle would also be applied by the American Founders as they formed the new nation of the United States. The Founders recognized in the U. S. Declaration of Independence that governments "derive their just powers from the consent of the governed...."

1 **Review: Checking Out the History**
2
3 Discuss questions in subgroups or whole group. As an option, the group may come up with main ideas or
4 insights from each question. Responses may be shared and discussed in the whole group.
5
6 1. What was the Protestant Reformation? What happened? What issues were at stake?
7
8
9
10
11 2. What were the effects or outcomes of the Reformation?
12
13
14
15
16 3. What were/are the main tenets of Protestants and Catholics? Of Calvinists?
17
18
19
20
21 4. What important writings came out of the Reformation and Counter-Reformation that would influence
22 Western and American political thought? Describe each.
23
24
25
26
27 5. What is "popular sovereignty" in your own words?
28
29
30
31
32 6. Who supported popular sovereignty during the Reformation era? What scriptures did they use to support it?
33 Cite both Catholic and Protestant examples.
34
35
36
37
38 7. How did the principle of popular sovereignty affect Western views of the church and civil government?
39
40
41
42
43 8. What basic Bible-based or Judeo-Christian principles are evident and important in this part of America's
44 heritage?
45
46

1 **Activity: The Biblical Basis of Popular Sovereignty**
2
3 After reviewing/discussing Chapter 1 of *Miracle of America*, think about the scriptural basis for popular
4 sovereignty provided by both Catholic and Protestant thinkers in history. In the chart below, list the scripture(s)
5 historically cited in support of popular sovereignty (with verse number and, optionally, text), the thinkers who
6 cite them, the meanings and/or main ideas of the verses in your own words, and a brief explanation of the
7 thinkers' views in your own words. Draw lines across the chart to separate verses and meanings as needed.
8

Popular Sovereignty			
Scripture Verses Cited	**Thinker(s)**	**Scripture Verse Meanings in your own words**	**Brief Explanation of Thinkers' Views in your own words**

1 **Call to Action**
2
3 Each person will reflect on and write his/her responses to the questions below. Responses may then be shared
4 and discussed in the group.
5
6 1. What, if anything, about the Protestant Reformation did you find unusual? Surprising/shocking?
7 Beneficial? Admirable? Courageous? Positive/negative? Why?
8 _____
9 _____
10 _____
11 _____
12
13 2. What influences of the Protestant Reformation and Counter-Reformation do you see today in society and
14 culture?
15 _____
16 _____
17 _____
18 _____
19
20 3. What do you think life would be like under "absolute rule"? Would you want to live under such rule?
21 _____
22 _____
23 _____
24 _____
25
26 4. What do you think are the benefits/positives, if any, of "popular sovereignty"? What are the
27 problems/negatives, if any?
28 _____
29 _____
30 _____
31 _____
32
33 5. Give several examples in your community or state and/or in our nation in which the principle of popular
34 sovereignty is demonstrated:
35 _____
36 _____
37 _____
38 _____
39
40
41

Chapter 2
The Pilgrims, the Mayflower Compact, and the First Thanksgiving in America

Attention must now be turned to the first settlers in the American colonies, in what will become the United States, to examine these settlers' and the Bible's influences in this new land. In particular, attention must be paid to the Pilgrims who arrived in 1620 and who planted some of the first seeds of Judeo-Christian thought and principles for the growth of a new nation. The Pilgrims by their Mayflower Compact—as well as the other Puritan groups that arrived soon after—activated in their new colonies the Bible-inspired principles of popular sovereignty, God's sovereignty, covenants, and self-government. These Bible-based principles became foundational to the early American colonies and ultimately to the new nation of the United States of America.

2.1 A Royal Charter for the Colony of Virginia

The Pilgrims were not the first settlers in what would become the original thirteen colonies of the United States. In 1606, King James I of England, prompted in part by Spain's and France's expansion in the New World, granted a royal charter to the Virginia Company of London to establish the colony of Virginia in North America. The company's charter laid out its goals to claim part of the continent, establish a new settlement, search for gold, civilize the natives, propagate the Christian religion to the natives, and find a route to Asia.[62] While the company's mission was largely motivated by commerce, the king also instructed the company to develop governing councils and to set up the Church of England in the new colony.[63] The colony of Virginia would become the first of the thirteen colonies that would become part of the United States of America.

Founded in 1607, Jamestown became the first permanent settlement in Virginia. The Virginia Company established the Anglican Church of England in the new settlement. Religious observances and church services were regularly practiced and conducted in Jamestown according to royal authority and out of personal conviction by some settlers.

In 1619, the colonists in Jamestown formed, according to their rights as Englishmen, a two-house or bicameral representative assembly to govern their colony. It would become the first bicameral assembly in America. The Virginia assembly was based on the British Westminster model of government—a monarchy in which the king and his councilors composed one house of government and a Parliament of representatives composed another house. This form was also practiced within Britain's Church of England. Similarly in Virginia, the governor, representing the king, and his councilors composed one house of the governing assembly while elected burgesses made up another house. A "burgess" was an elected or appointed representative of a town. Though limited in power since the Virginia Company could overrule its actions, this two-house assembly with its House of Burgesses also became the first form of representative government in America.

Also in 1619, the first African slaves were brought to Virginia for crop labor. Thus began the practice of slavery in the American colonies. Slavery was a moral as well as social-political issue with which many Americans struggled and contended in the colonies and future nation. Some colonies ended or attempted to end slavery during the Revolutionary era of the mid 1700s, but the issue would not be completely resolved in the new nation until the American Civil War of the 1800s.

When Virginia became a royal colony in 1624, it implemented a social-political system that combined church and civil government, as was typical at that time and historically in Europe. The Church of England became the official church of the colony, and, as such, the colony's civil government raised taxes to support the church and its clergy. The colonial government also regulated Christian morality through religious laws since the colony founders believed that religious uniformity promoted a moral, orderly society. Other bothersome religious sects and denominations were not permitted in the colony. Settlers generally accepted the authority of the Church of England and believed it represented the true Christian faith. Though the expression of Christian morality was lacking in many ways in the practices of many early colonists in Virginia, the colony would establish to a certain extent the presence and traditions of the Christian church in its culture and society.

2.2 The Pilgrims Come to America For Religious Freedom and Identify with the Israelites

Though Britain's Church of England, which had been under the Roman Catholic Church for centuries, implemented some moderate reforms and became Anglican Protestant during the Reformation, some English Protestants did not believe its reforms went far enough. The Reformation had given rise to a devout, austere group of Christians in England who called for more radical reform and purification of the Church of England. The "Puritans," as they were called, wanted to purify the church from within. They wanted to expel from the church what they saw as heresy and corruption in the church's doctrine and worship practices. One remnant of this group, though, believed the church was too corrupt to be restored, and they separated from it altogether. These "Separatists," as they were called, refused to conform to the church. King James and the Church of England would not tolerate their position, and the king declared, "I will make them conform themselves, or I will harrie them out of the land, or else do worse."[64] The Separatists' movement was outlawed, so a small group met secretly in a home in Scrooby, England. Then, to escape harassment, they moved to Leyden, Holland. Disillusioned by hardship and the secular society of Holland, they ultimately set sail for America after gaining permission from England to go to Virginia. They would become known as the Pilgrims. The Pilgrims' migration across the Atlantic on the *Mayflower* vessel in 1620 would prove to be an historic move.

The Pilgrims' primary reason for coming to America was religious freedom. They wanted freedom to believe and worship without harassment or persecution. The Pilgrims' concept of religious freedom was like others' of their time. They envisioned religious freedom in a community with a combined state and church and in which all those in their community shared the same beliefs and practices. Their concept did not mean tolerance of differing religious teachings and practices which they deemed a disturbance to the public order. Still, the Pilgrims, all freely sharing the same beliefs, sought freedom in America to set up their own uniform church and community as they chose. As early French historian Alexis de Tocqueville notes in his well-known 1835 observations of America, titled *Democracy in America*, the Pilgrims sought "some rude and unfrequented part of the world, where they could live according to their own opinions, and worship God in freedom...."[65] The Pilgrims also hoped, in the process, to advance the Gospel of Jesus Christ.[66]

In their voyage to America, the Pilgrims compared themselves to the Israelites in the Old Testament of the Bible. The Israelites, also known as Hebrews or Jews, were God's chosen people. In the book of Exodus, they escape from bondage in Egypt with God's help, wander in the desert wilderness, renew their covenant with God at Mount Sinai, and claim the Promised Land of Canaan. In his journal, *The History of Plymouth Settlement*, Pilgrim leader William Bradford compares the Pilgrim's voyage to America with the Israelites' migration:

Our fathers were Englishmen who came over the great ocean, and were ready to perish in this wilderness; but they cried unto the Lord, and He heard their voice, and looked on their adversity.... ... Yea, let them that have been redeemed of the Lord, show how He hath delivered them from the hand of the oppressor. When they wandered forth into the desert-wilderness, out of the way, and found no city to dwell in, both hungry and thirsty, their soul was overwhelmed in them. Let them confess before the Lord His loving kindess, and His wonderful works before the sons of men.[67]

Like the Israelites' Exodus from Egypt, the Pilgrims had left what they saw as an oppressive, degraded situation in Europe in order to create a new life in America. They were God's people, and America was their Promised Land.

2.3 The Pilgrims' God as Creator, Provider, and Supreme Ruler/Judge

Like other Christians, the Pilgrims and Puritans, were monotheists, believing in one God—the God of the Bible. This God, all-knowing and all-powerful, acts as Creator, Provider, and Supreme Ruler/Judge of the world. He is, as one reformer described Calvin's God, "the Creator, Preserver, and Governor of the world, and of every thing contained in it."[68]

The God of the Bible acts firstly as Creator. In Genesis 1 and 2, God creates the heavens, earth, creatures, and mankind. Notably, God creates Adam and Eve as the first man and woman, the beginning of the human race. God makes the human race unlike anything else in all creation. For God uniquely creates humans in His own image and likeness and gives them His direct breath of life, as found in Genesis 1:26-27 and Genesis 2:7. Genesis 1:26-27 states, "Then God said, 'Let Us make man in Our image, according to our likeness....' So God created man in His *own* image; in the image of God He created them; male and female He created them." Genesis 2:7 states, "And the LORD formed man *of* the dust of the ground, and breathed into his nostrils the breath of life; and man became a living being." As such, humans resembled God in their attributes and abilities of body and soul. They were God's representatives and reflection on earth. Moreover, just as God's life is immortal, humans also possessed immortal souls. The prophet Isaiah describes God as Creator in Isaiah 42:5: "Thus says God the Lord, Who created the heavens and stretched them out, Who spread forth the earth and that which comes from it, Who gives breath to the people on it, And spirit to those who walk on it...." Calvin refers to God as "Creator of heaven and earth" and "Creator and Architect of the world."[69] Even the Deists shared the view of God as Creator. The Deists, who gain prominence during the Enlightenment era of the 1600s and 1700s, believed in the Creator's existence as revealed by nature, though not by scriptural or divine revelation. God the Creator would be conspicuously acknowledged by the American Founders' in the United States' Declaration of Independence which states that all men "are endowed by their Creator with certain unalienable Rights...."

The Bible's God also acts as Provider. God as Provider fulfills the needs of mankind and His people. In the Old Testament, in Genesis 22, for example, God tests Abraham and instructs him to sacrifice his beloved son, Isaac, as a burnt offering. As father and son make their way to Mount Moriah for the sacrifice, Isaac asks about the offering, and Abraham replies with a statement about God's provision. Genesis 22:7-8 states, "Then he [Isaac] said, 'Look, the fire and the wood, but where *is* the lamb for a burnt offering?' And Abraham said, 'My son, God will provide for Himself the lamb for a burnt offering.'" Ultimately, in Genesis 22:13-14, as Abraham is about to slay Isaac, God halts the act and provides Abraham with a ram to sacrifice in place of the boy. Abraham calls the place "Jehovah-Jireh," which means in Hebrew "The Lord Will Provide."[70] In the New Testament, God provides His Son Jesus Christ as the ultimate sacrifice to redeem mankind from sin and eternal death. In 1 Corinthians 5:7, the Apostle Paul says, "Christ, our Passover, was sacrificed for us," and in Ephesians 5:2 he says, "Christ also has loved us and given Himself for us, an offering and a sacrifice to God...." In accordance with God's nature in the Bible, many early Americans referred to God as "Divine Providence." "Providence," derived from the word "provide," referred to God's overseeing of earthly events for His purposes and to meet human needs. Early Puritan writings supported this description from the Bible. For example, in his widely-read 1623 summary of Calvinism, entitled *Marrow of Theology*, Puritan William Ames alludes to Ephesians 1:11 to describe Providence as "the efficiency whereby he [God] provides for existing creatures in all things in accordance with the counsel of his will."[71] Similarly, in Ephesians 1:11, the Apostle Paul tells the church that they are "predestined according to the purpose of Him [God] who works all things according to the counsel of His will." Citing additional verses, Ames says that Providence is God's direct or indirect provision for His creatures.[72] It preserved God's creatures and governs them to their proper end.[73] The idea of Providence instilled in the Pilgrims and early Americans a belief that God would assist them in their godly endeavors. It gave them profound trust in God and great courage to face difficult challenges. The Pilgrims, for example, sought God's direction and aid in their voyage to America and in founding their new colony. Later, revolutionary-era Americans would rely heavily on God's provision during the American Revolution.

The God of the Bible further acts as Supreme Ruler or Judge of the world. As Supreme Ruler and Judge, God rules above all earthly authorities, and all humans are subjects of His earthly kingdom. He is "King of kings and Lord of lords" according to 1 Timothy 6:15, Revelation 17:14, and Revelation 19:16.[74] Psalm 97:1 affirms God's supreme rule over the earth: "The Lord reigns; Let the earth rejoice; Let the multitude of isles be glad!" The Pilgrims and Puritans, like other Christians, recognized God's supreme authority or "sovereignty" over all humans and earthly realms. God's sovereignty meant that all earthly spheres, institutions, and jurisdictions—including church, civil state or government, family, and individual—are under God's rule and law. Though these earthly spheres are distinct from one another, they are each accountable to God. The principle of God's sovereignty contrasted with some humanistic views that humans supremely rule in the place of God in the earthly realms.

Brutus' *Vindiciae* upholds the idea of God as Supreme Ruler and Judge from the Bible—citing Isaiah 48:11 and Psalm 2. In Isaiah 48:11, God says through the prophet Isaiah, "I will not give My glory to another," and in Psalm 2:9, God tells His Son, "You shall break them [the nations] with a rod of iron." Brutus elaborates on these verses, saying, "God never divests Himself of His power and authority. He holds a scepter in one hand to restrain raging kings and crush defiant ones, and in the other a pair of scales in order to weigh those who distribute right inequitably.... No more certain insignia of supreme command could be given." [75] Brutus also supports God's sovereignty based on Proverbs 8 and Job 12. Proverbs 8:15-16 conveys the words of God's Wisdom: "By me kings reign, And rulers decree justice. By me princes rule, and nobles, All the judges of the earth." Brutus explains from these verses God's sovereignty over all earthly authority:

> ...the Holy Scriptures teach that God rules by His own authority, but kings as if by sufferance of another....: God by Himself, and kings through God: that God exercises his own jurisdiction, but kings only a delegated one. ...that God's jurisdiction is immeasurable, whilst that of kings is measured; that God's sway...is infinite, whilst that of kings is limited; that the kingdom of God is not circumscribed by any frontiers, whilst on the contrary those of kings are restricted to specific regions and bounded by certain boundaries....[76]

This Bible-based view of God's sovereignty affected the early Pilgrims' and Puritans' religious and political views and their recognition of God as highest authority in various spheres of society like church and civil government. The Pilgrims believed in God's earthly rule over creation and nature, the human spirit, and human history. Though the world rebels against God's rule, obedience to it, they believed, produces blessing.[77] God as Supreme Judge, they further believed, rewards or punishes humans in this or the next life based on their decisions and actions in relation to God's rule and moral law. In his 1659 *A Holy Commonwealth*, English Puritan minister Richard Baxter strikingly expresses how God is Creator King over all men. He writes, "The World then is a Kingdom whereof God is the King, and the form of the Government is...an absolute Monarchy...with...Dominion or propriety of persons and things, by the Title of Creation,"[78] and "All men as men are the subjects of God's Kingdom, as to Obligation and Duty, and God will not ask the consent of any man to be so obliged."[79]

Moreover, the Pilgrims and Puritans as Christians also specifically expressed God in Christ's rule in the church. Pilgrim pastor Rev. John Robinson, for example, acknowledges Christ "as absolute and as entire a King as he is a Priest" in the church.[80] Puritan minister Rev. Thomas Hooker of Connecticut acknowledges Christ's headship in the church based on Isaiah 33:22 which states, "For the LORD *is* our Judge, The LORD *is* our Lawgiver, The LORD *is* our King; He will save us...." In his 1648 defense of the Puritan Congregational Church, known as the *Survey of the Summe of Church Discipline*, he writes, "The Church is the visible Kingdome in which Christ reigns, by the scepter of his word and ordinances, and the execution of discipline. To whomsoever he is a Head, over them he will be King. He is our King; He is our Lawgiver."[81] Other Puritans upheld Christ's headship based on other scriptures like 1 Kings 8:57-59, Acts 5:31, and Isaiah 9:6.[82]

The Pilgrims' belief in God as Supreme Ruler influenced their approach to forming a civil body in America. They acknowledged God as the highest authority in their charter, the Mayflower Compact. They validated their charter by God's authority, rather than by an earthly king's—"solemnly and mutually in the presence of God, and of one another." This validation became the sanction for their new colony. In coming to America, the Pilgrims and Puritans actually hoped to set up in some ways, though imperfect, God's kingdom rule on earth.[83] The Pilgrims' recognition of God's sovereignty set an important precedent for the direction of the Puritan colonies in New England and, ultimately, for the founding of the new nation. The American Founders would later also appeal to the "Supreme Judge of the world" in the Declaration of Independence.

2.4 The Mayflower Compact: The Pilgrims Practice Popular Sovereignty and Form of a Civil Body Under God

While the Pilgrims initially intended to sail to Virginia, upon arrival in America, they found themselves north of their destination and outside of England's colonial jurisdiction and charter. Realizing they were outside chartered territory, some non-Pilgrims or "strangers" on board the *Mayflower* talked of leaving the group and venturing out on their own. But the Pilgrims had selected every man on the trip according to his particular skills. They depended on one another for survival. So, while aboard the *Mayflower* vessel, they made an unprecedented decision to draft and sign their own charter. The Mayflower Compact, as it became known, was a written agreement or covenant among themselves under God to create a civil body and to enact just laws in their new colony of Plymouth. It was the first self-governing document of their colony. The contract, signed on November 11, 1620, by all heads of households, Pilgrims and non-Pilgrims alike, states:

> In the name of God. Amen. **We whose names are underwritten**, the loyal subjects of our dread Sovereign Lord, King James, by the grace of God, of Great Britain, France, and Ireland king, defender of the faith, etc., having undertaken, for the glory of God, and advancement of the Christian faith, and honor of our King and country, a voyage to plant the first colony in the Northern parts of Virginia, **do by these presents solemnly and mutually in the presence of God, and one of another, covenant and combine ourselves together into a civil body politic**, for our better ordering and preservation and furtherance of the ends aforesaid; and by virtue hereof to enact, constitute, and frame such just and equal laws, ordinances, acts, constitutions, and offices, from time to time, as shall be thought most meet and convenient for the general good of the Colony, unto which we promise all due submission and obedience. In witness whereof we have hereunder subscribed our names at Cape Cod the 11th of November, in the year of the reign of our sovereign lord, King James, of England, France, and Ireland the eighteenth, and of Scotland the fifty-fourth. Anno Domini 1620.[84]

By their Compact, the Pilgrims practiced popular sovereignty because they authorized the creation of a new civil body and colony—not by an absolute ruler but by the consensual agreement of those in their group. As with many reformers, their religious views inevitably affected their political views. Tocqueville affirms that Puritanism "was not merely a religious doctrine, but it corresponded in many points with the most absolute democratic and republican theories."[85] To be sure, the Pilgrims and Puritans, some historians note, did not see themselves as political protesters. They simply sought to be loyal to God's government in the world.[86] Seeing God's authority as residing in the people, the Pilgrims and Puritans, as Tocqueville describes, "continually exercised the rights of sovereignty; they named their magistrates, concluded peace or declared war, made police regulations, and enacted laws, as if their allegiance was due only to God."[87]

2.5 The Pilgrims Practice Biblical Covenants

In signing the Mayflower Compact, the Pilgrims applied the principle of covenants in the founding of their new colony. A covenant is a voluntary, moral agreement or pact between two or more free parties, usually for a religious or civil purpose. It is secured by an oath or promise. This binding agreement centered on the relationship between the parties involved and defines the responsibilities of the relationship. Each party in the pact promised to fulfill certain conditions. If one party breached the terms of the covenant, the injured party was released from its obligations.[88] A covenant could be made between humans and a higher authority like God or king. Or it could be made among humans who validate it by the higher authority of God or king who acts as a witness, sanctioner, or guarantor. "In its heart of hearts," says Daniel Elazar, "a covenant is an agreement in which a higher moral force, traditionally God, is either a direct party to or a guarantor of a particular relationship."[89] Covenants were often enacted when founding a new people or nation.[90] 13

With the help of the Reformation, the Bible—which tells the story of the ancient Israelites in the Old Testament and the early Christians in the New Testament—was the inspiration for the Pilgrims' use of covenants.[91] For in the Bible—which the Pilgrims read as God's inerrant Word—God often related with His people through covenants. The Israelites, in turn, often related with their rulers through these agreements. In the New Testament, the Christians entered into a spiritual covenant with God through Jesus Christ to become God's "new covenant" people. The Reformation had revived and articulated covenants as not only a religious but a political practice. The Pilgrims were undoubtedly influenced by these sources.

A brief look at some covenants in the Old Testament reveals their importance to the Israelites—and thus to the Pilgrims and Puritans in early America—as they relate with God, their rulers, and one another. Some scholars consider the first covenant in the Bible to be an implicit one between God and all mankind—found in Genesis 1 and 2.[92] As mentioned, in Genesis 1:26-28, God creates Adam and Eve as the first man and woman. Before their fall, God covenants with Adam and Eve, who represent all mankind. He expects them to obey His commands. God gives Adam a command and warning in the Garden of Eden in Genesis 2:15-17: "Then the LORD God took the man and put him in the garden of Eden to tend and keep it. And the LORD God commanded the man, saying, 'Of every tree of the garden you may freely eat; but of the tree of the knowledge of good and evil you shall not eat, for in the day that you eat of it you shall surely die.'" God also instills in mankind a moral and natural law, a Law of Love, by which they are to live with God and one another. Thus mankind is obligated at creation to keep God's law. God expects humans to honor His commands, carry out their duties, and follow His law as a kind of creation covenant. In this "covenant of works" based on human effort and righteousness, God promises mankind eternal life for obedience and eternal death for disobedience to His commands.[93] The Westminster Confession of 1646 acknowledges this creation covenant: "God gave Adam a law as a covenant of works, by which he bound him and all his posterity to personal, entire, exact and perpetual obedience, promised life upon the fulfillment, and threatened death upon the breach of it; and endued him with power and ability to keep it."[94] Unfortunately, Adam and Eve disobey God in the Garden of Eden in Genesis 3. Their disobedience leads to a break in their relationship with God, the fall and corruption of mankind, mankind's imperfect expression of God on earth, and death. While this covenant is still considered to be in effect today, it only serves to expose man's sinfulness and depravity.

After the fall of mankind, God institutes a new "covenant of grace" based not on human performance but on God's promise and on a person's faith in the promise. Later in Genesis, God covenants with faithful Abraham. Because Abraham has faith in God and His promises, and obeys Him accordingly, God responds in turn. Abraham's faith in God is attributed to him as righteousness. Genesis 15:6 says, "And he [Abraham] believed in the LORD, and He [God] accounted it to him for righteousness." In Genesis 15, 17, and 22, God promises that Abraham will become "a father of many nations," inherit the land of Canaan, and have a son with his barren wife, Sarah, in their old age. Genesis 17:1-14 reveals this covenant in which God says to Abraham,

I will make My covenant between Me and you, and will multiply you exceedingly. … As for Me, behold, My covenant is with you, and you shall be a father of many nations. … And I will establish My covenant between Me and you and your descendants after you. Also I give to you and your descendants after you the land in which you are a stranger, all the land of Canaan, as an everlasting possession; and I will be their God. … As for you, you shall keep My covenant, you and your descendants after you throughout their generations. This is My covenant which you shall keep, between Me and you and your descendants after you: Every male child among you shall be circumcised…and it shall be a sign of the covenant between Me and you.

Abraham believes God's promises. God seals His covenant with Abraham and his descendants, the Israelites, who become God's chosen people. Following God's command, Abraham circumcises every male in his household as a sign of this covenant.[95] True to His word, God provides Abraham and Sarah with a son, Isaac. When God tests Abraham, instructing him to sacrifice his son, Isaac, at Mount Moriah, Abraham again prepares to obey. But God stops the act and provides an animal for the sacrifice instead. For Abraham's complete faith and devotion, God reafffirms His covenant with Abraham in Genesis 22:15-18, responding, "I will multiply your descendants as the stars of the heaven and as the sand which is on the seashore" and "In your seed all the nations of the earth shall be blessed."[96]

Centuries later, God renews the Abrahamic covenant with Abraham's descendants—Moses and the Israelites—who have become very numerous. The Israelites receive from God at Mount Sinai the specific words or terms of this covenant to be God's people. These terms—the Ten Commandments—are written on stone tablets and part of God's moral law. This covenant renewal occurs after God frees the Israelites from bondage in Egypt where they have been held captive as slaves for 400 years. It is found in Exodus 20 and 34.[97] In the Ten Commandments, found in Exodus 20:1-17 of the Old Testament, God commands that His people have no other gods, make no idols, do not take His name in vain, keep the Sabbath rest, honor their fathers and mothers, do not murder, do not commit adultery, do not steal, do not bear false witness against their neighbors, and do not covet their neighbors.[98] In Exodus 34:27, God tells Moses to "'Write these words, for according to the tenor of these words I have made a covenant with you and with Israel.'"[99] Subsequently, the people of Israel enact covenants with their rulers in their nation to honor God and His commands. Their rulers agree to honor God's moral laws and rule justly, and the people agree to loyally submit to them. This practice of civil covenants between people and ruler in Israel later became important for the political reformers of the Reformation as well as the early Americans.

In the New Testament, God completes the new "covenant of grace" with all believers—both Jew and Gentile—through the mediator Jesus Christ. Both Old and New Testaments actually speak of the new covenant based not on human works but on God's covenant of redemption for those who simply have faith in Him. In the Old Testament, Christians note, the prophet Jeremiah speaks in Jeremiah 31:31-34 of a new covenant to come— written by God's spirit not on stone but on human hearts.[100] Jeremiah 31:31-34 states,

Behold, the days are coming, says the LORD, when I will make a new covenant with the house of Israel and with the house of Judah— not according to the covenant that I made with their fathers in the day *that* I took them by the hand to lead them out of the land of Egypt, My covenant which they broke, though I was a husband to them, says the LORD. But this *is* the covenant that I will make with the house of Israel after those days, says the LORD: I will put My law in their minds, and write it on their hearts; and I will be their God, and they shall be My people. No more shall every man teach his neighbor, and every man his brother, saying, 'Know the LORD,' for they all shall know Me, from the least of them to the greatest of them, says the LORD. For I will forgive their iniquity, and their sin I will remember no more.

1   The New Testament also speaks of a new covenant. In this covenant, Jesus Christ—deemed the Son of God
2   and the perfect man—fulfills God's law since God's people do not fulfill it due to their sinfulness and
3   imperfection. Indeed, by the law the people's sins are exposed, and they are justly sentenced to eternal death.
4   But Christ, as the perfect Lamb of God, acts as the ultimate substitute and sacrifice to redeem all mankind.
5   When Christ is crucified on the cross, the sin of the world transfers to Him, and He dies in the place of all
6   humans. Now, all humans can be free from eternal death and made spiritually alive simply by their faith in
7   Christ. Jesus Christ declares this new covenant when he offers wine to his disciples as a symbol of his
8   redemptive blood for mankind. Matthew 26:27-28 states, "Then He [Jesus] took the cup, and gave thanks, and
9   gave *it* to them [disciples], saying, 'Drink from it, all of you. For this is My blood of the new covenant, which
10 is shed for many for the remission of sins.'"[101] Hebrews 9:15 also reveals the new covenant: "And for this
11 reason He [Jesus] is the Mediator of the new covenant, by means of death, for the redemption of the
12 transgressions under the first covenant, that those who are called may receive the promise of the eternal
13 inheritance." In Romans 2:29, the Apostle Paul, echoing Jeremiah, says the new covenant is engraved in the
14 hearts of believers, sealed by a spiritual circumcision of the heart. Paul writes that "he is a Jew who is one
15 inwardly; and circumcision is that of the heart, in the Spirit, not in the letter...."[102] In this new "covenant of
16 grace" a person receives spiritual salvation and eternal life through faith in Jesus Christ.
17
18   The covenants in the Bible demonstrate the means by which God often relates with humans and how
19 humans may effectively and positively relate with one another. Covenants are a necessary practice that enables
20 fallible humans to secure mutual commitments to and from God as well as to and from one another. They result
21 in positive partnerships and outcomes. Civil covenants, some scholars point out, allow people in a community
22 to set up order and principles that will protect their rights and the cooperative, consensual exercise of power.[103]
23 When such binding agreements are upheld, they are a source of blessings. When they are broken, negative
24 consequences may result.
25
26   Covenants, as the reformers described them and as seen in the Bible, are normally enacted by free,
27 consenting parties. In the Bible, God only covenants with His people when they are free from bondage—
28 whether it be physical, political, or spiritual. In the Old Testament, God covenants with obedient Abraham
29 when Abraham is a nomadic freeman. God renews His covenant with the Israelites only after He has freed
30 them from captivity in Egypt. In the New Testament, God enters into a new covenant with those who by faith
31 in Christ become free from the spiritual bondage of sin and death. For Paul tells the church in Galatians 5:1,
32 "Stand fast therefore in the liberty by which Christ has made us free, and do not be entangled again with a yoke
33 of bondage." The covenant, says Elazar, "presupposes the independence and worth of each individual and the
34 truth that each person possesses certain inalienable rights, because only free people with rights can enter into
35 agreements with one another."[104] Only a free, consenting people can be responsible and accountable for making
36 and keeping a covenant. Covenants, therefore, assume the consent of the parties involved. Like popular
37 sovereignty, then, covenants further support the idea, as later found in the United States' Declaration of
38 Independence, that government derives just power from the "consent of the governed."
39
40   The ancient Biblical practice of covenants spread to other parts of the world through Jewish dispersion.
41 It led to the practice of covenant-based charters, contracts, and corporations in medieval Europe.[105] Charters—
42 agreements between people and king—were civil covenants. The Magna Carta or "Great Charter" of 1215, for
43 instance, was a civil covenant between Britain's king and subjects which secured certain rights for the people.
44 The charter for Virginia was also a civil covenant, being signed under the royal seal of the British Crown.
45 Notably, the practice of covenants expanded during the Protestant Reformation. During that movement,
46 reformers developed a covenant-based theology and political philosophy that impacted ideas of church, state,
47 and society.

1   The reformers were among the first of the modern era to write about Biblical covenants. German
2 reformer Johannes Oecolampadius was one of the first to do so. In 1525, he pointed out the creation covenant
3 between God and humans in Genesis.[106] Swiss reformer Heinrich Bullinger wrote one of the first books in the
4 church on covenants in 1534—entitled *A Brief Exposition of the One and Eternal Testament or Covenant of*
5 *God*. In it he defines the Biblical covenant and its basis in God's moral law, and he identifies the faithful seed
6 of Abraham as God's covenant people.[107]   Bullinger developed a "Covenant Theology," also known as
7 "Federalism." The word "federal" comes from the Latin word *foedus* which means "covenant."[108] Covenant
8 Theology asserts that all creation, humans, and human society—including civil government and politics—exist
9 in covenant with God and are subject to God's moral laws.[109]
10
11   Soon after Covenant Theology emerged, the idea of political or *civil* covenants also emerged in the
12 writings of the political reformers. The principle of *civil* covenants would be further developed as various
13 political thinkers of the Reformation era and after justified arguments for civil resistance against tyranny.
14 Theodore Beza, scholar and disciple of Calvin, recognized in his 1574 *On the Rights of Magistrates* a political
15 covenant that exists among people, rulers, and God. This covenant is a "twofold obligation." The first part of
16 this agreement is between God and people—in which both king and people promise to follow God's law. The
17 second part is between ruler and people—in which the king promises to rule justly and the people promise to
18 obey.[110] With this civil covenant, the ruler is accountable to the people, not just to God. If the king does not
19 abide by the terms of the covenant, the people may dethrone him.[111] Beza bases this civil covenant, in part, on
20 the Israelites' practices in the Bible. He cites the election of David as king in 2 Samuel 5:1-4 and the history of
21 King Joash in 2 Kings 11:4, 17 to support such covenants. 2 Samuel 5:3 tells of how David is made king by
22 covenant with the people: "Therefore all the elders of Israel came to the king at Hebron, and King David made
23 a covenant with them at Hebron before the LORD. And they anointed David king over Israel." 2 Kings 11—just
24 as 2 Chronicles 22-23—tells of how Athaliah usurps the throne unlawfully and is overthrown by the people.
25 The people authorize the rightful king by covenanting with young King Joash. 2 Kings 11:17 tells of the two-
26 fold covenant made among God, King Joash, and people as declared by the prophet Jehoiada: "Then Jehoiada
27 [the prophet of God] made a covenant between the LORD, the king [Joash], and the people, that they should be
28 the LORD's people, and *also* between the king and the people." Beza further supports the idea that the people
29 may dethrone a ruler who violates this covenant based on the overthrow of Athaliah for violating the civil
30 covenant with absolute rule and tyranny.
31
32   A few years after Beza's work was published, Brutus's 1579 political tract *Vindiciae* appeared with
33 more in-depth discussion about civil covenants in the civil state and society. Brutus elaborated on the two-fold
34 covenant between God, king, and people.[112] He also based civil covenants largely on the Bible and the practice
35 of the Israelites.[113] Just as Beza, Brutus supports the two-fold covenant from 2 Kings 11:17 and 2 Samuel 5:3,
36 among other verses. In such a covenant, says Brutus, God may judge the people if they breach their first
37 agreement to follow God's laws, while the people may judge the king for breach of the second agreement to
38 rule justly. If the king becomes unjust or tyrannical, the people may resist him. Breach of the second
39 agreement makes the agreement void, its obligations annulled.[114] After the release of the widely-read *Vindiciae*,
40 other writings affirmed civil covenants. In his 1593 *Laws of Ecclesiastical Polity*, Anglican clergyman Richard
41 Hooker affirmed the idea that rulers and subjects are bound by a compact.[115] In 1613, Francisco Suarez also
42 maintained in his *Defense of the Catholic Faith* that a king's power depends on a contract between ruler and
43 people.[116] In 1644, Presbyterian covenanter Rutherford similarly addressed covenants among God, king, and
44 people in his *Lex Rex*. He upheld the idea, based on scripture and reason, that kings are bound in covenant with
45 the people. Rulers are, therefore, accountable to the people, not just to God.[117]
46
47   Also during this time, in 1603, German Christian philosopher and political theorist Johannes Althusius
48 explicitly articulated the first comprehensive covenant-based political theory in his landmark work *Politica*
49 *Methodice Digesta—Politics Arranged Methodically* or *Politics Methodically Set Forth*.[118] In his theory, he

1 affirms that the people of a civil state hold civil power. He then asserts that the state and society are based on
2 covenantal agreements. Contracts in society start as simple ones in the single family and lead to more complex
3 ones in a province and state among people and leaders/government. Towns and provinces, for instance, are
4 formed by consentual associations. A state or commonwealth is a product of contracts between towns and
5 provinces.[119] Althusius' theory centers primarily on the God-infused commitments that link humans together in
6 order to create and maintain a harmonious, productive society. It views civil law as important but secondary—
7 the result of covenant relationships.[120] Covenants are naturally supported, he thought, by the fact that God, in
8 creating people with varying skills and aptitudes, binds people together by their need for one another.
9 Furthermore, politics allows people's abilities to be used to better society.[121] To support his theory, Althusius
10 combined Biblical, Roman, and common law using faith, reason, and experience. Notably, he drew largely
11 from the Bible, Covenant Theology, and *Vindiciae*.[122] Althusius' work became foundational, say some
12 scholars, to modern political thought on federalism and government in nations around the world.[123]
13
14 **Beza, Brutus, and Althusius were some of the first—if not *the* first—of the modern era to present**
15 **Bible-based civil covenants—a covenant-based theory for the civil state. Their ideas along with Covenant**
16 **Theology affected Western political thought. Covenant Theology or Federalism became part of Western**
17 **Judeo-Christian tradition.[124] The principle of civil covenants, say some scholars, became the basis for a**
18 **political theory of human rights.[125] Covenants provided a framework within which human rights were**
19 **protected. The concept was embraced by the Pilgrims and Puritans in the early American colonies.**
20 **Later, it would also be taken up and secularized by John Locke—who was influenced by Richard Hooker**
21 **and Rutherford—and, ultimately, by the American Founders when they created the federal government**
22 **of the United States.**
23
24 The Pilgrims applied the principle of covenants to form their new colony of Plymouth in America.
25 When the Pilgrims arrived in America, landing at Plymouth Rock, they were without a royal charter from the
26 British Crown. To found their new colony and to secure their religious freedom, they formed a civil covenant
27 among themselves before God—known as the Mayflower Compact. They had already practiced religious
28 covenants in their churches since they followed the Biblical covenants and covenant theology.[126] But now, for
29 the first time, they created a civil covenant, calling on God as witness.[127] The Mayflower Compact, which they
30 referred to as the "Plymouth Combination," states their act to "solemnly and mutually in the presence of God,
31 and one of another, covenant and combine ourselves together into a civil body politic." This civil agreement
32 was not merely a practical matter to create a civil body. By this act, the Pilgrims saw God as authorizing or
33 validating the founding of their colony. Early American statesman Daniel Webster observed that the Pilgrim's
34 pact invokes "a *religious* sanction and the authority of God on their *civil* obligations...."[128] The Mayflower
35 Compact was the first covenantal act in the American colonies. It would become the foundation for future civil
36 laws and constitutions and a precedent for the United States' Declaration of Independence as a national
37 compact.[129] The use of covenants in early America clearly reveals the Judeo-Christian roots of America's
38 heritage.
39
40 **2.6 The Pilgrims Create a Civil Self-Government**
41
42 The Pilgrims' Mayflower Compact differed from other charters in an important way. For while charters
43 were typically made between two politically unequal parties—king and people, ruler(s) and subjects—the
44 Mayflower Compact was made among persons of equal position in the group or community.[130] As such, it was
45 a strikingly new, democratic initiative of self-government among equals. "What was remarkable about this
46 particular contract," explains Paul Johnson, "was that it was not between a servant and a master, or a people and
47 a king, but between a group of like-minded individuals and each other, with God as a witness and symbolic co-
48 signatory."[131] The Pilgrims' covenant or compact created a *civil* self-government to govern their new colony *by*
49 *themselves*, under God. Such self-governing civil states did not exist at that time in the world. In attributing

authority to God and assuming equality and rights of humans under that authority, the compact was, as affirmed by some early American historians, rooted in Christian belief.[132]

The Pilgrims created their civil self-government largely based on their experience with church self-government. The Pilgrims' civil self-government, explains George Cheever, came from the "congregational independence and self-government under Christ" which they had practiced for many years in their self-governing or "congregational" churches.[133] They also based it on ideas that stemmed from the Reformation era including the Bible-based principles of popular sovereignty and covenants—both of which supported the idea of "the consent of the governed."

Some reformers had, in a sense, advocated for church self-government in their writings. Luther had argued for the right of church members to call councils for church accountability, reform, and correction. Citing Matthew 18:15-17, Luther says that all members are accountable to the Bible, to one another, and to the church. Furthermore, members are called to assemble to address issues in the church. Matthew 18:15-17, which references Deuteronomy 19:15, states,

> Moreover if your brother sins against you, go and tell him his fault between you and him alone. If he hears you, you have gained your brother. But if he will not hear, take with you one or two more, that "by the mouth of two or three witnesses every word may be established." And if he refuses to hear them, tell *it* to the church. But if he refuses even to hear the church, let him be to you like a heathen and a tax collector.

Luther consequently observes, "This passage commands each member to exercise concern for his fellow; much more is it our duty when the wrongdoer is one who rules over us all alike, and who causes much harm and offence to the rest by his conduct. And if I am to lay a charge against him before the church, then I must call it together."[134] Luther also cites 2 Corinthians 10:8 in which the Apostle Paul says to the church, "For even if I should boast somewhat more about our [Paul and Timothy's] authority, which the Lord gave us for edification and not for your destruction, I shall not be ashamed…." Citing this verse, Luther points out,

> No one in Christendom has authority to do evil, or to forbid evil from being resisted. The church has no authority except to promote the greater good. Hence, if the pope should exercise his authority to prevent a free council, and so hinder the reform of the church, we ought to pay no regard to him and his authority. … …for this authority of his would be presumptuous and empty. He does not possess it, and he would fall an easy victim to a passage of Scripture; for Paul says to the Corinthians, "For God gave us authority, not to cast down Christendom, but to build it up" [II Cor. 10:8].[135]

In his view of members' right and responsibility to call together the church to address church matters, Luther essentially demonstrates support for self-government. For the members are responsible for overseeing and governing the church.

Civil self-government had been encouraged by Rev. Robinson who drew from the Bible and the principles of popular sovereignty and covenants. In his farewell letter sent with the Pilgrims to America, Robinson, echoing Deuteronomy 1:13 and Romans 13:1-5, instructed the Pilgrims to set up a colonial civil self-government similar to that of their churches—characterized by equal standing among men, chosen godly magistrates, and obedience to chosen officials who are "Gods ordinance for your good." Robinson exhorts,

> Lastly, whereas you are to become a body politic, administering among yourselves civil government, and are furnished with persons of no special eminence above the rest, from whom you will elect some to the office of government, let your wisdom and godliness appear, not only in choosing such persons as

will entirely love and promote the common good, but also in yielding them all due honour and obedience in their lawful administrations; not beholding in them the ordinariness of their persons, but **God's ordinance for your good**.[136]

In Deuteronomy 1:13 Moses tells the people of Israel, "'Choose wise, understanding, and knowledgeable men from among your tribes, and I will make them heads over you.'" In Romans 13:3-4, the Apostle Paul tells the church, "[Civil] rulers are not a terror to good works, but to evil. Do you want to be unafraid of the [civil] authority? Do what is good, and you will have praise from the same. For he is God's minister to you for good." The Pilgrims implemented civil self-government in order to secure their religious freedom. It would allow them to create a society based on God's laws and to freely practice their beliefs and covenants as they chose. Indeed, their habit of self-government, points out Cheever, "was the cradle of a well-ordered civil, as well as religious liberty."[137]

2.7 Private Property and Perseverance in Adversity: The Pilgrims' Settlement at Plymouth and the First Thanksgiving

When the Pilgrims landed in America in 1620, they settled at Plymouth, in what would later become part of the colony of Massachusetts (around 1690). The Pilgrims faced many challenges during their first year in the New World. The winter climate was harsh, and many suffered sickness and disease. Food and shelter were hard to obtain in the winter, especially in their weak condition. Though most of the Pilgrims farmed, the soil in the region was poor and difficult to farm. Their food and supplies, therefore, were very limited. The Pilgrims experienced hunger and starvation during this time. In the harsh environment, half of the Pilgrims died during the first winter of their arrival.

Though the Native Americans were a constant threat, the Pilgrims met a native named Squanto who had been to Europe and spoke English well. Through Squanto, the Pilgrims were able to form peaceful relations with the Wampanoag natives and their chief, Massasoit. Squanto became an interpreter for the Pilgrims and taught them how to catch fish, fertilize the soil, and grow corn.

In the spring, the Pilgrims farmed their land and planted many crops. The following autumn, they reaped a small harvest. In the fall of 1621, the Pilgrims held three days of Thanksgiving to God for His provision and blessing. They celebrated with a feast and invited their Native American friends to join them in the celebration. They enjoyed corn, ground-nuts, various shellfish, fish, waterfowl, deer, turkey, and venison in the region. Pilgrim Edward Winslow described this event in his *Journal of the Pilgrims*:

> God be praised, we had a good increase of Indian corn, and our barley indifferent good…. Our harvest being gotten in, our governor sent four men on fowling, so that we might in special manner rejoice together after we had gathered the fruit of our labors…. And although it is not always so plentiful as it was at this time with us, by the goodness of God, we are so far from want that we often wish you partakers of our plenty.[138]

At first, food and supplies in Plymouth were shared and allocated among colonists in a communal system of distribution. In this system, everyone received the same portion of food and other necessities. The idea was that everyone would do equal work and thus equally divide the supply. Many Pilgrims, however, did not like this system of labor and distribution, which seemed unjust to them. For everyone did not or could not work to the same degree, contrary to the supposition. Those who worked harder did not receive more provision for oneself or one's family, and the older ones felt disrespected in being treated the same as the younger ones in labor, food, and clothes. In addition, allotted portions were difficult to regulate. Some, particularly the non-Pilgrim visitors, ate more than their fair share, further draining the colony's limited supplies. This system resulted in a lack of incentive to work and less overall productivity. With the colony again on the verge of starvation in 1623, Governor William Bradford parceled out land to the Pilgrims and let them farm their own land, for themselves and their own families, which led to increased farming. A similar system had been applied successfully in Jamestown, Virginia. This shift to a free, individualized economic system increased productivity and benefited the colony. Bradford describes this early economic shift in Plymouth in his journal. He writes,

> The failure of this experiment in communal service, which was tried for several years, and by good and honest men proves the emptiness of the theory of Plato and other ancients, applauded by some of later times, –that the taking away of private property, and the possession of it in community, by a commonwealth, would make a state happy and flourishing; as if they were wiser than God. For in this instance, community of property (so far as it went) was found to breed much confusion and discontent, and retard much employment which would have been to the general benefit and comfort. … If (it was thought) all were to share alike, and all were to do alike, then all were on an equality throughout, and one was as good as another; and so, if it did not actually abolish those very relations which God himself has set among men, it did at least greatly diminish the mutual respect that is so important should be preserved amongst them. Let none argue that this is due to human failing, rather than to this communistic plan of life in itself. I answer, seeing that all men have this failing in them, that God in His wisdom saw that another plan of life was fitter for them.[139]

In the Summer of 1623, the Pilgrims faced another trial. A drought threatened to destroy their crops and survival. In response, they arranged a public day of Fasting and Prayer to beseech God for mercy and rain and, as Pilgrim Edward Winslow expresses in his journal, "to humble ourselves together before the Lord."[140] On an appointed day, everyone gathered together, fasted, and prayed. The next day it began to rain for a span of fourteen days, and the crops and harvest were saved. The Pilgrims considered the event to be a direct provision from God. The natives observed these events in astonishment. Also at that time, the Pilgrims received word that supplies were headed their way. Rejoicing, they attributed the rain, plentiful harvest, and additional supplies to God and His providence.

In response to these events, the Pilgrims held a second, public day of Thanksgiving to God for His provision and blessings. Winslow describes the Pilgrims' day of Thanksgiving "wherein we returned glory, honor, and praise with all thankfulness, to our good God, which deals so graciously with us…."[141] Thus the Pilgrims overcame famine, and Plymouth Colony survived.

Pilgrim Governor William Bradford expressed the Pilgrims' experience of famine and provision as well as of faith during their early years in Plymouth in *A Fragment of a Poem About New England*. In this poem, Bradford refers to a scripture from Deuteronomy 8:3, Matthew 4:4, and Luke 4:4 which says that "man shall not live by bread alone, but by every word that proceeds from the mouth of God." He writes:

> Famine once we had--But other things God gave us in full store, As fish and ground nuts, to supply our strait, That we might learn on providence to wait; And know, by bread man lives not in his need, But by each word that doth from God proceed. But a while after plenty did come in, From his hand only who doth pardon sin. And all did flourish like the pleasant green, Which in the joyful spring is to be seen.[142]

1   Throughout their severe trials, the Pilgrims' faith comforted, encouraged, and strengthened them to
2 press on and to trust in God's deliverance and sustenance. Ultimately, they persevered through adversity and
3 gave thanks for God's mercy and provision.
4
5   Plymouth became very prosperous. The Pilgrims formed a community centered on the Bible and
6 practiced a self-governing or congregational church and civil government. Bradford reflects on the
7 Pilgrims' and God's success in settling Plymouth Colony: "Thus out of small beginnings greater things have
8 grown by His [God's] hand Who made all things out of nothing, and gives being to all things that are; and as
9 one small candle may light a thousand, so the light enkindled here has shone to many, yea, in a sense, to our
10 whole nation; let the glorious name of Jehovah have all the praise."[143] The Pilgrims' first Thanksgiving
11 would lead to calls by future leaders of the United States to recognize a day of thanks to God for national
12 blessings. It would initiate the observance of Thanksgiving Day in the new nation and become an enduring
13 value in the cultural and civil life of the United States.
14
15 **2.8 Conclusion: Early Bible-Based Influences in the Heritage of A Nation**
16
17   The Pilgrims were notable for their religious zeal, quest for religious freedom, and Bible-based
18 practices. Driven by their beliefs, they came to America and formed the Mayflower Compact—their first civil
19 covenant in America—among themselves under God. With this binding agreement among equals, they created
20 a civil, political body to govern their new colony of Plymouth. In the process, they applied the Bible-inspired
21 principles of popular sovereignty, God's sovereignty, covenants, and self-government that would become
22 foundational not only to the colony but to the future United States. These principles were rigorously drawn and
23 defended from the Bible by significant thinkers and writings of the church and the Protestant Reformation that
24 greatly impacted the Pilgrims and Puritans. Through these thinkers and their writings, a clear connection is
25 apparent between the Bible or Judeo-Christian thought and these American principles. The Mayflower
26 Compact gave root to the Pilgrim's colony. It would also become a foundational root for the future nation of
27 the United States and its founding documents—the Declaration of Independence and the Constitution. Along
28 with the first Thanksgiving, this extraordinary agreement among free equals would affect the nation's
29 formation, development, character, and values.

The Mayflower Compact

November 11, 1620

In the name of God, amen. We, whose names are underwritten, the loyal subjects of our dread sovereign Lord, King James, by the grace of God, of Great Britain, France, and Ireland, King, Defender of the faith, etc. Having undertaken for the glory of God, and advancement of the Christian faith, and the honor of our King and country, a voyage to plant the first colony in the northern parts of Virginia; do by these presents solemnly and mutually, in the presence of God and one another, covenant and combine ourselves together into a civil body politic, for our better ordering and preservation, and furtherance of the ends aforesaid; and by virtue hereof, do enact, constitute, and frame such just and equal laws, ordinances, acts, constitutions, and officers, from time to time, as shall be thought most meet and convenient for the general good of the colony; unto which we promise all due submission and obedience. In witness whereof, we have hereunto subscribed our names, at Cape Cod, the eleventh of November, in the reign of our sovereign Lord King James, of England, France and Ireland, the eighteenth, and of Scotland the fifty-fourth, Anno Dom. 1620.[144]

Mr. John Carver	Mr. Samuel Fuller	Edward Tilly
William Bradford	Mr. Christopher Martin	John Tilly
Mr. Edward Winslow	Mr. William Mullins	Francis Cook
Mr. William Brewster	Mr. William White	Thomas Rogers
Mr. Isaac Allerton	Mr. Richard Warren	Thomas Tinker
Capt. Miles Standish	John Howland	John Ridgdale
John Alden	Mr. Stephen Hopkins	Edward Fuller
John Turner	Digery Priest	Richard Clark
Francis Eaton	Thomas Williams	Richard Gardiner
James Chilton	Gilbert Winslow	John Allerton
John Craxton	Edmund Morgeson	Thomas English
John Billington	Peter Brown	Edward Dolen
Joses Fletcher	Richard Bitteridge	Edward Liester
John Goodman	George Soule	

1 **Review: Checking Out the History**
2
3 Discuss questions in subgroups or whole group. As an option, the group may come up with main ideas or
4 insights from each question. Responses may be shared and discussed in the whole group.
5
6 1. Why did the Pilgrims come to America? What do the reasons/motives suggest about the Pilgrims?
7
8
9
10
11 2. How did the Pilgrims' belief in God as sovereign ruler or king affect their religious and political worldviews
12 and actions?
13
14
15
16
17 3. Why did the Pilgrims want self-government and the ability to choose their magistrates? How did their views
18 of government compare/contrast with the societies from which they came?
19
20
21
22
23 4. The Pilgrims' basis for creating a civil covenant was drawn from what influences?
24
25
26
27
28 5. Considering the Bible scriptures on covenants, how might the Mayflower Compact compare/contrast with
29 the covenant between God and Israel in the Old Testament and/or between God and His believers in the New
30 Testament?
31
32
33
34
35 6. What basic Bible-based or Judeo-Christian principles are evident and important in this part of America's
36 heritage?
37
38

1 **Activity: The Mayflower Compact**
2
3 Read the Mayflower Compact. Consider how the Compact commits the Pilgrims to religion, government, and
4 civility. In the words of the compact or in your own words, write the phrases that correspond to each of these
5 areas of commitment in the boxes below.
6
7

The Mayflower Compact	In the name of God. Amen. We whose names are underwritten, the loyal subjects of our dread Sovereign Lord, King James, by the grace of God, of Great Britain, France, and Ireland king, defender of the faith, etc., having undertaken, for the glory of God, and advancement of the Christian faith, and honor of our King and country, a voyage to plant the first colony in the Northern parts of Virginia, do by these presents solemnly and mutually in the presence of God, and one of another, covenant and combine ourselves together into a civil body politic, for our better ordering and preservation and furtherance of the ends aforesaid; and by virtue hereof to enact, constitute, and frame such just and equal laws, ordinances, acts, constitutions, and offices, from time to time, as shall be thought most meet and convenient for the general good of the Colony, unto which we promise all due submission and obedience. In witness whereof we have hereunder subscribed our names at Cape Cod the 11th of November, in the year of the reign of our sovereign lord, King James, of England, France, and Ireland the eighteenth, and of Scotland the fifty-fourth. Anno Domini 1620.
Religion	
Government	
Civility	

8
9
10
11

1   **Call to Action**
2
3   Each person will reflect on and write his/her responses to the questions below. Responses may then be shared
4   and discussed in the group.
5
6   1. What, if anything, about the Pilgrims did you find unusual? Surprising? Admirable? Courageous? How or
7   in what ways might the Pilgrims serve as a positive example or role model for Americans?
8   _____
9   _____
10   _____
11   _____
12
13   2. What influences of the Bible and God's law do you see today in your community and in various sectors of
14   society?
15   _____
16   _____
17   _____
18   _____
19
20   3. Give several examples in today's society and culture in which contracts or covenants are used.
21   _____
22   _____
23   _____
24   _____
25
26   4. Give examples of stated or implied contracts, covenants, or agreements that exist in your own life such as
27   regarding your family, marriage, church, school, business, place of employment, goods, or services. In your
28   family, for example, you may have an agreement or rules for chores or expected behavior.
29   _____
30   _____
31   _____
32   _____
33
34

Chapter 3
The Puritans Create Bible Commonwealths in Early America

A decade after the Pilgrims arrived in North America, another group of English Puritans migrated to the same region, led by Puritan John Winthrop. Though they did not separate from the Church of England when the Pilgrims did, the Puritans shared many of the Pilgrims' radically reformed religious and political views. In coming to America, they also shared the same goals and desire for self-government. In America, the Puritans sought to develop a Bible-centered civil state where they could govern themselves and worship as they chose. They founded the colony of Massachusetts and later, led by Rev. Thomas Hooker, the colony of Connecticut. In the process of developing their colonies, they upheld the same beliefs and self-governing principles of the Pilgrims—covenants, God's sovereignty, and popular sovereignty. They endeavored to apply these ideas in their colonies. They also notably applied the civil principles and values of constitutions, Rule of Law, representative government, limited power, education, and a strong work ethic. They often derived and supported these concepts from the Bible and their religious beliefs. Ultimately, the Puritans' new endeavor at self-government and their application of Bible-inspired ideas in their colonies would shape American political thought and foundations. As their governing principles and values became rooted in the early colonies, they would become the seedbed and soil for the founding of the future nation, the United States of America.

3.1 John Winthrop and the Puritans Come to America with Their Charter and Found the Colony of Massachusetts

By the 1620s in England, the Puritans had gained political power in Parliament. But Anglican King Charles I of Britain, who came to the throne in 1625, held Catholic tendencies, and leaders in the Church of England opposed the Puritans. As a result, the Puritans did not find a favorable environment for their radical reformed views and their hopes for the church. Many Puritans began to migrate to North America. In 1629, King Charles granted a large group of reform-minded Puritans a royal charter to plant the colony of Massachusetts Bay in America. The charter granted authority to the Massachusetts Bay Company, a commercial venture overseen by Puritans, to govern the colony. These Puritans—about 700 of them on eleven ships—set sail to America and arrived in Massachusetts, near Plymouth, in 1630. Massachusetts would eventually absorb the Pilgrims' colony of Plymouth.

In a distinctive move, the Puritans *brought their charter with them* to America. This move assured those in the company who came overseas that they would manage the company themselves. In bringing along their charter, the Puritans contributed to the creation of a self-governing colony, note some historians, because the charter became the basis for the colony's first governing laws.[145] Since the British Crown did not closely supervise activities in America, but allowed for self-government through local governors, the colony operated independently of England.

Puritan John Winthrop led this first large group of Puritans who migrated to America. Winthrop, who had attended Trinity College at Cambridge, England, was a lawyer with strong religious beliefs. He sought religious freedom in America through the Massachusetts venture. During his trip to America on the vessel *Arbella*, Winthrop delivered his famous 1630 sermon, *A Model of Christian Charity*, exhorting the Puritans to fulfill their purpose to become a "city on a hill"—a godly example of a Bible-centered colony for the world to see. Winthrop's *Model* sermon would become one of the most well-known sermons of American history. Winthrop was elected governor of the colony of Massachusetts.

3.2 The Puritans Seek Religious Freedom and to Form a Bible Commonwealth, a "City On A Hill"

      The Puritans came to America in search of prosperity and, like the Pilgrims, for religious and political reasons. Winthrop laid out many of their specific reasons in his 1629 argument to migrate—"Reasons to Be Considered for Justifying the Undertakers of the Intended Plantation in New England." The Puritans hoped to escape not only economic hardship but worldly evils—what they saw as corruption of churches and schools in England and Europe. They also hoped to escape religious restrictions and oppression. They wanted freedom to worship differently than what was regulated by the official Church of England. They saw America as a place to find religious freedom and to purify and restore the church.[146] In addition, the Puritans also wanted to advance the Gospel and the reformed church as well as to increase and represent God's people on earth based on Genesis 1:28 in which God tells man to "'Be fruitful and multiply; fill the earth and subdue it.'"[147] Winthrop further indicates the Puritans' religious motives for coming to America in his *Model of Christian Charity* sermon. He states their hope to improve their lives, serve the Lord, comfort and increase the Body of Christ, be preserved from worldly corruptions, and, based on Philippians 2:12, work out their salvation in a godly environment, under godly laws.[148] In Philippians 2:12, the Apostle Paul exhorts Christians to "work out your own salvation with fear and trembling...." Such goals, the Puritans believed, could only be realized in America.

      The Puritans, in fact, had a great vision for their coming to America. In the free, autonomous environment of this new land, they hoped to create a new Bible commonwealth or Bible-centered civil state in which they could live according to their religious beliefs. Their community would be based on the Bible, covenants, and godly laws. Religious worship would be central to life.[149] Their group would be united by their shared identity as the Body of Christ. Alluding to Colossians 2, 1 Corinthians 12, and Ephesians 4, Winthrop describes this unity among themselves as "a Company professing ourselves fellow members of Christ, ...knitt together by this bond of love" and "allwayes having before our eyes our Commission and Community in the worke, ...as members of the same body, soe [so] shall wee keepe the unitie of the spirit in the bond of peace."[150] Similarly in the Bible, in Colossians 2:2, the Apostle Paul tells believers in Christ to learn the wisdom of God in Christ so that their hearts may be "knit together in love." Of the one Body of Christ, Paul states in 1 Corinthians 12:20, "But now indeed *there are* many members, yet one body." And in Ephesians 4:3, he exhorts believers to "keep the unity of the Spirit in the bond of peace." The Puritans' shared identity was the basis of their experience and desire to create a godly society.[151] A strikingly similar, yet secular expression of unity would later be found in the future United States' 1776 de facto motto, *E Pluribus Unum*, which means in Latin "Out of Many, One." Success of the Puritans' colony, Winthrop believed, would provide a godly model of a Bible-centered community—a "city on a hill"—for Europe and the world to emulate: "...[F]or wee must Consider that wee shall be as a Citty upon a Hill, the eies [eyes] of all people are upon us."[152]

3.3 The Puritans Identify With the Israelites and Practice Covenants

      Like the Pilgrims, the Puritans strongly identified with the ancient Israelites of the Bible who, with God's help, escaped captivity in Egypt and set their new nation in the Promised Land of Canaan. The Puritans who came to America similarly saw themselves as God's chosen people who had fled oppression in Europe and were called to set up a godly civil state in America, a New Israel. In his *Model* sermon, Winthrop links the Puritans with the Israelites. He exhorts his fellow Puritans, "...[T]he Lord will be our God and delight to dwell among us, as his owne people and will commaund a blessing upon us in all our wayes, ...wee shall finde that the God of Israell is among us...."[153] Abiding by the practice of the Israelites as well as Covenant Theology and the Pilgrims, the Puritans enacted covenants when they came to America.[154] In accordance with Covenant Theology, they deemed covenants as foundational to their colonies. They based their churches, civil states, and laws on these binding agreements. They also viewed all relationships in society in terms of such agreements. Such commitments were ingrained in their lives.[155] A successful colony, they believed, depended on them.

During the Puritans' voyage to America, Winthrop articulates in his *Model* sermon the Puritans' covenant with God and one another—like the one between God and the Israelites in the Bible—to follow God's moral law which he draws from the Bible—in Deuteronomy 30:16, Matthew 5:44, and Matthew 7:12. Jesus instructs His followers in Matthew 5:44 to "'love your enemies, bless those who curse you, do good to those who hate you, and pray for those who spitefully use you and persecute you'" and in Matthew 7:12 that "'whatever you want men to do to you, do also to them.'"[156] In Deuteronomy 30:6, Moses talks of loving God to the people of Israel: "'And the LORD your God will circumcise your heart and the heart of your descendants, to love the LORD your God with all your heart and with all your soul, that you may live.'" God's moral law, Winthrop reminds the others, means to "love the Lord our God, and to love one another to walke in his [God's] wayes and to keepe his Commaundments." Winthrop also cites the counsel of Micah 6:8 in instructing the Puritans to "to doe [do] Justly, to love mercy, to walke humbly with our God."[157] Their covenant was their commitment to love God and one another and to uphold justice and mercy in dealing with one another. Winthrop explicitly confirms their covenant for coming to America:

> Thus stands the cause betweene God and us, wee are entered into Covenant with him for this worke, wee have taken out a Commission, the Lord has given us leave to drawe our owne articles wee have professed to enterprise these Accions [actions] upon…, wee have…besought him of favour and blessing: Now if the Lord shall please to heare us, and bring us in peace to the place wee desire, then hath hee ratified this Covenant and sealed our Commission, [and] will expect a strickt performance of the Articles contained in it….[158]

The Puritans' earthly goal of this pact was to find a place of habitation and, there, to successfully set up their Bible Commonwealth and to live by God's law. Winthrop explains their purpose "to seeke out a place of Cohabitation and Consorteshipp under a due forme of Government both civill and ecclesiasticall." [159]

The Puritans, like the Pilgrims, enacted their pact with the consent of those in the group. Winthrop makes a point to say of their agreement that "for the work wee have in hand, it is by a mutuall consent through a speciall overruleing providence, and a more then an ordinary approbation [approval] of the Churches of Christ."[160] The Puritans had chosen this venture and compacted together by their own free will. Thus they honored not only the principle of covenants but also the principle of the consent of the governed. Their understanding that a covenant presupposed a voluntary agreement among free parties was, says Elazar, "one reason why the Puritans, even though aspects of their regime in Massachusetts would be considered repressive by contemporary democratic standards, can be regarded as the fathers of American liberty. Their application of the daring Bible-inspired idea that people are or ought to be free in order to make pacts with God became one of the bases for all people's claims to liberty in relation to one another."[161]

Their covenants had certain conditions, the Puritans believed, just like those of the Israelites. God's people are divinely blessed when they keep covenant with God and divinely punished when they disobey. God promises the Israelites blessings for abiding by His covenants, as in Exodus 34:10-11: "And He [God] said, 'Behold, I make a covenant. Before all your people I will do marvels such as have not been done in all the earth, nor in any nation; and all the people among whom you *are* shall see the work of the Lord. For it is an awesome thing that I will do with you. Observe what I command you this day." The Puritans thus encouraged adherence to and warned against breaking their covenant. They sought to do godly works in order to live, be blessed, and multiply. Otherwise, if they turned away from God and pursued selfish aims, they might be cursed.[162] Failure of their covenant would be a disgrace to God and man, but success would provide an example for others to follow.

The Puritans were not the only group who brought the practice of covenants to America. Other covenantal groups would also soon settle in this Promised Land including the German and Dutch Reformers,

French Huguenots, Scottish and European Presbyterians, and more.[163] Covenants would ultimately shape the new nation's founding documents—the Declaration of Independence and Constitution—and influence its system of civil government.

3.4 Thomas Hooker and the Puritans Found the Colony of Connecticut

Soon after the Puritans had settled in Massachusetts, some Puritans moved and formed the colony of Connecticut. One Puritan who became instrumental in founding Connecticut was Rev. Thomas Hooker. Hooker had grown up in England, attended the Puritan-oriented Emmanuel College in Cambridge, and had become a strong Puritan preacher. Due to harassment from authorities in England over his religious teachings, he had fled to Holland. In 1633, he migrated to Massachusetts to join his Puritan congregation. There, he pastored his congregation in New Towne, later named Cambridge, Massachusetts, and became a prominent leader in the colony. But Hooker soon fell out of favor in the colony due to his political differences with other leaders like Winthrop, though he was friends with Winthrop. So, in 1636, he and his congregation moved to a settlement outside of Massachusetts at Hartford. In 1637, his and other nearby groups founded the colony of Connecticut. On May 31, 1638, Hooker delivered an influential sermon before the Connecticut General Court based on Deuteronomy 1:13 in which he advocates for certain Bible-inspired governing principles of self-government—including popular sovereignty, consent of the governed, chosen representatives, and limited power. Hooker thus draws from the Bible in support of these principles. As a result of Hooker's sermon, popular sovereignty was asserted for the first time in the colonies.

In 1648, Thomas Hooker wrote his *Survey of the Summe of Church Discipline* to defend important principles of Puritan Congregational church doctrine and organization. Because the Puritans applied their form of church government to their civil government, Hooker's *Summe of Church Discipline* is important to understanding the civil governments of the early American colonies. *Summe* reveals the Bible-based thought behind various governing principles of Puritan and early American civil government.[164] Hooker is often described as "the father of American democracy" or "the first American democrat" for his support of republican/democratic principles in the early American colonies.[165]

3.5 The Puritans See the Need for Civil Government and Limited Power for Sinful Mankind

The Puritans believed what the Bible said about humans and human nature, which, in turn, affected their view of civil law and government. The reformers of the Protestant Reformation, who shared the same views of human nature, also likely influenced the Puritans' ideas of government. Because humans are sinful, they require civil government as well as limited power in society. According to the book of Genesis in the Bible, humans are created by God and made in God's image and likeness. At the same time, however, they are also sinful and corrupt due to the fall of Adam and Eve in the Garden of Eden as found in Genesis 2 and 3 and in Romans 5:12-14.[166] In Genesis 2 and 3, Adam and Eve are deceived and tempted by the evil serpent, Satan. They disobey God's command and eat a forbidden fruit. As a result, they become poisoned and corrupted with sin or ungodliness. Sin is a transgression or violation of God's moral law. Consequently, God casts Adam and Eve out of the Garden of Eden and sentences them to physical and spiritual death. Their immortal souls, without salvation, are condemned to hell or eternal separation from God. This fallen state of mankind afflicts all the descendants of Adam and Eve, the whole human race. In Romans 5:12 the Apostle Paul says that "through one man [Adam] sin entered the world, and death through sin, and thus death spread to all men, because all sinned...." Mankind's representation and reflection of God on earth is thus tainted and imperfect. In his 1563 *Bible Commentaries on Genesis*, Calvin vividly describes the Bible-based view of human sinfulness as a result of the evil forces of Satan against God in the world: "And, because he [Satan] could not drag God from his throne, he assailed man, in whom His [God's] image shone. He knew that with the ruin of man the most dreadful confusion would be produced in the whole world, as indeed it happened, and therefore he endeavored, in the person of man, to obscure the glory of God."[167] In his 1531 *Commentary on Galatians*,

1 Luther likewise observes that "the devil reigneth throughout the whole world, and enforceth men to all kinds of
2 horrible wickedness." He compares mankind's fallen nature to a "wild beast."[168] Puritan Winthrop affirms the
3 Bible's and Christian's view of man's sinfulness, observing that "…Adam Rent himselfe from his Creator, rent
4 all his posterity allsoe [also] one from another, whence it comes that every man is borne with this principle in
5 him to love and seeke himselfe only [only]…."[169] Echoing Luther, Winthrop in his *History of New England*
6 also calls humans' sinful nature a "wild beast" contrary to God.[170] Puritan minister and author Rev. Cotton
7 Mather reaffirms in his 1702 *Magnalia Christi Americana*, a church history of New England, the Bible-based
8 view of sin in human nature: "*Adam* was the *common root* of all *mankind*, and so his *first sin* is imputed unto
9 all his posterity…."[171] Because man's nature is sinful, his natural tendencies and desires lure him at times into
10 immorality, evildoing, rebellion, and lawlessness against God, self, and others.
11

12 　　　The Puritans saw that since humans are made in God's image yet corrupted by sin, they are made to be
13 free—and indeed naturally are free—but cannot have unlimited civil freedom to do evil in society. Fallen
14 humans require civil government to restrain their sinful nature, to protect their true rights and freedoms, and to
15 maintain peace in society. Winthrop, like the Reformers, favored civil freedom for citizens "to that only which
16 is good, just, and honest."[172] The restraint of evil in civil society, he believed, was the proper end and object of
17 civil government. The Puritans believed that civil government was ordained or decreed by God for these
18 purposes. The Bible specifically acknowledges the divine function of civil government in society to punish
19 what is evil and praise what is good. Civil government was God's approved earthly instrument for the
20 preservation and security of mankind. The Puritans' view of the God-ordained role of civil government was
21 undoubtedly affected by their Bible-centered religious beliefs and the ideas of the Reformation.
22

23 　　　Though the reformers faced a number of practical challenges in the church and civil governments of
24 their day, their assertion about the God-ordained role of civil government would be accepted and shared by
25 many. Reformers including Luther and Calvin based their view of civil government on the Bible—as presented
26 by the Apostle Paul in Romans 13 and by the Apostle Peter in 1 Peter 2. The reformers cited these verses to
27 show the divine role of civil government on earth. The Puritans likely viewed the role of civil government in
28 light of these same verses. In Romans 13:1-5 Paul states,
29

30 　　　Let every soul be subject to the governing authorities. For there is no authority except from God, and
31 　　　the authorities that exist are appointed by God. Therefore whoever resists the authority resists the
32 　　　ordinance of God, and those who resist will bring judgment on themselves. For rulers are not a terror to
33 　　　good works, but to evil. Do you want to be unafraid of the authority? Do what is good, and you will
34 　　　have praise from the same. For he is God's minister to you for good. But if you do evil, be afraid; for
35 　　　he does not bear the sword in vain; for he is God's minister, an avenger to *execute* wrath on him who
36 　　　practices evil. Therefore *you* must be subject, not only because of wrath but also for conscience' sake.
37

38 In 1 Peter 2:13-15, Peter states, "Therefore submit yourselves to every ordinance of man for the Lord's sake,
39 whether to the king as supreme, or to governors, as to those who are sent by him for the punishment of evildoers
40 and *for the* praise of those who do good. For this is the will of God, that by doing good you may put to silence
41 the ignorance of foolish men…." In his 1523 Reformation treatise, *Secular Authority: To What Extent It*
42 *Should Be Obeyed*, Luther acknowledges from these Bible verses the God-ordained role of civil government.
43 Before quoting Romans 13:1 and 1 Peter 2:13-14, he says, "We must firmly establish secular law and the
44 sword, that no one may doubt that it is in the world by God's will and ordinance."[173] In his *Commentaries on*
45 *Galatians*, Luther further addresses the role of civil government to restrain man's sinful nature and to preserve
46 peace, particularly so that religious faith could prosper:
47

48 　　　God hath ordained civil laws, yea all laws to punish transgressions. Every law then is given to restrain
49 　　　sin. …

...Therefore God hath ordained magistrates, parents, teachers, laws, bonds and all civil ordinances, that, if they can do no more, yet at the least they may bind the devil's hands.... ... This civil restraint is very necessary, and appointed of God, as well for public peace as for the preservation of all things, but specially lest the course of the Gospel should be hindered by the tumults and seditions of outrageous men.[174]

Calvin similarly explains in his 1563 *Institutes of the Christian Religion* that the civil officer is divinely called by God to protect the people from evil for the common good. Quoting Romans 13:4, Calvin writes,

"the minister of God to us for good;" we understand from this, that he [the civil officer] is divinely appointed in order that we may be defended by his power and protection against the malice and injuries of wicked men, and may lead peaceable and secure lives. But if it be in vain that he is given to us by the Lord for our protection, ...it clearly follows that we may appeal to him, and apply for his aid, without any violation of piety.[175]

Incidentally, Luther further points out from these same verses that the church—the spiritual power—is also subject to the civil government—the earthly or temporal power. Religious authorities are not exempt from civil authority and laws. He says,

Hence secular [civil] Christian authorities should exercise their office freely and unhindered and without fear, whether it be pope, bishop, or priest with whom they are dealing; if a man is guilty let him pay the penalty. What canon law [church law] says to the contrary is Romish presumptuousness and pure invention. For this is what St. Paul says to all Christians, "Let every soul (I hold that includes the pope's) be subject to the higher powers, for they bear not the sword in vain. They serve God alone, punishing the evil and praising the good" [Rom. 13:1-4]. And St. Peter [I Pet. 2:13, 15], "Be subject unto every ordinance of man for God's sake, whose will is that it should be so." ...
... The reason is that the social corpus of Christendom includes secular government as one of its component functions. ...
There is no longer any defense against punishment where sin exists. ... But God and the apostles made them [the religious authorities, brackets mine] subject to the secular "sword."[176]

The Puritans shared the Bible's and the reformers' view of the God-ordained role of civil government to restrain sin and to keep peace for the protection and preservation of mankind. As such they viewed government and politics as godly endeavors, and they were actively engaged in these spheres of society.[177] Following the Bible-based and reformed ideas of government, the Puritans set up civil government and constitutions of law in their colonies so that they could have godly commonwealths of peace, unity, and order. They also wanted communities in which the Gospel and religious faith could prosper. To be sure, the Puritans, say some writers, were actually more concerned about creating a godly society than a democratic one.[178] Their goal was to create societies conducive to a life and practice of Biblical faith. The Puritans of Connecticut, for example, specifically expressed in their constitution, the Fundamental Orders, the God-ordained role of civil government in society:

...[T]he word of God requires that to maintain the peace and union of such a people there should be an orderly and decent Government established according to God, to order and dispose of the affairs of the people...; [we] do therefore associate and conjoin ourselves to be as one Public State or Commonwealth; and do...enter into Combination and Confederation together, to maintain and preserve the liberty and purity of the Gospel of our Lord Jesus which we now profess, as also the discipline of the Churches, which according to the truth of the said Gospel is now practiced amongst us; as also in our civil affairs to be guided and governed according to such Laws....[179]

1   The Puritans thought that although civil government was needed to restrain evil among the people, a
2   need also existed to restrain and limit the power of civil authorities and governments themselves since they
3   were made up of imperfect humans. Boundaries had to be set for those in power. Indeed, the Puritans opposed
4   unlimited power of any kind—whether of kings, governors, aristocrats, priests, churches, or the people.[180] The
5   Puritans, therefore, supported limited power in their colonial church and civil governments. Puritan Rev. John
6   Cotton, a leading clergyman in Massachusetts, writes of the need to limit human power based on the Bible in a
7   1655 sermon he preached on "Limitation of Government." He cites Jeremiah 3:5 in which God, who judges the
8   people of Israel for their ungodly behavior, says, "Behold, you have spoken and done evil things, As you were
9   able." Cotton consequently warns,

11   Let all the world learn to give mortall men no greater power then they are content they [men] shall use,
12   for use it they will: and unless they be better taught of God, they will use it ever and anon…. No man
13   would think what desperate deceit and wickednesse there is in the hearts of men…. What, saith the Lord
14   in Jer. 3:5: *Though hast spoken and done evill things as thou couldst.* … There is a straine in a mans
15   heart that will sometime or other runne out to excesse, unlesse the Lord restraine it…. It is necessary
16   therefore, that all power that is on earth be limited, Church-power or other…. It is therefore fit for every
17   man to be studious of the bounds which the Lord hath set: and for the People, in whom fundamentally
18   all power lyes [lies], to give as much power as God in his word gives to men….[181]

20   The Puritans notably achieved limited power and government in their colonies by means of their
21   constitutions of law, Rule of Law, election of moral civil representatives, and consent of the governed. They
22   also divided power in their bicameral or two-housed governing assemblies. The Puritans' development of
23   constitutions was a particularly important contribution to limited power in their colonies and in the future
24   nation. The American Founders—possessing the same worldview of sinful man—would later secure certain
25   limits to power and civil government in the U. S. Constitution and Bill of Rights.

27 **3.6 The Puritans Create Democratic Civil Government with a State Religion**

29   Winthrop and Thomas Hooker held somewhat different ideas about the type of government that should
30   be implemented in the Puritan commonwealth in America. Winthrop favored a kind of "mixed government."
31   A mixed government typically has elements of democracy, aristocracy, and monarchy. A democracy is a state
32   in which civil power resides with the whole people. "Democracy" comes from a Greek term for "rule of the
33   people." Such a state is governed either directly by the people or through elected representatives. An
34   aristocracy is a state governed by a superior or privileged upper class or nobility. This class is sometimes
35   hereditary. Other times, it might consist of those who possess exceptional expertise, learning, knowledge,
36   character, and/or godliness. "Aristocracy" is based on a Greek word meaning "rule of the best." As mentioned
37   earlier, a monarchy is a state ruled by a sovereign monarch who typically comes to power by hereditary
38   succession. The Latin word "monarchy" is derived from Greek words meaning "rule of one." In mixed
39   government, some issues are decided by the majority of the people, others by a few, and still others by a sole
40   head. Winthrop specifically favored a "mixed aristocracy" in which the government practices elements of both
41   democracy and aristocracy. In Winthrop's notion of government, civil representatives are elected by the people.
42   These representatives possess a substantial amount of power and discretion to govern over the people. This
43   system is based on the idea that God has designated some persons to lead or govern the people, to be in charge
44   of others. Winthrop disliked mere democracy—of which, he thought, there was "no warrnt [warrant] in
45   scripture for it: there was no such Goverm' [government] in Israell."[182] He thought democracy violated God's
46   fifth commandment to "honor your father and mother."

In contrast, Hooker thought Winthrop's mixed aristocracy gave civil leaders too much authority, particularly over issues not specifically addressed in the Bible. Instead, he favored only democracy. For no man, he thought, is naturally subordinate to another. As such, the people may elect representatives for themselves and may also distinctly limit the powers of their representatives. These representatives possess only the powers assigned to them by the people. Thus leaders' powers were more limited in Hooker's democratic system than in Winthrop's mixed aristocratic system. While Winthrop and the colonists in Massachusetts debated their form of government, Hooker and others set up a democratic government in Connecticut. Massachusetts soon became more democratic as well, with more limited power for civil representatives.

To further grasp the kind of government practiced in the Puritans' colonies, it is also necessary to understand how the Puritans' commonwealths were different from a theocracy. A "theocracy" was a government that recognized God as ruler or head of the civil state. "Theocracy" comes from a Greek term that literally means "rule of God." Though the Puritans acknowledged the sovereignty of God abstractly, their commonwealth differed from a theocracy in literal practice. In a theocracy, the state is governed directly by God or by a civil leader who governs in the place of God and on God's direct authority. Such a leader is believed to receive divine revelation directly from God—like the prophet Moses who led the Israelites. Another type of theocracy could be a system in which a religious leader of a dominant religious group rules the state or in which a religious body rules above the civil body—as occurred in medieval Europe and in the Papal states, states under the Pope. In these systems, such religious rulers are not seen as prophets who receive divine revelation but as those who can interpret such received revelation or sacred text. The Puritan commonwealth, however, like the more modern monarchies of Europe, was not a theocracy in this practical sense since the Puritans' civil body governed above the church body. In this respect, the Puritans practiced a secular government. Their government, however, did have an official state religion and church. It was also strongly influenced by Bible-based principles.

Regarding the church-state relationship in the Puritans' commonwealths, the Puritans' experiences and history in Europe influenced their view of the relationship between civil state and church in their colonies in America. For centuries in Europe, the civil state was administratively tied to an official state church. In the European monarchies, the civil state often acted as an arm and financial support for the church, and the church often became an extension of the civil state. Monarchs sometimes claimed the right to appoint bishops in their territories. During the Reformation, a few reformers questioned the administrative tie between civil state and church, but no alternatives to this system were realized. Furthermore, many reformers still believed that the civil state and church should assist one another, though they differed in their ideas of how this assistance was carried out. Calvin thought the civil state should protect and support the church, and the church should pray for and advise the state. The purpose of both state and church were to protect and defend the people—whether in temporal or spiritual terms. Citing Isaiah 49:23 and 1 Timothy 2:1-2, Calvin writes of the roles of the state and church to assist one another:

> In like manner Isaiah, when he predicts that 'kings shall be nursing-fathers and queens nursing-mothers' to the Church [Isaiah 49:23], does not depose them from their thrones; but rather establishes them by an honourable title, as patrons and protectors of the pious worshippers of God: … But the most remarkable of all [testimonies] is that passage where Paul, admonishing Timothy that in the public congregation, 'supplications, prayers, intercessions, and giving of thanks be made for kings and for all that are in authority,' assigns as a reason, 'that we may lead a quiet and peaceable life in all godliness and honesty [1 Timothy 2:-1-2]:' language in which he recommends the state of the Church to their [kings'] patronage and defence.[183]

With this view, religious reformers like Calvin did not strongly challenge the traditional political structure of state and church. However, a few political-minded reformers like Luther questioned the ties between these two

1 institutions. Luther challenged this political structure as unbiblical and prone to corruption and tyranny. He
2 believed that both civil and religious authorities were called to "protect the populace" and "defend them by
3 means of their temporal and spiritual possessions."[184] He called for more administrative separation between the
4 two institutions to successfully achieve that end. His argument was quite radical for his time, though, and was
5 not implemented then. The Puritans similarly believed that the state and church should assist one another. In
6 implementing this idea, they maintained, in many ways, the long-held relationship between state and church
7 with which they were familiar in Europe.
8
9 As in Europe, the Puritans saw their civil state and church functioning closely together in their American
10 colonies. So as the Puritans set up their civil state, they also established their Congregational Church as the
11 official state church. The civil state financially supported the church. The state also implemented religious
12 laws and regulated religious doctrine in the colonies. Yet the Puritans, wary of the religious oppression they
13 had experienced in Europe, did apply somewhat more separation between state and church than in Europe
14 because they staffed these two institutions with different personnel. This notable difference was an early,
15 beginning move toward greater structural, administrative separation between the official church and the civil
16 government in America.
17
18 It is important to recognize both the Puritans' Bible-based notion of a cooperative state and church—as
19 drawn from Isaiah 49 and 1 Timothy 2—and how they implemented this idea based on their experiences. It
20 indicates, in part, why many Americans would later argue for a traditionally connected state and church in the
21 future states of the new nation. Still, over time, the distinction between the idea and the implementation would
22 become more significant. The traditional model for implementing a cooperative church and civil government
23 would be challenged by new, Bible-based views. As the colonies expanded and the new nation was formed, the
24 American understanding of the practical relationship between state and church would ultimately be
25 reinterpreted.
26
27 **3.7 God's Moral Law: The Puritans' Source of Moral Authority and Law**
28
29 The Puritans and other Christians believed that since the Bible was God's divinely-inspired written
30 Word, this sacred book acted as the Puritans' final word on civil and religious law in their commonwealths. It
31 was the bedrock of their morality and laws. The Bible contained the moral Law of God as expressed in the Ten
32 Commandments, the Two Great Commandments, and some other teachings of Moses, the prophets, Jesus
33 Christ, and the Apostles. Other ceremonial laws were practiced by the Israelites in their Jewish nation, but
34 those laws were not considered part of God's moral law, nor applicable to other peoples. In the Ten
35 Commandments found in Exodus 20:1-17 of the Old Testament, as mentioned earlier, God commands that His
36 people have no other gods, make no idols, do not take His name in vain, keep the Sabbath rest, honor their
37 fathers and mothers, do not murder, do not commit adultery, do not steal, do not bear false witness against their
38 neighbors, and do not covet their neighbors.[185] This moral law is summarized in the Two Great
39 Commandments—to love God and to love others—also known as the "Law of Love."
40
41 The two Great Commandments of love appear in both the Old and New Testaments. They are found in
42 Deuteronomy 6:5, 10:12, 11:1, 13, 22, 13:3, 30:6, 16, 20; Joshua 22:5, 23:11; Leviticus 19:17-18; Matthew
43 5:44, 7:12, 19:19, 22:37-40, Mark 12:30-33, Luke 10:27, John 13:34-35, Romans 13:8-10, Galatians 5:14,
44 and James 2:8. In Matthew 22:37-40, when Jesus is questioned by a religious leader about the greatest
45 commandment of the law, Jesus replies with the Two Great Commandments found in Deuteronomy 6:5 and
46 Leviticus 19:18: "'You shall love the Lord your God with all your heart, with all your soul, and with all your
47 mind.' This is *the* first and great commandment. And *the* second *is* like it: 'You shall love your neighbor as
48 yourself.' On these two commandments hang all the Law and the Prophets.'" In John 13:34-35, Jesus teaches
49 his disciples the Great Commandments, saying, "'A new commandment I give to you, that you love one
50 another; as I have loved you, that you also love one another.'" Calvin in his *Institutes* describes these two main

1   articles of God's moral law as "the true and eternal rule of righteousness, prescribed to men of all ages and
2   nations, who wish to conform their lives to the will of God."[186] The Puritans sought to uphold this Biblical
3   moral law in their colonies. In his *Model* sermon, as mentioned, Winthrop cites God's moral law from Matthew
4   5:44, Matthew 7:12, and Deuteronomy 30:16 as part of the Puritans' covenant with God and one another in
5   coming to America.

7   The Bible was the primary source of civil and religious law in the Puritan colonies. For example, the
8   General Court of Massachusetts instructed the committee that drafted the Massachusetts constitution to make
9   the laws of its commonwealth "as near the law of God as they can be."[187] The 1647 General Laws and Liberties
10   of Massachusetts specifically acknowledged the source of law from Old Testament Israel. It states,

12   So soon as God had set up political government among his people Israel, he gave them a body of laws
13   for judgement both in civil and criminal causes. These were brief and fundamental principles, yet withal
14   so full and comprehensive as out of them clear deductions were to be drawn to all particular cases in
15   future times... ... This has been no small privilege and advantage to us in New England that our
16   churches and civil state have been planted and grown up, like two twins, together like that of Israel in
17   the wilderness....[188]

3.8 The Puritans Uphold Rule of Law

21   The Puritans upheld "Rule of Law" in their colonies in accordance with the Bible. "Rule of Law" is the
22   the principle that all humans, including those in power, are subject to the law, that no one is above the law.[189]
23   This principle differed from "Ruler's Law" in which an absolute ruler or governing body may arbitrarily govern
24   over subjects without limit or accountability to the law. Rule of Law was not based on fallible, changing rulers
25   but on a constant law to which every person, including rulers, was accountable.   Rule of Law had been
26   recognized in Britain's Magna Carta or "Great Charter of the Liberties of England" of 1215 which asserted
27   various rights of Englishmen, though the principle was not always embraced by Britain's rulers. The Puritans
28   upheld Rule of Law in America because they believed it was consistent with the Bible. In the Bible, God sets
29   the moral law, and this law applies to everyone, not just to certain people or groups. The Puritans, in fact,
30   started to practice Rule of Law in their colonies before Rutherford's 1644 *Lex Rex* was released in Britain.

32   Rule of Law is related to the Bible-based idea of equity—of justness, impartiality, and fairness of law.
33   Some thinkers of the Reformation era had addressed the issue of equity in the Bible and its relevance to human
34   law. In his *Institutes*, John Calvin asserts that just as equity characterizes and purposes God's moral law, so
35   also it should characterize and purpose all human law. Calvin, for one, describes the equity of human beings in
36   the Bible, that all people are made in God's image and possess the human nature: "Scripture notes a twofold
37   equity.... Man is both the image of God and our flesh."[190] Calvin explains that God's moral law for all
38   mankind as well as the civil laws among the ancient Israelites in the Bible functioned with equity. He writes,

40   The moral law, ...being comprised in two leading articles, ...is the true and eternal rule of righteous,
41   prescribed to men of all ages and nations, who wish to conform their lives to the will of God. ... The
42   judicial law, given to them [the Israelites] as a political constitution, taught them certain rules of equity
43   and justice, by which they might conduct themselves in a harmless and peaceable manner towards each
44   other. ... What I have said will be more clearly understood, if in all laws we properly consider these two
45   things; the constitution of the law, and its equity, on the reason of which the constitution itself is
46   founded and rests. Equity, being natural, is the same to all mankind; and consequently all laws, on every
47   subject, ought to have the same equity for their end. Particular enactments and regulations, being
48   connected with circumstances and partly dependent on them, may be different in different cases, without
49   any impropriety, provided they are all equally directed to the same object of equity. Now as it is certain

that the law of God, which we call the moral law, is no other than a declaration of natural law, and of that conscience which has been engraven by God on the minds of men, the whole rule of this equity of which we now speak is prescribed in it. This equity therefore must alone be the scope and rule and end of all laws.[191]

Calvin explains how equity characterizes God's moral law, applicable to all people, as well as the Israelites' civil laws. The Israelites learn from the equity of their civil law how they should conduct themselves toward one another. Similarly, all people can learn from the equity of God's moral law the standard for human law and how to treat each another. Equity is necessary for just human law, and constitutions of law are made to uphold equity. Equity is, he says, "the reason of which the constitution itself is founded and rests."[192]

In his 1556 *Short Treatise of Political Power*, John Ponet also supports equity from the Bible—from Deuteronomy 1 and John 7. Directly referencing these verses, he writes, "When you sit to judge, you shall not have respect of persons, whether they be rich or poor, great or small: fear no man, for you execute the judgment of God, says the Holy Ghost by the mouth of Moses. Judge not after the outward appearance of man, but judge rightly, says Christ." Similarly, in Deuteronomy 1:17, Moses says to Israel's judges, "'You shall not show partiality in judgment; you shall hear the small as well as the great; you shall not be afraid in any man's presence, for the judgment *is* God's.'" In John 7:24, Jesus says to the people, "Do not judge according to appearance, but judge with righteous judgment."

The Puritans implemented Rule of Law in their colonies based on the principles of equity and judgment according to law found in the Bible and in Reformed writings. They applied equity and Rule of Law in their colonies with their newly-formed constitutions of law. This practice was beneficial and necessary because, while the Bible was the primary source of civil law in the Puritan colonies, the Puritans recognized that many civil issues were not literally or directly addressed in the Bible. Such issues were subject to the interpretation or discretion of their governors. Some colonists like Thomas Hooker feared that too much judicial discretion might lead to violations of law, justice, and civil rights. In response, the Puritans sought to create written codes of laws—or constitutions—to prevent arbitrary rule by governors and to articulate and secure their freedoms as shared by all colonists—both governors and governed. Hooker notably supported the need for a constant law over arbitrary rule—based on the Bible. In a letter to Winthrop, he argues for Rule of Law based on Deuteronomy 17:10-11, Acts 5:12-40, and Acts 4:18-20. Hooker writes,

> …[T]he question here grows—what rule the judge must have to judge by; secondly, who those counsellors must be.
> That in the matter which is referred to the judge, the sentence should lie in his breast, or be left to his discretion, according to which he should go, I am afraid it is a course which wants both safety and warrant. I must confess, I ever looked at it as a way which leads directly to tyranny, and so to confusion, and must plainly profess, if it was in my liberty, I should neither choose to live nor leave my posterity under such a government. … 17 Deut., 10, 11—Thou shalt observe to do according to all that they inform, according to the *sentence of the Law*. Thou shalt seek the Law at his mouth: not ask what his discretion allows, but what the Law requires. And therefore the Apostles [in the book of Acts], when the rulers and high priest passed sentence against their preaching, as prejudicial to the State, the Apostle Peter made it not dainty to profess and practice contrary to their charge, because their sentence was contrary to the law, though they might have pretended discretion and depth of wisdom and policy in their charge.[193]

Hooker believed that the Deuteronomy scriptures that indicate judgment according to the "sentence of the law" directly supported Rule of Law over arbitrary rule. The Acts 4 and 5 scriptures that he mentions tell of how the religious rulers, though seemingly wise, issue an improper judgment (contrary to God's law) against the

1 Apostles when they follow their own discretion. Hooker thus illustrates the need for a consistent law by which
2 to judge civil matters. Hooker favored a civil government operating under clearly defined laws, not under
3 arbitrary rulers who might rule in error by their discretions. The best protection for order, justice, and human
4 rights, he therefore thought, was Rule of Law.
5
6 The Bible-based principle of Rule of Law influenced the Puritans to define the civil laws of their
7 community's constitution. A constitution was an outline of civil laws agreed upon by those in the community.
8 A constitution would make civil law regular or evenly enforced, not arbitrarily applied based on who was in
9 power. Indeed, Rule of Law naturally led to constitutions.[194]
10

3.9 The Puritans Create Constitutions of Law

12
13 When the Puritans arrived in Massachusetts, they did not yet have a complete, formal set of civil laws
14 for their colonies. They set about immediately to debate and decide the civil laws of their new commonwealth,
15 and they often looked to their colony's royal charter to determine many of their civil rights and laws. The
16 charter laid out certain governing rules for the colony. Additionally, the Massachusetts Company had promised
17 settlers in the new colony all the rights of Englishmen as granted by English law including Rule of Law and
18 "due process" of law—in which no one can be denied his or her rights without proper legal procedure and just
19 judgment according to the law of the land.[195] From these points of reference, the colonists in Massachusetts
20 closely guarded their rights. Indeed, early Massachusetts was, says Johnson, a "remarkably argumentative and
21 politically conscious society...."[196] The first voting election and use of secret ballots occurred in Salem,
22 Massachusetts, in 1634.
23
24 In 1639, the Puritans in Connecticut drafted a first, comprehensive framework of written laws, agreed
25 upon by the colonists, known as the Fundamental Orders of Connecticut. It became the first complete, written
26 constitution in history. It was also, essentially, the first complete self-government by the people. The
27 constitution was inspired by Thomas Hooker's May 31, 1638 speech which he delivered to the Connecticut
28 General Court—in which Hooker argued in favor of self-government via popular sovereignty, consent of the
29 governed, representative government, and limited power. The Puritans in Connecticut consequently created by
30 their constitutions a civil republic/democratic style of self-government in their colony that secured these
31 principles. Their constitution included Rule of Law, elections and term limits for chosen representatives, voting
32 rights and secret ballot, due process of law, trial by jury, no taxation without representation, prohibitions against
33 cruel and unusual punishment, and other individual rights and limits to power. It maintained some of the
34 Pilgrims' Plymouth laws of 1636 (which had upheld consent, elections, term limits, and due process).
35 Connecticut would later become known as "the Constitution State" for being the first colony to develop a
36 complete constitution to govern itself. The Fundamental Orders would become a model for constitutions in
37 other colonies. It prompted the colonists in Massachusetts, for example, to create a more formal and complete
38 set of written laws, their own constitution—the Massachusetts Body of Liberties of 1641—which secured many
39 of the same rights and restraints.
40
41 In creating written constitutions, the Puritans followed the Israelites' practice of written laws in the
42 Bible. The Israelites' Ten Commandments, for example, are engraved in stone. Similarly, the Puritans wrote
43 down all of their civil covenants and constitutions of law.[197] Indeed, the written word was very important to
44 them. The Puritan's practice of written laws would mean that the founding documents and laws of the United
45 States—including the Mayflower Compact, Declaration, Constitution, and Bill of Rights—would also be in
46 written form.

In keeping with the Israelites' practice of covenants, the Puritans founded their constitutions of law on covenants among the people. They articulated these agreements in their constitutions. Reminiscent of the Mayflower Compact, the Fundamental Orders state that the people "do therefore associate and conjoin ourselves to be as one Public State or Commonwealth; and do…enter into Combination and Confederation together…."[198] The Orders also state that governors elected to rule are to be voted in by freemen—adult male church members—who had taken an "Oath of Fidelity" to the colony. Governors then swear an oath to rule justly according to the law. In the Massachusetts Body of Liberties, the colonists approve their laws with their "sollemne consent" by which they "doe [do] therefore this day religiously and unanimously decree and confirme" them."[199] Covenants secured and protected the Puritans' laws and responsibilities to the community.

The Puritan constitutions—and the governing principles found in them—would lay the groundwork for Rule of Law, individual rights, and covenant-based state constitutions in the future nation of the United States. The future state constitutions would, in turn, serve as models for the United States' federal government and constitution.

3.10 Thomas Hooker and the Puritans Assert Popular Sovereignty

The Puritans—Thomas Hooker in particular—introduced and defended the principles of popular sovereignty and consent of the governed in Connecticut. Popular sovereignty is, as discussed earlier, the idea that God gives civil authority to the people as a whole, not to a particular individual, group/class, or lineage of humans. The people may choose governors by their consent and limit the power of these rulers. Popular sovereignty is a basis for democracy/republicanism. In asserting popular sovereignty, Hooker was likely influenced by his Bible-based religious beliefs and the ideas of the Reformation. Hooker believed in Martin Luther's Reformed idea of the "priesthood of all believers" in the church and, therefore, of church power. Hooker's view of church power led to his similar view of civil power. Hooker first articulates the principle of popular sovereignty in his influential court speech in Connecticut, asserting that "the foundation of authority is laid, firstly, in the free consent of the people."[200] In his 1648 *Summe of Church Discipline*, he continues to defend these principles from nature and the Bible, echoing earlier thinkers and reformers and citing scriptures. In this work, he applies these principles to the church and, subsequently, to the civil state. All representatives, he asserts, have only the power given to them by the general court.

As indicated earlier, the "priesthood of all believers" is the idea, asserted by reformer Luther, that all believers in the church have equal standing and ministry responsibilities before God. Luther addresses this topic in his 1520 Reformation writing, *Appeal to the Ruling Class of German Nationality*. He bases this idea on scriptures like 1 Peter 2:9-10 and Revelation 5:9-10. Notably, he also affirms this view from Matthew 16, to which Thomas Hooker also refers. In Matthew 16:19 (and Matthew 18:18), when the Apostle Peter declares that Jesus Christ is the Messiah, Jesus responds to Peter, "'And I will give you the keys of the kingdom of heaven, and whatever you bind on earth will be bound in heaven, and whatever you loose on earth will be loosed in heaven.'" Many religious leaders in the Roman church had asserted that this verse meant that Peter alone and therefore the pope alone—who represents Peter according to the Roman church—possessed these keys of power or certain spiritual abilities and authority in the church. Luther, however, believed that Jesus was speaking of the spiritual abilities of *all* believers in the church—like the abilities to receive and lead others to spiritual salvation, to perform spiritual services, and to interpret scripture. Luther explains in his writings that Jesus's words are "said to Christians individually and collectively," that Christ "hath given the keys to his Church," and that "the treasures of the church are the keys of the church, and are bestowed by the merits of Christ."[201] Luther elaborates that the keys of power belong to the whole church, not only to the pope and clergy. Referencing Matthew 16:18-19 and John 17:9, he further explains,

...[I]f they [religious leaders in the Roman church] claim that St. Peter received authority when he was given the keys [Matthew 16:18-20, brackets mine]—well, it is plain enough that the keys were not given to St. Peter only, but to the whole Christian community. ... ...Christ did not pray for Peter only, but for all apostles and Christians. As He said in John 17 [:9, 20], "Father, I pray for those whom Thou hast given me, and not only them, but for all those who believe on me through their word." Surely these words are plain enough.[202]

Thomas Hooker shared Luther's reformed view of the priesthood of all believers. In his *Summe of Church Discipline*, Hooker also cites Matthew 16:19 to support his position on church power. Like Luther, he takes from this verse that all Christians in the church have equal spiritual responsibilities and thus spiritual authority. Hooker explains that the "keys" mentioned by Jesus in this verse are a sign of delegated power to oversee church affairs and necessities. These keys of power are entrusted to the whole church as a "single society" who *share* the power since all Christians share the same spiritual commission and responsibilities which issue from that power. As such, the power of the keys belongs firstly or directly with the whole church. The church may then, by consent, assign some power to governors or leaders. Thus the church's power to elect and admit governors comes *before* the existence of governors or leaders.[203] Drawing from this idea of church power, Hooker saw a similar application to civil power in the civil state. Just as believers are equal in the church, he believed, so are citizens equal in the state. And just as authority in the church resides with all the believers, not with any particular one, authority in the civil state likewise resides with all the citizens. Citizens may similarly elect governors to oversee their civil affairs.

Since all people are equal in nature and standing as human beings in the civil state and as Christians in the church, Thomas Hooker continues to explain, legitimate church and civil authority can only come from the consent of the whole people. Hooker remarks of church power, *"No man by nature hath Ecclesiasticall power over another…. If then nature gives not this: …it comes not by constraint; therefore it must come by mutual and free consent."*[204] Church power among naturally equal church members, he points out, is legitimized by consent. Civil power is also granted this way. When the people voluntarily select and subject to a church or civil officer, the people give that officer the legal right to govern over them. Hooker explains, *"Those in whose choice it is whether any shall rule over them or no; from their voluntary subjection it is, that the party chosen hath right, and stands possessed of rule and authority over them."*[205] The people's election of a civil officer or body to govern over them is seen as God's sanction or approval of that civil authority. This practice enables the people to choose governors for themselves who allow them to fulfill their covenant responsibilities toward God and one another. Hooker's and the Puritans' support for popular sovereignty and consent in the civil state significantly influenced the governance of early American colonies like Connecticut and Massachusetts. It also later influenced the future states and nation of the United States.

3.11 The Puritans Choose Representatives to Govern, Implement Representative Government

The Puritans elected civil officers to govern in their colonies rather than having their rulers rule absolutely by hereditary succession as often occurred in Europe. Both Winthrop and Thomas Hooker supported representative government. The people's practice of choosing representatives to govern largely reflected the ideas of popular sovereignty and consent. It also reflected in some ways the Israelites' practice of selecting rulers in ancient Israel—firstly when Israel is governed by judges and then later, to some extent, when the nation comes under the rule of kings. The principle of representative government actually demonstrates the main characteristic of a "republic"—a country governed by elected representatives of its people. A republic serves a number of practical needs. Namely, it provides approved, godly, qualified men to govern and to represent the people in the civil state—particularly helpful when the gathering of the whole people is impractical and inefficient. The elected civil officers in the republican style colonies in America served as

1   representatives of the people, who governed by laws, not as absolute rulers who came to power by birthright
2   and who ruled with unlimited, arbitrary power.

3   The election of rulers by the people put into action the principle of popular sovereignty. Under the
4   principle of election, some rulers might be confirmed by covenant or agreement, voted in, selected by draw, or
5   otherwise *directly* chosen or elected by the people. Other rulers might be appointed by those chosen leaders—
6   and thus *indirectly elected* by the people. Both methods are forms of election. As the Bible verses in this
7   section will show, ancient Israel in the Bible also practices some methods of election (though their leaders
8   represent God, not the people). The Puritans also looked to their example.

10   Before they came to America, the Puritans had assigned religious leaders in their churches. Now, in
11   their colonies in America, they followed the pattern of their churches and elected civil leaders for their
12   commonwealths. In his *Summe of Church Discipline*, which sums up Puritan church doctrine, Thomas Hooker
13   explains the idea of election based on popular sovereignty. Though Hooker is writing about church leaders, the
14   Puritans adopted the same thinking for their civil leaders. Hooker writes,

16   There is *an act of power put forth in election. … Election*…implies two things; 1. The *choice* on the
17   peoples part: 2. The *acceptation* of the call on his [the pastor's] part. … *…[T]heir giving of him
18   authority* over them, their calling and by willing *subjection*, delivering up themselves to be ruled by him
19   in Christ, *is an act of Power. … Hence* the *power* that the *Pastor* hath, extends no *larger* nor further
20   then *his own* people; he hath no more then what they give, no more but this: for their subjection is onely
21   [only] from themselves.[206]

23   Such political authority granted to a chosen ruler could be limited or removed by the people based on popular
24   sovereignty. Hooker expresses this point in his Connecticut court sermon: "They [the people] who have power
25   to appoint officers and magistrates, it is in their power, also, to set the bounds and limitations of the power and
26   place unto which they call them."[207] Hooker's point is reminiscent of that of medieval Catholic theologian
27   Thomas Aquinas who had expressed, "If any society of people have a right of choosing a king, then the king so
28   established can be deposed by them without injustice, or his power can be curbed, when by tyranny he abuses
29   his regal power."[208]

31   The Puritans further supported the idea of chosen representatives to govern based on the practices of
32   ancient Israel—firstly under the judges and then later under the kings. They found examples of this idea in
33   Exodus 18, Deuteronomy 1 and 17, and 2 Chronicles 19. The story behind the Israelite's election of
34   representatives in Deuteronomy 1 is found in Exodus 18. In Exodus 18:13-27, Jethro, the father-in-law of
35   Moses, watches Moses serving all day long as the only judge for all the people. When Jethro asks why Moses
36   does it alone, Moses replies that the people come to him to seek God's counsel. Moses moderates the people's
37   disputes according to God's law and statutes. But Jethro advises Moses to select wise, godly men to share the
38   burden of judging the people's affairs, a task too difficult and tiresome for Moses alone. Following Jethro's
39   advice, Moses educates the people in God's law and their responsibilities. He then appoints 70 elders or judges
40   to share in the responsibility of governing the nation and to represent the people. Exodus 18:13-27 states,

42   And so it was, on the next day, that Moses sat to judge the people; and the people stood before Moses
43   from morning until evening. So when Moses' father-in-law [Jethro] saw all that he did for the people,
44   he said, "What *is* this thing that you are doing for the people? Why do you alone sit, and all the people
45   stand before you from morning until evening?"
46   And Moses said to his father-in-law, "Because the people come to me to inquire of God. When
47   they have a difficulty, they come to me, and I judge between one and another; and I make known the
48   statutes of God and His laws."

So Moses' father-in-law said to him, "The thing that you do *is* not good. Both you and these people who *are* with you will surely wear yourselves out. For this thing *is* too much for you; you are not able to perform it by yourself. [19] Listen now to my voice; I will give you counsel, and God will be with you: Stand before God for the people, so that you may bring the difficulties to God. And you shall teach them the statutes and the laws, and show them the way in which they must walk and the work they must do. Moreover you shall select from all the people able men, such as fear God, men of truth, hating covetousness; and place *such* over them *to be* rulers of thousands, rulers of hundreds, rulers of fifties, and rulers of tens. And let them judge the people at all times. Then it will be *that* every great matter they shall bring to you, but every small matter they themselves shall judge. So it will be easier for you, for they will bear *the burden* with you. If you do this thing, and God *so* commands you, then you will be able to endure, and all this people will also go to their place in peace."

So Moses heeded the voice of his father-in-law and did all that he had said. And Moses chose able men out of all Israel, and made them heads over the people: rulers of thousands, rulers of hundreds, rulers of fifties, and rulers of tens. So they judged the people at all times; the hard cases they brought to Moses, but they judged every small case themselves.

In the subsequent account of this process of appointing judges—in Deuteronomy 1:9-18—Moses instructs the people of Israel to select wise, godly men from among their tribes whom he will then appoint as rulers over their tribes. The people approve this process and select such worthy men. These selected leaders serve as judges for the people according to God's law. This process of election and appointment of rulers by Moses and the people is demonstrated when Moses says to the people in Deuteronomy 1:13-15, "'**Choose wise, understanding, and knowledgeable men from among your tribes, and I will make them heads over you.' And you answered me and said, 'The thing which you have told *us* to do *is* good.' So I took the heads of your tribes, wise and knowledgeable men, and made them heads over you, leaders of thousands, leaders of hundreds, leaders of fifties, leaders of tens, and officers for your tribes**."[209]

The Puritans also noticed that judges are similarly appointed by the king of Israel after the nation comes under the rule of kings as found in 2 Chronicles 19 and Deuteronomy 17. In 2 Chronicles 19:4-11, Jehoshaphat, the king of Judah, appoints judges in all the cities of Judah to govern according to God's law.[210] 2 Chronicles 19:5-7 states, "Then he [Jehoshapat] set judges in the land throughout all the fortified cities of Judah, city by city, and said to the judges, 'Take heed to what you are doing, for you do not judge for man but for the LORD, who *is* with you in the judgment. Now therefore, let the fear of the LORD be upon you; take care and do *it,* for *there is* no iniquity with the LORD our God, no partiality, nor taking of bribes.'" Deuteronomy 17:8-11 explains how the people must honor the sentence of judgments given by the chosen judges who follow God's law.[211]

Interesting to note, some political writings of the Reformation of the 1500s and 1600s had also supported the idea of chosen representatives based on the practices of Israel under the kings. One such tract that supported this idea was *Vindiciae Contra Tyrannos* by the anonymous Stephen Brutus. The Puritans were likely, if indirectly, familiar with and influenced by this well-known tract. Brutus in *Vindiciae* defends the principle of elected representatives based on the Biblical books of Numbers, Exodus, 1 Chronicles, and 2 Samuel. From these books, he describes Israel's use of officers to manage the king's house, the commonwealth, and the towns and cities. He tells how the elders, representing the people, deliberate on issues of the nation. He also points out how King David consults with the elders on important civil and religious matters of the nation. Brutus observes,

But from the time when kings began to extend their frontier…, and the whole people could not assemble in one place without confusion, officers in the kingdom were instituted to protect…the rights of the people…. …

We see this to have been the arrangement…in the Israelite kingdom, which, in the judgement of almost all political thinkers, was the best constituted. The king had his butlers, his serving men, his chamberlains, and his mayors of the palace or stewards, who looked after his household. And the kingdom had its officers, seventy-one elders and the leaders elected by individual tribes, to take care of the commonwealth in time of peace or war; and then its magistrates in individual towns, each to protect the cities of the kingdom, as the former did the whole kingdom [Numbers 11:16, Exodus 24:1]. If the gravest matters had to be deliberated upon, these officers convened, and nothing which pertained to the highest affairs of the commonwealth…could be determined without their being consulted. Thus David convoked them when he wanted Solomon to be invested with the kingdom, when he wanted the constitution…which he had restored to be examined and approved, when the Ark was to be moved, and so on [1 Chronicles 29:1, 2 Samuel 5:3, 1 Chronicles 11:3, 1 Chronicles 13:1-5]. Because they [officers or elders] represent the whole people, the whole people was then said to have been assembled.[212]

Some leading Puritans in the colonies—including Thomas Hooker of Connecticut as well as John Winthrop and John Cotton of Massachusetts—were instrumental in defending governance by chosen representatives based on some of these Bible verses and understandings. Hooker argues in his Connecticut court sermon that "the choice of public magistrates belongs unto the people, by God's own allowance."[213] He cites Deuteronomy 1:13 to support this point. Cotton likewise cites Deuteronomy 1:13, 15, and 17 in his 1641 *An Abstract of the Laws of New England* to support the choosing of representatives—that "ALL magistrates are to be chosen."[214] These particular verses in Deuteronomy, the Puritans believed, clearly demonstrated the principle of chosen representatives based on the consent of the people, for in these verses the people explicitly approve the election process, responding to Moses, "'The thing which you have told *us* to do *is* good.'" In addition, in a letter to Winthrop, Hooker refers to 2 Chronicles 19 and Deuteronomy 17:10-11 in support of chosen representatives to govern for the people. Hooker concludes from these verses that the best states are governed by chosen representatives:

> …[A] general counsel, chosen by all, to transact businesses which concern all, I conceive, under favor, most suitable to rule and most safe for relief of the whole. This was the practice of the Jewish church, directed by God, Deut. 17:10, 11; 2 Chron., 19; and the approved experience of the best ordered States give in evidence this way.[215]

Moreover, since the power of election is with the people, the Puritans noted, the people have a responsibility to exercise election in godliness and according to God's law. Hooker points out in his Connecticut court sermon that "…The privilege of election, which belongs to the people, therefore must not be exercised according to their [the people's] humors, but according to the blessed will and *law of God*."[216] Following God's law, the Puritans sought to choose moral, godly representatives to administer God's rule among the people. For God-fearing men possessed the morality necessary to govern justly. The religious and moral convictions of representatives, the Puritans believed, positively affected their actions and restrained their sinful tendencies while they were in power. Religious belief was a means for self-evaluation and self-restraint. It also imposed a high moral standard on those in power. Furthermore, godly leaders could influence or correct the views and acts of immoral or unjust leaders.

The Puritans cited a number of scriptures on the issue to elect godly rulers. They cited Exodus 18:21 in which Jethro instructs Moses to choose able, God-fearing men as rulers: "Moreover you shall select from all the people able men, such as fear God, men of truth, hating covetousness; and place *such* over them *to be* rulers…."[217] Cotton cites this verse in a letter of correspondence and also in his *Abstract* to support the idea to choose God-fearing men to govern, "the ablest men and most approved amongst them."[218] Rev. Samuel Willard, a colonial clergyman who was born in Massachusetts, also affirms the importance of godly virtue in rulers in his 1694 printed election sermon *The Character of a Good Ruler*. He describes virtues for leaders from the Bible relating to honesty, truthfulness, righteousness, equity, lawfulness, justness, knowledge, wisdom, humility, conscientiousness, piety, faithfulness, integrity, steadfastness, benevolence, selflessness, and public-mindedness. These virtues, he says, stem from the idea in 2 Samuel 23:3 that good rulers "must be just, ruling in the fear of God" as well as from Exodus 18:21; Deuteronomy 1:17, 16:19, and 17:18-19; and Psalms 75:10 which indicate such characteristics of a godly ruler.[219] Puritan theologian and later founder of Rhode Island, Roger Williams believed a non-religious man could possess moral, godly qualities but affirmed the benefits of religious conviction in civil officers for moral, godly ruling. In his 1644 *Bloudy Tenent of Persecution for Cause of Conscience*, he cites on this point 1 Peter 1:15 in which the Apostle Peter expresses God's desire that Christians act in a godly manner—"but as He who called you *is* holy, you also be holy in all *your* conduct." From this verse, Williams observes that Christianity teaches believers "to act in their several callings, to a higher ultimate end, from higher principles, in a more heavenly and spiritual manner... ... A Christian pilot...acts from a root of the fear of God and love of mankind in his whole course. ...[H]is aim is more to glorify God, than to gain his pay, or make his voyage."[220] Williams thus also cites 1 Peter 2:15 which states, "For this is the will of God, that by doing good you may put to silence the ignorance of foolish men...."

In the mind of the Puritans, it made sense that their civil representatives should be godly and moral since these officers act as servants of God to administer God's justice among the people. These officers are to serve and benefit the good of the people, and the people are to submit to them as divinely sanctioned authority. Ultimately, both governors and governed are responsible to God. Hooker supports this idea of godly rulers in his *Summe of Church Discipline* based on Matthew 22:13 and Romans 13:3-4. He writes that both church and civil leaders are responsible for leading and ruling justly for God:

> But the Lord Christ, as a King of infinite mercy as well as wisdome, he provides for the outward good and comfort of all his houshold and subjects, in regard of their estates, that they may be maintained, and their health also, and so their lives preserved in a prosperous condition, and to this end he hath appointed Officers.... ... Matt. 22.13. *Then said the King unto his Servants*; the word is...used also to express the administratio of the civil Magistrate, *Rom*.13.4. when their administratios are considered as under God, being his servants, *he is the Minister of God to thee for good*....[221]

In accordance with their Bible-based beliefs, the Puritans implemented representative government in their colonies. For one, they elected governors to oversee their colonies. Then, in 1634, the Puritan freemen or voters of Massachusetts elected their first Assembly of Representatives to help govern their colony. In 1636, the Puritans of Connecticut elected representatives for their own General Court. In 1644, Massachusetts separated its representative assembly into two houses—the House of Assistants and House of Deputies—to form a bicameral General Court. The General Court held legislative, executive, and judicial power to make, implement, and interpret laws. Alluding to Colossians 3:14 and Matthew 12:25, Winthrop encourages the two branches of the court to operate in love since "Love is the Bond of perfection, & a kingdome or house divided cannot stand."[222] This bicameral assembly, found first in Virginia and then in Massachusetts, is the origin of the two branches of congress—the Senate and House of Representatives—in the future United States.[223] By applying the principle of chosen representatives in their colonies, the Puritans contributed to the development of representative self-government in the future states and nation of the United States. They, consequently, contributed to the new nation's formation as a republic.

3.12 The Puritans Support Education for Bible Literacy

The Puritans strongly supported education. Literacy, they believed, is necessary in order to read and understand the Bible and its principles. Literacy and education were also important to them because a civil republican/democratic self-government require informed, knowledgeable voters and representatives who understand the laws of the colony. Literacy and education also provide communities with competent citizens of various professions. The Puritans, therefore, wanted to spread knowledge to everyone for the benefit of the community. The Puritans felt so strongly about Bible literacy that they passed education laws requiring sizeable towns to set up schools and to require that reading and writing be taught. The Massachusetts School Act of 1642 required all children to be taught to read and write by their parents or schoolmasters. The Old Deluder Satan Act of 1647 required communities and towns to set up and fund grammar schools and hire schoolmasters. The act intended to prevent Satan, "the Old Deluder," from deceiving people with illiteracy and keeping them from reading the Bible. The Puritans' Old Deluder law became the basis for the public school system in America.

The Puritans' support for Bible education and the Old Deluder Law was influenced by the Protestant Reformation and their reformed views about the church and the Bible. The Puritans held the view that all believers in Christ, not just church leaders or clergy, may read and interpret the Bible. This view stemmed from two Reformation concepts—"the priesthood of all believers" and *sola scriptura. Sola scriptura*, Latin for "scripture alone," is the Reformed idea that the Bible—as the inspired, infallible Word of God—is the highest, final source of authority on Christian faith, doctrine, and practice. The Bible is the speaking and teaching, the authority of God. This idea is found in 2 Timothy 3:16: "All Scripture *is* given by inspiration of God, and *is* profitable for doctrine, for reproof, for correction, for instruction in righteousness...." All earthly religious authorities and interpretations of scripture are, therefore, subject to correction by the Holy Scriptures.

From these two concepts, the priesthood of all believers and *sola scriptura*, Luther and the reformers opposed the old traditional church practice in which only the pope and clergy could read and interpret the Bible. For such a practice, he saw, had led to unbiblical errors, heresies, and corruptions in the church. He argued, instead, that all Christians have the ability and responsibility to read, understand, interpret, teach, and correct with the Bible. Referencing 1 Corinthians 14:30, John 6:45, Matthew 16:18-20, John 17, 1 Corinthians 2:15, 2 Corinthians 4:13, 2 Corinthians 3:17, 1 John, 4:1, and Galatians 2:11, he observes,

The Romanists [religious leaders in the Roman church] profess to be the only interpreter of Scripture, even though they never learn anything contained in it their lives long. They claim authority for themselves alone, juggle with words shamelessly before our eyes, saying that the pope cannot err as to the faith, whether he be bad or good; although they cannot quote a single letter of Scripture to support their claim. Thus it comes about that so many heretical, unchristian, and even unnatural laws are contained in the canon [church, brackets mine] law.... ... In such a case, what is the need or the value of Holy Scripture? Let it be burned, and let us be content with the ignorant gentlemen at Rome.... ...
But lest we fight them with mere words, let us adduce Scripture. St. Paul says, I Corinthians 14 [:30, brackets editor's], "If something superior be revealed to any one sitting there and listening to another speaking God's word, the first speaker must be silent and give place." What would be the virtue of this commandment if only the speaker, or the person in the highest position, were to be believed? Christ Himself says, John 6 [:45], "that all Christians shall be taught by God." ... Has not the pope made many errors? Who could enlighten Christian people if the pope erred, unless someone else, who had the support of Scripture, were more to be believed than he?
Therefore it is a wicked, base invention, for which they cannot adduce a tittle of evidence in support, to aver that it is the function of the pope alone to interpret Scripture, or to confirm any particular interpretation. ...
In addition, as I have already said, each and all of us are priests because we all have the one faith, the one gospel, one and the same sacrament; why then should we not be entitled to taste or test, and to judge what is right or wrong in the faith? How otherwise does St. Paul's dictum stand, I Corinthians 2 [:15], "He that is spiritual judges all things and is judged by none," and II Corinthians 4 [:13], "We all have the one spirit of faith"? Why then should we not distinguish what accords or does not accord with the faith quite as well as an unbelieving pope? These and many other passages should give us courage and set us free. ... We ought to march boldly forward, and test everything the

Romanists do or leave undone [1 John 4:1, brackets mine]. We ought to apply that understanding of the Scriptures which we possess as believers, and constrain the Romanists to follow, not their own interpretation, but that which is in fact the better. ... ...St. Paul upbraided St. Peter as a wrongdoer [Gal. 2:11, brackets editor's]. Hence it is the duty of every Christian to accept the implications of the faith, understand and defend it, and denounce everything false.[224]

Luther and the reformers upheld the ability and responsibility of all Christians to read, understand, interpret, teach, and correct with the Bible. Consequently, they knew the Bible had to be accessible to all the people. They thus set about translating the Bible into the common languages of the people. They also recognized the need and value of teaching the Bible to young people in schools. Luther protested the degraded state of schools of his day that did not teach the Bible to students. He emphasized this need for Bible teaching in schools and the consequences for neglecting it. Referencing Proverbs 22:6 and Lamentations 2:11-12, Luther expresses,

> Above all, the most important and most usual teaching, in both the universities and the lower schools, ought to be concerned with the Holy Scriptures; beginning with the gospels for the young boys. Would to God also that each town had a girls' school where, day by day, the girls might have a lesson on the gospel.... ...
>
> Oh! how unwisely we deal with our poor young folk, whom we are commanded to train and instruct [Prov. 22:6]! But we shall have to give a serious account of our stewardship, and explain why we have not set the Word of God before them. Their lot is that of which Jeremiah speaks in Lamentations 2, "Mine eyes do fail with tears, my bowels are troubled, my liver is poured upon the earth, for the destruction of the daughter of my people, because the young children and the sucklings swoon in the streets of the city. They say to their mothers, Where is corn and wine? When they swooned as the wounded in the streets of the city, when their soul is poured out into their mothers' bosom" [Lam. 2:11]. We fail to notice the present pitiful distress of the young people. Though they live in the midst of a Christian world, they faint and perish in misery because they lack the gospel in which we should be training and exercising them all the time.[225]

The Puritans in America shared these Bible-based views of the reformers. Since all believers are priests and ministers of God, and since the Bible is the final authority on Christian doctrine, the Puritans thought, all believers in the church should read and know the Bible. The Puritans likewise thought that all Christians have the ability and responsibility to read, understand, interpret, teach, and correct with the Bible. As such, they also shared the reformers' view of the need for Bible accessibility, literacy, and education among the people. The Puritans had an awareness that if the people do not read and know the Bible, they could be led astray by false teachings, heresies, and corrupt teachers as had occurred in the Roman church in Europe prior to the Reformation. Consequently, they required the formation of schools and Bible education in their colonies in America.

American schools thus began in the 1600s to insure Bible literacy. As expected, the Bible was the core of learning in schools, and children were educated from a Christian worldview. Local governments could determine what prayers and religious observances were said in their schools. The *New England Primer*, the first reader in America, included Bible truths, stories, poems, hymns, and prayers, many by future founders of the nation. This textbook was used for over a century by settlers. Schools multiplied, and low tuition due to market competition also made higher education for the general population possible.[226] The building of the printing press in the colonies in 1639 led to mass printing of books and sermons in America, which further enhanced literacy and education.

The Puritans founded many of the first colleges and universities in America, and they did so with a strong Christian purpose. The Puritans founded the first college, Harvard University, in Massachusetts in 1636 to train ministers of the Gospel. Graduates pursued fields like ministry, politics, law, and medicine for the glory of God. Harvard's rules and precepts declared, "Let every Student be plainly instructed, and earnestly pressed to consider well, the maine end of his life and studies is, *to know God and Jesus Christ which is eternall life*, John 17:3 and therefore to lay *Christ* in the bottome, as the only foundation of all found knowledge and Learning."[227] In 1701, the Puritans founded Yale University in Connecticut as the third college in the colonies. It purposed "to plant, and under the Divine blessing, to propagate in this wilderness the blessed reformed Protestant Religion, in the purity of its order and worship...."[228] The Puritans began Dartmouth College in 1750 as a school to train ministers and missionaries to the Native Americans. Colleges founded in other colonies by other Christian groups in the 1600s and 1700s also had a religious focus. The Anglicans, for example, founded the second college in the colonies, College of William and Mary, in Virginia in 1693. It was founded partly "to the end that the Church of Virginia may be furnished with a seminary of ministers of the gospel, and that the youth may be piously educated in good letters and manners, and that the Christian faith may be propagated amongst the Western Indians, to the glory of Almighty God...."[229] These and future schools shaped the leaders and thinkers of early America including the Founding Fathers and presidents of the future United States of America.

The Puritan's emphasis on education influenced the public school system, widespread literacy, and the idea of an informed citizenry in America. Nearly all white men in early America were literate and knew the Bible. The direct understanding of the Bible by many promoted strong religious convictions among colonists. "It explains why New England religion was so powerful a force in people's lives," Johnson observes, "and of such direct and continuing assistance in building a new society from nothing. They were colonists for God, planting in His name."[230] The Puritans' belief in the Bible as God's Word and the need for literacy led to the creation of the most educated, literate society in the world.[231] The Puritan emphasis on education would further shape the future United States as an educated society that promoted education for all citizens. Schools and universities in the new nation would be modeled after early American schools.

3.13 The Puritans Value a Bible-Based Work Ethic

In their New England colonies, the Puritans practiced and valued a strong work ethic of hard work, industry, discipline, diligence, frugality, reliability, perseverance, sobriety, efficiency, self-sufficiency, and the living of one's life as a service and glory to God. The principle of work, the Puritans believed, is a consequence of Adam and Eve's fall in Genesis. It is based on Genesis 3:17-19 in which God requires fallen human beings to work for their sustenance. In Genesis 3:17 God says to Adam, "'Because you have heeded the voice of your wife, and have eaten from the tree of which I commanded you, saying, 'You shall not eat of it': Cursed *is* the ground for your sake; In toil you shall eat *of* it All the days of your life." As such, the Puritans viewed work as an obligation with moral, social, and economic value. Work could benefit the individual, family, society, and God. The Puritans, like Calvin, saw not only the need for and benefits of labor to sustain mankind but also humans' need for work in order to avoid Satan's evils and temptations that came through idleness and sloth. Since mankind is assigned by God to work, the godly, moral man has a strong work ethic.

In the first colony of Virginia, colony leader Captain John Smith had encouraged a strong, Bible-based work ethic among the settlers, for hardship, idleness, and greed had plagued those first colonists in Virginia. Such challenges threatened the colony's success and existence. Smith observed that many settlers did not want to work or lacked proper skill or experience to survive in the harsh environment. Many settlers spent their time searching for gold rather than farming. As a result, Smith implemented a Christian work ethic based on 2 Thessalonians 3:10 in which the Apostle Paul says to believers, "If anyone will not work, neither shall he eat." Smith likewise announced to the settlers, "[Y]ou must obey this now for a Law, that he that will not worke shall

1   not eate (except by sicknesse he be disabled:) for the labours of thirtie or fortie honest and industrious men shall
2   not be consumed to maintaine an hundred and fiftie idle loyterers [loiterers]."[232] Smith's Biblical reference and
3   Bible-based view of work reflected that of Luther who had also cited 2 Thessalonians 3:10 in his Reformation
4   writings. Luther writes in his *Appeal to the Ruling Class,*
5

6   He who has chosen poverty, ought not to be rich; but if a man chooses wealth, let him put his hand to the
7   plough and get his wealth for himself out of the earth. It is sufficient if the poor are decently provided
8   for, in such a way that they do not die of hunger or cold. It is not seemly that one man should live in
9   idleness on the labours of his fellows, or possess wealth and luxury through the hardships which others
10   suffer, as is the prevailing, perverse custom. St. Paul says, "If a man will not work, neither shall he eat"
11   [II Thess. 3:10, brackets editor's]. God has commanded no one to live at another man's expense, except
12   preachers and administrating priests for the sake of their spiritual labours [1 Corinthians 9:14, brackets
13   mine].[233]
14

15   In addition, Luther cites 1 Corinthians 9:14 in which Paul tells the believers that "the Lord has commanded that
16   those who preach the gospel should live from the gospel." In other words, those whose work as ministers may
17   receive their living from this work.
18

19   The American colonies attracted those in Britain and Europe, Smith explained, because they gave
20   colonists who were willing to work opportunities to create better, fulfilling lives for themselves and their
21   families. In his 1616 *Description of New England,* he writes of the opportunity in America: "[H]ere every man
22   may be master of his owne labour and land. …[I]f he have nothing but his hands, he may set up this Trade; and
23   by industry quickly grow rich…."[234] Smith expressed the joy of working in a free environment for oneself and
24   one's posterity, with social mobility. He elaborates, "…[I]f hee have but the taste of vertue [virtue], and
25   magnanimity, what to such a minde can bee more pleasant then planting and building a foundation for his
26   posterity, got from the rude earth by God's blessing and his owne industry without prejudice to any…."[235] In
27   expressing the opportunities in America for those who would work, Smith encouraged many in Britain to come
28   to America, causing Virginia and other colonies to grow. Smith's Christian view of work would later be found
29   in the Puritan work ethic.
30

31   A strong work ethic was a part of Puritan life and society and aligned with the Puritans' Christian
32   beliefs. Work was a duty, the Puritans saw, that allowed for mankinds's provision and prosperity, benefited self
33   and society, helped man avoid evil, and fulfilled God's assignment and purposes. The Bible encouraged work
34   and diligence. Citing 1 Timothy 1:12 and 1 Corinthians 7:19-20, John Cotton addresses in a sermon, "Christian
35   Calling," God's calling for humans to work:
36

37   Faith drawes the heart of a Christian to live in some warrantable calling; as soone as ever a man begins
38   to looke towards God, and the ways of his grace, he will not rest, till he find out some warrantable
39   Calling and imployment…. …Paul makes it a matter of great thankfulnesse to God, that he had given
40   him ability, and put him in place where he might doe him service, 1 Tim. 1. 12. … *As God hath called*
41   *every man, so let him walke,* 1 Cor. 7. 19, 20. This is the cleane worke of faith, hee would have some
42   imployment to *fill the head and hand with.*[236]
43

44   The Puritan work ethic was strongly supported and exemplified by future American Founder Benjamin
45   Franklin, who learned the values of his Puritan father. In addition to being a Founder of the United States,
46   Franklin was also an author, printer, postmaster, theorist, scientist, inventor, satirist, musician, statesman, and
47   diplomat. Indeed, Franklin was one of the most well-known figures in the American colonies due to his many
48   accomplishments. Franklin, like the Puritans, saw work as an important duty. In his writings, The *Way to*
49   *Wealth* and *Poor Richard's Almanac,* Franklin promotes the benefit and reward of work, citing the Bible

1 extensively. He observes, "'He that hath a trade hath an estate; and he that hath a calling, hath an office of
2 profit and honor'" and "'God gives all things to industry.'"[237] He also remarks that "'industry gives comfort,
3 and plenty, and respect'" and that "'God helps them that help themselves.'"[238] Sloth and idleness, he thought,
4 are to be avoided: "'Be ashamed to catch yourself idle, when there is so much to be done for yourself, your
5 family, your country, and your God.'"[239] Franklin supports the principle of work with many other Bible
6 scriptures including Ecclesiastes 9:10, Proverbs 10:14, 1 Thessalonians 4:11, and Proverbs 18:9. Ecclesiastes
7 9:10 states, "Whatever your hand finds to do, do *it* with your might...." Proverbs 18:9 states, "He who is
8 slothful in his work is a brother to him who is a great destroyer."[240]
9
10 In the spirit of Calvin, the Puritans, however, also reminded themselves of the need, while working, to
11 ultimately depend on God for all needs and provision. They maintained a balanced view of self-sufficent work
12 and of trust in God for blessings. Calvin similarly expresses this belief in God's provision in his Reformation-
13 era *Bible Commentaries on Psalms*:
14
15 ...[W]e shall enter upon our worldly avocations in a right way when our hope depends exclusively upon
16 God, and our success in that case will correspond to our wishes. But if a man, taking no account of God,
17 eagerly makes haste, he will bring ruin upon himself by his too precipitate course. ...[I]n executing
18 what God has enjoined upon them, they [humans] should always begin with prayer and calling upon his
19 [God's] name, offering to him their labors that he may bless them.[241]
20
21 Franklin expressed well the Puritan belief in God's ultimate provision. He instructs others who wish to become
22 prosperous to not only work diligently but also to humbly seek God for provision, stating,
23
24 ...[D]o not depend too much upon your own industry, and frugality, and prudence, though excellent
25 things; for they may all be blasted without the blessing of heaven; and, therefore, ask that blessing
26 humbly, and be not uncharitable to those [who] at present seem to want it, but comfort and help them.[242]
27
28 While humans work, they are to firstly rely on God because blessings ultimately come from God and earthly
29 riches may be fleeting. Further, many blessings are spiritual, not earthly. Franklin thus exhorts, "Those who
30 depend upon God shall not want, even in a desert."[243] For this idea of reliance on God, Franklin cites Proverbs
31 11:28, Psalms 32:10, Proverbs 3:6, and Proverbs 13:25.[244] Proverbs 3:6 states, "In all your ways acknowledge
32 Him, and He shall direct your paths." Proverbs 11:28 states, "He who trusts in his riches will fall, but the
33 righteous will flourish like foliage." The Puritan work ethic gave value to work as a godly duty but prioritized
34 God as the source and provider of all good things.
35
36 The Puritans, in fact, did prosper economically in America. Some Puritans like clergyman Rev. Cotton
37 Mather of Massachusetts believed this prosperity was due to continued worship and service of Christ. Though
38 the pursuit of wealth later became more important for some than the pursuit of godliness, say some historians,
39 the church and the Bible continued to play an important role in society.[245] The Puritan regard for the Bible-
40 based virtues of diligence, industry, and frugality, early Americans knew, were important for prosperity and
41 success in America. The Bible-based or Puritan work ethic would continue to be an important aspect of
42 American life in the future United States. It would influence American ideas of industry and capitalism and
43 provide a foundation for an American view of work.[246]
44
45 **3.14 Challenges in the Puritans' Bible Commonwealths: The Dilemmas of Religious Laws and Religious**
46 **Dissent**
47
48 In seeking to form a Bible Commonwealth, or civil state, the Puritans were undoubtedly influenced by
49 their experiences in Europe as well as by the ancient Israelites. The Puritans' experiences and identification

with the Israelites presented both challenges and benefits when it came to forming their Bible Commonwealths. In practically implementing their Bible-centered civil states, the Puritans struggled with their religious laws and religious conformity.

The Puritans defined religious freedom as freedom from religious error or heresy. It was freedom to voluntarily set up their own church and community based on their own beliefs rather than be forced to conform to an official church with which they disagreed. To be sure, the Puritans, much like their European forebears, were supporters of religious conformity in accordance with their own Congregational church which they named the official church in their colonies. They did not tolerate different religious sects and denominations in their colonies. Indeed, such a concept was largely unheard of and unpracticed in that time in Europe from whence they came. Religious uniformity or conformity was, the Puritans thought, the only way to preserve the church's faith, protect the church from corruption and heresy, and keep the community spiritually pure. Religious conformity was also necessary, they believed, to preserve the political and social order. Since many Puritans generally shared many of the same beliefs, such views of conformity were widely accepted and did not pose any problems initially. In time, however, some Puritans with differing religious views emerged and began to vocalize their opinions and beliefs. But the Puritans did not tolerate religious dissent—the expressed difference of opinion and/or refusal to conform to the official or established church. Dissenters, they thought, could undermine the peace, order, and stability of the community. As such, dissenters had to keep quiet about their differing beliefs or else leave the community. The Puritans in Massachusetts banished a number of bothersome religious dissenters from their colony including Roger Williams, who would found the colony of Rhode Island, and Anne Hutchinson, who for her unorthodox beliefs was tried, convicted, and expelled from the colony. Hutchinson and her supporters moved to Rhode Island. It is important to note that the Puritans, as they saw themselves, did not force anyone to conform to their beliefs, as often occurred in Europe, but gave non-conformists the freedom to leave the community and follow their own paths. One had free choice in the matter. Puritans like lawyer and minister Nathaniel Ward responded to qualms about intolerance by stating that those with differing beliefs "shall have free Liberty to keep away from us."[247] Religious tolerance for dissenters within the community remained outside the norm.

In their attempt to follow the example of the Israelites, the Puritans directly applied the nation practices of ancient Israel in their commonwealth. As such, they directly adopted Israel's Old Testament religious laws for their colony. This approach led to harsh moral and religious civil laws within the community—which were easily passed since most colonists agreed on them. Thus the Puritans' early laws and constitutions, while promoting many civil republican/democratic ideas, also gave the death penalty or severe punishments for religious offenses and immoral acts like idolatry, blasphemy, adultery, homosexuality, sodomy, witchcraft, murder, smiting of parents, and kidnapping. Such laws bring to mind the notorious Salem witch trials of 1692 and 1693 in which numerous colonists accused of witchcraft were imprisoned or executed by the civil court. Though the convictions were an unjust reaction to mass hysteria, they were based on the view that the colony should follow the religious laws of ancient Israel.[248] Actually, similarly harsh laws existed in Europe and elsewhere and were somewhat typical of the time.

The Puritans deeply struggled with how to shape their civil state and laws according to the Bible. They saw, say some scholars, two different spiritual approaches in the Old and New Testaments. Their circumstances, they knew, differed from those of the ancient Israelites, yet they also believed God's covenants and Word—the Bible—were relevant to their present situation.[249] The difficulty they experienced in implementing their Christian state was evidenced, says Johnson, in the changing governing approaches of Winthrop. Though Winthrop was greatly respected, his governance in early Massachusetts was considered by some to be too harsh and was sometimes challenged. His leadership raised issues of freedom and authority and the governor's role in implementing laws in a Christian manner. Further questions arose over how to balance

1   law, order, and justice with Christian mercy.[250] The Puritans wrestled increasingly over time with such issues of
2   religious law and governance.
3
4   Despite these challenges of the Puritans' direct application of Old Testament religious laws, the
5   Puritans' Bible Commonwealths had some benefits. For one, due to the Puritans' widely shared Judeo-
6   Christian beliefs and efforts to create Bible Commonwealths, high moral standards characterized Puritan life.
7   Communities gathered in towns or villages where church, government, and defense were grouped. The church
8   hall was centrally located for public worship, and the church service was central to society. The sermon was the
9   most influential form of communication in New England, and the Bible was the main source of sermons. The
10 Puritans' beliefs and moral lifestyle positively influenced Puritan views of self, family, community, work,
11 respect for laws and rights, concern for the poor, and reverence for God.[251] In fact, daily and community life,
12 observes one historian, naturally supported the religious laws of the colonies.[252] The Puritans' morality was so
13 rigorous, says Mark Noll, that "almost all Americans since have been forced to react to it in some way."[253] The
14 Puritans would make radical Protestantism normal in America, say some historians, and give the future nation
15 of the United States a strong moral rigor.[254] In the 1800s, Puritan morality was often credited for the new
16 nation's success.
17
18 **3.15 Conclusion: A Civil Society Practicing Many Bible-Based and Republican/Democratic Principles**
19
20   Though they saw their work as incomplete, the Puritans attempted to create a society in America
21 centered on their Bible-based or Judeo-Christian beliefs. These beliefs provided a source of strength for them
22 as well as a purpose and vision for America. Their Judeo-Christian worldview and beliefs affected everything
23 they did in church, government, state, and society. In following their religious beliefs and worldview, the
24 Puritans implemented and promoted many self-governing principles and civic values in their colonies that were
25 Bible-based and Bible-supported. Though they struggled with issues of religious law and religious dissent in
26 their colonies, many of their key governing principles and civic values proved democratic, effective, and
27 enduring. The Puritans implemented the enduring civic principles and values of God's sovereignty, covenants,
28 constitutions, Rule of Law, popular sovereignty and consent, representative government, law and order, limited
29 power, the Biblical role of God-ordained government, literacy and education, and a strong work ethic. Such
30 principles would begin to promote freedom, equality, individual rights, and just constitutional republicanism in
31 early America. These ideas and practices would become the Puritans' valuable legacy. Indeed, they would
32 become foundational to American political thought and to the new states and nation of the United States of
33 America. Because the Puritans' civic ideas and practices were so strongly influenced by their religious beliefs,
34 the Puritans' greatest legacy might arguably be their Bible-based worldview and faith.
35

Church Covenant & Consent
as a Basis for Civil Self-Government

The application of covenants and consent as a basis for self-government are found in the openings of the Puritan constitutions—the Fundamental Orders of Connecticut and the Massachusetts Body of Liberties.

The Fundamental Orders of Connecticut of 1639

Excerpt of Opening:

"Forasmuch as it hath pleased Almighty God by the wise disposition of his divine providence so to order and dispose of things that we the Inhabitants and Residents of Windsor, Hartford and Wethersfield are now cohabiting and dwelling in and upon the River of Connectecotte and the lands thereunto adjoining; and well knowing where a people are gathered together the word of God requires that to maintain the peace and union of such a people there should be an orderly and decent Government established according to God, to order and dispose of the affairs of the people at all seasons as occasion shall require; **do therefore associate and conjoin ourselves to be as one Public State or Commonwealth; and do for ourselves and our successors and such as shall be adjoined to us at any time hereafter, enter into Combination and Confederation together,** to maintain and preserve the liberty and purity of the Gospel of our Lord Jesus which we now profess, as also, the discipline of the Churches, which according to the truth of the said Gospel is now practiced amongst us...."[255]

Excerpt of First Order:

"1. It is Ordered, sentenced, and decreed, that there shall be yearly two General Assemblies or Courts, the first shall be called the Court of Election.... ...Whereof one to be chosen Governor.... ...provided always there be six chosen besides the Governor, **which being chosen and sworn according to an Oath recorded for that purpose, shall have the power to administer justice according to the Laws here established, and for want thereof, according to the Rule of the Word of God; which choice shall be made by all that are admitted freemen and have taken the Oath of Fidelity,** and do cohabit within this Jurisdiction having been admitted Inhabitants by the major part of the Town wherein they live or the major part of such as shall be then present...."[256]

Massachusetts Body of Liberties of 1641

Excerpt of Opening:

"The free fruition of such liberties, immunities, and privileges as humanity, civility, and Christianity call for as due to every man in his place and proportion without impeachment and infringement hath ever been and ever will be the tranquillity and stability of churches and commonwealths. And the denial or deprival thereof, the disturbance if not the ruin of both.

We hold it therefore our duty and safety whilst we are about the further establishing of this government to collect and express all such freedoms as for present we foresee may concern us, and our posterity after us, **and to ratify them with our solemn consent.**

We do, therefore, this day religiously and unanimously decree and confirm these following rights, liberties, and privileges concerning our churches and civil state to be respectively, impartially, and inviolably enjoyed and observed throughout our jurisdiction for ever."[257]

Review: Checking Out the History

Discuss questions in subgroups or whole group. As an option, the group may come up with main ideas or insights from each question. Responses may be shared and discussed in the whole group.

1. Why did the Puritans come to America? What did they seek to do?

2. How did the Puritans' view of God as the source of power and liberties affect their understanding and view of rule of law?

3. Why did the Puritans practice covenants in their church, state, and society?

4. How did the Puritans' Judeo-Christian beliefs affect their beliefs about earthly governing power and free consent of the governed? Explain how these views led to and supported the practice of electing civil representatives.

5. What was the Puritans' Judeo-Christian view of man and his condition? How did they view the worth of the individual?

6. How did the Puritans' view of man affect their view, form, and practice of self-government?

7. Why did the Puritans' prioritize education? Why did they set up schools?

8. How did the Puritans' view daily, worldly work? Why?

9. What was the basis for the Puritans' constitutions? What were the aims and benefits of constitutions?

10. In what ways did the Puritans begin to implement greater separation between church and civil government in their colonies than previously existed?

11. What basic Bible-based or Judeo-Christian principles are evident and important in this part of America's heritage?

1 **Activity: The Massachusetts Body of Liberties and Our Rights Today**
2
3 In the chart below, review the rights outlined in the Massachusetts Body of Liberties that still endure today.
4 Match each law to the corresponding right in the U. S. Bill of Rights in the next column. You may draw a
5 connecting line between them, color code them, etc. Both columns are listed in random order.
6

Massachusetts Body of Liberties, 1641	U. S. Bill of Rights, 1791
8. No man's cattle or goods of what kind soever shall be pressed or taken for any public use or service, unless it be by warrant grounded upon some act of the General Court, nor without such reasonable prices and hire as the ordinary rates of the country do afford. And if his cattle or goods shall perish or suffer damage in such service, the owner shall be sufficiently recompensed.	**Amendment VI.** In all criminal prosecutions, the accused shall enjoy the right to a speedy and public trial, by an impartial jury….
12. Every man, whether inhabitant or foreigner, free or not free, shall have liberty to come to any public Court, Council, or Town meeting, and either by speech or writing to move any lawful, seasonable, and material question, or to present any necessary motion, complaint, petition, Bill, or information….	**Amendment V.** …nor shall any person be subject for the same offence to be twice put in jeopardy of life or limb….
26. Every man that finds himself unfit to plead his own case in any court shall have liberty to employ any man against whom the Court does not except, to help him….	**Amendment V.** …nor shall [any person] be compelled in any criminal case to be a witness against himself….
29. In all actions at law it shall be the liberty of the plaintiff and defendant by mutual consent to choose whether they will be tried by the Bench or by a Jury….	**Amendment VIII.** …nor cruel and unusual punishments inflicted.
42. No man shall be twice sentenced by civil justice for one and the same crime, offense, or trespass.	**Amendment V.** …nor shall private property be taken for public use without just compensation.
45. No man shall be forced by torture to confess any crime against himself….	**Amendment VI.** In all criminal prosecutions, the accused shall enjoy the right…to have the assistance of counsel for his defence.
46. For bodily punishments we allow amongst us none that are inhumane, barbarous, or cruel.	**Amendment I.** Congress shall make no law…abridging…the right of the people peaceably to assemble, and to petition the Government for a redress of grievances.

2. Every person within this jurisdiction…shall enjoy the same justice and law that is general for the plantation, which we constitute and execute one toward another without partiality or delay. **41.** Every man that is to answer for any criminal cause…his cause shall be heard and determined at the next court that hath proper cognizance thereof, and may be done without prejudice of justice.	**Amendment IV.** The right of the people to be secure in their persons, houses, papers, and effects, against unreasonable searches and seizures, shall not be violated, and no Warrants shall issue, but upon probable cause…. **Amendment V.** No person shall…be deprived of life, liberty, or property, without due process of law….
1. No man's life shall be taken away, …no man's person shall be arrested, restrained, …nor any ways punished, …no man's goods or estate shall be taken away from him, nor any way indamaged under color of law or countenance of authority, unless it be by virtue or equity of some express law of the country…. **18.** No man's person shall be restrained or imprisoned by any authority whatsoever, before the law hath sentenced him thereto….	**Amendment VII.** In suits of common law…the right of trial by jury shall be preserved….

1

Call to Action

Each person will reflect on and write his/her responses to the questions below. Responses may then be shared and discussed in the group.

1. While many Puritan principles endure in the United States, some of their laws no longer exist. Which Puritan laws or ideas no longer exist in the United States, from your observation? Why do you think that is the case?

_____

_____

_____

_____

2. How has the Puritan view and practice of inter-connection between the Bible and civil government endured and/or changed in modern American life, in your observation?

_____

_____

_____

_____

3. In what ways do the Puritans' Judeo-Christian beliefs and principles influence various spheres of modern American government, society, and life today, from your observation? Give examples.

_____

_____

_____

_____

4. How or to what extent do your spiritual or religious beliefs affect your views of civil government and politics? Give some examples.

_____

_____

_____

_____

5. How do you benefit today in your daily life from the Judeo-Christian principles and individual rights held by the Puritans and/or outlined in their constitutions?

_____

_____

_____

_____

Chapter 4
Freedom of Conscience and Religious Tolerance in Early America

While the idea of freedom of conscience—freedom of belief and conviction—was advanced by the Reformation and existed in Europe in the 1500s and 1600s, it was not embraced by everyone and was very restricted in actual practice, manifesting in only partial, contested, temporary ways. However, the Bible-based arguments made for it by some religious and political reformers were quite similar to those later made by individuals who directly impacted American thought and settlement in the 1600s and 1700s. Drawing on the Bible, American Puritan dissenter Roger Williams and Quaker William Penn played important roles in advancing freedom of conscience and religious tolerance in America during this time. Their arguments for religious tolerance and freedom of conscience were strongly rooted in the Bible. Based on conviction, they attempted to practice and experiment with these principles by forming new, tolerant colonies. Also, Williams began to express a new, though not widely-held, idea about the relationship between church and civil government—with greater separation between these institutions as a way to protect freedom of conscience. Decades later, secular Enlightenment philosopher John Locke took a strikingly similar position on freedom of conscience and religious tolerance, also based on the Bible. Locke's secular writings on this topic influenced the views of many in England and America. They later informed many founding-era Americans on the issues. The idea of freedom of conscience that developed over time among certain European reformers, dissidents in America, and Enlightenment-era thinkers was strongly rooted in the Bible. It is found in a developing process of Western thought that helped move American colonists and colonizers toward justifications for and experiences in greater religious tolerance. The first experiments at religious tolerance that took place in the newly-founded colonies of Rhode Island, Pennsylvania, Maryland, and others were notable and real, if imperfect or incomplete, testimonies of this largely unpracticed idea. They brought the issue of freedom of conscience to the forefront of the American mind.

4.1 The Reformers Recognize Two Kingdoms—Spiritual and Civil

During the Protestant Reformation in the 1500s, reformers Martin Luther and John Calvin addressed not only religious reforms in the church but also some political reforms. They broached the ideas of freedom of conscience and greater distinction between church and civil government. Luther and Calvin basically recognized two distinct kingdoms—a civil one and a spiritual one—that concern the life of man. The civil kingdom is in the earthly realm of man and concerns man's physical life and relationship with other men in society. The spiritual kingdom is in the heavenly realm of God and concerns man's religious beliefs and relationship with God. To these reformers, these two kingdoms have distinct rulers and jurisdictions.[258]

Luther in Germany believed that men should be able to freely choose their religious beliefs and that the Bible supports this position. Civil government, he thought, has no authority to force religious belief on men. Only God has authority over men's consciences or beliefs. He opposed the use of physical punishments and tortures to coerce men in their religious beliefs. Religious heresy, he thought, is an issue of the mind and ought to be corrected with books. Regarding the two kingdoms, Luther believed that in the earthly realm, men are regulated in society in their outward behavior toward others by a general moral Law of Nature and by civil laws. In the spiritual realm, God's spiritual law regulates and discerns the inner condition of the souls, hearts, minds, consciences, and beliefs of believers. Luther saw this difference as the basis for a distinction between civil government and church roles in society, though the functions of government and church were very much combined in his day. Luther thus supported freedom of conscience or religious belief. Luther's ideas were not accepted in his day but would be asserted by many later political writers in Europe and would eventually influence American political thought.

Calvin, located in Geneva, Switzerland, shared many of Luther's views not only of religious reform but of more distinct roles of church and civil government. Calvin, like Luther, recognized a civil kingdom and a spiritual kingdom. He acknowledged a Natural Law governing man's outward behavior in civil society as well as a spiritual law governing man's inner conscience in the spiritual realm. Calvin states,

> ...[I]n man government is twofold: the one spiritual, by which the conscience is trained to piety and divine worship; the other civil, by which the individual is instructed in those duties which, as men and citizens, we are bound to perform.... To these two forms are commonly given the not inappropriate names of spiritual and temporal jurisdiction, intimating that the former species has reference to the life of the soul, while the latter relates to matters of the present life, not only to food and clothing, but to the enacting of laws which require a man to live among his fellows purely, honourably, and modestly. The former has its seat within the soul, the latter only regulates the external conduct. We may call the one the spiritual, the other the civil kingdom.[259]

The state has authority to regulate over external, temporal things like one's body, behavior, and property, he proposed, while only God has authority over inner spiritual, eternal matters like one's religious belief. Calvin, like Luther, contemplated the idea of freedom of conscience. Luther's and Calvin's religious and political ideas influenced political thinkers who would, ultimately, influence early Americans on political and religious freedom.

4.2 Roger Williams and a Quest for Religious Purity

Puritan dissident Roger Williams, often considered one of America's greatest early democrats, was a pioneer of Christian religious freedom in America. Williams, a Puritan pastor in Salem, Massachusetts, believed in God's supreme rule and limitation of human power. Yet he differed from traditional Puritan thinking and Governor John Winthrop in many ways, though the two men liked one another. Much like the Pilgrims, Williams thought it was necessary to separate from the existing church (in his case the Puritans' Congregational church in Massachusetts) in order to establish a more pure one. He separated himself from both the Anglican and Congregational state churches.

Williams was an advocate of freedom of conscience and of greater distinction between church and civil government. The official church in Massachusetts, to him, was impure due to its combined church and government and its oppressive practices to regulate religious beliefs and doctrine. Such characteristics, to Williams, did not accurately reflect New Testament church rule, law, and practice. Williams bemoaned the initial combining of church and government in 313 A. D. by the first Christian Roman Emperor, Constantine I. Though supportive of Christianity, this combination, Williams pointed out, soon led to an impure, corrupt church.[260] To address this impurity, the church needed to separate from the civil government with regard to its institutional administration and legal jurisdiction. True religion, Williams believed, required worship without state interference. These radical concepts—more radical than those of most Christians of his day—were motivated by Williams's search for greater religious purity in the church and Christian life. The separation he sought, explain some scholars, turned over understandings of the time not only of state church establishments but of the church itself.[261] Williams was banished from Massachusetts for his dissident beliefs and founded the religiously tolerant colony of Rhode Island.

In 1644 Williams wrote *The Bloudy Tenent of Persecution for the Cause of Conscience* in support of freedom of conscience and against religious coercion and persecution. The Bible was a foundational source of his arguments. Some of his arguments were similar to Luther's. Williams advocated for free thought and conscience because it was, he believed, the only means to true faith and religion. His ideas raised questions and challenges but endured and solidified over time. In response to Williams, Puritan John Cotton wrote in 1647 *The Bloudy Tenent, Washed, and Made White in the Bloude of the Lambe* to argue against some of Williams's views. Cotton supported, for example, the implementation of Old Testament law and religious conformity. In

1 response to Cotton, Williams wrote his 1652 *The Bloody Tenent yet More Bloody: by Mr. Cotton's Endeavor to*
2 *Wash it White in the Blood of the Lambe* in which he reasserted his views.
3
4 **4.3 The Westminster Confession Supports Freedom of Conscience**
5
6   The Westminster Confession of Faith of 1646, the core statement of faith for the Reformed churches in
7 English-speaking countries, aspired to freedom of conscience, just as Williams and some of the reformers and
8 their political writings did. Referencing numerous Biblical scriptures, the Confession asserts that "God alone is
9 the Lord of the conscience [James 4:17], and hath left it free from the doctrines and commandments of men,
10 which are in any thing contrary to his word, or beside it, in matters of faith or worship [James 4:12, Romans
11 14:4, Acts 4:19, Acts 5:29, 1 Corinthians 7:23, Matthew 23:8-10, 2 Corinthians 1:24, Matthew 15:9]."[262] In the
12 mid-1600s, the principle of religious freedom was introduced in many churches in Britain and America, if not
13 yet fully, practically realized in their civil states and church-state establishments.
14
15 **4.4 William Penn and a Quest for Religious Freedom**
16
17   William Penn, a Quaker, was another of America's most notable advocates of religious freedom. Son of
18 British naval officer Sir William Penn, young Penn believed all had the God-given right to choose how to
19 worship and with whom to fellowship. In England he was expelled from a church for views not aligning with
20 the Church of England. He was sent to France by his father to shake his non-conformity but there, studying
21 among persecuted Huguenots, became a stronger dissenter. As a Quaker, or one who often shook when hearing
22 the Bible, he believed in the Inner Light of Christ and criticized formal external religion. He traveled Europe
23 visiting Quakers and met philosopher John Locke. When Quakers and Catholics were persecuted in Britain,
24 Penn became an advocate for religious freedom and was imprisoned. He corresponded with Roger Williams of
25 Rhode Island and protested to colonial authorities when Quakers in Massachusetts were mistreated.
26
27   Penn's, like Williams's, idea of religious freedom differed from Puritan leader John Winthrop's and
28 other Puritans. Winthrop sought a homogeneous or conformed Christian society free from religious error in
29 which only Puritan practices were allowed and other sects kept differing beliefs to themselves. In contrast,
30 Penn wanted to allow Christian heterogeneity or differences in belief and worship. Like the Puritans, Penn
31 favored a peaceful, ordered colony of godly people, but he believed that the fundamentals of Christianity are
32 more important than denominational differences. He was later instrumental in forming other religiously tolerant
33 colonies in America that would become Pennsylvania, New Jersey, and Delaware.
34
35   In 1670, Penn wrote *A Great Case of Liberty of Conscience Debated and Defended by the Authority of*
36 *Reason, Scripture, and Antiquity* in support of freedom of conscience and against religious coercion and
37 persecution as violating the Bible and human birthrights. Some of Penn's views reflected those of Luther's and
38 Williams's. Penn argues that religious coercion discredits the honor of God, the meekness of the Christian
39 religion, the authority of Scripture, the privilege of nature, the principles of common reason, the well-being of
40 government, and the learning of wise men of historical and modern times. Coercive practices are ill-natured
41 and ungodly, unnatural, unlawful, irrational, and ruinous of government and society.[263] The Bible, he argues,
42 supports religious tolerance. Citing the Bible extensively, he declares the intention of his writing to "take the
43 righteous holy God to record, against all objections that are ignorantly or delightedly raised."[264] One early
44 historian called Penn's treatise "the completest exposition of the theory of toleration" of the time.[265]
45

4.5 John Locke and Religious Tolerance

British Enlightenment philosopher, physician, and civil servant John Locke—later influential to the American Founders and the Declaration of Independence—was also a relatively early proponent of religious tolerance and freedom of conscience. Though Locke was a secular thinker of the Enlightenment era, he asserted, decades later, a remarkably similar position as Williams and Penn on the issues of religious tolerance and freedom of conscience in society. Like them, he also drew from the Bible to support his positions. Locke, who attended Oxford University, favored the use of man's reason to search for and understand truth in life and society. This rational search was, he believed, part of man's God-given purpose. Locke's sensible views may have influenced his support for religious tolerance as necessary for man's search for truth. Incidentally, in 1669, Locke wrote the Constitution for the colony of Carolina in America, supporting freedom of conscience.

In the wake of the Reformation and religious persecution in England and Europe, Locke wrote his *Letters Concerning Toleration*—his 1689 *Letter Concerning Toleration*, 1690 *Second Letter Concerning Toleration*, and 1692 *Third Letter Concerning Toleration*—in defense of religious tolerance from a Bible-based viewpoint. Freedom of conscience is, Locke essentially believed, a God-given, natural right. Like Puritan English author John Milton, Locke believed that religious oppression is contrary to the Bible. Religious regulation, Locke argues, should be outside the concern and realm of the civil government. The use of the civil government to impose religious beliefs or practices is unauthorized and ineffective because only God can fully ascertain religious truth and accurately judge a person's faith or religious belief. Moreover, religious freedom is the only means by which people can arrive at genuine Christian faith. Locke believed that truth—in his mind, the Christian Gospel—can prevail amidst other ideas. In his 1707 *A Paraphrase and Notes on the Epistles of St. Paul*, Locke further defends religious tolerance as an aspect and act of Christian charity or love. In his 1695 *The Reasonableness of Christianity*, Locke argues that the teachings of Christianity are compatible with reason. Locke's writings on these issues influenced the views of many in England and in colonial America. They would be studied by many American Founders and would inform the Founders' approach to the issue of religion in the future United States.

4.6 Freedom of Conscience and Religious Tolerance Defined

Conscience is understood in the religious tolerance writings of this time to be the place of man's inner beliefs and convictions, if not belief itself. Freedom of Conscience is the God-given, natural right and freedom of man to believe or disbelieve a doctrine as he chooses and to lawfully exercise that belief in visible worship. Worship is often based on what God or the belief requires. The neglect of true worship due to fear or favor of mortal man is often seen to be sinful and to incur God's wrath. Freedom of conscience allows for true worship consistent with man's heart and mind. Such worship is honored in the Bible since God desires worship from a sincere heart. The spiritual realm of the conscience is distinct from the external, secular, or temporal (earthly or temporary) realm.[266]

Religious tolerance in these writings means the allowing of religious practice and worship of differing religious beliefs in society within the bounds of civil order and peacekeeping. In contrast, religious coercion means the forceful imposition on people to profess certain things to be true or false, to act or not act a certain way with regard to religious belief, and to worship or not worship a certain way. Refusal to follow these dictates often results in punishments or penalties.

4.7 The Dilemma of Religious Freedom in a Combined Church-State System

Though Luther and Calvin in Europe as well as the early Puritans in America supported freedom of conscience in theory, they often had difficulty applying this principle in the existing system of a combined church and state establishment. For no earthly civil government existed in those times that allowed for total religious freedom. Calvin suggested that people have freedom to believe as they choose. But he also believed, as most people of his day, that civil government may suppress what is deemed heretical religious views or practices, for the common good of a society. This had been the role of the government for centuries. As both a religious and political leader in Geneva, Calvin had suppressed some dissident views. The Puritans in America shared many of these views, seeing religious freedom as consistent with religious conformity. Though many religious and political reformers favored the idea of freedom of conscience, the entrenched church-state system and mindset of their time did not allow for the consistent, practical application of this idea whenever people's religious views began to collide. Nevertheless, the Bible-based justifications for freedom of conscience asserted by the reformers in Europe are important to understanding, in part, those later made by Williams and Penn in America and then by Locke. The Bible-based support of this concept plays an important role in a developing process and move of Western thought and action toward religious freedom.

Puritan dissidents in America, Williams, Penn, and Cecil Calvert, would be the first colonists to experiment with greater freedom of conscience and religious tolerance in a society. America's free environment and new colonies made such experiments feasible. Amos and Gardiner observe, "The Protestant Reformation in Europe and in the American colonies forced people to reexamine the traditional merger between church and government. America in particular was to become the test case for resolving the tension between religious freedom and social conformity."[267]

4.8 Old Testament Literal Religious Law vs. New Testament Grace and Spiritual Law: Religious Laws Not to Be Applied to the Civil State

The Puritans accepted religious intolerance in the American colonies, Williams and Locke noted, due to their experience of uniform state churches in England and Europe. They also accepted a literal application of Old Testament religious law.[268] In the Old Testament, the ancient Israelites are regulated in their religious worship and practices by the civil state. The Puritans' colonies in America likewise enforced religious conformity to their official church, with religious laws taken literally from Old Testament law given to the Israelites before Christ came. Thus religious or moral offenses had harsh penalties. However, Williams disagreed with these practices in the colonies. Differences existed, he saw, between the Old Testament Israelites and the American colonists in the New Testament age of the church. In the New Testament age, he believed, Old Testament religious laws should be interpreted and applied only spiritually in the church, not physically in the civil state. The religious laws of ancient Israel and Judah are meant to be types or shadows for God's spiritual people, the church, in the New Testament. "…[T]hose former types of the land, of the people, of their worships [of Israel and Judah]," Williams explains, "were types and figures of a spiritual land, spiritual people, and spiritual worship under Christ."[269]

Old Testament civil-religious laws should only be applied spiritually to religious matters in the New Testament, Williams argues, because Moses as God's Old Testament law-giver is comparable to Jesus Christ in the New Testament who is not a civil officer but a spiritual figure. Moses is a Christ figure, cites Williams, as indicated in Deuteronomy 18:15 and Acts 3:22. In Acts 3:20-22 the Apostle Peter, quoting Deuteronomy, says to the Jews, "…He [God] may send Jesus Christ…. For Moses truly said to the fathers, '*The Lord your God will raise up for you a Prophet like me from your brethren.*'" Peter clearly affirms a comparison between Moses and Christ. Williams thus asserts, "…[W]e find expressly a spiritual power of Christ Jesus in the hands of his saints, ministers, and churches, to be the true antitype of those former figures [of the Old Testament] in all the prophecies concerning Christ's spiritual power."[270] In other words, God's people in the New Testament are to approach Old Testament religious laws not as civil laws but with a view of the laws' spiritual significance to their relationships with God.

The Israelites' legal penalties and punishments for disobedience to Old Testament religious laws, Williams concludes, are not to be paralleled in the New Testament age amongst all peoples and nations but are unique to that nation and age only. For Christ is the fulfillment and end of such laws in the New Testament. Citing Romans 10:4, James 2, John 3:18, and 1 John 5:12, Williams writes,

> …[T]he great and high reward or punishment of the keeping or breach of these laws to Israel, was such as cannot suit with any state or kingdom in the world beside. The reward of the observation was life, eternal life. The breach of any one of these laws was death, eternal death, or damnation and separation from the presence of the Lord. So Rom. x. [Romans 10], James ii [James 2]. Such a covenant God made not before nor since with any state or people in the world. For, Christ is the end of the law for righteousness to every one that believeth, Rom. x.4 [Romans 10:4]. And, he that believeth in that Son of God, hath eternal life; he that believeth not hath not life, but is condemned already, John iii. [John 3:18] and 1 John v [1 John 5:12].[271]

Williams essentially reveals the contrast between the Old and New Testaments as broached by Christian thinkers like John Calvin. Calvin had put forth in his 1536 *Institutes of the Christian Religion* the idea that the Old Testament blessings of the Israelites are a picture, figure, or foreshadow of the forthcoming New Testament spiritual blessings of all believers of Christ. While the Old Testament applies to the Jews in a temporal, earthly setting, the New Testament applies to all believers in Christ, Jew and Gentile, in a spiritual, heavenly setting. The Old Testament is of the letter, but the New Testament is of the spirit. The Old Testament enacts laws and punishments for sin, keeping men in fear and bondage under sin, but the New Testament provides the fulfillment of God's law and the merciful redemption of mankind from sin through Jesus Christ, providing joy and liberty for all. While the Old Covenant of law is temporary, the New Covenant of grace is eternal. Calvin illustrates this contrast with Jeremiah 31:31-34 and 2 Corinthians 3:5-6. [272] In 2 Corinthians 3:5-6, for example, the Apostle Paul writes, "Not that we are sufficient of ourselves to think of anything as *being* from ourselves, but our sufficiency *is* from God, who also made us sufficient as ministers of the new covenant, not of the letter but of the Spirit; for the letter kills, but the Spirit gives life."

Locke later echoes Williams' view that Old Testament religious laws apply only to ancient Israel, not to other nations or civil states, nor to nations or states in the New Testament age of the Gospel. The New Testament Gospel and church in the Bible, he acknowledges, have no such civil state with religious laws. Locke recognizes a distinction between morals laws that are and are not to be enforced in a Christian-influenced nation. Only disruptions of civil peace and order or offenses against other men or the civil state should be, he argues, of concern to the civil government. He illustrates in his *Letter Concerning Toleration*,

> Now whosoever maintains that idolatry [which is condemned in the first of the Ten Commandments] is to be rooted out of any place by laws, punishments, fire, and sword, may apply this story to himself. …
>   But idolatry, say some, is a sin and therefore not to be tolerated. If they said it were therefore to be avoided, the inference were good. But it does not follow that because it is a sin it ought therefore to be punished by the magistrate. For it does not belong to the magistrate to make use of this sword in punishing everything, indifferently, that he takes to be a sin against God. Covetousness, uncharitableness, idleness, and many other things are sins by the consent of men, which yet no man ever said were to be punished by the [civil] magistrate. The reason is because they are not prejudicial to other men's rights, nor do they break the public peace of societies. Nay, even the sins of lying and perjury are nowhere punishable by laws; unless, in certain cases, in which the real turpitude of the thing and the offence against God are not considered, but only the injury done unto men's neighbours and to the commonwealth. And what if in another country, to a Mahometan or a Pagan prince, the Christian religion seem false and offensive to God; may not the Christians for the same reason, and after the same manner, be extirpated there?

But it may be urged farther, that by the law of Moses, idolaters were to be rooted out. True indeed, by the law of Moses; but that is not obligatory to us christians. Nobody pretends that every thing, generally, enjoined by the law of Moses, ought to be practised by christians. But there is nothing more frivolous than that common distinction of moral, judicial, and ceremonial law, which men ordinarily make use of. For no positive [civil] law whatsoever can oblige any people but those to whom it is given. "Hear, O Israel," sufficiently restrains the obligation of the law of Moses only to that people. And this consideration alone is answer enough unto those that urge the authority of the law of Moses, for inflicting of capital punishments upon idolaters. But however, I will examine this argument a little more particularly.

The case of idolaters, in respect of the Jewish commonwealth, falls under a double consideration. The first is of those who, being initiated in the Mosaical rites, and made citizens of that commonwealth, did afterwards apostatize from the worship of the God of Israel. These were proceeded against as traitors and rebels, guilty of no less than high treason. For the commonwealth of the Jews, different in that from all others, was an absolute theocracy; nor was there, or could there be, any difference between that commonwealth and the Church. The laws established there concerning the worship of One Invisible Deity were the civil laws of that people and a part of their political government, in which God Himself was the legislator. … But there is absolutely no such thing, under the gospel, as a christian commonwealth. There are, indeed, many cities and kingdoms that have embraced the faith of Christ, but they have retained their ancient forms of government; with which the law of Christ hath not at all meddled. He, indeed, hath taught men how, by faith and good works, they may attain eternal life. But he instituted no commonwealth. He prescribed unto his followers no new and peculiar form of government, nor put he the sword into any magistrate's hand, with commission to make use of it in forcing men to forsake their former religion, and receive his.[273]

Based on the contrast between Old and New Testaments, Christian thinkers like Williams as well as Locke asserted that religious laws should not be implemented in the civil state. Such religious laws are spiritual matters that concerned the believer and his relationship with God. In the New Testament age, civil states and civil officers are to regulate only civil matters and to protect the bodies and goods of the people, not spiritual or soul causes.

4.9 God as Creator, Ruler, and Judge of Conscience

With their view of the civil and spiritual kingdoms, some reformers like Luther, Calvin, John Ponet, and Stephen Brutus had suggested that God is the sole judge of man's conscience. For one's conscience is under God's righteous rule in the spiritual realm. Because the civil power has no power over the spiritual realm, they argued, the civil power and man-made civil laws have no right to intrude on a person's conscience.[274] They cited various Bible verses in support of this point. These views and Bible verses were taken up by Williams and Penn as they argued for freedom of conscience and religious tolerance.

Luther and Ponet note Jesus's distinction between earthly civil governments and God's spiritual government in Matthew 22:21 when Jesus tells the Pharisees, "'Render therefore to Caesar the things that are Caesar's, and to God the things that are God's.'" Civil government and laws, they explain, have power to regulate over some things like the protection of a person's physical body and the regulation of person's outward actions. However, only God has the rightful authority and ability to judge a person's inner convictions and beliefs of the spiritual realm. Luther says in his 1523 *Secular Authority: To What Extent It Should Be Obeyed*,

Christ Himself made this nice distinction and summed it all up briefly when He said, "Give unto Caesar the things that are Caesar's, and unto God the things that are God's" [Matt. 22:21]. If, then, imperial power extended to God's kingdom and power, and were not something by itself, He would not thus have made it a separate thing. For, as was said, the soul is not under Caesar's power; he can neither teach nor guide it, neither kill it nor make it alive, neither bind it nor loose it, neither judge it nor condemn it, neither hold it nor release it, which he must do had he power to command it and impose laws upon it....[275]

Luther expresses a desire to see the civil government and the church tend to their proper, distinct spheres of authority—temporal and spiritual respectively. The secular judges, he thought, should only deal with earthly matters of "money, property, life, and honour" while the church should only be concerned with "matters of faith and good morals."[276] These distinct roles are a matter not only of purity but of jurisdiction. It is unbiblical, he thought, when one sphere oversteps its bounds into the other. It often leads to corruption and tyranny. Citing the same verse in Matthew, Ponet presents a similar argument in his 1556 *Short Treatise on Political Power* of a distinction between civil and spiritual realms. Civil government rules in the physical realm while God rules in the spiritual realm. He writes,

> "Yield unto Caesar, those things that be Caesar's," says Christ, "and unto God the things that be God's." Civil power is a power and ordinance of God, appointed to certain things, but no general minister over all things. God has not given it power over the one and best of man, that is, the soul and conscience of man, but only over the other and the worst part of man, that is, the body, and those things that belong unto the temporal life of man. And yet over that part [the conscience]…he has not only not given man the whole power, and stripped himself of all the authority, but also he has reserved to Himself the power thereof.[277]

In his 1579 *Vindiciae Contra Tyrannos*, Stephen Brutus likewise acknowledges a distinction between mankind's rule in the earthly, temporal realm and God's rule in the spiritual realm. With allusion to Matthew 22:21 and additional references to 1 and 2 Chronicles, Exodus, Isaiah, and Daniel, he asserts God as ruler of conscience, religious rights, and limits to civil power. He explains,

> Man is made up of body and soul: God formed the body and also infused the soul. Therefore He alone could use both of them with absolute right. But if He freely granted to kings that they might use the bodies and goods of their subjects only for the subjects' preservation, they ought clearly to remember that the use was conceded, not the abuse. For above all, they have nothing which they may requisition [*imperent*] from the soul under the title of tribute, who themselves are bound to profess their own souls as liable to pay tribute to God. The king takes tribute or dues [census] from the body and from those things which are acquired or cultivated by the agency of the body; and God from the soul in particular, which actually exercises its functions through the body. To the former type of tribute belong renders in kind, money payments, and other dues both real and personal; to the latter, sacrifices, congregations, and divine worship both private and public. These two tributes are so different and distinct that neither impedes the other; the fisc of God deprives Caesar's fisc of nothing, but each one keeps its rights.[278]

Humans and civil government cannot have authority over other people's consciences, Luther further argues, due to their obvious lack of discernment of or power over it. Earthly forces have no ability to determine a soul's fate or to discern or change the hearts of others. They cannot see and therefore cannot properly judge a person's inner soul. Among other verses, Luther references Matthew 10:28, Psalm 7:8-9, Acts 10 and 15:8, Jeremiah 17:9, Romans 13:1-7, and 1 Peter 2:3 on this point. He explains,

> Worldly government has laws which extend no farther than to life and property and what is external upon earth. For over the soul God can and will let no one rule but Himself. Therefore, where temporal power presumes to prescribe [religious] laws for the soul, it encroaches upon God's government and only misleads and destroys the souls. …

When a man-made [religious] law is imposed upon the soul, in order to make it believe this or that, as that man prescribes, there is certainly no word of God for it. ...

Again, consummate fools though they are, they must confess that they have no power over souls. For no human being can kill a soul or make it alive, conduct it to heaven or hell. And if they will not believe us in this, Christ indeed will certify strongly enough to it, since He says in Matthew 10 [:28, brackets editor's], "Fear not them which kill the body and after that have power to do naught; but rather fear Him Who after He has killed the body has power to condemn to hell." I consider that here it is sufficiently clear that the soul is taken out of all human hands and is placed under the power of God alone. ...

Besides, we can understand how any authority shall and may act only where it can see, know, judge, change and convert. For what kind of judge would he be who should blindly judge matters which he neither heard nor saw? Tell me, how can a man see, know, judge, condemn and change hearts? This is reserved for God alone, as Psalm 7 [:9] says, "God trieth the heart and reins"; likewise, "The Lord shall judge the people" [Ps. 7:8]; and Acts 15 [:8], "God knoweth the hearts"; and, Jeremiah 17 [:9 f.], "Wicked and unsearchable is the human heart; who can know it? I the Lord, who search the heart and reins." A court ought and must be quite certain and clear about everything, if it is to pass sentence. But the thoughts and intents of the heart can be known to no one but God; therefore it is useless and impossible to command or compel any one by force to believe one thing or another. ...

You reply, But Paul said in Romans 13 [:1], "Every soul shall be subject to power and authority," and Peter says, "We should be subject to every ordinance of man" [I Pet. 2:13]. I answer, That is just what I want! These sayings are in my favor. St. Paul speaks of authority and power. Now, you have just heard that no one but God can have authority over souls. Hence Paul cannot be speaking of any obedience except where there can be corresponding authority. From this it follows that he does not speak of faith, and does not say that secular authority should have the right to command faith, but he is speaking of external goods, and that these are to be set in order and controlled on earth. This his words also clearly indicate, when he prescribes the limits to both authority and obedience, and says, "Render to every one his dues, tribute to whom tribute is due, custom to whom custom; honor to whom honor; fear to whom fear" [Rom. 13:7]. You see, temporal obedience and power apply only externally to tribute, custom, honor and fear. Likewise when he says, "The power is not a terror to good, but to evil works" [Rom. 13:4], he again limits the power, so that it is to have the mastery not over faith or the Word of God, but over evil works."

This is what St. Peter also desires, when he says, "Ordinance of man" [I Pet. 2:13]. Human ordinance cannot possibly extend its authority to heaven and over souls, but belongs only to earth, to the external intercourse of men with each other, where men can see, know, judge, sentence, punish, and acquit.[279]

Some Reformers concluded that while people are subject to civil authority, if this authority tries to regulate people's religious beliefs or books, it should not be obeyed. For civil authority does not have such right or power. Luther, Calvin, and Ponet note godly individuals in the Bible who refuse to worship falsely against conscience when commanded by civil or religious authorities. Luther cites Acts 5:29 in which the Apostle Peter and Jesus' other disciples disobey the public authorities who forbid them from preaching the Gospel.[280] When questioned by the authorities about their disobedience, Peter and the others answer, "'We ought to obey God rather than men.'" Calvin in his *Institutes* and Ponet in his *Short Treatise* point out examples in Daniel 3 and 6. In Daniel 3, godly Israelites Shadrach, Meshach, and Abednego refuse to obey King Nebuchadnezzar's order to worship a golden calf. For this order violated their conscience of belief. The king tells them that if they disobey the order they will be thrown into a fiery furnace. They respond in Daniel 3:17-18, "'[O]ur God whom we serve is able to deliver us from the burning fiery furnace, and He will deliver us from your hand, O king. But if not, let it be known to you, O king, that we will not serve your gods, nor will we worship the gold image which you have set up." God, in the end, protects the men from harm in the furnace. In

Daniel 6, the godly prophet Daniel disobeys King Darius' misguided edict that forbids praying to God. Daniel, who prayed to God daily, refuses to obey the order according to his conscience of belief, despite the penalty of being thrown into a lion's den for disobedience. Daniel 6:10 states, "Now when Daniel knew that the writing [order] was signed, he went home. And in his upper room, with his windows open toward Jerusalem, he knelt down on his knees three times that day, and prayed and gave thanks before his God, as was his custom since early days." Daniel is cast into the lion's den for his disobedience, but God protects him from the lions. In these verses, freedom of conscience, says Calvin and Ponet, supercedes the ungodly restrictive religious laws imposed by the authorities.[281] Citing Daniel 6:22, Calvin states, "On this principle Daniel denied that he had committed any crime against the king in disobeying his impious decree [Daniel 6:22]; because the king had exceeded the limits of his office, and had not only done an injury to men, but, by raising his arm against God, had degraded his own authority."[282] In addition to these verses, Calvin refers to Galatians 5.[283] In Galatians 5:1, Paul says to the church, "Stand fast therefore in the liberty by which Christ has made us free, and do not be entangled again with a yoke of bondage." Calvin thought that such verses support the argument that "chains ought not to be imposed on consciences, which are subject to the government of God alone."[284] The Reformers thus presented a line of argument for God's sole rule over conscience based on the words and actions of godly people in the Bible. Religious worship, they suggested, belongs under God's dominion or jurisdiction, not under that of earthly public authorities. When public authorities interfere with religious worship, they abuse their jurisdiction.

In the 1600s, when American colonizers Roger Williams and William Penn began to advocate for greater freedom of conscience and religious tolerance, they drew from some of the same scriptures as the Reformers as well as developed additional arguments from other verses. Williams and Penn asserted that God alone—not any human or earthly authority—is creator and judge of a person's conscience. Referring to Psalms 2:9 and Acts 2:36, Williams asserts that "...God anointed Jesus to be the sole King and Governor of all the Israel of God in spiritual and soul causes."[285] Penn similarly argues that religious coercion or force usurps God's "incommunicable right of government over conscience." God does not give any person or earthly power such authority to force or punish anyone on religious belief. Penn concludes from Matthew 22:21 that God "has reserved to himself that empire from all the Caesars on earth" and "shall judge all by Jesus Christ; and...no man is so accountable to his fellow-creatures."[286]

Williams and Penn also point out that God is the author of a person's faith. As such, religious coercion denies God as the source of faith by suggesting that humans can create, change, or conjure it. Faith is the gift of God. Quoting Job 32:8, Penn expresses, "'For the Inspiration of the Almighty gives understanding: and faith is the gift of God,' says the divine writ."[287] Faith as the gift of God is also indicated in Ephesians 2:8 which states "For by grace you have been saved through faith, and that not of yourselves; *it is* the gift of God...." and in Hebrews 12:2 which states, "...looking unto Jesus, the author and finisher of *our* faith...." Coercion, Penn thought, defeats "God's work of Grace, and the invisible operation of his eternal Spirit, (which can alone beget faith, and is only to be obeyed, in and about religion and worship) and attributes men's conformity to outward force and punishment."[288] True faith and understanding could not be forced or obtained by physical, earthly force but comes from God who speaks to a person's heart—which only God can change. As a result, God is sole ruler of conscience. People answer only to God, not to earthly human institutions like religious or civil bodies, for their spiritual beliefs.[289] For God, says Penn, "will not give his honour to another, and to him only, that searches the heart and tries the reins, it is our duty to ascribe the gifts of understanding and faith, without which none can please God."[290]

Williams, like the Reformers, similarly concludes from the books of Daniel 3 and 6 and Acts 4 and 5 that laws violating freedom of conscience should not be obeyed. He points out from Daniel 3 and 6, like Calvin and Ponet, how the godly men Shadrach, Meshach, and Abednego as well as the prophet Daniel disobey unlawful orders that violate their religious beliefs.[291] Williams also cites Acts 4 and 5, as Luther did Acts 5, in which Jesus' disciples follow their consciences and preach the Gospel against the orders of the public authorities. In Acts 4:18-20, when the Apostles Peter and John are commanded by the religious authorities not to speak or teach about Jesus, the apostles answer, "'Whether it is right in the sight of God to listen to you more than to God, you judge. For we cannot but speak the things which we have seen and heard.'" A similar event occurs in Acts 5:27-29. Both times, their responses support their right to preach according to conscience. Williams observes, "God's people have been immoveable, constant, and resolved to the death, in refusing to submit to false worships, and in preaching and professing the true worship, contrary to the express command of public authority."[292]

The Bible, the reformers as well as Williams and Penn saw, clearly indicates a distinction between civil government and God's spiritual government. Civil powers have authority over earthly matters, but God rules over people's consciences as part of a spiritual realm. Only God can rule over a person's conscience because only God can properly affect, discern, and judge it. What is more, only God can instill faith. As a result, earthly authorities or laws that violate conscience should not be obeyed. This point is affirmed by the fact that godly people in the Bible assert their right to freedom of conscience even when it counters earthly authorities and laws. In fact, on several occasions in the Bible, God seems to confirm His authority in the spiritual realm of conscience by delivering His followers from the earthly punishments assigned to them for disobeying public orders. In the book of Daniel, God supernaturally protects Shadrach, Meshach, and Abednego from the fiery flames of the furnace. He also shuts the lion's mouth so that the prophet Daniel is not harmed in the lion's den. In Acts 5:17-20, an angel of God frees Peter and the other apostles from prison and admonishes them to continue preaching their message, saying, "'Go, stand in the temple and speak to the people all the words of this life.'" Clearly, all people and all authorities are subject to the higher rule of God who provides freedom of conscience to all.[293]

4.10 Religious Coercion as Contrary to the Biblical Teachings of Christ

In addition to their primary argument that God is ruler of conscience, Williams, Penn, and later Locke asserted that religious coercion is contrary to the New Testament teachings of Christ and His followers on life, peace, meekness, gentleness, forbearance, and charity. For one, God outrightly condemns religious persecution and the killing of God's people. Williams cites Revelation 6:9 for its illustration of God's judgment against such persecution and killing of God's people who, for their beliefs, stood "against the worship of the states and times." In Revelation 6:9, the Apostle John describes his heavenly vision of the martyrs of God who ask God for justice: "...I [the Apostle John] saw under the alter the souls of those who had been slain for the word of God and for the testimony which they held. And they cried with a loud voice, saying, 'How long, O lord, holy and true, until You judge and avenge our blood on those who dwell on the earth?'" Based on this verse, says Williams, the "doctrine of persecution for cause of conscience is proved guilty of all the blood of the souls crying for vengeance under the alter."[294]

Furthermore, the Christian way in the New Testament, saw Williams and Penn, is about seeking to save human souls and bodies as Christ admonishes in Luke 9:54-56.[295] Luke 9:54-55 states,

> And when His [Jesus'] disciples James and John saw *this* [that the Samaritans did not receive Jesus] they said, "Lord, do You want us to command fire to come down from heaven and consume them, just as Elijah did?" But He turned and rebuked them, and said, "You do not know what manner of spirit you are of. For the Son of Man [Jesus Christ] did not come to destroy men's lives but to save *them*."

Jesus Christ desires the saving of life—spirit, soul, and body—not the destroying of life by religious coercion. Williams comments on these verses in Luke 9:

[I]f the civil magistrate be a Christian, a disciple, or follower of the meek Lamb of God, he is bound to be far from destroying the bodies of men for refusing to receive the Lord Jesus Christ: for otherwise he should not know, according this speech of the Lord Jesus, what spirit he was of, yea, and to be ignorant of the sweet end of the coming of the Son of man, which was not to destroy the bodies of men, but to save both bodies and souls, vers. 55, 56. ... ...[T]he end of the Lord Jesus' coming [was] not to destroy men's lives, but to save them.[296]

Also, to follow the teachings of Christ, those in leadership over other believers, explains Williams, Penn, and Locke, should be meek, gentle, peaceable, and charitable, not oppressive and violent. Williams affirms the attribute of peace in Jesus Christ: "...The God of Peace, the God of Truth will shortly seal this truth, and confirm this witness, and make it evident to the whole world, that the doctrine of persecution for cause of conscience, is most evidently and lamentably contrary to the doctrine of Christ Jesus the Prince of Peace."[297] Penn and Locke cite meekness in Matthew 20:25-26 and Luke 22:25-27 in which Jesus tells His disciples, "whoever desires to be great among you, let him be your servant" and "he who governs [let him be] as he who serves." Penn further cites gentleness and peaceableness in 1 Timothy 3:2-3 and 2 Timothy 2:24-25 in which the qualities of a godly leader are described: "A bishop then must be blameless, ...sober-minded, of good behavior, hospitable, able to teach; ...not violent, not greedy for money, but gentle, not quarrelsome, not covetous...." Penn also cites the "golden rule" of Matthew 7:12 and Luke 6:31 which states, "[W]hatever you want men to do to you, do also to them...."[298] In his 1690 *Second Letter Concerning Toleration*, Locke affirms the Gospel as "mild, and gentle, and meek, and apter to use prayers and intreaties, than force, to gain a hearing."[299]

Locke sees charity—love, benevolence, and forbearance toward others—as a Christian trait that is essential to the argument for religious tolerance. In his *Paraphrases on the Epistles of St. Paul*, he defines charity from 1 Corinthians 13:1-10 as gentle and benign benevolence and long-suffering toward others, with an awareness of man's fallibility and imperfection. Modern Bible translations of these verses often call this trait "love." Locke paraphrases verses 3-10:

And if I bestow all I have, in relief of the poor, and give myself to be burnt, and have not charity, it profits me nothing. Charity is long-suffering, is gentle and benign, without emulation, insolence, or being puffed up; Is not ambitious, nor at all self-interested, is not sharp upon others failings, or inclined to ill interpretations: Charity rejoices with others, when they do well; and, when any thing is amiss, is troubled, and covers their failings: Charity believes well, hopes well of every one, and patiently bears with every thing. Charity will never cease, as a thing out of use; but the gifts of prophecy, and tongues, and the knowledge whereby men look into, and explain the meaning of the scriptures, the time will be, when they will be laid aside as no longer of any use. For the knowledge we have now in this state, and the explication we give of scripture, is short, partial, and defective. [300]

Based on such verses, religious coercion, Locke as Williams and Penn believe, is contrary to charity and the character of Christ. Locke expresses in his *Letter Concerning Toleration*, "That any man should think fit to cause another man, whose salvation he heartily desires, to expire in torments, and that even in an unconverted state, would, I confess, seem very strange to me, and, I think, to any other also. But nobody, surely, will ever believe that such a carriage can proceed from charity, love or goodwill," and "...[N]o man can be a Christian without charity and without that faith which works, not by force, but by love."[301] In his 1692 *Third Letter for Toleration*, Locke praises "those generous principles of the gospel, which so much recommend and inculcate universal charity, and a freedom from the inventions and impositions of men in the things of God...."[302]

In addition, Jesus Christ and the Apostles, say Williams and Penn, do not call for religious coercion or physical violence to win converts. They support the peaceful evangelizing of the Gospel and seek the voluntary acceptance of it by others. They also practice the use of reason to defend the Gospel. This method to spread the Gospel is suitable for and effective in the spiritual realm. As the earthly civil state is regulated by material force, says Williams echoing Luther, God and the church fight the battle of faith with spiritual force. He derives this view from 2 Corinthians 10:4-6 in which the Apostle Paul tells the church, "The weapons of our warfare *are* not carnal but mighty in God for pulling down strongholds, casting down arguments and every high thing that exalts itself against the knowledge of God, bringing every thought into captivity to the obedience of Christ." Williams elaborates on the need to fight spiritual error with spiritual tools: "[A]gainst these spiritual strongholds in the souls of men, spiritual artillery and weapons are proper, which are mighty through God to subdue and bring under the very thought to obedience, or else to bind fast the soul with chains of darkness, and lock it up in the prison of unbelief and hardness to eternity."[303] Luther had likewise asserted from 2 Corinthians 10:4-6 that heresy and spiritual warfare must be fought with the Word of God, not with the iron sword and physical punishments: "Heresy can never be prevented by force. ... Heresy is a spiritual matter, which no iron can strike, no fire burn, no water drown. God's Word alone avails here."[304] In fact, the Word of God or the Bible describes itself as the spiritual weapon or tool—a two-edged sword—to deal with spiritual issues or errors. Hebrews 4:12 states, "For the word of God is living and powerful, and sharper than any two-edged sword, piercing even to the division of soul and spirit, and of joints and marrow, and is a discerner of the thoughts and intents of the heart." Alluding to Hebrews 4:12 and Revelation 1 and 3, Williams reflects on the Word of God as the spiritual sword to fight spiritual battles:

> Although the [civil] magistrate by a civil sword might well compel that national church to the external exercise of their national worship: yet it is not possible, according to the limits of the civil magistrate versus the work of the Spirit, to compel whole nations to true repentance and regeneration, without which…the worship and holy name of God is profaned and blasphemed. An arm of flesh and sword of steel cannot reach to cut the darkness of the mind, the hardness and unbelief of the heart, and kindly operate upon the soul's affections…. This work performs alone that sword out of the mouth of Christ, with two edges, Rev. i and iii.[305]

Paul calls believers to use peaceful means and spiritual tools—namely the Word of God—to win souls for Christ. Souls must freely accept the Gospel. Religious laws could force men to engage in certain religious practices but could not address or touch the inner man or his spiritual condition and belief. In the Christian way, Williams concludes, it is not only effective and appropriate but also godly and honorable to fight spiritual warfare with spiritual artillery.[306] Luther accordingly expresses of the Word of God, "I will preach it, teach it, write it, but I will constrain no man by force, for faith must come freely without compulsion."[307]

In addition, Paul uses reason when effective to capture his audiences. In Acts 17:2, 17 and Acts 18:4, 8, notes Williams, Paul reasons and debates with the people—Jews and Gentiles—regarding the Gospel of Christ.[308] Acts 17:16-17 says, "Now while Paul waited for them at Athens, his spirit was provoked within him when he saw that the city was given over to idols. Therefore he reasoned in the synagogue with the Jews and with the Gentile worshipers, and in the marketplace daily with those who happened to be there." This point is similar to that of Luther who had argued that heresy is overcome with books, not physical punishments. Luther had stated, "Heretics ought to be persuaded by argument, and not by fire; and this was the way of the early Fathers. If it were wise policy to suppress heretics by burning them, then the executioners would be the most learned teachers on earth. We should have no need to study books any longer, for he who could overthrow his fellow by violence would have the right to burn him at the stake."[309]

Clearly, the Apostles' teachings in the New Testament, Williams notes, show that God does not require or favor religious coercion and violence in the physical, earthly realm. To gain believers, Christians should speak, write, reason, and debate their beliefs in society, often drawing from scripture.

4.11 Religious Coercion Opposes the Order of Nature

Another argument for freedom of conscience and religious tolerance advocated by Penn was belief that religious coercion opposes the order of nature. It does so because it is contrary to man's spiritual nature and natural faculties, destroys man's natural affection for others and self, and discounts God's goodness toward man. Coercion unnaturally denies man's God-given capacities of faith, intellect, and choice. Penn states,

> If God Almighty has made of one blood all nations, as himself has declared, and that he has given them both senses corporeal and intellectual, to discern things and their differences, so as to assert or deny from evidences and reasons proper to each; then where any one enacts the belief or disbelief of any thing upon the rest, or restrains any from the exercise of their faith, to them indispensable, such an one exalts himself beyond his bounds, enslaves his fellow-creatures, invades their right of liberty, and so perverts the whole order of nature.

In addition, religious coercion, says Penn, denies man's natural instinct and privilege with which he is born to relate with God, his Creator—"that instinct of a Deity, which is so natural to him, that he can be no more without it, and be, than he can be without the most essential part of himself." Coercion confounds man's relationship with a personal, loving, compassionate God. Further, in persecuting fellow man, man's natural affection for others and for himself as a man are destroyed. Religious coercion is thus an enemy of nature.[310]

4.12 Religious Coercion Opposes Reason

Williams, Penn, and Locke also asserted that religious coercion opposes the principle of reason. It does so by imposing unjustified penalties, creating false religion and worship, robbing rewards of faith and salvation, and removing intellectual freedom and real religious expression.

Firstly, religious coercion is not justifiable since fallible man could not be certain of religious truth outside of faith. Coercions, Penn stated, "impose an uncertain faith, upon with certain penalties."[311]

Secondly, intellectual freedom is beneficial because it allows men to arrive at genuine Christian faith. Religious force or coercion in a state or nation has negative spiritual effects on people including religious hypocrisy, spiritual blindness, and hardness of heart. Coerced worship creates hypocrites out of previously conscientious yet weaker people because they are forced to worship outwardly in a way inconsistent with their true, inward convictions of heart and mind.[312] Luther had asked of the authorities, "Why then would they constrain people to believe from the heart, when they see that it is impossible? In this way they compel weak consciences to lie, to deny, and to say what they do not believe in their hearts...."[313] "True it is," Williams similarly bemoans in his *Bloudy Tenent*, citing Isaiah 10, "the sword may make, as one the Lord complained, Isa. x., a whole nation of hypocrites...."[314] Penn expresses the same idea: "Force may make an hypocrite; it is faith, grounded upon knowledge, and consent, that makes a Christian."[315] A man who accepts a religion by force and against his own judgment—"by another man's choice, not his own"—does not truly possess that religion. Since men do not believe on the basis of force but on truth, religious coercion thus subverts true religion. In such a context, men will more likely not believe due to the force, which obliges them to obey rather than dispute. "...[F]aith in all acts of religion is necessary," says Penn, and requires understanding, judgment, and free will.[316]

Thirdly, truth—in particular, the Christian Gospel—can prevail amidst other ideas. Based on the Bible, truth does not need the help of men or man's force, for it holds its own qualities and strength. Locke makes this argument in his *Second Letter Concerning Toleration*, stating,

But of this you have an experiment in its [the Christian Religion's] first appearance in the world, and several hundreds of years after. It was then "better preserved, more widely propagated, in proportion, and rendered more fruitful in the lives of its professors," than ever since; though then jews and pagans were tolerated, and more than tolerated by the governments of those places where it grew up. I hope you do not imagine the Christian Religion has lost any of its first beauty, force, or reasonableness, by having been almost two thousand years in the world; that you should fear it should be less able now to shift for itself, without the help of force. I doubt not but you look upon it still to be "the power and wisdom of God for our salvation;" and therefore cannot suspect it less capable to prevail now, by its own truth and light, than it did in the first ages of the church, when poor contemptible men, without authority, or the countenance of authority, had alone the care of it. This, as I take it, has been made use of by christians generally, and by some of our church in particular, as an argument for the truth of the christian religion; that it grew, and spread, and prevailed, without any aid from force, or the assistance of the powers in being; and if it be a mark of the true religion, that it will prevail by its own light and strength; but that false religions will not, but have need of force and foreign helps to support them, nothing certainly can be more for the advantage of true religion, than to take away compulsion every-where.... ... The inventions of men in religion need the force and helps of men to support them. A religion that is of God wants not the assistance of human authority to make it prevail.[317]

Locke's position on intellectual freedom and true religion would be adopted later by many American Founders including James Madison and Benjamin Franklin.

Fourthly, taking away man's intellectual freedom is inhumane because it makes men into animals, which no one has the right to do. Hindering intellectual freedom reduces man's faculties unnaturally. Penn alludes to Daniel 4:19-34 in which God temporarily removes proud King Nebuchadnezzar's reason as a punishment, making him like a beast. Removing intellectual freedom, Penn asserts, "does not unbrute us, but unman us: for take away understanding, reason, judgment, and faith, and, like Nebuchadnezzer, let us go graze with the beasts of the field."[318]

Fifthly, forced religion frustrates the Biblical rewards that come with man's free choice to believe—such as eternal life. Coercion deludes or compels a man out of biblical, eternal rewards given to the faithful since he is still unsaved from eternal punishment by his false or insincere worship.[319] Penn, much like Luther, conveys this point: "[U]nreasonable are those imposers, who secure not the imposed or restrained from what may occur to them, upon their account [before God in eternity]; and most inhuman are those persecutors that punish men [on earth] for not obeying them, though to their utter ruin."[320]

Sixthly, faith is confounded when men cannot freely act by it but are forced to evade conscience and to act or worship on doubt. Penn declares, "That which most of all blackens the business, is persecution: for though it is very unreasonable to require faith where men cannot chuse but doubt, yet, after all, to punish them for disobedience, is cruelty in the abstract: for we demand, Shall men suffer for not doing what they cannot do? must they be persecuted here if they do not go against their consciences, and punished hereafter if they do?"[321] A person's faith cannot be properly expressed and acted upon in a coercive or oppressive environment. Religious coercion is thus irrational.

Seventhly, the use of external force and punishments for religious coercion is irrational because they are inappropriate and ineffective methods to address inward spiritual or intellectual matters of human beings. Such external persecutions cannot convince a person's understanding or change a person's mind or belief. Penn describes "the monstrous arguments they have to convince an heretick" such as fines, "clubs, staves, stocks, pillories, prisons, dungeons, exiles, &c. in a word, ruin to whole families; as if it were not so much their design to convince the soul, as to destroy the body." Only spiritual or intellectual means can convince and persuade a person in religious matters. For example, Penn declares,

> …[T]he understanding can never be convinced, nor properly submit, but by such arguments as are rational, persuasive, and suitable to its own nature; something that can resolve its doubts, answer its objections, enervate its propositions. But to imagine those barbarous…instruments of clubs, fines, prisons, &c. with that whole troop of external and dumb materials of force, should be fit arguments to convince the understanding, scatter its scruples, and finally convert it to their religion, is altogether irrational, cruel, and impossible.[322]

Locke similarly opposes the irrational use of temporal or physical punishments to change men's minds and beliefs:

> The care of souls cannot belong to the civil magistrate, because his power consists only in outward force: but true and saving religion consists in the inward persuasion of the mind, without which nothing can be acceptable to God. And such is the nature of understanding, that it cannot be compelled by outward force. Confiscation of estate, imprisonment, torments, nothing of that nature can have any such efficacy as to make men change the inward judgment that they have framed of things.[323]

4.13 Religious Coercion Opposes Good Government's Purpose and Character

Penn also makes the argument that religious coercion contradicts good government's purpose and nature of justice, prudence, and fidelity. Good government, he asserts, is based on justice and fairness to all and the Biblical golden rule to "do unto others as you would have them do unto you." A just government gives proportional penalties for crimes. External punishment for intellectual error, however, is unjust, being disproportionate to the offense. Penn bases this reasoning on Titus 3:9-11 which says, "But avoid foolish disputes, geneaologies, contentions, and strivings about the law; for they are unprofitable and useless. Reject a divisive man after the first and second admonition, knowing that such a person is warped and sinning, being self-condemned." According to the Bible, Penn thought, the state should avoid improper or vain methods to convert or influence others in religious matters. Also, coercion in earthly government, Penn thought, unjustly invades the domain of heavenly government. Furthermore, to have men support an oppressive government but receive no protection from it and by it lose their liberty and properties—"to enrich those that ruin them"—is, Penn asserts, unjust and unequal.[324] Religious coercion is thus contrary to the intended, just nature and purpose of government.

Coercion contradicts good government's prudence, Penn thought. Government should uphold human rights and immutable laws over temporary, changeable laws dependent on those in power. Temporal laws, he asserts, cannot invalidate fundamental, immutable, agreed upon rights, laws, and constitutions of the people—the foundation of government. Temporal laws of religious coercion are futile and destructive of government. They turn faith and religion into a state policy subject to the humors, interests, and conveniences of rulers. They also often encourage vice among the people. For in seeing reverent men persecuted, irreverent men learn it is better to be as they themselves are. Such laws only make subjects invective.[325] Penn remarks, "…[F]orce never yet made either a good Christian, or a good subject."[326] Religious tolerance, Penn thought, produces peace and order while coercion and intolerance create disturbance and disunity.[327]

Religious coercion is also, Penn believed, contrary to the felicity or fidelity of government for the common good. In stripping the necessities of life from individuals and families, persecution does not benefit but destroys families, rights, peace, unity, trade, wealth, revenue, strength, and power in society. It ruins the country. Conversely, good government, Penn saw, according to Romans 13, is hard only on evil and evildoers,

1 not on moral, godly, law-abiding people. Government could not require all people to share the same faith and
2 worship, Penn concludes, in order to benefit under the same civil law. It could not refuse law and life to those
3 who do not conform religiously.[328]
4
5 **4.14 Freedom of Conscience Within Civil Peace and Order**
6
7 **Freedom of conscience, Williams and Penn emphasized, should be upheld by the civil state and**
8 **citizens within the bounds of civil peace and order.** Civility and Christianity, they believed, could flourish
9 together in a tolerant state. Strife, Williams found, was generally ungodly, unlawful, and negative based on
10 Romans 12:18. Citing Romans 12:18, Williams observes that "there is a possibility of keeping sweet Peace in
11 most cases, and, *if it be possible*, it is the express command of God that Peace be kept, Rom. xii."[329] One
12 should determine whether strife is necessary or godly. Civil peace, Williams believed, was godly and should be
13 maintained based on Romans 13 and the call of believers to submit to good or godly authorities and to keep
14 civil peace and order. Romans 13:1-5 states of good government,
15
16   Let every soul be subject to the governing authorities. For there is no authority except from God, and
17   the authorities that exist are appointed by God. Therefore whoever resists the authority resists the
18   ordinance of God, and those who resist will bring judgment on themselves. For rulers are not a terror to
19   good works, but to evil. … For he is God's minister to you for good. But if you do evil, be afraid; for
20   he does not bear the sword in vain; for he is God's minister, an avenger to *execute* wrath on him who
21   practices evil. Therefore *you* must be subject, not only because of wrath but also for conscience' sake.
22
23 One should abide by the just civil laws of the state while practicing freedom of conscience and tolerance. Penn
24 assures, "We are pleading only for such a liberty of conscience as preserves the nation in peace, trade, and
25 commerce; and would not exempt any man, or party of men, from not keeping those excellent laws, that tend to
26 sober, just, and industrious living."[330] God's people are to exercise freedom of conscience, Williams affirms,
27 "not daring either to be restrained from the true, or constrained to false worship; and yet without breach of the
28 civil or city peace, properly so called."[331] The Bible, Williams believed, clearly supports the right to freedom of
29 conscience and practice within the bounds of civil peace, order, and just laws.
30
31   To be sure, God's people, in upholding conscience and defending against oppression, would at times
32 find themselves in disruptions. Though not the intentional cause of disruption, they might accidentally become,
33 according to Luke 12:51, as Williams tells, "the occasion of great contentions and divisions, yea, tumults and
34 uproars, in towns and cities where they have lived and come; and yet neither their doctrine nor themselves
35 arrogant nor impetuous, however so charged: for thus the Lord Jesus discovereth men's false and secure
36 suppositions, Luke xii. 51, *Suppose ye that I am come to give peace on the earth? I tell you, nay; but rather*
37 *division…*."[332] In exercising and defending freedom of conscience and religious tolerance, God's people might
38 find themselves in battles or meeting with opposition. Further, the defense of innocent people against earthly
39 oppression, Williams also believed, is godly and necessary. Citing Psalm 73 and Job 29, he states, "…[I]t is
40 necessary, honorable, godly, &c., with civil and earthly weapons to defend the innocent, and to rescue the
41 oppressed from the violent paws and jaws of oppressing, persecuting Nimrods, Psal. lxxiii. Job xxix."[333]
42 Conflicts should not be sought out by God's people but are sometimes unavoidable.
43
44 **4.15 A Call for Greater Separation Between Church and Civil Government**
45
46   To preserve freedom of conscience and the church's purity, Roger Williams proposed the radical idea of
47 greater separation between church and civil government. He saw the church as a pure garden that needs to be
48 separated from the impure world in order to preserve its purity. Williams held a more radical, practical view of
49 separation than the Puritans who thought the church should function together with the civil government.

1 Williams believed the government and church should actually have more separate, independent functions in
2 society in order to keep the church pure. His idea challenged views of that time regarding the role and function
3 of the church and government in the world.[334]
4
5   To be sure, the Bible and Christians in history had always viewed the civil government and church as
6 two distinct institutions based on John 18:36 in which Jesus points out two kingdoms—of God and of the
7 world—in stating, "'My kingdom is not of this world.'" They also based it on Matthew 22:21 in which Jesus,
8 distinguishing between civil government and church and what should be offered to each, says to the Pharisee
9 religionists questioning Him, "'Render therefore to Caesar the things that are Caesar's, and to God the things
10 that are God's.'"[335] In portraying this distinction, Christians in the 1500s depicted the church as a pure garden
11 enclosed from the wilderness and impurities of the fallen world. This image was based on a physical and
12 metaphorical contrast in Exodus between the Israelite's Promised Land of Canaan and the Sinai desert
13 wilderness where the Israelites wandered before reaching their destination. It was also based on the biblical
14 Garden of Eden in Genesis and on the picture of a pure bride in Song of Songs 4:12 which states: "A garden
15 enclosed *Is* my sister, my spouse, A spring shut up, A fountain sealed."[336] Some Catholic believers practiced
16 monastery living with such images in mind. Many Christians also adopted the metaphorical image for Israel
17 itself and for the church as God's people. English Protestant minister Nehemiah Rogers in 1623 describes the
18 church as a garden in the same way that Israel is God's vineyard in Isaiah 5. In Isaiah 5:1-2, 7 the prophet
19 Isaiah writes of Israel as God's vineyard:
20
21   Now let me sing to my Well-beloved A song of my Beloved regarding His [God's] vineyard: My Well-
22   beloved has a vineyard On a very fruitful hill. He dug it up and cleared out its stones, And planted it
23   with the choicest vine. He built a tower in its midst, And also made a winepress in it; So He expected *it*
24   to bring forth *good* grapes.... ... For the vineyard of the LORD of hosts *is* the house of Israel, And the
25   men of Judah are His pleasant plant.
26
27 Rogers describes the church similarly: "'God hath taken it [the church] in out of the vast wilderness of this
28 wretched world, and hath imparked it with the pales of his mercy, and separated it from all other grounds
29 whatsoever, to be a Vineyard for himself.'"[337] Church and government were thus historically acknowledged
30 and portrayed as distinct from one another.[338]
31
32   Williams saw the Judeo-Christian metaphorical distinction between church and world as a more radical,
33 practical one than others. He uses a "wall of separation" metaphor to describe the church's proper separation
34 from the world. This wall represents a protection for the purity of the church and Christian life.[339] The
35 combined roles and functions of civil government and church had been the rule and practice in England and
36 Europe for centuries. It had led to the practice of state church establishments. But Williams believed this
37 practice mixed the church with the world, making it impure. Since state church establishments mandated
38 religious practices for all, they wrongly mixed Christians and non-Christians together in the church and gave a
39 false appearance of salvation among non-Christians. This outward religious conformity led to impurity and
40 hypocrisy in the church. The New Testament, Williams thought, does not support a coerced, mixed church tied
41 to worldly powers. Furthermore, the true church is spiritual and not confined to believers in one state, nation, or
42 territory. State church establishments, he thought, confuse the civil and spiritual realms and corrupt the church.
43
44   A church tied to the civil government, Williams believed, neglects the church's proper separation from
45 the world practiced among Jews and Christians in the Bible and brings impurity. In Isaiah 5, for example, God
46 warns of the removal of Israel's garden wall due to the bad fruits of injustice, unrighteousness, and
47 oppression.[340] In Isaiah 5:3-6, the prophet Isaiah expresses God's disappointment with His corrupted vineyard:

"And now, O inhabitants of Jerusalem and men of Judah, Judge, please, between Me and My vineyard. What more could have been done to My vineyard That I have not done in it? Why then, when I expected *it* to bring forth *good* grapes, Did it bring forth wild grapes? And now, please let Me tell you what I will do to My vineyard: I will take away its hedge, and it shall be burned; *And* break down its wall, and it shall be trampled down. I will lay it waste; It shall not be pruned or dug, But there shall come up briers and thorns. I will also command the clouds That they rain no rain on it."

The breaking down of the garden wall, thought Williams, is God's punishment for religious oppression and unrighteousness. When Israel or the church becomes corrupt, God in punishment tears down its wall and turns it into a wilderness wasteland. Referring to Israel's or the church's contact with the world and alluding to Isaiah 5:3-6, Williams observes,

> …[T]he church of the Jews under the Old Testament…and the church of the Christians under the New Testament…were both separate from the world; …When they have opened a gap in the hedge, or wall of separation, between the garden of the church and the wilderness of the world, God hath ever broke down the wall itself, removed the candlestick, &c. and made his garden a wilderness, as at this day. And that therefore if he will ever please to restore his garden and paradise again, it must of necessity be walled in peculiarly unto himself from the world, and that all shall be saved out of the world are to be transplanted out of the wilderness of the world, and added unto his church or garden.[341]

The wall exists to protect the church garden from the wilderness of the world. Williams expresses concern about the corruption in Isaiah 5:3-7 in which the wall of God's people is completely broken down as divine punishment. He, like other "Separationists," argues that churches and congregations should separate from what are thought to be impure, established state churches. He also opposes a state church that mixes Christians and non-Christians together. State church establishments threaten individual freedom and the purity of the believers. Williams believed civil government should regulate only civil offenses, and the church should only regulate church or religious matters.

In continuing a combined church and civil government in America, the Puritans, to Williams, did not adequately purify the church. The Puritan church had mixture with the world and in its congregation, he thought. Though the Puritans deemed all those in their congregations to be Christians, the need for religious regulation or coercion, to Williams, proved the mixture. He observes,

> …[B]y compelling all within their jurisdiction to an outward conformity of the church worship, of the word and prayer, and maintenance of the ministry thereof, they evidently declare that they still lodge and dwell in the confused mixtures of the unclean and clean, of the flock of Christ and the herds of the world together—I mean, in spiritual and religious worship.[342]

That men were legally required to abide by a certain belief and worship, Williams notes, suggested they had differing beliefs and views about worship.

Separation between church and civil government, Williams believed, is the solution to remove religious coercion and to preserve freedom of conscience necessary for religious purity. Churches in America, he asserts, should be separate from the government rather than government-supported, official national churches. Separation, he thought, would protect church and government from each other—the church from corruption, ambitions, vices, and power lusts of men, and the state from "the most un-Christian Christendom."[343] Separation would make the church a voluntary institution, purifying the mixture of Christians and non-Christians in it. In the absence of religious coercion, truth would prevail over error in a free exchange of ideas, and the Bible-based ideal of a state could be realized.[344] Separation would also eliminate conflicts between church and government in religion and politics which had characterized religious wars in England and Europe. Williams, however, did not oppose Christian principles in government.

Civil government and church, as separated, Williams and later Locke assert, should maintain separate jurisdictions and functions. Civil government and church officers should have separate roles and responsibilities. The government and its officers should oversee civil matters and the welfare and protection of men's bodies while the church and its officers should oversee spiritual matters and the welfare of souls, which were ultimately in the jurisdiction of Christ and His heavenly kingdom. Williams affirms that "as the civil magistrate hath his charge of the bodies and goods of the subject: so have the spiritual officers, governors, and overseers of Christ's city or kingdom, the charge of their souls, and soul-safety."[345] The responsibilities of the church and government need to be distinct and separate, Williams argues, based on Acts 20:26. The government has only an earthly jurisdiction while God and the church have a heavenly jurisdiction. Citing Acts 20:26, Williams explains,

> ...[W]oe were it with the civil magistrate...if together with the common care and charge of the commonwealth...the blood of every soul that perisheth should cry against him; unless he could say with Paul, Acts xx. [Acts 20:26] (in spiritual regards) *I am clear from the blood of all men*, that is, the blood of souls, which was his charge to look after, so far as his preaching went, not the blood of bodies which belongeth to the civil magistrate.[346]

The civil government and its officers should oversee only civil matters, argued Williams, Penn, and Locke, because they did not have power over conscience or religious matters. Locke explained that the civil government and earthly rulers should only oversee temporal, not spiritual matters:

> The commonwealth seems to me to be a society of men constituted only for the procuring, preserving, and advancing their own civil interests.
>
> Civil interest I call life, liberty, health, and indolency of body; and the possession of outward things, such as money, lands, houses, furniture, and the like.
>
> It is the duty of the civil magistrate, by the impartial execution of equal laws, to secure unto all the people in general, and to every one of his subjects in particular, the just possession of these things belonging to this life. ...
>
> Now that the whole jurisdiction of the magistrate reaches only to these civil concernments; and that all civil power, right, and dominion, is bounded and confined to the only care of promoting these things; and that it neither can nor ought in any manner be extended to the salvation of souls; these following considerations seems to me abundantly to demonstrate.
>
> First, Because the care of souls is not committed to the civil magistrate, any more than to other men. It is not committed unto him, I say, by God; because it appears not that God has ever given any such authority to one man over another, as to compel any one to his religion. Nor can any such power be vested in the magistrate by the consent of the people; because no man can so far abandon the care of his own salvation, as blindly to leave it to the choice of any other, whether prince or subject, to prescribe to him what faith or worship he shall embrace. For no man can, if he would, conform his faith to the dictates of another. All the life and power of true religion consists in the inward and full persuasion of the mind; and faith is not faith, without believing. Whatever profession we make, to whatever outward worship we conform, if we are not fully satisfied in our own mind that the one is true, and the other well-pleasing unto God, such profession and such practice, far from being any furtherance, are indeed great obstacles to our salvation. For in this manner, instead of expiating other sins by the exercise of religion, I say in offering thus unto God Almighty such a worship as we esteem to be displeasing unto him, we add unto the number of our other sins, those also of hypocrisy, and contempt of his Divine Majesty.[347]

Since the government and its officers do not have power in religious matters, says Williams, to have the state enforce religious laws is futile and inappropriate. Locke explains, "For laws are of no force at all without penalties, and penalties in this case [of spiritual matters] are absolutely impertinent, because they are not proper to convince the mind…."[348] Religious belief and worship cannot be regulated by the government because they are of the spiritual realm.

To further support the limits of state authority in judging religious matters, Williams and Penn cite Matthew 13:24-44, Jesus' parable of the wheat and tares growing in a field, representing true and false believers respectively, in the voluntary church. Jesus tells in Matthew 13:27-30,

> So the servants of the owner came and said to him, "Sir, did you not sow good seed in your field? How then does it have tares [weeds]?" He said to them, "An enemy has done this." The servants said to him, "Do you want us then to go and gather them up?" But he said, "No, lest while you gather up the tares you also uproot the wheat with them. Let both grow together until the harvest."

When tares or weeds—representing idolators, false worshippers, anti-Christians—are sown among the wheat—representing true Christians—in the field of the voluntary church, Christ does not allow the government or any man to try to discern or weed them out. Christ tolerates the tares to grow up among the true Christians until His harvest in His heavenly kingdom.[349] The state, Williams concludes, should not judge men's consciences or religious matters, for Christ will judge men in His heavenly kingdom. It could use laws and the sword to maintain peace and order and to defend the common good, but it could not coerce religious conversions or punish heretics. Williams affirms, "…[A]s the civil state keeps itself with a civil guard, in case these tares shall attempt ought against the peace and welfare of it let such civil offences be punished; and yet, as tares opposite to Christ's kingdom, let their worship and consciences be tolerated."[350] In the same way, the civil government is called to regulate public civil peace and order and to protect against "injury done unto men's neighbours, and to the commonwealth" but has no calling or authority to constrain or restrain people to or from worship. The proper civil government actually functions to protect conscience and the sacred relationship between God and the individual.[351]

It is important to note that the ideas of separation between civil government and church that arose in the 1600s and 1700s, even as Williams defined it, did not typically mean a complete separation of these spheres and their functions in society as is understood in present-day separation. Their distinctiveness was still seen as compatible with a civil state that had an official religion.[352] The government was still expected to support and protect the church, and the church was to provide moral guidance to the government. Only, it presented the idea that the government was not to mandate religious practice. Before the 1800s, few supported separation in any modern sense except a small number of European Enlightenment secularists mistrustful of institutional churches and clergy and a small number of religious dissenters in America. For many believed the church was to minister in the world, though not be of the world.

4.16 The Colony of Rhode Island and Freedom of Conscience

Rev. Roger Williams was opposed by the Puritans in Massachusetts due to his dissident views, dislike of the conforming churches, and strong reactions to views with which he disagreed. Puritan leaders believed he threatened religious uniformity, and he was banished from the colony in 1635.

In 1643, Williams founded Rhode Island as a religiously tolerant colony—"a shelter for persons distressed of conscience"—with laws supporting greater separation of church and civil government and freedom of conscience.[353] The colony did not establish a state church, did not enforce religious opinion, and viewed God alone as ruler of conscience. Rhode Island's 1663 charter includes a statement about free religious opinion:

1   "…[N]oe person within the sayd colonye, at any tyme hereafter, shall bee any wise molested, punished,
2   disquieted or called in question, for any differences in opinione in matters of religion, and doe not actually
3   disturb the civill peace…."[354] Similar statements appeared in charters and constitutions of other colonies.
4
5   Rhode Island's government was, as stated in the 1647 laws of the colony, "democratical; that is to say, a
6   government held by the free and voluntary consent of all, or the greater part of the free inhabitants."[355] While
7   having freedom of conscience, a settler was to submit to civil laws or the will of the majority in civil or secular
8   matters. To be sure, Rhode Island's leaders struggled with how to create an ordered society with religious
9   freedom and found the differing religious groups with differing practices to be burdensome. Catholics, Jews,
10   and atheists did not have full rights, though their religious opinions and consciences were tolerated. Yet Rhode
11   Island was the first colony in America to attempt separation between church and government and where
12   freedom of conscience was a human right. The colony became a refuge for religious dissidents who fled from
13   religious intolerance or persecution.   Quakers, Antinomians, Baptists, Catholics, Jews, and many other
14   dissenting groups and individuals including Puritan dissident Ann Hutchinson settled in the colony. The colony
15   also initiated the practice of religious competition.[356]
16

17   **4.17 The Colony of Maryland and the Religious Toleration Act**
18
19   The colony of Maryland, settled in 1634, was the one colony among the original thirteen colonies in
20   America with a significant Catholic population. It was founded by George Calvert and his son Cecil, the First
21   and Second Lords Baltimore. George Calvert, a Catholic convert who was Secretary of State under King James
22   I of England, had to resign his post upon refusal to swear allegiance to the Church of England at the succession
23   of King James's son, King Charles I. To repay the Calverts for loyal service to his father and himself, King
24   Charles gave the Calvert family a large grant of land in America. Maryland, named in honor of Charles' French
25   Catholic queen, Henrietta Maria, served as a haven for persecuted Catholics. Despite its Catholic origins,
26   Maryland's population was largely Protestant, and Protestant settlers were not antagonized for their beliefs.
27   Maryland had no state church originally, though later it established a tolerant Anglican state church. Maryland
28   would later become home to the first Catholic Bishop in the United States and, for a long time, the center of
29   American Catholicism. Maryland, like other Christian settlements, had missions for Native Americans.
30
31   The Religious Toleration Act was issued in Maryland in 1649 by Cecil Calvert to protect Catholic
32   interests against the Puritan English parliament during the Puritan Revolution in England. More a protection
33   than a commitment to religious tolerance, the act, resembling Rhode Island's charter was nonetheless a notable
34   step toward religious freedom because it made religious tolerance a law.[357] It prohibited hostile or derogatory
35   language or labels regarding the religion of others and allowed for free practice of religion, enacting that "noe
36   person or persons whatsoever within this Province…professing to believe [sic] in Jesus Christ, shall from
37   henceforth bee any waies troubled, Molested or discountenanced for or in respect of his or her religion nor in
38   the free exercise thereof within this Province…nor any way compelled to the beleife or exercise of any other
39   Religion against his or her consent, soe as they be not unfaithfull to the Lord Proprietary, or molest or conspire
40   against the civill Government established…."[358] The law, also called the Act Concerning Religion, was the
41   first law on religious tolerance in America and influenced religious tolerance laws in other colonies.
42
43   **4.18 The Colony of Carolina Supports Freedom of Conscience**
44
45   In the 1660s, King Charles II supported the development of the American colony of Charleston. In
46   1663, eight noblemen, led by Anthony Ashley Cooper, Lord Shaftesbury, founded the colony of Carolina. The
47   area surrounding Charleston was named Carolina based on the Latin word for Charles, *Carolus*. King Charles
48   appointed his advisor, Lord Shaftesbury, to draft a constitution for the colony. And Lord Shaftesbury, in turn,
49   recruited Locke to draft the document. Locke, who adhered to the reformed ideas of Luther, Calvin, and the

Puritans, supported freedom of conscience. Though the colony of Carolina had an Anglican state church, the Constitution of Carolina of 1669, written by Locke for the colony of Carolina, notably supported freedom of conscience and greater religious rights for settlers and dissidents. It granted legal rights to all religious groups who acknowledged a Creator and prohibited religious harassment, stating "No person whatsoever shall disturb, molest, or persecute another for his speculative opinions in religion or his way of worship."[359]

4.19 The Colony of Pennsylvania, a "Holy Experiment" in Religious Tolerance for a Moral People

Though disapproving of Penn's dissident views, King Charles II granted young William Penn a royal charter or title of land in colonial America in 1681 to repay a debt owed to Penn's father, Sir William, and to remove Penn and his protests from England. King Charles named the land Pennsylvania, meaning "Penn's woods" or "Penn's forest," to honor Penn's father who had been a friend of the Crown. Young Penn hoped both for revenue on the land to pay off debts and to establish a colony for religious freedom in America. He founded Pennsylvania as a "tolerance settlement" for persecuted Christians in Europe, calling it a "Holy Experiment" in religious and civil freedom to be an example for Christians everywhere. The colony had no state church.

Pennsylvania was open to Christians of all denominations and sects. Settlers were simply required to possess the Christian faith but could believe in and practice denominational or sectarian differences as they chose. Like the Puritans, Penn envisioned a peaceful, ordered colony inhabited by godly people. But the fundamentals of Christianity, regarded as the one true religion, overrode denominational differences, he believed. The colony accepted religious pluralism, Frank Lambert says, as "the many faces of a common Christianity and the foundation of a society where sectarians would cooperate with each other for the public good."[360] It was based on the assumptions that colonists would live piously and put public good above private interest. Penn hoped the environment would allow colonists to pursue and find true faith in God.

Penn recruited Christians of all sects from England and Europe. Due to his recruiting efforts and the attraction of a tolerance settlement, refugees from many parts of Europe came to the new colony. They included those of the Protestant Reformation, European religious wars, and English Civil War as well as some non-Christians. Christian groups that came included Mennonites, Lutherans, Reformed, Moravians, Presbyterians, Roman Catholics, Huguenots, Baptists, Dunkers, Quakers, Methodist Episcopalians, and others. This mix of religious sects in Pennsylvania was often called by colonists "a great mixt multitude." Pennsylvania became one of the most influential examples of religious freedom in New England and the most religiously tolerant place in the world.[361]

Pennsylvania's Frame of Government of 1682 laid out the terms of the "Holy Experiment." Penn believed government should maintain peace, order, and other necessary affairs. He set up a government of civil and religious freedom, placing power in the hands of the people and in their consent on goverance and laws. The preface to the colony's Frame of Government declares, "'*Any government is free to the people under it* (whatever be the frame) *where the laws rule, and the people are a party to those laws*, and more than this is tyranny, oligarchy, or confusion.'"[362] Colonists were self-governed, made and enforced laws, and prospered through industry. Penn also implemented fair treatment and rights of Native Americans.

While the Puritans in Massachusetts adopted elements they knew from England such as a state church establishment, religious conformity, and limited religious tolerance, Pennsylvania departed from such state church uniformities.[363] Like Rhode Island, it did not establish a government-supported church. It forbid irreverence against God but did not impose religious conformity to one sect. No one could be persecuted for religious beliefs or practices. One had to be a Christian to become a citizen or hold public office in the colony, yet no denominational or sectarian restrictions existed. This was a notable development. The colony gave much religious freedom to its Christian citizens. The colony essentially provided, says David Gibbs, Jr., "not freedom *from* religion, but freedom *of* religion—not a separation of government from all religion, but a government that respected the religious consciences of all its citizens."[364]

Though supportive of religious tolerance, Penn emphasized the need for godly, moral people in government and society. Good, workable government, Penn thought, required not only good laws but good people. Good people mattered more than good laws, he thought, and that a government run by moral people was greater than the form of government. In the preface of Pennsylvania's 1682 Frame of Government, he elaborated on the need for moral people and leaders in government:

> Let men be good, and the government cannot be bad; if it be ill, they will cure it. But, if men be bad, let the government be never so good, they will endeavor to warp and spoil it to their turn.
>
> I know some say, let us have good laws, and no matter for the men that execute them: but let them consider, that though good laws do well, good men do better: for good laws may want good men, and be abolished or evaded [invaded in Franklin's print] by ill men; but good men will never want good laws, nor suffer ill ones. It is true, good laws have some awe upon ill ministers, but that is where they have not power to escape or abolish them, and the people are generally wise and good: but a loose and depraved people (which is the question) love laws and an administration like themselves. That, therefore, which makes a good constitution, must keep it, viz: men of wisdom and virtue....[365]

Godly, moral people must obey laws to live freely while good government must respect people's freedom through just rule, for, as Penn expounds, "liberty without obedience is confusion, and obedience without liberty is slavery."[366]

4.20 The Struggle with Sectarian Issues in Civil Government and Public Policy

Though Pennsylvania enjoyed religious freedom, it struggled with sectarian issues in government and public policy. For religious sects disagreed on public policy and how to govern the colony. To prevent one group from imposing its denominational beliefs on the entire colony through public policy, Penn invited public officers of diverse denominations to serve in the early government. The Quaker Party, however, gained and held a legislative majority in the governing assembly in the 1680s until the mid 1700s and legislated their own sectarian beliefs. Penn instructed the Quakers to put aside sectarian interests for the good of society, but the ruling Quaker Party disagreed among themselves on whether to cede, distribute, or share power. Thus a sectarian group with majority power abandoned Penn's vision of a religiously differentiated but harmonious Christian society.

Two Quaker policies that stirred opposition were the refusals to take civil oaths or military action to protect the colony. Since Quakers did not take civil oaths, the Quaker Party legally exempted Quakers from taking oaths as citizens, officeholders, jurors, witnesses, etc. Instead, Quakers gave an affirmation of loyalty to the civil power. Military affairs drew the most criticism and became a major issue due to wars in Europe at the time and hostile native attacks in the colony. As absolute pacifists, the Quakers refused to form policy on defense or take military action for any reason, though other colonists viewed defense and a military as imperative. To non-Quakers who saw defense as a necessity to society and a non-issue to faith, the Quaker's refusal to protect citizens due to sectarian beliefs unacceptably subjected everyone to mortal danger.[367] The defense issue led to the end of Quaker governance.

The forming of public policy in the name of religious freedom, and freedom of conscience thus became problematic for Pennsylvania. Freedom of conscience and religion essentially enabled the majority religious group in power to impose its beliefs on society in a similar manner as a state church.[368] Despite its struggles, though, Penn's unprecedented experiment in Pennsylvania would provide a strong example for America and the future United States in religious freedom and tolerance.

4.21 The English Toleration Act of 1689

Around this time in England, Protestant groups feared that King James II and his male heir would establish the Catholic Church. In an effort to fight Catholic tendencies, the various Protestant groups united. Upon the encouragement of the Protestants, William of Netherlands, who was married to King James's Protestant daughter, Mary, seized the English crown in the Glorious Revolution of 1688. William and Mary thus became the Protestant sovereigns of England. Subsequently, in 1689, British Parliament passed the Toleration Act of 1689 that allowed freedom of worship to Protestant non-conformists—like Congregationalists, Presbyterians, Quakers, and Baptists—who dissented from the Church of England but who pledged allegiance to Britain. This act maintained the favored position of a state church, like the Church of England, but allowed Protestant non-conformists to worship where and as they chose and to select their ministers. Their worship houses had to be registered and their teachers licensed. The act notably excluded tolerance of Catholics, non-trinitarians, and atheists. It also excluded all dissenters from voting and holding public office. The act was applied in the British colonies in America—including New England—by charter or governor. Consequently, most of the colonies in America became more tolerant of Protestant dissenters and non-conformists. However, tolerance colonies like Rhode Island, Pennsylvania, and New Jersey went beyond the act to prohibit the establishment of official churches and to allow more diverse religious expression. Still, only Pennsylvania and Maryland allowed Catholics freedom of worship. Some historians consider Locke's *Letters Concerning Toleration* to be the philosophical influence behind the English act. Locke had similarly applied tolerance to Protestant non-conformists coexisting with a state church. Many colonists in America accepted Locke's view of tolerance.[369]

4.22 Conclusion: The Religious Landscape of the Thirteen Colonies

By 1732, thirteen colonies had formed in North America: Virginia, Massachusetts, Maryland, Connecticut, Rhode Island, North Carolina, South Carolina, New York, New Jersey, New Hampshire, Pennsylvania, Delaware, and Georgia. The Puritans' Congregational Church was established in New England. The Anglican Church was established in the southern colonies. The middle colonies had a Christian pluralism, often unharmonious, of various Christian denominations. Acceptance of religious tolerance and freedom of conscience grew and spread in these colonies in the 1700s. Though most colonists in the early 1700s—about 85% of 500,000 inhabitants in North America—lived in colonies with an official state church, the Congregational Church or the Anglican Church, state churches gradually granted more tolerance for other denominations in their colonies.[370] Many colonists including Thomas Jefferson, James Madison, and John Adams, future Founders of the United States, began to view freedom of conscience as more important than religious conformity. They also began to see politics differently. As religious toleration became more widespread, observes Jon Meacham, so did the support and acceptance of more democratic ideas. "For people who chose their own spiritual path," Meacham writes, "wondered why they could not choose their own political path as well."[371] Indeed, the American colonies became increasingly tolerant and democratic. Shaped by and rooted in Bible-based or Judeo-Christian thought by its earliest supporters in America, the principles of religious tolerance, freedom of conscience, and separation of church and civil government would become, a century later, widely accepted and practiced principles in American thought and law. Religious freedom for all and separation of church and government would eventually be fully realized, successfully implemented, and secured by the Founding Fathers in the United States Constitution and Bill of Rights.

The Thirteen Colonies, Christian and Denominationally Diverse, 1600s-1700s

Name of Colony	Date Founded	Founder(s)	Region	Religion / Church	Status in 1775 Pre-Revolution
Virginia	1606	Virginia Company of London	Southern	Anglican Church est., relig conformity	Royal
Massachusetts (Plymouth fd 1620, merges w/MA 1691)	1629	Puritans, Plymouth founded by Pilgrims	New England	Congregational Church est., relig conformity	Royal (loses charter 1684, new charter 1691)
Maryland	1634	George and Cecil Calvert, Lords Baltimore	Southern	Tolerant of Catholics & Protestants, later weak Anglican Church est.	Proprietary
Connecticut (New Haven merges w/CT 1662)	1637	Thomas Hooker and Mass. Puritan emigrants	New England	Congregational Church est., relig conformity	Royal
Rhode Island	1643	Roger Williams	New England	No est. church, non-sectarian, pluralistic, tolerant of Protestants	Royal
Maine (merges w/MA 1652, secedes from MA 1820)	1622	Sir Ferdinando Gorges	New England	Congregational Church est., tolerant of Protestants	Royal
North Carolina (Carolina separates 1712)	1663	Eight English Nobles led by Anthony Ashley Cooper, Lord Shaftesbury	Southern	Weak Anglican Church est.	Royal
South Carolina (Carolina separates 1712)	1663	Eight English Nobles led by Anthony Ashley Cooper, Lord Shaftesbury	Southern	Weak Anglican Church est.	Royal
New York	1664	James, Duke of York, bro. of King Charles II	Middle	Weak Anglican Church est., pluralistic	Royal
New Jersey	1664	Two Nobles, Sir George Carteret and Lord John Berkeley	Middle	No est. church, non-sectarian, pluralistic	Royal
New Hampshire	1629	Capt. John Mason	New England	Congregational Church est., relig conformity	Royal
Pennsylvania	1681	William Penn	Middle	No est. church, non-sectarian, pluralistic	Proprietary
Delaware (merges w/PA 1682, sep. legislature 1701)	1664	James, Duke of York	Middle	No est. church, pluralistic	Proprietary
Georgia	1732	Gen. James Oglethorpe	Southern	Weak Anglican Church est., tolerant of Christians & Jews	Royal

Review: Checking Out the History

Discuss questions in subgroups or whole group. As an option, the group may come up with main ideas or insights from each question. Responses may be shared and discussed in the whole group.

1. How did the experiences of Roger Williams, William Penn, and Cecil Calvert influence their views about religious tolerance and freedom of conscience?

2. How did the beliefs of William and Penn differ from those of the Puritans? How were they similar?

3. What main points from the Bible and other sources were used by Williams, Penn, and Locke to argue against religious coercion and in support of religious tolerance and freedom of conscience?

4. Why do you think Williams and Penn based their arguments against religious intolerance and coercion largely on the Bible and Judeo-Christian principles?

5. Where did early ideas of separation of church and civil government originally come from? What did the concept mean?

6. Why were the colonies of Rhode Island, Pennsylvania, and Maryland significant?

7. How were these colonies similar to and/or different than earlier American colonies? How did they and the ideas of their founders affect the other colonies?

8. What other factors at this time influenced the American colonies and their positions on religious tolerance and freedom of conscience?

9. What Bible-based or Judeo-Christian principles are evident and important in this part of America's heritage?

1 **Activity: Roles of Church and Government**
2 Review the list of items that are (or are not) a right, role, or responsibility in America **today**. Consider which
3 sector(s)—church, government, both, or neither—has/have the right, role, or responsibility for each item.
4 Check the column(s) which apply. Some items may not have checks.
5

Right / Role / Responsibility (today)	Right or Role of the Church	Right or Role of Government (local, state, natl)
To teach church doctrine		
To maintain the peace		
To establish and protect religious freedom		
To raise money for social services		
To support objective education about religion		
To recite the Bible in a devotional manner		
To convert people to faith		
To meet the social needs of the community		
To burn heretics at the stake		
To read and refer to the Bible		
To pray in meetings		
To preach the Gospel		
To require a particular religion for all people or members		
To vote or hold elections on teaching the Bible in schools		
To hold meetings on teaching the Bible in schools		
To discuss or teach morals and ethics		
To imprison one for having a non-conformist faith		
To display the ten commandments or other scriptures		
To abide by the laws of the land		
To compel religious conversion by force or punishment		
To require forms of worship for all religious groups		

To defend religious expression in the public square		
To endorse a particular political candidate or party		
To discuss politically sensitive issues		
To provide objective information on elections		
To provide objective information on all political candidates		

1
2

1 **Call to Action**
2
3 Each person will reflect on and write his/her responses to the questions below. Responses may then be shared
4 and discussed in the group.
5
6 1. What indications of the legacies of Williams, Penn, Calvert, and/or Locke are apparent to you in American
7 life today?
8 _____
9 _____
10 _____
11 _____
12
13 2. How is Williams's idea of separation of church and state similar to and/or different than the idea as it is
14 often understood today?
15 _____
16 _____
17 _____
18 _____
19
20 3. How are you impacted today by the assertion of freedom of conscience?
21 _____
22 _____
23 _____
24 _____
25
26 4. Why do religious dissidents come to America?
27 _____
28 _____
29 _____
30 _____
31
32 5. How are the United States' governments today similar to and/or different than America's early colonial
33 governments?
34 _____
35 _____
36 _____
37 _____
38
39 6. From your observation, what benefits and effects does religious tolerance and freedom of conscience have
40 on modern American society? What current issues or concerns are raised with regard to these principles?
41 _____
42 _____
43 _____
44 _____

Chapter 5
The Great Awakening, An Evangelical Revival in the American Colonies

In the 1700s, the thirteen colonies in America, which had formed distinct religious identities, encountered population growth, geographic expansion, and new ideas. The influx of European immigrants to America expanded settlements beyond existing boundaries and into the frontier where few ministers and churches existed. Immigrants brought various beliefs and Christian denominations with them, and existing churches and parishes could no longer contain the settlers and their views. In addition, many colonists became economically independent and prosperous by obtaining free or cheap land and by their labor and industry. Such events at this time fostered a new attitude, says H. Richard Niebuhr, of "practical individualism."[372] These changes made the colonies more religiously diverse and pluralistic, introduced religious competition, and challenged assumptions about state church establishments.[373] The colonies, says Niebuhr, saw "a new world of emancipated individuals who had become their own political masters to an uncommon degree," where "absolute individuals had replaced absolute kings and absolute churches."[374] It was onto this scene that a Christian evangelical revival arrived that would significantly impact culture, society, and politics in colonial America: the Great Awakening. The Great Awakening would move pre-revolutionary colonists toward greater regard for human dignity, equality, and rights; greater religious pluralism and religious tolerance; a democratic and independent spirit, and a shared identity rooted in Bible-based beliefs and values.

5.1 The Great Awakening Emerges in the Early 1700s

The Great Awakening was an evangelical revival of Christianity that swept through the American colonies in the early to mid 1700s and influenced societal changes in religion and politics. It was called *great*, say historians, because it affected many regions and aspects of colonial life, and it was an *awakening* because it led to increased spiritual life and devotion among Americans.[375] The Awakening, says Johnson, had European roots among German immigrants thankful "for their delivery from European poverty and their happy coming into the Promised Land."[376] It was influenced by the European pietist movement that began in German and Prussian principalities and spread to the Netherlands and England at the turn of the 1700s.[377] The Awakening represented the first time non-English-speaking immigrants influenced American intellectual life.[378] Pietism, a German concept, emphasized a holy life over doctrinal disputes, personal religious experience, self-examination, and individual transformation. The Awakening had pietistic elements in emphasizing personal religious conversion and a godly life due to an inner change of heart. Many colonists made personal decisions about their beliefs. Individuals practiced prayer, Bible reading, and personal exhortation.[379] The Awakening crossed different theologies and denominations in its teachings. Some revival views were new takes on Puritan views or new altogether. The Awakening continued the Protestantism of the 1600s but emphasized new ideas in a changing society.[380] For one, while God's sovereign rule was the focus of the first period of Protestantism in Puritan America, the heavenly kingdom of Christ became a dominant idea of the Awakening. This kingdom had to do with Christ's redemption or liberation of man from sin and reconciliation of believers to God.[381]

Several leaders were prominent in the Great Awakening. The Awakening began largely with Congregational minister Solomon Stoddard of Northampton, Massachusetts, and German Reformist minister Theodore Frelinghuysen of New Jersey. Stoddard and Frelinghuysen held revival meetings that sparked many dramatic religious conversions. Others then preached on being "born again." Two "intercolonial" or "national" leaders of the Awakening were Puritan theologian Jonathan Edwards and Anglican pastor George Whitefield.

The Awakening cut across denominational lines and spread through rural areas and towns in all regions. During the peak of revival in the 1740s, churches grew daily. In New England, 25,000 to 50,000 people joined churches out of a population of 300,000, with 3 out of 4 colonists likely affected.[382]

5.2 Jonathan Edwards—Theologian of the Great Awakening

Jonathan Edwards (1703-1758) is considered by some historians to be the most important theologian of early America and the Great Awakening and the first major thinker in American history.[383] A Puritan Congregationalist and Calvinist, Edwards attended Yale and was a minister in Massachusetts and a president of Princeton. In Northampton, Massachusetts, in 1734, Edwards preached a series of sermons on man's need for repentance and justification by faith alone, and despite his plain preaching, hundreds of people converted and the whole town was affected. The revival, lasting till the early 1740s, spread to other areas by traveling ministers and word of mouth. Edwards wrote many influential sermons and works during and in response to the Great Awakening, providing a theological foundation for the revival. Edwards influenced George Whitefield and Methodism founder John Wesley and became known internationally for his writings.

Edwards's widely-read sermons and other works presented many foundational Christian themes including God's sovereignty, the wrath and love of God, original sin, man's need for repentance and Christ's salvation, justification by faith, personal conversion, the human will, divine love and happiness, the beauty and virtue of God, equality before God, spiritual transformation, the kingdom of Christ, and the purpose of God's creation. *Sinners in the Hands of an Angry God* was his best-known revival sermon of 1741, depicting the wrath of God and hope of Christ.

Edwards's teachings became a doctrine of love and an equalizer for all people, say historians. Edwards' main message and appeal, says Johnson, "is that love is the essence of the religious experience."[384] Christianity was a religion in which humanity found God's love and grace in Christ. This Christianity was for all people who wished to live fulfilling, purposeful lives.

5.3 George Whitefield—The Modern, Democratic Preacher of the Great Awakening

George Whitefield (1714-1770) was the most notable preacher of the Great Awakening who turned local revivals into an American "national" movement. A Calvinist and Anglican, Whitefield was a Church of England minister who studied at Oxford University in the early 1700s with Methodism Founders John and Charles Wesley. Whitefield, known as the "Grand Itinerant," was the first man to travel up and down the east coast in America, preaching in all 13 American colonies. As an itinerant preacher, he traveled through more colonies than anyone of his time. After visiting Georgia in 1738 to help found an orphanage, he made the first continental tour of the colonies in 1740, from Boston, Massachusetts, to Savannah, Georgia. Whitefield possessed rhetorical and dramatic gifts and skills and spoke with great power. He had a loud, clear voice that could be heard among thousands in large gatherings. He spoke in church halls, streets, and marketplaces. This "Divine Dramatist," as he was called, attracted enormous crowds of many thousands. During his 1740 tour, he addressed huge crowds daily for over a month. His 1740 tour, says Noll, was "one of the most remarkable episodes in the whole of American Christianity" and "the key event of the Great Awakening."[385] Whitefield made seven continental tours of the colonies in thirty years, between 1739 and 1770. His "trafficking for the Lord," as he called it, spread revival throughout the colonies. Whitefield became one of the first public figures known throughout the thirteen colonies. He was, says Noll, "the single best-known religious leader in America of that century...."[386]

Whitefield preached against stale religion. He admired the "good old Puritans" for bringing Protestant Christianity to America, yet he increasingly spoke against those he saw as unconverted preachers serving in state churches and elsewhere. Though Whitefield never left the Anglican Church, he criticized the Church of England for its spiritual and moral deadness and failure to preach on Christ's salvation. He was banned from the Anglican Church for his preachings and criticisms. Disregarding parish boundaries, he preached wherever possible.   He appealed to all denominations including Anglicans, Puritans, Calvinists, and Catholics, disregarding their differences. All churches were influenced by his efforts.

Whitefield's preaching, like American revivalism over the next two centuries, centered on inner conversion and the need for New Birth or to be "born again" in Christ. People needed to recognize their sinfulness and repent to God in order to receive salvation in Christ. This salvation depended on faith, not good behavior.   Whitefield sought genuine religious experience.   The real, "heartfelt conversions Whitefield facilitated, even more than the changes he brought to the practice of religion," observes Noll, "are why he was such an important figure in his age and why his legacy has remained at the heart of the history of Christianity in America."[387]

American Founder Benjamin Franklin, also a well-known figure in the colonies and a printer of Whitefield's sermons and journals, was intrigued by Whitefield's preaching and integrity, though he disagreed with some of his views. The two men maintained a friendship. When Whitefield had no place to preach, Franklin helped build a hall in Philadelphia for him and clergy of any denomination.   Franklin describes Whitefield's influence during the Awakening: "It was wonderful to see the change soon made in the manners of our inhabitants. From being thoughtless or indifferent about religion, it seem'd as if all the world were growing religious, so that one could not walk thro' the town in an evening without hearing psalms sung in different families of every street."[388]

Whitefield significantly changed the cultural form and standard of colonial preaching and became a model for modern evangelists.[389] Previously preachers read sermons for long periods. Whitefield, however, practiced an innovative approach to preaching using rhetorical and emotional skills, media, and marketplace dynamics. He often memorized his sermons, preached extemporaneously, and spoke with charisma. Interested in the stage as a youth, he dramatically varied his voice and gestured, and he appealed to emotions and the heart.[390] Whitefield also used new media like the new colonial newspapers, including Franklin's *Pennsylvania Gazette*, to spread the gospel and raise publicity for preaching tours. Franklin offered news coverage and connections to other publishers, and together they created a subscription of Whitefield's messages. Whitefield further used commercial market techniques such as advertising and publicity practices to create advance publicity for his tours.[391] Whitefield's enthusiastic preaching and practices changed expectations, perceptions, and demands of preachers.   Previously congregations sought leaders with formal training and traditional orthodoxy. Now they looked for leaders with emotion, enthusiasm, and charisma.[392]

Whitefield's approach to preaching led to a more modern, democratic style of Christianity and political life in America as well as more unified, interconnected colonies.[393] Though an Anglican, Whitefield was not interested in church hierarchy. His style and form of ministry supported the religious power of the people. He believed that every person—regardless of class, wealth, education, or prestige—could choose Jesus Christ. Though he was seemingly unaware of its political implications, Whitefield's ministry had democratic elements that influenced a more democratic spirit in American life, churches, and politics.[394] Whitefield thus facilitated a new social emphasis in both religion and politics.   Also, due to his preaching tours, Whitefield played a significant role, say some scholars, in the development of spiritual, political, and geographical unity among the colonies and in inter-colonial communication.[395] These would be important influences prior to the American Revolution.

5.4 The Value and Dignity of the Human Being

The Revivalists gave more weight to the Judeo-Christian idea that the individual human being possesses inherent dignity and value. While the early Puritan colonists had shared this perspective, the Revivalists raised more awareness of it in society. They did so indirectly by simply affirming and acting on basic concepts in the Bible that supported human dignity—like seeing human beings as made in God's image and likeness and as

1   possessing the potential for spiritual salvation. These beliefs influenced the American view of the dignity,
2   value, and rights of the individual. The fact that the Bible had become accessible to everyone from the time of
3   the Reformation also strengthened people's notion of the importance of the individual and of the individual's
4   rights to spiritual and civil freedom.[396]
5

6   Revivalists affirmed that humans reflect God in being made in God's image and likeness. Genesis 1:26-
7   27 states, "Then God said, 'Let Us make man in Our image, according to Our likeness....' So God created man
8   in His *own* image; in the image of God He created him; male and female He created them." Genesis 2:7 states,
9   "And the LORD God formed man *of* the dust of the ground, and breathed into his nostrils the breath of life; and
10   man became a living being." In his Reformation-era *Bible Commentaries on Genesis*, the reformer Calvin, who
11   influenced some Revivalists like Edwards, shows mankind's significance in pointing out from these verses that
12   God counsels with His three persons or "Trinity"—Father, Son, and Holy Spirit—before creating Adam. God
13   says, "'Let Us make man...'" Thus mankind is a product of God's wisdom and goodness.[397] In addition, the
14   human body and soul reveal godly aspects. The human body, Calvin illustrates, is a scientific wonder—a
15   "microcosm" or "miniature world."[398] And the human soul possesses abilities of mind, emotion, will, and
16   conscience. The soul, for example, can remember the past, discover and explore the universe, and invent works
17   of art. All these aspects evidence God's agency in mankind—that "the human race are a bright mirror of the
18   Creator's works" and possess "excellent gifts with which he [God] has endued us attesting that he is our
19   Father."[399] In his *Miscellaneous Observations*, Edwards likewise observes that humans are God's "principal
20   part of the visible creation"—evident in that God has created the earth for human habitation and has given
21   humans dominion over His creation.[400] Edwards also observes that the human soul can "have understanding,
22   and are voluntary agents, and can produce works of their own will, design, and contrivance, as God does."[401]
23

24   The Revivalists also affirmed God's moral law in the human conscience. Every person has a
25   "conscience," Edwards affirmed, a sense of good and evil, of right and wrong. This conscience approves virtue
26   and disapproves vice. Yet it does not depend on a person's spiritual awareness of God. It is based on an innate
27   sense of equality, justice, and a natural Law of Love to treat others as oneself. It functions properly when a
28   person is enlightened and his or her private interests, errors, prejudices, and sensual appetites are set aside.[402]
29   Moreover, humans reflect God when they act morally. Edwards writes in his *Freedom of the Will*, "Herein very
30   much consists the natural image of God; as his spiritual and moral image, wherein man was made at first,
31   consisted in that moral excellency, that he was endowed with."[403] Many viewed the human conscience, notes
32   Edwards in his *Nature of True Virtue*, as evidence of a universal moral sense among mankind.[404]
33

34   Most notably, Revivalists emphasized that the human soul is immortal like God. On the human soul,
35   Calvin had stated, God "engraved his own image, to which immortality is annexed."[405] Humans are given life
36   directly by God's breath as stated in Genesis 2:7. Considering mankind's godly soul traits, Calvin responds,
37   "What shall we say but that man bears about with him a stamp of immortality which can never be effaced?"[406]
38   That humans are given life by and reflect God is, he says, "incomparably the highest nobility."[407] In his *Soul's
39   Immortality*, Edwards likewise cites numerous scriptures to support the idea of the soul's immortality—2
40   Corinthians 12:2-4 and 5:6-9, Acts 7:59, Matthew 10:28, Hebrews 12:22-23, 2 Peter 1:13-14, 1 Thessalonians
41   5:9-10, Philippians 1:21-23, 1 Peter 3:19-20, Ecclesiastes 12:7, Luke 23:43, Luke 16:22-23, and Revelation
42   5:9-10, 6:9-10, 7:13-15.[408] In Ecclesiastes 12:7, Solomon says of the human body and soul, "The dust will
43   return to the earth as it was, And the spirit will return to God who gave it." In Matthew 10:28, Jesus instructs
44   His disciples, "Do not fear those who kill the body but cannot kill the soul. But rather fear Him [God] who is
45   able to destroy both soul and body in hell." In 1 Thessalonians 5:9-10, the Apostle Paul exhorts the church,
46   "God did not appoint us to wrath, but to obtain salvation through our Lord Jesus Christ, who died for us, that
47   whether we wake [live bodily] or sleep [die bodily], we should live together with Him." In Luke 23:43, Jesus
48   comforts the contrite, confessing criminal crucified on a cross next to His: "'Assuredly, I say to you, today you
49   will be with Me in Paradise.'" Edwards asserts that the human soul is "capable of existence and thought, and

1 according to abundant scriptural declarations, actually enjoying them both, when the body is dead." What is
2 more, the soul will be accountable to God in a future state of rewards and punishments.[409]

3   Another crucial element of human worth, to Revivalists, is the soul's potential to obtain salvation through
4 Jesus Christ. For God—in the crucifixion of His son, Jesus Christ, as told in the Gospels of Matthew, Mark,
5 Luke, and John—has paid a great price for the redemption of human souls. As Edwards notes in his *Wisdom of*
6 *God*, God in Christ "endured so much to purchase salvation for them" in order to "bestow eternal life on them
7 for whom he purchased it."[410] Moreover, God gains much glory in redeeming humanity from the Fall in the
8 Garden of Eden that separates mankind from God. Edwards explains,

9   The power of God more gloriously appears in man's being actually saved and redeemed in this way. In
10   his being brought out of a state of sin and misery, into a conformity to God; and at last to the full and
11   perfect enjoyment of God. This is a more glorious demonstration of divine power, than creating things
12   out of nothing…. To produce a new creature is a more glorious effect, than merely to produce a
13   creature. –Making a holy creature, a creature in the spiritual image of God, in the image of the divine
14   excellencies, and a partaker of the divine nature—is a greater effect than merely to give being.[411]

15 In redeeming the human soul, God also receives glory in overcoming great opposition—from mankind's sinful
16 state and from God's enemy, Satan. Citing Colossians 2:15, Edwards observes,

17   Power never appears more illustrious than in conquering. Jesus Christ, in this work, conquers and
18   triumphs over thousands of devils, strong and mighty spirits, uniting all their strength against him. …
19   Col. ii. 15, "And having spoiled principalities and powers, he made a show of them openly, triumphing
20   over them in the cross."[412]

21 The human soul is the place where this spiritual battle occurs, where a person's eternal fate is decided by his or
22 her faith in or denial of Christ. Ultimately, the saved human soul glorifes God and His Trinity, justice, holiness,
23 truth, mercy, and love.[413] In return, the redeemed soul receives the goodness, favor, peace, honor, richness, and
24 happiness of God. It receives eternal life with God, rather than eternal death apart from God. It enjoys a love
25 relationship and fellowship with God.[414] This Bible-based view of the individual's potential for spiritual
26 salvation highlights the worth of the human being in God's eyes.

27   Other scriptures in the Bible also illustrate the great worth of humans to God. In his *Commentaries on*
28 *Matthew, Mark, and Luke*, Calvin alludes to Matthew 10:28-31 and Luke 12:6, which are similar verses. In
29 Matthew 10:29-31, Jesus says to His disciples, "'Are not two sparrows sold for a copper coin? And [yet] not
30 one of them falls to the ground apart from your Father's will. But the very hairs of your head are all numbered.
31 Do not fear therefore; you are of more value than many sparrows.'" Calvin explains from these verses the value
32 of human life to God: "There is hardly any thing of less value than sparrows, (for two were then sold for a
33 farthing, or, as Luke states it, five for two farthings,) and yet God has his eye upon them to protect them, so that
34 nothing happens to them by chance. Would He who is careful about the sparrows disregard the life of men?"[415]
35 Such verses supported the Bible believers' view that God assigns great worth to a human life.
36
37   Though the Awakening was not an explicitly political movement, Revivalists, perhaps more than the
38 early Puritans, affirmed the value of the individual in the church and, subsequently, in the civil state. Rev.
39 Thomas Hooker had reasoned that the individual believer is the first, visible expression of the church. The
40 church is composed of believers in Christ. Individuals are important to the larger group because they make up
41 that body. Hooker points out in his 1648 *Summe of Church Discipline* that "the *exist[ence]* and *working* of
42 Churches and Officers is *only* to be seen, as it…appears, & is expressed in the *individuals*. As when God
43 makes…*Officer* by election, erects a *Church*, it's a *particular Church* and *individuall Officer*; therefore the
44 individuall *there* first exists, and the *generall* in the *individuall*."[416] The church, Hooker emphasized, is a body

of distinct individuals who compose, preserve, express, and represent the church. As the Puritans applied aspects of their church government to their civil government, they assigned a similar value to the citizen as the first, visible expression and representation of their civil state. Subsequently, Revivalists in the 1700s placed even more emphasis on the individual's value, role, and rights in church, society, and state.

The increased awareness of the value and dignity of the human being that occurred during the Great Awakening was important to understanding, at least in part, the value of the individual and of human life in American society and in the future nation. It supported individual rights and love, compassion, and respect for others. Soon after the Great Awakening, Franklin, in his 1758 *The Way to Wealth*, expresses the best contemporary American view of the worth of the human being: "If the globe were one mass of pure gold, if the stars were so many *jewels* of the finest order, and the sun a *ruby*, they were less than nothing when compared with the infinite value of one soul."[417] Many colonial laws and, ultimately, the future United States would recognize and protect the rights and freedoms of the individual human being.

5.5 All Men Equal Before God

Revivalists saw Christianity as an equalizer or non-respecter of persons regardless of race, gender, social status, economic standing, education, position, wealth, or power.[418] Despite differences, all men are in the same fallen moral state. Edwards explains in his *Doctrine of Original Sin*,

> Things were wisely so established, that all [men] should naturally be in one and the same *moral state*; and not in such exceeding different states, as that some should be perfectly *innocent* and holy, but others *corrupt* and wicked; some needing a Saviour, but others needing none; some in a confirmed state of perfect *happiness*, but others in a state of public condemnation to perfect and eternal *misery*; some justly exposed to great calamities in this world, but others by their innocence raised above all suffering. Such a vast diversity of state would by no means have agreed with the natural and necessary constitution and unavoidable situation and circumstance of the world of mankind....[419]

Christ's salvation is needed by and available to everyone. Alluding to Galatians 6:15, Edwards expresses human equality in Christ in his *Treatise Concerning Religious Affections*: "For in Christ Jesus neither circumcision [Jew], nor uncircumcision [Gentile], neither high profession, nor low profession, neither a fair story, nor a broken one, avails any thing; but a new creature."[420] In Christianity, all men are sinful despite any differences among them, and all could find love and hope in Christ.[421]

In New England, in fact, all kinds of people were affected by the revival. Edwards noticed. "The work in this town, and some others about us," he describes in his *Narrative of Surprising Conversions*, "has been extraordinary on account of the universality of it, affecting all sorts, sober and vicious, high and low, rich and poor, wise and unwise; it reached the most considerable families and persons to all appearance, as much as others."[422] After witnessing many conversions, he thus exhorts all diverse people to praise and honor God in his *Thoughts on the Revival*: "God doubtless now expects, that all sorts of persons in New England, rulers, ministers and people, high and low, rich and poor, old and young, should take great notice of his hand, in this mighty work of his grace, and should appear to acknowledge his glory in it, and greatly rejoice in it, everyone doing his utmost, in the place that God has set them in, to promote it."[423]

God makes no distinction among men, says Edwards, so that men depend on and credit God, not themselves, for redemption. Citing 1 Corinthians 1 and Romans 11:35-36, he explains in his work, *Concerning Efficacious Grace,*

It is evident by what the apostle Paul says, 1 Cor. i., latter end, that the entireness and universality of our dependence on God, is that which cuts off occasion of boasting; as, our receiving our wisdom, our holiness, and redemption through Christ, and not through ourselves.... ...God has contrived to exclude our glorying; that we should be wholly and every way dependent on God, for the moral and natural good that belongs to salvation; and that we have all from the hand of God, by his power and grace. ... And that such a universal dependence is what takes away occasion of taking glory to ourselves...is manifest from Rom. xi. 35, 36 "Or who hath first given unto him [God], and it shall be recompensed to him [man] again? For of him [God], and to him, and through him, are all things; to whom be glory for ever and ever, Amen."[424]

1 Corinthians 1:21-31 states,

> For since, in the wisdom of God, the world through wisdom did not know God, it pleased God through the foolishness of the message preached to save those who believe. ... Because the foolishness of God is wiser than men, and the weakness of God is stronger than men. For you see your calling, brethren, that not many wise according to the flesh, not many mighty, not many noble, *are called.* But God has chosen the foolish things of the world to put to shame the wise, and God has chosen the weak things of the world to put to shame the things which are mighty; and the base things of the world and the things which are despised God has chosen, and the things which are not, to bring to nothing the things that are, that no flesh should glory in His presence. But of Him you are in Christ Jesus, who became for us wisdom from God—and righteousness and sanctification and redemption—that, as it is written, "He who glories, let him glory in the LORD."

Man is redeemed not by his own merits or qualities but by God due to His glorious attributes. Romans 9:15-16 and Romans 11, Edwards also cites, similarly show salvation from God over man's efforts. Romans 9:15-16 states, "For He[God] says to Moses, '*I will have mercy on whomever I will have mercy, and I will have compassion on whomever I will have compassion.*' So then *it is* not of him who wills, nor of him who runs, but of God who shows mercy."

God's act of redemption through Christ, saw Edwards, is superior to all of man's distinctions, efforts, and works.[425] "[I]n the apostle's [Paul's] account," Edwards states, "a benefit's being of our works, gives occasion for boasting, and therefore God has contrived that our salvation shall not be of our works, but of mere grace, Romans 3:27, Eph. 2:9. And that neither the salvation, nor the condition of it, shall be of our works, but that, with regard to all, we are God's workmanship and his creation...."[426] Romans 3:27 states, "Where *is* boasting then? It is excluded. By what law? Of works? No, but by the law of faith." Ephesians 2:8-10 states, "For by grace you have been saved through faith, and that not of yourselves; *it is* the gift of God, not of works, lest anyone should boast. For we are His workmanship...." God demonstrates this principle of salvation by faith over human efforts by saving people of all distinctions, seeing them as equal in value and in need and reception of grace.

5.6 "Born Again" Individual Spiritual Conversion

While "rationalism"—the application of reason as the only basis for one's opinions or beliefs—emerged in Europe from the Enlightenment, Revivalists in America acknowledged God-given reason but adhered to spiritual faith. Revivalists like Edwards agreed that humans are naturally capable of reasoning, judgment, and discernment of arguments for God's existence. However, Edwards believed that while people could discern some truth about God by reason, only a "born again" spiritual conversion experience could convince a person about God. A "born-again" conversion involves the Spirit of God birthing or instilling spiritual faith in a person's heart and spirit. This new, spiritual birth of mind, heart, and spirit, says Edwards, is indicated in John

1 3:3 when Jesus tells the inquiring pharisee Nicodemus, "'Most assuredly, I say to you, unless one is born again,
2 he cannot see the kingdom of God.'" When Nicodemus questions how an old man can be born a second time
3 from his mother's womb, Jesus replies in John 3:5-6, "'Most assuredly, I say to you, unless one is born of water
4 and the Spirit, he cannot enter the kingdom of God. That which is born of the flesh is flesh, and that which is
5 born of the Spirit is spirit.'"[427] This new birth is also, Edwards says, like a "circumcision of the heart" as
6 foretold by Moses in Deuteronomy 30:6: "'And the Lord thy God will *circumcise thy heart*, and the *heart* of
7 thy seed, to love the Lord thy God with all thine heart, and with all thy soul.'" Being spiritually reborn or
8 regenerated of God, Edwards explains, citing Romans 2:28-29, involves an internal change of heart, not just an
9 external religion:

11 　　　Regeneration is that whereby men come to have the character of true Christians; as is evident, and as is
12 　　　confessed; and so is *circumcision of heart*; for by this men become Jews *inwardly*, or Jews in the
13 　　　spiritual and *Christian sense…*, as of old *proselytes* were made Jews by circumcision of the flesh. Rom.
14 　　　ii. 28, 29, "For he is not a Jew, which is one outwardly; neither is that circumcision, which is outward in
15 　　　the flesh: but he is a Jew, which is one inwardly; and *circumcision* is that *of the heart*, in the spirit and
16 　　　not in the letter, whose praise is not of men, but of God."[428]

18 An individual is changed from within. Personal conversion emphasized a fundamental aspect of Christianity in
19 which the individual, practicing self-examination and private judgment, personally relates with and is
20 responsible before God.　This individualistic perspective stimulated personal prayer, Bible reading, and
21 Christian fellowship and weakened traditional links between individuals and established state churches.[429]

23 ## 5.7 The Judeo-Christian Law of Love

25 　　　Revivalists affirmed the Judeo-Christian Law of Love—to love God and others—known as the two
26 Great Commandments in the Old and New Testaments. It is expressed by Jesus, Edwards cites in his *Treatise*
27 *Concerning Religious Affections*, in Matthew 22:37-40: ""'You shall love the LORD your God with all your
28 heart, with all your soul, and with all your mind.'　This is *the* first and great commandment.
29 And *the* second *is* like it: 'You shall love your neighbor as yourself.'"" [430] The second part is often referred to
30 as the "golden rule," of treating others as one wishes to be treated. Matthew 7:12 expresses it, "Whatever you
31 want men to do to you, do also to them." Revivalists also embraced religious affections that expressed
32 Christian love in their worship of God and in their service toward others. Godly affection is important in
33 religion, Edwards thought, since true faith produces affections of the soul, and man's affections are "the spring
34 of men's actions."[431] Love could build the church, he asserts, based on Ephesians 4:16 in which the church in
35 Christ "causes growth of the body for the edifying of itself in love."[432] Lively, emotional church practices of
36 singing, praising, prayer, writing, reading, and preaching are, therefore, desirable as they can affect the heart.[433]
37 While emotionalism was viewed with suspicion by some Puritans and traditionalists, revivalists generally
38 welcomed it. Revivalists thus applied Puritan ideas of holy living in a new way.[434]

40 　　　A secular acknowledgement of the Bible-based idea to love others came from Enlightenment-era
41 philosopher John Locke who was very influential to founding-era Americans. In 1689, Locke had written an
42 important treatise on government—his *Second Treatise of Civil Government*—which strongly influenced the
43 early Americans and their Founders. In this treatise, Locke cites Anglican theologian Richard Hooker's 1593
44 work on church governance, *Laws of Ecclesiastical Polity*, to present a rational idea for love of others in society
45 that reflected the Bible-based principle. From the reasonable standpoint given by Locke, mutual love and
46 respect among people in society had a basis in the equality of humans before God and in natural reason. Since
47 all men are created by and equal before God, people have a duty to impartially love and respect one another.
48 Locke writes in his *Second Treatise*,

This equality of men by Nature, the Judicious [Richard] Hooker looks upon as so evident in itself, and beyond all question, that he makes it the foundation of that obligation to mutual love amongst men on which he builds the duties they owe one another, and from whence he derives the great maxims of justice and charity. His words are:—

> "The like natural inducement hath brought men to know that it is no less their duty to love others than themselves, for seeing those things which are equal, must needs all have one measure; if I cannot but wish to receive good, even as much at every man's hands, as any man can wish unto his own soul, how should I look to have any part of my desire herein satisfied, unless myself be careful to satisfy the like desire, which is undoubtedly in other men weak, being of one and the same nature: to have any thing offered them repugnant to this desire must needs, in all respects, grieve them as much as me; so that if I do harm, I must look to suffer, there being no reason that others should shew greater measure of love to me than they have by me showed unto them; my desire, therefore, to be loved of my equals in Nature, as much as possible may be, imposeth upon me a natural duty of bearing to themward fully the like affection. From which relation of equality between ourselves and them are as ourselves, what several rules and canons natural reason hath drawn for direction of life no man is ignorant. (Eccl. Pol. lib. i.)"[435]

It is simply reasonable or logical, say Locke and Hooker, for a person in society to treat others in the same way that he or she desires to be treated, for people have similar natures and desires. One has no reason to expect better treatment from others than what one practices toward them.

Edward's Bible-based view of the "golden rule" went further than the rational one given by Richard Hooker and Locke.[436] Edwards saw the practice of impartial, altruistic, or godly love toward others as the ground of godliness and virtue.[437] Edwards points out, "The Scriptures do represent true religion, as being summarily comprehended in love, the chief of the affections, and fountain of all other affections."[438] God wants humans to live with genuine, fervent love of heart. For love toward others is the sum of God's laws. Drawing from Romans 13:8-10, Matthew 22:37-40, 1 Timothy 1:5, James 2:8, and Galatians 5:14, Edwards elaborates,

> As to that Excellence, that Created Spirits partake of; that it is all to be resolved into Love, none will doubt, that knows what is the Sum of the Ten Commandments; or believes what the Apostle [Paul] says, That Love is the fulfillment of the Law [Romans 13:8-10]; or what Christ says, That on these two, loving God and our neighbor, hang all the Law and the Prophets [Matthew 22:37-40]. This doctrine is often repeated in the New Testament. We are told that the End of the Commandment is Love [1 Timothy 1:5]; that to Love, is to fulfil the Royal Law [James 2:8]; and that all the Law is fulfilled in this one word, Love [Galatians 5:14].[439]

Love, to revivalists, is expressed not only by affection but by action.[440] Edwards declares, "Love is an active principle.... Reason teaches, that a man's actions are the most proper test and evidence of his love."[441] Any religious or moral philosophy, Edwards thought, that lacks regard for and love of God and others as its source of virtue is flawed.[442]

5.8 The Unalienable Right to Freedom of Conscience

Many Revivalists asserted the idea that all men have a natural or God-given right to freedom of conscience or religious belief. Locke's views on freedom of conscience as expressed in his *Letters Concerning Toleration* apparently affected the views of many on this issue. Locke's essay, *A Letter Concerning Toleration*, published in America in 1742, was often referenced by religious non-conformists who advocated for greater religious freedom.[443] In addition to these essays, Locke's *Second Treatise of Government* asserted the natural or God-given rights of humans—as created by God—to life, liberty, and property. Since humans have a natural

1 right to their persons and property, many Revivalists thought, they also have a natural right to freedom of
2 conscience.
3
4   In 1744, Congregationalist minister and Yale College rector Elisha Williams wrote a revival-era
5 pamphlet, *The Essential Rights and Liberties of Protestants*, defending freedom of conscience as an unalienable
6 right. Echoing Roger Williams, William Penn, and especially Locke, he affirms that as all men have an
7 "unalienable right" to their persons and property, they also have an unalienable right to conscience or religious
8 belief according to God's moral law or the Law of Nature.[444] An "unalienable right" is an unremovable or
9 irrevocable right. It cannot be taken away or transferred from one person to another. The right of conscience,
10 Elisha Williams argues, is a sacred and unalienable right based on the nature of humans as reasonable, moral,
11 and accountable beings before God. It is also based on the fact that true religious belief does not exist without
12 understanding and choice. Thus all people, Williams wrote, have the right and responsibility to search the holy
13 scriptures and to choose and assess their own beliefs. Williams asserts,
14
15   The members of a Civil State do *retain their natural Liberty or Right of judging for themselves in*
16   *Matters of Religion*. Every man has an equal Right to follow the Dictates of his own *Conscience* in the
17   Affairs of *Religion.* **Every one is under an indispensable Obligation to *search the Scriptures* for**
18   **himself (which contains the whole of it) and to make the best Use of it he can for his own**
19   **Information in the Will of GOD, the Nature and Duties of Christianity.** And as every Christian is so
20   bound; so he has an *unalienable Right* to *judge* of the *Sense and Meaning* of it, and to follow his
21   Judgment wherever it leads him; even an equal Right with any Rulers be they Civil or Ecclesiastical.—
22   This I say, I take to be an original Right of the humane Nature, and so far from being given up by the
23   Individuals of a Community that it cannot be given up by them if they should be so weak as to offer it.
24   **Man by his Constitution as he is a *reasonable* Being capable of the Knowledge of his MAKER; is a**
25   ***moral & accountable* Being: and therefore as every one is accountable for himself, he must reason,**
26   **judge and determine for himself.** That Faith and Practice which depends on the Judgment and Choice
27   of any other Person, and not on the Person's own Understanding Judgment and Choice, may pass for
28   Religion in the Synagogue of *Satan*, whose Tenet is that Ignorance is the Mother of Devotion; but with
29   no understanding Protestant will it pass for any Religion at all. No Action is a religious Action without
30   Understanding and Choice in the Agent. Whence it follows, the Rights of Conscience are sacred and
31   equal in all, and strictly speaking unalienable. This *Right* of *judging every one for himself in Matters of*
32   *Religion* results from the Nature of Man, and is so inseperably connected therewith, that a Man can no
33   more part with it than he can with his *Power* of *Thinking*: and it is equally reasonable, for him to attempt
34   to strip himself of the *Power* of *Reasoning*, as to attempt the vesting of another with this Right. And
35   whoever invades this Right of another, be he *Pope* or *Caesar*, may with equal Reason assume the other's
36   Power of Thinking, and so level him with the Brutal Creation.—A Man may alienate some Branches of
37   his Property and give up his Right in them to others; but he cannot transfer the *Rights* of *Conscience*,
38   unless he could destroy his rational and moral Powers, or substitute some other to be judged for him at
39   the Tribunal of GOD.[445]
40
41   Further, since God is the author and source of faith, says Williams, earthly authorities have no real or
42 assumed power to influence or judge others' beliefs. When humans take on a role to govern and judge the
43 consciences of other people, they govern outside of their rightful authority, dominion, and purpose. God as
44 Creator or Christ, as the Head of the Church, is the sole authority who has the ability, power, and right to reach,
45 convict, and judge a person's conscience.[446] Williams elaborates on this point: "…[N]o other Authority which
46 has yet been or ever shall be set up, has any Manner of Right at all to govern and direct our *Consciences* in
47 *religious* Matters. … …[I]f CHRIST be the *Lord* of the *Conscience*, the sole King in his own Kingdom; then it
48 will follow, that *all such* as in any Manner or Degree *assume* the Power of directing and governing the
49 Consciences of Men, are justly chargeable with *invading* his rightful Dominion; He [God] alone having the

1 Right they claim."[447] Even while Christians, especially church leaders, have a duty to explain the scriptures and
2 teach the laws, mind, and will of Christ, God alone could instill faith and conviction in a person.

5.9 Eternal Happiness Found in God

The sense or affection of happiness was a reoccurring theme of Edwards. To Edwards, happiness is important in religious matters and has a spiritual dimension. Like love, happiness, he thought, is found in and part of God. Happiness consists not just of a person's own contentment apart from God but of joy and pleasure found in God. He elaborates,

> …[T]he special end of man does not only respect him as consisting in his own happiness as separate from God, and as having nothing to do with him, or in his own happiness consisting in the enjoyments of the visible world. The happiness of the greater part of mankind, in their worldly enjoyments, is not great enough or durable enough to prove such a supposition, as that the end of all things in the whole visible universe is only that happiness. Therefore, nothing else remains, no other supposition is possible, but that man's special end, or that which he is made for, respects the Creator, or is something wherein he has immediately to do with his Creator.[448]

True happiness, Edwards thought, goes beyond the visible, temporal world and involves the eternal, spiritual one. It addresses a person's eternal happiness and need for salvation from his or her miserable, fallen state in nature and from an eternal death separated from God. The goal of human life is, therefore, to pursue eternal salvation as happiness. Humans are created, revivalists believed, to seek and find eternal happiness in God. Regarding mankind's call to seek God, Edwards refers to one Scottish Enlightenment theologian George Turnbull's response in his *Christian Philosophy* based on Philip 2:12-13:

> Turnbull's explanation of Philip ii. 12, 13, "Work out your own salvation with fear and trembling, for it is God that worketh in you both to will and to do his own good pleasure,' is this (*Christian Philosophy*, p. 96, 97): 'Give all diligence to work out your salvation; for it is God, the Creator of all things, who, by giving you, of his good pleasure, the power of willing and doing, with a sense of right and wrong, and reason to guide and direct you, hath visibly made it your end so to do. Your frame shows, that to prepare yourselves for great moral happiness, arising from a well cultivated and improved mind suitably placed, is your end appointed to you by your Creator. Consider, therefore, that by neglecting this your duty, this your interest, you contemn and oppose the *good will of God towards you, and his design in creating you.*'"[449]

God in Jesus Christ, Edwards believed, is the key to eternal happiness.[450] Christ's suffering and death is for the happy redemption of man from sin.[451] Christ "procures a title to us for happiness," says Edwards in his *History of the Work of Redemption.* "The satisfaction of Christ is to free us from misery, and the merit of Christ is to purchase happiness for us."[452] The "chief happiness of mankind," he affirms, is "knowledge, service, and enjoyment of the living God…."[453]

5.10 The Godly Purpose of Moral Government

In the process of addressing spiritual and sometimes social matters, revival theologian Edwards also developed awareness and ideas about the purpose of civil government in society. God sets up human moral governments, as all creation, for the good of man, Edwards thought. He cites Mark 2:27-28, for example, in which Jesus tells a Pharisee or Jewish religionist that "'The Sabbath was made for man, and not man for the Sabbath. Therefore the Son of man is also the Lord of the Sabbath.'" Edwards elaborates, "Christ mentions…the reason why the Son of man is made Lord of the Sabbath, that 'the Sabbath was made for man.'

1   And if so, we may in like manner argue, that *all things* were made for man, that the Son of Man is made Lord of
2   all things."[454] Edwards saw that God has created certain things, like the weekly day of rest, for the need and
3   benefit of people. Such things are not then to become unfitting religious regulations for the sake of the ritual
4   itself, defeating its intended purpose for mankind. In the same way, civil government, suggests Edwards, is thus
5   created by God for man, not man for government.[455]   God is concerned with civil government, Edwards
6   believed, because mankind, as central to God's creation and purpose, needs moral regulation and civil order in
7   society. Edwards says in his *Miscellaneous Observations*,

> 9   If God be concerned how things proceed in the world he has made, he will be so chiefly in that part of
> 10   his world that he has set his heart most upon. ... And therefore God will not leave the world of
> 11   mankind to themselves, without taking any care to govern and order their state so, that this part of the
> 12   world may be regulated decently and beautifully, that there may be good order in the intelligent,
> 13   voluntary, active part of God's creation....; ...he will take care that the world of mankind be well
> 14   regulated with respect to its moral state; and so will maintain a good moral government over the world
> 15   of mankind.[456]

17   Specifically, God ordains moral human governments—personal and corporate, private and public—
18 Edwards thought, for restraint of mankind's sinful nature, to uphold human rights and justice, and for
19 mankind's protection and preservation.[457]   Such reasons for government are evident, like many things, by
20 observing its natural cause, design, and function.[458] In the design and function of families, for example, one can
21 see that parents are to nourish their children, and children are to be subject to their parents. But if a man
22 murders his children or children murder their parents, this act opposes the Creator's aims.[459] In the design and
23 function of a civil state, one can see that a civil officer should uphold justice and protect the rights of his
24 countrymen, but if he acts unjustly or oppresses and abuses the people, he opposes God's aim. While immoral
25 or ungodly governments often do not secure human rights or preservation, moral governments generally seek to
26 abide by the godly design and function of government.

28   The ultimate purpose of human moral governments, thought Edwards, is to allow humans an opportunity
29 to fulfill the purpose for which God has created them—to have a relationship with God.[460] Edwards expresses,

> 31   Now the greatest thing that men are capacitated for, by their faculties, more than the beasts, is that they
> 32   are capable of having intercourse with their Creator, as intelligent and voluntary agents. They are
> 33   capable of knowing him, and capable of esteeming and loving him, and capable of receiving instructions
> 34   and commands from him, and capable of obeying and serving him, if he be pleased to give commands
> 35   and make a revelation of his mind.[461]

37   Further, moral civil governments, says Edwards, properly reflect God's heavenly government of rewards
38 and punishments and mankind's relationship with God. In a fallen world where injustice, oppression, and
39 unrighteousness exist, visible moral governments confirm, demonstrate, and reflect God's heavenly kingdom
40 rule of just rewards and happiness for the righteous along with punishments and misery for the unrighteous.[462]
41 For the Bible says that one day God will remedy injustice and oppression on earth as stated in Ecclesiastes 3:17:
42 "'God shall judge the righteous and the wicked.'"[463] God's kingdom rule is also seen, Edwards notes, in
43 Ecclesiastes 8:11-13 and 12:13-14 and in Proverbs 12:28, 13:14, and 11:30. The day of God's judgment will
44 be, says Edwards, "the time appointed for the highest exercises of God's authority as moral governor of the
45 world; and is, as it were, the day of the consummation of God's moral government, with respect to all his
46 subjects in heaven, earth and hell."[464]   Moral government also illustrates an aspect of an individual's
47 relationship with God in that a person must be clothed with submission before God.[465] Thus moral human
48 government, in many ways, gives people a concrete illustration of God's heavenly rule.[466]

5.11 Revival Effects on Church, State, and Society: A New Church Landscape

The Great Awakening revitalized all churches in the mid 1700s. It led to church upheavals and splits, yet it energized both old and new churches across all denominations.[467] With revival, American churches fell into two broad groups—traditionalists or Old Lights and revivalists or New Lights—with respect to the priority of the individual, church, society, and/or state. Each group viewed itself as a part of the English dissenting tradition.

Evangelical Revivalists, or New Lights, sought individual conversions of believers and to purify the church of non-Christians and unbiblical doctrine. Revivalists who benefited from state churches generally favored the state church system, while those who did not benefit from such establishments generally opposed them. While the former group, or moderates, did not advocate for church-state separation, some were willing to relinquish some church authority over society in order to purify state churches. They saw that government coercion of external acts of worship did not necessarily make people become believers. The latter group, or radicals, supported church-state separation and opposed government support of churches. They believed state churches had negative effects, for state concerns could potentially override church needs. They left the state churches and formed new independent churches. The church, they believed is governed and judged by God and the Bible, not the state. The state has no jurisdiction in religious matters but serves to enforce moral and civil laws for a peaceful society. Many New Lights made dissent respectable again in the 1700s after being stigmatized prior to revival.

Traditionalists, or Old Lights, sought to protect and promote the Puritan concept of a unified Christian state and society and to uphold the church-state establishment. The Puritan church state focused less on individual conversion and the covenant of grace and more on a covenanted society. They believed, as the early colonies had initially believed, that national or state churches are necessary to promote religion and to mediate spiritual salvation in society. They wanted churches open to the whole society in order to influence the culture in godly ways. They saw unregulated religion as divisive, undermining order and stability in society. Moderates appreciated the Awakening's religious renewal but feared it might destroy a uniform Christian society. Radicals opposed the revival as outdated and harmfully emotional. They held a more liberal view of Christianity. They saw reason as the solution to the revival's emotionalism. Some radicals left Christianity for Unitarianism, a non-trinitarian theology and step toward agnosticism. Old Lights held many pulpits and influenced religious liberalism in America.[468]

In the changing religious environment, revival weakened church-state establishments and laws, providing more lenient church states and greater religious tolerance in the colonies.[469] While legislators did not always remove state church laws, they provided ways for more sects to preach and minister. Many revivalists opposed paying taxes to a state church, and some were exempted from church taxes or could pay their own ministers. Other laws restricting revival activities had little effect. Unlicensed revival preachers defied civil and church authorities, laws, and boundaries to preach wherever they could. In Connecticut, notably, due to political protest and debate, the legislature removed itinerant preacher licensing laws in the colony and exempted New Light groups from paying taxes to the colony's state church. As colonies became more tolerant, state churches became, says Richard Bushman, "neither an agency of social control nor a symbol of community coherence, but only the religion of the majority." In the place of established state churches, a more secular civil state became, he says, "the sole institution binding society" and "the symbol of social coherence."[470] Those clergymen or churches that tried to reassert their state authority met with arguments from lawyers, political Whigs, and other colonists in defense of individual right of conscience. Though colonists disagreed about religion and politics, many agreed on having the freedom to define or choose their faith and beliefs. Despite religious regulations and laws in some colonies, colonists began to see religious choice as an individual right.[471]

1   The Great Awakening gave American religion and all churches in the 1700s a more American flavor and
2   renewed life.[472]   Churches became more Americanized—less formal and outward, more evangelical,
3   individualistic, pietistic, pragmatic, egalitarian, moralistic yet tolerant, and laity-empowering.[473]   Revived
4   churches pursued "security of structures and liberation in the Holy Spirit," says Noll, a combination of opposing
5   forces that became "quintessentially American."[474]   Though the revival did not stop the increasing
6   secularization of society, it energized evangelism and the spiritual life of churches. The Christian church as a
7   whole gained members, energy and enthusiasm, outreach in society, public action, and responsibility.[475]   The
8   key verse to describe American Christianity, says one historian, was Revelation 21:5 in which God states,
9   "'Behold, I make all things new.'"[476]

10

11   The 1700s were a time of unparalleled church and congregational growth. Independent churches and
12   denominations formed and grew alongside state churches. Many Christian denominations expanded without
13   colonial government support. They formed new congregations and built church buildings more than ever
14   before, some resulting from spiritual revival. Many groups formed church councils in the colonies to oversee
15   church affairs.

16

17   **5.12 Revival Effects on Church, State, and Society: Religious Choice in a Free Marketplace of Ideas**

18

19   As a result of the Great Awakening and societal changes, including a growing number of dissenters and
20   religious groups, American religious society developed into a free "marketplace of ideas" that shifted away
21   from regulated religion, monopoly churches, and ideas of one dominant sect toward religious pluralism. To
22   traditionalists, religious competition and choice undermined the idea of one true denomination and fragmented
23   the church and Christian unity. To revivalists, though, regulated religion and a conformed state church were
24   impractical in a pluralistic society. In the religious marketplace, colonists as empowered individuals now had
25   increased religious choice, and religious groups now competed for new members or souls by persuasion, not
26   coercion. Churches now had to attract voluntary members and adapt their preaching and worship styles with
27   laity preferences in mind. Colonists could voluntarily select a church suited to their beliefs, needs, and tastes.
28   Revival challenged many to make choices about their religious beliefs. Colonists increasingly preferred non-
29   state churches to state churches. While over 60 percent of congregations were in an official state church in the
30   early 1700s, less than 30 percent were in a state church in the late 1700s.[477]

31

32   **5.13 Revival Effects on Church, State, and Society: Empowering of the Church Laity**

33

34   During the Awakening, colonists as laity or non-clergy church members were also empowered by a new
35   model of church leadership.[478] This new church leadership model changed assumptions about clergy and laity
36   and empowered the laity.[479] Revival leaders challenged the laity to examine their own beliefs and relationship
37   with God. They discouraged dependence on clergy to perform religious duties and encouraged people to
38   practice their religion on their own. Colonists were reminded that they didn't need a preacher to converse with
39   God but could connect with Him directly. To be sure, some laymen, in adopting secular ideas that questioned
40   Christianity, went in directions disapproved by revival leaders. But revival mostly created stronger fervor for
41   Christianity among colonists. In addition, revival evangelists believed few clergymen had preached on the New
42   Birth or been converted. Many urged the laity to reject unconverted clergy. Many laymen voted out ministers
43   deemed unconverted or left churches to form new ones. More rigorous standards of being "born again" were
44   demanded for clergy in their personal lives. Also, revival leaders' disregard for preacher license laws and
45   church boundaries added a political dimension to the revival that further empowered the church laity.[480]

46

5.14 Revival Effects on Church and Society: Education, Missions and Humanitarianism, Women in Church and Society, and a Gospel for All People

The Awakening in America had a number of effects that influenced and shaped American life and society. The revival continued the Puritan emphasis on education, propelled the missionary and humanitarian movements, led to women's increased involvement in church and society, and spread the Gospel to all groups of people in society. These movements would come to characterize American society, culture, and life in significant ways.

Awakeners, like the Puritans, encouraged education to promote Bible reading, prepare ministers of the gospel, and train laymen. To encourage Bible study, revival preachers provided basic education to their flocks, particularly in rural areas with few if any schools. Since colleges and public schools were largely supported by Christian individuals and groups, revivalists defended their interests in education against state churches. Since education was Bible-centered and Bible study required reading, Bible knowledge was equated with general knowledge. The basic literacy rate among white males in New England was nearly 100% in the late 1700s. Several evangelical colleges founded in the mid 1700s including Princeton, Brown, Rutgers/Queens, and Dartmouth took up ideas of the revival as well as greater religious freedom. Brown's charter for religious freedom upheld "absolute and uninterrupted liberty of conscience" and admitted students of all Christian denominations.[481] The church Sunday school movement, initially a humanitarian endeavor, also began to grow.

The Awakening also stimulated the missionary movement and humanitarianism. Humanitarian societies of the early 1800s that helped the poor, sick, needy, or unfortunate stemmed from Christian thought and revival. Humanitarian causes, says Niebuhr, "became the rallying point of ardent souls who had been kindled by the gospel of the kingdom of Christ."[482]

Women became more active in religion during and after the Awakening as denominations expanded. Previously, women could not directly influence church life as men could. They could not conduct formal meetings or hold church offices. Such restrictions reflected secular life in which women could not vote and lost property rights upon marriage. But in the late 1600s and 1700s, women made up the majority of church membership in all denominations and regions. While men continued to exercise religious authority, women's increased religious activities from this period on altered the exclusive predominance of men in American churches and religion. Some denominations supported greater women's activism, giving women more direct church roles, the ability to vote on congregational matters, and management of philanthropic groups.[483]

Though the Awakening did not address the issue of slavery, it brought the gospel more directly to all classes and groups of people including often disregarded Native Americans as well as African-Americans, many of whom were slaves. Some revivalists became missionaries to the Native Americans or evangelized among black slaves. Also, the revival's emphasis on personal religious experience resonated with blacks and even resembled African religions. Faith gave some purpose and hope to slaves. Some found spiritual liberation even while in slavery. Though disadvantaged, churches by and for blacks gradually appeared. The first continuing black church was Silver Bluff Church in Aiken County, South Carolina, where African-American preacher David George established a congregation in 1773 or 1774. When revivalist preacher George Whitefield died, Phyllis Wheatley, an emancipated slave and America's first published black poet, wrote her first published poem as a memorial to Whitefield. It addressed the hope Whitefield brought to African-Americans.

An anti-slavery movement did not form during the Awakening due to the growing use of slaves on crops and the impending American Revolution which demanded the attention of revivalists.[484] Evangelicals focused more on freeing slaves and providing for their needs than on addressing the institution of slavery. Nevertheless, the Awakening, in supporting the idea that all men are created equal before God, opened the Bible and Gospel to African-Americans.[485] The Bible-based view of equality would begin to pave the way to freedom for all men.

5.15 Revival Influences on Unity, Democracy, and Revolution

The Great Awakening had political undercurrents that affected society prior to the American Revolution in the areas of American unity, democratic equality, and political freedom. As America's first "national" or inter-colonial event, say historians, the Awakening created a new national awareness and identity in America in the mid 1700s by facilitating spiritual, political, and geographical unity among the colonies. Though many churches and denominations became more fragmented during this time, American colonists were able to forge a common identity by their largely shared beliefs and values—which led to their greater sense of unity as a people. It created this solidarity through inter-colonial communication, preaching tours, and shared spiritual experiences.[486] During their first 150 years, the colonies were self-contained and had little contact with one another. Colonial charter conflicts were addressed directly with England. An exception was the 1643 New England Confederation of Puritan Colonies that united some colonies for safety. When the Awakening came, ministers like Whitefield traveled the colonies to preach, and others discussed and corresponded about revival with colonists and ministers in different colonies. Revival thus increased communication and common shared experiences among Americans, making the colonies more spiritually and politically unified and distinct from Europe.[487] The revival, explains Ellis Sandoz, prompted the "experiential formation of the rudiments of an *American* community of shared convictions rooted in faith rising above and beyond colonial and merely British identities."[488] With greater communication and reinforced similarities among regions, revival also decreased geographical separation.[489] Changing geographical perceptions made parish and colonial boundaries seem less relevant. As such, the revivals were not only an awakening to God but to national consciousness.[490]

The Great Awakening, historians indicate, politically influenced democratic ideas and challenged traditional church-state relations before and during the American Revolution.[491] The beliefs and characteristics of the Awakening supported democratic ideas and revolution. The beliefs that humans are made in God's image and equal in God's eyes supported human dignity, equality, and natural rights and led to more democratic thinking. In addition, the revival's empowering of the church laity encouraged democratic and revolutionary ideas. To be sure, revivalists recognized the sinfulness of man and opposed unlimited natural liberty in civil society. Yet they did not think that man was hopelessly sinful and required to live without any freedom. Humans in God's image, revivalists believed, have godly virtues and God's laws in their hearts and minds which qualified man for freedom and citizenship in a state. Revivalists did not fear freedom for humans in society. In America and England, Niebuhr asserts, "the Christian enlightenment stood beside the rational enlightenment in the battle for democracy."[492] Some historians, in fact, describe the Awakening as the "democratic republicanism of the 1770s."[493]

While revivalists did not directly address civil or political issues like the Puritans, their quest for spiritual liberty benefited the move toward political liberty and democracy. For revivalists used terms in public discussion such as *liberty, freedom, virtue, tyranny, bondage,* and *slavery* in a spiritual context with regard to personal, spiritual liberation from sin through Christianity's salvation. These terms were then applied to the concept of political liberty prior to and during the American Revolution. "It was easy, when the tyrant became Parliament rather than sin," say Noll and others, "to make fruitful use of the capital which these terms had acquired in the revival."[494] These liberty themes, they elaborate, "undergirded the struggle for American independence from Great Britain and the spirit of independence, and...led to a belief that if the Revolution was grounded in the Awakening, then it must also be a work of God."[495]

As colonists began to see themselves as Americans, they became more wary of official state churches with ties to Europe like the Church of England. European religious leaders did not understand American religion, and the Church of England's lack of support for the revival raised further suspicions. When tensions arose between America and Britain in the 1700s prior to the revolution, revivalists' suspicion of the Church of England became another reason to distrust the British.[496] Revivalists also resisted taxes supporting official state churches. The experience gave colonists experience in challenging authority and in being revolutionaries for liberty.[497]

Indeed, the Awakening and the American Revolution, considered by historians to be the two most significant events of the 1700s, had important connections.[498] The Awakening was, some historians argue, the primary influence in the Revolution.[499] It provided much of the religious grounding for the war. The Revolution could not have occurred without the Awakening's religious belief and thought. For the Revolution was, Johnson asserts, a religious event in its origins, a fact that would shape it "from start to finish and determine the nature of the independent state it brought into being." The revival, Johnson describes, was a "proto-revolutionary event, the formative event in American history, preceding the political drive for independence and making it possible."[500]

To be sure, while the Great Awakening had unifying and democratic elements that influenced the colonies and the American Revolution, it did not offer a workable Christian socio-political model or theory for civil society to replace the regulated church state system of the Puritans.[501] As American religion diversified, revivalists focused on evangelism and spiritual life rather than on a Bible-based framework for civil society. Yet no political concept for the civil state could address the religious diversity in America in which no one Christian or religious group ruled or dominated. "They seemed to think," Noll and others observe, "that if they could...be successful at evangelism, the problems of politics would take care of themselves. But they didn't."[502] The task of formulating a civil state for America's largely Christian yet denominationally, religiously diverse society would lie with the future American Founders of the United States. Revivalists would support the creation of a democratic nation.

5.16 Conclusion: The Great Awakening—A Significant Event in American Society

The Great Awakening was a significant event in American history that had lasting effects on American culture, society, and politics. In the words of a Virginia newspaper of 1745, it "turn'd the World upside down."[503] It supported the value and dignity of the human being, equality, promoted goodwill and happiness in humanity, and gave purpose to government, society, and the world. It provided new cultural models of public speaking and evangelism. It created religious competition in a free marketplace and ultimately revived all churches.[504] It offered to individuals personal conversion, religious choice, and a new church leadership model that empowered the church laity and weakened state church establishment laws.[505] It influenced a democratic spirit and colonial unity and raised national consciousness by which colonists started to identify themselves as Americans.[506] In challenging spiritual oppression, it favored political freedom. The Awakening helped to lay a foundation for American political independence and religious freedom.[507] It would help to prepare colonists for the forming of a new kind of Christian nation.[508]

1
2
3
4
5
6
7
8
9

Excerpt of
On the Death of the Reverend George Whitefield – 1770

An Elegiac Poem On the Death of that Celebrated Divine, and Eminent Servant of Jesus Christ, the Reverend and Learned Mr. George Whitefield [509]

by Phillis Wheatley (1753-1784),
a 17-year-old African-American servant girl

When his *Americans* were burden'd sore,
When Streets were crimson'd with their guiltless Gore,
Unrivall'd Friendship in his Breast now strove;
The Fruit thereof was Charity and Love.
Towards *America*—Couldst thou do more
Than leave thy native Home, the *British* Shore,
To cross the great *Atlantic*'s wat'ry Road,
To see *America*'s distress'd abode?
Thy Prayers, great Saint, and thy incessant Cries,
Have pierc'd the Bosom of thy native Skies!
Thou, Moon, hast seen, and ye, bright Stars of Light,
Have witness been of his Requests by Night.
He pray'd that Grace in every Heart might dwell:
He long'd to see *America* excel;
He charg'd its Youth to let the Grace Divine
Arise, and in their future Actions shine;
He offer'd THAT he did himself receive,
A greater Gift not GOD himself can give:
He urg'd the Need of HIM to every one;
It was no less than GOD's co-equal SON.
Take HIM, ye wretched, for your only Good;
Take HIM, ye starving Souls, to be your Food.
Ye Thirsty, come to his Life-giving Stream:
Ye Preachers, take him for your joyful Theme:
Take HIM, "my dear *Americans*," he said;
Be your Complaints in his kind Bosom laid:
Take HIM ye *Africans*, he longs for you;
Impartial SAVIOUR, is his Title due;
If you will choose to walk in Grace's Road,
You shall be Sons, and Kings, and Priests to GOD.

Review: Checking Out the History

Discuss questions in subgroups or whole group. As an option, the group may come up with main ideas or insights from each question. Responses may be shared and discussed in the whole group.

1. What were some important ideas and beliefs of the Great Awakening?

2. How/In what ways did the Awakening influence culture, society, and politics or the civil state in America?

3. How did the Great Awakening influence the kind of Christian nation America would become? What kind of nation did it help create? How would America differ from other Christian nations?

4. How/In what ways did the Great Awakening help pave the way or contribute to American independence?

5. What basic Bible-based or Judeo-Christian principles are evident and important in this part of America's heritage?

1 **Activity: Causes and Effects of the Great Awakening**
2 Consider important ideas or events related to the Great Awakening or time period and their religious, social, and
3 political effects. Write these effects, if any, in the appropriate columns.
4

The Great Awakening	Religious Effects	Social Effects	Political Effects
The Christian emphasis on individual and personal spiritual conversion			
The view of Christian love or charity as the sum of all virtue			
The view of God and Christianity as an equalizer of all people			
The traveling and preaching of ministers among all colonies in America			
The religious choice created by a free marketplace of ideas			
The Christian view of freedom or liberty from sin			

5
6

Call to Action

Each person will reflect on and write his/her responses to the questions below. Responses may then be shared and discussed in the group.

1. Describe a period in your personal life when you experienced a new insight or change of heart or mind with regard to an important issue or approach in your life. How did this experience affect your life?

_____

_____

_____

_____

2. Describe the moral, cultural, social, and/or political condition of our nation today as you see it.

_____

_____

_____

_____

3. How might a religious revival today help our nation morally, culturally, socially, and politically? What do you think would be the effects of a movement like the Great Awakening in our nation today?

_____

_____

_____

_____

4. What do you believe is the contribution of leaders who have studied the Bible to our nation?

_____

_____

_____

_____

5. In light of this discussion, what are some qualities of good citizens of our nation? What might you do to become a better citizen and help others do the same?

_____

_____

_____

_____

6. How might you help the nation to uphold, renew, or return to its Bible-based, moral roots?

_____

_____

_____

_____

Chapter 6
The Bible-Centered Debate on Revolution

6.1 Introduction: The American Revolution

Since they first arrived in America, the American colonists had enjoyed English rights under British law. These rights came from their colonial charters, the Magna Carta of 1215, and the English Bill of Rights of 1689. The Magna Carta upheld the Rule of Law, the principle that no ruler or public official is above the law. Since all were equally subject to the law, no one could rule arbitrarily. The "Great Charter" also upheld due process of law. Colonists had also enjoyed minimal supervision from Britain. They were therefore free to set up their own assemblies and govern themselves. By the 1700s, the American colonies had formed and lived by self-governed, elective, representative colonial assemblies for nearly 150 years.

In the 1760s and 1770s, however, changing political circumstances with Britain challenged the American colonists' way of life. Tensions arose between colonists and Britain as King George III and British Parliament, failing to recognize the colonists' governing assemblies, imposed regulations on colonial trade and commerce in America. While colonists tried to avoid conflict with Britain, they questioned Britain's right to intrude in their affairs after a century of very little interference.[510] As colonists protested, Britain only tightened its control, escalating conflict. Opposition to British rule was strongest in Boston. Following the Boston Tea Party of 1773, British Parliament attempted to revoke the charter of Massachusetts and submit the colony to British rule.[511] Avid defenders of their rights, colonists saw British policies and taxes as unjust violations of their rights and civil law. They had serious concerns about corruption, the loss of Rule of Law and their freedoms, the possibility of an enforced national church, and subservience to Britain. The rights violated by the British, colonists cited, included no taxation without representation, trial by jury, innocence until proven guilt, due process of law, freedom of travel in peacetime, no quartering of troops in private homes in peacetime, and no standing army in peacetime without consent. The church issue that concerned colonists was the possibility that Britain might impose the national Church of England in the colonies, for the church had proposed to appoint a bishop in America. Though not supported by the British government and never realized, the proposal was seen as a threat to remove religious tolerance gained during the Great Awakening and to persecute religious dissenters. The issue, say historians, added to anti-British sentiment.[512]

Since colonists had no elected representative in British Parliament, they had no say on laws enacted by Britain. As Britain's policies became more intrusive in America, colonists' lack of representation or justification by British law or Crown to claim it, left them in a powerless position by which to assert themselves and their rights as free Englishmen. When Parliament denied violations of colonists' rights and claimed that Americans were indirectly represented in Britain, early American minister Rev. Stephen Johnson responded as many Americans: "Tis ridiculous to common sense that two millions of free people can be represented by a representative elected by no one of them."[513] The Americans, in fact, wanted more than representation overseas. They wanted to govern themselves.

In 1774, American representative delegates from the colonies convened as the first national governing assembly in the First Continental Congress in Philadelphia to represent and unify the colonies, create a militia, and rebuff Britain's policies. Led by radical delegates Samuel Adams and John Adams of Massachusetts and Patrick Henry and Richard Henry Lee of Virginia, the Congress issued a "Declaration of Rights and Grievances." This proclamation declared that the colonists were entitled to life, liberty, and property based on the laws of nature, the English constitution, and their charters and compacts. They did not forfeit English rights when migrating to America. Nor did they give power to any earthly authority to remove these rights. They also had a right to participate in legislative councils that enacted laws in the colonies. They were entitled, in fact, to exclusive power in their colonial assemblies over internal policies and taxation. All legislation and taxes were to be enacted by themselves, with their consent. King George III, however, rejected this proclamation and

1 responded, "The New England governments are now in a state of rebellion; blows must decide whether they are
2 to be subject to this country or to be independent." After hearing this response, and with the first shots fired on
3 the battlefield, Benjamin Franklin, intermediary between Britain and America, was convinced that peace was no
4 longer possible and told associates that the only real safety for America was as a free country. In a last effort to
5 avoid full-blown war with Great Britain, the Second Continental Congress adopted the "Olive Branch Petition"
6 in 1775 that affirmed American allegiance to Britain and implored the king for a peaceful resolution. The king,
7 however, rejected this petition as well. Its rejection sent a message to many colonists that they had to choose
8 between complete independence or complete submission to British rule. For their independence and freedom,
9 the American colonists would have to fight.
10
11 　　　　William Prescott of Massachusetts reflected the thinking of Americans favoring independence: "We
12 think if we submit to these [Britain's] regulations, all is gone. Our forefathers passed the vast Atlantic, spent
13 their blood and treasure, that they might enjoy their liberties, both civil and religious, and transmit them to their
14 posterity. Their children have waded through seas of difficulty, to leave us free and happy in the enjoyment of
15 English privileges. Now, if we should give them up, can our children rise up and call us blessed? Is a glorious
16 death in defense of our liberties better than a short infamous life, and our memories to be had in detestation to
17 the latest posterity?"[514] The Americans would pledge their lives, fortunes, and honor for their cause.
18
19 　　　　Following the first battles at Lexington and Concord between the American colonists and the British
20 army, delegates met at the Second Continental Congress. Finding peace with Britain impossible, they drafted
21 the Declaration of Independence of 1776, declaring themselves a new, independent nation. The colonies thus
22 joined together to become the United States of America.
23
24 **6.2 The Influence of the Bible on the Founding Era**
25
26 　　　　The Bible had a definite influence on the American Revolution. Colonists debated fiercely over whether
27 revolution was acceptable according to the Bible. While some colonists opposed revolution as unbiblical, many
28 supported it as Biblical. Those who opposed revolution were often called "loyalists." Those who supported
29 revolution were often called "patriots" or "Whigs" after the pro-reform political party in England. Many patriot
30 revolutionary leaders, congressional delegates, founders, clergy, and other colonists spoke and wrote in support
31 of the cause of liberty from the Bible—educating, uniting, and mobilizing Americans for the cause and its
32 principles. The fact that the Bible was intensively debated and discussed among American Christians revealed
33 its importance to and influence on the revolutionary generation and the Revolution itself.
34
35 　　　　In confirmation of this point, a notable study by Donald Lutz as discussed in his *Origins of American*
36 *Constitutionalism* shows that the Bible was the most frequently cited source in the political literature of 1760-
37 1805 that influenced American political thought. This literature includes both secular writings and sermons.
38 The European thinkers most influential to American political thought—including Charles de Montesequieu,
39 John Locke, and William Blackstone—cited or drew from the Bible or a Judeo-Christian worldview in their
40 writings. Other influential Bible-based thinkers included Algernon Sidney, Samuel Pufendorf, and Edward
41 Coke.[515] Writers most often referred to sections in the Bible on covenants and on God's promises to Israel. The
42 most frequently cited Old Testament books were, in order, Deuteronomy, Isaiah, Genesis, Exodus, and
43 Leviticus. The most frequently cited writings of the New Testament were, in order, those of Paul—particularly
44 his epistle or letter to the Romans on the issue of obedience to authorities—Peter, and John (his Gospel). Other
45 frequently cited passages came from Joshua, 1 and 2 Samuel, 1 and 2 Kings, and the Gospel of Matthew.[516]
46 Due to the frequency of Biblical citations, Lutz observes, "When reading comprehensively in the political
47 literature of the war years, one cannot but be struck by the extent to which biblical sources used by ministers
48 and traditional Whigs undergirded the justification for the break with Britain, the rationale for continuing the
49 war, and the basic principles of Americans' writing their own constitutions."[517] Thus, in addition to Whig

1 revolutionary political thought and other influences, the Bible was, as confirmed by statistical and contextual
2 research, a significant influence in the founding of America.
3
4   The frequent use of the Bible, by both believers and non-believers, in the public and private writings of
5 the founding era reveals the Bible's strong cultural influence in society during that time. Founding-era
6 Americans' frequent references to the Bible in their public discourse, says Daniel Dreisbach, "reveals as much
7 about the Bible's place in the hearts and minds of their audiences as it does about them."[518] The Bible was, he
8 says, "the most authoritative, accessible, and familiar literary text in America."[519] It was the "lingua franca" of
9 the late 1700s.[520] Many Americans held a deep spiritual or moral belief in the Bible.[521] They saw it as relevant
10 to all areas of life and society. As such, Americans used the Bible in various rhetorical, literary, and theological
11 ways for political, cultural, and spiritual purposes to reach a biblically literate audience who viewed the Bible as
12 a central text in society, culture, and religious faith.[522] The King James Version was the most widely used
13 English translation of the Bible during the founding era.[523] Many founding-era Americans, like earlier
14 colonists, looked to the ancient nation of Israel in the Bible as a model for republican government.[524] They also
15 saw in the Bible a God who cared about mankind and human events, and they searched this book to understand
16 how God might be involved in their nation's development.[525] Many Americans sought to align their political
17 principles with Biblical moral principles.[526]
18
19   Also, though some scholars have thought that the founding-era generation was largely "unchurched,"
20 recent scholarship indicates that at the beginning of the Revolution, in the 1760s and 1770s, the majority of
21 America's 3 million colonists were active in churches. According to recent, rigorous research findings, 56-80%
22 of the white population were active in churches during this period. The largest percentages were found in the
23 northern colonies, with lower percentages in the southern colonies. One historian calculates that the average
24 colonial church-goer would have listened to approximately 7,000 sermons in his or her lifetime. What is more,
25 recent findings indicate that the majority of colonial churches were of the Reformed Calvinist tradition. 82% of
26 New Englanders were active in Congregational Churches alone, not including other Reformed denominations.
27 In 1776, Reformed churches accounted for more than half of all churches in the colonies—84% in New
28 England, 51% in the middle colonies, and 58% in the southern colonies.[527] Some historians estimate that three-
29 fourths of American colonists were connected with the Reformed tradition and denominations.[528] In fact, many
30 American Founders who signed the Declaration of Independence came from Reformed Christian backgrounds
31 including John Adams, Samuel Adams, Josiah Bartlett, Abraham Clark, William Ellery, William Floyd, Lyman
32 Hall, John Hancock, John Hart, Philip Livingston, Thomas McKean, Samuel Huntington, Robert Treat Paine,
33 Roger Sherman, James Smith, Richard Stockton, Matthew Thornton, William Whipple, William Williams,
34 James Wilson, John Witherspoon, and Oliver Wolcott.[529] The unorthodox Declaration signer Benjamin
35 Franklin was actually raised in a Congregationalist family. Charles Carroll, the only Catholic, also notably
36 signed the Declaration. Other historians affirm these findings. Sandoz affirms, "The fact of the matter is that
37 the best recent scholarship supports the proposition that the Christian perspective was alive, well, and
38 flourishing in the [founding] period and that it was central to many of its major events."[530]
39
40   Many American patriots drew from the Bible to support the American Revolution. Many saw revolution
41 as a just war for a just cause. In line with Reformed political thought, they believed that the people had a moral
42 right and obligation, a sacred duty to defend their freedoms against tyranny. While loyalists upheld submission
43 to authority, patriots focused on civil government's God-ordained purpose to protect and preserve the rights of
44 the people and the common good, not to abuse or oppress the people. They felt no obligation to submit to such
45 immoral civil governments. Patriots also drew from other known historical and contemporary Bible-based
46 arguments for resistance to tyranny to support their position. They pointed to God's favoring of freedom for
47 His people in the Bible, popular sovereignty, civil covenants, obedience to God's moral law above human law,
48 ancient Israel's history of resistance to oppressive rulers, and the lawfulness of defensive war.

Many historical Reformed, Bible-based writings including Ponet's *Short Treatise* and Brutus' *Vindiciae* influenced these ideas of resistance in American political thought of the revolutionary era. Indeed, the Reformation era of the 1500s and 1600s had been, says Harold Laski, "one long research into the terms of political obedience."[531] Since the Congregationalist Puritans and Presbyterians espoused the views of the Reformation and its resistance theory, the American Revolution was often referred to by loyalist supporters of King George III as the "Presbyterian Rebellion." One loyalist Rev. William Jones tells the British government that the Revolution had been instigated by Presbyterians who were "Calvinists by profession, and Republicans in their politics" and that "this has been a Presbyterian war from the beginning...."[532] Another loyalist in New York writes in 1774, "I fix all the blame for these extraordinary *American* proceedings upon them [the Presbyterians]. ... Believe me the Presbyterians have been the chief & principal instruments in all these flaming measures...."[533] Declaration signer and second U. S. president John Adams later reflects on and affirms the influence of Reformed political thought on the American Founding, stating, "I love and revere the memories of Huss Wickliff Luther Calvin Zwinglius Melancton and all the other reformers how muchsoever I may differ from them all in many theological metaphysical & philosophical points. As you justly observe, without their great exertions & severe sufferings, the USA had never existed."[534] Whether rightly or wrongly applied, the political principles of the American Revolution were, says Gary Amos, an "inheritance left to colonial Americans by earlier generations of Christian writers." It was a heritage of Western political theory that had developed over centuries.[535]

6.3 The Debate: Bible-Based Submission to Authority and Concept of Government

While many Christian colonists of the revolutionary era believed the Bible commanded obedience to authority and opposed resistance, many others believed resistance was consistent with the Bible and Christian teaching. Both loyalist and patriot Americans used Biblical themes to oppose or defend revolution. Many voices in the colonies contributed to the debate over revolution including loyalist and patriot clergy, political leaders, and Christian colonists. They largely debated over justification of war based on Romans 13:1-7 and 1 Peter 2:13-17 with regard to the Biblical mandate to submit to civil authority. Luther had presented these verses in his 1523 Reformation treatise, *Secular Authority: To What Extent It Should be Obeyed* as the basis for civil government. Calvin had also presented them in his *Institutes* to indicate the honor and obedience that men are to afford to their governors.[536] The Apostle Paul in Romans 13:1-7 states:

> *Let every soul be subject to the governing authorities. For there is no authority except from God, and the authorities that exist are appointed by God. Therefore whoever resists the authority resists the ordinance of God, and those who resist will bring judgment on themselves. For rulers are not a terror to good works, but to evil. Do you want to be unafraid of the authority? Do what is good, and you will have praise from the same. For he is God's minister to you for good. But if you do evil, be afraid; for he does not bear the sword in vain; for he is God's minister, an avenger to execute* wrath on him who practices evil. Therefore *you* must be subject, not only because of wrath but also for conscience' sake. For because of this you also pay taxes, for they are God's ministers attending continually to this very thing. Render therefore to all their due: taxes to whom taxes *are due*, customs to whom customs, fear to whom fear, honor to whom honor.

The Apostle Peter in 1 Peter 2:13-17 states:

> Therefore submit yourselves to every ordinance of man for the Lord's sake, whether to the king as supreme, or to governors, as to those who are sent by him for the punishment of evildoers and *for the* praise of those who do good. For this is the will of God, that by doing good you may put to silence the ignorance of foolish men—as free, yet not using liberty as a cloak for vice, but as bondservants of God. Honor all *people*. Love the brotherhood. Fear God. Honor the king.

To Loyalists, including many Anglican ministers, Romans 13 taught complete, unlimited submission to authority and civil government without exception. Such was the traditional interpretation in the church. Loyalists supported obedience to civil authority regardless of the government's form or actions. This submission included the paying of taxes. They thus opposed the American Revolution and resistance to the British government. Anglican Rev. Jonathan Boucher, for example, preached from 1763 to 1775 against resistance. He argues, "To resist and to rebel against a lawful government, is to oppose *the ordinance of God*, and to injure or destroy institutions most essential to human happiness."[537] Alluding to Romans 13, he asserts that resistance is inconsistent with the Bible and church doctrine:

> But whatever doctrines any particular administration, governed only by human policy, may see fit to avow or disavow, the word of God, like mount Zion, *abideth fast for ever*; and the doctrine of "non-resistance" is unquestionably "a tenet of our Church." It is the uniform doctrine of the Articles, the Liturgy, the Injunctions, and Canons, and Homilies; in one of which I find the following strong words: "Lucifer was the first author and founder of rebellion; which is the first, the greatest, and the root of all other sins. Kings and princes, as well the evil as the good, do reign by God's ordinance; and subjects are bound to obey them, and for no cause to resist, or withstand, or rebel, or make any sedition against them, although they be wicked men. It were a perilous thing to commit unto subjects the judgment, which prince is wise, which government good; and which otherwise. A rebel is worse than the worst prince, and a rebellion worse than the worst government of the worst prince that hath hitherto been."[538]

Citing the Apostle Peter, Boucher continues to argue against resistance:

> Having, then, my brethen, thus long been *tossed to and fro* in a wearisome circle of *uncertain traditions*, or in speculations and projects still more uncertain, concerning government, what better can you do than, following the Apostle's advice, *to submit yourselves to every ordinance of man, for the Lord's sake; whether it be to the King as supreme, or unto GOVERNORS, as unto them that are SENT by him for the punishment of evil-doers, and for the praise of them that do well? For, so is the will of God, that with well-doing ye may put to silence the ignorance of foolish men: as free, and not using your liberty for a cloke of maliciousness, but as the servants of God. Honour all men: love the brotherhood: fear God: honour the king.*[539]

Loyalist Anglican Samuel Seabury of New York, also alluding to Peter, similarly argues for Christian Americans "to wipe off those Asperations and ill Impressions which the Ignorance and foolish Men had brought upon the Christian Religion, by pretending that their Christian Liberty set them free from the Subjection to civil Government."[540] Christians are to obey government, Seabury argued, "whether it be exercised by KINGS as Supreme, or by Governors sent by them and acting by their Authority." He also states,

> When St. Peter and St. Paul wrote their Epistles, they were under the Government of Heathen Emperors and Magistrates, who persecuted them, and the other Christians—depriving them of their Possessions, beating and banishing and killing them—without any Crime proved against them, but merely because they were Christians. And yet it was to these Emperors and Magistrates—even to Nero and Caligula—that the Apostles commanded Honor and Respect, at all Times; and whenever it could be done consistently with Obedience to God, Duty and Submission.[541]

Loyalist Anglican Rev. Charles Inglis of New York believed Christian obedience to government is what "distinguish[ed] themselves from others and manifest[ed] the native Excellence and Spirit of their Religion."[542] Inglis points out that Peter wrote his epistles, including 1 Peter 2, when Nero, who persecuted Christians, was the emperor of Rome. Inglis concludes that "the personal character of the Magistrate was not to interfere with the Civil Duty of the Subject. Even when bad, it did not dissolve the Obligation of the latter."[543] Early Christians, the loyalists pointed out, remained subject to the public authorities even when those authorities were

1   evil. These Christians did not speak of or arrange political rebellion but continued to assert submission to civil
2   authority.
3
4   The American Patriots, on the other hand, opposed passive obedience and *unlimited* submission to
5   government, especially to evil government and tyranny.   While they believed that *good* or *moral* civil
6   government is God-ordained and should be submitted to, they did not believe in absolute submission to an
7   absolute government, particularly when the government does not properly represent or benefit the people.
8   Romans 13, they thought, clearly speaks of submission to a *good* or *moral* government—a government that is
9   "not a terror to good works, but to evil" and a "minister to you for good." 1 Peter 2 likewise speaks of
10 submission to a *good* or *moral* government sent "for the punishment of evildoers and for the praise of those who
11 do good." These verses clearly do not call for submission to evil or immoral governments. In fact, in revealing
12 the *moral* purpose of *good* government, they actually *support resistance* to *immoral* governments. As such,
13 patriots believed resistance to tyrannical authority is a natural right and justified based on the same Bible verses.
14 In addition, Patriot Americans and clergy emphasized the early Puritan view that the people of America are
15 God's chosen people—the New Israel—and thus that God sides with the cause of freedom. Patriot clergy often
16 blended Biblical themes with Whig revolutionary politics, linking spiritual and political themes. They applied
17 Locke's political ideas in their messages and sermons to support revolution and independence. The Patriots
18 thus supported the American Revolution and saw it as in line with the Bible.
19
20 Many patriot clergy, known as the "Black Regiment" for their black robes, and revolutionary leaders
21 drew from the Bible's concept of government to justify resistance to tyrannical authority. One of the most
22 outspoken patriot clergymen was Boston Congregationalist preacher Rev. Jonathan Mayhew. Mayhew, who
23 had attended Harvard, believed resistance to tyranny is a Christian duty. Mayhew's *Discourse Concerning*
24 *Unlimited Submission* of 1750 became one of the most well-known and widely-read sermons of the
25 revolutionary period in support of resistance based on Romans 13 and other Bible verses. While Mayhew was
26 not an orthodox Christian, his *Discourse*, like other messages of that time, reflected Reformed political thought
27 of resistance to tyranny.[544] It addressed not only religious but political freedoms, asserting that the people could
28 resist a government that was religiously oppressive. It was written prior to the American Revolution at a time
29 when fear had emerged among many Americans that the Church of England—which in the 1700s had moved
30 away from the doctrines of the American Puritan churches—was planning to send an Anglican bishop to
31 America to oversee the New England churches. Though written 25 years before the Revolution, Mayhew's
32 sermon proved to be very affecting to revolutionary-era Americans in general and very influential to the
33 Patriots. It set off a public debate in Boston newspapers on the issue of Christian obedience to authority.
34 American Founder John Adams would note the influence of Mayhew's sermon on the American Revolution:
35 "If the orators on the 4th of July really wish to investigate the principles and feelings which produced the
36 Revolution, they out [ought] to study this pamphlet [James Otis's 1762 *A Vindication of the Conduct of the*
37 *House of Representatives of the Province of Massachusetts Bay*], and Dr. Mayhew's sermon on passive
38 obedience and non-resistance, and all the documents of those days."[545] Though Mayhew's *Discourse* was
39 written primarily to defend religious freedom, many historians affirm that it was an impetus of the American
40 Revolution.[546] One early historian called it the "MORNING GUN OF THE REVOLUTION."[547]
41
42 Mayhew argues from Romans 13:1-8 that Christians are not called to submit to an oppressive ruler but,
43 rather, have a duty to resist tyranny. Mayhew supports just authority and government for the good of society
44 and the judgment of evil. Christians are to submit to *just* governments, which are ordained by God, regardless
45 of their form—monarchy, aristocracy, or republic. However, tyrannical governments were not to be absolutely
46 submitted to, he argues, because they contradict the Law of Nature, reason, and the meaning of Romans 13.
47 Romans 13 concerns submission to just rulers who do *good*, not to tyrants who ruin nations and lives and do
48 evil. The Apostle Paul's instruction to Christians in Romans 13 to submit to those in authority does not apply in
49 the context of oppressive governments and tyrants.

Mayhew further argues that unjust, immoral civil authorities are not among the authorities to which Christians are to submit because such authorities do not fulfill their proper end and work contrary to God's purpose. Mayhew, as other patriots, saw Romans 13 as supporting resistance to such authorities in order to protect the nation from slavery, misery, and ruin. Referring to Romans 13:1-7, Mayhew asserts that when a ruler is tyrannical, "we are bound to throw off our allegiance to him, and to resist; and that according to the tenor of the apostle's argument in this passage."[548]   For God does not desire His people to live under oppression. God promises His people freedom. "Rulers have no authority from God to do mischief," Mayhew argues. Referencing 2 Corinthians 12:7, he further asserts, "It is blasphemy to call tyrants and oppressors God's ministers. They are more properly 'the messengers of Satan to buffet us.'"[549] Also citing 2 Samuel 23:3, Mayhew asserts,

> No rulers are properly God's ministers but such as are "just, ruling in the fear of God." When once magistrates act contrary to their office, and the end of their institution, --when they rob and ruin the public, instead of being guardians of its peace and welfare, --they immediately cease to be the ordinance and ministers of God and no more deserve that glorious character than common pirates and highwaymen. So that, whenever that argument for submission fails which is grounded upon the usefulness of magistracy to civil society, --as it always does when magistrates do hurt to society instead of good, --the other argument, which is taken from their being the ordinance of God, must necessarily fail also; no person of a civil character being God's minister, in the sense of the apostle, any further than he performs God's will by exercising a just and reasonable authority, and ruling for the good of the subject.[550]

Mayhew concludes from Romans 13 that the people are not obliged to submit to evil, tyrannical authorities that do not support the public good. Quite the contrary, the people have a duty to defend against tyrannical authorities for the good of society and to guard their God-given freedoms. He asserts,

> Thus, upon a careful review of the apostle's [Paul's] reasoning in this passage [Romans 13:1-8], it appears that his arguments to enforce submission are of such a nature as to conclude only in favor of submission to such rulers as he himself describes; i.e., such as rule for the good of society, which is the only end of their institution. Common tyrants and public oppressors are not entitled to obedience from their subjects by virtue of anything here laid down by the inspired apostle.[551]

Based on this reasoning, Mayhew supports the refusal to submit to oppressive rulers if submission leads to the ruin of society and the public good. In fact, people should do the opposite. Mayhew adds that revolution and resistance to tyranny do not ruin society or the public good but actually preserve society from ruin:

> I now add, further, that the apostle's argument is so far from proving it to be the duty of people to obey and submit to such rulers as act in contradiction to the public good, and so to the design of their office, that it proves the direct contrary. For, please to observe, that if the end of all civil government be the good of society; if this be the thing that is aimed at in constituting civil rulers; and if the motive and argument for submission to government be taken from the apparent usefulness of civil authority, --it follows, that when no such good end can be answered by submission, there remains no argument or motive to enforce it; and if, instead of this good end's being brought about by submission, a contrary end is brought about, and the ruin and misery of society effected by it, here is a plain and positive reason against submission in all such cases, should they ever happen. And therefore, in such cases, a regard to the public welfare ought to make us withhold from our rulers that obedience and submission which it would otherwise be our duty to render to them.[552]

6.4 God's Desire for Freedom, Not Slavery, for His People

American patriot clergy and revolutionaries supported resistance to British tyranny based on the Bible-based view that God desires freedom—literal and spiritual—rather than bondage for His people. Patriot revolutionaries supported the cause of liberty and independence by applying this notion of freedom—as found in the Bible and in the early Puritans' mission in America—to the political context of the American colonies. Like the Puritans of the early 1600s, Americans of the revolutionary era similarly compared themselves to the Israelites and God's believers in the Bible. They saw America as a Promised Land of religious and civil liberty for God's people. Though their concept of liberty was broader, their mission remained rooted in Judeo-Christian thought. They cited the Israelites' escape from slavery in Egypt and their coming into the Promised Land of Canaan in the Old Testament book of Exodus. When the evil Pharaoh of Egypt refuses to obey God and free the captive Israelites, God sends plagues upon Egypt. These plagues demonstrate that all men and rulers are subject to God and His laws and that God ordains liberty for His people. Various ministers drew a connection between the enslaved Israelites of the Bible and the oppressed colonists. Enslaving God's people—as ministers like Rev. Stephen Johnson of Lyme, Connecticut, warned in 1766—is a great sin in God's sight. It violates mankinds' natural rights and God's covenant with his people.[553] In a 1776 sermon, Congregational minister Rev. Samuel Cooper of Boston—like Puritan John Cotton before him in his *God's Promise to His Plantation*—cites 2 Samuel 7:10 and the idea that America has a just cause for freedom against Britain based on God's promise and covenant with them. God's protection of His people's liberties, he asserts, is confirmed from Deuteronomy 33:29: "Happy art thou, O Israel: who is like unto thee, O People saved of the Lord, who is the Shield of thy Help, and the Sword of thine Excellency. Thine Enemies will be found Liars unto Thee, and Thou shalt tread upon their high Places."[554] Patriot Americans cited God's favor of liberty for the Israelites as support for their revolutionary cause.

Patriot clergy and revolutionaries also supported the cause of freedom over slavery from other verses in the New Testament in which God's people are spiritually freed from the bondage and condemnation of sin through Jesus Christ. Ministers cited Galatians 5:1 in which the Apostle Paul declares, "Stand fast therefore in the liberty by which Christ has made us free, and do not be entangled again with a yoke of bondage." Reformer Martin Luther had cited this verse during the Reformation, stating, "When we were baptized, we were set free, subject only to God's Word. Why should any man use human words and make us prisoner? As St. Paul says, 'Ye are bought with a price; become not bond-servants of men' [I Cor. 6:20; Gal. 5:1], namely, of those who rule according to man-made laws."[555] The Bible uses words like "slavery," "bondage," "deliverance," "freedom," and "liberty" to describe this spiritual liberation. Ministers compared spiritual liberty with political liberty using symbols, metaphors, and double meanings. They supported political liberty with such comparisons. Galatians 5:1 was often invoked during the revolution and became an American motto. The Bible's principle of liberty—both spiritual and political—became an American principle of religious and civil liberty. God evidently desires freedom—literal and spiritual—for His people and expects His people to seek and defend it.

The Bible-based arguments for freedom asserted by patriot Americans drew attention to the social institution of slavery that existed at that time in the American colonies. Many colonists, particularly in the south, depended on slaves for crop labor. These slaves, largely African-American, did not have any rights and were often subject to cruel, inhumane treatment and poor living conditions. As calls for freedom from British oppression increased, so did calls by many Americans for an end to the slave trade. The Great Awakening of the 1740s had also facilitated the belief that all men are created free and equal before God and can receive salvation through the Gospel of Christ. The issue of slavery thus became a more frequent topic in political pamphlets and publications in America, particularly in New England and the middle colonies.[556]

An increasing number of Americans asserted that slavery violated God's moral law and human rights. Slaves were often bought and sold as property and considered by others to have no human rights or dignity.

Also, children and descendants of slaves were typically considered slaves as well. Some clergymen and Christians increasingly protested the practice of slavery. Rev. Samuel Cooke of Cambridge, Massachusetts, for example, preached on slavery in 1770, stating that God "is no respecter of persons" and that "we, the patrons of liberty, have dishonored the Christian name, and degraded human nature nearly to a level with the beasts that perish…."[557] Declaration signer and educator Benjamin Rush, alluding to the Puritans, denounces slavery in his 1773 tract, "On Slave Keeping," calling Americans to oppose "a vice which degrades human nature… Remember the eyes of all Europe are fixed upon you, to preserve an asylum for freedom in this country after the last pillars of it are fallen in every other quarter of the globe."[558] Baptist minister Rev. John Allen of Boston, who also strongly opposed slavery, asserts in his 1772 *An Oration on the Beauties of Liberty, or The Essential Rights of the Americans* that slavery violates the Laws of God and Nature and the natural rights of mankind. Allen, citing Isaiah 58:6, exhorts, "Loose the bands of wickedness, undo the heavy burdens, let the oppressed go free." [559] In 1774, Congregationalist preacher Rev. Levi Hart of Connecticut preached a sermon against slavery as ungodly. Citing John 8:36, he beseeches colonists to "bid adieu to the kingdom of darkness, the cause of tyranny and oppression, enlist under the captain of the Lord's host, fight under his banner, you may be sure of victory, and liberty shall be your lasting reward, for whom the Son maketh *free* shall be *free indeed*."[560]

Calls to end slavery arose in response to the revolutionary call for American freedom from British oppression. Richard Wells of Philadelphia asks in 1774 how Americans could "reconcile the exercise of SLAVERY with our *professions of freedom*. … [W]hat arguments can we advance in *their* [slaves'] favor which will not militate against ourselves, whilst England remains superior by land and by sea?" For colonists to disengage in the practice of slavery would "breathe such an independent spirit of liberty, and so corroborate our own claims that I should dare to hope for an intervening arm of Providence to be extended in our favor."[561] Levi Hart posed, "When, o when shall the happy day come, that Americans shall be consistently engaged in the cause of liberty?" Congregationalist theologian Samuel Hopkins of Rhode Island, Hart's mentor and a student of Jonathan Edwards, also raised objections to slavery. To him, the cause of American liberty and the cause against slavery were the same. In 1776, he sent a pamphlet to the Continental Congress asking how they and Americans, so adverse to enslavement by British Parliament, could overlook the slavery of African-Americans "who have as good a claim to liberty as themselves." America's struggle for liberty, he thought, could never be fully realized while slavery continued. He warned of God's judgment and called for repentance.[562]

While the slave trade did not end at this time, such revolutionary and religious ideas promoted pre-revolutionary efforts to abolish the institution as early as 1767. In Massachusetts, in 1771 and 1774, the colony's legislature voted to abolish the slave trade, though the law was vetoed. Also at this time, the Continental Congress pledged to discontinue the slave trade in the colonies. The colonies of Rhode Island and Connecticut declared that slaves imported into these states would become free. Delaware prohibited the importation of slaves. Pennsylvania ended the slave trade by taxation. In 1775, the Quakers formed the first anti-slavery society in the western world. In 1776, Congress voted to prohibit the importation of slaves into the thirteen colonies. Slavery was, says Bernard Bailyn, "subjected to severe pressure as a result of the extension of Revolutionary ideas, and it bore the marks ever after. As long as the institution lasted the burden of proof would lie with its advocates to show why the statement 'all men are created equal' did not mean precisely what it said: *all* men, 'white or black.'"[563]

Slavery was not abolished prior to the American Revolution due to the growing use of slaves on crops and the impending war which occupied the attention of Americans.[564] The social and moral issue of slavery was one that would see and take more time, attention, events, and history. It would reemerge and come to the forefront in the United States with the American Civil War in the mid-1800s.[565] The American quest for freedom and the ideas and principles contained in the Declaration of Independence, however, would lay the ground-work for the later fight for equality and equal rights for all citizens.

6.5 Thomas Paine's *Common Sense*: Popular Sovereignty and God's Opposition to Absolute Rule

Many patriot Americans supported the defense of liberty as a natural right in accordance with the Bible-based principle of popular sovereignty—in which the people possess political power and in which all humans are created equal, given dominion by God, and cannot be ruled over by others without consent. Many refuted the Divine Right of Kings—the absolute or unlimited rule of a monarch or earthly power over their nation. God was to be their Supreme Ruler and King. Their view reflected that of historical Bible-inspired thinkers, both Catholic and Protestant, on right to resistance based on popular sovereignty and civil covenants. It was also reminiscent of that of 1600s secular English author John Milton who, drawing on popular sovereignty and Psalm 149, expresses,

> So that if it is by God that kings now-a-days reign, it is by God too that the people assert their own liberty; since all things are of him, and by him. I'm sure the scripture bears witness to both; that by him kings reign, and that by him they are cast down from their thrones. And yet experience teaches us, that both these things are brought about by the people, oftener than by God. Be this right of kings, therefore, what it will, the right of the people is as much from God as it. And whenever any people, without some visible designation of God himself, appoint a king over them, they have the same right to put him down, that they had to set him up at first. **And certainly it is a more godlike action to depose a tyrant than to set up one**: And there appears much more of God in the people, when they depose an unjust prince, than in a king that oppresses an innocent people. Nay, **the people have a warrant from God to judge wicked princes; for God has conferred this very honour upon those that are dear to him, that celebrating the praises of Christ their own king, 'they shall bind in chains the kings of the nations, (under which appellation all tyrants under the gospel are included) and execute the judgments written upon them that challenge to themselves an exemption from all written laws,' Psalm cxlix.**[566]

Defending liberty, for the Patriots, meant defending God's moral law and mankind's God-given freedom. It was a godly duty. "Freedom was a part of God's moral law," John Adams expresses. "We have a right to it, derived from our Maker."[567]

One of the most influential tracts of the American Revolution was political pamphleteer Thomas Paine's 1776 pamphlet *Common Sense*. This pamphlet did more than support resistance to tyranny. It refuted absolute rule and the Divine Right of Kings in support of popular sovereignty. Paine questioned not only the king's policies but also the legitimacy of the king's rule and power. To do this, he took references from the Bible that were found in Reformed Christian political writings including Ponet's *Short Treatise* and Rutherford's *Lex Rex* and put these ideas fresh into the minds of revolutionary-era Americans. Paine, who came to Philadelphia from England in 1774, argued that the American cause should be one not just of revolution against taxes but of independence. Selling more than 500,000 copies, this pamphlet, more than any other revolutionary writing, paved the way for the Declaration of Independence.

Paine questioned the authority of King George III and absolute rulers on Biblical grounds in favor of representative government like that of the ancient Israelites of Moses.[568] Since all men are equal by creation, Paine argues, the presumptive, nonconsensual rule of one man or governing body over other men is unnatural. Though Paine was a religious skeptic, he argued his point by referring to God's disapproval of Israel's adoption of kings as found in 1 Samuel 8 and as referenced in Reformed Christian writings like *Short Treatise* and *Lex Rex*. Paine argues against monarchy by citing ancient Israel's history and experience under the judges and then under the kings. The Israelite's request in 1 Samuel 8 and Judges 8:22-23 to have a king like other nations, Paine recounts, is contrary to God's desire for His people, for God himself was to be their king as declared by Gideon and the prophet Samuel. Excerpting 1 Samuel 8:6-9, Paine writes of God's disapproval of absolute rulers and powers among men:

The hankering which the Jews had for the idolatrous customs of the Heathens, is something exceedingly unaccountable; but so it was, that laying hold of the misconduct of Samuel's two sons who were entrusted with some secular concerns, they [Jews] came in an abrupt and clamorous manner to Samuel, saying *behold thou art old, and thy sons walk not in thy ways, now make us a king to judge us like all the other nations*. And here we cannot but observe that their motives were bad, viz. that they might be *like* unto other nations, *i. e.* the Heathens, whereas their true glory laid in being as much *unlike* them as possible. *But the thing displeased Samuel when they [the Israelites] said, give us a king to judge us; and Samuel prayed unto the Lord, and the Lord said unto Samuel, Hearken unto the voice of the people in all that they say unto thee, for they have not rejected thee, but they have rejected me, THEN I SHOULD NOT REIGN OVER THEM. According to all the works which they have done since the day that I brought them up out of Egypt, even unto this day; wherewith they have forsaken me and served other Gods; so do they also unto thee. Now therefore hearken unto their voice, howbeit, protest solemnly unto them and show them the manner of the king that shall reign over them, i.e. not of any particular King, but the general manner of the Kings of the Earth whom Israel was so eagerly copying after. ... and ye shall cry out in that day because of your king which ye shall have chosen, AND THE LORD WILL NOT HEAR YOU IN THAT DAY. ... This accounts for the continuation of* Monarchy; neither do the characters of the few good kings which have lived since, either sanctify the title, or blot out the sinfulness of the origin; the high encomium given of David takes no notice of him *officially as a King*, but only as a *Man* after God's own heart.[569]

The reformed writings *Short Treatise* and *Lex Rex* also cite 1 Samuel 8 on this point about God's disapproval of an absolute king or earthy power among men. Ponet's *Short Treatise* tells of how the prophet Samuel speaks against kings "to scare the people, that they should not go about to alter the order and policy that God had ordained: which if they did, they should feel what a plague it were to have a king given in God's fury."[570] Rutherford's *Lex Rex* states that the prophet Samuel, upon the Israelites' request for a king, warns them that in seeking a king to rule over them they would suffer under tyranny. Rutherford writes,

> ...[T]hat he [Samuel] is dissuading them from suiting a king is clear from the text. (1.) Because he saith, Give them their will; but yet protest against their unlawful course. (2.) He biddeth the prophet lay before them the tyranny and oppression of their king; which tyranny Saul exercised in his time, and the story showeth. (3.) Because how ineffectual Samuel's exhortation was is set down, ver. 19, "Nevertheless they would not obey the voice of Samuel, but said, Nay, we will have a king over us." If Samuel had not been dehorting them from a king, how could they be said in this to refuse to hear the voice of Samuel?"[571]

Like the Israelites, Paine suggests, Americans are not destined to be arbitrarily ruled by an earthly absolute ruler, body, or power that might oppress them. God is their king and provider of freedoms. Possibly alluding to Rutherford's *Lex Rex*, Paine expressed,

> But where say some is the King of America? I'll tell you friend, he reigns above; and doth not make havoc of mankind…. Yet that we may not appear to be defective even in earthly honours, let a day be solemnly set a part for proclaiming the Charter; let it be brought forth placed on the Divine Law, the Word of God; let a crown be placed thereon, by which the world may know, that so far as we approve of monarchy, that in America THE LAW IS KING. For as in absolute governments the King is law, so in free countries the law ought to be king; and there ought to be no other.[572]

6.6 God's Preference for Ancient Israel's "Republic" Over Absolute Monarchy

To support the idea of independence, some patriot Americans spoke of departing from the old autocratic, monarchic order of government and of creating a new republican order of government in America. They looked to Israel's ancient nation and history in the Bible to support this position.[573] They pointed out God's apparent preference for what they described as a "republic" for the nation of Israel. Though the nation of Israel in the Bible is a theocracy with God as king, it resembles a republic, they thought, because it has no earthly absolute king and it appoints representatives to govern (though these representatives represent God the king, not the people). Ministers and revolutionaries cited Judges 8, 1 Samuel 8, and 1 Kings 12 in support of a republican form of government as God's preference for His people. These verses reveal Israel's 400-year history of peace and prosperity under the Israelite's original government with judges, God's disapproval of their desire for earthly absolute kings "like the other nations" who ruled not for God but on their own behalf, and Israel's division and suffering under various evil kings. Support for a republic grew following a 1775 sermon given before the Massachusetts legislature by Harvard College president Samuel Langdon.[574] Langdon outlines the qualities of Israel's original form of government before absolute monarchy:

> The Jewish government, according to the original constitution which was divinely established, if considered merely in a civil view, was a perfect Republic. The heads of their tribes, and elders of their cities, were their counselors and judges. They called the people together in more general or particular assemblies, took their opinions, gave advice, and managed the public affairs according to the general voice. Counsellors and judges comprehend all the powers of that government; for there was no such thing as legislative authority belonging to it, their complete code of laws being given immediately from God by the hand of Moses. And let them who cry up *the divine right of Kings* consider, that the only form of government which had a proper claim to a divine establishment was so far from including the idea of a King, that it was a high crime for Israel to ask to be in this respect like other nations; and when they were gratified, it was rather as a just punishment of their folly…than as a divine recommendation of kingly authority.
>
> Every nation, when able and agreed, has a right to set up over themselves any form of government which to them may appear most conducive to their common welfare. The civil Polity of Israel is doubtless an excellent general model, allowing for some peculiarities; at least some principal laws and orders of it may be copied, to great advantage, in more modern establishments.[575]

When the kingdom of Israel becomes divided and disordered under absolute monarchy, notes Langdon, God promises restoration of Israel as found in Isaiah 1:26. He cites Isaiah 1:26 at the beginning of his sermon, which states, "'I [God] will restore your judges as at the first, And your counselors as at the beginning. Afterward you shall be called the city of righteousness, the faithful city.'" Langdon points out to the Massachusetts legislature the potential opportunity in the revolution to create a new republic:

> Who knows but in the midst of all the distresses of the present war to defeat the attempts of arbitrary power, God may in mercy restore to us our judges as at first, and our counselors as at the beginning.
>
> On your wisdom, religion, and public spirit, honored gentlemen, we depend, to determine what may be done as to the important matter of reviving the form of government, and settling all the necessary affairs related to it in the present critical state of things, that we may again have law and justice, and avoid the danger of anarchy and confusion.[576]

Paine's *Common Sense* inspired many Americans with the idea of founding an independent republic. Revolutionary leader and Declaration signer Samuel Adams writes in a 1785 letter to Declaration signer Richard Henry Lee of his belief that God prefers a republic for America: "I firmly believe that the benevolent Creator designed the republican Form of Government for Man."[577] Republicanism was the form of government, many patriot Americans thought, most preferred by God for Biblical Israel and thus for America.

6.7 The Terms of Civil Covenants and the Right of Resistance

To further support resistance to Britain, patriot Americans recognized the terms of civil covenants—in particular, that a breach of the civil covenant by a ruler, due to unjust rule, releases the people from their allegiance to that ruler. They believed that Britain's unlawful policies were grounds for their release from their civil obligations to Britain. In fact, they had a legitimate right to resist Britain in order to set up just rule. Moreover, many Americans, like the early Puritans, believed that God had a special covenant with America as His people, the New Israel. Therefore, God favored and would protect freedoms in America. As discussed earlier, the principle of civil covenants had emerged from the Bible and in Bible-based writings before and during the Reformation.

The terms of civil covenants and the case for resistance in such contexts can actually be found in medieval times, before the Reformation. It arose in 1075-1122 during the Gregorian Reform or papal revolution begun by Pope Gregory VII to free the church from secular political powers and to make itself a self-governing body. In his 1085 *Liber ad Gebehardum*, a letter to Bishop Gebehard of Salzbury, one Alsatian monk Manegold of Lautenbach (1030-1103) argues that Emperor Henry IV could be deposed because he breaks his contract with the people in ruling unjustly. In examining the covenantal relationship between ruler and subjects in the Bible, Manegold articulates the terms of the political pact between ruler and subjects. He also argues that the king may be dismissed or resisted if he does not fulfill his covenantal duties.[578] He presents the *Lex Regia* or royal law as a pact or contract between king and subjects. This pact reflects the Old Testament covenants in Israel between king and people to authorize the king's rule. For the kings of Israel are authorized by the people through covenants. Though these rulers are selected by God, they are appointed by the people through a covenant and do not possess authority until this appointment and covenant are made. In 2 Samuel 5:3, for example, the people of Israel covenant with King David. Though David has already been chosen by God, his authority is not activated until the people appoint and covenant with him. 2 Samuel 5:3 states, "Therefore all the elders of Israel came to the king at Hebron, and King David made a covenant with them at Hebron before the Lord. And they appointed David king over Israel." In such a pact, the people elect their ruler or king by an agreement that validates the ruler's authority. The ruler has a duty to rule justly as indicated in Romans 13:1-5 in which rulers are to do good, not evil. The people have a duty to obey in accordance with 1 Peter 2:13-17 which exhorts Christians to submit themselves to and honor the governing authorities, using their freedom not for vice but for service to God. The power of the ruler, however, is not absolute but restrained by laws. If the king rules unjustly or becomes tyrannical, the people are released from the pact and their duty to obey because the ruler breaches the agreement. Manegold explains this pact between rulers and subjects:

> When he who has been elected for the coercion of the wicked and the defense of the upright has begun to foster evil against them, to destroy the good, and himself to exercise most cruelly against his subjects the tyranny which he ought to repel, is it not clear that he deservedly falls from the dignity entrusted to him and that the people stand free of his lordship and subjection, when he has been evidently the first to break the compact for whose sake he was appointed? … [H]e who attempts not to rule men, but to drive them into confusion, [is] deprived of all the authority and dignity which he has received over men. … It is one thing to reign, another to exercise tyranny in the kingdom. For as faith and reverence ought to be given to emperors and kings for safeguarding the administration of a kingdom, so certainly, for good reason, if they break into the exercise of tyranny, without any breach of faith or loss of piety no fidelity or reverence ought to be paid them …. "King" is not the name of a nature, but of an office, like "bishop," "priest," or "deacon." And when any of these is deposed for good reasons from the office committed to him, he is no longer what he was, nor afterwards is the honor due to the office to be paid to him …. Since no one can make himself emperor or king, for this one thing the people raises someone above itself: that he govern and rule them according to just government, giving to each what he deserves, cherishing the pious, destroying the impious, weighing out justice for all. But if he ever breaks the pact under which he was elected, he will have brought about the disruption and confusion of

the very things he was set up to control [*corrigere*], and by every just and reasonable consideration absolves the people from the duty of subjections, since it was he who first deserted his oath [*cum fidem prior ipse desereurit*] by which they were bound by mutual fidelity.... If he persists, not in governing the kingdom, but under the appearance of governing, practises tyranny, destroys justice, upsets the peace, and deserts his faith, then the taker of the oath [of allegiance] is absolved from the binding force of his oath, and it is free for the people to depose him and to select another.[579]

In his *Liber Contra Wolfelmum*, Manegold further argues that breach of the pact by the king warrants resistance by the people through other legitimate authorities. He bases his arguments on 1 Peter 2:13, 2 Chronicles 22:10-11 and 23:11-15, and 2 Kings 11:17-20 in which the ancient Israelites depose a tyrannical ruler through the recognized authorities of their nation. In 2 Chronicles 22-23, Athaliah, mother of King Ahaziah, unlawfully makes herself queen of Israel when her son dies. She tries to kill the royal line of Judah so that no one else can take the throne. But the godly high priest Johoiada intervenes to restore the legitimate king of Israel. Johoiada hides the rightful successor, infant Joash, who survives. When Joash is 7, Jehoiada covenants with the leaders of Israel—the lower magistrates—to remove Athaliah from the throne and to crown Joash as king. The lower civil officials arrest and execute Athaliah and crown Joash. The people ratify the revolution and authorize their rightful king by covenanting with King Joash.[580]

Historians note that political pacts are derived from covenants. Manegold's idea of political pacts is derived from and close to covenantalism, says Elazar, since "any compacts entered between ruler and ruled were under God, who served at the very least as witness and guarantor."[581] Elazar also asserts that "both compacts and contracts are derived from covenant...."[582] Manegold's covenantal pact supports resistance to tyranny. Manegold bases this position on popular sovereignty or the God-given earthly political power of the people to set up and choose their governments and governors by consent. Manegold also looks to the example of Jesus in the Bible for this principle of resistance to tyranny, stating, "'For he who bade all to obey the powers, chose rather to die than yield to Nero, thus teaching us by his example that when we cannot obey God and the secular power, we should obey God rather than men.'"[583] Manegold asserts the idea that rebellion to tyrants is obedience to God. Manegold's pact in Liber ad Gebehardum, says John Keane, "proposed a view of kingship that was utterly original for its time."[584] Because of his articulation of political pacts or contracts, Manegold is considered by many scholars to be the first social contract theorist.[585]

The idea of covenants or pacts between subjects and rulers was further developed and asserted by political writers of the Reformation era in the 1500s and 1600s in order to justify resistance to tyrannical political authority. "Justification of resistance to an unjust ruler based on the idea of popular sovereignty," explains Olga Babaeva, "became a keystone of the theory of social contract and legitimized the battles of the Protestant Reformation."[586] Some French Huguenot political writers who favored popular sovereignty and a contract between the civil ruler or state and the people included Philippe de Mornay, Hubert Languet, Theodore de Beza, Francois Hotman, and the anonymous writer(s) of Vindiciae, Stephen Brutus. These writers are often referred to as "Monarchomachs" and viewed as early developers of social contract theory. Reformation writers cited and referenced the Bible extensively—using Manegold's verses and many others—to ground the ideas of covenants and resistance to tyranny.

The 1579 Reformation tract Vindiciae Contra Tyrannos identifies two covenants between God, king, and people in a civil state and society as exemplified among the ancient Israelites, God's chosen covenant people, and maintained in the Gospel of the Bible. The first is between God and king/people—that the king and people will be God's people and follow His law. The second is between king and people—that the king will rule justly by God's law for the good of the people and the people will faithfully obey.[587]

In Brutus's first covenant, the king and people take an oath to secure the pure, proper worship of God— that "the king would rule in such a way that he would allow the people to serve God and would keep it to God's

1 law" and that "the people would wish to obey the king in such a way that it should nevertheless defer to God
2 first." In this pact, "the king and the people, like promissory parties, swore to maintain the law of God, and
3 bound themselves with a solemn oath to worship God above all...."[588] The first covenant is derived from 2
4 Kings 11:17 and 2 Chronicles 23:16 in which a covenant is made between God (represented by the high priest
5 Jehoiada), the people, and king Joash to be God's people. 2 Kings 11:17 states, "Then Jehoiada made a
6 covenant between the LORD, the king, and the people, that they should be the LORD's people, and *also* between
7 the king and the people." It is also derived from 2 Kings 23:2-3 in which king Josiah and the people enter into a
8 covenant with God. Other supporting scriptures include Deuteronomy 29, 30, and 31 in which Moses explains
9 the terms of the covenant to the Israelites and orders the agreements or law of God to be kept in the Ark of the
10 Covenant. In Joshua 24:1-15, 25-28, Joshua presents to the people their covenant with God, which the people
11 confirm. When Saul is anointed king, the prophet Samuel acknowledges a covenant of king and people with
12 God in 1 Samuel 12:13-14, 22, 25.[589] In 2 Chronicles 15:12, 13, King Asa, under the direction of the prophet
13 Azariah, summons the whole people to Jerusalem to seal a covenant with God.[590] Both king and people are
14 bound to and responsible for this covenant with God to insure it is upheld among the whole people.[591] The
15 blessings or punishments that come from honoring or breaching this covenant applies to both king and people.
16 If they honor their covenant with God, they will be blessed. If they betray it, as Joshua states in Joshua 24:1-15,
17 25-28, they will be scattered and ruined.[592]   Given this responsibility, the consent of the whole people is
18 required to seal the covenant.[593] Brutus asserts that the covenant practice of the Old Testament Israelites also
19 applies to the New Testament age of the Gospel, though the kingdom is different. While Israelites are bound to
20 uphold the law, Christian rulers and nations are bound to propagate the Gospel. The covenant principle and its
21 conditions are the same.[594]
22
23   In Brutus's second covenant between king and people, the people stipulate and ask whether the king will
24 rule justly according to the law, and the king agrees to do so. The people agree to faithfully obey the king as
25 long as he rules justly. If the king breaches the agreement, the people are absolved from their duty to obey
26 him.[595] The second covenant is derived from Deuteronomy 17 and 1 Samuel 10:25 in which Saul, when he is
27 made king, is presented with God's royal law. In 2 Samuel 5:3 and 1 Chronicles 11:3, David covenants with
28 the elders of Israel, representing the people, and is anointed king. In 2 Chronicles 23:3 and 2 Kings 11:17, Joash
29 is made king by covenant with the people as declared by the priest Jehoiada. Then, in 2 Kings 23:3, King Josiah
30 promises to follow God's law.[596] "In all these places it is said that the covenant is established by the whole
31 people...," says Brutus. "In this way the creation of the king was settled. For the people made the king, not the
32 king the people. So there is no doubt that the people stipulated, and the king promised...."[597]
33
34   The condition of Brutus' covenants is, as identified in the Bible, adherence to just rule and God's law—
35 love of God and neighbor—as stated in the two Great Commandments and implied in the Ten Commandments.
36 It deals with piety and justice. Of the two tables of the Ten Commandments, says Brutus, "the first comprises
37 the worship of God, and the second the duty towards neighbors: the first, I say, piety; and the second, justice
38 united with charity...."[598] The covenants of a nation are judged accordingly. Brutus explains, "In the first
39 [covenant], the king promises to obey God piously; in the second, to command the people justly. In the former,
40 he promises to care for the glory of God; in the latter, for the welfare of the people. In the former the condition
41 is, 'If you observe my law'; in the latter, 'If you render to every individual his right.'" God judges the people
42 for breach of the first covenant while the people serve as judge of their king for breach of the second.[599] In the
43 second, if the king is unjust or tyrannical, the people can resist him. If the king breaches the second covenant
44 and becomes a tyrant, the covenant becomes void, and lower officers or representatives of the people can
45 interpose against the king and suppress his tyranny.[600]
46
47   Rutherford's 1644 *Lex Rex*, like *Vindiciae*, also acknowledges two political covenants in the state
48 between God and nation, and king and people. Breach of the second covenant by the king means the people are
49 no longer under the compact's obligation to obey the king. Rutherford's views are built on covenant or
50 compact theory of government, widely known from the *Vindiciae*. Rutherford presented his views during and

1 influenced the Puritan Revolution in England. *Lex Rex* would influence Locke and his social contract theory
2 and thus the American founding.
3
4   Political theorist Johannes Althusius is credited by some historians as one of the first to articulate the
5 modern social contract for society and government, a comprehensive political philosophy of covenant, in his
6 1603 *Politica Methodice Digesta*, translated as *Politics Arranged Methodically* or *Politics Methodically Set
7 Forth*. Althusius asserts that the people are sovereign in the state and that society was based on consentual
8 agreements. Althusius drew largely from the Bible, reformed covenant theology, and *Vindiciae*. Althusius
9 states that "no realm or commonwealth has ever been founded or instituted except by contract entered into one
10 with another, by covenants agreed upon between subjects and their future prince, and by an established mutual
11 obligation that both should religiously observe."[601] Althusius' covenant-based political theory was a notable
12 step, say some historians, to modern federalism or federal government.[602]

13   Before and during the American Revolution, civil covenants played a part in Bible-based arguments for
14 the American cause of freedom and resistance to Britain. Covenants, patriot revolutionaries and clergy argued,
15 aligned with the American cause because they could only be enacted by a free people and were based on
16 popular sovereignty and consent of the governed.   The relationship between the British Crown and the
17 American colonies had been based on a type of covenant as indicated by the colonial charters.   But the
18 American colonists viewed the British Crown as violating its promise to rule in favor of their rights, protection,
19 preservation, and well-being (though British King George III, of course, thought the colonists were the ones
20 who had seditiously breached covenant). The British government's breach of covenant meant to Americans that
21 it lost its authority in the colonies. Colonists believed they had the right to defend themselves.

22   Many Americans believed that God had a special covenant with America and that America was the New
23 Israel, the land of God's people. This covenant could not be practiced in an environment of tyranny or
24 oppression because it required God's Word to be authoritative and His people to freely and voluntarily commit
25 to its principles. God desired His people to be free and would protect His people's freedom. God's desire for
26 His people's freedom is confirmed in the book of Exodus when God leads the Israelites out of captivity in
27 Egypt. For these reasons, Americans believed that God disliked passive subjection to tyranny among His
28 people. It threatened their covenant with Him. Seeing themselves as God's people, Americans believed they
29 could successfully resist British tyranny because God would favor, aid, and protect them and their liberties.
30 Ministers, particularly in New England, preached on the subject of God's protection of liberty for Americans
31 based on their covenant with God.   For example, Congregationalist minister Rev. Judah Champion of
32 Connecticut, preached, "The most high has gloriously owned the cause of liberty, in New-England, and will
33 continue to own it, unless we so abuse, as to sin away our privileges."[603] Congregational minister Rev. Edward
34 Barnard of Massachusetts preached a 1776 sermon on Psalm 122:1-6 regarding compacts and the defense of
35 liberties. Psalm 122:1-6 states, "Jerusalem is built As a city that is compact together, Where the tribes go up,
36 The tribes of the LORD, To the Testimony of Israel, To give thanks to the name of the LORD. For thrones are
37 set there for judgment, The thrones of the house of David." Barnard asserted that the colonies were similarly
38 compacted together. He believed that Israel's history showed that God "gave them political laws as well as
39 religious institutions whereby their liberty was secured beyond the possibility of reversal by an arbitrary
40 monarch."[604] The Americans saw their covenant with God and with one another as support for their cause of
41 liberty.

42 **6.8 Obedience to God Over Man: Civil Laws Contrary to God's Moral Law Should Not Be Obeyed**
43
44   Another Bible-based argument taken up by patriot Americans to defend their cause was the principle
45 that all humans and human laws are subject to God's moral law—summed up in the two Great Commandments
46 to love God and others. All human laws are measured by God's moral law. As such, tyrannical or unjust civil
47 laws that are contrary to God's higher, universal law should not be obeyed.   This idea was supported by

Reformed thought and writings like Luther's *Secular Authority*, Calvin's *Institutes*, Ponet's *Short Treatise*, and Brutus's *Vindiciae*.   It was also asserted in Bible-based revolutionary writings like Mayhew's sermon, *Discourses Concerning Unlimited Submission*.   Because patriot Americans saw British policies as unjust violations of moral law, they believed they had no obligation to obey them.

Calvin had stated in his *Institutes* that though men are generally to submit to their governors, they are not to obey their governors when their commands are contrary to the commands of God: "The Lord, therefore, is the King of kings; who, when he hath opened his sacred mouth, is to be heard alone, above all, for all, and before all…. If they [man's rulers] command any thing against him [God], it ought not to have the least attention; nor, in this case, ought we to pay any regard to all that dignity attached to magistrates; to which no injury is done when it is subjected to the unrivalled and supreme power of God."[605] Calvin cites Daniel 6:22 as support for religious freedom, in which the prophet Daniel disobeys an impious decree of King Darius to prohibit prayers. Calvin also cites Acts 5:29 and 1 Corinthians 7:23 in support of obedience to God over men and ungodly laws, stating,

> But since this edict has been proclaimed by that celestial herald, Peter, "We ought to obey God rather than men:" [Acts 5:29] let us console ourselves with this thought, that we truly perform the obedience which God requires of us, when we suffer any thing rather than deviate from piety. And that our hearts may not fail us, Paul stimulates us with another consideration; that Christ has redeemed us at the immense price which our redemption cost him, that we may not be submissive to the corrupt desires of men, much less be slaves to their impiety. [1 Cor. 6:23][606]

In fact, civil laws and rulers that uphold the standard of God's moral law, thought the patriots, lead to freedom from oppression for the people. In his *Short Treatise of Political Power*, reformer John Ponet sums up God's moral law as the Two Great Commandments of the Bible—to love God and others—which, by their nature, support freedom over oppression by their nature. Citing Matthew 22:37-40, Matthew 7:12, and John 13:34-35, Ponet states,

> And the wonderful providence of God is herein to be well noted and considered, of all such as love and fear God, that in all places and counties where God's word has been received and embraced, there for the time the people followed God, no tyranny could enter, but all the members of the body sought the prosperity and wealth of one another, for God's word taught them to do this. You shall love the Lord your God (it says) above all things, and your neighbor as yourself [Matthew 22:37-40]. And, what you will have men do unto you, do you also to them [Matthew 7:12]. The fruits of His word is to love one another [John 13:34-35], whatever state or degree in this world they be in. And the state of the policies and commonwealths have been disposed and ordained by God, that the heads could not (if they would) oppress the other members.[607]

The *Vindiciae*, also citing the Bible extensively, supports resistance to tyranny and for civil covenants in government between rulers and the people. The tract, like Ponet's, asserts that rulers and civil governments are bound by and subject to God and His moral law. This universal moral law originates in the Bible and is encompassed in the Two Great Commandments. The *Vindiciae* asserts, as mentioned, "By the law of God, which we are discussing, we understand the two tables of the law handed to Moses, which, like hard and fast limits, ought to circumscribe the authority of all princes. The first comprises the worship of God, and the second duty towards neighbours: the first, I say, piety; and the second, justice united with charity, from which the preaching of the Gospel does not in the least detract, but to which, on the contrary, it lends authority."[608]

All men and rulers, Ponet and Brutus' *Vindiciae* assert, are subject to God's moral law. Rulers—as "ministers of the laws, and not the law itself"—are, Ponet asserts, to be subject to and uphold God's law. Ponet exhorts from Psalm 2:12, "The Holy Ghost said by the mouth of a king and a prophet: 'And now you kings

1   understand, and be learned you that judge the earth. Serve the Lord in fear, and rejoice with trembling. Kiss
2   the Son (that is, receive with honor), lest the Lord become angry, and you lose the way, when His wrath shall in
3   a moment be kindled."[609] Various rulers in the Bible, including disobedient and jealous Saul in 1 Samuel
4   15:10-34 and idolatrous Jeroboam in 1 Kings 14:1-14 are examples of rulers who, in disobeying God's laws and
5   commandments, lost their kingdoms and inheritances. Rulers are also subject to all the human civil laws of
6   their state. They do not have absolute power over their subjects. *Vindiciae* also asserts rulers' subjection to
7   God and His laws: "So kings are the vassals of the King of kings, invested with the sword as a symbol of royal
8   authority, in order that with that sword they should uphold divine law, protect the good and destroy the bad. ...
9   A vassal accepts law and conditions from the superior lord; the king from God, ordering that he should always
10 observe His law and keep it before his eyes. ... In a like manner the king swears to command according to the
11 prescriptions of divine law."[610]
12
13   In addition to opposition against religious coercion, Luther and Ponet assert that human laws contrary to
14 God's moral law should not be made or obeyed by people. Kings and rulers are to rule by divine law. Luther
15 believed the civil government should not be obeyed when it requires one to do wrong. Luther made this point
16 in his Reformation writings based on Acts 5:29, posing, "But when a prince is in the wrong, are his people
17 bound to follow him then too? I answer, No, for it is no one's duty to do wrong; we ought to obey God Who
18 desires the right, rather than men [Acts 5:29].[611] Based on Romans 13:1-5, Acts 4:19-20, and Acts 5:27-29,
19 Ponet notes, civil governors are ordained by God to do good, not evil, and have authority only to make godly
20 laws for the common good. For the Apostle Peter explicitly states than men are to obey God rather than men.
21 Ponet similarly writes,
22
23   Christian men ought well to consider and weigh men's commandments, before they be hasty to do them,
24   to see if they are contrary or repugnant to God's commandments and justice: which if they be, they are
25   evil and cruel, and ought not to be obeyed. ... Saint Paul (the teacher of obedience) teaches that civil
26   power and princes are not ordained to be a terror to those that do well but to those that do evil, and will
27   not the men should do whatever the power? "Do that which is good, and you shall have praise for it:
28   for it is the minister of God ordained for your benefit, not to your destruction. But if you do that which
29   is evil, then fear: for it carries not the sword in vain: for it is the minister of God, an avenger and
30   executioner, to punish him that does evil [Romans 13:1-5, brackets mine]." And therefore it is ordained
31   that evil might be taken away. ... But if the ministers of the civil power command you to dishonor
32   God, to commit idolatry, to kill an innocent, to fight against your country, to give or lend what you have,
33   to the mind of subversion and destruction of your country, or to maintain them in their wickedness, you
34   ought not to do it, but to leave it undone: for it is evil, and God (the Supreme and Highest Power) will
35   not have you do it. The apostles in time of persecution did not only give us an example of what to do
36   when the worldly powers would have them to follow their proceedings, but also left us a lesson to do so.
37   God must be obeyed (they say) rather than men [Acts 4:19-20, 5:27-29]. And this lesson even from the
38   beginning before it was written, was by the Holy Ghost printed in man's heart.[612]
39
40   Ponet notes additional Bible references to support the principle to obey God's law over human law.
41 Throughout the Bible, many Prophets, Apostles, and believers choose not to follow evil laws and orders
42 contrary to God's law but disobeyed them, often unto persecution and/or death. In Exodus 1:15-21, for
43 example, when Pharoah commands the Hebrew midwives to kill all the male Hebrew babies, the midwives,
44 fearing God who commands not to kill, leave the order undone. In 1 Kings 18:4, 13, when evil queen Jezebel
45 orders the prophets of God to be killed to silence their opposition to her idols, the chief officer Obadiah, who
46 fears God, "did clean contrary to her commandment, and hid and preserved a hundred of the prophets in caves."
47 In 1 Samuel 22:11-17, when evil king Saul orders his servants to kill the godly priest Abimelech and his family
48 out of hatred for future king David, the God-fearing servants flatly disobey the king's unlawful order. These
49 laws also included those violating freedom of conscience and belief. In Daniel 3, godly Shadrach, Mesach, and
50 Abednego disobey King Nebechadnezer's order to worship a golden calf. Though they are thrown into a fiery

1 furnace as a result, God protects them. In Daniel 6, the prophet Daniel disobeys King Darius' misguided order
2 to refrain from praying to God. Though Daniel is cast into a lion's den for his disobedience, God protects him.
3 The Apostle Paul also suffers persecution and martyrdom for disobeying orders to refrain from preaching the
4 gospel.[613]
5
6 Ponet believed that a person's duty to obey God over human laws is affirmed by Matthew 6:33 in which
7 the Apostle Matthew exhorts "in all things to seek first the Kingdom of God." To support this point, Ponet—
8 alluding to the teachings of Christ and the Apostle Paul in Matthew 10:38, Matthew 5:10-12, and 2 Timothy
9 3:12—rhetorically asks,
10
11   Why did not the Prophets, the Apostles, and so many thousands of martyrs follow the wicked tyrant's
12   commandments and proceedings, but resisted them, and with their blood testified, that they allowed
13   them not? But all these holy men's doings in confessing and obeying the highest power, God, and not
14   the inferior powers in wicked and evil things, are commended and left by the Holy Ghost to us in Holy
15   Christ to follow and do the same. If men's laws and commandments were a sufficient warrant to men,
16   to do whatever is commanded them: tell me (I pray you) to what purpose is suffering of persecution so
17   often repeated, so earnestly taught, so highly commended in Scripture? Christ says: "He that does not
18   take up his cross and follow me, is not mete for me [Matthew 10:38, brakcets mine]." And again:
19   "Blessed be those that suffer persecution for righteousness sake, for theirs is the kingdom of Heaven.
20   Blessed are you when men shall curse you, and persecute you, and speak all evil against you, living for
21   my sake: be glad and rejoice, for your reward is plentiful in Heaven. So did they persecute the Prophets
22   that were before you [Matthew 5:10-12]." And the Apostle [Paul] says: "All that live godly in Christ
23   Jesus, shall suffer persecution [2 Timothy 3:12]." And so in a great number of places in Scripture.[614]
24
25   Brutus in *Vindiciae*, like Ponet, similarly asserts that all men should obey God over man. Brutus in
26 *Vindiciae* states:
27
28   For if God is in the position of superior lord, and the king in that of vassal, who would not decree that
29   the lord should be obeyed rather than the vassal? If God commands this, and the king the opposite, who
30   would judge that man a rebel who denied obedience to the king against God? Who would not rather
31   condemn a man for rebellion if he were more reluctant to obey God, or were to obey the king in this
32   matter? In short, if the king on the one hand and God on the other were to summon us to do service,
33   who would not decide that the king should be abandoned in order that we might fight for God? So not
34   only are we not obliged to obey a king commanding something contrary to God's law, but also if we
35   should obey we would be rebels [to God]....[615]
36
37 Similarly, Brutus, like Ponet, supports lawful resistance to rulers in defense of God's law by observing
38 examples in the Old and New Testaments. Brutus and Ponet cite similar verses. In the Old Testament, in 1
39 Kings 18:4, Obadiah disobeys King Ahab and Jezebel's order to kill the prophets of God. Instead, Obadiah
40 conceals and feeds the prophets. In 1 Kings 18:17, 40, when king Ahab commands the people to sacrifice to the
41 idol Baal, the prophet Elijah criticizes king and people and calls for the priests of Baal to be killed. Elijah seeks
42 to restore the worship of the true God. In Daniel 3:18, the faithful Shadrach, Meshach, and Abednego
43 disobeyed the order of ungodly King Nebuchadnezzar to worship an idol. In Daniel 6:10, the prophet Daniel
44 disobeys king Darius's misguided order to refrain from prayer to God. Brutus observes in the New Testament,
45 in Acts 4:19, that the Apostles disobeyed an order to refrain from preaching the Gospel.[616] He cites Romans
46 13:1 and 4—"'Let every soul be subject to the higher power, for there is none except God'" and "'The prince is
47 a minister of God for our good in order to do justice.'" Whenever the Apostles instruct Christians to obey the
48 earthly authorities, it is always with an admonishment that God is to be obeyed firstly. Brutus explains, "It
49 might be sufficiently concluded from these words that God is to be obeyed rather than the king. For if the king
50 is to be obeyed on account of God, it certainly cannot be against God."[617] In support of this point, Brutus also

observes Romans 13:7 and Matthew 22:21 which state respectively, "'Render tribute to whom tribute is due, honour to whom honour, and fear to whom fear'" and "Render to Caesar those things which are Caesar's, and to God those things which are God's.'" He also observes 1 Peter 2:17-18: "'Fear God, honour the king. Servants [servi], obey masters [domini], even the irascible ones.'"[618] Brutus notes from these verses the principle to obey God over man, stating, "The tribute and honour are Caesar's, and the fear is God's."[619] Brutus concludes, "These precepts should be observed in the order in which they are stated. Clearly, just as servants are not bound to obey masters if they command anything contrary to the directives of the king, so also subjects are not obliged to obey kings, if they order anything against the law of God."[620]

Ponet points out from the Bible that though people may be tested and killed for obeying God over human regulations, their souls will be saved in eternity. Citing Matthew 10:28, Ponet says, "For the princes (do they the worst they can) can but take from men their goods and lives: but God can take from us both goods and body, and cast both body and soul into hell."[621] Men must trust and commit all ends to God. "We must obey God rather than man, for whose sake if we lose both goods and life, we ought to rejoice, that we be called to serve him, and not doubt, as He is able to recompense it, so will He (according to His promise) reward it."[622] Luther's, Ponet's, and Brutus's points would also support religious liberty.

During the American Revolution, Rev. Jonathan Mayhew asserts in his 1750 influential revolutionary sermon, *Discourses Concerning Unlimited Submission*, this Reformed position that men are to obey God over civil rulers when such rulers command anything contrary to God and His moral law. He asserts that "no civil rulers are to be obeyed when they enjoin things that are inconsistent with the commands of God. All such disobedience is lawful and glorious; particularly if persons refuse to comply with any *legal establishment of religion*, because it is a gross perversion and corruption...."[623]

6.9 Human Law Contrary to God's Law Should Be Actively Resisted

Patriot Americans believed that unjust laws should not only not be obeyed but should be actively resisted—for the benefit of the people and to maintain a just state and government. Unjust or tyrannical rule and laws contrary to God's moral law or civil justice need to be removed. People have a responsibility to defend, protect, and preserve a just civil state and society for the good of mankind. As such, the Patriots asserted active resistance to Britain because of what they saw as unjust rule and policies.

Ponet's *Short Treatise* affirms this point, stating, "To this it may be answered that evil customs (be they never so old) are not to be suffered, but to be utterly abolished: and none may prescribe to do evil, whether king or subject."[624] Civil governors and governments are ordained by God for good, justice, and the prosperity and benefit of the people and state, not for injustice or the state's ruin. Ponet affirms, "For next after God, men be born to love, honor, and maintain their country."[625] Just as the governor is ordained by God to uphold justice and restrain evil, so are governors punished and/or corrected for their vices by the people's representatives. Ponet further explains this responsibility of both rulers and the people and their representatives to check evil and tyranny:

> ...[W]here justice is not executed...there cannot be, but a most corrupt, ungodly, and vicious state, which although it prosper for a season, yet no doubt at length they may be sure, that unto them shall come that came to Sodom, Gomorrah, Jerusalem, and such other, that were utterly destroyed. And on the other side, where the nobility and people look diligently and earnestly upon their authorities, and do see the same executed on their heads and governors, making them to yield account of their doings; than without fail will the princes and governors be as diligent to see the people do their duty. And so shall the commonwealth be godly, and prosper, and God shall be glorified in all. But you will say, that if the nobility, and those that be called to common Councils, and should be the defenders of the people, will not or dare not execute their authority: what is then to be done? The people be not so destitute of

remedy, but God has provided other means, that is to complain to some minister of the word of God, to whom the keys be given to excommunicate not only common people for all notorious and open evils: but also kaisers, kings, princes, and all other governors, when they spoil, rob, undo, and kill their subjects without justice and good laws.[626]

If a tyrannical king or ruling body violates God's moral law, Brutus in *Vindiciae* also asserts, the tyrannical power may be resisted or removed by the people according to that higher law. The people were obliged, in fact, to resist tyrants based on this universal law. He states, "In the first place, natural law [*ius Naturale*] teaches us to preserve and protect our life and liberty—without which life is scarcely life at all—against all force and injustice [*iniuria*]. … So he who disputes whether it is lawful to fight back seems to be fighting nature itself."[627] And "If someone should try to infringe this law [*ius*] by force or deceit, we are all obliged to resist him because he violates the society to which he owes everything, and because he undermines the country to which we are bound by nature, laws, and oath."[628]

Influenced by historical Christian writings like *Short Treatise* and *Vindiciae* and by revolutionary era writings, American patriots saw God's moral laws above human laws according to the Bible. Human laws that violated God's moral law, they argued, are not to be obeyed but actively resisted. These views supported the American cause of liberty.

6.10 Ancient Israel's Resistance to Oppressive Rulers and Division as a Nation

Patriot clergy and revolutionaries also found support for their resistance to Britain and for independence from ancient Israel's resistance to oppressive rulers and division as a nation. Israel's national division in the Bible takes place during the reign of Kings Jeroboam and Rehoboam, as found in 1 Kings 12 and 2 Chronicles 13.

In 1 Kings 12, King Solomon's son and successor, Rehoboam, is named king of Israel. But Rehoboam rejects his elders' advice, refuses to listen to the people, and imposes oppressive policies and harsh taxes on the people. As a result, the ten northern tribes of Israel revolt and name Jeroboam their king. Rehoboam's southern kingdom consists of the one or two tribes in Judah. 1 Kings 11 reveals an earlier prophecy to Jeroboam of this event and how God will give Jeroboam the northern kingdom but never the southern one. In 1 Kings 11:30-37, Jeroboam is told by God through the prophet Ahijah that Jeroboam will be the new king of the northern tribes of Israel. However, God will let Solomon's son, Rehoboam, rule the tribes of Judah in the south:

> "…[T]hus says the LORD, the God of Israel: 'Behold, I will tear the kingdom out of the hand of Solomon and will give ten tribes to you [Jeroboam] (but he [Solomon's son Rehoboam] shall have one tribe for the sake of My servant David, and for the sake of Jerusalem, the city which I have chosen out of all the tribes of Israel), because they [Judah] in the south have forsaken Me, and worshiped [false gods]…, and have not walked in My ways to do *what is* right in My eyes and *keep* My statutes and My judgments, as *did* his father David. However I will not take the whole kingdom out of his hand…. And to his [Solomon's] son I will give one tribe, that My servant David may always have a lamp before Me in Jerusalem, the city which I have chosen for Myself, to put My name there. So I will take you, and you shall reign over all your heart desires, and you shall be king over Israel."

As predicted, Jeroboam is placed over the northern tribes of Israel, and Rehoboam flees to Jerusalem and sets up the smaller southern kingdom of Judah. However, Jeroboam becomes idolatrous and leads the people into idolatrous practices. Later, as revealed in 2 Chronicles 13, Jeroboam goes to war against the succeeding king of Judah, Abijah. 2 Chronicles 13:12 tells how King Abijah warns Jeroboam that an attack on the smaller Judah will not succeed against God's will. 2 Chronicles 13:12,18 provides his warning and the outcome:

"Now look, God Himself is with us [Judah] as *our* head, and His priests with sounding trumpets to sound the alarm against you [Jereboam's Israel]. O children of Israel, do not fight against the Lord God of your fathers, for you shall not prosper!' … Thus the children of Israel were subdued at that time; and the children of Judah prevailed, because they relied on the Lord God of their fathers."

Though Jeroboam's northern army is larger than Judah's, it is unsuccessful and takes many losses due to God's protection of Judah.

Some influential historical reformed Christian political writings, including Ponet's *Short Treatise* and Rutherford's *Lex Rex*, cite the divided kingdoms of Israel under kings Jeroboam and Rehoboam to support resistance to tyranny. These writings influenced American political thought. *Short Treatise* cites the two kings Jeroboam and Rehoboam as examples of rulers who are punished by God for their tyranny and/or idolatry: Ponet writes,

Rehoboam, because he would reign as a tyrant and not be subject to law or counsel, had ten tribes of his kingdom taken away from him, and given to Jeroboam: who also did not content himself to be subject to God's written word and law, but fell to his own idolatrous inventions, and caused his subjects to follow his proceedings: was stripped completely from the inheritance of his crown, that his seed was utterly rooted out.[629]

In *Lex Rex*, Rutherford also references the Biblical accounts of Jeroboam and Rehoboam and their sins, writing that Jeroboam in his idolatry "made Israel to sin" and that Rehoboam loses the ten tribes of Israel "due to oppression."[630]

Patriot Americans similarly drew from Israel's history of divided kingdoms, citing lessons of both kings in order to support their cause of freedom. They found in both sides of Israel's conflict justification for their revolution and independence. They identified, for one, with the revolt of the northern tribes against Rehoboam and his harsh taxes. They likewise sought revolution against the British government and its oppressive policies. They also feared religious oppression, whether it was a real threat or not. They believed that their cause was similarly justified.[631] Yet Americans also identified with the undefeated southern tribes of Judah. Like Judah with its smaller but victorious army due to God's protection, Americans called for trust in God for victory against the stronger British forces. Rev. William Emerson, in a sermon on 2 Chronicles 13:12, for example, addresses Israel's divided kingdom and the right of rebellion as it related to America's cause.[632] He discusses the right of the Americans, like the Israelites, to revolt against oppressive laws. He also discusses the warning of King Jeroboam's defeat for attacking Judah, relating these events to Britain's King George III and the American colonies respectively. "Through his oppressive policies and disregard for the people, Rehoboam illustrated the evils of tyranny and the right of the northern tribes to revolt," explains Harry Stout. "By introducing false gods in the north and engaging in an unsuccessful war with Judah (unsuccessful because he made war over the prohibitions of God's prophets), Jeroboam illustrated how a king with superior armies could not defeat his countrymen to the south because God would not allow it."[633] America's stand against Britain also stirred metaphors of David defeating the giant Goliath in 1 Samuel 17. These Biblical precedents, say historians, helped to justify the American cause of liberty and prepared Americans for war.[634]

6.11 The Lawfulness of Defensive War

Many American patriots, citing the Bible extensively, believed that defensive war is just and lawful before God. They argued that the American Revolution was approved by God to defend their God-given liberties and rights. Patriot clergy often cited the Bible for examples and explanations to support defensive war and the preservation of their freedoms and rights.

1   Early American minister Rev. David Jones of Pennsylvania, in his 1775 sermon *Defensive War in A Just*
2 *Cause Sinless*, for example, asserts that the oppressed have a duty to defend their liberties based on the Old
3 Testament. Jones compares a number of defensive wars of the Old Testament with the American Revolution—
4 Abram rescuing Lot from the four kings in Genesis 14, Moses defending Israel against the Amorites in
5 Numbers 21:21-25, Joshua and the Israelites in the Promised Land, the Judges who deliver Israel from
6 oppression and bondage, David defeating Goliath, the Jews defending their wall against enemies in Nehemiah
7 4, and others. Jones cites, for example, Genesis 14 in which Abram, later called Abraham, arms himself and his
8 servants to rescue his nephew Lot who has been taken captive by four kings. The godly Melchizedeck, a high
9 priest of God and Christ figure in the Old Testament, even praises Abraham's battle success, saying in Genesis
10 14:19-20, "'Blessed be Abram of God Most High, Possessor or heaven and earth; And blessed be God Most
11 High, Who has delivered your enemies into your hand.'" "This passage," says Jones, "proves not only that this
12 [support for defensive war] was Abram's belief, but also that Melchizedeck, priest of the most high God,
13 Melchizedeck, the brightest type of Christ, was fully of the same opinion, and therefore may be admitted as
14 evidence in favour of a defensive war."[635] Jones concludes from these examples "that in some cases, when a
15 people are oppressed, insulted, and abused, and can have no other redress, it then becomes our duty as men,
16 with our eyes to God, to fight for our liberties and properties; or in other words, that a defensive war is sinless
17 before God; consequently to engage therein, is consistent with the purest religion."[636]

19   In his 1775 sermon, *A Self-Defensive War Lawful*, Presbyterian pastor Rev. John Carmichael of
20 Pennsylvania also believed resistance was justified under certain unavoidable circumstances. Carmichael
21 reasons that when, in the New Testament, Jesus tells His followers to "turn the other cheek," it is a proverbial
22 expression. It means that "we should be ready to put up with a good deal of ill-usage, before we would create
23 disturbance, yea that we should do anything consistent with our own safety." When Jesus teaches us to "love
24 your enemies," says Carmichael, he "can't possibly [have] meant that we should love them better than
25 ourselves—that we should put it in the enemy's power to kill us, when we have it in our power to save our own
26 life, by killing the enemy." Jesus does not intend, he explains, "to forbid us to use lawful and proper means of
27 self-preservation." In the case of the American Revolution, says Carmichael, Americans had born Britain's
28 abuses patiently, but now they had to defend their way of life.[637]

6.12: Conclusion: The Bible as Central to American Thought and Debate

32   Americans of the revolutionary era were a largely religious people who regarded the Bible and its
33 principles and values as central to their society and culture. Their strong adherence to the Bible and its
34 principles would be the cause of great debate, argument, exploration, and study prior to the American
35 Revolution. The Americans held strong opinions about revolution against Britain—which they argued for or
36 against based on their interpretations of the Bible. Loyalist Americans opposed resistance to Britain based on
37 the Bible's instruction of submission to civil authority. But other Americans, patriots or Whigs, supported
38 revolution and independence from Britain based on the Bible's *specific* instruction to submit to *moral* or *good*
39 civil authority. They believed the Bible supported resistance to immoral or unjust governments and laws that
40 did not fulfill the moral purpose for which God had ordained civil authority. The patriots also supported their
41 position with a number of other historical and contemporary Bible-based assertions for resistance to tyranny.
42 Their arguments pertained to God's desire for His people's freedom, popular sovereignty, God's opposition to
43 absolute rule by humans, civil covenants, obedience to God's moral law over human law, ancient Israel's
44 resistance to oppressive rulers, and the lawfulness of defensive war. Subsequently, the phrase "Rebellion to
45 Tyrants is Obedience to God" became a motto of the American Revolution. As a result, many Americans
46 favored the forming of an American military. In a sermon on 2 Chronicles 13:12, Rev. William Emerson,
47 chaplain in the Revolutionary Army preached, "…[O]ur Military Preparation here for our own Defense is not
48 only excusable but justified in the Eyes of the impartial World: nay, for should we neglect to defend ourselves
49 by military Preparation, we never could answer it to God and to our own Consciences or the rising
50 [generations]."[638] The fierce debate among Americans over resistance to Britain revealed the strong influence

1   of the Bible on American political thought and action during the Revolutionary era and on Americans' founding

2   of a new nation.

3

Review: Checking Out the History

Discuss questions in subgroups or whole group. As an option, the group may come up with main ideas or insights from each question. Responses may be shared and discussed in the whole group.

1. What Bible-based issue(s) did many Christian and other Americans fiercely debate regarding political revolution? Explain the differing viewpoints/interpretations.

2. What Bible-based arguments did patriot revolutionary Americans and influential historical thinkers and writings use to support and justify resistance to tyranny and revolution?

3. Why did the institution of slavery become an increasingly common topic of discussion prior to the American Revolution?

4. What Bible-based principles or justifications in support of revolution are presented in Thomas Paine's *Common Sense*? Why was this pamphlet so revolutionary?

5. How did Americans' identification with the Israelites affect their views of revolution? Provide relevant events/passages from the Bible.

6. What did the debate on revolution suggest about the influence or role of the Bible in American life, government, politics, and culture during the Founding era?

7. What basic Bible-based or Judeo-Christian principles are evident and important in this part of America's heritage?

1 **<u>Activity: Bible-Based Justification For Revolution</u>**
2 In your own words, explain/describe the following Biblical principles or arguments used by many patriot
3 Americans to justify and support the revolution. Provide the relevant scripture verse(s) for each argument.
4
5

Bible-Based Principle or Argument	Explain this Principle or Argument and How It Was Used to Support or Justify Revolution	Key Bible Verse(s) or Passage(s) if applicable
Submission to authority and the Biblical concept of government		
Justness of a war or cause		
Freedom over slavery		
God as King: No earthly absolute power		
Obedience to God and God's law over man and human law		
Right to resist tyranny according to the Law of Nature and God		
Civil Covenants and Social Contracts		

6
7

Call to Action

Each person will reflect on and write his/her responses to the questions below. Responses may then be shared and discussed in the group.

1. What new understanding do you have about the influence of the Bible on American political thought of the revolutionary era and on the American Revolution?

_____

_____

_____

_____

2. Do you think Americans today assign the same level of value, importance, and accountability to the Bible in society as revolutionary-era Americans did? Why or why not? What, if anything, has changed?

_____

_____

_____

_____

3. Do you personally assign a level of value, importance, and accountability to the Bible in your own life and actions? Why or why not?

_____

_____

_____

_____

4. Do you think it is important for citizens to adhere to and stand up for certain Bible-based and/or moral principles and standards in their lives and in society? What are the benefits for having such a measure of accountability? The consequences for not having such a measure of accountability?

_____

_____

_____

_____

5. What do you/could you do to help support and promote Bible-based and/or moral principles and accountability in your own life as well as in your community, state, and nation?

_____

_____

_____

_____

Chapter 7
The Rationale of America's Revolution

7.1 The American Quest for Self-Government, Lack of a National Model, and New Justification for Liberty

The American quest for self-government, practically unknown in history, challenged and questioned an existing authoritarian government model known for centuries throughout the world. Americans wanted to create their own laws, not have Britain impose laws on them.

The American position that favored complete self-governance was highly controversial and questioned by some. Anglican loyalist Samuel Seabury, for example, like other loyalists, saw this position as a threat to law and order, responding that "'The position that we are bound by no laws to which we have not consented either by ourselves, or our representatives, is a novel position, unsupported by any authoritative record of the British constitution, ancient or modern. It is republican in its very nature, and tends to the utter subversion of the English monarchy.'"[639] To Seabury and others, such a position would only lead to chaos and anarchy, for if one person "has a right to disregard the laws of the society to which he belongs, all have the same right; and then government is at an end."[640]

While Seabury's argument was valid, the American colonies had proved self-government was possible. In unprecedented circumstances, they had governed themselves by their colonial assemblies for generations without falling into disorder and anarchy. Since British law and rule did not validate the American experience, colonists were compelled to look for justification of their freedoms and sovereignty elsewhere, outside of British law and known governmental practice. "If England insisted that New England's conception of liberty and sovereignty was wrong," reflects Stout of their thinking, "then the British constitution…would have to be removed." In this predicament, the Americans, true to character, were heading into uncharted territory. They, says Stout, "found themselves propelled down paths none had dared travel before to a destination none could clearly perceive."[641] Yet they were sure of their means to get there. They believed that men possessed the right to choose their form of government and governors. Constitution signer and future U. S. Secretary of Treasury Alexander Hamilton's later expression during the ratification of the U. S. Constitution about choice in government likely reflected the thoughts of Americans of the revolution. Hamilton writes in Federalist Paper 1, "…[I]t seems to have been reserved to the people of this country, by their conduct and example, to decide the important question, whether societies of men are really capable or not of establishing good government from reflection and choice, or whether they are forever destined to depend for their political constitutions on accident and force."[642]

Ultimately, the Americans would look to a higher source—God and the Bible—and a higher law—the Law of Nature and Nature's God—for the basis of their freedoms, rights, and nation. They would appeal to sacred scriptural revelation, reason, and nature. While the Americans' Declaration of Independence of 1776 may have been influenced by Enlightenment rationalist thinking in some ways, it contained concepts that Americans understood largely from Bible-based or Judeo-Christian ideas and perspectives. Such concepts included God as Creator and Supreme Judge of the world, the universal Law of Nature and Nature's God, mankind's moral sense, God-given unalienable rights, the social contract as derived from covenants, and God as Divine Providence. A Judeo-Christian ethic and worldview of God and mankind shaped the American rationale and justification for self-government and human rights. "Without this metaphysical background," observes Michael Novak, "the founding generation of Americans would have had little heart for the War of Independence. They would have had no ground for believing that their seemingly unlawful rebellion actually fulfilled the will of God—and suited the laws of nature and nature's God."[643] This Bible-based worldview and faith provided the moral support and courage to Americans for carrying out the American Revolution. Perry Miller expressed, "A pure rationalism such as his [Thomas Jefferson's] might have declared the independence

1 of these folk [Americans], but it could never have inspired them to fight for it."[644] The Judeo-Christian ethic
2 provided moral justification as well as exceptional moral strength, courage, and nobility to the American
3 colonists to defend their cause of liberty and independence when all odds were against them.
4
5 Congress appointed a committee to draft the Declaration of Independence. It included John Adams of
6 Massachusetts, Benjamin Franklin of Pennsylvania, Robert Livingston of New York, Roger Sherman of
7 Connecticut, and Thomas Jefferson of Virginia.   Jefferson, the primary writer of the Declaration, held
8 unorthodox beliefs as a "theistic rationalist," as Gregg Frazer calls him—a rationalist who believed in a Creator
9 God involved in human affairs and appreciated the morality of the Bible.   Though Jefferson was not an
10 orthodox Christian, he presented principles and ideas in the Declaration to appeal to and to reflect the thinking
11 of Americans at large, many of whom were orthodox Christians and church-goers.[645] Jefferson, in fact, states
12 that the Declaration is a reflection of the ideas of the whole American people and of various sources influential
13 at the time:
14
15   Neither aiming at originality of principle or sentiment, nor yet copied from any particular and previous
16   writing, it [the Declaration] was intended to be an expression of the American mind.... All its authority
17   rests then on the harmonizing sentiments of the day, whether expressed in conversation, in letters,
18   printed essays, or in the elementary books of public right, as Aristotle, Cicero, Locke, Sidney, etc.[646]
19
20 Jefferson expressed ideas in the Declaration that Americans understood and upon which most Americans
21 agreed. Indeed, when it came to laying the philosophical principles upon which to found their civil society,
22 even the theistic rationalist's belief in a Creator God and concern for a moral society meshed quite well with the
23 Biblical values of most Americans. Also, many of the secular writers that Jefferson drew from were themselves
24 influenced to some degree by the Bible and/or Bible-based thinkers. What is more, the philosophical concepts
25 and language conveyed in the Declaration were read by the majority of the people from a Biblical or Judeo-
26 Christian worldview. For these reasons, it is important to recognize how the concepts in the Declaration were
27 understood by many or most Americans and how these ideas reflected the identity, beliefs, principles, and
28 values of a largely religious people.[647]
29
30 **7.2 The Creator God: The Basis of Authority, Law, and Rights for Mankind**
31
32 The Declaration notably acknowledges a Creator of mankind. It draws from a Bible-based or Judeo-
33 Christian worldview and concept of God, just as early Americans had always done. Most of the Founders,
34 whether or not they held orthdox Christian beliefs, acknowledged such a Creator God. Their view of a Creator
35 God of mankind is essential to understanding their perspective on the law, rights, and value assigned to human
36 beings.
37
38 Declaration and Constitution signer, legal professor, and Supreme Court Justice James Wilson, for
39 example, explains in his 1790-1791 *Lectures on Law* how the Creator God is the basis for all authority and law.
40 He cites Swiss legal and political theorist Jean-Jacques Burlamaqui's 1748 *Principles of Natural Law* on the
41 point. Influenced by the Scottish Enlightenment, Burlamaqui was often quoted in political sermons of the
42 founding era in America. His *Principles* was often used as a textbook. Wilson paraphrases Burlamaqui and his
43 allusion to Acts 17:28:
44
45   "Properly speaking, there is only one general source of superiority and obligation. God is our creator:
46   in him we live, and move, and have our being [Acts 17:28]: from him we have received our intellectual
47   and our moral powers: he, as master of his own work, can prescribe to it whatever rules to him shall
48   seem meet. Hence our dependence on our Creator: hence his absolute power over us. This is the true
49   source of all authority [Burl. 83. 87]."[648]

Wilson affirms this idea that the Creator of mankind is the ultimate ruler over and law-maker of mankind. Humans have an obligation to this Creator and His laws which are made to preserve moral order, and their own man-made laws should necessarily reflect the Creator's for the same purpose. Wilson writes that Burlamaqui's idea "contains a solemn truth, which ought to be examined with reverence and awe. It resolves the supreme right of prescribing laws for our conduct, and our indispensable duty of obeying those laws, into the omnipotence of the Divinity."[649] Wilson also states, "That our Creator has a supreme right to prescribe a law for our conduct, and that we are under the most perfect obligation to obey that law, are truths established on the clearest and most solid principles."[650]

James Madison—primary drafter of the Constitution, author of the Bill of Rights, and fourth U. S. president—also acknowledged the importance of the principle of a Creator God as essential to the order and benefit of mankind. He observes, "…[T]he belief in a God All Powerful wise & good, is so essential to the moral order of the World & to the happiness of man, that arguments which enforce it cannot be drawn from too many sources nor adapted with too much solicitude to the different characters & capacities to be impressed with it."[651]

In acknowledging the Creator God, the Declaration also upheld the value and rights of the individual human being. According to the Bible, the individual possessed intrinsic value. The individual has value in being created by and for God, made in God's image and likeness, and possessing an immortal soul as indicated in Genesis 1 and 2. In addition, humans are able to receive spiritual salvation and have a relationship with God as indicated in the New Testament. The individual's value in the eyes of God became the basis for man's dignity and natural rights.[652] Expressing the individual's value as God's creation, Russell Kirk states, "Every person has a soul, a distinct essence. That soul is precious to God. Though all sinners, still all of us are the children of God, and able to experience His love, if we do not turn our faces away from Him."[653] Man's value as God's creation, he affirms, is the source of man's dignity and rights. He elaborates,

> This creature called man, who contains a spark of immortal life that is his personality, possesses dignity. That dignity is conferred upon him by God; and without God, there can be no human dignity. By 'the dignity of man,' Christians mean that every living person is entitled to be treated as a son of God, with respect for his personality. No matter how debauched or hideous or stupid a man may seem, he is entitled to certain rights and privileges…because he *is* a man…. …[I]f we treat them [men] with indignity, in some sense we are insulting God. … From this concept of the dignity of man—a dignity that exists only through our relationship with God—there has grown up a recognition of what are called 'natural rights.' These are the rights that all men and women are entitled to: rights that belong to them simply because they participate in human dignity.[654]

7.3 The Law of Nature: The Universal Moral Law of Mankind

While the early Puritans and Awakeners acknowledged the Law of Nature and the Law of God, they generally relied on the British constitution and their colonial charters for the protection of their rights in the American colonies. Such British laws and constitution sufficed for their needs. Likewise in the mid-1700s, the American colonists again relied on the British constitution and their charters to defend their rights when King George III and British parliament began to impose more interfering, oppressive policies in the American colonies. But when the British Crown and government rejected the colonists' petition for certain rights and freedoms and announced that the colonies were in rebellion and must be controlled by force, the colonists could no longer defend themselves by British law. So instead, the Americans appealed to God and His higher law. They came to justify their rights and freedoms no longer by the British constitution or any other human law but solely by a higher law based on the Bible, human nature, common sense, and reason. As such, they shifted their focus from human law to natural and divine law. The early Americans appealed to these higher laws, which they called "the Law of Nature and Nature's God," in the Declaration of Independence. It was their last hope in defense of their God-given freedoms.

The Americans, like various thinkers in Europe, recognized a general Law of Nature in the world that applied to all humans, a law which had been recognized for centuries. The Law of Nature, or Natural law, is understood as an eternal, unchangeable, universal moral law given by God to all mankind as created in His image, to which all people and nations are subject at all times. This law is naturally revealed in a person's right reason and conscience or moral sense. It is considered a general, rational version of God's moral law revealed in the Bible. The Law of Nature, like God's Law, cannot be repealed, abolished, or altered by any man or earthly power. It simply exists as the will of God. To deny it is sinful and unjust. The aim of Natural Law is the morality and preservation of mankind and the fulfillment of God's purposes. Originating from the Creator God, this law rules over mankind before any human laws or civil states existed. It is superior to all man-made laws. It sets down standards of right and wrong, ethical truths, norms, and rules of governance in society. As such, just man-made laws reflect this higher law. As applied to political societies, it is sometimes referred to as the Law of Nations. This law would become a moral foundation and a source of natural, unalienable rights for all people.[655]

Some historical thinkers who directly or indirectly influenced the American Founders on Natural Law included Cicero in ancient classical times, the medieval schoolmen like Augustine and Aquinas, and the modern-era Edward Coke, William Blackstone, Samuel Pufendorf, Richard Hooker, Thomas Reid, and John Locke.

The earliest use of the Law of Nature purportedly came from ancient Roman philosopher Marcus Tullius Cicero (106-43 BC) in his 54-51 BC *The Republic* as reported in 3 A. D. by Lucius Lactantius, the Christian Roman author and advisor to first Christian Roman Emperor Constantine I. Cicero was the first to articulate a universal, eternal moral law of God that ruled over all men. He defined this moral law as man's "right reason" from God. Various thinkers through history as well as the founding-era Americans adopted Cicero's idea of God's universal moral law as "right reason." Cicero states,

> There is a true law, a right reason, conformable to nature, universal, unchangeable, eternal, whose commands urge us to duty, and whose prohibitions restrain us from evil. Whether it enjoins or forbids, the good respect its injunctions, and the wicked treat them with indifference. This law cannot be contradicted by any other law, and is not liable either to derogation or abrogation. Neither the senate nor the people can give us any dispensation for not obeying this universal law of justice. It needs no other expositor and interpreter than our own conscience. It is not one thing at Rome and another at Athens; one thing to-day and another to-morrow; but in all times and nations this universal law must for ever reign, eternal and imperishable. It is the sovereign master and emperor of all beings. God himself is its author, --its promulgator, --its enforcer. He who obeys it not, flies from himself, and does violence to the very nature of man. For his crime he must endure the severest penalties hereafter, even if he avoid the usual misfortunes of the present life.[656]

Philo Judaeus, a first-century Hellenistic Jew from Alexandria, Egypt, was the first to use the term "Law of Nature" to describe God's universal moral law. Philo mixed Hebrew thought with Greek terms to develop "Law of Nature." The concept of "Law of Nature" emerged, then, just before the first century or during the time of the Gospel and New Testament. It became part of Western Christian tradition.[657]

Various thinkers and reformers through history wrote on the Law of Nature from a Bible-based or pro-God worldview. These thinkers would, in part, influence Americans in their understanding of the Law of Nature as it appears in the Declaration. These philosophers included, among others, Edward Coke, Samuel Pufendorf, and William Blackstone.

British Chief Justice and legal scholar Sir Edward Coke greatly influenced British law and the British constitution as well as legal education in America. Coke upheld the British common law of the 1600s as the supreme law in British courts and Parliament. Coke's view of authoritative common law was based on and supported Natural Law. In his influential eleven volumes of *Law Reports* of the early 1600s, he laid out principles of English law through commentaries on court decisions. In 1628-1644, Coke wrote his four volumes of *Institutes of the Lawes of England*, a foundational text of British common law. American Founders and leaders John Adams, John Quincy Adams, Thomas Jefferson, John Jay, Patrick Henry, Daniel Webster, and others read Coke. For example, Jefferson writes to Madison, "You will recollect, that before the Revolution, Coke Littleton [the first volume of Coke's *Institutes*] was the universal elementary book of law students, and a sounder whig never wrote, nor of profounder learning in the orthodox doctrines of the British constitution, or in what were called English liberties."[658] Constitution signer John Rutledge of South Carolina thought Coke's *Institutes* seemed "to be almost the foundation of our law."[659] Coke's *Institutes* was, says Sandoz, a "reigning textbook for America's lawyers."[660] Coke's *Institutes* and *Reports* were, Sandoz also says, "the cornerstone and much of the legal edifice of legal education in eighteenth-century America."[661] With Coke's *Institutes*, Sandoz points out, "came a sturdy and intricate historical jurisprudence to augment the jurisprudence of divine and Stoic natural law that played such a key role in cogently justifying [Americans'] departure from the realm of England."[662]

Baron Samuel von Pufendorf was a German jurist, professor, and historian known for his defense of the Law of Nature and his *Of the Law of Nature and Nations*. Son of a Lutheran pastor, Pufenforf attended Leipzig University, a Lutheran school. In 1672, he published his major work *Of The Law of Nature and Nations* and an excerpt from it in 1698 entitled *The Whole Duty of Man According to the Law of Nature*. In these works, Pufendorf based the Law of Nature and human laws on a Bible-based worldview. He was instrumental to making the Law of Nature an internationally recognized Law of Nations, the basis of international law. The "Law of Nations" would be recognized in Section 1, Article 8 of the United States Constitution. He also formed a just war theory. Philosopher John Locke recommended Pufendorf's works for legal education and as reading for young people. Pufendorf influenced Blackstone, Montesquieu, and Scottish Enlightenment thought. He would become influential to American Founders like Thomas Jefferson, James Madison, and Alexander Hamilton.

William Blackstone was a British lawyer, judge, and member of parliament who wrote the influential *Commentaries on the Laws of England*, published between 1765 and 1769, the best known description of the doctrines of English law, much of which drew from the canon law of the Catholic church.[663] Blackstone's *Commentaries* became the basis of legal education in America and England and was widely studied in the American colonies. His *Commentaries* were based on his university lectures on English common law at Oxford, the first lectures on common law ever delivered in a university. One of his goals in teaching common law, as he stated in a notice of his lectures in 1753, was to "compare them with the Laws of Nature and of other Nations."[664] Blackstone acknowledged the Law of Nature in the beginning of his *Commentaries*, which, says Kirk, "confirmed Americans in their appeal to a justice beyond parliamentary statute, not altogether to Blackstone's relish." One of the most frequently cited secular thinkers of the American founding era, Blackstone affirmed for Americans the Law of Nature as the highest law. Blackstone's idea of the Law of Nature reflected the ideas of Cicero and the medieval Christian scholastics or Schoolmen like Thomas Aquinas and Francisco Suarez, Jean-Jacques Burlamaqui, Richard Hooker, and Samuel von Pufendorf.[665]

The American Founders who wrote and signed the Declaration also largely understood and affirmed the Law of Nature as presented by British lawyer William Blackstone. Blackstone defined Natural Law in Judeo-Christian terms as the law and will of the Creator God and the moral law of right and wrong to which all men are accountable. In his *Commentaries on the Laws of England*, which sold as many copies in America as in England, he explains this higher law:

Man, considered as a creature, must necessarily be subject to the laws of his creator, for he is entirely a dependent being. ... And consequently, as man depends absolutely upon his maker for every thing, it is necessary that he should in all points conform to his maker's will.

This will of his maker is called the law of nature. For as God, when he created matter, and endued it with a principle of mobility, established certain rules for the perpetual direction of the motion; so, when he created man, and endued him with freewill to conduct himself in all parts of life, he laid down certain immutable laws of human nature, whereby that freewill is in some degree regulated and restrained, and gave him also the faculty of reason to discover the purport of those laws. ...

But as he [God] is also a being of infinite *wisdom*, he has laid down only such laws as were founded in those relations of justice.... These are the eternal, immutable laws of good and evil, to which the creator himself in all his dispensations conforms; and which he has enabled human reason to discover, so far as they are necessary for the conduct of human actions. Such among others are these principles: that we should live honestly, should hurt nobody, and should render to every one his due....

But if the discover of these first principles of the law of nature depended only upon the due exertion of right reason...the world would have rested content in mental indolence, and ignorance it's inseparable companion. As therefore the creator is a being, not only of infinite *power*, and *wisdom*, but also of infinite *goodness*, he has been pleased so to contrive the constitution and frame of humanity, that we should want no other prompter to inquire after and pursue the rule of right, but only our own self-love, that universal principle of action. For he has so intimately connected, so inseparably interwoven the laws of eternal justice with the happiness of each individual, that the latter cannot be attained but by observing the former. ...

This law of nature, being coeval with mankind and dictated by God himself, is of course superior in obligation to any other. It is binding over all the globe in all countries, at all times; no human laws are of any validity if contrary to this: and such of them as are valid derive all their force, and all their authority, mediately or immediately, from this original.[666]

Enlightenment philosopher John Locke confirms in his important 1689 *Second Treatise of Government*, influential to early Americans, the Law of Nature as found in and validated by man's reason: "The state of Nature has a law of Nature to govern it, which obliges every one, and reason, which is that law, teaches all mankind who will but consult it, that being all equal and independent, no one ought to harm another in his life, health, liberty, or possessions...."[667]

The early Americans based their unalienable rights, liberty, and national independence on the Law of Nature. This universal moral law plays a significant role in the Judeo-Christian influence on the American founding. For many of the Founders, like the philosophers they read, recognized and validated this law as appearing in the Bible. They also understood this law as aligning with the Law of God or the "Law of Nature's God."

7.4 The Law of Nature in the Bible

Many early Americans likely recognized that the Law of Nature appears in the Bible. Their views about this law in the Bible were undoubtedly influenced by historical Judeo-Christian thought. For many of the medieval and modern thinkers they read or knew of, like Augustine and those who came after, had identified this law in scripture. The medieval and modern Christian Church—including the Catholic church and the Reformed Protestant church—as well as Christian or pro-God Enlightenment thinkers had recognized the Law of Nature in Romans 1 and 2—specifically Romans 2:14-15. In Romans, the Apostle Paul identifies a Natural Law present in all human hearts.[668] Paul writes in Romans 2:14-15:

...[F]or when Gentiles [non-Jews], who do not have the law, by nature do the things in the law, these, although not having the law, are a law to themselves, who show **the work of the law written in their**

hearts, their conscience also bearing witness, and between themselves *their* thoughts accusing or else excusing *them*….

This universal law of mankind written on human hearts is God-given and validated by man's reason and an innate moral sense also known as conscience. Due to the Bible's acknowledgement of the Law of Nature, early Americans and the American founders surely acknowledged this law as compatible with Judeo-Christian beliefs.

In his *Confessions* of 397-8, Saint Augustine, Bishop of Hippo, alluding to Romans 2:15, recognizes God's moral creation law or Law of Nature—to love God and man—as naturally present within men, "written in men's hearts, which iniquity itself cannot blot out."[669] By the 1000s, the Catholic Church recognized a Law of Nature in its theology and canon law. In his well-known 1200s *Summa Theologica*, Italian Dominican priest and theologian Thomas Aquinas identifies the Law of Nature in man's reason. He also bases this law on Romans 2:14-15, interpreting these verses to mean, "*Although they [non-Jews] have no written law, yet they have the natural law, whereby each one knows, and is conscious of, what is good and what is evil.*"[670] Like Augustine, Aquinas saw the Law of Nature as "written in the hearts of men."[671]

During the Protestant Reformation, the Law of Nature was also identified from Romans 2:14-15 by the Reformed churches and Calvin in his 1536 *Institutes of the Christian Religion*. Calvin, whose theology influenced the American Puritans and Awakeners, observes,

> If the Gentiles have the righteousness of the law naturally engraven on their minds, we certainly cannot say that they are altogether blind as to the rule of life. Nothing, indeed, is more common, than for man to be sufficiently instructed in a right course of conduct by natural law, of which the Apostle here speaks.[672]

Also alluding to Romans 2:14-15, John Ponet's 1556 *Short Treatise on Political Power*—which John Adams recognized as influencing Locke and Sidney and American political theory—affirms God's moral law within man's heart, stating, "For it is no private law to a few or certain people, but common to all: not written in books, but grafted in the hearts of men: not made by man, but ordained of God… and (as St. Paul says) man's conscience bearing witness of it."[673]

In his 1623 explanation of Reformed doctrine, *The Marrow of Theology*, Puritan philosopher William Ames—who, like Calvin, influenced the Puritans in America—also affirms the Law of Nature in man's heart and conscience from Romans 2 and as matching the written Law of God.[674]

In his 1593 *Laws of Ecclesiastical Polity*, Anglican theologian Richard Hooker, who influenced philosophers Blackstone and Locke, similarly recognizes the Law of Nature in Romans 2 and as known by man's reason. Drawing from Augustine and Aquinas, he aptly describes the Law of Nature as a moral law universally agreed upon by all men and able to be known from man's reason. From this law, humans may naturally grasp the basic morals of right and wrong, good and evil. He writes,

> …[T]hose [natural] laws are investigable by reason, without the help of revelation, supernatural or divine. …[T]he knowledge of them is general, the world hath always been acquainted with them…. It is not agreed upon by one, or two, or few, but by all; …but this law is such that being proposed no man can reject it as unreasonable and unjust. Again, there is nothing in it but any man, having natural perfection of wit and ripeness of judgment, may by labour and travail find out. And to conclude, the general principles thereof are such as it is not easy to find men ignorant of them. Law rational, therefore, which men commonly use to call the law of Nature, meaning thereby the law which human nature knoweth itself in reason universally bound unto, which also for that cause may be termed most

fitly the law of reason, this law, I say, comprehendeth all those things which men by the light of their natural understanding evidently know, or at leastwise may know, to be beseeming or unbeseeming, virtuous or vicious, good or evil for them to do.[675]

From canon church law, the Law of Nature became part of Christian legal thought and English common law. Having studied Roman and canon church law, English jurist Henri de Bracton addresses the Law of Nature in his 1200s *The Laws and Customs of England*, which would influence English legal thought in the 1400s and 1500s. In the 1400s, English lawyer Sir John Fortescue gives a legal application to the Law of Nature in his treatise on English law, *In Praise of the Laws of England*.[676]

British Chief Justice Edward Coke affirms the Bible-based view of the Law of Nature in British legal thought. Referencing Romans 2:14 and Romans 13:1, Coke expounds in his *Reports*:

> The law of nature is that which God at the time of creation of the nature of man infused into his heart, for his preservation and direction; and this is *lex aeterna*, the moral law, called also the law of nature. And by the law, written with the finger of God in the heart of man, were the people of God a longtime governed, before the law was written by Moses, who was the first reporter or writer of law in the world. The Apostle [Paul] in the Second Chapter to the Romans saith, ... [While the nations who do not have the law do naturally the things of the law.] ... [T]herefore the law of God and nature is one to all. ... This law of nature, which indeed is the eternal law of the Creator, infused into the heart of the creature at the time of his creation, was two thousand years before any laws written, and before any judicial or municipal laws."[677]

British constitutional law recognized the Law of Nature as the basis by which to create and judge human laws. If man-made laws are unjust or do not uphold the rights of the people, the people may appeal to the higher law.

The Law of Nature in Reformed thought also influenced political reformers in Britain. Scottish Presbyterian minister Samuel Rutherford wrote of the Law of Nature and God in his 1644 Puritan political treatise, *Lex Rex*, which influenced Locke. Kings and rulers are, he asserted, bound by the Law of Nature as well as human, civil laws. Political theory and civil government, he saw, must be based on the Law of Nature and God.

Some Enlightenment thinkers also viewed the Law of Nature with a Bible-based or Judeo-Christian worldview that, consequently, contributed to American thought on the concept. One such thinker, Christian German Enlightenment philosopher Samuel Pufendorf, in his *Of the Law of Nature and Nations*, recognizes God as the source of this universal law and believes this law aligns with God's moral law in the Bible. The Law of Nature, Pufendorf asserts, is written by God in human hearts or consciences and can be understood by human reason as indicated in Romans 2:14-15. Pufendorf states,

> The Laws of Nature would have a full and perfect Power of binding Men, altho' GOD ALMIGHTY had never propos'd them anew in his Reveal'd Word. For Man was under Obligation to obey his Creator, by what means so ever he was pleas'd to convey to him the Knowledge of his Will. ... ...[T]he Divine Law is of equal Obligation, whether it is discover'd to Men either by GOD Himself in a visible Shape, and with the Resemblance of Human Voice, or by Holy Men peculiarly inspir'd from Heaven; or whether, lastly, it be work'd out by Natural Reason from the Contemplation of Human Condition. ... ...[O]n that account they are justly attributed and referr'd to GOD, the Author of Nature.[678]

Alluding to Romans 2:14-15, Pufendorf also affirms,

...[T]he Law of Nature is to be drawn from Man's Reason; flowing from the true Current of that Faculty, when unperverted. On which account the Holy Scriptures declare it to be written on the Hearts of Men. This we judge to be a most manifest Truth, that although the sacred Writings do throw in a more enlarged Light to direct us in the clearest View of Nature's Law: Yet the same Law may without that extraordinary Assistance be found out and solidly demonstrated, by the bare force of Reason, such as God first implanted and still preserves in Mankind.[679]

Locke also recognized the Law of Nature in Romans 1 and 2 in his *Reasonableness of Christianity*. Citing Romans 2:14-15, he states,

But the Law given by *Moses* being not given to all Mankind. How are all men sinners; since without a Law there is no Transgression? To this the Apostle [Paul], v. 14. Answers, *For when the Gentiles which have not the Law, do* (i. e. find it reasonable to do) *by nature the things contained in the Law; these having not the Law, are a Law unto themselves: Which shew the work of the Law written in their hearts, their Consciences also bearing witness, and amongst one another their thoughts accusing or excusing.* By which, and other places in the following Chapter, 'tis plain, that under the Law of Works is comprehended also the Law of Nature, knowable by Reason as well as the Law given by *Moses*.[680]

Though the Law of Nature was supported by rationalists, most early Americans, like these Bible-based thinkers, likely acknowledged this higher law in the Declaration as aligning with Biblical truth and their Judeo-Christian worldviews and beliefs.

7.5 The Law of Nature's God: The Written Law of God in the Bible

The "Law of Nature's God" also expressed in the Declaration was likely understood by the early Americans and Founders as referring to and/or corresponding with God's moral law as can also be found in the teachings of the Bible—in God's two Great Commandments to love God and others. These commandments are revealed by Moses and the Prophets to the Israelites in the Old Testament and through Jesus and the Apostles in the New Testament. As mentioned earlier, they are found in many Bible verses including Deuteronomy 6:5, Leviticus 19:18, Matthew 22:37-40, and Matthew 7:12.[681] In Matthew 22:37-40, Jesus, referencing Deuteronomy 6:5 and Leviticus 19:18, states: "'*You shall love the Lord your God with all your heart, with all your soul, and with all your mind.*' This is *the* first and great commandment. And *the* second is like it: '*You shall love your neighbor as yourself.*' On these two commandments hang all the Law and the Prophets." In Matthew 7:12, Jesus states, "Therefore, whatever you want men to do to you, do also to them, for this is the Law and the Prophets." God makes His nature and moral law known through these Two Great Commandments and Jesus Christ who, says Kirk, "set the example for the conduct of all human life."[682]

Early American statesman, educator, and author of the *American Spelling Book* and the *American Dictionary*, Noah Webster describes this moral law of God:

The duties of men are summarily comprised in the Ten Commandments, consisting of two tables. One comprehending the duties which we owe immediately to God—the other, the duties we owe to our fellow men. Christ himself has reduced these commandments under two general precepts, which enjoin upon us, to love the Lord our God with all our heart, with all our soul, with all our mind and with all our strength—and to love our neighbor as ourselves. On these two commandments hang all the law and the prophets—that is, they comprehend the substance of all the doctrines and precepts of the Bible, or the whole of religion.[683]

The divine commandments of God's moral law revealed in the Bible were, some thinkers recognized, unlike any other laws in history that originated with man. Instead, they were, says Kirk, "an unveiling of truth

1 not obtained through simple experience in this world" and a "communication of knowledge from some source
2 that transcends ordinary human perception." They revealed to the Israelites the existence of one God, God's
3 covenant with His people, and a moral law and order for their lives and society—including man's duty towards
4 and relationship with God and others.[684] These laws consequently revealed man's moral nature, sinful and
5 imperfect condition, and need for law and order. This divine revelation compelled the Israelites to depart from
6 their ancient order of rule and polytheism or worship of many gods and to embrace a Judaic order and
7 monotheism or worship of one God.   Furthermore, it became influential to civilizations worldwide and
8 permanently changed and influenced the worldviews of mankind. Mankind now has a new perspective and
9 purpose related to God, man, and life. This new moral understanding led John Adams to express,

11   ...[T]he Hebrews have done more to civilize men than any other nation. If I were an atheist, ...I should
12   still believe that fate had ordained the Jews to be the most essential instrument for civilizing the nations.
13   ...that chance had ordered the Jews to preserve and propagate to all mankind the doctrine of a supreme,
14   intelligent, wise, almighty sovereign of the universe, which I believe to be the great essential principle of
15   morality, and consequently all civilization.[685]

17   The spirit of God's moral law in the Bible was not to be confused with the literal religious, ceremonial,
18 and political laws enacted by the ancient Israelites. The Israelites' literal laws applied only to the ancient
19 Jewish nation. But God's eternal moral law applied to all mankind at all times. Locke explains, "But the Moral
20 part of *Moses'* Law, or the Moral Law, (which is every where the same, the Eternal Rule of Right) obliges
21 Christians and all Men every where, and is to all Men the standing Law of Works.'"[686]

23   As will be demonstrated in the next sections, many early Americans undoubtedly identified the "Law of
24 Nature's God" as expressed in the Declaration as God's moral law as it is expressed in the Great
25 Commandments in the Bible.

7.6 The Law of Nature and Nature's God: One Universal Moral Law Expressed Two Ways

29   Many early Americans, like the philosophers they read, likely viewed the Law of Nature and the Law of
30 God in the Declaration as one universal moral law expressed in two ways. These two expressions made up a
31 "two-fold" moral law, as Amos describes it—one as a natural or rational law written on men's hearts and one as
32 a written law in the Holy Scripture or Bible. The Law of Nature is God's "general" revelation of His moral law
33 as naturally present in a person's reason, heart, and conscience. The Law of God is God's "special" or
34 "specific" revelation of his moral law as written in the Bible. The content for both is the same, and the general
35 is subject to the specific. This moral law became known as the Law of Nature and God. It has long been
36 recognized as correlating with the Bible.[687]

38   In the 1300s, medieval Bible scholars connected the Law of Nature with the written Law of God, seeing
39 them as the same law. They called this two-fold moral law the "law of nature and of God" to acknowledge its
40 two expressions—natural and written. The phrase presented God's law in the same order and timing in which
41 God revealed it to man historically—first in general in creation and then specifically in Holy Scripture.[688]

43   John Calvin had affirmed in his *Institutes* that the Law of Nature and the Law of God are the same moral
44 law. This moral law is revealed in the Bible's Ten Commandments and the first two Great Commandments.
45 Calvin states,

47   The moral law, therefore, with which I shall begin, being comprised in two leading articles, of which
48   one simply commands us to worship God with pure faith and piety, and the other enjoins us to embrace
49   men with sincere love; this law, I say, is the true and eternal rule of righteousness, prescribed to men of

all ages and nations, who wish to conform their lives to the will of God. For this is his eternal and immutable will, that he himself be worshipped by us all, and that we mutually love one another.[689]

Calvin further writes of this divine moral law,

> Now as it is certain that the law of God, which we call the moral law, is no other than a declaration of natural law, and of that conscience which has been engraven by God on the minds of men, the whole rule of this equity of which we now speak is prescribed in it. This equity therefore must alone be the scope and rule and end of all laws.[690]

Alluding to Romans 2:14-15, Calvin elaborates on God's divine moral law as the same as Natural Law:

> …[T]he very things contained in the two tables are, in a manner, dictated to us by that internal law, which, as has been said already, is in a manner written and stamped on every heart. For conscience, instead of allowing us to stifle our perceptions, and sleep on without interruption, acts as an inward witness and monitor, reminds us of what we owe to God, points out the distinction between good and evil, and therefore convicts us of departure from duty.[691]

In his *Short Treatise*, Ponet affirms these two expressions of God's moral law.[692] Alluding to these Bible verses, Ponet observes,

> This rule [of one God] is the law of nature, first planted and grafted only in the mind of man…. God set this rule forth in writing the Decalogue, or the Ten Commandments: and after that, reduced by Christ our Savior to just two commands: You will love the Lord your God above all things, and your neighbor as yourself. The latter part He also expounded on: Whatever you would want done unto yourself, do that unto others. In this law is compiled all justice, the perfect way to serve and glorify God, and the right means to rule each and every man: and the only stay to maintain every commonwealth. This is the touchstone to try every man's works, whether he is king or beggar, whether he be good or evil. By this all men's laws will be discerned, whether they be just or unjust, godly or wicked.[693]

Puritan leader John Winthrop likewise identifies God's two-fold moral law in his well-known 1630 sermon, *A Model of Christian Charity*, delivered to the Puritans as they sailed to America. Winthrop observes,

> There is likewise a double Lawe by which wee are regulated in our conversacion one towardes another: in both the former respects, the lawe of nature and the lawe of grace, or the morrall lawe or the lawe of the gospel…. By the first of these lawes man as he was enabled soe withal [is] commaunded to love his neighbor as himeselfe upon this ground stands all the precepts of the morrall lawe, which concernes our dealings with men.[694]

The Westminster Confession of Faith and Catechisms of 1647, the Church of England's Reformed creed written also recognizes God's two Great Commandments as revealing the universal moral law to which all mankind since Adam is covenantally bound and subject by God. The Confession of Faith recognizes this moral law of God both as a Law of Nature and as conveyed in the moral commandments of the Bible, applying to all humans:

God gave Adam a law as a covenant of works, by which he bound him and all his posterity to personal, entire, exact and perpetual obedience, promised life upon the fulfillment, and threatned death upon the breach of it; and endued him with power and ability to keep it.

II. This law, after his fall, continued to be a perfect rule of righteousness; and, as such, was delivered by God upon mount Sinai in ten commandments, and written in two tables *b*; the four first commandments containing our duty towards God, and the other six our duty to man *c*. ...

V. The moral law doth for ever bind all, as well justified persons as others, to the obedience thereof *h*; and that not only in regard of the matter contained in it, but also in respect of the authority of God the Creator who gave it *i*. Neither doth Christ in the gospel any way dissolve, but much strengthen this obligation *k*.[695]

In his *Laws of Ecclesiastical Polity*, Richard Hooker recognizes God's moral law and the two ways of knowing it—generally and particularly. Alluding to Hebrews 4:12, he states,

The first principles of the law of Nature are easy, hard it were to find men ignorant of them: but concerning the duty which Nature's law doth require at the hands of men in a number of things particular, so far hath the natural understanding even of sundry whole nations been darkened, that they have not discerned no not gross iniquity to be sin. Again, being so prone as we are to fawn upon ourselves, and to be ignorant as much as may be of our own deformities, without the feeling sense whereof we are most wretched...how should our festered sores be cured, but that God hath delivered a law [in scripture] as sharp as the two-edged sword, piercing the very closest and most unsearchable corners of the heart, which the law of Nature can hardly, human laws by no means, possible reach unto?[696]

In his *Reasonableness of Christianity*, Locke affirms the Law of Nature and the Law of God as two expressions of the same moral law of God.[697] Locke describes this moral law as the "law of God and nature."[698] Both parts of this law are compatible since the Law of Nature requires men to obey the Law of God—"it being a part of the Law of Nature, that man ought to obey every Positive Law of God, whenever he shall please to make any such addition to the Law of His Nature. But the Moral part of *Moses'* Law, or the Moral Law, (which is every where the same, the Eternal Rule of Right) obliges Christians and all Men every where, and is to all Men the standing Law of Works."[699] This moral law of Nature and God is, Locke saw, the basis of society. Locke elaborates on the measure of man's morality by and man's duty to follow God's moral law in his *Essay Concerning Human Understanding*:

The divine law, whereby I mean that law which God has set to the actions of men, whether promulgated to them by the light of nature, or the voice of revelation. That God has given a rule whereby men should govern themselves, I think there is nobody so brutish as to deny. He [God] has a right to do it; we are his creatures; he has goodness and wisdom to direct our actions to that which is best; and he has power to enforce it by rewards and punishments, of infinite weight and duration in another life; for nobody can take us out of his hands. This is the only true touchstone of moral rectitude; and by comparing them to this law it is that men judge of the most considerable moral good or evil of their actions; that is, whether as duties or sins, they are like to procure them happiness or misery from the hands of the Almighty.[700]

Blackstone, like others drawing on historical Christian thought, also saw the Law of Nature and the Law of God as the same single law. This law could be known partially by man's imperfect reason and completely by the Bible. Due to man's imperfect reason, Blackstone says the Bible's clear revelation of this higher moral law is needed:

And if our reason were always, as in our first ancestor [Adam] before his transgression, clear and perfect, unruffled by passions, unclouded by prejudice, unimpaired by disease or intemperance, the task [of discerning God's law and will] would be pleasant and easy; we should need no other guide but this [reason]. But every man now finds the contrary in his own experience; that his reason is corrupt, and his understanding full of ignorance and error.

This [corruption] has given manifold occasion for the benign interposition of divine providence; which, in compassion to the frailty, and the imperfection, and the blindness of human reason, hath been pleased, at sundry times and in divers manners, to discover and enforce its laws by an immediate and direct revelation. The doctrines thus delivered we call the revealed or divine law, and they are to be found only in the holy scriptures.[701]

Christian Enlightenment philosopher Samuel Pufendorf, who influenced Blackstone and early Americans, closely examines in his 1672 *Of the Law and Nature of Nations* the Bible's Two Great Commandments—to love God and man—as the primary focus of God's universal moral law for all men and nations. Of man's first duty to love God, Pufendorf expresses, "Amongst *Connate* Obligations, such as are planted, as it were, in our *Being*, the most Eminent is that which lies on all Men with respect to Almighty God, the supream Governor of the World; by Virtue of which we are bound to adore his Majesty, and to obey his Commandments and his Laws."[702] He also states in his 1673 *On the Duty of Man and Citizen According to the Natural Law*, a summary of his ideas presented in *Of the Law of Nature and Nations*, of man's first duty to love God:

And the Mind of Man is oblig'd, from a consideration of this his [God's] Power and Goodness, to fill it self with all that Reverence towards him, of which its Nature is susceptible. Hence it is, that it is our Duty to *love* him, as the Author and Bestower of all manner of Good; to *hope* in him, as from whom only all our Happiness for the future does depend; to *acquiesce* in his Will, he doing all things for the best, and giving us what is most expedient for us; to *fear* him, as being most powerful, and the offending whom renders us liable to the greatest Evil; lastly, in all things most humbly to *obey* him, as our Creator, our Lord, and our Best and Greatest Ruler.[703]

Such expressions of love, Pufendorf describes, include thanking God for blessings, obeying Him, admiring and celebrating His greatness, offering prayers to Him, observing one's oaths under God, speaking of God and His name in reserve and not in vain, not arguing about His nature and government, worshipping Him in public and private, and keeping the Laws of Nature and God.

Of man's second duty to love others, Pufendorf observes, man is not to injure others. He explains,

We come now to those Duties which are to be practis'd by *one man towards another*. Some of these proceed from that *common Obligation* which it has pleas'd the Creator to lay upon all men in general;....
...
Among those Duties we account *Absolute*, or those of every man towards every man, this has the first place, that *one do no wrong to the other*.... It is also the *most necessary*, because without it *Human Society* cannot be preserv'd.[704]

However, man's duty to love others involves more than just refraining from injuring others. It also involves expressing benevolence or goodwill toward others for the good of society. He states,

Among the Duties of one Man towards another, which must be practiced for the sake of *Common Society*, we put in the *third* place this, *That every man ought to promote the good of another, as far as conveniently he may*. For all Mankind being by Nature made, as it were, *akin* to each other; such a Relation requires more than barely abstaining from offering injury and doing despight to others; it is not therefore sufficient that we neither hurt nor despise our Fellows, but we ought also to do such *good*

Offices to others, or mutually to communicate the same, as that common *brotherly Love* may be kept up among Men.[705]

Man is called to these duties toward God and man in society, says Pufendorf, because man is created by and for God to worship Him, achieve His purposes, and to be a useful member of society: "For Man not being born for Himself alone, but being therefore furnish'd with so many excellent *Endowments*, that he may set forth his *Creator's* Praise, and be rendred a fit Member of *Human Society*; it follows hence, that it is his *Duty*, to cultivate and improve those Gifts of his Creator which he finds in himself, that they may answer the end of their *Donor*; and to contribute all that lies in his power to the benefit of *Human Society*."[706]

The Law of Nature, Pufendorf acknowledges, is limited to the sphere of man's present life and peace and society on earth. It does not address or secure eternal spiritual salvation for men, which not reason but only a supernatural divine faith could do.[707]

The American Founders drew from the Bible, various philosophers through history, and their experiences to understand God's two-fold moral law. The Law of Nature and Nature's God as expressed in the Declaration was understood by Americans to be the moral foundation and obligation of mankind and civil society. This universal moral law is only truly workable, Americans thought, when it is based on a Creator God. For without God, humanistic Natural Law is flawed. For example, God's absence in the Natural Law aspect of self-preservation could lead to inequality, survival of the fittest, slavery, and oppression. With God in Natural Law, the dignity, equality, freedom, and rights of all men are secured. Moreover, most Americans and influential thinkers believed that the teachings of the Bible supported, enhanced, and aligned with this law. "[F]aith permeated philosophy and lifted it above its own limitations," explains Novak.[708] The moral and intellectual weakness of Natural Law was uplifted and perfected by God's moral law as expressed in the teachings of Judeo-Christianity. Declaration signer and second U. S. president John Adams notably proclaims the dignity and freedom of man as uplifted by a God-centered moral law:

> Let us see delineated before us the true map of man. Let us hear the dignity of his nature, and the noble rank he holds among the works of God,—that consenting to slavery is a sacrilegious breach of trust, as offensive in the sight of God as it is derogatory from our own honor or interest or happiness,—and that God Almighty has promulgated from heaven, liberty, peace, and good-will to man![709]

7.7 Self-Evident Truth and Common Sense

In addition to the Law of Nature and Nature's God, the idea of self-evident truth and common sense contributed to the American Founders' worldview, knowledge, and justification for the natural rights of man and just government. It was the view that some truths do not require complex reasoning or evidence to prove. Some truths are obvious to and understood by all. Self-evident truths were also known as "first principles" or axioms upon which other truths are based. They are reflected in the Declaration which states, "We hold these truths to be self-evident, that all men are created equal, that they are endowed by their Creator with certain unalienable Rights, that among these are Life, Liberty, and the pursuit of Happiness."

The view that some truth or knowledge is self-evident is found among Christian Bible scholars through history. Saint Augustine in the 400s, Saint John of Damascus in the 700s, and Thomas Aquinas in the 1200s all expressed ideas related to self-evident truth. It was later expressed by Enlightenment-era thinkers including Richard Hooker, John Locke, and Thomas Reid.

In his 1265-1274 *Summa Theologica*, Aquinas, essentially expressing the idea of Romans 2:14-15, acknowledged that some truths are "naturally implanted" in men and therefore self-evident. Aquinas views the existence of God and Truth, for example, as self-evident. Drawing from Saint John and his *De Fide Orthodoxa*

1   or *The Orthodox Faith*, he states, "These things are said to be self-evident to us the knowledge of which is
2   naturally implanted in us, as we can see in regard to first principles. But the Damascene [St. John] says that, *the*
3   *knowledge of God is naturally implanted in all*. Therefore the Existence of God is self-evident."[710] The first
4   principles of the Law of God are, says Aquinas, the two Great Commandments of the Bible. He writes, "For the
5   first and principal precepts of the [Old Testament] Law are *Thou shalt love the Lord thy God*, and, *Thou shalt*
6   *love thy neighbour*, as stated in Matth. xxii. 37, 39." Such general principles of the Law of God and Nature are
7   self-evident—they "need no further promulgation after being once imprinted on the natural reason to which
8   they are self-evident; as, for instance, that one should do evil to no man, and other similar principles...."[711]

10   Richard Hooker, influenced by Augustine and Aquinas, also saw that some principles in the Law of
11   Nature are self-evident. He states in his *Ecclesiastical Polity*, "For to make nothing evident of itself unto man's
12   understanding were to take away all possibility of knowing anything...." and "Wherefore as touching the law of
13   reason, this was, it seemeth, St. Augustine's judgment, namely, that there are in it some things which stand as
14   principles universally agreed upon, and that out of those principles, which are in themselves evident, the
15   greatest moral duties we owe towards God or man may without any great difficulty be concluded." [712]

17   Though a rationalist, Locke, influenced by Hooker, recognized the existence of a self-evident truth that
18   does not need rational proof as indicated in his influential 1690 *Essay Concerning Human Understanding*.
19   Locke asserts,

21   There are a sort of propositions, which under the name of maxims and axioms, have passed for
22   principles of science; and because they are self-evident, have been supposed innate, although nobody
23   (that I know) ever went about to show the reason and foundation of their clearness or cogency. ...
24   Knowledge, as has been shown, consists in the perception of the agreement or disagreement of ideas:
25   now, where that agreement or disagreement is perceived immediately by itself, without the intervention
26   or help of any other, there our knowledge is self-evident. This will appear to be so to any one, who will
27   but consider any of those propositions, which, without any proof, he assents to at first sight.... ... So
28   that in respect of identity, our intuitive knowledge reaches as far as our ideas. ... To which, if we add
29   all the self-evident propositions which may be made about all our distinct ideas, principles will be
30   almost infinite, at least innumerable, which men arrive to the knowledge of at different ages....[713]

32   Locke viewed the existence of a Creator God as self-evident, for example, based on the existence of natural
33   creation. Creation obviously reveals a Creator. Citing Acts 14:17 and Romans 1:20, he asserts, "[F]or I judge it
34   as certain and clear a truth, as can any where be delivered, that 'the invisible things of God are clearly seen from
35   the creation of the world, being understood by the things that are made, even his [God's] eternal power and
36   Godhead."[714] This natural knowledge and intuition differs from the supernatural faith of the Holy Spirit.[715]
37   Locke did not view the Law of Nature, understood by reason, as necessarily the same as innate, self-evident
38   truth, which required no reason.

40   Thomas Reid was a Scottish Enlightenment professor and pastor in Scotland who asserted a theory of
41   knowledge based on common sense. This theory supported the idea of self-evident truths. Reid asserted that
42   man's knowledge and understanding begins with real-life common sense, including an innate moral sense in
43   man's heart or conscience. Man has an intuitively discerned moral sense, he asserts, that acted as his moral
44   receptor, regulator, or medium in moral matters just as the five human senses served as faculties by which man
45   understands and interacts with the visible, physical world. Reid introduced this idea in his 1764 *An Inquiry into*
46   *the Human Mind, on the Principles of Common Sense*. He later asserts it in his 1785 *Essays on the Intellectual*
47   *Powers of Man* and 1788 *Essays on the Powers of the Human Mind*. Alluding to the parable of the talents in
48   Matthew 25:14-29, he explains in his *Essays on the Powers of the Human Mind*,

Some knowledge of duty and of moral obligation is necessary to all men. Without it they could not be moral and accountable creatures, nor capable of being members of civil society. It may therefore be presumed, that nature has put this knowledge within the reach of all men. Reasoning and demonstration are weapons which the greatest part of mankind never was able to wield. The knowledge that is necessary to all, must be attainable by all. We see it is so in what pertains to the natural life of man.

Some knowledge of things that are useful, and things that are hurtful, is so necessary to all men, that without it the species would soon perish. But is it not by reasoning that this knowledge is got, far less by demonstrative reasoning. It is by our senses, by memory, by experience, by information; means of knowledge that are open to all men, and put the learned and unlearned, those who can reason and those who cannot, upon a level.

It may, therefore, be expected from the analogy of nature, that such a knowledge of morals as is necessary to all men, should be had by means more suited to the abilities of all men than demonstrative reasoning is.

This, I apprehend, is in fact the case. When men's faculties are ripe, the first principles of morals, into which all moral reasoning may be resolved, are perceived intuitively, and in a manner more analogous to the perceptions of sense than to the conclusions of demonstrative reasoning. ...

Of such propositions, there are some that are self-evident to every man that has a conscience; and these are the principles from which all moral reasoning must be drawn. They may be called the axioms of morals. ... ...[B]ecause he who has but one talent in reasoning, and makes the proper use of it, shall be accepted, as well as he to whom God has given ten [Matthew 25:14-29].[716]

Reid's common-sense theory of knowledge supported the existence of self-evident truths, axioms, or moral "first principles" as found in the Law of Nature. Such truths or principles, Reid thought, are commonly known or intuited by all men by their innate moral sense. These truths or principles are so obvious that they do not require rational proof or evidence other than themselves, though they can be tested by reason. They are automatically accepted. They are, Reid acknowledges, implanted by God in man's heart or conscience. Reid explains man's moral faculty and obligation to follow the moral principles it conveys:

If a man had not the faculty given him by God of perceiving certain things in conduct to be right, and others to be wrong, and of perceiving his obligation to do what is right, and not to do what is wrong, he would not be a moral and accountable being.

If a man be endowed with such a faculty, there must be some things which, by this faculty, are immediately discerned to be right, and others to be wrong; and therefore there must be in morals, as in other sciences, first principles, which do not derive their evidence from any antecedent principles, but may be said to be intuitively discerned.[717]

In drafting the Declaration, the American Founders were influenced by these ideas of self-evident truths and common sense.[718] Their view that some principles of the Law of Nature are revealed by common sense and self-evident truths supported the natural rights of man.[719] American Founders including James Wilson, Rev. John Witherspoon, and Thomas Jefferson recognized man's innate moral sense or common sense and self-evident truths.

Wilson—echoing Richard Hooker, Reid, and Aquinas—expounds on self-evident truth and common sense, stating,

...[L]et us embrace the philosophy which dwells with common sense.

This philosophy will teach us, that first principles are in themselves apparent; that to make nothing selfevident, is to take away all possibility of knowing any thing; that without first principles, there can be neither reason nor reasoning; ...that, consequently, all sound reasoning must rest ultimately on the principles of common sense—principles supported by original and intuitive evidence.[720]

Jefferson affirmed his adherence to and use of common sense in the Declaration in presenting the American arguments for revolution and independence. He writes in a letter,

> But with respect to our rights, and the acts of the British government contravening those rights, there was but one opinion on this side of the water. All American Whigs thought alike on these subjects. When forced, therefore, to resort to arms for redress, an appeal to the tribunal of the world was deemed proper for our jurisdiction. This was the object of the Declaration of Independence. Not to find out new principles, or new arguments, never before thought of, not merely to say things which had never been said before; but to place before mankind the common sense of the subject, in terms so plain and firm as to command their assent, and to justify ourselves in the independent stand we are compelled to take.[721]

Jefferson believed all men have a God-given "moral sense" for virtuous behavior. He frequently, specifically acknowledges this moral sense in man:

> ...[H]ow necessary was the care of the Creator in making the moral principle so much a part of our constitution as that no errors of reasoning or of speculation might lead us astray from its observance in practice. ... These good acts give us pleasure...[b]ecause nature hath implanted in our breasts a love of others, a sense of duty to them, a moral instinct, in short, which prompts us irresistibly to feel and to succor their distresses....[722]

This innate moral sense, Jefferson believed, is found in man's heart and conscience. It is by this moral sense in man, and as revealed in the Bible, that God's moral law was validated and preserved in man and in society. This moral law is exemplified, Jefferson thought, in the moral life of Jesus. Jefferson writes,

> The practice of morality being necessary for the well-being of society, He [God] has taken care to impress its precepts so indelibly on our hearts that they shall not be effaced by the subtleties of our brain. We all agree in the obligation of the moral precepts of Jesus and nowhere will they be found delivered in greater purity than in his discourses [in the Bible].[723]

With such a view of man's innate moral sense, Jefferson expresses the idea in the Declaration: "We hold these Truths to be self-evident...."

7.8 The Law of Nature and Nature's God: Defended and Upheld During the Revolutionary Era

The American Founders of the revolutionary era based man's natural rights and responsibilities and their new nation and government on reason, conscience, and God's moral law. The Americans turned to the Law of Nature and Nature's God as the higher law that justified their resistance to oppressive British policies and supported their rights and freedoms. The United States' Declaration of Independence referred to the Laws of Nature and Nature's God as the highest law upon which the new nation was founded.

Prior to and during the American Revolution, colonists increasingly protested British policies as violations of the moral Law of Nature and God. In 1764, for example, revivalist and lawyer James Otis of Boston makes this argument in his political pamphlet *The Rights of the British Colonies Asserted and Proved*:

> But if every prince since *Nimrod* had been a tyrant, it would not prove a right to tyrannize. There can be no prescription old enough to supercede the law of nature and the grant of God Almighty, who has given to all men a natural right to be *free*, and they have it ordinarily in their power to make themselves so if they please.[724]

To Otis as other revolutionaries, God is the supreme authority, and the Law of Nature is the highest law and basis of human law. Earthly powers have no absolute authority to violate such law. Otis adds,

> To say that Parliament is absolute and arbitrary is a contradiction. ... The Supreme power in a state...belongs alone to God. Parliaments are in all cases to *declare* what is for the good of the whole; but it is not the *declaration* of Parliament that makes it so. There must be in every instance a higher authority, viz., GOD. Should an act of Parliament be against any of his natural laws, which are *immutably* true, *their* declaration would be contrary to eternal truth, equity, and justice, and consequently void: and so it would be adjudged by the Parliament itself when convinced of their mistake.[725]

In 1765, the House of Representatives of Massachusetts similarly affirms that men have unalienable rights based on the Law of Nature and God:

> 1. *Resolved*, That there are certain essential rights of the British Constitution of government, which are founded in the law of God and nature, and are the common rights of mankind;--therefore,
> 2. *Resolved*, That the inhabitants of this Province are unalienably entitled to those essential rights in common with all men: and that no law of society can, consistent with the law of God and nature, divest them of those rights.[726]

Samuel Adams of Boston, known as the "father of the American Revolution," was a significant contributor to the ideas of the Law of Nature and God during the revolution. In 1772, he presents a report to the Committee of Correspondence in Boston called *The Rights of Colonists* in which he recognizes the Law of Nature and God as the source and foundation of man's natural rights. This powerful report, drawing from Locke, outlines important concepts of the natural rights of colonists as men, Christians, and subjects. It asserts that these rights have been violated and supports resistance against the British. Citing Locke in his preface of *Letter Concerning Toleration*, Adams asserts, "'Just and true liberty, equal and impartial liberty,' in matters spiritual and temporal is a thing that all men are clearly entitled to by the eternal and immutable laws of God and nature, as well as by the law of nations and all well-grounded municipal laws, which must have their foundation in the former."[727] Later republished by Franklin, Adams's report impacted other revolutionary writings. Prompted by Adams' report, Congress, in 1774, drafted a *Declaration of Rights and Grievances*, listing the violations of natural rights of the British against colonists.

Of James Otis' and Samuel Adams' influence on the colonists in resisting British policies prior to the American Revolution, John Adams, alluding to the Reformation, observes,

> If Otis was Martin Luther, Samuel Adams was John Calvin. If Luther was rough, hasty, and loved good cheer, Calvin was cool, abstemious, polished, and refined, though more inflexible, uniform, and consistent. The people in Boston, New York, Philadelphia, Charleston, and everywhere else, arose like a hurricane, and bore down the stamp act and the stamps, their officers and principal abettors, as nullities.
> This open resistance by force was a virtual declaration, by the people of all the colonies, of their independence on parliament, and on the crown too, whenever that crown should cease to defend and protect their fundamental laws and essential liberties....[728]

The principle of the Law of Nature and God as the source of man's rights in revolutionary writings was reflected, according to John Adams, in the ideas of the early Congress and in the Declaration. John Adams writes in a letter, "As you justly observe, there is not an idea in it [the Declaration of Independence] but what had been hackneyed in Congress two years before. The substance of it is contained in the declaration of rights and the violations of those rights, in the Journals of Congress, in 1774. Indeed, the essence of it is contained in a pamphlet, voted and printed by the town of Boston, before the first Congress met, composed by James Otis, as I suppose, in one of his lucid intervals, and pruned and polished by Samuel Adams." [729]

Founding-era Americans, like the philosophers they read, understood the Law of Nature as confirmed by Romans 2 and as aligning with God's moral law in the Bible. In fact, many American Founders directly linked the Law of Nature to the Law of God, the Two Great Commandments, in the Bible. In his *Lectures on Law*, Wilson, for example, affirms the universal Law of Nature of mankind as described in Romans. The Law of Nature, says Wilson, is written on man's heart and conscience by God. Alluding to Romans 2:14-15, he states,

> Laws may be promulgated by reason and conscience, the divine monitors within us. They are thus known as effectually, as by words or by writing: indeed, they are thus known in a manner more noble and exalted. For, in this manner, they may be said to be engraven by God on the hearts of men: in this manner, he is the promulgator as well as the author of natural law.[730]

In his 1792 address to the Massachusetts legislature, Samuel Adams also recognizes the Law of Nature as described in Romans 2 and as aligning with God's two Great Commandments. He states, "...[A]ll men are equally bound by the laws of nature, or to speak more properly, the laws of the Creator:—they are imprinted by the finger of God on the heart of man. Thou shall do no injury to thy neighbor, is the voice of nature and reason, and it is confirmed by written revelation [the Bible]."[731]

In his 1796 Senate notes, John Adams, possibly drawing from Pufendorf, directly connects the Law of Nature with the two Great Commandments of the Bible, stating, "One great advantage of the Christian Religion is, that it brings the great principle of the Law of nature and nations, —Love your neighbor as yourself, and do to others as you would that others should do to you, —to the knowledge, belief, and veneration of the whole people."[732]

Declaration signer, Continental Congress delegate, Princeton president, and Presbyterian minister Rev. John Witherspoon similarly preached a sermon on the two Great Commandments of the Bible as the universal moral law:

> The sum of the moral law is, "Thou shalt love," &c. The whole is contained under these heads, especially the first of them, from which the other is a corollary. ... If we take the sense of the second table, by itself, we shall see the same thing very plainly, "Thou shalt love thy neighbor as thyself;" or which is the same thing, "whatsoever ye would, that men do unto you, do ye the same unto them." Is this unreasonable? Is any man's reason so perverted, or his conscience so depraved, as to complain of this, as an unjust, or oppressive law. ... Would you be satisfied to hear any man trace out a system of moral duty, and make any alteration in these? Yet they are the whole in substance; wherever these are, every thing will follow of course. If you love God supremely, and your neighbor as yourselves, you will neglect no duty to the one or the other.[733]

Wilson elaborates in his *Lectures on Law* on the two-fold nature of God's moral law as many founding-era Americans likely understood it. He affirms that this moral law is the "will of God."[734] It is communicated to us as *Natural Law* by reason and conscience (the moral sense in us) or the "divine monitors within us" and as divinely *revealed law* by the Holy Scriptures or "the sacred oracles, the divine monitors without us." Both of these laws, natural and revealed, for mankind and nations come from God and make up God's moral law.[735] He states,

> That law, which God has made for man in his present state; that law, which is communicated to us by reason and conscience, the divine monitors within us, and by the sacred oracles, the divine monitors without us...has been called natural; as promulgated by the holy scriptures, it has been called revealed

law. … But it should always be remembered, that this law, natural or revealed, made for men or for nations, flows from the same divine source: it is the law of God.

Both natural and revealed law, he emphasizes, are necessary for fully understanding God's moral law. He further explains, "The law of nature and the law of revelation are both divine: they flow, though in different channels, from the same adorable source. It is, indeed, preposterous, to separate them from each other. The object of both is—to discover the will of God—and both are necessary for the accomplishment of that end."[736] God's universal moral law, Wilson asserts, upholds the maxims to obey God, to injure no man, and to faithfully fulfill one's engagements.[737]

Citing John 13:34-35, American Founder Benjamin Rush likewise observes the importance of the Bible's Two Great Commandments of love as the foundation of moral law. He acknowledges this moral law as revealed in the Gospel of Jesus Christ and achievable only by God's grace. He advises,

> Let us not be wiser than our Maker. If moral precepts alone could have reformed mankind, the mission of the Son of God into our world, would have been unnecessary. He came to promulgate a system of *doctrines*, as well as a system of morals. The perfect morality of the gospel rests upon a *doctrine*, which, though often controverted, has never been refuted, I mean the vicarious life and death of the Son of God. This sublime and ineffable doctrine delivers us from the absurd hypotheses of modern philosophers, concerning the foundation of moral obligation, and fixes it upon the eternal and self moving principle of LOVE. It concentrates a whole system of ethics in a single text of scripture. "*A new commandment I give unto you, that ye love one another, even as I have loved you.*"[738]

The two Great Commandments of love, Rush surmises, reveals God's moral law for man. He further writes in his spiritual book, *The Road to Fulfillment*, "These two commandments taken together form a complete summary of the spiritual law of the relations between God and man. All other spiritual laws are commentaries on them—detailed instructions on how they are best complied with…."[739]

Many early Americans and Founders clearly understood the higher moral law expressed in the Declaration—the "Laws of Nature and Nature's God"—as God's moral law found in natural reason and conscience as well as in the Bible. This law had been similarly phrased and used by Bible and legal scholars for centuries. It resembled Locke's and Samuel Adam's Christian use of the phrase, and it corresponded with the revolutionary and legal thought of the Continental Congress and the American Founders.[740] The Declaration's Law of Nature and Nature's God, says Amos, "*makes the Bible a fundamental part of the legal foundation of America. By referring to the Bible in two distinct ways, the phrase 'laws of nature and of nature's God' incorporates by reference the moral law of the Bible into the founding document of our country!*"[741]

The Americans' resort to the Law of Nature and God to justify their rights and position during the revolution was, observes Kirk, "the extreme medicine of a people lacking any other means of redress."[742] Without it, the American Revolution probably would never have taken place. The Law of Nature and Nature's God was the Founders' last but strongest appeal in defense of the natural freedoms and rights of Americans.

7.9 The Law of Nature and God: A Foundation and Standard for Just Government and Human Civil Law

The Law of Nature and God in the Declaration was, to the American Founders as to various historical thinkers, the foundation and standard for free, just government and human civil law. For it served as the basis of man's natural rights and the limits of earthly power. Just government and human laws could only exist when they are founded on and adhere to this higher law. This higher law became the basis of the United States Constitution and its civil laws.

Reformed thinkers affirmed this idea. John Calvin had also suggested that Christian nations and states abide by the Bible's two Great Commandments of love as framework of all civil law and order. He writes in his *Institutes,*

> …[T]he precepts and duties of love remain of perpetual obligation, notwithstanding the abolition of all these judicial ordinances. If this be true, certainly all nations are left at liberty to enact such laws as they shall find to be respectively expedient for them; provided they be framed according to that perpetual rule of love, so that, though they vary in form, they may have the same end.[743]

A just nation's civil government and laws are, says Calvin, to abide by God's commandments—the essence of the Law of Nature and God.

God's universal moral law, Ponet similarly asserts in his *Short Treatise*, are the basis and guide for man's just government and civil law. Alluding to Acts 17:24-28, Psalm 100:3, Exodus 6:7, Hebrews 2:10, and Isaiah 9:6-7, Ponet writes,

> …[S]uch [people of God] were desirous to know the perfect and the only governor of all, constrained to seek further than themselves, and so at length to confess, that it was one God that ruled all. By Him we live, we move, and we have our being [Acts 17:24-28]. He made us, and not we ourselves. We are His people, and the sheep of His pasture [Psalm 100:3]. He made all things for man: and man He made for Himself, to serve and Glorify Him [Hebrews 2:10]. He has taken upon Himself the order and government of man, His chief creature, and prescribe a rule to him, how he should behave himself, what he should do, and what he may not do [Isaiah 9:6-7].[744]

Man's just government and civil order are guided by and reflect in many ways God's Biblical standard and moral order.

Enlightenment-era thinkers influential to the American Founding including Charles de Montesequieu, William Blackstone, Richard Hooker, John Locke, and Algernon Sidney all affirmed this principle that just governments and laws are based on the higher law.

In his *Spirit of the Laws*, French philosopher Charles Baron de Montesquieu, the most cited secular thinker of the American founding era, asserts the value of the Law of Nature and God to civil government and law, observing, "The Christian religion, which ordains that men should love each other, would, without doubt, have every nation blest with the best civil, the best political laws; because these, next to this religion, are the greatest good that men can give and receive."[745] Montesquieu makes a connection between the Biblical moral law and just civil government and law: "…[W]e shall see that we owe to Christianity, in government, a certain political law; and in war, a certain law of nations—benefits which human nature can never sufficiently acknowledge."[746]

In his *Commentaries*, British lawyer and jurist William Blackstone also confirms the Law of Nature and God as the basis of human government and law: "Upon these two foundations, the law of nature and the law of revelation, depend all human laws; that is to say, no human laws should be suffered to contradict these."[747]

In his *Laws of Ecclesiastical Polity*, Richard Hooker affirms the idea that the origin of human law comes from the higher laws. He writes, "'Human Laws…have…higher Rules to be measured by, which rules are two, the Law of God and the Law of Nature. So that laws human must be made according to the general laws of Nature, and without contradiction unto any positive law of scripture, otherwise they are ill made.'"[748] To Hooker, God's Word in the Bible is the highest law upon which all human law must be based.

Locke, citing the above passage of Hooker in his *Second Treatise of Civil Government*, also asserts the origin of human law from the higher Law of Nature and God.[749] Locke further explains that the authority of man-made laws rests on the higher moral law. He states,

> ...[T]he Obligations of the law of Nature cease not in society, but only in many cases are drawn closer, and have, by human laws, known penalties annexed to them to enforce their observation. Thus the law of Nature stands as an eternal rule to all men, legislators as well as others. The rules that they [legislators] make for other men's actions must, as well as their own and other men's actions, be conformable to the law of Nature—i.e., to the will of God, of which that [Law] is a declaration, and the fundamental law of Nature being the preservation of mankind, no human sanction can be good or valid against it.[750]

In his 1698 influential essay, *Discourses Concerning Government,* British theorist Algernon Sidney shares the view that free governments can only rightly exist if they are founded on the Law of Nature: "If it be said that every nation ought in this to follow their own constitutions, we are at an end of our controversies; for they ought not to be followed, unless they are rightly made: They cannot be rightly made, if they are contrary to the universal law of God and nature."[751]

The American Founders, like these pro-Christian thinkers, saw the Law of Nature and God in the Declaration as God's higher moral law and the God-authorized standard and criterion for all just civil government and law. Human laws, they believed, are not authorized merely by the earthly power or the people's majority. All just human laws must conform to and abide by the higher moral law. Otherwise they are invalid, unjust, tyrannical, and not to be obeyed. During the Revolution, the Americans had resisted British laws which they viewed as unjust in violating this higher law. The Declaration reaffirmed this higher law as the standard authorized by God for all earthly government and law. In the Declaration, the Founders would uphold the "Laws of Nature and Nature's God" as the basis for man's equality, man's natural, unalienable rights, and the American cause for independence. The Americans would later create their constitutional government and civil laws based on a commitment to this Biblical moral law.

Wilson observes the importance of religion or, more specifically, the Bible and God's moral law to the foundation and forming of the United States' civil law: "Human law must rest its authority, ultimately, upon the authority of that law, which is divine. ..... Far from being rivals or enemies, religion and law are twin sisters, friends, and mutual assistants. Indeed, these two sciences run into each other. The divine law, as discovered by reason and moral sense, forms an essential part of both."[752]

Statesman Hamilton, in seeing the influence and importance of Christianity on the forming of the nation, desired to form a "Christian Constitutional Society" to support both the Christian religion and the United States. He writes in 1775 of the influence of the Bible on the Declaration's natural, unalienable rights and civil liberty in his 1775 writing, *The Farmer Refuted*:

> The fundamental source of all your errors, sophisms, and false reasonings, is a total ignorance of the natural rights of mankind. Were you once to become acquainted with these, you could never entertain a thought, that all men are not, by nature, entitled to a parity of privileges. You would be convinced, that natural liberty is a gift of the beneficient Creator, to the whole human race; and that civil liberty is founded in that; and cannot be wrested from any people, without the most manifest violations of justice. *Civil liberty is only natural liberty, modified and secured by the sanctions of civil society.* It is not a thing in its own nature, precarious and dependent on human will and caprice; but it is conformable to the constitution of man, as well as necessary to the well-being of society.
> Upon this principle, colonists, as well as other men, have a right to civil liberty. For, if it be conducive to the happiness of society (and reason and experience testify that it is), it is evident, that

every society, of whatsoever kind, has an absolute and perfect right to it, which can never be withheld without cruelty and injustice.[753]

Continental Congress delegate, Constitution signer, third U. S. Secretary of War, and founder and president of Baltimore Bible Society, James McHenry of Maryland also expresses the value of the Bible and its moral law to civil government, law, and society:

> All Christians allow that the Old and New Testaments taken together, are the only books in the world which clearly reveal the nature of God, contain a perfect law for our government, propose the most powerful persuasions to obey this law, and furnish the best motives for patience and resignation, under every circumstance and vicissitude of life. Even those writers who deny their divinity, have yet acknowledged that the matters contained in them are, at least, calculated to make mankind wiser and better. These surprising and salutary effects the scriptures have unequivocally produced, and whenever they are read and attended to, will continue to produce. Facts so fully ascertained and so clearly demonstrating the great importance of circulating the sacred writings have (within these few years past) called the attention of men more particularly to this subject, and given rise to the establishment of Societies whose object is to encourage their circulation....[754]

U. S. Supreme Court Justice, Harvard Law Professor, and author of *Commentaries on the Constitution of the United States*, Joseph Story similarly saw the importance of the Bible and its commandments to the foundation of American civil law. In his 1829 induction speech as Harvard law professor, he states,

> One of the beautiful boasts of our municipal jurisprudence is, that Christianity is a part of the common law, from which it seeks the sanction of its rights, and by which it endeavours to regulate its doctrines. .... There never has been a period, in which the common law did not recognise Christianity as lying at its foundations.[755]

Sixth U. S. President and U. S. Secretary of State John Quincy Adams, son of John Adams, would later aptly observe that the Declaration committed Americans to the Biblical moral law. He affirms in his July 4th oration, "From the day of the declaration, the people of the North American union and of its constitutent states, were associated bodies of civilized men and christians, in a state of nature; but not of anarchy. They were bound by the laws of God, which they all, and by the laws of the gospel, which they nearly all, acknowledge as the rules of their conduct."[756]

The Declaration's Law of Nature and Nature's God—which includes God's Biblical commands of justice, righteousness, and brotherly love—became the commitment and foundation of a new people and nation. It also served as the foundation of the new nation's civil laws and government as would later be created with the United States Constitution. The Constitution, in its legal approach and spirit, would be founded on the Judeo-Christian moral law of the Bible as indicated in the Declaration of Independence.

7.10 Algernon Sidney and John Locke, Natural Rights Philosophers of the American Revolution

Two thinkers who had a primary, significant influence on founding-era Americans and the principle of civil liberty were Enlightenment philosophers John Locke and Algernon Sidney. These philosophers articulated from the Bible and historical Christian writings Bible-based principles of liberty, equality, popular sovereignty, covenants, and natural rights. Locke and Sidney emphasized the principles that all men are equal and possess certain God-given, unalienable, natural rights. They believed that civil government should protect the natural rights of men. Locke and Sidney also upheld covenant-based social contract theory.

British Philosopher John Locke and his 1689 *Two Treatises of Civil Government* played a significant role in the development of American political thought in asserting republican principles as based on and derived from historical Christian writings and the Bible. In his *First Treatise of Civil Government,* Locke refutes the Divine Right of Kings and absolute monarchy and asserted the equality of all men and popular sovereignty. In his *Second Treatise of Civil Government*, Locke presents the concepts of equality, popular sovereignty, consent of the governed, covenant-based social contracts, God-given natural rights, and the right of revolution. With these concepts, Locke's *Second Treatise* developed a Natural Law philosophy and resistance theory that aligned with Reformation-era revolutionary theory as found in Brutus' *Vindiciae* and Rutherford's *Lex Rex*.[757] Locke asserted that man has God-given natural rights and that the purpose of civil government is to protect these rights. Governments that abandoned this purpose could be overthrown and changed by the people. Locke, like the earlier reformers, supported a social contract theory of government and presented this theory in more secular terms. Locke presented these ideas in a clear, understandable form which the American Founders would later look to in order to justify the American Revolution. Locke's writings provided the American Founders with many principles that they would include in the United States' Declaration of Independence.

Algernon Sidney was an English parliamentarian, political philosopher, and Protestant Christian of the late 1600s who supported popular sovereignty and the right to revolution. Sidney was a member of the Whig party—the pro-reform political party in England that stood against the Divine Right of Kings and absolute rule and in favor of popular sovereignty and natural rights. The Whigs raised opposition to the British crown. Sidney argued for this position in his well-known 1698 essay, *Discourses Concerning Government*. In this writing, he supported popular sovereignty based on consent of the people, resistance theory, and covenant-based social contract theory held by the religious and political reformers. He believed the Bible and the Law of God and Nature supported these principles. Sidney cited the Bible extensively as well as Bellarmine and Suarez for popular sovereignty. Sidney was arrested on the belief that he was guilty of treason. At his trial, passages of his *Discourses* were presented as evidence of his views on revolution. Due to this writing, he was sentenced to death. Sidney was executed for allegedly plotting to overthrow the king. Sidney was viewed by Whigs as a great republican Whig martyr. Like Locke, Sidney's political ideas were influential to the American Founders. His *Discourses* later became popular in America as a "textbook of revolution" during the American Revolution.[758] When discussing the influences on the revolution, the Founders often mentioned Locke and Sidney together. Jefferson cited Sidney as one of his sources in writing the Declaration of Independence. As an important influence to American political thought and the Declaration, Sidney, says Lutz, "combines reason and [Biblical] revelation in his analysis, and thus shows how easily the Declaration can be an expression of earlier, biblically based American constitutional thought."[759]

Locke's *Second Treatise on Civil Government* and Sidney's *Discourses Concerning Government* presented a secularized political philosophy of natural rights and right of resistance that was applied by the American revolutionaries. Their ideas aligned with Americans' Bible-inspired worldview and political situation. Jefferson applied their ideas in the Declaration. Locke and his *Letters Concerning Toleration* also influenced the American Founders like Jefferson and Madison on the issue of religious tolerance.

7.11 All Men As Equal and Popular Sovereignty

One principle of the Law of Nature that the Founders notably mentioned in the Declaration is that all men are equal. The Declaration states, "We hold these truths to be self-evident: that all men are created equal…." Equality refers to every individual's innate moral value and position in nature, before God, and in the civil state. This principle came from the Bible and was recognized and emphasized during the Great Awakening. God and Christianity, revivalists emphasized, view all men as equal before God. Equality, in fact, emerged with Christianity. For God in the Bible does not distinguish among men based on wealth, power, rank, status, or success. All are loved by Him, in a fallen state, and dependent on Him. God judges all men equally.[760]

Since all men are equal, earthly political power resided with the people—hence the concept of popular sovereignty. The principle of popular sovereignty or the idea that earthly power resides with the people was found in many historical Bible-based writings including those of medieval churchmen Aquinas, Bellarmine, and Suarez and in Reformed writings—Ponet's *Short Treatise*, Brutus's *Vindiciae*, and Rutherford's *Lex Rex*. It was further addressed by Richard Hooker in his *Laws of Ecclesiastical Polity*. It was also addressed by early Puritan Rev. Thomas Hooker in the early Puritan colony of Connecticut. This principle of popular sovereignty, among other principles, was taken up by Locke and Sidney who aligned with these historical writings.

Locke and Sidney affirmed the social and political equality of humans. Refuting the Divine Right of Kings as asserted by political theorist and King James I's court theologian Robert Filmer, they supported the position of Bellarmine and Suarez. No rank or power pre-exists among humans, Locke noted, in which one is naturally over or under the authority of another. Locke's 1689 *First Treatise on Government* refutes the assertion that Adam is the first king and that the king of England is a direct heir of Adam. Locke aims to show that when God creates Adam and mankind, God does not make Adam or any other person superior to others in rank or rule simply by inheritance or succession. People are naturally free and equal. Therefore, the state of mankind in society, Locke asserts, is rightly one of freedom and equality and equal rights among men. He observes,

> But if Creation, which gave nothing but a being, "made" not Adam "prince of his posterity," if Adam (Gen. i.28 [Genesis 1:28]) was not constituted lord of mankind, nor had a "private dominion" given him, exclusive of his children, but only a right and power over the earth and inferior creatures, in common with the children of men; … if all this be so, as I think, by what has been said, is very evident, then man has a "natural freedom"…since all that share in the same common nature, faculties, and powers are in nature equal, and ought to partake in the same common rights and privileges, till the manifest appointment of God, who is "Lord over all, blessed for ever," can be produced to show any particular person's supremacy, or a man's own consent subjects him to a superior.[761]

Locke speaks of the natural state of man before civil society as being *"a state of perfect freedom* to order their actions, and dispose of their possessions and persons, as they think fit, within the bounds of the law of nature, without asking leave, or depending upon the will of any other man."[762] Locke, citing Richard Hooker, then goes on to assert that all men as created by God are equal before their Maker and in accordance with reason and self-evident truth. He writes,

> A state also of equality, wherein all the power and jurisdiction is reciprocal, no one having more than another, there being nothing more evident than that creatures of the same species and rank, promiscuously born to all the same advantages of Nature, and the use of the same faculties, should also be equal one amongst another, without subordination or subjection, unless the lord and master of them all [God] should, by any manifest declaration of his will, set one above another, and confer on him, by an evident and clear appointment, an undoubted right to dominion and sovereignty.
>   5. This equality of men by Nature, the judicious [Richard] Hooker looks upon as so evident in itself, and beyond all question, that he makes it the foundation of that obligation to mutual love amongst men on which he builds the duties they owe one another, and from whence he derives the great maxims of justice and charity. His words are:--
>   "The like natural inducement hath brought men to know that it is no less their duty to love others than themselves, for seeing those things which are equal, must needs all have one measure…"[763]

Drawing on Calvinist and historical Christian thought, Locke speaks of man's equality as leading to every man's natural right to freedom—"that equal right that every man hath to his natural freedom, without being subjected to the will or authority of any other man."[764]

In his *Discourses Concerning Government*, Sidney cites Bellarmine on the Bible-based grounds for popular sovereignty in opposition to Filmer's support for the Divine Right of Kings and absolute monarchy. Sidney, like Bellarmine and *Vindiciae*, asserts that God is the source of power, all men are equal, and earthly power belongs to the people or multitude. Sidney writes,

> In the next place he [Filmer] recites an argument of Bellarmine, That "it is evident in Scripture God hath ordained powers; but God hath given them to no particular person, because by nature all men are equal; therefore he hath given power to the people or multitude." I leave him to untie that knot, if he can;....
> ... I take Bellarmine's argument to be strong;... ... ...I may justly insist upon it... ... It is hard to imagine, that God, who hath left all things to our choice, that are not evil in themselves, should tie us up in this; and utterly incredible that he should impose upon us a necessity of following his will, without declaring it to us. Instead of constituting a government over his people, consisting of many parts, which we take to be a model fit to be imitated by others, he might have declared a word, that the eldest man of the eldest line should be king; and that his will ought to be their law. This had been more suitable to the goodness and mercy of God, than to leave us in a dark labyrinth, full of precipices; or rather, to make the government given to his own people, a false light to lead us to destruction. ... We see nothing in scripture, of precept or example, that is not utterly abhorrent to this chimera. The only sort of kings mentioned there with approbation, is such a one "as may not raise his heart above his brethren [Deuteronomy 17]." If God had constituted a lord paramount with an absolute power, and multitudes of nations were to labour and fight for his greatness and pleasure, this were to raise his heart to a height, that would make him forget he was a man. Such as are versed in scripture, not only know, that it neither agrees with the letter or spirit of that book; but that it is unreasonable in itself....[765]

God does not assign absolute rulers or forms of government over men, asserts Sidney, but rather the choice of rulers and government belongs to the people or multitude, made up of men who are all equal in position. Earthly civil power is given by God to the people.

The Founders are aligned with such views of equality among men and popular sovereignty and conveyed them in the Declaration. In the spirit of Locke and Sidney, Rush similarly refers to the Bible as the source of equality among men. In his essay, *Of the Mode of Education Proper in a Republic*, he states,

> A Christian cannot fail of being a republican. The history of the creation of man, and of the relation of our species to each other by birth, which is recorded in the Old Testament, is the best refutation that can be given to the divine right of kings, and the strongest argument that can be used in favor of the original and natural equality of all mankind.[766]

John Adams also recognizes the influence of Christianity on equality in his *Notes on a Debate in the Senate*: "The Christian religion is, above all the religions that ever prevailed or existed in ancient or modern times, the religion of wisdom, virtue, equity, and humanity....; it is resignation to God, it is goodness itself to man."[767] Wilson also recognizes human equality, stating, "As in civil society, previous to civil government, all men are equal; so, in the same state, all men are free. In such a state, no one can claim, in preference to another, superiour right: in the same state, no one can claim over another superiour authority."[768] Jefferson affirms the equality of men in a 1826 letter:

> All eyes are opened, or opening, to the rights of man. The general spread of the light of science has already laid open to every view the palpable truth that the mass of mankind has not been born with saddles on their backs, nor a favored few booted and spurred, ready to ride them legitimately, by the grace of God. These are grounds of hope for others. For ourselves, let the annual return of this day, forever refresh our recollections of these rights, and an undiminished devotion to them.[769]

Equality further aligned with the Rule of Law in which all men are equally subject to the law—both Natural and human law. Americans also supported social equality in contrast to a rigid class system. This idea meant that no man's life is restricted or determined by class or position based on circumstances of birth, but rather individuals has an equal right and opportunity to build and better their lives through their work and efforts.

The Founders' Declaration affirms the source of power as from God and the equality of all men in stating, "all men are created equal." The Declaration also asserts the power or popular sovereignty of the people to choose their rulers and form their government: "That to secure these rights, Governments are instituted among Men, deriving their just powers from the consent of the governed, that whenever any Form of Government becomes destructive of these ends, it is the Right of the People to alter or abolish it, and to institute new Government...." With equality and popular sovereignty, the people had the authority and right to form a self-governing nation. The Declaration states the American people's intent to "assume among the Powers of the earth, the separate and equal station to which the laws of Nature and of Nature's God entitle them...."

7.12 God-Given Unalienable Rights: Life, Liberty, Religious Freedom, and the Pursuit of Happiness

Another principle taken up by the American Founders in the Declaration was the idea that the Creator God endows every human being with natural, unalienable rights. Unalienable rights are the inherent rights of man that cannot be sold, bought, or taken away by any man, power, or human law without just cause. Doing so violates the Law of Nature. These rights are a God-given birthright of all men. They cannot be removed or alienated from man. God's creation and value of man, man's God-given authority, and Rule of Law, many early Americans saw, led to the view of the unalienable rights of man. Such rights included life and liberty. The unalienable rights of men came from the Bible-based view that man as an individual was made by God in His image and holds dominion over the earth as indicated in Genesis 1 and 2.[770] They were also based on the Bible-based view that man as God's creation and "workmanship" is made for God's, not another man's, purpose as indicated in Ephesians 2:10. Unalienable rights such as liberty, explains one scholar, allow man to live according to his God-given nature, to freely obey God and His laws, and to have relationship with God.[771]

The American principle of God-given rights differed from earlier ideas that rights originated from a king or man-made law. During the revolution, Americans could not claim the source of their rights as from king or British law, for the colonists were essentially questioning and challenging these authorities. Instead, the Founders invoked the Creator God and the Law of Nature as the source of man's natural rights. Government, they held, secures but does not grant these rights. These rights are, as Founders Samuel Adams and Jefferson describe, the gift of God. Jefferson writes, "The God who gave us life, gave us liberty at the same time: the hand of force may destroy, but cannot disjoin them."[772] He also declared, "And can the liberties of a nation be thought secure when we have removed their only firm basis, a conviction in the minds of the people that these liberties are of the gift of God? That they are not to be violated but with His wrath?"[773] The Declaration proclaims that these rights are God-given, "that they [men] are endowed by their Creator with certain unalienable rights; that among these are life, liberty, and the pursuit of happiness." Men may ultimately defend these natural rights in the duty of self-preservation. The Founders did also make legal arguments for their position, and they knew they had to create new civil laws for themselves to uphold their principles and values.

The Founders' ideas of the individual, natural rights to life, liberty, and property were influenced by Locke and Sidney. Locke and Sidney's ideas aligned with the Bible. Bible-based medieval Christian thought on unalienable rights developed in the 1100s and 1200s. The Bible-inspired principle of unalienable rights was first articulated by medieval Christian lawyers dealing with property law in the Christian Church. Medieval lawyers viewed property or, in Latin, "dominium" as a right. In the 1200s, the word "property" was used to refer to one's material goods or estates which were transferable or "alienable." Such property could be sold, bought, transferred, etc. With regard to the property of one's person, such as one's life, however, the lawyers developed the concept of non-transferrable or "unalienable" property. Such sacred property of personhood could not be sold, bought, transferred, etc. without violating the Law of Nature and God. The right to life thus became a sacred, unalienable right of man.[774] In the 1300s and 1400s, liberty also came to be viewed as a property of man and an unalienable right based on Genesis 1 and 2. For from Genesis, Archbishop Richard Fitzralph asserted that mankind's God-given dominion over the earth is an authority given to mankind. French scholar Jean Gerson asserted in his 1402 *De Vita Spirituali Animae* that man's dominion is not only an authority but a capability. He then argued that liberty, necessary for man to exercise dominion, is a property and natural right of man. Soon after, Dominican theologians defined liberty as unalienable on the basis that it could not be rightfully sold, bought, or taken away without just cause. These thinkers acknowledged the link between the Law of Nature and unalienable rights and recognized life and liberty as natural, unalienable rights.[775]

Man's unalienable rights were essentially derived from man's Bible-inspired, unalienable duties to God. In Genesis 1 and 2, humans are created to live their lives for God—to abide by God's rule and law, represent and reflect God's image on earth, serve as a steward over God's creation and for God's authority, and carry out his duties and dominion on earth. Every person has a responsibility to God. Man is called to honor the image of God in himself and others and to resist attempts against his own duty to God. Man was also not to interfere with others' righteous efforts to fulfill their duties to God and dominion on earth. Man is to abide by the Law of Nature or the Law of Love, not injuring others or interfering in their duties. This point is demonstrated in the case of Adam and Eve's children, Cain and Abel. In Genesis 4, Abel brings a good offering to God, but Cain brings an unacceptable one. In his anger and jealousy, Cain kills his brother Abel. God punishes Cain, showing that Cain has violated a moral law. These verses helped to illustrate that man's duties to God become man's natural, unalienable rights.[776]

Christian thinkers also supported man's unalienable rights with the Bible-based view that man as God's creation is God's, not another man's, possession for His purpose based on Ephesians 2:10. Ephesians 2:10 states, "For we are His [God's] workmanship, created in Christ Jesus for good works, which God prepared beforehand that we should walk in them." Alluding to Ephesians 2:10, Calvin in his *Institutes* observes that man as God's workmanship or creation is made for God's purpose and use: "For how can the idea of God enter your mind without instantly giving rise to the thought, that since you are his workmanship, you are bound, by the very law of creation, to submit to his authority?—that your life is due to him?—that whatever you do ought to have reference to him?"[777] He also states, "It is now easy to understand the doctrine of the law, viz., that God, as our Creator, is entitled to be regarded by us as a Father and Master, and should, accordingly, receive from us fear, love, reverence, and glory; nay, that we are not our own, to follow whatever course passion dictates, but are bound to obey him implicitly, and to acquiesce entirely in his good pleasure."[778]

Other Calvinists similarly wrote about human beings as God's workmanship, called to fulfill their duties to God. In his *Short Treatise*, Ponet writes on man as God's workmanship made to serve God:

> God is the highest power, the power of powers, from Him is derived all power. All people are His servants made to serve and glorify Him. All other powers are but His ministers, set to oversee that everyone behaves himself, as he should towards God, and to do those things, that he is justly commanded to do by God.
>
> Whatever God commands man to do, he ought not to consider the matter, but be straight to obey the commander. For we are sure, what He commands, is just and right: for from Him, that is, all together just and right, no injustice nor wrong can come.[779]

Ponet further states that "…God (to testify that He has also power of the body) has many times in all ages mightily and miraculously delivered His people from the power of tyrants: as the Israelites from Pharaoh….

So that we see God to be the Supreme Power of the whole man, as well to punish as to deliver at His own will."[780]

Stephen Brutus's political tract *Vindiciae Contra Tyrannos* also asserts that God as Creator is proprietor of heaven and earth and that man is God's workmanship and possesses certain duties to God. Citing various scriptures, Brutus elaborates on these points that humans are God's possession and property:

> …God created heaven and earth out of nothing, so by right He is truly the lord [*dominus*] and proprietor [*proprietarius*] of heaven and earth. But those who inhabit the earth are, as it were, his tenants and copyholders [*coloni & emphyteutae*]; those who have jurisdiction on earth and preside over others for any reason, are beneficiaries and vassals [*beneficiarii & clientes*] of God and are bound to receive and acknowledge investiture from Him. In short, God is the only proprietor and the only lord: all men, of whatever rank they may ultimately be, are in every respect his tenants [*coloni*], bailiffs, officers, and vassals. The more ample the proceeds they receive, the larger the dues they owe; the greater the authority they attain, the more strictly they are bound to render an account [*rationem reddere*]; the more distinguished the honour they gain, the heavier the burdens for which they are liable.
>
> This is taught throughout Holy Scripture, and has always been recognized by all the pious and even by some of the most outstanding heathen. King David says: 'The earth is the Lord's, and the fullness thereof' [Psalm 24/Psalm 23 (vulgate)]. And lest men should sacrifice their ploughshares, the earth never gives forth without rain from heaven. For this reason God required from His followers that the first of all the fruits be devoted to Him, and even the heathen have of their own accord made offerings, by which they might profess themselves to be tenants and Him to be truly Lord. 'Heaven is the throne of the Lord', says King Solomon, 'and the earth His footstool.' [Isaiah 66:1] Therefore, since all kings are beneath His feet, it is not surprising if God is called King of kings and Lord of lords, whereas all kings—who are constituted to administer jurisdiction—are referred to as ministers of His kingdom [1 Kings 8]. 'Through Me', says the wisdom of God, 'kings rule, and princes judge the earth.' [Wisdom 6:1, 2, Proverbs 8:15] 'And if they fail to do so, I loose the sword-belts of kings and tie a girdle around their loins.' [Job 12:16]. …
>
> For the same reason the people itself is always said to be the people and inheritance of God, and the king the administrator of His inheritance and leader of God's people—which title is expressly applied to David, Solomon, Hezekiah, and other pious princes [1 Samuel 9:16, 10,1, 2 Samuel 6:21, 2 Kings 20:5, 2 Chronicles 1:9]. When the covenant [*foedus*] is ratified between God and the king, it is done on this condition: that the people should be and should remain forever the people of God [2 Kings 11:17, 2 Chronicles 33:16]. Without doubt this was to demonstrate that God does not deprive Himself of His property [*proprietas*] and possession when He hands over the people to kings, but that it is conveyed in order to be ruled, cared for, and nurtured, just as he who chooses a shepherd for his flock nonetheless remains its owner [*dominus*]. This was patently recognized by the pious kings David, Solomon, Jehoshaphat, and others… [2 Chronicles 22:6].[781]

Brutus refers to all men of every rank—both individually and as a whole people in civil society—as God's possession and possessing certain duties to God. Though Brutus does not explicitly refer to man's individual, natural rights here based on man as God's possession, the idea is prompted by and can be implicitly derived from his Judeo-Christian view of and regard for people.

Since humans are created by God, Bible-based thinkers believed, men have duties to God. They are made to serve God. Man possesses natural, unalienable rights in order to fulfill those duties. As a result, unalienable rights became part of Western Christian thought.

Since it was recognized that man possesses natural, unalienable rights, it was also believed that the people and civil governments have no authority to make or consent to civil laws that violate those rights. A just government protects these rights. American Puritan dissident and founder of Rhode Island Roger Williams conveys this idea that men are stewards of God. He says in his 1644 *Bloudy Tenent of Persecution,*

> For in a free state no Magistrate hath power over the bodies, goods, lands, liberties of a free people, but by their free consents. And because free men are not free Lords of their owne estates, but are only stewards unto God, therefore they may not give their free consents to any Magistrate to dispose of their bodies, goods, lands, liberties, at large as themselves please, but as God, the sovereign Lord of all, alone. And because the word is a perfect rule, as well of righteousness as of holiness, it will be therefore necessary that neither the people give consent, nor that the Magistrate take power to dispose of…[these possessions], but according to the laws and rules of the word of God.[782]

Such Bible-based or Judeo-Christian views of people's ownership by and duties to God and their consequent unalienable rights would characterize, influence, and become part of the thinking of American colonists.

In his *Discourses Concerning Government,* Sidney similarly asserts the God-given rights of men such as liberty, stating, "The Liberty of a people is the Gift of God and nature."[783] As God's creation, Sidney asserts, man is naturally free and possesses certain natural rights of freedom. Sidney believed that man's natural rights come from God. Humans naturally possess liberty, he says, due to the fact that people are created by God, not other men:

> The creature having nothing, and being nothing but what the Creator makes him, must owe all to him, and nothing to any one from whom he has received nothing. Man therefore must be naturally free unless he be created by another power than we have yet heard of… This liberty therefore must continue, till it be either forfeited or willingly resigned….[784]

Since God makes man equal and free, says Sidney, such natural value and existence no person or power may rightly seize or destroy. Man's right to liberty was further demonstrated, he thought, by man's nature and Genesis 11:1-9 in which God scatters the men of Babel by different languages throughout the world, with no one group ruling the others. He explains,

> But because I cannot believe God hath created man in such a state of misery and slavery….I am led to a certain conclusion, that every father of a family is free and exempt from the domination of any other, as the seventy-two that went from Babel were.[785]

All men are free and equal as they are in the Bible. Sidney further states of unalienable rights, "If any man ask, how nations come to have the power of doing these things, I answer, that liberty being only an exemption from the dominion of another, the question ought not to be, how a nation can come to be free, but how a man comes to have a dominion over it; for till the right of dominion be proved and justified, liberty subsists, as arising from the nature and being of a man."[786]

Locke introduces a modern doctrine of God-given natural rights of "Life, Liberty, and Estate"—which he generally calls Property.[787] To Locke, Property involves a man's person and possessions—his life, liberty, body and health, labor and industry, and material goods.[788] Locke based these rights on the belief that men as created by God are God's possession, designed for His purpose and use. Locke, like Calvin, referred to the Apostle Paul's view of man as God's workmanship in Ephesians 2:10. Alluding to this verse, Locke writes of man as God's property:

> …for Men being all the workmanship of one omnipotent and infinitely wise Maker; all the Servants of one sovereign Master, sent into the world by His order and about His business; they are His property, whose workmanship they are[,] made to last during His, not one another's pleasure. And, being

furnished with like faculties, sharing all in one community of Nature, there cannot be supposed any such subordination among us that may authorize us to destroy one another, as if we were made for one another's uses…. Every one as he is bound to preserve himself, and not to quit his station wilfully, so by the like reason, when his own preservation comes not in competition, ought he as much as he can *to preserve the rest of mankind*, and may not unless it be to do justice on an offender, take away, or impair the life, or what tends to the preservation of the life, the liberty, health, limb, or goods of another.[789]

In other words, man is created for God's, not another man's, use. Man must therefore honor his and others' natural rights, for all men are, ultimately, God's property.

Drawing from Locke, Samuel Adams identifies these natural rights in his revolutionary pamphlet, *Rights of Colonists*, as life, liberty, property, and religious freedom, along with the defense of these rights. Since God gives man life and dignity, man has a natural right to life. Since man has God-given reason and free will to reflect and choose, man has a natural right to liberty—including political and religious liberty. Man also has a right to property—of himself and his beliefs, possessions, and labor—for his survival. Adams also supported religious freedom, stating,

As neither reason requires, nor religion permits the contrary, every Man living in or out of a state of civil society, has a right peaceably and quietly to worship God according to the dictates of conscience. … In regard to Religion, mutual toleration in the different professions thereof, is what all good and candid minds in all ages have ever practiced; and both by precept and example inculcated on mankind. It is now generally agreed among Christians that this spirit of toleration in the fullest extent consistent with the being of civil society 'is the chief characteristical mark of the true church' & …such toleration ought to be extended to all whose doctrines are not subversive of society.[790]

Adams summarizes his defense of colonists' rights by stating their origin in God and nature—and in God's moral law: "'Just and true liberty, equal and impartial liberty' in matters spiritual and temporal, is a thing that all Men are clearly entitled to, by the eternal and immutable laws Of God and nature, as well as by the law of Nations, & all well grounded municipal laws, which must have their foundation in the former."[791] Adams further asserted that man's rights are found in the Bible. He defends, "These [rights] may be best understood by reading and carefully studying the institutes of the great Lawgiver and head of the Christian Church [Jesus Christ]: which are to be found closely written and promulgated in the *New Testament*."[792]

In the Declaration, Jefferson draws from Locke's property of person—life and liberty—and the idea that they are unalienable rights. Jefferson does not, however, list property in the sense of estate or fortune as an unalienable right because Jefferson, like thinkers of the Scottish Enlightenment—including Francis Hutcheson, David Hume, and Jean-Jacques Burlamaqui—believed man's possessions, goods, and fruits of labor are transferrable or exchangeable—alienable—property that may be bought or sold, transferred or exchanged, as man chooses in order to sustain and better his life. For example, in his 1755 *A System of Moral Philosophy*, Hutcheson states, "Our rights are either alienable, or unalienable. The former are known by these two characters jointly, that the translation of them to others can be made effectually, and that some interest of society, or individuals consistently with it, may frequently require such translations. Thus our right to our goods and labours is naturally alienable."[793] Garry Wills links Jefferson's view of alienable property and rights with that of Hutcheson: "Jefferson's views on property, rights, and the social nature of man fit perfectly the Hutchesonian background; and this explains his refusal to put property among the 'inalienable rights' of his Declaration. For him, property is the transferable commerce of those who have pledged moral 'fidelity' to each other and have an equal stake in the public good."[794]

Wilson likewise supports the idea of individual, unalienable rights in his *Lectures on Law* and in his 1793 court decision *Chisholm vs. Georgia*.[795] In his *Lectures*, he observes that all humans possess natural rights which are upheld by God's moral law and the Law of Nature. He writes,

> The natural rights and duties of man belong equally to all. Each forms a part of that great system, whose greatest interest and happiness are intended by all the laws of God and nature. These laws prohibit the wisest and the most powerful from inflicting misery on the meanest and most ignorant; and from depriving them of their rights or just acquisitions. By these laws, rights, natural or acquired, are confirmed, in the same manner, to all; to the weak and artless, their small acquisitions, as well as to the strong and artful, their large ones.[796]

In his court decision, Wilson alludes to Genesis, Psalm 139:14 in which the individual is described as "fearfully and wonderfully made," and Ephesians 2:10 in which the individual is described as God's "worksmanship." He thus defends from the Bible a person's God-given dignity and individual rights which are to be protected by civil government. At the same time, he rues mankind's history of unjust usurpation of God and oppression of human rights by unjust earthly powers. He states,

> MAN, fearfully and wonderfully made, is the workmanship of his all perfect CREATOR: A State; useful and valuable as the contrivance is, is the inferior contrivance of man; and from his native dignity derives all its acquired importance. …
> … …[L]aws derived from the pure source of equality and justice must be founded on the CONSENT of those, whose obedience they require. The sovereign, when traced to his source, must be found in the man.[797]

Wilson suggests that man's individual, unalienable rights come from God and are to be defended by civil government. "What Wilson establishes here," explains Daniel Robinson, "is that the dignity accorded to the state is parasitic on the dignity enjoyed by persons. To whatever extent actions by the state constitute a diminution of the dignity of the individual, to that same extent the standing of the state is itself diminished."[798] Because the state consisted of the people, if the state diminishes the rights and dignity of the individual, it basically also diminishes the rights and dignity of the state itself.

The principle of God-given, natural, unalienable rights was central to the Declaration and later to the Constitution. The Declaration would include the truth that all men "are endowed by their Creator with certain unalienable rights, that among these are Life, Liberty, and the Pursuit of Happiness." It was, says Steven Waldman, the "best argument that Judeo-Christian tradition influenced the creation of our nation."[799] The Bible was the only original, ancient source to include all the principles embodied in the Declaration.[800] The Bible and the Declaration link the Law of Nature and natural, unalienable rights.

7.13 The God-Given Right to Pursue Happiness

The American Founders' recognition of the pursuit of happiness as a natural right of man in the Declaration had a number of likely pro-Christian influences. The idea of the pursuit of happiness as right emerged in the 1700s among the "moral-sense" philosophers, many of the Scottish Enlightenment, who recognized the innate, moral desire in man for good versus evil in one's life.[801] Scottish Enlightenment thinker Francis Hutcheson had described man's innate desire for good as a right to pursue it, stating in his 1747 *A Short Introduction to Moral Philosophy,* "The several rights of mankind are therefore first made known by the natural feelings of their hearts, and their natural desires, pursuing such things as tend to the good of each individual or those dependent on him: and recommending to all certain virtuous offices."[802]

Swiss legal and political theorist Jean-Jacques Burlamaqui, who was influenced by Hutcheson and the Scottish Enlightenment, saw man's universal desire for good versus evil in life as a desire for "happiness." Happiness comes from the Bible and was used to describe man's blessedness on earth or in heaven. The concept of happiness is similar to the idea of blessedness. Blessedness appears in the "beatitudes" or "blesseds" of Matthew 5.[803] Burlamaqui was the first theorist to articulate the pursuit of happiness as a natural human right. As all men universally desire happiness, he saw, all men have a natural right to pursue and acquire happiness. Burlamaqui addressed the right to pursue happiness in his *Principles of Natural Law*. Burlamaqui explains the natural right of man to pursue happiness and goodness in life:

> …God by creating us, proposed our preservation, perfection, and happiness. This is what manifestly appears, as well by the faculties with which man is inriched, which all tend to the same end; as by the strong inclination that prompts us to pursue good, and shun evil. God is therefore willing, that everyone should labor for his own preservation and perfection, in order to acquire all the happiness of which he is capable according to his nature and state.[804]

Blackstone and Pufendorf more specifically believed that man's happiness is found in man's relationship with God, in living by and obeying God and His law. This is man's purpose in life and gives man a sense of well-being. In his 1765 *Commentaries*, Blackstone stated that God has "so intimately connected, so inseparably interwoven the laws of eternal justice with the happiness of each individual, that the latter cannot be attained but by observing the former; and, if the former be punctually obeyed, it cannot but induce the latter."[805] Blackstone basically aligned with Pufendorf on the matter. Pufendorf had stated in his *Of the Law of Nature and Nations* "that by Order of the Divine Providence it so falls out, that by a Natural Consequence our Happiness flows from such Actions as are agreeable to the Law of Nature, and our Misery from such as are repugnant to it."[806]

Many moral sense philosophers believed that the primary goal of civil government is the people's happiness. Hutcheson writes, "But as the end of all civil power is acknowledged by all to be the safety and happiness of the whole body; any power not naturally conducive to this end is unjust; which the people, who rashly granted it under an error, may justly abolish again when they find it necessary to their safety to do so."[807]

A number of sources and occasions in early and revolutionary America addressed the idea of happiness. In most cases, the early American view of happiness was seen as a moral pursuit. And, at times, it was understood as relating to matters not only temporal and secular but also divine and eternal. Revivalist theologian of the Great Awakening, Jonathan Edwards, for example, believed man's happiness is found in God—specifically, in Christ's eternal salvation of man from his fallen, sinful condition and eternal condemnation. Man's goal in life was to pursue this eternal salvation and happiness in God.

American statesman George Mason along with Wilson also saw the pursuit of happiness as a natural, unalienable right. George Mason's 1774 and 1776 Virginia Declaration of Rights included the idea of happiness as a natural right, stating,

> 1. That all men are by nature equally free and independent, and have certain inherent rights, of which, when they enter into a state of society, they cannot, by any compact, deprive or divest their posterity; namely, the enjoyment of life and liberty, with the means of acquiring and possessing property, and pursuing and obtaining happiness and safety.[808]

Wilson similarly asserts that because God created man out of His goodness and holds goodwill towards man, man has a natural right to pursue happiness or blessedness. Wilson states,

By his goodness, he [God] proposes our happiness: and to that end directs the operations of his power and wisdom. Indeed, to his goodness alone we may trace the principle of his laws. Being infinitely and eternally happy in himself, his goodness alone could move him to create us, and give us the means of happiness. The same principle, that moved his creating, moves his governing power. The rule of his government we shall find to be reduced to this one paternal command—Let man pursue his own perfection and happiness.[809]

Wilson also asserts that because God has given mankind a natural desire for happiness, the pursuit of happiness is a natural human right. He states,

Nature has implanted in man the desire of his own happiness; she has inspired him with many tender affections towards others, especially in the near relations of life; she has endowed him with intellectual and with active powers; she has furnished him with a natural impulse to exercise his powers for his own happiness, and the happiness of those, for whom he entertains such tender affections. If all this is true, the undeniable consequence is, that he has a right to exert those powers for the accomplishment of those purposes, in such a manner, and upon such objects, as his inclination and judgment shall direct; provided he does no injury to others; and provided more publick interests do not demand his labours. This right is natural liberty. Every man has a sense of this right. Every man has a sense of the impropriety of restraining or interrupting it.[810]

Wilson observed that the purpose of government and the cause for independence from Britain was, ultimately, the people's happiness. He makes this point in his 1774 *Considerations on the Nature and Extent of the Legislative Authority of the British Parliament*. Citing Burlamaqui, he asserts that, based on the Law of Nature, government is created to increase the people's happiness:

All men are, by nature, equal and free: no one has a right to any authority over another without his consent: all lawful government is founded on the consent of those who are subject to it: such consent was given with a view to ensure and to increase the happiness of the governed, above what they could enjoy in an independent and unconnected state of nature. The consequence is, that the happiness of the society is the *first* law of every government c [2. Burlamaqui 32, 33.].

This rule is founded on the law of nature: it must control every political maxim: it must regulate the legislature itself d [1. Blackstone's Commentaries 41.]. The people have a right to insist that this rule be observed; and are entitled to demand a moral security that the legislature will observe it. If they have not the first, they are slaves; if they have not the second, they are, every moment, exposed to slavery. ...

Let me now be permitted to ask—Will it ensure and increase the happiness of the American colonies, that the parliament of Great Britain should possess a supreme, irresistible, uncontrolled authority over them? Is such an authority consistent with their liberty? Have they any security that it will be employed only for their good? Such a security is absolutely necessary.[811]

These and other sources likely influenced Jefferson and his inclusion of the idea of the "pursuit of happiness" as an unalienable right in the Declaration of Independence. Such sources also likely influenced Americans' Judeo-Christian understanding of the pursuit of happiness as a moral pursuit, not a hedonistic one.

Jefferson found in Wilson and the moral sense philosophers the gauge of a government's legitimacy—the people's happiness.[812] A state that does not support man's liberties and the good of society and deprives man of happiness, he thought, operates contrary to its aim and authority. Jefferson would thus write in the Declaration, "...[W]henever any Form of Government becomes destructive of these ends, it is the Right of the People to alter or to abolish it, and to institute new Government, laying its foundation on such principles, & organizing its powers in such form, as to them shall seem most likely to effect their Safety and Happiness."

The American Founders saw "happiness" as a purpose of government and the pursuit of happiness as a God-given natural right of humans. These views were asserted in the Declaration. Based on their Judeo-Christian worldviews, influences, and assertions, the early Americans likely saw the pursuit of happiness not only as a natural right but also as a moral pursuit of good or blessedness versus evil in life—with an awareness that man's well-being comes from obedience to God and His moral laws. Furthermore, the Founders themselves also most likely had in mind not only an earthly, temporal happiness but an eternal, spiritual one. Indeed, Jefferson would later speak in his presidential Inaugural Address of both temporal and eternal happiness:

> Let us, then, with courage and confidence pursue our own federal and republican principles; our attachment to our union and representative government. ...acknowledging and adoring an overruling Providence, which by all its dispensations, proves that it delights in the happiness of man here and his greater happiness hereafter....[813]

While government could not guarantee the acquiring of personal happiness in men, early Americans thought it could avoid creating hindrances to pursuing it.[814]

7.14 The Purpose of Civil Government to Enforce the Law of Nature and to Preserve Man's Natural Rights and Property

Civil government's proper purpose, the Founders held, is to enforce the Law of Nature and to protect and secure man's natural rights—not to grant or deny them—in order to better citizens' lives, ensure their survival, and increase their happiness. In just civil government the Rule of Law and natural rights are secured for every individual. Governments that do not protect these rights could be overthrown by the people.[815]

Philosopher Pufendorf asserts in his *Of the Law of Nature and Nations* that government is ordained by God to regulate and uphold the Law of Nature and God in society. He observes,

> ...[B]oth the States themselves, and the chief Government erected in them, are suppos'd to proceed from God, as the Author of the Law of Nature. For not those things alone are from God, which He institutes and ordains by his own immediate Act, without the Concurrence or Interposition of Men; but those likewise which Men themselves, by the Guidance of good Reason, according as the different Circumstances of Times and Places required, have taken up in order to the fulfilling of some Obligation, laid upon them by God's Command (a). And, in as much as the Law of Nature cannot, amongst a great Multitude, be conveniently exercis'd, without the Assistance of Civil Government; 'tis manifest, that God, who imposed the said Law on Human Race, did command likewise the establishing of Civil Societies, so far as they serve for Instruments and Means of improving and inforceing the Law of Nature. And hence likewise it is, that God, in the Holy Scriptures, expressly approves of such Government, acknowledging and confirming it, as his own Appointment....[816]

Locke explains the purpose of government to preserve man's rights and restrain evil among men:

> If man in the state of Nature [without civil society] be so free, as has been said, if he be absolute lord of his own person and possessions, equal to the greatest and subject to nobody, why will he part with his Freedom, this empire, and subject himself to the dominion and control of any other power? To which it is obvious to answer, that though in the state of Nature he hath such a right, yet the enjoyment of it is very uncertain, and constantly exposed to the invasion of others; for all being kings as much as he, every man his equal, and the greater part no strict observers of equity and justice, the enjoyment of the property he has in this state is very unsafe, very unsecure. This makes him willing to quit this condition which, however free, is full of fears and continual dangers; and it is not without reason that he seeks out

and is willing to join in society with others who are already united, or have a mind to unite for the mutual preservation of their lives, liberties and estates, which I call by the general name—property.[817]

The purpose of government, Locke asserted, is to preserve and protect man's rights and property—man's life, liberty, and estate—to which all men, as created by God, have an equal right. This property includes man's own self or person, labor, land, family, and possessions.[818] For this purpose God provides the natural earth as common to all men for their subsistence and provision. The Bible, notes Locke, citing Psalms 115:16, "gives us an account of those grants God made of the World to Adam, and to Noah, and his sons, it is very clear, that God, as king David says (Psalm cxv. 16), 'has given the earth to the children of men,' given it to mankind in common."[819] Civil society and government are developed by humans to protect their persons, property, labor, land, and other possessions.

Locke addresses the need for and purpose of government for the preservation of mankind and lawful restraint of man's evil behaviors in a society in which all men are equal and free:

> 7. …[A]ll men may be restrained from invading other's rights, and from doing hurt to one another, and the law of Nature be observed, which willeth the peace and preservation of all mankind, the execution of the law of Nature is in that state put into every man's hands, whereby every one has a right to punish the transgressors of the law to such a degree as may hinder its violation. For the law of Nature would, as all other laws that concern men in this world, be in vain if there were nobody that in the state of Nature had a power to execute that law, and thereby preserve the innocent and restrain offenders; and if any one in the state of Nature may punish another for any evil he has done, every one may do so. For in that state of perfect equality, where naturally there is no superiority or jurisdiction of one over another, what any may do in prosecution of that law, every one must needs have a right to do.[820]

The Law of Nature had to be enforced in civil law and society, and all men were to be equally protected under the law.

Sidney also asserts that the purpose of just civil government and society is to protect man's natural rights, which are otherwise at risk, for mankind's survival and benefit. Sidney explains it,

> Reason leads them to this: no one man or family is able to provide that which is requisite for their convenience or security, whilst every one has an equal right to every thing, and none acknowledges a superior to determine the controversies, that upon such occasions must continually arise, and will probably be so many and great, that mankind cannot bear them.[821]

Men create governments for their own good, Sidney asserts, for justice and protection. He further states, "But if governments arise from the consent of men, and are instituted by men according to their own inclinations, they do therein seek their own good; for the will is ever drawn by some real good, or the appearance of it" and "The only ends for which government are constituted, and obedience rendered to them, are the obtaining of justice and protection; and they who cannot provide for both, give the people a right of taking such ways as best please themselves, in order to their own safety."[822]

The Declaration asserts the purpose of government to defend and uphold the Law of Nature and man's natural rights of life, liberty, and the pursuit of happiness in stating, "That to secure these rights, Governments are instituted among Men, deriving their just powers from the consent of the governed….

7.15 The Natural Right to Resist Tyranny and Oppression

Based on the American view of man's God-given natural rights and of the role of government to protect those rights, early Americans and the Founders asserted their right to resist tyranny when such natural rights were violated. The American Founders largely drew from Locke's articulation of social contract theory and the people's right to resist tyranny. Locke asserted that the people have the right to overthrow tyrannical governments that violate their natural rights to life, liberty, and property. Tyranny was understood as the unauthorized exercise of power and making of laws by a civil authority beyond the just law and its right and trust and to another's harm. It was the use or altering of power without the people's consent or authority. It was also the use of power for one's own private, separate interests or passions, not for the public good. In such circumstances of continued abuses, asserted Locke, the people have the right to resist the civil authority, dissolve the government, and constitute a new governing body as they think best for their rights, safety, good, and preservation.[823] Self-preservation and self-defense are, Locke recognized, part of the Law of Nature.

Locke's revolutionary theory essentially aligned with historical Christian revolutionary theory as found in, among other sources, *Vindiciae* and *Lex Rex*. Locke, however, was less concerned about the process of revolution as addressed by Rutherford and more concerned about its moral justification.[824]

The American Founders applied this revolutionary theory in the Declaration as articulated by Locke. Locke asserts,

> But if a long train of abuses, prevarications, and artifices, all tending the same way, make the design visible to the people, and they cannot but feel what they lie under, and see whither they are going, it is not to be wondered that they should then rouse themselves, and endeavour to put the rule into such hands which may secure to them the ends for which government was at first elected....[825]

Government's purpose is to uphold the Law of Nature, protect man's natural s rights and freedom, and restrain evil. The Declaration echoed Locke in asserting man's right to resist tyranny and oppression, stating,

> ...whenever any Form of Government becomes destructive of these Ends, it is the Right of the People to alter or to abolish it, and to institute new Government, laying its Foundation on such Principles, and organizing its Powers in such Form, as to them shall seem most likely to effect their Safety and Happiness. Prudence, indeed, will dictate that Governments long established should not be changed for light and transient Causes; and accordingly all Experience hath shewn, that Mankind are more disposed to suffer, while Evils are sufferable, than to right themselves by abolishing the Forms to which they are accustomed. But when a long train of abuses and usurpations, pursuing invariably the same Object, evinces a design to reduce them under absolute Despotism, it is their right, it is their duty, to throw off such Government, and to provide new Guards for their future security. Such has been the patient Sufferance of these Colonies; and such is now the Necessity which constrains them to alter their former Systems of Government.

7.16 Social Contract Theory and Consent of the Governed

The practice of covenants in the Bible led to the development of a more secularized social contract theory that would ultimately influence the American Founding. Social contracts were seen as voluntary compacts or oaths of mutual obligation between subjects and their rulers/governments for various political purposes, usually to form a state under certain laws or to authorize a ruler. Social contracts were derived from and resembled the Biblical covenants. The Biblical practice of covenants would lead to the development of pacts in medieval times and social contracts in the Enlightenment era in the 1600s and 1700s. It was seen in Reformed Christian political writings of *Vindiciae* and *Lex Rex*. It was also seen in the social contract theory

1 presented by Thomas Hobbes in his 1651 *Leviathan* and Locke in his *Second Treatise of Civil Government*.[826]
2 George Klosko affirms that "the ancient texts of the Christian Bible provided material for contractualists,
3 especially in the Old Testament discussions of God's covenants with the children of Israel."[827]

4   Though Hobbes supported absolute monarchy, an idea that Locke and the American Founders would
5 refute, Hobbes nevertheless rooted social contracts in the Biblical covenants practiced by the Israelites. He
6 states, "God is king of all the earth by His power; but of His chosen people He is king by covenant."[828] Hobbes
7 outlines the covenants God made with Abraham, Moses, and the Israelites in the Old Testament in Genesis 17
8 and with believers in Christ in Romans 4 in the New Testament:

9   …I find the "kingdom of God" to signify, in most places of Scripture, a "kingdom properly so named,"
10 constituted by the votes of the people of Israel in peculiar manner; wherein they chose God for their king
11 by covenant made with Him, upon God's promising them the possession of the land of Canaan…. …
12   After this it pleased God to speak to Abraham, and (Gen. xvii. 7,8) to make a covenant with him
13 in these words, "I will establish my covenant between me, and thee, and thy seed after thee in their
14 generations, for an everlasting covenant, to be a God to thee, and to thy seed after thee; and I will give
15 unto thee, and to thy seed after thee, the land wherein thou art a stranger, all the land of Canaan for an
16 everlasting possession." In this covenant "Abraham promiseth for himself and his posterity, to obey as
17 God, the Lord that spake to him; and God on His part promiseth to Abraham the land of Canaan for an
18 everlasting possession." And for a memorial, and a token of this covenant, He ordaineth (Gen. xvii.II)
19 the "sacrament of circumcision." This is it which is called the "old covenant" or "testament;" and
20 containeth a contract between God and Abraham; by which Abraham obligeth himself, and his posterity,
21 in a peculiar manner to be subject to God's positive law; for to the law moral he was obliged before, as
22 by an oath of allegiance. And though the name of "King" be not yet given to God, or of "kingdom" to
23 Abraham and his seed: yet the thing is the same; namely, an institution by pact, of God's peculiar
24 sovereignty over the seed of Abraham; which in the renewing of the same covenant by Moses, at Mount
25 Sinai, is expressly called a peculiar "kingdom of God" over the Jews: and it is of Abraham, not of
26 Moses, St. Paul saith (Rom. iv. II) that he is the "father of the faithful;" that is, of those that are loyal,
27 and do not violate their allegiance sworn to God, then by circumcision, and afterwards in the "new
28 covenant" by baptism.[829]

29

30   Hobbes also recognized the covenants the Israelites made with their rulers as in 2 Kings 23:1-3 in which
31 King Josiah covenants with God and the people.[830] This verse states,

32

33   Now the king [Josiah] sent them to gather all the elders of Judah and Jerusalem to him. The king went
34 up to the house of the LORD with all the men of Judah, and with him all the inhabitants of Jerusalem—
35 the priests and the prophets and all the people, both small and great. And he read in their hearing all the
36 words of the Book of the Covenant which had been found in the house of the LORD. Then the king
37 stood by a pillar and made a covenant before the LORD, to follow the LORD and to keep His
38 commandments and His testimonies and His statutes, with all *his* heart and all *his* soul, to perform the
39 words of this covenant that were written in this book. And all the people took a stand for the covenant.

40

41   Sidney also recognized and applied Bible-based covenant theory to civil society and the relationship
42 between the civil state and the people. He states that "a civil society is composed of equals, and fortified by
43 mutual compacts…."[831] He acknowledged the old and new covenants of the Bible and the practice of the
44 Israelites in choosing and covenanting with their kings. No man becomes king until chosen by the people.

45

46   Sidney cites the Israelites' practice of choosing and covenanting with their kings as, for example, David
47 in 2 Samuel 2 and 5, Jeroboam in 1 Kings 12, Joas in 2 Chronicles 23, and Ammon in 2 Chronicles 33. He
48 writes that "all Judah came to Hebron, and made David their King: …and anointed him king over them, and he

made a covenant with them before the Lord. When Solomon was dead, all Israel met together in Sechem; and ten tribes, disliking the proceedings of Rehoboam, rejected him, and made Jeroboam their king."[832] Citing 2 Chronicles 23 and 2 Chronicles 33 respectively, he also illustrates how the people of Israel overthrow the usurper Queen Athaliah and covenant with and crown King Joash:

> And both the examples of Joas and Josiah prove, that neither of them came in by their own right, but by the choice of the people. "Jehoiada [the priest] gathered the Levites out of all the cities of Judah, and the chief of the fathers of Israel, and they came to Jerusalem: and all the congregation made a covenant with the king in the house of God, and brought out the king's son, and put upon him the crown, and gave him the testimony, and made him king;" whereupon they slew Athaliah. "And when Ammon was slain, the people of the land slew them that had conspired against king Ammon; and the people of the land made Josiah his son king in his stead"....[833]

Sidney further emphasized that covenants, compacts, or contracts can only occur among free men who possess natural rights, being entered into voluntarily by men:

> This shewing the root and foundation of civil powers, we may judge of the use and extent of them, according to the letter of the law, or the true intentional meaning of it; both which declare them to be purely human ordinances, proceeding from the will of those who seek their own good; and may certainly infer, that since all multitudes are composed of such as are under some contract, or free from all, no man is obliged to enter into those contracts against his own will, nor obliged by any to which he does not assent; those multitudes that enter into such contracts, and thereupon form civil societies, act according to their own will: those that are engaged in none, take their authority from the law of nature; their rights cannot be limited or diminished by any one man, or number of men; and consequently whoever does it, or attempts the doing of it, violates the most sacred laws of God and Nature.[834]

Sidney goes on to mention that a compact between ruler and people is mutually binding and that if one breaches the contract, the other is released from it—that "all contracts are of such mutual obligation, that he who fails of his part, discharges the other. If this be so between man and man, it must needs be so between one and many millions of men...."[835]

Referring to 1 Samuel 16, 2 Samuel 2:1-17, and 1 Chronicles 11:1-3, Sidney also emphasizes that the people have a right to change or remove their rulers and government if they breach the covenant or compact due to tyranny:

> If David, tho design'd by God to be king, and anointed by the hand of the prophet, was not king till the people had chosen him, and he had made a covenant with them; it will, if I mistake not, be hard to find a man who can claim a right which is not originally from them. And if the people of Israel could erect, and pull down, institute, abrogate, or transfer to other persons or families, kingdoms more firmly established than any we know, the same right cannot be denied to other nations.[836]

Locke developed a more secularized social contract theory of government that influenced American political thought and the American Founding. Locke firstly refuted the absolute divine right of kings in his *First Treatise*. In his *Second Treatise*, he laid out a social contract theory between rulers and ruled based on popular sovereignty and consent of the governed.

In Locke's social contract theory, each individual, free and equal before God, possesses certain God-given natural rights such as life, liberty, and property. God as Creator is the source of man's natural rights, and all men equally possesses these rights.[837] In a state of nature, before or outside of civil government and society, says Locke, man is unable to protect these rights which are always threatened by others because they are unable to be enforced. In this insecure state, each person voluntarily agrees to give up some of his natural freedom in order to form a civil government and society to protect and enforce the rights of men and to ensure survival. Men contract together to accept the authority and laws of a social order and civil body or sovereign. Each person willingly submits himself to the rule of this earthly civil power and laws in order to secure their rights and benefits for themselves and to better their lives. Locke's social contract theory was a secularized application of earlier Bible-based covenants and pacts. Locke addresses this practice and purpose of social contracts:

> Men being, as has been said, by nature, all free, equal, and independent, no one can be put out of this estate, and subjected to the political power of another without his own consent, which is done by agreeing with other men, to join and unite into a community for their comfortable, safe, and peaceable living, one amongst another, in a secure enjoyment of their properties, and a greater security against any that are not of it. … When any number of men have so consented to make one community or government, they are thereby presently incorporated, and make one body politic, wherein the majority have a right to act and conclude the rest.[838]

The purpose of socially-contracted civil governments are to preserve and protect man's rights. Men enter society and give up some of their rights in order to form a civil society, says Locke, "only with an intention in every one the better to preserve himself, his liberty and property (for no rational creature can be supposed to change his condition with an intention to be worse)…."[839] In the civil state, man's rights and freedoms are limited only to the extent that is necessary for the good of society. If an earthly authority violates man's natural rights he can be overthrown. A ruler's authority can be limited or removed by the people, and tyranny can be resisted. In sum, legitimate civil government is formed by consent or voluntary agreement in which free, equal men join together to form a civil state and society in order to secure and preserve their God-given rights. Notably, Locke's view of social contract aligned with the Bible-based worldview, as found in Genesis, that man was fallible and prone to violating the rights of others in a state of nature if left unrestrained. Locke's theory would be taken up by the American Founders.

Locke's social contract theory was based on consent of the governed. This principle meant that civil government derives authority and power from the people's voluntary agreement, not from force or illegitimate power, and by just rule according to the Laws of Nature. Consent was the legitimizing authority of the people to form civil states and laws—based on the idea of popular sovereignty—though a contract was not necessary with consent. No governing body holds rightful authority without this consent. Abuse of this authority meant the people can reform the government or remove those in power. Locke addressed the need for consent in all contracts. He says, "…[T]hat which begins and actually constitutes any political society is nothing but the consent of any number of freemen capable of majority, to unite and incorporate into such a society. And this is that, and that only, which did or could give beginning to any lawful government in the world."[840]

While Locke's social contract theory did not require religion to function in a civil society, it was derived from Biblical covenants and historical, Bible-based Christian thought. Locke's social contract was influenced by the Bible, his Protestant experience and education, and Christian political writings including Rutherford's *Lex Rex* and Richard Hooker's *Laws of Ecclesiastical Polity*.[841] Citing Hooker, Locke affirms consent of the people as the God-given authorization of civil laws in civil society:

> "The lawful power of making laws to command whole politic societies of men, belonging so properly unto the same entire societies, that for any prince or potentate of what kind soever upon earth, to exercise the same of himself, and not by express commission immediately and personally received from God, or else by authority derived at the first from their [the people's] consent, upon whose persons they impose Laws, it is no better than mere tyranny. Laws they are not, therefore, which public approbation hath not made so."[842]

Social contracts reflected the sacred covenants practiced by God's people in the Bible and by the Pilgrims and Puritans in early America. The Pilgrim's Mayflower Compact of 1620, Puritan John Winthrop's "City on a Hill" sermon, and the Puritan law covenants and constitutions set forth the practice of covenants in America. The charters of the early colonies had also been viewed as types of covenants or contracts upholding English rights under the British constitution. Some revolutionary-era Americans would describe these charters, as Rev. Samuel Webster of Massachusetts preached, as "a solemn covenant between [the king] and *our fathers*...in the same manner that King David stood engaged by the covenant of the people." These charters, explained Rev. Moses Mather of Connecticut, were supposed to limit government power and secure the people's rights.[843] To revolutionary patriot Americans, however, King George III and the British government had violated its charters with American colonists, and, therefore, the ties between America and Britain were dissolved.

Prior to the American Revolution, Samuel Adams, drawing on Locke, affirmed in his *Rights of Colonists* the reasons for and conditions of social contracts to protect and preserve man's God-given natural rights. His writings helped to bring Locke's social contract theory freshly into American political thought during the revolutionary era. Adams declares,

> When men enter into Society, it is by voluntary consent; and they have a right to demand and insist upon the performance of such conditions, And previous limitations as form an equitable *original compact*. Every natural Right not expressly given up or from the nature of a Social Compact necessarily ceded remains. All positive and civil laws, should conform as far as possible, to the Law of natural reason and equity. ... In the state of nature, every man is under God, Judge and sole Judge, of his own rights and the injuries done him. By entering into society, he agrees to an Arbiter or indifferent Judge between him and his neighbors....[844]

Locke's social contract theory influenced American political thought during the founding era and was applied in the Declaration of Independence and later the U. S. Constitution. The social contract entered into by Americans in their founding documents became the basis for a new people, nation, and government in the new nation of the United States. In creating a new nation by a social contract and in the presence of and under God, Americans essentially practiced the Bible-based principle of covenants in their new nation and its founding documents—the Declaration and Constitution. Indeed, the founding documents of the United States make up and function as a national covenant or compact.[845]

The Declaration—as an agreement on the creation of a new people and nation—and later the U. S. Constitution—as an agreement on the nation's civil government and laws—reflected the two specific covenants needed to form a civil state, as supported and outlined in Samuel von Pufendorf's Enlightenment-era writings on the Law of Nature. In his 1698 *The Whole Duty of Man According to the Law of Nature*, an excerpt of his 1672 *Of the Law and Nature of Nations,* 1703, German jurist and historian Pufendorf specifies two modern covenants or contracts among a people to establish a civil state—one to create the civil state and another to create the form or type of government. A covenant is also made with those chosen to govern in the state. He elaborates,

> Moreover, that any Society may grow together after a regular Manner, there are requir'd Two *Covenants*, and One Decree, or *Constitution*. For, first, Of all those many, who are suppos'd to be in a Natural Liberty, when they are join'd together for the forming a constituting any Civil Society, every Person enters into Covenant with each other, That they are willing to come into one and the same lasting Alliance and Fellowship, and to carry on the Methods of their Safety and Security by a common Consultation and Management among themselves: In a Word, That they are willing to be made Fellow Members of the same Society. To which Covenant, it is requisite, that All and singular Persons do consent and agree, and he that does not give his Consent, remains excluded from such Society.

> After this *Covenant*, it is necessary, that there should be a *Constitution* agreed on by a publick Decree, setting forth, what *Form* of *Government* is to be pitch'd upon. For 'till this be determined, nothing with any Certainty can be transacted, which may conduce to the publick Safety.
>
> After this Decree concerning the *Form* of *Government*, there is Occasion for another *Covenant*, when he or they are nominated and constituted upon whom the Government of this Rising Society is conferr'd; by which Covenant the Persons that are to govern, do oblige themselves to take Care of the Common Safety, and the other Members do in like manner oblige themselves to yield Obedience to them; whereby also all Persons do submit their Will to the Will and Pleasure of him or them, and they do at the same Time convey and make over to him or them the Power of making Use of and applying their united Strength, as shall seem most convenient for the Publick Security. And when this Covenant is duly and rightly executed, thence at last arises a *complete* and *regular Government*.[846]

In social contracts, affirms Lutz, men agree firstly "to form a society and be bound by the majority in collective decisions" and secondly "on the form of government to have."[847] These two covenants could be seen respectively in the Declaration and later in the Constitution. The Declaration and Constitution are derived from the covenant or compact tradition of the early American colonies, historical Christian thought, and the theories of Locke and Sidney.

In applying compact theory in their Declaration, the Americans closely adhered to the Bible-based principle of covenants. The Declaration acknowledges the people's consent, stating that "Governments are instituted among Men, deriving their just powers from consent of the governed." Like a covenant, the document also appeals to God:

> We, therefore, the Representatives of the United States of America, in General Congress, Assembled, appealing to the Supreme Judge of the world for the rectitude of our intentions, do, in the Name, and by Authority of the good People of these Colonies, solemnly publish and declare, That these United Colonies are, and of Right ought to be Free and Independent States....

The Declaration also concludes with a pledge among the people, with God as witness and guarantor: "And for the support of this Declaration, with a firm reliance on the Protection of Divine Providence, we mutually pledge to each other our Lives, our Fortunes, and our sacred Honor."

Elazar notes the correlation between covenant- or contract-based societies and the Bible: "What is common to all political societies rooted in the covenant idea is that they have drawn their inspiration proximately or ultimately from its biblical source. ... [W]e have not found any developed covenantal tradition that is not derived from the Bible."[848] Americans, for example, identified with the Israelites in their Exodus from Egypt and receiving of the Ten Commandments from Moses to become the Jewish people. Elazar states, "Revolutions take things apart; covenants reassemble them through conscious acts of consent. Where frontiers and revolutions coincide, as in the exodus of ancient Israel and the founding period of the United States, covenant ideas tend to become the informing ideas of the peoples and politics in question."[849]

The American Revolution, says Elazar, "translated the concept [of covenant] into a powerful instrument of political reform but only after merging it with the more secularized idea of compact. American constitutionalism is a product of that merger."[850] Biblically-derived covenants "acquired fully separate political justification," says Elazar, "which, through Locke, Montesquieu, and the covenanter settlers of America, became the basis for the formation of the United States as reflected in the preambles of the Declaration of Independence, the U. S. Constitution, and the American state constitutions."[851] And the Americans still made a point to create a contract, though secularized, in the presence of and under God, in the spirit of a true covenant. "...[I]f all the Biblical and Christian sources in history for compact theory were removed," concludes Amos, "the Declaration could not have been written the way it was."[852]

7.17 The Influence of Locke and Sidney on the Revolution

Revolutionary-era Americans and the Founders specifically acknowledged the strong influence of Locke and Sidney on civil liberty and the political thought of America's revolution and founding. For example, the works of Locke and Sidney were in the libraries of many American Founders including Jefferson, Franklin, and Hamilton. They appeared on Jefferson's library list. In his *Commonplace Book*, his student collection of excerpts, Jefferson cites Locke. On May 8, 1825, Jefferson wrote a letter about the sources of the Declaration: "All its authority rests then on the harmonizing sentiments of the day, whether expressed in conversation, in letters, printed essays, or in the elementary books of public right, as Aristotle, Cicero, Locke, Sidney, etc.[853] In addition, in a May 30, 1790, letter to a prospective law student, Jefferson recommends Locke's *Second Treatise* for reading, stating, "Locke's little book on Government, is perfect as far as it goes."[854] In a June 11, 1807, letter, Jefferson lists Locke and Sidney among several sources of reading he recommends on civil government. Jefferson writes,

I think there does not exist a good elementary work on the organization of society into civil government: I mean a work which presents in one full and comprehensive view the system of principles on which such an organization should be founded, according to the rights of nature. For want of a single work of that character, I should recommend Locke on Government, Sidney, Priestley's Essay on the First Principles of Government, Chipman's Principles of Government, and the Federalist [Papers].[855]

In addition, Locke and Sidney were influential among the clergy and often cited in political sermons in Boston during the revolutionary era. Revolutionary clergyman Rev. Jonathan Mayhew, for example, was greatly influenced by Locke's writings.[856] In a 1754 election sermon, Mayhew named Locke and Sidney as significant sources of American civil liberty and part of his education at Harvard:

Having been initiated in his youth, in the doctrines of civil liberty, as explained and inculcated by Plato, Demosthenes, Cicero, and other renowned persons among the ancients, and such as Sidney, Milton, Locke, and Hoadly, among the moderns, I approved them—they appeared rational and just: and having also learned, from the holy scriptures, that wise, and brave, and virtuous men were always the friends of liberty…I was thus led to conclude that freedom as a great blessing.[857]

Benjamin Rush likewise expressed the importance Americans placed on Locke in his 1777 *Observations on the Government of Pennyslvania*: "Mr. Locke is an oracle as to the *principles*, Harrington and Montesquieu are the oracles as to the *forms* of government."[858]

John Adams also notes in his 1787 *A Defense of the Constitutions of Government of the United States of America* the influence of Sidney and Locke on the American founding. He states,

Americans, too, ought for ever to acknowledge their obligations to English writers, or rather have as good a right to indulge a pride in the recollection of them as the inhabitants of the three kingdoms. The original plantation of our country was occasioned, her continued growth has been promoted, and her present liberties have been established by these generous theories.

There have been three periods in the history of England, in which the principles of government have been anxiously studied, and very valuable productions published, which, at this day, if they are not wholly forgotten in their native country, are perhaps more frequently read abroad than at home.

The first of these periods was that of the Reformation…. The "Short Treatise of Politicke Power…compyled by John Poynet…," …contains all the essential principles of liberty, which were afterwards dilated on by Sidney and Locke. …

The third period was the [Glorious] Revolution of 1688 [in England], which produced Sidney, Locke, Hoadley, Trenchard, Gordon, Plato, Redivivus…and others without number. The discourses of Sidney were indeed written before, but the same causes produced his writings and the Revolution.

Americans should make collections of all these speculations, to be preserved as the most precious relics of antiquity….[859]

John Adams further praises the merit of Sidney in a September 17, 1823, letter to Jefferson:

I have lately undertaken to read Algernon Sidney on Government. … As often as I have read it and fumbled it over, it now excites fresh admiration [surprise] that this work has excited so little interest in the literary world. As splendid an edition of it as the art of printing can produce, as well for the intrinsic merits of the work, as for the proof it brings of the bitter sufferings of the advocates of liberty from that time to this, and to show the slow progress of moral, philosophical, and political illumination in the world, ought to be now published in America.[860]

On March 4, 1825, the Board of Visitors of the University of Virginia, directed by Jefferson, adopted a resolution to include the works of Locke and Sidney in the school's curriculum. The resolution stated,

Whereas, it is the duty of this Board to the government under which it lives, and especially to that of which this University is the immediate creation, to pay special attention to the principles of government which shall be inculcated therein, and to provide that none shall be inculcated which are incompatible with those on which the Constitutions of this State, and of the United States were genuinely based, in the common opinion; and for this purpose it may be necessary to point out specially where these principles are to be found legitimately developed: Resolved, that it is the opinion of this Board that as to the general principles of liberty and the rights of man, in nature and in society, the doctrines of Locke, in his "Essay concerning the true original extent and end of civil government," and of Sidney in his "Discourses on government," may be considered as those generally approved by our fellow citizens of this, and the United States….[861]

Lutz affirms the importance of Locke and Sidney for their clear articulation of many long-held ideas of Americans, which Americans drew upon during the founding era:

[T]he sentiments, ideas, and commitments found in Locke and Sidney existed also in American colonial writing [such as Thomas Hooker and Roger Williams] long before these two English theorists published their great works. … On the other hand, the manner of expressing these ideas and commitments in the Declaration of Independence rested heavily upon the writings of Sidney and Locke, as well as Burlamaqui and Vattel, though mediated by two slightly earlier documents written by prominent Americans.[862]

The language of the Declaration is much like Locke's, says Lutz, "because the Americans enthusiastically fastened upon his clear, efficient vocabulary for expressing what they had already been doing for years."[863]

7.18 God As Supreme Judge of the World and "No King But King Jesus"

Most Americans had always held the Judeo-Christian belief that God is Creator and the highest governing authority over man based on Isaiah 33:22: "For the Lord is our Judge, The Lord is our Lawgiver, The Lord is our King; He will save us." All men, including human earthly authorities, are subject and responsible to and judged by God. During the revolution, Americans appealed to God and His sovereign rule for the moral uprightness of their cause. The Declaration of Independence included an appeal "to the Supreme Judge of the world for the rectitude of our intentions." Describing the God of the Bible, this name and phrase, says Waldman, expressed "a classically biblical vision of God's stature, disposition, and involvement" in the lives of men.[864] Americans appealed to God as highest ruler for faith, justification, protection, and success in challenging the most powerful nation in the world at that time.

"Supreme Judge" was a name for God that Americans had learned from the Bible and various Bible-based thinkers. The American Founders possibly drew their description of God in the Declaration from Locke and Judges 11. Locke had referred to God as "Supreme Judge" based on such a description of God in Judges 11. In Judges 11:27, 32, when no earthly authority exists to whom the Israelites can appeal against their enemies in battle, they appeal to God as the judge of all men to decide the outcome—giving victory to the army in the right and defeat to the army in the wrong. Subsequently, God judges the outcome of the war between the armies of Israel, led by Jephthah, and the armies of Ammon. Locke states,

> 21. To avoid this *state of war* (wherein there is no appeal but to heaven, and wherein every the least difference is apt to end, where there is no authority to decide between the contenders) is one great reason of men's puttings themselves into society, and quitting the state of nature: for where there is an authority, a power on earth, from which relief can be had by *appeal*, there the continuance of the *state of war* is excluded, and the controversy is decided by that [earthly] power. Had there been any such court, any superior jurisdiction on earth, to determine the right between Jephtha and the Ammonites, they had never come to a *state of war*: but we see he [Jephtha] was forced to appeal to heaven. "The Lord the judge (says he) be judge this day between the children of Israel and the children of Ammon," Judg. xi. 27. and then prosecuting, and relying on his *appeal*, he leads out his army to battle: and therefore in such controversies, where the question is put, *who shall be judge*? It cannot be meant, who shall decide the controversy; every one knows what Jephtha here tells us, that *the Lord the judge* shall judge. Where there is no judge on earth, the appeal lies to God in heaven. That question then cannot mean, who shall judge, whether another hath put himself in a *state of war* with me, and whether I may, as Jephtha did, *appeal to heaven* in it? of that I myself can only be judge in my own conscience, as I will answer it, at the great day, to the supreme judge of all men."[865]

If no earthly judge exists for a time on earth, God in heaven still serves as Supreme Judge, and men could appeal to this Supreme Judge according to their consciences which also judged. The Declaration's reference to God as "Supreme Judge," some say, may have come from Locke's Biblical reference. Says Amos, "If the drafters of the Declaration were aware of that passage in Locke and meant to follow it, this means they were asking God to miraculously deliver the Continental Army from the British if the British were in the wrong."[866] The Declaration's reference to a Supreme Judge demonstrated Americans' belief in an active God who governed in the affairs of men.

As the American colonies took up arms in 1775 against the strongest power on earth, the Continental Congress publicly besought God for protection, wisdom, and justice in the war. For example, in their 1775 "Declaration on Taking Arms" report following the battles of Concord, Lexington, and Bunker Hill, Congress publicly appeals to God as Supreme Judge and Ruler of the universe:

> With an humble confidence in the mercies of the supreme and impartial Judge and Ruler of the universe, we most devoutly implore his divine goodness to protect us happily through this great conflict, to dispose our adversaries to reconciliation on reasonable terms, and thereby to relieve the empire from the calamities of civil war.[867]

In 1778, after repeated attempts to reconcile with Britain, Congress declares its "solemn appeal to the tribunal of unerring wisdom and justice: to that Almighty Ruler of Princes, whose kingdom is over all" and to "that God who searcheth the hearts of men, for the rectitude of our intentions…."[868]

In acknowledging the Supreme Judge of the world, Americans also acknowledged God as highest ruler in their new nation. Revolutionary minister Rev. Jonathan Mayhew expresses this belief, preaching, "And while I am speaking of loyalty to our earthly Prince, suffer me just to put you in mind to be loyal also to the supreme ruler of the universe, by whom kings reign, and princes decree justice."[869] During the signing of the Declaration, Samuel Adams echoes this Bible-based principle of God as highest ruler: "We have this day restored the Sovereign to Whom alone Men ought to be obedient: He reigns in Heaven, and with a propitious Eye beholds his Subjects assuming that freedom of thought, and dignity of self-direction, which he bestowed on them. From the rising to the setting Sun, may his Kingdom come."[870] It was this American mindset of God as Supreme Ruler that gave Americans courage to fight and gave rise to the battle cry "No King But King Jesus" among many revolutionaries and evangelicals during the revolution.

7.19 The Protection of God as Divine Providence

"Divine Providence" was understood by revolutionary-era Americans as a name for and function of the Judeo-Christian God of the Bible as a provider. Unlike the Deist's view of a distant God uninvolved in the world, this God is actively involved in the lives, events, and affairs of men to fulfill His divine purpose. He cares for people and their needs. This God could work in nature and in the hearts of men. He could coordinate with man's free will. He could even use harmful, destructive, immoral, unlawful people or events for His greater good and purpose. In sum, Divine Providence was understood as God's care for His people and operation in the world by His sovereign power. God's role as Divine Providence was a Bible-based teaching understood by all Christians since the early Christian church. It was acknowledged by Augustine, Aquinas, Luther, Calvin, and the early American Puritans. Rev. John Witherspoon explains the idea of Providence as was understood by Americans in his writing on the "Dominion of Providence":

> He [God] overrules all his creatures, and all their actions. ... ...It is the duty of every good man to place the most unlimited confidence in divine wisdom, and to believe that those measures of providence that are most unintelligible to him, are yet planned with the same skill, and directed to the same great purposes as others....[871]

Jefferson also expresses Americans' belief that God governs over the nation and world: "We are not in a world ungoverned by the laws and the power of a superior agent. Our efforts are in His hand, and directed by it; and He will give them their effect in his own time."[872] In a 1781 proclamation, the Continental Congress affirms God's providence, declaring that "At all times it is our duty to acknowledge the over-ruling providence of the great Governor of the universe, and devoutly to implore his divine favour and protection."[873] The Declaration conveys the American faith and trust in an active God in expressing "a firm Reliance on the Protection of divine Providence."

7.20 The Declaration: A National Compact for a New People and Nation

The Declaration of Independence that the American Founders signed in 1776 was as a social contract for a new nation, the United States of America. As a social contract, the Declaration essentially applied compact or covenant theory. It was a voluntary agreement among the diverse colonists of the thirteen American colonies to become a new people and nation.[874] It was also an agreement among Americans of the principles they would uphold as a people and nation. The Declaration, says Lutz, aimed to "create a people, define the kind of people they are or wish to become, and establish a government."[875] The Declaration was a covenant or compact presenting the nation's values to the people.[876] That its authority was derived by consent and unanimity among the people made it a social compact, says Lutz, based on Locke's social contract theory and colonial constitutional traditions. Those who signed the Declaration "spoke for the people and made it the people's compact by their proxy," Lutz explains."[877] In calling on God as witness and guarantor, with an appeal to the

"Supreme Judge of the world," the Declaration was also a type of covenant among the people before and under God as was the Pilgrim's Mayflower Compact.[878]

American colonists became nationally unified by the Declaration, says Paul Johnson, gaining a new "American political consciousness" and a "distinctive national voice."[879] New Englanders, observes Stout, "broadened their redemptive horizons to include all American patriots."[880] Revolutionary leader Patrick Henry reflected this change of perspective among Americans in stating, "The distinction between Virginians, Pennsylvanians, New Yorkers, and New Englanders, are no more. I am not a Virginian, but an American."[881] As such, the American Revolution, as Stout asserts, "involved far more than questions of taxes and representation; it meant nothing less than the reformation and reconstruction of American society."[882]

To maintain unity among Americans, the American Founders used general, non-sectarian descriptions for God in the Declaration like "Nature's God," "Creator," "Supreme Judge," and "Divine Providence." These names for God appealed to Americans of various beliefs—Secularists, Deists, Jews, and Christians alike—in order to reflect the religious or denominational diversity of Congress and the nation, avoid theological differences, and maintain unity.[883] Though these descriptions were more general than some Judeo-Christian ones, they were very compatible with a Bible-based worldview—indeed, clearly Judeo-Christian. The God of the Declaration thus became, says Meacham, "the God of America's public religion."[884]

7.21 The Bible and American Courage: The Continental Congress and the People Rely on God

The Judeo-Christian religious belief was in many ways the driving force behind those who championed American freedom and independence during the American Revolution. The Declaration's view of God, man, law, and nature—including its explicit mention of God as "Creator," Lawgiver, "Divine Providence" and "Supreme Judge of the world"—revealed the Bible-based worldview and Judeo-Christian God of the American Founders and revolutionaries. American patriot revolutionaries and clergy, the American Founders, the First Continental Congress, General George Washington, and the Continental Army found courage to fight for liberty and independence against the strongest power in the world by their faith in God and their conviction that they were doing the right thing. Americans relied heavily on God as "Divine Providence" and "Supreme Judge" for success during the Revolutionary War. Without Americans' faith and trust in God, the Revolutionary War would not have happened.

The Continental Congress played a large role in promoting a reliance on God in the American colonies throughout the American Revolution. Congress began their sessions with prayer, appointed congressional and military chaplains, followed covenant theology in their proclamations for days of prayer and fasting, exhorted Continental Army troops to practice godly behavior, endorsed the publication of Bibles, attributed success of the American cause to God, and called for thanksgiving and religious revival among Americans.

When the Continental Congress first convened in Philadelphia in 1774 to deal with the colonies' escalating conflict with Britain, their first motion was to seek God's guidance through prayer. Though of differing church denominations and initially reluctant to the idea, the men decided to pray together after Samuel Adams declared that he was no bigot and could pray with any virtuous, pious man who was also a patriot. Congressional chaplain Rev. Jacob Duché read from Psalm 35, the scripture of the day in the *Book of Common Prayer*, and led a prayer. The devotional greatly encouraged the delegates facing war. John Adams describes its encouraging effect on the delegates in a letter to his wife, Abigail: "You must remember this was the next morning after we heard the horrible rumor of the cannonade of Boston. I never saw a greater effect upon an audience. It seemed as if Heaven had ordained that Psalm to be read on that morning. After this, Mr. Duché, unexpected to everybody, struck out into an extemporary prayer, which filled the bosom of every man present." The experience, Adams further notes, "had an excellent effect upon everybody here."[885] The tradition of opening congressional sessions in prayer continues to this day. Congress did not favor or patronize any one

1 particular church denomination. They appointed chaplains of various denominations and attended services at
2 various churches.
3
4   During the Revolutionary War, Congress and the people sought and relied on God intensely for help,
5 protection, guidance, and success. Congress proclaimed days of Fasting and Thanksgiving, calling on the
6 nation to confess and repent of their sins, practice charity among themselves, go to church, and pray to God for
7 His favor, protection, and victory over British tyranny. In doing so, Congress frequently described God, His
8 attributes, and His relationships with humans in Judeo-Christian or Bible-based terms, often alluding to Bible
9 scriptures. Additionally, Congress practiced Judeo-Christian "covenant theology," as did the early Pilgrims and
10 Puritans, as a war strategy to secure God's favor during the American Revolution. Covenant theology asserted
11 that God forms an agreement or covenant with His people in which He blesses, protects, and rewards them
12 when they are faithful and obedient and punishes them when they are unfaithful and disobedient. Disobedience
13 could bring calamity or curse, but prayer, confession, and repentance stir God's mercy and forgiveness. This
14 covenant acknowledged the Judeo-Christian belief that people need to humbly turn to God and confess their
15 sins in order to obtain God's mercy and forgiveness. People also needed to offer thanksgiving to God, with
16 gratitude for His blessings. For example, Leviticus 26:40-42, 2 Chronicles 7:14, and 1 John 1:9 speak of
17 confession to God. In Leviticus 26:40-42, God says concerning the Israelites, "'But if they confess their
18 iniquity…then I will remember My covenant with Jacob, and My covenant with Isaac and My covenant with
19 Abraham I will remember. I will remember the land.'" In 2 Chronicles 7:14, God tells King Solomon, "If My
20 people who are called by My name will humble themselves, and pray and seek My face, and turn from their
21 wicked ways, then I will hear from heaven, and will forgive their sin and heal their land." In 1 John 1:9, the
22 Apostle John says to the church, "If we confess our sins, He [Christ] is faithful and just to forgive us *our* sins
23 and to cleanse us from all unrighteousness." In Philippians 4:6, the Apostles Paul and Timothy exhort the
24 church to show thanksgiving to God as they pray, saying, "Be anxious for nothing, but in everything by prayer
25 and supplication, with thanksgiving, let your requests be made known to God…." The covenant doctrine, "one
26 of the signature statements of the New England Puritans," says James Hutson, was embraced by most Christians
27 in America.[886] During the Revolutionary War, Congress revealed their covenant theology beliefs and practices
28 in their public resolutions and proclamations. They encouraged true religion, piety, and morality among
29 citizens. Such holiness and purpose, they thought, would lead to continued blessings in the nation. Ultimately,
30 Congress affirmed many of the Bible-based principles and values of America's history and founding.
31
32   In 1775, Congress declares the first national day of "public humiliation, fasting and prayer" to beseech
33 God's favor. Their resolution states,
34
35   As the great **Governor of the World**, by his **supreme and universal Providence**, not only **conducts**
36   **the course of nature** with unerring wisdom and rectitude, but frequently **influences the minds of men**
37   to serve the wise and gracious purposes of his providential government; and it being, at all times, our
38   **indispensable duty devoutly to acknowledge** his **superintending providence**, especially in times of
39   impending danger and public calamity, to reverence and adore his **immutable justice** as well as to
40   implore his **merciful interposition for our deliverance**:
41   This Congress, therefore, considering the present critical, alarming and calamitous state of these
42   colonies, do earnestly recommend that Thursday, the 20th day of July next, be observed, by the
43   inhabitants of all the English colonies on this continent, as a day of **public humiliation, fasting and**
44   **prayer**; that we may, with united hearts and voices, unfeignedly **confess and deplore our many sins**;
45   and offer up our joint **supplications** to the **all-wise**, **omnipotent**, and **merciful Disposer of all events**;
46   humbly beseeching him to **forgive our iniquities**, to remove our present calamities, to **avert those**
47   **desolating judgments**, with which we are threatened…. That these colonies may be ever under the
48   **care and protection of a kind Providence**, and be prospered in all their interests That the **divine**
49   **blessing may descend and rest** upon all our civil rulers, and upon the representatives of the people, in
50   their several assemblies and conventions, that they may be **directed to wise and effectual measures** for

preserving the union, and securing the just rights and priviledges of the colonies; That **virtue and true religion may revive and flourish throughout our land**; And that all America may soon behold a **gracious interposition of Heaven**, for the redress of her many grievances, the restoration of her **invaded rights**, a reconciliation with the parent state, on terms constitutional and honorable to both; And that her civil and religious priviledges may be secured to the latest posterity.

And it is recommended to Christians, of all denominations, to **assemble for public worship**, and to **abstain from servile labor and recreations on said day**.[887]

In a 1776 Resolution, Congress urges Americans to observe a day of humiliation, fasting, and prayer, "that we may, with united hearts, **confess and bewail our manifold sins and transgressions**, and, by a sincere **repentance** and amendment of life, appease his [God's] **righteous** displeasure, and, through the **merits and mediation of Jesus Christ**, obtain his **pardon and forgiveness**; humbly **imploring his assistance** to frustrate the cruel purposes of our unnatural enemies...." It further declares, "...[I]t becomes the indispensable **duty** of these hitherto free and happy colonies, with true penitence of heart, and the most reverent devotion, publickly to **acknowledge the over ruling providence of God**; to **confess and deplore our offences** against him; and to supplicate his interposition for averting the threatened danger, and prospering in our strenuous efforts in the cause of freedom, virtue, and posterity." It also calls on "the **Lord of Hosts**, the **God of Armies**, to animate our officers and soldiers with invincible fortitude, to **guard and protect** them in the day of battle, and to crown the continental arms, by sea and land, with victory and success...."[888]

Their 1778 Congressional Resolution assigns a day for public thanksgiving and praise:

It having pleased **Almighty God**, through the course of the present year, to bestow many great and manifold **mercies** on the people of these United States; and it being the indispensible **duty of all men gratefully to acknowledge their obligations to him** for benefits received;

Resolved, That it be and hereby is recommended to the legislative or executive authority of each of the said states to appoint Wednesday the 30th of December next to be observed as a day of public **thanksgiving and praise**; that all people may with united hearts, on that day, express a just sense of **unmerited favours**; particularly in that it hath pleased him by his **over-ruling providence** to support us in a **just and necessary war**, for the **defence of our rights and liberties**, by affording us seasonable supplies for our armies; by disposing the heart of a powerful monarch [of France] to enter into alliance with us, and aid our cause, by defeating the councils and evil designs of our enemies, and giving us victory over their troops; and by the continuance of that union among these states which, by his blessing, will be their future strength and glory.

And it is further recommended, that, together with **devout thanksgiving**, may be joined a **penitent confession of our sins**, and **humble supplication for pardon, through the merits of our Saviour [Philippians 4:6]**; so that, under the **smiles of Heaven**, our public councils may be directed, our arms by land and sea prospered, our liberty and independence secured, our schools and seminaries in learning flourish, our trade revived, our husbandry and manufactures increased, and the hearts of all impressed with undissembled piety, with benevolence and zeal for the public good.[889]

Their 1779 Resolution of the Continental Congress calls for fasting, humiliation, and prayer to God:

...that **he [God] will be pleased to avert** those impending calamities which **we have but too well deserved**: that he will **grant us his grace to repent of our sins, and amend our lives, according to his holy word**: that he will continue that wonderful **protection** which hath **led us through the paths of danger and distress**: ...that he will grant us **patience in suffering**, and **fortitude in adversity**: that he will inspire us with **humility** and moderation, and **gratitude** in prosperous circumstances: that he will give **wisdom** to our councils, firmness to our resolutions, and victory to our arms. ... That he will bountifully continue his **paternal care** to the commander in chief, and the officers and soldiers of the

United States: that he will grant the **blessings of peace** to all contending nations, **freedom to those who are in bondage**, and **comfort to all the afflicted**: that he will **diffuse useful knowledge, extend the influence of true religion**, and give us that **peace of mind, which the world cannot give**: that he will be our **shield in the day of battle**, our **comforter in the hour of death**, and our **kind parent** and **merciful judge** through time and through **eternity**.[890]

A 1780 Congressional Resolution states,

WHEREAS **Almighty God**, in the righteous dispensation of his **providence**, hath permitted the continuation of a cruel and desolating war in our land; and it being at all times the **duty of a people to acknowledge God** in all ways, and more especially to **humble themselves before him** when evident tokens of his displeasure are manifested; --to acknowledge his **righteous government**; **confess**, and **forsake their evil ways**; --and **implore his mercy**:-- *Resolved*, That it be recommended to the United States of America to set apart Wednesday the 22d day of April next, to be observed as a day of **fasting, humiliation, and prayer**; --that at one time and with one voice the inhabitants may acknowledge the righteous dispensations of **Divine Providence**, and **confess their iniquities and transgressions**, for which the land mourneth; that they may implore the **mercy and forgiveness of God**; and beseech him that vice, prophaneness, extortion, and **every evil, may be done away**; and that we may be a **reformed** and **happy** people....[891]

In a 1782 call for fasting, humiliation, and prayer, Congress asks citizens to pray so that "our joint **supplications** may then ascend to the **Throne of the Ruler of the Universe**, beseeching Him to diffuse a spirit of universal reformation among all ranks and degrees of our citizens; and make us a holy, that so we may be a happy people..."[892]

Every year during the war, Congress applied covenant theology in its days of humiliation, prayer, fasting, believing Americans' repentance for their sins and practice of moral behavior would strengthen colonists' moral and spiritual resolve and bring God's favor, assistance, and victory over the British. John Adams hoped from such proclamations of prayer and fasting so that "Millions will be upon their knees at once before their great Creator, imploring his forgiveness and blessing, his smiles on American councils and arms."[893] In calling for such days of fasting, humiliation, and prayer, Congress hoped, as in its 1781 proclamation, that God would see to it "that the blessings of peace and liberty may be established on an honourable and permanent basis, and transmitted inviolate to the latest posterity..."[894]

In addition, the Continental Congress, along with U. S. presidents, declared the first National Thanksgiving Day in the nation to acknowledge God's continued assistance and mercy and to secure and thank God for His blessings. In 1777, Congress issued the first national Thanksgiving Proclamation, approving a resolution to set apart a day for thanksgiving and praise to God and to secure God's blessings over the nation. It refers to God both in general terms as Providence and Benefactor and in specific terms as Jesus Christ. It states,

Forasmuch as it is the indispensable **duty of all men to adore the superintending providence of Almighty God**; to acknowledge with **gratitude** their obligation to him for **benefits received**, and to **implore such farther blessings** as they stand in need of; and it having pleased him in his **abundant mercy** not only to continue to us the innumerable bounties of his common **providence**, but also **smile upon us** in the prosecution of a **just and necessary war**, for the **defence and establishment of our unalienable rights and liberties**; ... [I]t is therefore recommended to the legislative or executive powers of these United States, to set apart Thursday, the eighteenth day of December next, for solemn **thanksgiving and praise**; that with one heart and one voice the good people may express the grateful feelings of their hearts, and consecrate themselves to the service of their **divine benefactor**; and that together with their sincere acknowledgements and offerings, they may join the **penitent confession of**

1   **their manifold sins**, whereby they had forfeited every favour, and their **humble and earnest**
2   **supplication that it may please God, through the merits of Jesus Christ, mercifully to forgive and**
3   **blot them out of remembrance**....[895]
4
5   In this first Thanksgiving proclamation, Congress, citing Romans 14:17, also recognizes the benefits of
6   thanksgiving to God "to prosper the means of religion for the promotion and enlargement of that kingdom
7   which consisteth 'in **righteousness, peace and joy in the Holy Ghost**.'" The Continental Congress issued a
8   Thanksgiving proclamation every year from 1777 through 1784.
9   Congress' 1779 Thanksgiving Proclamation praises God, "above all, that he hath diffused the **glorious**
10 **light of the gospel**, whereby, through the **merits of our gracious Redeemer**, we may become the **heirs of his**
11 **eternal glory**...." It calls for a day of thanksgiving to God for His favor and protection of the United States
12 and, among other things, that "he would grant to his church the plentiful effusions of **divine grace**, and pour out
13 his **holy spirit** on all ministers of the **gospel**; that he would bless and prosper the means of education, and
14 spread the **light of christian knowledge** through the remotest corners of the earth" and "establish the
15 independence of these United States upon the **basis of religion and virtue**, and support and protect them in the
16 enjoyment of peace, liberty and safety."[896]
17
18   The U. S. Presidents would later issue national Thanksgiving Proclamations. The first U. S. President,
19 George Washington, issued the first presidential Thanksgiving Proclamation in 1789. Assigning November 26
20 as Thanksgiving Day, Washington's 1789 proclamation states,
21
22   Whereas it is the **duty of all Nations to acknowledge the providence of Almighty God**, to **obey his**
23   **will**, to be **grateful for his benefits**, and **humbly to implore his protection and favor**; and whereas
24   both Houses of Congress have, by their joint Committee, requested me "to recommend to the people of
25   the United States a day of Public Thanksgiving and Prayer, to be observed by **acknowledging with**
26   **grateful hearts the many and signal favours of Almighty God**, especially by affording them an
27   opportunity peaceably to **establish a form of government for their safety and happiness**;"
28   Now, therefore, I do recommend and assign Thursday, the twenty-sixth day of November next,
29   to be devoted by the people of these States to the service of that great and glorious **Being**, who is the
30   **Beneficent Author of all the good that was, that is, or that will be**; that we may then all unite in
31   rendering unto him our sincere and humble thanks for his kind **care and protection** of the people of this
32   country, previous to their becoming a nation; for the **signal and manifold mercies**, and the favorable
33   **interpositions of his providence**, in the course and conclusion of the late war; for the great degree of
34   tranquility, union, and plenty, which we have since enjoyed; for the peaceable and **rational manner** in
35   which **we have been enabled to establish Constitutions of Government** for our safety and **happiness**,
36   and particularly the national one now lately instituted; for the **civil and religious liberty** with which we
37   are blessed, and the means we have of **acquiring and diffusing useful knowledge**; and in general for all
38   the great and various **favours**, which **he hath been pleased to confer** upon us.
39   And, also, that we may then unite in most **humbly offering our prayers and supplications** to
40   the great **Lord and Ruler of Nations**, and **beseech him to pardon our national and other**
41   **transgressions**; to enable us all, whether in public or private stations, to perform our several and relative
42   duties properly and punctually; to render our National Government a blessing to all the people, by
43   constantly being a government of **wise, just, and constitutional laws, discreetly and faithfully**
44   **executed and obeyed**; to protect and guide all sovereigns and nations (especially such as have shown
45   kindness to us), and to **bless** them with good governments, **peace** and concord; to promote the
46   knowledge and practice of **true religion and virtue**, and the increase of science, among them and us;
47   and, generally, to grant unto all mankind such a degree of temporal prosperity as he alone knows to be
48   best.[897]

1 Later, in 1863, during the Civil War, U. S. President Abraham Lincoln would make Thanksgiving a national
2 annual holiday celebrated on the last Thursday of November. His proclamation invites fellow citizens to
3 observe the holiday and similarly reflects Bible-based or Judeo-Christian ideas:

5   I do, therefore, invite, my fellow-citizens in every part of the United States, and also those who are at
6   sea and those who are sojourning in foreign lands, to set apart and observe the last Thursday of
7   November next as a day of **thanksgiving and praise** to our **beneficient Father who dwelleth in the**
8   **heavens**. And I recommend to them that, while **offering up the ascriptions justly due to him** for such
9   singular **deliverances and blessings**, they do also, with **humble penitence** for our **national**
10   **perverseness and disobedience**, **commend to his tender care** all those who have become widows,
11   orphans, mourners, or sufferers in the lamentable civil strife in which we are unavoidably engaged, and
12   fervently **implore the interposition of the almighty hand to heal the wounds of the nation [2**
13   **Chronicles 7:14]**, and to **restore** it, as soon as may be consistent with the **Divine purposes**, to the full
14   enjoyment of peace, harmony, tranquility, and union.[898]

16 Today, thanksgiving is celebrated annually on the fourth Thursday in November.

18   In addition, Congress approved the appointment of civil and military chaplains. Civil chaplains in
19 Congress provided spiritual support and direction to congressional members and national leaders. In 1775,
20 Congress, along with General George Washington, created and approved a paid Military Chaplain Corps in the
21 Continental Army. Military chaplains were enlisted in order to provide spiritual strength and moral support for
22 troops. Congress appointed chaplains of different denominations.

24   Also in line with covenant thought, Congress, along with General Washington, instructed military troops
25 to attend church and practice moral behavior in order to maintain God's favor. In the American Articles of War
26 governing military conduct in the Continental Army during the Revolutionary War, adopted in 1775 and revised
27 in 1776, Congress included protocols focused on the moral and religious development and practice of troops. In
28 Section 1 of the Articles, Article 2 earnestly recommended that all officers and soldiers attend Divine Service
29 and gave reprimands for indecent or irreverent behavior in places of worship. Article 3 issued penalties for
30 profane cursing and swearing. Article 4 in the 1776 Articles of War also gave punishments to chaplains who
31 abandoned their troops.[899] Additionally, Congress demanded virtuous behavior of the men on Naval ships,
32 requiring in Article 1 of the 1775 Rules for the Regulation of the Navy for commanders to present themselves
33 as examples of honor and virtue and to check and correct dissolute, immoral behavior. Article 2 required
34 commanders to make sure that divine service was performed twice a day on board and a sermon was preached
35 on Sundays. Article 3 gave penalties for cursing, blaspheming God, and drunkenness.[900] Of Congress'
36 emphasis on moral behavior of troops during the war, Hutson observes, "It is difficult to overemphasize
37 Congress' concern for the spiritual condition of the armed forces, for the covenant mentality convinced it that
38 irreligion in the ranks was, of all places, the most dangerous, for God might directly punish a backsliding
39 military with defeat, extinguishing in the process American independence."[901]

41   Congress also supported the importation and publication of Bibles during the war. Because the conflict
42 between Britain and the American colonies had interrupted the supply of Bibles from Great Britain, in 1777
43 Congress authorized the U. S. Committee of Commerce to import 20,000 Bibles from continental Europe.
44 While this legislation was not passed due to war events, in 1782, Congress officially endorsed the printing of an
45 American Bible by Philadelphia printer Robert Aitken and recommended it to the people.   It was the first
46 English language Bible published in the American colonies.

48   When the Americans won the Revolutionary War, Congress as many Americans attributed victory to
49 God. In an Address of the Congress to the Inhabitants of the United States of America in 1778, for example,

Congress acknowledges the Providence of God, in whom Americans had trusted, for success in the nation's cause:

> ...[O]ur dependence was not upon man; it was upon Him who hath commanded us to love our enemies, and to render good for evil. And what can be more wonderful than the manner of our deliverances? How often have we been reduced to distress, and yet been raised up? When the means to prosecute the war have been wanting to us, have not our foes themselves been rendered instrumental in providing them? This hath been done in such a variety of instances, so peculiarly marked, almost by the direct interposition of Providence, that not to feel and acknowledge his protection would be the height of impious ingratitude.
>
> At length that God of battles, in whom was our trust, hath conducted us through the paths of danger and distress to the thresholds of security.[902]

The United States' Peace Treaty with Great Britain, made at the end of the Revolutionary War in 1783, recognizes God as a part of the peace process. Signed by U. S. delegates John Adams, Benjamin Franklin, and John Jay, the peace treaty begins, "In the name of the Most Holy and Undivided Trinity. It having pleased the Divine Providence to dispose the hearts of the most serene and most potent Prince GEORGE the Third, by the Grace of God King of Great-Britain, France, and Ireland...and of the UNITED STATES OF AMERICA, to forget all past misunderstandings and differences that have unhappily interrupted the good correspondence and friendship which they mutually wish to restore...."[903]

The Continental Congress' encouragement of religious faith and moral virtue during the Revolutionary War reflected the spirit of revolutionary-era Americans. Congress' notable priority and investment in the spiritual life of Americans during this time likely influenced the war and Americans in many positive, profound ways. Hutson notes, "...[R]emarkable was the energy Congress invested in encouraging the practice of religion throughout the new nation, energy that far exceeded the amount expended by any subsequent American national government."[904]

7.22 The Bible and American Courage: General George Washington and the Continental Army Rely on God

George Washington, Commander General of the Continental Army, also maintained a strong reliance on God throughout the American Revolution. As his small, ragtag army of colonists fought against the strongest nation and army on earth, Washington looked to God for strength, encouragement, and success. Washington saw the American cause as a just cause. God, he believed, favors nations that uphold freedom, justice, and the Laws of Nature and God. Washington's faith in God and in the justness of the American cause influenced his continual prayer and supplication for God's guidance and protection, his endurance during the trials of war, and his trust in God for the best outcome.

Washington, like the Continental Congress, relied on his faith and trust in God during the war and encouraged his troops to do the same. During the Battle of Long Island in 1776, for example, Washington directed his troops, "Let us therefore rely upon the goodness of the cause, and the Aid of the supreme Being, in whose hands Victory is, to animate and encourage us to great and noble Actions...."[905] On December 18, 1777, during the harsh winter in Valley Forge, Pennsylvania, a time of severe trial and suffering for the troops, Washington and his men observed a day of thanksgiving and praise to God for His blessings and to seek God's continuing sustenance for the American cause. Washington orders,

> To-morrow being the day set apart by the honorable Congress for public thanksgiving and praise, and duty calling us all devoutly to express our grateful acknowledgements to God for the manifold blessings he has granted us, the General directs, that the army remain in its present quarters, and that the chaplains

perform divine service with their several regiments and brigades; and earnestly exhorts all officers and soldiers, whose absence is not indispensably necessary, to attend with reverence the solemnities of the day.[906]

Army chaplain Rev. Israel Evans delivered a sermon for the occasion on December 18, 1777. Washington later wrote to Evans, thanking him for his ministry to the troops during this difficult time, saying, "…[I]t will ever be the first wish of my heart to aid your pious endeavours to inculcate a due sense of the dependence we ought to place in that all-wise and powerful Being, on whom alone our success depends…."[907] Washington was a man who regularly prayed and depended on God. During the war, as in his life, Washington relied on his faith and trust in God's Providence to sustain him, his troops, and the American cause. He writes in a letter to his cousin, "I look upon every dispensation of Providence as designed to answer some valuable purpose, and hope I shall always possess a sufficient degree of fortitude to bear without murmuring any stroke which may happen…."[908]

Adhering to covenant theology, Washington believed God is influenced by the prayers and conduct of men. To win the war, his army needed to be prepared not only militarily but spiritually and morally in order to gain the "favor of divine providence"—and victory.[909] In accordance with his religious convictions and the acts of Congress, Washington enforced religious discipline and moral behavior in his army. He ordered daily officer-led prayer, Sunday rest and church attendance, moral conduct, and the appointment of and respect for military chaplains in the Continental Army. Among his troops, he forbid cursing, swearing, offensive oaths, profanity, blaspheming, gambling, and drunkenness, believing such behavior would alienate God's care and favor over their cause. He also banned conduct that might offend citizens upon whose support they depended.[910] Washington encouraged his men to act as Christians to represent the nation and to maintain God's blessings and favor. For Washington, like the Continental Congress, recognized the need for spiritual support and God's blessings during the war. He exhorts his troops, "The blessing and protection of Heaven are at all times necessary, but especially so in times of public distress and danger. The General hopes and trusts, that every officer and man will endeavor to live and act as becomes a Christian soldier, defending the dearest rights and liberties of his country."[911]

Washington encouraged his troops to be attentive to their duties to God. He admonishes, "While we are are duly performing the duty of good soldiers, we certainly ought not to be inattentive to the higher duties of religion. To the distinguished character of a Patriot, it should be our highest glory to add the more dist-inguished character of a Christian."[912] With such orders for moral conduct and church attendance among his troops, Washington hoped to encourage morality and to "implore the blessings of Heaven upon the means used for our safety and defence."[913] Otherwise, he and his troops "can have little hope of the blessing of heaven on our arms, if we insult it by our impiety and folly…."[914]

During the war, Washington sometimes attributed military defeats to immorality, and he attributed successes to God. Recognizing America's mission and God's provision, he states, "The signal instances of Providential goodness which we have experienced, and which have almost crowned our arms with complete success, demand from us, in a peculiar manner, the warmest returns of gratitude and piety to the Supreme Author of all Good."[915] Of various favorable events and successes during the war, Washington wrote in a letter to Brigadier-General Nelson, saying, "The hand of Providence has been so conspicuous in all this, that he must be worse than an infidel that lacks faith, and more wicked, that has not gratitude enough to acknowledge his obligations."[916] Following the victory at the battle of Yorktown, he orders his troops to attend Divine Service in gratitude of God's assistance for the American cause: "Divine service is to be performed to-morrow in the several brigades and divisions. The Commander-in-chief earnestly recommends, that the troops not on duty should universally attend, with that seriousness of deportment and gratitude of heart, which the recognition of such reiterated and astonishing interpositions of Providence demand of us."[917] At the end of the war, he stated in his general orders that "the chaplains with the several brigades will render thanks to Almighty God for all his mercies...."[918] In reflecting on the successful outcome of the war, Washington and the American Founders thoroughly believed that the Revolution was won by the blessing and assistance of God or Divine Providence.

Americans' faith in God and in their just cause gave them great courage to fight the largest military force in the world. The American Founders and revolutionaries, the Continental Congress, General George Washington, and the Continental Army all declared and demonstrated a strong reliance on the Judeo-Christian God of the Bible for protection and success during the American Revolution. Indeed, the American Founders' Declaration of Independence would make an unwavering appeal of their cause for freedom to the "Supreme Judge of the World for the Rectitude of our Intentions" and "with a firm reliance on the protection of Divine Providence." It was this appeal and faith that would encourage them to "mutually pledge to each other our Lives, our Fortunes, and our sacred Honor."

7.23 Conclusion: A New Nation Founded on Bible-Based Principles

The success of the American Revolution led to a new nation—the United States of America—with a Bible-inspired self-government never before realized in the world. This nation was based on the Bible and historical Judeo-Christian thought. It was uniquely founded on the Law of Nature and Nature's God, equality, popular sovereignty, compacts, consent of the governed, and God-given natural rights. It upheld the belief in a Creator and Supreme Judge who assigns value and freedom to the human being, governs over all men with a universal moral law, ordains government to uphold this moral law and protect man's rights, and desires man to fulfill his God-given purpose.

While Judeo-Christianity was not the only influence on the revolution and Declaration, the principles in the Declaration are derived in large part from the Law of Nature and the Bible. Amos explains,

> ...[T]he theory of the revolution was "Christian" in the sense that the principles of the American Revolution, whether rightly or wrongly applied, were an inheritance left to colonial Americans by earlier generations of Christian writers. ...[W]ithout the Bible and Christianity, the Declaration could not have been written at all, since it depends so heavily on the Judeo-Christian stream of political thought.[919]

Sandoz acknowledges the Bible-based underpinnings of the Declaration, stating,

> The Declaration of Independence is a primary text for any understanding of Americanism and a concise, creedal statement of its meaning. But to be rightly understood it must be placed in the biblical context.... The evocation of transcendent divine Being in the Creator-creaturely relationship and the sense of providential governance of human affairs beyond any sectarian divisions are authoritatively communicated therein, as is also an anthropology hinting of man as *imago dei* [in the image of God] and as, thereby, indelibly stamped with Liberty, expressed in the rhetorical mode of inalienable rights reflective of the Creator's salient attributes. The 'Lockean' liberal political theory therein advanced thus ontologically foots on this anthropology as demanding consent for legitimacy of laws and of government itself, whose powers are thus inherently limited and whose cardinal purpose is *salus populi*: to serve its citizenry and not they it. The Declaration expressed the Whig consensus of Americans at that time, Jefferson later said.[920]

Lutz affirms the influence of historical Christian thought and the Protestant Reformation on the revolution: "What has often been called the fruit of the American Revolution was in reality the result of radically extending the logic inherent in the Protestant Reformation, especially as the process occurred in colonial America."[921] Noll also affirms the influence of Reformed Christian and political thought on the Revolution and its rationale, which Americans would embrace. He writes,

...[O]ne of the reasons the War for Independence succeeded was that Protestants sacralized its aims as from God. The Protestantism that performed this sacralization did so with fragments of theology left over from the Puritan past. Some of those fragments pointed toward evangelicalism, some did not. But had not this Revolutionary-era Protestantism already been mostly cured of historic Christian antagonism toward republican theory and already mostly won over to commonsense moral reasoning, it would not have been able to provide such material assistance to the cause of independence. As it was, however, the patriots' message was embraced by a religious community whose own religious history prepared it for the receiving that message. In turn, the Revolutionary message that precipitated a democratic revolution was already marked by its association with a certain kind of Protestant religion, even as its effects transformed the social, economic, and political axioms by which Americans ordered their lives.[922]

John Adams saw a correlation between these American Bible-based beliefs and worldview and the American Revolution. Adams acknowledged the importance of the Protestant Reformation as well as Bible-based thinkers to ideas of civil and religious liberty and civil government in his 1787 *Defense of the Constitutions of Government of the United States of America.* He states, as cited in parts earlier,

Americans, too, ought for ever to acknowledge their obligations to English writers, or rather have as good a right to indulge a pride in the recollection of them as the inhabitants of the three kingdoms. The original plantation of our country was occasioned, her continued growth has been promoted, and her present liberties have been established by these generous theories.

There have been three periods in the history of England, in which the principles of government have been anxiously studied, and very valuable productions published, which, at this day, if they are not wholly forgotten in their native country, are perhaps more frequently read abroad than at home.

The first of these periods was that of the Reformation.... The "Short Treatise of Politicke Power...compyled by John Poynet...," ...contains all the essential principles of liberty, which were afterwards dilated on by Sidney and Locke. ...

The second period was the Interregnum, and indeed the whole interval between 1640 and 1660. In the course of those twenty ears, not only Ponnet and others were reprinted, but Harrington, Milton, the *Vindiciae contra Tyrannos*, and a multitude of others, came upon the stage.

The third period was the [Glorious] Revolution of 1688 [in England], which produced Sidney, Locke, Hoadley, Trenchard, Gordon, Plato, Redivivus...and others without number. The discourses of Sidney were indeed written before, but the same causes produced his writings and the [English] Revolution.

Americans should make collections of all these speculations, to be preserved as the most precious relics of antiquity, both for curiosity and use. There is one indispensable rule to be observed in the perusal of all of them; and that is, to consider the period in which they were written, the circumstances of the times, and the personal character as well as the political situation of the writer.[923]

John Adams further acknowledges the importance of the Reformation to religious liberty, with many of its proponents exiled in Geneva: "Let not Geneva be forgotten or despised. Religious liberty owes it much respect, Servetus notwithstanding. JA. 1813. Vol. VI."[924]

John Adams would later observe the influence of the philosophical, religious-influenced views of the American people on the American Revolution, writing in a 1818 letter to publisher Hezekiah Niles:

The Revolution was effected before the war commenced. The Revolution was in the minds and hearts of the people; a change in their religious sentiments of their duties and obligations. While the king, and all in authority under him, were believed to govern in justice and mercy, according to the laws and constitution derived to them from the God of nature and transmitted to them by their ancestors, they thought themselves bound to pray for the king and queen and all the royal family, and all in authority under them, as ministers ordained of God for their good; but when they saw those powers renouncing all the principles of authority, and bent upon the destruction of all the securities of their lives, liberties, and properties, they thought it their duty to pray for the continental congress and all the thirteen State congresses, & c. … *This radical change in the principles, opinions, sentiments, and affections of the people, was the real American Revolution.*[925]

Before the Civil War erupted in the mid 1800s in America, which led to the abolition of slavery, President Abraham Lincoln would speak at Independence Hall of the Declaration's significance in securing God-given liberty and rights for all men. Lincoln expresses,

I have never had a feeling, politically, that did not spring from the sentiments embodied in the Declaration of Independence. I have often pondered over the dangers which were incurred by the men who assembled here and framed and adopted that Declaration. I have pondered over the toils that were endured by the officers and soldiers of the army who achieved that independence. I have often inquired of myself what great principle or idea it was that kept this Confederacy so long together. It was not the mere matter of separation of the colonies from the motherland, but that sentiment in the Declaration of Independence which gave liberty not alone to the people of this country, but hope to all the world, for all future time.[926]

Statesman John Quincy Adams would also later recognize and articulate the United States' founding on Judeo-Christian principles. In 1837, he poses,

Why is it that, next to the birthday of the Saviour of the World, your most joyous and most venerated festival returns on this day [July 4th]? … Is it not that, in the chain of human events, the birth-day of the nation is indissolubly linked with the birth-day of the Saviour? That it forms a leading event in the progress of the gospel dispensation? Is it not that the Declaration of Independence first organized the social compact on the foundation of the Redeemer's mission upon earth? That it laid the corner stone of human government upon the first precepts of Christianity…?[927]

American Founder James Madison would later write of the achievements of the American Revolution and the formation of the United States as unparalleled in history: "Happily for America, happily we trust for the whole human race, they pursued a new and more noble course. They accomplished a revolution which has no parallel in the annals of human society. They reared the fabrics of governments which have no model on the face of the globe. They formed the design of a great Confederacy, which it is incumbent on their successors to improve and perpetuate."[928]

John Adams expressed hope in the Declaration's endurance for future generations, saying: "I am well aware of the toil, and blood, and treasure, that it will cost us to maintain this declaration, and support and defend these States. Yet, through all the gloom, I can see the rays of ravishing light and glory. I can see that the end is more than worth all the means, and that posterity will triumph in that day's transaction, even although we should rue it, which I trust in God we shall not."[929]

The glory of the Declaration, founding-era Americans knew, largely resided in the Judeo-Christian God of the Bible and His universal moral law. Without God and His Word, Americans would not have had a cause, rationale, or revolution. The Bible was, the Founders strongly believed, the source or root from which the Declaration of Independence and the United States of America were ultimately brought into existence.

Excerpts from

The Unanimous Declaration of the Thirteen United States of America In Congress, July 4, 1776

U. S. National Archives and Records Administration
www.nara.gov

"When, in the course of human events, it becomes necessary for one people to dissolve the political bands which have connected them with another, and to assume, among the powers of the earth, **the separate and equal station to which the laws of nature and of nature's God entitle them**, a decent respect to the opinions of mankind requires that they should declare the causes which impel them to the separation."

"**We hold these truths to be self-evident: that all men are created equal; that they are endowed by their Creator with certain unalienable rights; that among these are life, liberty, and the pursuit of happiness. That, to secure these rights, governments are instituted among men, deriving their just powers from the consent of the governed.**
That, whenever any form of government becomes destructive of these ends, it is the right of the people to alter or to abolish it and to institute new government, laying its foundation on such principles and organizing its powers in such form as to them shall seem most likely to effect their safety and happiness. Prudence, indeed, will dictate that governments long established should not be changed for light and transient causes; and accordingly all experience hath shown that mankind are more disposed to suffer, while evils are sufferable, than to right themselves by abolishing the forms to which they are accustomed. But when a long train of abuses and usurpations, pursuing invariably the same object, evinces a design to reduce them under absolute despotism, it is their right, it is their duty, to throw off such government, and to provide new guards for their future security.   Such has been the patient sufferance of these colonies; and such is now the necessity which constrains them to alter their former systems of government. The history of the present king of Great Britain is a history of repeated injuries and usurpations, all having in direct object the establishment of an absolute tyranny over these states. To prove this, let facts be submitted to a candid world."

"**W**e, therefore, the Representatives of the United States of America, in General Congress assembled, **appealing to the Supreme Judge of the world for the rectitude of our intentions**, do, in the name, and by authority of the good people of these colonies, solemnly publish and declare, That these United Colonies are, and of right out to be, free and independent states; that they are absolved from all allegiance to the British crown, and that all political connection between them and the state of Great Britain, is and ought to be, totally dissolved; and that, as free and independent states, they have full power to levy war, conclude peace, contract alliances, establish commerce, and to do all other acts and things which independent states may of right do. **And for the support of this declaration, with a firm reliance on the protection of Divine Providence, we mutually pledge to each other our lives, our fortunes, and our sacred honor.**"

Signers of the Declaration of Independence

Connecticut
Samuel Huntington
Roger Sherman
William Williams
Oliver Wolcott

Delaware
Thomas McKean
George Read
Caesar Rodney

Georgia
Button Gwinnett
Lyman Hall
George Walton

Maryland
Charles Carroll
Samuel Chase
Thomas Stone
William Paca

Massachusetts
John Adams
Samuel Adams
Elbridge Gerry
John Hancock
Robert Treat Paine

New Hampshire
Josiah Bartlett
Matthew Thornton
William Whipple

New Jersey
Abraham Clark
John Hart
Francis Hopkinson
Richard Stockton
John Witherspoon

New York
William Floyd
Francis Lewis
Philip Livingston
Lewis Morris

North Carolina
Joseph Hewes
William Hooper
John Penn

Pennsylvania
George Clymer
Benjamin Franklin
Robert Morris
John Morton
George Ross
Benjamin Rush
James Smith
George Taylor
James Wilson

Rhode Island
Stephen Hopkins
William Ellery

South Carolina
Thomas Heyward, Jr.
Thomas Lynch, Jr.
Arthur Middleton
Edward Rutledge

Virginia
Carter Braxton
Benjamin Harrison
Thomas Jefferson
Francis Lightfoot Lee
Richard Henry Lee
Thomas Nelson, Jr.
George Wythe

The History *of*
Thanksgiving Day

The Pilgrims of Plymouth Colony landed in Massachusetts on the *Mayflower* in the fall of 1620. They did not have time to build proper shelter or to plant and harvest crops before the brutal winter arrived. During that first winter, nearly half of the Pilgrims died from disease or starvation. The following year, with the help of the local natives, the Pilgrims had a good harvest. They thanked God for the harvest with three days of prayer and feasting in the fall of 1621.

During the Revolutionary War, the Continental Congress proclaimed days of Fasting and Thanksgiving, calling on the nation to confess and repent of their sins, offer thanksgiving, and pray to God for His favor, protection, and victory over the British. This practice reflected their Covenant Theology. In these and later proclamations, Congress frequently described God, His attributes, and His relationships with humans in Judeo-Christian or Bible-based terms, often alluding to Bible scriptures.

In 1777, the Continental Congress declares the first National Thanksgiving Day of the new nation to acknowledge God's continued assistance and mercy and to secure and thank God for His blessings. The proclamation states,

> Forasmuch as it is the indispensable **duty of all men to adore the superintending providence of Almighty God**; to acknowledge with **gratitude** their obligation to him for **benefits received**, and to **implore such farther blessings** as they stand in need of; and it having pleased him in his **abundant mercy** not only to continue to us the innumerable bounties of his common **providence**, but also **smile upon us** in the prosecution of a **just and necessary war**, for the **defence and establishment of our unalienable rights and liberties**; ... [I]t is therefore recommended to the legislative or executive powers of these United States, to set apart Thursday, the eighteenth day of December next, for solemn **thanksgiving and praise**; that with one heart and one voice the good people may express the grateful feelings of their hearts, and consecrate themselves to the service of their **divine benefactor**; and that together with their sincere acknowledgements and offerings, they may join the **penitent confession of their manifold sins**, whereby they had forfeited every favour, and their **humble and earnest supplication that it may please God, through the merits of Jesus Christ, mercifully to forgive and blot them out of remembrance**....[930]

The Congress issues a Thanksgiving proclamation every year from 1777 to 1784.

After the colonists had won their independence from Great Britain, the new Congress of the United States asks President George Washington to "recommend to the people of the United States a day of public thanksgiving and prayer to be observed by acknowledging with grateful hearts the many signal favors of Almighty God, especially by affording them an opportunity peaceably to establish a form of government for their safety and happiness." In November of 1789, Washington issues the first presidential Thanksgiving proclamation of the new nation:

> Whereas it is the **duty of all Nations to acknowledge the providence of Almighty God**, to **obey his will**, to be **grateful for his benefits**, and **humbly to implore his protection and favor**; and whereas both Houses of Congress have, by their joint Committee, requested me "to recommend to the people of the United States a day of Public Thanksgiving and Prayer, to be observed by **acknowledging with grateful hearts the many and signal favours of Almighty God**, especially by affording them an opportunity peaceably to **establish a form of government for their safety and happiness**;"

Now, therefore, I do recommend and assign Thursday, the twenty-sixth day of November next, to be devoted by the people of these States to the service of that great and glorious **Being**, who is the **Beneficent Author of all the good that was, that is, or that will be**; that we may then all unite in rendering unto him our sincere and humble thanks for his kind **care and protection** of the people of this country, previous to their becoming a nation; for the **signal and manifold mercies**, and the favorable **interpositions of his providence**, in the course and conclusion of the late war; for the great degree of tranquility, union, and plenty, which we have since enjoyed; for the peaceable and **rational manner** in which **we have been enabled to establish Constitutions of Government** for our safety and **happiness**, and particularly the national one now lately instituted; for the **civil and religious liberty** with which we are blessed, and the means we have of **acquiring and diffusing useful knowledge**; and in general for all the great and various **favours**, which **he hath been pleased to confer** upon us.

And, also, that we may then unite in most **humbly offering our prayers and supplications** to the great **Lord and Ruler of Nations**, and **beseech him to pardon our national and other transgressions**; to enable us all, whether in public or private stations, to perform our several and relative duties properly and punctually; to render our National Government a blessing to all the people, by constantly being a government of **wise, just, and constitutional laws, discreetly and faithfully executed and obeyed**; to protect and guide all sovereigns and nations (especially such as have shown kindness to us), and to **bless** them with good governments, **peace** and concord; to promote the knowledge and practice of **true religion and virtue**, and the increase of science, among them and us; and, generally, to grant unto all mankind such a degree of temporal prosperity as he alone knows to be best.[931]

Later, the governors of the states proclaim Thanksgiving Days.

In 1863, during the Civil War, President Abraham Lincoln makes Thanksgiving a national annual holiday to be celebrated on the last Thursday in November. His proclamation invites fellow citizens to observe the holiday:

I do, therefore, invite, my fellow-citizens in every part of the United States, and also those who are at sea and those who are sojourning in foreign lands, to set apart and observe the last Thursday of November next as a day of **thanksgiving and praise** to our **beneficent Father who dwelleth in the heavens**. And I recommend to them that, while **offering up the ascriptions justly due to him** for such singular **deliverances and blessings**, they do also, with **humble penitence** for our **national perverseness and disobedience**, **commend to his tender care** all those who have become widows, orphans, mourners, or sufferers in the lamentable civil strife in which we are unavoidably engaged, and fervently **implore the interposition of the almighty hand to heal the wounds of the nation**, and to **restore** it, as soon as may be consistent with the **Divine purposes**, to the full enjoyment of peace, harmony, tranquility, and union.[932]

Thanksgiving is now celebrated every year on the fourth Thursday in November.

1   **Review: Checking Out the History**
2
3   Discuss questions in subgroups or whole group. As an option, the group may come up with main ideas or
4   insights from each question. Responses may be shared and discussed in the whole group.
5
6   1. Why did the Americans seek independence from Britain? What laws and rights were violated by Britain?
7
8
9
10
11 2. What is the "Law of Nature and Nature's God"? What are the principles/commandments of Christianity that
12 are the sum of and reflect the spirit of the Law of God and Nature?
13
14
15
16
17 3. What natural rights were identified by Samuel Adams and the Declaration? Why is the Bible and Judeo-
18 Christianity important with regard to natural rights?
19
20
21
22
23 4. Why did the Founders justify their rights and freedoms and their defense of them by the Law of Nature and
24 Nature's God? What was the benefit of justification by this higher law?
25
26
27
28
29 5. Thomas Jefferson and the Founders drew from the Bible as well as many philosophers to draft the
30 Declaration of Independence. What does this fact indicate about the American Founders and their beliefs and
31 values?
32
33
34
35
36 6. What basic Bible-based or Judeo-Christian principles are evident and important in this part of America's
37 heritage?
38
39
40

1 **Activity 1: Concepts in the Declaration of Independence**
2
3 Consider the Christian and philosophical concepts incorporated in the Declaration of Independence. In the
4 appropriate columns, give the source(s) from which each concept was derived and the concept's meaning,
5 explanation, and/or context in your own words.
6

Concept in Declaration of Independence	Principle or Idea	Meaning, Explanation, and/or Context in your own words
"When...it becomes necessary for one people...to assume...the...station to which the laws of nature and of nature's God entitle them...."		
"We hold these truths to be self-evident: that all men are created equal...."		
"...They [men] are endowed by their Creator...."		
"...They [men] are endowed...with certain unalienable rights...."		
"...that among these [rights] are life, liberty, and the pursuit of happiness."		
"...To secure these [unalienable] rights, governments are instituted among men...."		
"...Governments...deriving their just powers from the consent of the governed."		
"When a long train of abuses and usurpations...evinces...to reduce them under absolute despotism, it is their right...to throw off such a government...."		
"...To institute a new government, laying its foundation on such principles and organizing its powers in such form as...most likely to effect their safety and happiness."		
"...appealing to the Supreme Judge of the world for the rectitude of our intentions...."		
"...with a firm Reliance on the Protection of Divine Providence...."		

7
8

1 **Activity 2: A Government and People Encouraging Voluntary Prayer, Fasting, and Thanksgiving**
2
3 Review the Continental Congress Resolutions and Proclamations on prayer, fasting, and thanksgiving found in
4 Chapter 7 and in the handout, "The History of Thanksgiving Day." Consider the Bible-based or Judeo-
5 Christian ideas and/or Bible verses reflected in the **bold** words and phrases of these proclamations. In the left
6 column of the table below, select and write 5-10 of these **bold** words and phrases. In the right column, identify
7 and describe the Bible-based principles/ideas and/or Bible verses <u>alluded to</u> or <u>reflected</u> in these words and
8 phrases. Use a separate sheet of paper as needed. Discuss.
9

Continental Congress Resolution/Proclamation Word or Phrase	Description of Bible-Based Principle/Idea and/or Bible Verse(s)
1.	
2.	
3.	
4.	
5.	
6.	
7.	
8.	
9.	
10.	

10

Call to Action

Each person will reflect on and write his/her responses to the questions below. Responses may then be shared and discussed in the group.

1. What new understandings do you have of the Declaration of Independence? What principles have you discovered in the Declaration?

_____

_____

_____

_____

2. How does the protection of unalienable rights to life, liberty, and the pursuit of happiness acknowledged in the Declaration affect your civic and personal life today? What might your life be like without these rights?

_____

_____

_____

_____

3. Why is it important for you as a citizen to understand the principles of the Declaration?

_____

_____

_____

_____

4. Do you think that most citizens today understand these principles? What is the cost of not understanding and perpetuating these principles to future generations?

_____

_____

_____

_____

5. Why is it important that the nation's Bible-based or Judeo-Christian roots be maintained? Do you think they are being preserved today? Why or why not?

_____

_____

_____

_____

6. What do you/could you do to help share and discuss with those in your church, school, or community about our nation's founding principles and God-given rights and freedoms?

_____

_____

_____

_____

Chapter 8
The Making of A Nation Under God

Following the victory of the American Revolution and the birth of a new, independent nation—the United States of America—the American Founders set about forming the nation's governmental and legal framework with the United States Constitution of 1787. They drew their concepts of rights, freedom, government, society, and religion from the Bible-based principles that shaped the Declaration, the state constitutions, and America's colonial history and experience. The American republic reflected Bible-inspired principles, says one educator, in both its structure and spirit.[933] The Constitution upheld and reflected the enduring Bible-based principles of civil covenant and social contract, representative and constitutional self-government, Rule of Law, the Laws of Nature and Nature's God as the standard for civil law, limited power in government, value of the individual, God-given natural rights, and separation of church and civil government. It created a new form and order of government for the nation—a constitutional republic with separated powers and checks and balances—and a free, pro-Christian society unique to history and the world. The Constitution, as a national founding document, became along with the Declaration, the nation's compact among the people of the United States of America and under God.

8.1 The Debate Over State Church Establishments, and Religious Freedom As a Natural Right

In the United States, the new states, formerly colonies, drafted new state constitutions of self-government based on their colonial constitutions, history, and experience. Americans, however, still differed in their definitions of religious freedom, which often meant to them religious tolerance, and in their views of state church establishments in which the state gave financial support and/or legal privileges to one official religious group or church. The relationship between church and government, including the establishment of an official church, was a source of intense conflict in many states. While all the states had become more religiously tolerant in the 1700s, nine of the thirteen states still had an official church. Most Americans saw the importance of religion—namely Christianity—in society, but they disagreed over how to preserve and encourage it in a free society and how to practically implement civil government in a Christian context. Some supported the continuing of official or established churches in their states while others supported complete disestablishment or separation of church and government in which no religious group or church would receive financial support or legal privileges from the state. As they drafted their constitutions, state delegates engaged in intense ideological battle over the issue. Heated debates arose in states with official churches like New England's Massachusetts, Connecticut, and New Hampshire where Puritan Congregationalism was established and in the southern states of Virginia, Maryland, the Carolinas, and Georgia where Anglicanism was established. The issue was less intense in middle colonies with no official churches like Rhode Island, Pennsylvania, New Jersey, and Delaware which began as pluralistic, though somewhat disunified, Christian societies. "The American revolution of religion began," explains A. James Reichley, "in the battle over religious clauses in the state constitutions."[934]

To supporters of state church establishments, an official church is essential for preserving, promoting, and teaching religion—specifically Christianity—in free society. In turn, it promotes unity, peace, order, morality, virtue, restraint of vices, and happiness. It helps support and maintain a strong Christian society. Separation of church and government along with new competition among religious sects and denominations would be the downfall of Christianity, they thought, promoting chaos and confusion, disturbance and disunity in society.[935] Government officials are to be, they traditionally held, the "nursing fathers" of the church, tending to its welfare, as interpreted from Isaiah 49:23 which states: "Kings shall be your foster fathers, And their queens your nursing mothers...." In the 1700s, they viewed the role of the nursing fathers as one no longer to enforce religious uniformity and doctrine as in the 1600s but to maintain financial support for official churches and to protect freedom of conscience. Tolerant establishments promote religious freedom, they held, because they typically allowed religious dissenters to organize their own churches, choose ministers, and pay church

1 taxes to a religious group of their choice. Pious individuals, they thought, should find no threat or violation of
2 conscience in submitting to the authority of a tolerant establishment.

4   In contrast, supporters of separation, typically dissenters and some secularists, agreed about the
5 importance of religion in society but favored total religious freedom—not just toleration—with complete
6 disestablishment or separation between church and government. Some of their arguments were Bible-based and
7 reflected those of early proponents of separation, Roger Williams, William Penn, and John Locke.

9   Separationists extended the argument beyond government support of religion to religious freedom as a
10 natural right and to a need to distinguish between state and church jurisdictions. For example, Awakening
11 convert and Baptist leader Rev. Isaac Backus of Connecticut and Massachusetts proposed in his 1779
12 *Declaration of Rights of the Inhabitants of Massachusetts Bay* that religious freedom is a natural right and that
13 government's role is to protect such rights. He states,

15   As God is the only worthy object of all religious worship, and nothing can be true religion but a
16   voluntary obedience unto his revealed will, of which each rational soul has an equal right to judge for
17   himself, every person has an unalienable right to act in all religious affairs according to the full
18   persuasion of his own mind, where others are not injured thereby. And civil rulers are so far from
19   having any right to empower any person or persons, to judge for others in such affairs, and to enforce
20   their judgements with the sword, that their power ought to be exerted to protect all persons and societies,
21   within their jurisdiction from being injured or interrupted in the free enjoyment of this right....[936]

23 In a 1784 *Petition Against the Religious Assessment Bill,* a group of Separationist citizens in Virginia who
24 opposed government support for religion similarly recognize the natural right of religious freedom as "the
25 privileges which by Nature they are said to be intitled to...."[937] In his 1785 *Memorial and Remonstrance*
26 *Against Religious Assessments*, U. S. Bill of Rights author James Madison of Virginia presents well many of the
27 arguments of the Separationists. Madison compares the fight for religious freedom to the American Revolution,
28 as a battle over human rights.[938] If the government supports religion, he warns, it could also potentially have
29 the power to regulate church taxes, select its church of choice, and regulate church doctrine—which could
30 potentially lead to religious oppression. Government regulation of religion was unacceptable, he believed,
31 because religious freedom is a natural right—a God-given, unalienable or unremoveable right—of mankind. As
32 religious freedom is a gift of God and nature, the state has no authority or judgment over it when it does not
33 violate civil liberties. The government's role is simply to protect religious freedom. Madison asserts in his
34 *Memorial and Remonstrance,*

36   The Religion then of every man must be left to the conviction and conscience of every man; and it is the
37   right of every man to exercise it as these may dictate. This right is in its nature an unalienable right. It
38   is unalienable; because the opinions of men, depending only on the evidence contemplated by their own
39   minds, cannot follow the dictates of other men: It is unalienable also; because what is here a right
40   towards men, is a duty towards the Creator. ... This duty is precedent...to the claims of Civil Society.
41   Before any man can be considered as a member of Civil Society, he must be considered as a subject of
42   the Governor of the Universe.... We maintain therefore that in matters of Religion, no man's right is
43   abridged by the institution of Civil Society, and that Religion is wholly exempt from its cognizance.[939]

45 Madison argues that religious freedom naturally existed before civil society. As such, one's religious beliefs
46 should have no effect on one's civil liberties. Religious freedom is outside the authority of the civil
47 government.

49   Separationists opposed even tolerant establishments and any government authority over religion. They
50 pointed out that even tolerant state church establishments violate or threaten men's natural right to religious

1   freedom and overstep the bounds of civil government.[940] For if the government has authority over religion and
2   the power to grant religious tolerance, it also has power to remove it. The government could then possibly
3   impose a different belief, intolerance, persecution, or other oppressions. Madison was concerned about
4   government authority over religion for this reason. He asserts,

6   Who does not see that the same authority which can establish Christianity, in exclusion of all other
7   Religions, may establish with the same ease any particular sect of Christians, in exclusion of all other
8   Sects? That the same authority which can force a citizen to contribute three pence only of his property
9   for the support of any one establishment, may force him to conform to any other establishment in all
10   cases whatsoever?[941]

12 A government with authority to grant religious rights and laws could remove or change them. Backus shared
13 this concern, explaining that though a current ruler or political power may enforce Christianity, earthly states
14 can change, and a state power that at one time supports Christians may at another time persecute them.
15 Consequently, Separationists wanted to do away with the view that church and government are tied together.
16 Madison affirmed the role of a separate government to protect—not grant—religious freedom for all men:
17 "…[A] government will be best supported by protecting every citizen in the enjoyment of his Religion with the
18 same equal hand which protects his person and his property; by neither invading the equal rights of any Sect,
19 nor suffering any Sect to invade those of another."[942] Only complete administrative separation between church
20 and government could insure and preserve man's God-given, natural right to religious freedom.

22   Separationists further argued that state church establishments are not Biblical. Such establishments are
23 contrary to the spirit of the Gospel. Early proponents of separation, Williams, Penn, and Locke had earlier
24 argued that religious coercion is contrary to the teachings of Christ on life, faith, peace, meekness, gentleness,
25 forbearance, and charity or love. Locke had asserted in his *Letter Concerning Toleration* that "If the gospel and
26 the apostles may be credited, no man may be a Christian without charity, and without that faith which works,
27 not by force, but by love."[943] Founding-era Separationists like Madison similarly argues that religious
28 intolerance and oppression are contrary to "Christian forbearance, love and charity" as found in 1 Corinthians
29 13:1-10, Ephesians 4:1-3, and Colossians 3:12-14.[944] In 1 Corinthians 13:7, the Apostle Paul tells the church
30 that love (or charity) "bears all things, believes all things, hopes all things, endures all things." In Ephesians
31 4:1-3, Paul says to the church, "I, therefore, the prisoner of the Lord, beseech you to walk worthy of the calling
32 with which you were called, with all lowliness and gentleness, with longsuffering, bearing with one another in
33 love…." In Colossians 3:12-14, Paul says, "Therefore, as *the* elect of God, holy and beloved, put on tender
34 mercies, kindness, humility, meekness, longsuffering; bearing with one another, and forgiving one another….
35 But above all these things put on love, which is the bond of perfection." Like Madison, Declaration writer and
36 Separationist Thomas Jefferson of Virginia—who was strongly influenced by Locke's *Letters Concerning
37 Toleration*—also expresses this idea in his endorsed 1776 *Notes on Religion* that "accdg [according] to the spirit
38 of the gospel, charity, bounty, liberality is due" to all.[945]

40   Additionally, Separationists thought that state church establishments are not Biblical because they are
41 contrary to the Bible-based view that Christ and his kingdom are not dependant on earthly powers. In the Bible,
42 early Christianity has no state religion in the places where it emerges, and the early Christian church does not
43 grow by means of a state church establishment and state financial support. Locke had made this argument in his
44 *Letter Concerning Toleration*. The founding-era Separationists in Virginia looked to the example in the Bible
45 of *voluntary* financial support of the early church. Alluding to Matthew 22:21 in which Jesus says "'Render to
46 Caesar the things that are Caesar's, and to God the things that are God's,'" their petition states, "Christ the head
47 of the Church has left plain Directions concerning Religion, and the manner of supporting its Teachers which
48 should be by free Contributions…. Let religious Societies Manage the affairs of Religion and Government
49 exercise it's Concern about the Civil Right and Temporal privileges of Man."[946] The Separationists in Virginia

1 also observed that while early Christianity and the early Christian church does not have government support, the
2 Christian faith and church flourishes during that time. Their petition declares,

4   Certain it is that the Holy Author of our Religion not only supported and maintained his Gospel in the
5   world for several hundred years without the aid of Civil Power, but against all the powers of the Earth.
6   The excellent purity of it's precepts and the unblamable behavior of it's Ministers (with the divine
7   Blessing) made it's way thro all opposition.[947]

9 Madison similarly asserted that early Christianity survives on its own without government support. Such
10 support does not exist in the Bible. Madison asserts,

12   [A state church establishment] is not requisite for the support of the Christian religion. To say that it is,
13   is a contradiction to the Christian Religion itself; for every page of it [the Bible] disavows a dependence
14   on the powers of this world: it [establishment] is a contradiction to fact; for it is known that this
15   Religion both existed and flourished, not only without the support of human laws, but in spite of every
16   opposition from them; and not only during the period of miraculous aid, but long after it had been left to
17   its own evidence and the ordinary care of Providence. Nay, it is a contradiction in terms; for a Religion
18   not invented by human policy, must have pre-existed and been supported, before it was established by
19   human policy.[948]

21 Based on the Bible and the early Christian church, Christianity existed apart from and did not depend on man-
22 made civil laws and force. Thus the Bible, separationists believed, supported separation of church and civil
23 government.

25   Moreover, some founding-era Separationists took up the argument broached by Reformers and early
26 proponents of disestablishment in America that human civil government cannot have authority over religious
27 belief because the government obviously lacks power over it. Reformed thinkers like Luther, Ponet, and Brutus
28 as well as Williams, Penn, Locke had suggested that earthly civil government is unable to touch, judge, or
29 determine the fate of man's inner soul. Consequently, government has no authority over man's conscience or
30 religious belief. Religious regulation by the civil government, therefore, opposed reason and the proper role of
31 government. Reminiscent of these earlier arguments, Jefferson addresses this argument in his *Notes on*
32 *Religion*. He writes,

34   Each church being free, no one can have jurisdn [jurisdiction] over another one, not even when
35   the civil magistrate joins it. … Every church is to itself orthodox; to *others* erroneous or heretical. …
36   The care of every man's soul belongs to himself. … Laws provide against injury from others;
37   but not from ourselves. God himself will not save men against their wills. …
38   If the magistrate command me to bring my commodity to the publick store house I bring it
39   because he can indemnify [compensate or insure] me if he erred & I thereby lose it; but what
40   indemnification can he give one for the kdom [kingdom] of heaven?
41   I cannot give up my guidance to the magistrates, bec. [because] he knows no more the way to
42   heaven than I do, & is less concerned to direct me right than I am to go right. If the Jews had followed
43   their Kings, among so many, what number would have led them to idolatry? …
44   The commonwealth is 'a Society of men constituted for protecting their civil interests.'
45   *Civil interests* are 'life, health, indolency of body, liberty and property.' That the magistrate's
46   jurisdn [jurisdiction] extends only to civil rights appears from these considns [considerations].[949]

48   To many separationists, religion in society should prosper or decline based on its merits, and good
49 religion like Christianity could prevail in a free exchange of ideas, without government support. This argument
50 reflected Locke's who had asserted in his *Letter Concerning Toleration* that true religion or Christianity could

1   defend itself by its light and evidence amidst other ideas and views and that truth "has no such way of
2   prevailing, as when strong arguments and good reason are joined with the softness of civility and good
3   usage."[950] Alluding to Hebrews 12:2, Locke states in his *Second Letter Concerning Toleration* that "It is not for
4   the magistrate or any-body else, upon an imagination of its usefulness, to make use of any other means for the
5   salvation of men's souls, than what the author and finisher of our faith hath directed…."[951] Similarly alluding
6   to Hebrews 12:2, Madison argues that establishments only weaken Christians' "pious confidence in its
7   [Christianity's] innate excellence and the patronage of its Author [God]" and conveyed this doubt to others.
8   True faith trusts in God, the "Author and Finisher of our faith" of Hebrews, for its endurance.[952] Madison later
9   reaffirms, "…[T]here are causes in the human breast, which ensure the perpetuity of religion without the aid of
10   law…."[953] Separationist Franklin of Pennsylvania shares this view in a letter, stating: "When a religion is
11   good, I conceive it will support itself, and when it does not support itself, and God does not take care to support
12   it, so that its professors are obliged to call for help of the civil powers, 'tis a sign, I apprehend, of its being a bad
13   one."[954] This argument is also reminiscent to one in the New Testament in which the Pharisee Gamaliel advises
14   his fellow religionists to not fight against Jesus' disciples and the Gospel. In Acts 5:38-39, Gamaliel
15   admonishes, "And now I say to you, keep away from these men [Jesus' disciples] and let them alone; for if this
16   plan or this work is of men, it will come to nothing; but if it is of God, you cannot overthrow it—lest you even
17   be found to fight against God." Many Separationists thought that Christianity, without government support,
18   would gain strength and favor based on its qualities and virtues. Jefferson similarly asserts in his *Notes on
19   Religion*, "Truth will do well enough if left to shift for herself. … She has no need of force to procure entrance
20   into the minds of men. Error indeed has often prevailed by the assistance of power or force. Truth is the proper
21   & sufficient antagonist to error."[955]
22

23   Separationists supported their argument that religion could survive without government financial aid by
24   citing examples of American colonies where religion had flourished without an official religion, like
25   Pennsylvania. The Separationist citizens in Virginia observes, "That religious Establishment and Government
26   are linked together, and that the latter cannot exist without the former, is Contrary to experience. Witness the
27   state of Pennsylvania, wherein no such Establishment hath taken place; their Government stands firm; and
28   which of the neighbouring States has better members, of brighter morals, and more upright character?"[956]
29   Jefferson likewise writes in his 1785 *Notes on the State of Virginia* that establishments are not needed for
30   religion like Christianity to flourish and that the absence of government regulation does not create fanaticism or
31   disorder. He also observes the peace and order of Pennsylvania where all religious groups are voluntarily
32   supported by their members, stating, "Religion is well supported; of various kinds indeed, but all good enough;
33   all sufficient to preserve peace and order; or if a sect arises whose tenets would subvert morals, good sense has
34   fair play, and reason laughs it out of doors, without suffering the State to be troubled with it."[957] Contrary to
35   fears, colonies and states without official churches did not suffer fanaticism or disorder due to greater religious
36   freedom, and churches and religious groups were adequately sustained by voluntary support. Independent,
37   voluntary churches and a just government that protects religious freedom are, separationists affirmed, most
38   beneficial to religion and civil society.[958]

39   Like Luther and Penn, Separationists also argued that state church establishments, despite their well-
40   intentioned aim, have negative and corrupting effects on religion and civil government, as history confirmed.
41   Establishments often violated conscience and produced weak, corrupt, insincere, and/or violent religion.
42   Williams had argued from Isaiah, "True it is, the sword may make, as one the Lord complained, Isa. x., a whole
43   nation of hypocrites…."[959] Penn had likewise declared that "Force may make an hypocrite; it is faith, grounded
44   upon knowledge, and consent, that makes a Christian."[960] Citing Romans 14:23, Jefferson similarly expresses
45   in his *Notes on Religion*, that establishments often promote false, not true religion:

46   No man has *power* to let another prescribe his faith. Faith is not faith witht [without] believing. No man
47   can conform his faith to the dictates of another. The life & essence of religion consists in the internal
48   persuasion or belief of the mind. External forms of worship, when against our belief are hypocrisy &

impiety. Rom. 14. 23 "he that doubteth is damned, if he eat, because he eateth not of faith: for whatsoever is not of faith, is sin."[961]

The Separationists in Virginia also pointed out the negative effects of establishments. Like Williams, they lamented the mixing of civil government and church in the 300s by ancient Roman Emperor Constantine I. Though well-intentioned, this combination, they thought, led to corrupt religion and church. They observe, "Nor was it better for the Church when Constantine first established Christianity by human Law's. True: there was rest from persecution. But how soon over Run with Error, Superstition, and Immorality; how unlike were Ministers then, to what they were before, both in orthodoxy of principle and purity of Life."[962] Such establishments would only serve to "Call in many Hirelings whose chief motive would be temporal Interest."[963] Madison in his *Memorial and Remonstrance* similarly observes the corrupting results of establishments in history: "During almost fifteen centuries, has the legal establishment of Christianity been on trial. What have been its fruits? More or less in all places, pride and indolence in the Clergy, ignorance and servility in the laity; in both, superstition, bigotry and persecution."[964] Establishments are negative for civil government, they thought, in encouraging religious and political tyranny rather than civil government's proper role as guardian of the people's liberties.

Like Williams, many Separationists thought that church and government would remain more pure when separate. Madison later expresses this view, reminiscent of Williams: "...[R]eligion & Government will both exist in greater purity the less they are mixed together."[965] Disestablishment of church and government is a benefit to both institutions.

The ideas of religious freedom as a natural right and of separation of church and government were reinforced by Americans' views of equality and freedom as expressed in the Declaration of Independence. To many Americans, state church establishments violated equality of rights among men and were contrary to America's fight for freedom. After the American Revolution, religious dissenters who had fought for freedom in the war would not tolerate religious discrimination by fellow Americans. They asserted their religious rights in the new nation. Catholics, for example, who had previously lacked freedom of worship in many Protestant colonies, asserted their equal religious rights as citizens. Catholic statesman Charles Carroll of Maryland declared, "...[F]reedom and independence—acquired by the united efforts, and cemented with the mingled blood of Protestant and Catholic fellow-citizens, should be equally enjoyed by all."[966] Citing the Virginia Declaration of Rights of 1776, Madison shared this view of complete religious freedom based on equality, arguing in his *Memorial and Remonstrance*:

> If 'all men are by nature equally free and independent,' all men are to be considered as entering Society on equal conditions; as relinquishing no more, and therefore retaining no less, one than another, of their natural rights. Above all are they to be considered as retaining an 'equal title to the free exercise of Religion according to the dictates of Conscience.' ... If this freedom be abused, it is an offense against God, not against man....[967]

Religious freedom was thus recognized and accepted by many Americans as a natural right of all citizens. The belief that religious freedom is a natural right and the Separationists' opposition to establishments influenced not only by the practical needs of an increasingly pluralistic society but also a strong Bible-based, historical, and revolutionary view among Americans of God-given rights and freedoms.

8.2 Virginia's "Free Exercise of Religion" and the Gradual Elimination of Establishments in the States

One of the most notable moves to disestablish government and church took place early on in Virginia. While establishment supporters wanted to set up a tolerant Episcopal state church, Separationists including Virginia delegates and American Founders James Madison, Thomas Jefferson, and George Mason as well as a growing majority of evangelicals revivalists and dissenters fought for total disestablishment and won. This victory led to complete disestablishment of church and government and total religious freedom in Virginia.

Madison, who would later draft the U. S. Constitution and Bill of Rights, introduced in Virginia total separation of church and civil government with a radical new expression of complete religious freedom, not just toleration, as a God-given right—the "free exercise of religion." Written by Madison and Mason, the religion clause of the Virginia Declaration of Rights of 1776 declares,

> XVI. That religion, or the **duty which we owe to our Creator** and the manner of discharging it, can be directed by reason and conviction, not by force or violence; and therefore, all men are equally entitled to the **free exercise of religion, according to the dictates of conscience**; and that it is **the mutual duty of all to practice Christian forbearance, love, and charity towards each other**.[968]

Madison's "free exercise of religion" provided complete religious freedom in Virginia, a colony that previously had a state church. This concept influenced laws and constitutions in other states, says Waldman, and "shift[ed] the terms of the [establishment] debate from toleration to liberty."[969] The Virginia Declaration's mention of the duties owed to the Creator God and "Christian forbearance, love, and charity" were specific references to the Bible—such as Genesis, 1 Corinthians 13, Ephesians 4:1-3 and Colossians 3:12-14—and the argument of some Separationists that the Bible supported religious freedom. Madison later provided such a Bible-based argument for "Christian forbearance, love and charity" and the "free exercise of Religion" in his *Memorial and Remonstrance*.[970] Virginia's Bible-based "free exercise" phrase would be adopted in Madison's and the American Founders' "Religion Clause" in the First Amendment of the U. S. Bill of Rights.

In 1786, Thomas Jefferson's *Virginia Statute for Religious Freedom* was approved, making separation between church and civil government a law in Virginia. Jefferson's bill was passed a few months after Madison wrote his *Memorial and Remonstrance*, due to majority support among the people. The bill—radical for that time—eliminated religious laws and taxes or government involvement in religion, placed all religious groups on equal standing, and declared religion a voluntary pursuit of individuals and churches. It created a state open to all sects and religions and had no religious requirement for officeholders. It asserted the separation between civil rights and religious conviction—that civil rights do not depend on one's religious convictions. In this bill, Jefferson asserts that God intends for mankind to be free and to have religious freedom and that religious freedom is a natural right. He also asserts that religious beliefs should not affect a person's civil rights. He writes,

> **Well aware that Almighty God hath created the mind free; that all attempts to influence it by temporal punishments or burdens, or by civil incapacitations, tend only to beget habits of hypocrisy and meanness, and are a departure from the plan of the Holy Author of our religion,** who being Lord both of body and mind, yet chose not to propagate it by coercions on either, as was in his Almighty power to do; …[T]o compel a man to furnish contributions of money for the propagation of opinions which he disbelieves, is sinful and tyrannical; …[O]ur civil rights have no dependence on our religious opinions, more than our opinions, in physics or geometry; …[I]t is time enough for the rightful purposes of civil government, for its officers to interfere when principles break out into overt acts against peace and good order; …[T]ruth is great and will prevail if left to herself, that she is the proper and sufficient antagonist to error, and has nothing to fear from the conflict, unless by human interposition disarmed of her natural weapons, free argument and debate, errors ceasing to be dangerous when it is permitted freely to contradict them.
>
> *Be it therefore enacted by the General Assembly*, That no man shall be compelled to frequent or support any religious worship, place or ministry whatsoever, nor shall be enforced, restrained, molested, or burdened in his body or goods, nor shall otherwise suffer on account of his religious opinions or

belief; but that all men shall be free to profess, and by argument to maintain, their opinions in matters of religion, and that the same shall in no wise diminish, enlarge, or affect their civil capacities.

...[W]e are free to declare, and do declare, that the rights hereby asserted are of the natural rights of mankind, and that if any act shall be hereafter passed to repeal the present or narrow its operation, such act will be an infringement of natural right.[971]

Jefferson's bill reflected the thought of the 1700s that God has created humans and their minds to worship freely.[972] The approval of Jefferson's statute, says Lambert, provided "a truly revolutionary religious freedom" and was "one of the most revolutionary moments in the entire American Revolution."[973] Jefferson considered the statute one of his greatest achievements.[974]

To be sure, Virginia's complete disestablishment of church and civil government was the exception, not the rule, among states. Most states, like Massachusetts, still had more limited religious freedom and official state churches and/or church taxes, though state churches in the 1700s were quite tolerant and often allowed citizens to pay taxes to the church of their choice. Most states also maintained religious requirements for public officers to be Christian and/or Protestant.

After the American Revolution, the states of the new nation gradually, voluntarily moved away from strict state church establishments. To varying degrees, states increased religious tolerance through tolerant or partial establishments or in some cases provided complete religious freedom by separating church and government. Southern states disestablished the Anglican Church of England with its ties to the British Crown, renaming it the Episcopal Church. New England states weakened establishment ties between the Congregational Church and the state. All Protestant denominations had more equal legal status. Citizens could choose where to send their church taxes and how to practice their Christian beliefs. Also, in many states, religious tests for public officers were relaxed. Most states only required public officers to be Protestant Christians, regardless of sect or denomination, who believed in a future existence of rewards and punishments. This requirement was based on the belief that public officers must have high moral standards grounded in Christianity.

In the late 1700s and early 1800s, with increasing religious diversity, many states of the new nation voluntarily eliminated state church establishments without any mandate from the U. S. Constitution.[975] In the 1800s, all states disestablished church and government and removed religious qualifications for public office. Though establishments were eventually declared unconstitutional, the states phased out establishments on their own before then. Church states had fallen out of favor and new forms of government were being learned and practiced.

It is important to note, however, that despite the gradual disestablishment of government and church in the states of the new nation, nearly all the post-revolutionary state constitutions from the late 1700s onward continued to acknowledge God and the need for religion in society. Almost all of the states included references to God in their new state constitutions. Their constitutions either invoked the favor and guidance of God or expressed gratitude for His blessings of liberty. In a 1892 court case *Church of the Holy Trinity v United States*, Supreme Court Justice David J. Brewer notes the inclusion of God in the states' constitutions, observing:

If we examine the constitutions of the various states we find in them a constant recognition of religious obligations. Every constitution of every one of the forty-four states contains language which either directly or by clear implication recognizes a profound reverence for religion and an assumption that its influence in all human affairs is essential to the wellbeing of the community.[976]

The states would continue to acknowledge God in their foundings and as essential to their civil and religious liberties.

1   The progress toward religious freedom and disestablishment of church and government in the early
2 colonies and in the states of the new nation was important nationally because state constitutions provided
3 precedents for the U. S. Constitution and federal government. The American Founders looked to the state
4 constitutions for practical models when creating the U. S. Constitution and federal government.
5
6 **8.3 A National Compact: Creation and Adoption of the United States Constitution and Bill of Rights**
7
8   Once the new nation of the United States was born, the Americans set about forming a new national
9 government for the new nation. The Articles of Confederation, adopted by the states in 1781, governed the
10 nation following independence in 1783. However, by 1787, the Articles were no longer sufficient for the states'
11 and nation's needs. This state-controlled central government, the Founders saw, was subject to local state
12 interests, left the nation open to internal rebellion and external invasion, and did not secure civil and religious
13 freedom. The nation needed a stronger national government to attend to national issues and the national public
14 good and to balance the state powers. Consequently, delegates from each state convened at the Constitutional
15 Convention at Independence Hall in Philadelphia in 1787 to revise the Articles. They drafted the United States
16 Constitution and formed the United States federal government.
17
18   Many of the delegates at the Constitutional Convention, point out historians, were brought up in a
19 Reformed Christian tradition—such as Abraham Baldwin, Gunning Bedford, William Blount, William Davie,
20 Oliver Ellsworth, Nicholas Gilman, Nathaniel Gorham, William Houston, Jared Ingersoll, John Langdon, John
21 Lansing Jr., William Livingston, Alexander Martin, James McClurg, James McHenry, William Paterson, Roger
22 Sherman, Caleb Strong, Hugh Williamson, James Wilson, and Robert Yates. While not all of these delegates
23 played a large role or signed the Constitution, some like Ellsworth, Paterson, Sherman, and Wilson served on
24 important committees and engaged in notable debates.[977] James Madison might also have been influenced by
25 the Reformed tradition to some degree, considering that he studied under American Founder and Presbyterian
26 minister John Witherspoon at Princeton. Catholics Daniel Carroll and Thomas Fitzsimons were also delegates
27 at the Convention and signed the Constitution.
28
29   The word "Constitution" is derived from the word "constitute" which means, says Lutz, "to establish,
30 ordain, or appoint…[a] legal form or status." Constitution referred to the "action of making, establishing,
31 decreeing, or ordaining something, usually…by a superior civil or ecclesiastical authority." It was used
32 historically to set limits to civil or ecclesiastical jurisdiction. It established something, usually a framework of
33 government or laws. It gave this framework legal status, described its organization, identified the sovereign
34 power, set limits, and described its foundational principles. In America today, the word "constitution" usually
35 refers specifically to the U. S. Constitution—the framework of the government and law of the United States.
36 While the British constitution was made up of thousands of documents, the United States Constitution consisted
37 of a single document.
38
39   While the Declaration was an agreement among Americans of the philosophical principles they would
40 uphold—the "who" and "why"—as a people and nation, the U. S. Constitution would subsequently create and
41 describe a workable form of government—the "how"—to practically order this new nation and implement its
42 principles. The Constitution upheld and applied the Declaration's Bible-inspired principles and values, with the
43 Constitution's Preamble reaffirming these principles.
44
45   In drafting the Constitution, the Founders formed a "federal" government for the new nation. The word
46 "federal," as mentioned earlier, comes from the Latin word *foedus*, meaning covenant. It had been used by
47 Reformation thinkers in Covenant Theology and applied by the early Puritans. It also appeared in the
48 Westminster Confession. The idea of covenants had come from Biblical covenants. In forming and organizing
49 a government for the new nation, the American Founders and James Madison, chief architect of the
50 Constitution, saw and described the new central government in widely-understood Calvinist or covenantal terms

1 as a "federal" government. This government consisted of a covenantal pact or agreement among the states in
2 and to the union. Just as in sacred religious covenants, this secularized federal union referred to an essentially
3 permanent, unbreakable bond.[978] It united the many states as one nation, with one national government. From
4 this concept came the nation's later motto, "From Many, One." The Founders thus described this new central
5 government as a federal government. They saw the U. S. Constitution as a written covenant of laws, thus
6 describing it as a federal constitution.[979]

8 The civil government and laws of the Constitution would be rooted in the same Bible-based principles
9 and universal moral law of the Declaration of Independence. For the Declaration provided the philosophical
10 groundwork for the "nuts and bolts" of the Constitution's framework of civil laws. The Constitution would thus
11 also uphold and reflect Judeo-Christian values in its civil government and law. The Constitution applied the
12 principles of covenant and social contract, Rule of Law, representative and constitutional self-government, the
13 Law of Nature and Nature's God, separation of powers, limited government, separation of church and
14 government, value of the individual, and God-given natural rights. The 1890 Missouri Bar Association aptly
15 expressed the Constitution's roots in the Declaration and its principles: "…[T]he Declaration of Independence
16 was taken as a basis [for the Constitution], and under the advice of Mr. Jefferson, that convention formulated
17 and adopted a constitution which has been the wonder and admiration of the world."[980] Sandoz affirms this
18 idea: "The philosophical foundation of the Bill of Rights is set forth in the Declaration of Independence's first
19 sentences, especially the announcement of 'certain unalienable rights' grounded in the 'laws of nature and
20 nature's God.'"[981] "If the social compact represented by the Declaration of Independence had not still been in
21 effect," Lutz explains, "there would have been no basis for a new national constitution."[982] These two national
22 founding documents—the Declaration and the Constitution—together became, says Lutz, the United States of
23 America's national compact—a contractual agreement among the people to form a new nation and
24 government.[983]

26 Drafting the Constitution was a difficult task and prompted many Founders' reliance on God. Delegates
27 fought contentiously over states' rights and other issues, and resolution seemed impossible. During this time, in
28 the summer of 1787, after the convention had deadlocked for weeks, Franklin gave an impassioned speech
29 reminding delegates to pray for God's guidance and direction for the new nation. Alluding to many Bible
30 verses including Job 12:25, James 1:17, Matthew 10:29-31, Luke 12:6-7, Psalm 127:1, Genesis 11:1-9,
31 Deuteronomy 28:37, and others, Franklin exhorted the delegates to remember God's aid during the revolution
32 and to seek his assistance again. He states,

34 In this situation of this Assembly, groping as it were in the dark [Job 12:25] to find political truth, and
35 scarce able to distinguish it when presented to us, how has it happened, Sir, that we have not hitherto
36 once thought of humbly applying to the Father of lights [James 1:17] to illuminate our understandings?
37 In the beginning of the Contest with G. Britain, when we were sensible of danger we had daily prayer in
38 this room for the divine protection.—Our prayers, Sir, were heard, & they were graciously answered.
39 All of us who were engaged in the struggle must have observed frequent instances of a superintending
40 providence in our favor. To that kind providence we owe this happy opportunity of consulting in peace
41 on the means of establishing our future national felicity. And have we now forgotten that powerful
42 friend? or do we imagine that we no longer need his assistance? I have lived, Sir, a long time, and the
43 longer I live, the more convincing proofs I see of this truth—*that God Governs in the affairs of men* [see
44 Daniel 4:17]. And if a sparrow cannot fall to the ground without his notice, is it probable that an empire
45 can rise without his aid [Matthew 10:29-31, Luke 12:6-7]? We have been assured, Sir, in the sacred
46 writings, that "except the Lord build the House they labour in vain that build it [Psalm 127:1]." I firmly
47 believe this; and I also believe that without his concurring aid we shall succeed in this political building
48 no better than the Builders of Babel [Genesis 11:1-9]: We shall be divided by our little partial local
49 interests; our projects will be confounded; and we ourselves shall become a reproach and bye word
50 down to future ages [Deuteronomy 28:37, 1 Kings 9:7, 2 Chronicles 7:20, Psalm 44:14]. And what is

worse, mankind may hereafter from this unfortunate instance, despair of establishing Governments by Human wisdom, and leave it to chance, war and conquest.[984]

Since God had answered their prayers during the revolution, Franklin offered, the Founders could rely on God to help them construct the nation. The delegates did not call for a clergyman because some like Hamilton did not wish to send a signal to the public that the convention was in trouble. Yet the Founders recognized the value of prayer for the nation.

The Constitution's Preamble states that the aim of the Constitution is "to form a more perfect Union, establish Justice, insure domestic Tranquility, provide for the common defense, promote the general Welfare, and secure the Blessings of Liberty to ourselves and our Posterity." The Constitution provides for national security while maintaining state autonomy.   The Constitution gave the federal government "enumerated powers" which means that the government only holds the powers explicitly assigned to it by the Constitution. All other powers not assigned to it remain with the states and people.   Thus the federal government is decentralized and balances power with the states.

The constitutions of the new states, formerly colonies, drafted from 1776 to 1783, were the first modern constitutions and provided models for the U. S. Constitution, as American Founder John Adams indicates in his *Defense of the Constitutions of Government of the United States*.[985] The state constitutions were, observes Lutz, "the culmination of a long development" of government and law over two centuries of American colonial experience and selected European and American ideas. These state constitutions and American constitutional history began with the early Puritan covenants and constitutions of self-government of the 1600s.[986]   The Puritan colonial constitutions, according to Toqueville, laid the "groundwork of modern constitutions." Thus key general governing principles from the Puritans' early covenants and constitutions like the Fundamental Orders of Connecticut and the Massachusetts Body of Liberties were applied in the state and federal constitutions of the new nation.[987] Some of the principles laid down in early Puritan constitutions includes Rule of Law, constitutional government, power and consent of the people, value of the individual, due process of law, trial by jury, no taxation without representation, prohibition against cruel and unusual punishment, elected or appointed representatives, and voting by secret ballot. The general Bible-based worldview of the early Americans was also retained in the state and federal constitutions of the new nation. The state constitutions influenced the national constitution and became an important part of the federal system of government in maintaining the rights of the states and balancing the national government.[988] As a result, the U. S. Constitution was influenced by the laws, customs, and experiences of America's early colonial and revolutionary history and by an American popular consensus of moral and social beliefs.[989]

The Constitution was submitted to the states for approval and ratification by the people. Ratification debates occurred between Federalists—Constitution supporters—and Anti-Federalists—Constitution opposers. Anti-Federalists feared the Constitution would create an over-powerful central government that Congress would overstep its bounds. During the debates, federal delegates James Madison, Alexander Hamilton, and John Jay wrote letters to the public, appearing in newspapers under the pseudonym Publius, to defend and explain the meanings and principles in the Constitution. The 85 published letters became known as *The Federalist Papers*. Ultimately, the Constitution was ratified by the delegates with the condition that a Bill of Rights would be added.

On September 17, 1787, the United States Constitution was adopted by the Constitutional Convention in Philadelphia, Pennsylvania. It was approved and ratified by eleven state conventions.

The Bill of Rights was added to the Constitution to limit and specify the powers of government and to protect and preserve individual and state rights. It insured the protection of individual liberties. Drafted by Madison and ratified in 1791, the Bill of Rights contains the first Ten Amendments to the Constitution. It was

1   written due to concerns among Anti-Federalists that without explicit mention of what the federal government
2   could *not* do, the government might potentially acquire more power and violate individual freedoms—including
3   religious freedom—and states' rights. They sought a clear, explicit mention of rights that could not be violated.
4   Though Federalists assured them that such rights were not endangered due to the Constitution's enumerated
5   powers, lack of a Bill of Rights endangered the Constitution's ratification by the states. So the delegates agreed
6   to the Bill of Rights. The first Ten Amendments of the Bill lists specific individual rights that the federal
7   government could not take away. These rights include freedom of religion, speech, press, and peaceable
8   assembly; the right to petition the government; the right to bear arms; the right against quartering of troops; the
9   right against unreasonable search and seizure; due process of law; trial by jury; and the restriction against
10   excessive bail and fines or cruel or unusual punishment. The 9th and 10th Amendments explicitly reaffirmed the
11   Constitution's enumerated powers. The Bill of Rights originally applied only to the federal government, not to
12   the states.

14   While Madison was a primary author of the Bill of Rights, a number of men who attended Reformed
15   churches and held religious faith were involved in the formation of this document. This group included Fisher
16   Ames, Abraham Baldwin, Egbert Benson, Benjamin Bourne, Elias Boudinot, Oliver Ellsworth, Jonathan Elmer,
17   Abiel Foster, Nicholas Gilman, Daniel Hiester Jr., Daniel Huger, Benjamin Huntington, James Jackson, John
18   Langdon, William Paterson, James Schureman, Philip Schuyler, Roger Sherman, William Smith, Caleb Strong,
19   Jeremiah Wadsworth, Hugh Williamson, Paine Wingate, and Henry Wynkoop. Some like Ames, Baldwin,
20   Boudinot, Ellsworth, Huntington, and Paterson were closely involved in this process.[990]

8.4 Why Government Is Necessary: Sinful Man's Need for Restraint

24   The American understanding of the need for a government, including a central federal government, was
25   based on experience under the Articles of Confederation and on a Bible-based or Judeo-Christian concept of
26   human nature—the sinfulness of man—as recognized by early American Puritans and Awakeners. According
27   to the Bible, history, and experience, man is inherently sinful, depraved, and corrupt. Even moral, religious, or
28   rational men are, at times, immoral and irreligious. Therefore, all men and institutions require some restraint by
29   civil government and laws. In Jeremiah 17:9 the Lord states, "'The heart is deceitful above all things, And
30   desperately wicked; Who can know it?'" Romans 3:23 states, "…for all have sinned and fall short of the glory
31   of God…." Likewise, in Federalist Paper 37, Madison writes of the "infirmities and depravities of the human
32   character" and in Federalist Paper 55 of the "degree of depravity in mankind."[991] Hamilton observes in
33   Federalist Paper 78 the "folly and wickedness of mankind" and the "depravity of human nature."[992] Locke had
34   also held the view that man is fallible and in need of protection of rights.

36   Though man is made to be free, civil government and laws are clearly necessary, the Founders believed,
37   to restrain men's vices. Hamilton expresses in Federalist Paper 15, "Why has government been instituted at all?
38   Because the passions of men will not conform to the dictates of reason and justice without constraint."[993]
39   Further, in governing and restraining the behaviors of imperfect men, the government itself as administered by
40   men also needs restraints on its power. Madison affirms in Federalist Paper 51,

42   But what is government itself but the greatest of all reflections on human nature? If men were angels,
43   no government would be necessary. … In framing a government which is to be administered by men
44   over men, the great difficulty lies in this: you must first enable the government to control the governed;
45   and in the next place oblige it to control itself.[994]

47   Jefferson agreed, writing later in 1798, "In questions of powers, then, let no more be heard of confidence in
48   man, but bind him down from mischief by the chains of the Constitution."[995] Sandoz affirms, "Let us not
49   overlook the great secret that a *sound map of human nature* (as John Adams insisted) uniquely lies at the heart
50   of the Constitution of the United States and its elaborate institutional arrangements."[996]

The Constitution, as Madison thought, addressed the problems of sinful man in a free republic. As he states in Federalist Papers 39 and 60, the Constitution checks the evil behaviors of men, the "tyranny of the majority" or the power of the majority position in local governments, and the power of factions or special interest groups by means of elected and appointed representatives and a presidential electoral system. The large territory and population of the American republic itself, thought Madison, would also naturally diffuse the power of factions by the large number of competing interests.

The Founders' belief in original sin led them to view government as necessary but not to be overly trusted, for it could be taken over by corrupt men. The Founders were influenced by Judeo-Christian thought on this governing principle. Madison, as a good many founders, was also likely influenced by his teacher-mentor John Witherspoon, an advocate of Reformed political theory, whom Madison studied under at Princeton. Their worldview of human nature would explain the necessity and form of the United States' government that the American Founders put together.

8.5 The Purpose of American Government: The Protection and Preservation of the Individual's God-Given Unalienable Rights

The Founders upheld and protected the natural rights of the individual in the U. S. Constitution and Bill of Rights. The Bill of Rights was written to confirm and protect individual rights. The notion of individual rights stemmed from Americans' Bible-based worldview that humans as created by and in the image of God have intrinsic value and God-given unalienable rights that civil government, society, and man are bound to honor.

Madison, like Locke, believed that the right of property contained all other God-given or natural human rights. He thought that unalienable rights such as life, liberty, conscience, faculty, labor, and the pursuit of happiness are essentially property rights. For all such factors are the inherent property of a man's person as a human being. Madison defined property as Blackstone did in his *Commentaries* as "'that dominion which one man claims and exercises over the external things of the world, in exclusion of every other individual'" but goes on to define it more broadly as "every thing to which a man may attach a value and have a right; and *which leaves to every one else the like advantage*."[997] In his well-known 1792 essay, "Property," Madison writes, "In a word, as a man is said to have a right to his property, he may be equally said to have a property in his rights."[998]

Government's purpose, explains Madison, is to protect the individual's property—whether of his person or possession. He writes in his 1792 essay on "Property," "Government is instituted to protect property of every sort; as well that which lies in the various rights of individuals, as that which the term particularly expresses."[999] He concludes, "If the United States mean to obtain or deserve the full praise due to wise and just governments, they will equally respect the rights of property, and the property in rights: they will rival the government that most sacredly guards the former; and by repelling its example in violating the latter, will make themselves a pattern to that and all other governments."[1000]

During the ratification of the Constitution, American Founder, statesman, and lawyer John Jay expressed the equal rights and protections of the individual citizen in Federalist Paper 2, stating, "To all general purposes we have uniformly been one people; each individual citizen everywhere enjoying the same national rights, privileges, and protection."[1001]

Madison asserts the protection of individual rights as the basis and check of all governmental aims in Federalist Paper 51: "…[T]he constant aim [in setting up the government] is to divide and arrange the several offices in such a manner as that each may be a check on the other—that the private interest of every individual may be a sentinel over the public rights." Madison also supports the protection of individual rights in society

1 itself by its diversity: "Whilst all authority in it [the federal republic of the United States] will be derived from
2 and dependent on the society, the society itself will be broken into so many parts, interests and classes of
3 citizens, that the rights of individuals, or of the minority, will be in little danger from interested combinations of
4 the majority."[1002]

5 Declaration and Constitution signer, law professor, and Supreme Court Justice James Wilson later
6 asserts this principle of individual value and its basis for civil government in his 1790-1791 *Lectures on Law*.
7 He observes of civil government,

8 The dread and redoubtable sovereign [highest ruler or ruling power], when traced to his ultimate and
9 genuine source, has been found, as he ought to have been found, in the free and independent man....
10 This truth, so simple and natural, and yet so neglected or despised, may be appreciated as the first and
11 fundamental principle in the science of government.[1003]

13 The United States' new federal government and laws supported and protected individual rights. While
14 in a pure democracy the majority represents the group, as Rosalie Slater points out, in America's constitutional
15 republic the majority represents the individual—"regardless of whether he agrees or disagrees with the action of
16 the majority. His position is not eliminated by the majority overruling him."[1004] In America's republic, agrees
17 Felix Morley, "this new government must be strong enough to preserve 'the rights of the minority,'
18 continuously jeopardized 'in all cases where a majority are united by a common interest or passion.'"[1005] To
19 protect the individual against the majority, the Constitution, affirms James Beck, "threw about the individual the
20 solemn circle of the law."[1006] Self-government in a republic, early historian Richard Frothingham further
21 affirms, is

23 not simply a custom, in the units termed municipalities or States, of managing their local affairs; but a
24 degree of freedom in the individual to engage in the various pursuits of life, unrecognized elsewhere at
25 the period when the Republic was formed, and yet unknown where centralization prevails, whether he
26 chooses to act by himself or in association for civil or religious purposes; and this self-government exists
27 in union with the fulfillment of every obligation demanded by the nation.[1007]

29 The American republic was clearly a nation, government, and society that upheld the value, dignity, and rights
30 of the individual. The first Ten Amendments to the Constitution, the Bill of Rights, affirms some individual
31 human rights, naming some specific rights, in order to protect them. The Ninth Amendment goes further to
32 reassert the God-given unalienable rights of the individual, whether *stated* or *unstated*. The Amendment reads,
33 "The enumeration in the Constitution, of certain rights, shall not be construed to deny or disparage others
34 retained by the people." American government served to protect the God-given unalienable rights of the
35 individual and of the people.

8.6 Constitutional Law and Government: Popular Sovereignty

39 The United States Constitution and Bill of Rights were rooted in the Bible-based principle of popular
40 sovereignty—that the people as a whole are the earthly source of civil authority and political power as
41 appointed by God. Constitutional Convention delegate and Constitution signer Charles Pinckney of South
42 Carolina affirms popular sovereignty during the ratification of the Constitution: "We have been taught here [in
43 America] to believe that *all power, of right, belongs to the people*—that it flows immediately from them, and is
44 delegated to their officers for the public good—that our rulers are the servants of the people, amenable to their
45 will, and created for their use."[1008] The U. S. Constitution's Preamble explicitly affirms popular sovereignty in
46 stating that "We the People" establish the Constitution. The Tenth Amendment of the Bill of Rights also
47 explicitly affirms popular sovereignty by affirming that the people assign specific powers to the government.
48 The Tenth Amendment states respectively, "The powers not delegated to the United States by the Constitution,

nor prohibited by it to the States, are reserved to the States respectively, or to the people." The Founders' U.S. government maintained the principle that just civil governments only hold power specifically granted to it by the people. The people are the earthly source of civil authority and power.

8.7 Constitutional Law and Government: Rule of Law

The United States Constitution upheld and applied the Bible-based concepts of covenant and constitutional law and government—the laws of the land agreed to among the people—which were practiced by the ancient Israelites, in English common law, and in the early American Puritan colonies. Constitutional law and government were ultimately applied in the founding of the new nation, in its Declaration and Constitution. Constitutional law and government were characterized by a covenant or agreement among the people to the laws of the land and Rule of Law or equity in the application of these laws. Constitutional law presupposed that the law rules above all men, all being imperfect, and all men are equally accountable to it, regardless of person or position. No man is above the law.

Constitutional law was also based on Rule of Law. This law was applied impartially, not arbitrarily. It naturally held every individual citizen including all rulers and representatives, equally accountable under the law, guarding against arbitrary rule and interests in government. It was based on the equality of all men before God and of equity of law—the fair and impartial application of the law to all men. Such equity was part of the Laws of Nature and of God and necessary for just human law.

The early American Puritans had practiced Rule of Law in their colonial laws and constitutions based on their beliefs and view of the Bible. The Awakeners had similarly acknowledged the equal position of all men before God in the Bible and the need and ability of all to receive spiritual salvation by the Gospel. As such, the early Americans had abided by Rule of Law and equity in both their civil and religious lives. Thus, the founding-era Americans found in the Bible and in the experiences and history of the early Americans a precedent of Rule of Law.

In addition, British law provided a precedent. Chief Justice of England Sir Edward Coke, who played a major role in defending Rule of Law over Ruler's Law or the Divine Right of Kings in England in the 1600s, was also influential to American political thought on the principle of Rule of Law. Early English historian Sir William Holdsworth notes that Coke's writings including his *Institutes of the Lawes of England* and his *Law Reports* "preserved for England and the world the constitutional doctrine of rule of Law" and became "the turning-point in English constitutional history."[1009] The Americans had studied Coke's position on Rule of Law and adopted it in their civil government. Sandoz affirms,

> The constitutional form authoritative at the time of the American founding was powerfully shaped by Coke, former attorney general and lord chief justice of England, who led a successful resistance against the extension of the royal prerogative and the attendant establishment of absolutism and rule of divine right that saved rule of law and constitutionalism for England and the modern world, as Sir William Holdsworth emphasized. Decisive for the continuity of this vision of liberty through law and limited government was the education of subsequent generations of lawyers, including the American revolutionary generation and beyond, by Coke's *Institutes* and *Reports*.[1010]

In his influential 1689 *Second Treatise of Civil Government*, Locke elaborates on Rule of Law in rationalist, secular terms. To do this, Locke draws from and secularizes Rutherford's 1644 *Lex Rex* which asserts that law is king, that all rulers are subject to the law. Locke bases this principle on the Law of Nature, the natural rights of all men, the purpose of government for the good of man and society, and the need for a set, consistent civil law for the people. He states,

136. ...[T]he legislative or supreme authority cannot assume to itself a power to rule by extemporary arbitrary decrees, but is bound to dispense justice and decide the rights of the subject by promulgated standing laws, and known authorized judges. ...

137. Absolute arbitrary power, or governing without settled standing laws, can neither of them consist with the ends of society and government, which men would not quit the freedom of the state of Nature [a state before or outside civil society] for, and tie themselves up under were it not to preserve their lives, liberties, and fortunes; and by stated rules of right and property to secure their peace and quiet. It cannot be supposed that they should intend, had they a power so to do, to give any one or more an absolute arbitrary power over their persons and estates, and put a force into the magistrate's hand to execute his unlimited will arbitrarily upon them; this were to put themselves into a worse condition than the state of Nature, wherein they had a liberty to defend their right against the injuries of others.... ... And, therefore, whatever form the commonwealth is under, the ruling power ought to govern by declared and received laws, and not by extemporary dictates and undetermined resolutions.... ... For all the power the government has, being only for the good of the society, as it ought not to be arbitrary and at pleasure, so it ought to be exercised by established and promulgated laws, that both the people may know their duty, and be safe and secure within the limits of the law, and the rulers, too, kept within their due bounds, and not be tempted by the power they have in their hands to employ it to purposes, and by such measures as they would not have known, and own not willingly.[1011]

Rule of Law, says Locke, is a natural right of all men in civil society and required in a just civil government.

Rule of Law protected the rights of all citizens from arbitrary power. It subjected every citizen, ruler, body, power, and authority to the law of the land. The Bible-aligned constitutional principles of Rule of Law and equity influenced American political thought and were applied in the U. S. Constitution. Toqueville aptly observed how the U. S. Constitution adhered to the Bible-aligned principle of equity or Rule of Law, stating, "Christianity, which has declared that all men are equal in the sight of God, will not refuse to acknowledge that all citizens are equal in the eye of the law."[1012]

8.8 A Constitutional Republic: A Government Aligned with Bible-Based Principles and Values

The Founders laid out in the Constitution a self-government—a constitutional republic. America's constitutional republic was administered through written constitutions of law, public institutions, and representatives. In a republic, the people hold the political power and self-govern through elected or appointed representatives. If public officials or representatives, accountable to the people, violate their jurisdictions or do not fulfill their proper duties, they can be removed and their authority transfers back to the people.[1013] The American republic thus reflected the American, Bible-inspired principles of the sovereignty of God, popular sovereignty, limited government, Rule of Law, and elected representatives.

A republic, the Founders believed, was the most suitable form of government for the United States because it was compatible with their Bible-inspired, American values of freedom, equality, natural rights, peace, justice, and benevolence. In Federalist Paper 39, founder James Madison expresses the American choice of republicanism due to its support of freedom and rights:

The first question that offers itself is whether the general form and aspect of the government be strictly republican. It is evident that no other form would be reconcilable with the genius of the people of America; with the fundamental principles of the Revolution; or with that honorable determination which animates every votary of freedom to rest all our political experiments on the capacity of mankind for self-government.[1014]

American Founder Benjamin Rush notes in a 1800 letter to Jefferson the shared values of Christianity and republicanism: "I have always considered Christianity as the *strong ground* of republicanism. ...[M]any of its precepts have for their objects republican liberty and equality as well as simplicity, integrity, and economy in government."[1015] Author and statesman Noah Webster affirms republicanism as aligning with Bible-based values, stating, "...[T]he genuine source of correct republican principles is the Bible, particularly the new Testament, or the Christian religion," and "...[T]he religion which has introduced civil liberty, is the religion of Christ and His apostles, which enjoins humility, piety and benevolence; which acknowledges in every person a brother, or a sister, and a citizen with equal rights. This is genuine Christianity, and to this we owe our free Constitutions of Government."[1016] Early historian Benjamin F. Morris observes in 1864 the shared values of Christianity and the constitutional republic: "These fundamental objects of the [Preamble of the] Constitution are in perfect harmony with the revealed objects of the Christian religion. Union, justice, peace, the general welfare, and the blessings of civil and religious liberty, are the objects of Christianity, and always secured under its practical and beneficient reign."[1017] Oppressive government and tyranny that often arose from absolute power, they believed, is anti-Christian in nature. Montesquieu perhaps shared some of their thoughts when he expressed how Christianity aligned well with free self-government rather than with oppressive governments of absolute power, stating, "The Christian religion is a stranger to mere despotic power. The mildness so frequently recommended in the gospel is incompatible with the despotic rage with which a prince punishes his subjects, and exercises himself in cruelty."[1018] Christianity and the Bible, he thought, support just government and esteem values and virtues like freedom, equality, rights, justice, peace, and benevolence. Americans saw republicanism as the political answer for their new nation and a Bible-based, pro-Christian society.

It is important to note that republicanism to many Americans was not an end in itself but also a means to preserve purity and virtue in the people and church. It would let the people freely continue their religious lifestyle and honor their covenant with God. As such, Americans differed in their mindset from the pagan republicans of ancient Greece and Rome.[1019]

8.9 A Constitutional Republic: A Government for a Virtuous People

A republic, the American Founders knew, requires virtuous citizens in order to endure and to function justly and successfully. More than a monarchy or autocracy, a republic, in giving more responsibility to citizens to govern themselves, requires citizens to exercise civic consciousness and to practice moral virtue in their lives and society in order for civil society to work properly. Consequently, the Founders continually exhorted the people of the need to maintain virtue. Declaration and Constitution signer Franklin remarks, "...[O]nly a virtuous people are capable of freedom. As nations become corrupt and vicious, they have more need of masters."[1020] American Founder Richard Henry Lee states, "It is certainly true that a *popular government* cannot flourish without *virtue* in the people...."[1021] Bill of Rights contributor George Mason affirms, "Justice and virtue are the vital principles of republican government."[1022] Washington in his Farewell Address notes that "virtue or morality is a necessary spring of popular government.—The rule indeed extends with more or less force to every species of Free Government."[1023] Madison similarly expresses the need for virtue in free or freedom-loving governments: "Is there no virtue among us? If there be not, we are in a wretched situation. No theoretical checks—no form of government can render us secure. To suppose that any form of government will secure liberty or happiness without any virtue in the people, is a chimerical idea."[1024]

Though the Founders recognized the sinfulness of mankind, they also acknowledged or presumed an amount of moral virtue and capability in man and in America's republican self-government. In Federalist Paper 55, Madison states,

> As there is a degree of depravity in mankind which requires a certain degree of circumspection and distrust, so there are other qualities in human nature which justify a certain portion of esteem and confidence. Republican government presupposes the existence of these qualities in a higher degree than

any other form. Were the pictures which have been drawn by the political jealousy of some among us faithful likenesses of the human character, the inference would be that there is not sufficient virtue among men for self-government; and that nothing less than the chains of despotism can restrain them from destroying and devouring one another.[1025]

In Federalist Paper 76, Hamilton affirms, "The institution of delegated power implies that there is a portion of virtue and honor among mankind, which may be a reasonable foundation of confidence. And experience justifies the theory. It has been found to exist in the most corrupt periods of the most corrupt governments."[1026]

The American constitutional republic assumes that the American people are a virtuous people. John Adams stresses the necessity and assumption of virtue in the people of the American republic, writing, "…[W]e have no government armed with power capable of contending with human passions unbridled by morality and religion. … Our Constitution was made only for a moral and religious people. It is wholly inadequate to the government of any other."[1027] American Founder Samuel Adams writes in a 1778 letter, "Whether America shall long preserve her Freedom or not, will depend on her Virtue."[1028] Lutz elaborates on this point that the American republic requires a moral people:

> If a people can be trusted to choose the good once it is distinguished from what is not, they must therefore possess certain qualities that incline them to the good. Logically prior to those two, and most fundamental to popular government, is the assumption that the American people are a virtuous people— that they are able and willing to seek the common good. It could be no other way. If the people are corrupt or lack the virtues necessary for popular control of government, it would be foolish to ever speak of popular control, no matter how strong one's belief in free will, the importance of consent, or the existence of natural rights. The people must be virtuous, or all is for naught."[1029]

Edward Rauchut, citing Robert George, further explains the need for virtue and morality among the citizenry:

> Because our nature is fallen, because we have a tendency to do wrong, our freedom and our very form of government are dependent on the maintenance of our virtue. The checks and balances built into our government may make it much more difficult to do wrong, just as a lock on a door discourages us from committing a robbery. But such checks are only checks. Only a moral people will remain a free people. As Princeton University's Robert P. George recently noted, 'as our founders warned, a people given over to license will be incapable of sustaining republican government. For republican government— government by the people—requires a people who are prepared to take responsibility for the common good, including the preservation of the conditions of liberty.' …
> …[W]e, as citizens, are obliged to live the sort of virtuous lives that can sustain the freedoms our government was invented to secure. With freedom, in short, comes this moral responsibility.[1030]

The Founders based their system of republican self-government on the presumption that the people, despite man's imperfection, would exercise restraint, virtue, and morality in order to achieve and maintain just civil self-government and liberty. It was with this view that Franklin, when asked following the Constitutional Convention what kind of government the Founders had given the people, responded, "A republic, if you can keep it."

Furthermore, the people needed not only to be virtuous but were required to assess virtue and character in those running for public office and when electing or appointing public officials in order to have just, moral civil representatives. This point was taught in the Bible and practiced by the early Puritans. Recognizing the importance of virtue in the people and their representatives, Samuel Adams exhorts,

He therefore is the truest friend to the liberty of his country who tries most to promote its virtue, and who, so far as his power and influence extend, will not suffer a man to be chosen into any office of power and trust who is not a wise and virtuous man. ... The sum of all is, if we would most truly enjoy this gift of Heaven, let us become a virtuous people....[1031]

During the Constitutional Convention, Franklin specifically cites a Bible-based standard of virtue for representatives. Alluding to Jethro's counsel to Moses in Exodus 18:21, Franklin, reports Madison, states a "dislike of every thing that tended to debase the spirit of the common people. ... We should remember the character which the Scripture requires in Rulers, that they should be men hating covetousness."[1032] Similarly, in Federalist Paper 57, Madison emphasizes the need for virtuous representatives in a republic: "The aim of every political constitution is, or ought to be, first to obtain for rulers men who possess most wisdom to discern, and most virtue to pursue, the common good of the society; and in the next place, to take the most effectual precautions for keeping them virtuous whilst they continue to hold their public trust."[1033] Noah Webster, echoing the early colonists' and the Founders' views on the importance of moral men in government, explains in his 1832 *History of the United States* the need to elect or appoint godly representatives in government according to Exodus 18:21. He states,

> When you [the people] become entitled to exercise the right of voting for public officers, let it be impressed on your mind that God commands you to choose for rulers, *just men who will rule in the fear of God.* The preservation of a republican government depends on the faithful discharge of this duty; if the citizens neglect their duty and place unprincipled men in office, the government will soon be corrupted.... If a republican government fails to secure public prosperity and happiness, it must be because the citizens neglect the divine commands, and elect bad men to make and administer the laws.[1034]

Both the people and their representatives needed to be virtuous. Only a virtuous people and representatives would enable the American republic to work successfully and to endure.

The question, to the Founders, was how to ensure public virtue for a successful, workable republic. The Founders, says Waldman, "were fairly obsessed with the question of how to instill enough virtue into citizens that a republic could flourish. Institutions that could imbue personal and communal values...were viewed as essential building blocks for democracy."[1035] In this regard, church and civil government, they imagined, would cooperate with one another in the nation.

8.10 The Value of Religion, Particularly the Bible, for a Virtuous People

The virtue required in the citizens of a free republic is cultivated, many Founders believed, by religion, particularly Biblical Christianity. Religion as the source of morality is necessary to sustain a just republic in which citizens have more freedom and responsibility than in autocratic governments. More freedom requires more virtue in the people. Americans considered Christianity—with its teaching of a future state of rewards and punishments and a Law of Love—to be a powerful source of man's virtue and of self-restraint or self-regulation of man's behavior. By instilling internal restraints and desires in man to live a godly life, it strengthens men's virtues and restrains their vices more than civil laws. Christianity espouses and fosters noble virtues in man that benefit a self-governing society. It fosters a value of human dignity, freedom, equality, love of fellow man and community, benevolence, good citizenship, public service, personal and social responsibility, lawfulness, peace and order, diligence and industry, and more. It discourages vice, immorality, corruption, lawlessness, and violence in men. Even rationalist and secularist Americans recognized the importance of the "Laws of Nature and Nature's God" in the Declaration in order to uphold a moral order in society. Time and again American leaders and the Founders emphasized the importance of religion to America's republic. Religion, they saw, is a primary source of virtue and thus a basis of liberty and free government.

Enlightenment philosopher Pufendorf thought that religion is *"in truth the utmost and firmest bond of Human Society."*[1036] Religion preserves the consciences of men. It allows men to trust one another's integrity and removes perpetual anxiety and suspicion in society of being deceived or injured by others. It restrains men from committing crimes. It alleviates mistrust and fear among rulers and subjects. It creates internal stability in the civil society and state. It causes men in society to do right, fulfill their duties, uphold justice, and not always seek personal advantage. It also encourages men to do glorious and noble acts.[1037]

Rush aptly expressed the relationship of religion to a republic, stating, "…[T]he only foundation for a useful education in a republic is to be laid in Religion. Without this there can be no virtue, and without virtue there can be no liberty, and liberty is the object and life of all republican governments."[1038] Early American David Ramsay, who served as a South Carolina delegate to the Continental Congress, similarly states, "Remember that there can be no political happiness without liberty; that there can be no liberty without morality; and that there can be no morality without religion."[1039] John Adams also stresses the importance of religion for virtue and republicanism, writing, "Statesman, my dear Sir, may plan and speculate for liberty, but it is religion and morality alone, which can establish the principles upon which freedom can securely stand. The only foundation of a free constitution is pure virtue…."[1040] American Founder George Washington agrees with this view, observing,

> Of all the dispositions and habits which lead to political prosperity, religion and morality are indispensable supports. In vain would that man claim the tribute of patriotism who should labor to subvert these great pillars of human happiness—these firmest props of the duties of men and citizens. … Let it be simply asked, where is the security for property, for reputation, for life, if the sense of religious obligation desert the oaths which are the instruments of investigation in courts of justice? And let us with caution indulge the supposition that morality can be maintained without religion. Whatever may be conceded to the influence of refined education on minds of peculiar structure, reason and experience both forbid us to expect that national morality can prevail in exclusion of religious principles.[1041]

Christianity taught the first early American settlers important virtues, says Slater, that helped them to endure and survive hardship in early Virginia, Plymouth, and Massachusetts.[1042] Founding-era Americans, like the Puritans, saw the necessity of virtue in the people and their representatives and believed religion, specifically the Bible and Christianity, is the key to instilling this virtue.

The American Founders favored the Bible and Judeo-Christianity in particular for the nation and society because this belief system addresses not only man's outward behavior but goes further to address his inner heart condition and motives that influence and precede his actions. It thus recognizes a higher standard of virtue and self-government than the mere outward regulation of civil laws. Jesus addresses not only a person's outward behavior but his inner condition. He also upholds the two Great Commandments of love—the internal as well as external Law of Love—as found in Matthew 22:37-40.[1043] Jesus, for example, says to his disciples in Matthew 5:21-22, "You have heard that it was said to those of old, *'You shall not murder*, and whoever murders will be in danger of the judgment.' But I say to you that whoever is angry with his brother without a cause shall be in danger of the judgment."[1044] This Biblical teaching of love and inner morality could more effectively regulate a person's outward actions than mere civil laws and, as a result, could prevent violations of civil law which originate internally, in man's heart. Without such internal restraints, man's behavior must be regulated by outward, costly, time-consuming, and generally reactive enforcements and punishments. Reformer John Calvin had noted this benefit of Christianity and its inward morality:

> At the outset, it was proved that in the [Biblical] Law human life is instructed not merely in outward decency, but in inward spiritual righteousness. …[A] human [civil] lawgiver does not extend his care beyond outward order, and, therefore, his injunctions are not violated without outward acts. But God,

whose eye nothing escapes, and who regards not the outward appearance so much as purity of heart, under the prohibition of murder, adultery, and theft, includes wrath, hatred, lust, covetousness, and all other things of a similar nature.   Being a spiritual Lawgiver, he speaks to the soul not less than the body.[1045]

Montesquieu similarly observes the Bible and Judeo-Christianity's effective internal regulation of man: "The principles of Christianity, deeply engraved on the heart, would be infinitely more powerful than the false honour of monarchies, than the humane virtues of republics, or the servile fear of despotic states."[1046] Jefferson also valued the Biblical Law of Love and New Testament Christianity that addressed man's inward morality, not just outward behavior. He contrasts these with the often outward Old Testament regulations: "The precepts of philosophy and of the Hebrew code, laid hold of actions only. He [Jesus] pushed his scrutinies into the heart of man; erected his [man's] tribunal in the region of his thoughts, and purified the waters at the fountain head."[1047] Witherspoon observes Christianity's effective inner morality:

> …[T]here is not only an excellence in the Christian morals, but a manifest superiority in them, to those which are derived from any other source.… … The love of God; humility of mind; the forgiveness of injuries; and the love of our enemies. … The law of God is not contracted into governing the outward conduct, but reaches to the very heart.… … The excellence of the Scripture doctrine appears from its efficacy. By this I mean the power it hath over the mind, and its actual influence in producing that holiness it recommends.[1048]

U. S. Secretary of State and Sixth U. S. President John Quincy Adams, writing to his son, elaborates on the importance of the Bible and Judeo-Christianity's internal regulation of the human heart by the Law of Love to government and society:

> Human legislators can undertake only to prescribe the actions of men: they acknowledge their inability to govern and direct the sentiments of the heart; the very law styles it a rule of civil conduct, not of internal principles.… It is one of the greatest marks of Divine favor bestowed upon the children of Israel, that the legislator [God] gave them [His children] rules not only of action but for the government of the heart.[1049]

The teachings of the Bible, early Americans recognized, reach man's thoughts, feelings, motives, and intentions before they manifest in outward behavior. Civil and moral laws could not address the heart, but the Bible and its two Great Commandments of love could.

Many Founders and most Americans thus regarded the Bible and Judeo-Christianity as foundational and necessary to a just republic because this belief system effectively promoted virtue and regulated man's conduct. It was exceptionally beneficial to a free, self-governing state and society. For these reasons, while the Founders implemented total religious freedom and saw the value of differing religions, they strongly recommended the Bible and Christianity to all citizens. Reflecting early Americans' thinking, early historian Benjamin F. Morris writes, "The state must rest upon the basis of religion, and it must preserve this basis, or itself must fall. But the support which religion gives to the state will obviously cease the moment religion looses its hold upon the popular mind."[1050]

Religion, particularly that of the Bible and Judeo-Christianity, founding-era Americans knew, was a highly effective source of virtue for men and society. Indeed, without such virtue in the people, the republic could not endure. As such, the American Founders sought to encourage religion and Christianity in their families and in society in every way possible. John Quincy Adams writes to his son of virtue and self-government from the Bible, citing Matthew 22:37-40 and Luke 10:27:

You must soon come to the age when you must govern yourself. ... You know the difference between right and wrong. You know some of your duties, and the obligation you are under of becoming acquainted with them all. It is in the Bible, you must learn them, and from the Bible how to practice them. Those duties are to *God*, to your *fellow creatures*, and to *yourself*. "Thou shalt love the Lord thy God, with all thy heart, and with all thy soul, and with all thy mind, and with all thy strength, and thy neighbor as thyself" (Luke x, 27; Matt. xxii, 40). On these two commandments (Jesus Christ expressly says) "hang all the law and the prophets."[1051]

Congregationalist minister Timothy Dwight also asserts the social value of Judeo-Christian virtue: "From the moral and religious instructions, the cogent motives of duty, and the excitements to decent, amiable, and useful conduct, which it [Christianity] furnishes, it establishes, perhaps more than any single thing, good order, good morals and happiness public and private. It makes good men; and good men must be good citizens."[1052] Alluding to Proverbs 29:2, Constitution signer and U. S. Supreme Court Justice William Paterson likewise recognizes the virtuous influence of Judeo-Christian principles on the people and their representatives, observing, "Religion and morality...[are] necessary to good government, good order, and good laws; for 'when the righteous are in authority, the people rejoice.'"[1053] In his presidential Inaugural Address, second U. S. President John Adams affirms the role of Christianity in virtuous leadership, stating that "a decent respect for Christianity [was] among the best recommendations for public service."[1054] Noah Webster also observes Judeo-Christianity's restraint on man's sinful tendencies: "All the miseries and evils which men suffer from vice, crime, ambition, injustice, oppression, slavery and war, proceed from their despising or neglecting the precepts contained in the Bible."[1055] U. S. Supreme Court Justice Joseph Story refers to the benefits of Judeo-Christianity to morality when he writes,

> The promulgation of the great doctrines of religion, the being, and attributes, and providence of one Almighty God; the responsibility to him for all our actions, founded upon moral freedom and accountability; a future state of rewards and punishments; the cultivation of all the personal, social, and benevolent virtues; —these can never be matters of indifference in any well ordered community. It is, indeed, difficult to conceive, how any civilized society can well exist without them.[1056]

Many Founders and Americans consequently expressed Judeo-Christianity's value to America's just republic and to the preservation of man's rights and freedoms based on its benefits of virtue and morality among the people. Declaration signer Charles Carroll emphasizes the republic's foundation on Christian virtue:

> [W]ithout morals a republic cannot subsist any length of time; they therefore who are decrying the Christian religion, whose morality is so sublime and pure...are undermining the solid foundation of morals, the best security for the duration of free governments.[1057]

American Founder James McHenry asserts the need for the Bible in American society to preserve public and private virtue:

> ...[P]ublic utility pleads most forcibly for the general distribution of the Holy Scriptures. The doctrine they preach, the obligation they impose, the punishment they threaten, the rewards they promise, the stamp and image of divinity they bear, which produces a conviction of their truths, can alone secure to society, order and peace, and to our courts of justice and constitutions of government, purity, stability, and usefulness. In vain, without the Bible, we increase penal laws and draw intrenchments around our institutions. Bibles are strong intrenchments.[1058]

Noah Webster affirms the destiny of Christianity and virtue in a free state and society:

No truth is more evident to my mind, than that the Christian religion must be the basis of any government intended to secure the rights and privileges of a free people.[1059]

Referencing Psalm 11:3, "If the Foundations Be Destroyed, What Can the Righteous Do?," geographer and Rev. Jedidiah Morse warns of the collapse of the republic if Christianity is removed from its base, preaching,

> To the kindly influence of Christianity we owe that degree of civil freedom, and political and social happiness which mankind now enjoy. ... Whenever the pillars of Christianity shall be overthrown, our present republican forms of government, and all the blessings which flow from them, must fall with them.[1060]

Even rationalist Jefferson saw Christianity as a religion most conducive to free thought and to a free state and society. He expresses,

> ...The Christian religion, when divested of the rags in which they [the clery] have enveloped it, and brought to the original purity and simplicity of its benevolent institutor, is a religion of all others most friendly to liberty, science, and the freest expansion of the human mind.[1061]

Founder Rush cites Christianity as an exceptional belief system for morality in the republic, stating,

> ...[T]he religion I mean to recommend in this place, is that of the New Testament. ... [A]ll its doctrines and precepts are calculated to promote the happiness of society, and the safety and well being of civil government.[1062]

Declaration signer John Hancock encourages Christianity and its virtue for the well-being of the free state:

> Sensible of the importance of Christian piety and virtue to the order and happiness of a state, I cannot but earnestly commend to you every measure for their support and encouragement that shall not infringe the rights of conscience, which I rejoice to see established by the Constitution on so broad a basis....[1063]

Americans and the Founders viewed Biblical Christianity as the moral foundation of America's free, prosperous, happy republic. The need for such religion and virtue in society was, says some scholars, one reason the Founders enacted the "free exercise of religion" in the First Amendment and encouraged religion in society.[1064]

8.11 Separation of Powers and Checks and Balances: Limited Power in Government and No Earthly Absolute Power

Because they believed the Bible's view that man's nature is sinful and corruptible by power, the American Founders believed that the nation needed a civil government that limited and balanced power. The Founders created a civil government with separation of powers and a system of checks and balances that divided power within three separate branches—legislative, executive, and judicial—each possessing legal powers and restraints. Each branch checked and balanced the powers of the other branches. If one branch became corrupt, the other just branches would keep it and the government in line. Thus no earthly absolute power or ruler existed. The powers of any public office or political body were limited by a counterbalancing power.

The Founders were influenced by the ideas of French Christian philosopher Charles de Montesquieu (1689-1755) as well as Judeo-Christian thought from the Bible on this principle and mechanism of separation of powers. Montesquieu was the most frequently cited secular thinker of the American Founding era.[1065]

1   Montesquieu shared the Bible-based view that man is sinful and prone to corruption, making consistently
2   upright leadership unlikely and abuse of power, tyranny, corruption, and excess very likely when power is
3   unrestrained. Due to man's imperfect nature and frequent departure from God's moral law, he thought, man
4   needs governing laws in society. In his well-known and highly influential 1748 classic *The Spirit of the Laws*
5   he explains this point:

7   As an intelligent being, he [man] incessantly transgresses the laws established by God, and changes
8   those of his own instituting. He is left to his private direction, though a limited being, and subject, like
9   all finite intelligences, to ignorance and error: even his imperfect knowledge he loses; and as a sensible
10   creature, he is hurried away by a thousand impetuous passions. Such a being might every instant forget
11   his Creator; God has therefore reminded him of his duty by the laws of religion. Such a being is liable
12   every moment to forget himself; philosophy has provided against this by the laws of morality. Formed
13   to live in society, he might forget his fellow-creatures; legislators have, therefore, by political and civil
14   laws, confined him to his duty.[1066]

16   To govern over and by sinful man, power must be limited, Montesquieu believed, by separating it and
17   setting up checks and balances for it. Montesquieu articulates in his *Spirit of the Laws* the principle of
18   separation of powers and checks and balances to limit power and to restrain man in government. He observes,
19   "But constant experience shows us that every man invested with power is apt to abuse it, and to carry his
20   authority as far as it will go. ... To prevent this abuse, it is necessary from the very nature of things that power
21   should be a check to power."[1067]

23   So that government does not become tyrannical, Montesequieu articulates three distinct, separate
24   branches in government—legislative, executive, and judicial. What made Montesquieu's theory unique was its
25   assertion of a separate *judicial* branch, something that had not been clearly articulated or practiced before. He
26   writes,

28   When the legislative and executive powers are united in the same person, or in the same body of
29   magistrates, there can be no liberty; because apprehensions may arise, lest the same monarch or senate
30   should enact tyrannical laws, to execute them in a tyrannical manner.
31   Again, there is no liberty, if the judiciary power be not separated from the legislative and
32   executive. Were it joined with the legislative, the life and liberty of the subject would be exposed to
33   arbitrary control; for the judge would be then the legislator. Were it joined to the executive power, the
34   judge might behave with violence and oppression.
35   There would be an end of everything, were the same man or the same body, whether of the
36   nobles or of the people, to exercise those three powers, that of enacting laws, that of executing the public
37   resolutions, and of trying the causes of individuals.[1068]

39   Montesquieu recognized the fallible nature of man and incorporated it as a necessary factor into his concept of
40   civil government. In order to remain free and just, each function of government needs to reside in a separate
41   branch so as to limit its power.

43   The American Founders shared Montesquieu's view of sinful man and the need for separate powers.
44   They also valued his theory of three separate branches of government. Montesquieu thus became a key
45   authority for the American Founders on forms of government and on constructing the United States' new
46   republican government. Rush pointed out the value of Montesquieu to the Founders in his 1777 *Observations
47   on the Government of Pennyslvania*: "Mr. Locke is an oracle as to the *principles*, Harrington and Montesquieu
48   are the oracles as to the *forms* of government."[1069] In a May 30, 1790, letter to a prospective law student,
49   Jefferson recommends Montesquieu's *Spirit of the Laws*, stating: "...[I]n the science of government,

Montesquieu's Spirit of Laws is generally recommended.   It contains, indeed, a great number of political truths...."[1070]

In their desire to depart from the centuries-old experience of absolute power and tyrannical government, the American Founders applied Montesquieu's theory, something never done before, and formed a republic with three separate branches—legislative, executive, and judicial—to make, implement, and interpret laws respectively. The Founder's creation of a separate judicial branch of courts was unprecedented in history. This branch independently interpreted and judged constitutional law.   Madison cites the above excerpt from Montesquieu in Federalist Paper 47 to defend three separate branches in the U. S. government.[1071] Madison agrees that "The accumulation of all powers, legislative, executive, and judiciary, in the same hands, whether of one, a few, or many, and whether hereditary, self-appointed, or elective, may justly be pronounced the very definition of tyranny" and "...[T]he preservation of liberty requires that the three great departments of power should be separate and distinct."[1072] Continental Army General, Constitution signer, and first U. S. President George Washington also affirms in his 1796 presidential Farewell Address the need for separation of powers due to man's imperfection, noting, "A just estimate of that love of power, and proneness to abuse it, which predominates in the human heart, is sufficient to satisfy us of the truth of this position.—The necessity of reciprocal checks in the exercise of political power, by dividing and distributing it into different depositories, and constituting each the Guardian of the Public Weal [Will] against invasions by the others, has been evinced...."[1073] Freedom for man is best protected, the Founders saw, with a government of limited, separated powers and checks and balances. Separation of powers functions as a kind of back-up plan of restraint among imperfect men.

Other checks and balances were also structured into the American system. Term limits were applied within each branch. These limits to power kept representatives in authority within their proper bounds and accountable to one another and to the people.[1074] Laws in the Constitution and Bill of Rights checked the rule of the majority by securing individual rights. Majority rule was, says Slater, "trusted with power only so far as is absolutely essential to the working of republican institutions."[1075] With separation of powers and checks and balances in place in the American system, note scholars, the positive benefits of civil government were achieved while the potential negatives were minimized.[1076]

Checks and balances also naturally existed in American society, noted Madison, in the differing interests or factions among the people. These checks and balances in society also worked to manage clashing interests for the public good, Madison pointed out, by checking and balancing one interest against another.[1077] In this sense, Madison saw religious pluralism as an important part of society in a republic. He notes, "In a free government the security for civil rights must be the same as that for religious rights. It consists in the one case in the multiplicity of interests, and in the other in the multiplicity of sects."[1078] Further, the multiplicity of sects actually benefited religious freedom. "Extend the sphere and you take in a greater variety of parties and interests," Madison observes in Federalist Paper 10. "[Y]ou make it less probable that a majority of the whole will have a common motive to invade the rights of other citizens...."[1079] Religious pluralism worked as a check in society since a variety of religious sects, denominations, or factions kept one group from overly dominating to the detriment of the public good.

The Bible-based principle of separation of powers and checks and balances became, says Gordon Wood, a "dominant principle of the American political system."[1080] State and local governments would also similarly apply separation of powers and checks and balances. Early British jurist James Bryce later reflects on the Bible-based view of human nature and its influence on the U. S. Constitution in his 1919 *The American Commonwealth*:

Some one has said that the American Government and Constitution are based on the theology of Calvin and the philosophy of Hobbes. This at least is true, that there is a hearty Puritanism in the view of human nature that pervades the instrument [U. S. Constitution] of 1787. It is the work of men who believed in original sin, and were resolved to leave open for transgressors no door which they could possibly shut. ... The aim of the Constitution seems to be not so much to attain great common ends by securing good government as to avert the evils which will flow, not merely from a bad government, but from any government strong enough to threaten the pre-existing communities or the individual citizen.[1081]

The United States' system of separation of powers and checks and balances, with its three branches of government unprecedented in history, reflected the Bible-based worldview of mankind. Edward Rauchet explains, "...[O]ur Founding Fathers' view of human nature in many ways determined the form of government they created. Because they assumed that our human nature is fallen, a government was designed to accommodate that notion of human nature."[1082] Sandoz affirms the connection between a Bible-based worldview of man and limited power:

> Merely mortal magistrates, no less than self-serving factions..., must be restrained artfully by a vast net of adversarial devices if just government is to have any chance whatever of prevailing over self-serving human passions while still nurturing the liberty of free men. To attain these noble ends in what is called a government of laws and not of men, it was daringly thought, perhaps ambition could effectively counteract ambition and, as one more *felix culpa*, therewith supply the defect of better motives. This is most dramatically achieved, at least in theory, through the routine operations of the central mechanism of divided and separated powers and of checks and balances that display the genius of the Constitution and serve as the well-known hallmark of America's republican experiment itself. *All of this would have been quite inconceivable without a Christian anthropology, enriched by classical political theory and the common law tradition, as uniquely imbedded in the habits of the American people at the time of the founding and nurtured thereafter.*[1083]

The Founders believed that man is fallible and power corrupts. Thus, government power must be limited and checked in order to maintain good, just government. Separation of powers and checks and balances were put in place within the branches of the central government and between the national and state governments in the federal system. While government relied on virtuous people to operate successfully, it provided a safeguard in the form and structure of government to protect against corruption. The American republican mechanism of separation of powers and checks and balances successfully endures today.

8.12 The First Amendment's Religion Clause: Separation of Church and Government, Religious Freedom as a Natural Right, and the Encouragement of Religion

A primary concern for Americans in the new nation was the issue of religion—religious freedom and the relationship between church and government. Knowing its importance, the Founders addressed this issue in the First Amendment of the Bill of Rights. The First Amendment's Religion Clause determined the relationship between church and government as well as religious rights at the national level. It states, "Congress shall make no law respecting an establishment of religion or prohibiting the free exercise thereof." The two parts of the Religion Clause are often referred to as the "No Establishment" clause and the "Free Exercise" clause. The Religion Clause's disestablishment of church and government and complete religious freedom were a radical new approach and departure from the centuries-old practice of nations in which church and government were tied together. The Religion Clause was based on the view that religious freedom was a natural right based on early American thought and experience in freedom of conscience, the Laws of Nature and Nature's God, and the Christian precepts of faith, forbearance, and charity or love.

The "No Establishment" Clause means that the national government cannot establish a national church or denomination and cannot regulate or financially support religion or a religious group with privileged laws or taxes. It affirms the distinction between church and government as two separate but complimentary spheres—but in harmony, not at odds. In separating or disestablishing the church and government on the national level, the Founders—for the most part very religious, spiritual men who were, says Meacham, "personally motivated and inspired by religious convictions"—did not view national disestablishment of church and civil government as irreligious, anti-religious, or bad for religion. Quite the contrary, they saw that it would protect the religious rights of all citizens in a large, religiously diverse society like America. For a multiplicity of religious sects and denominations was an outcome of a large nation. In such a setting, an established national church is not practical or favorable. Since the United States was a nation of multiple sects, the Founders saw, religious freedom was necessary. Separation on the national level was the only practical way to solve the issue of religious dissension and to unite religious groups in the religiously pluralistic nation. Justice Joseph Story, in his 1834 text, *The Constitutional Class Book: Being a Brief Exposition of the Constitution of the United States*, explains the reasoning behind the No Establishment Clause and the benefits of separation to both state and church:

> We are not to attribute this prohibition of a national religious establishment to an indifference to Religion in general, and especially to Christianity (which none could hold in more reverence, than the framers of the Constitution) but to a dread by the People of the influence of ecclesiastical power in matters of Government.... It was also obvious, from the numerous and powerful sects in the United States, that there would be perpetual temptations to struggles for ascendency in the national councils, if any one might thereby found a permanent, and exclusive national [church-government] establishment of its own; and religious persecutions might thus be introduced to an extent utterly subversive of the interests, and good order of the Republic. The most effectual mode of suppressing the evil was, in the view of the people, to strike down the temptations to its introduction.[1084]

Total disestablishment of church and government, the Founders believed, is the most practical way to protect religious rights of individuals, avoid corruption and abuse of power in church and government, and unite citizens in a large, religiously diverse nation.

Perhaps in this mindset of disestablishment and to facilitate understanding and relations among other nations, the United States government later discontinued the practice of the Continental Congress of officially calling the U. S. a "Christian nation." In its 1797 Treaty of Tripoli, an international treaty between the U. S. and the Muslim nation of Tripoli, the U. S. states that it is not founded on the Christian religion. The government likely wanted to indicate to the world and other (Muslim) nations that the United States was a religiously free, diverse new nation that respected the religious rights of all people and did not intend to engage in religious wars.[1085]

While the No Establishment Clause prohibited the establishment of a national church, it allowed free public religious expression in society and government as well as non-established cooperation between church and government. It allowed government and its representatives to encourage religion and non-sectarian Christianity without coercion. Indeed, the first U. S. Congress that wrote and approved the First Amendment found the argument compatible with early public religious practices (enacted by the Continental Congress and Washington) including opening prayers in Congress, national days of prayer and thanksgiving to God, appointment of chaplains in the military and Congress, and acts encouraging morality and religion in the armed forces, states, and schools. The first U. S. Congress continued many of these practices.

Chief Justice Story explains in his 1833 *Commentaries on the Constitution of the United States* that while public worship of God and support of religion was not part of the policy or law of the national government, religion—specifically Christianity—could and should be encouraged. He writes,

Probably at the time of the adoption of the constitution, and of the amendment to it, now under consideration, the general, if not the universal, sentiment in America was, that Christianity ought to receive encouragement from the state, so far as was not incompatible with the private rights of conscience, and the freedom of religious worship. An attempt to level all religions, and to make it a matter of state policy to hold all in utter indifference, would have created universal disapprobation, if not universal indignation.[1086]

In his *Democracy in America*, Tocqueville confirms the importance of religion, notably Christianity, to state and society in America, even with disestablishment of church and government in the nation. He writes, "Religious institutions have remained wholly distinct from political institutions, so that former laws have been easily changed whilst former belief has remained unshaken. Christianity has therefore retained a strong hold on the public mind in America...."[1087]

While most Americans opposed the establishment of a national religion, they favored religion and government's encouragement of it in society. The Religion Clause expresses, confirms Kirk, "the general sense of the American people on the relationship between State and Church. And that sense was not an arid secularism, hostile toward the religious consecration of the civil social order."[1088] Legislators still saw themselves as the "nursing fathers" of the church, but in a more limited sense in which they could encourage non-sectarian Christianity or religion for the good of society.[1089] The No Establishment Clause was compatible with church-government cooperation and free religious expression in civil society.

The "Free Exercise" Clause means that religious freedom—both to believe and to worship—is a God-given, natural, unalienable right of man based on the Laws of Nature and Nature's God and so outside the authority of federal government, church, or any earthly power. It was governed only by God and by man's choice and conviction. The clause provides total religious freedom, not just tolerance, for all Americans. It welcomes, promotes, accommodates, and protects all religion and religious expression in the nation to the extent that religious doctrines, authorities, and adherents do not violate civil rights, disturb civil peace, or endanger the safety and order of the nation's free civil society.

Total religious freedom of the Free Exercise Clause, the Founders believed, was the best means of protecting the natural religious rights of citizens and of promoting true religion and faith. For example, first U. S. President Washington writes in 1790 to a Hebrew congregation in Newport of total religious freedom, not just toleration, as a natural right:

It is now no more that toleration is spoken of as if it were the indulgence of one class of people that another enjoyed the exercise of their inherent natural rights, for, happily, the Government of the United States, which gives to bigotry no factions, to persecution no assistance, requires only that they who live under its protection should demean themselves as good citizens in giving it on all occasions their effectual support.[1090]

Jefferson also writes of support for total religious freedom as natural right: "I write with freedom, because, while I claim a right to believe in one God, I yield as freely to others that of believing in three. Both religions, I find, make honest men, and that is the only point society has any right to look to."[1091]

Total religious freedom also encouraged, the Founders believed, true religious belief and worship. When American Founder James Madison, as the fourth U. S. president, issues a Prayer and Thanksgiving Proclamation for the nation, he acknowledges the religious freedom of the people and called them to pray if they chose out of faith:

If the public homage of a people can ever be worthy the favorable regard of the Holy and Omnisicent Being to whom it is addressed, it must be that in which those who join in it are guided only by their free choice, by the impulse of their hearts and the dictates of their consciences....[1092]

The Free Exercise Clause resembled Madison's and Mason's religion clause in the 1776 Virginia Declaration of Rights with its "free exercise of religion," expressed duties to God, and practice of "Christian Forbearance, Love, and Charity towards each other." This correlation suggests that Madison's Free Exercise Clause was inspired by the same Judeo-Christian principles as Virginia's religion clause and as Madison's *Memorial and Remonstrance* in upholding a Christian view of the duties owed to God and of "Christian love, forbearance, and charity" as found in 1 Corinthians 13, Ephesians 4:1-3 and Colossians 3:12-14.[1093] For many of these Founders believed, in line with Locke's thinking, that the Christian teachings of faith, forbearance, and charity or love support and justify religious freedom.

Biblical Christianity, early Americans and the philosophers who influenced them understood, is conducive to religious and civil liberty because it recognizes man's natural religious rights and esteems virtues of faith, forbearance, and charity. It supports people of all faiths to believe and worship freely and peacefully. Tocqueville similarly notes the harmonious and mutually beneficial relationship between the Christian religion and freedom in America. "The Americans," he observes, "combine the notions of Christianity and of liberty so intimately in their minds, that it is impossible to make them conceive the one without the other...."[1094] American civilization, he elaborates,

> is the result...of two distinct elements, which in other places have been in frequent hostility, but which in America have been admirably incorporated and combined with one another. I allude to the spirit of Religion and the spirit of Liberty. ... These two tendencies...are far from conflicting; they advance together, and mutually support each other. Religion perceives that civil liberty affords a noble exercise to the faculties of man, and that the political world is a field prepared by the Creator for the efforts of the intelligence. Contented with the freedom and the power which it enjoys in its own sphere, and with the place which it occupies, the empire of religion is never more surely established than when it reigns in the hearts of men unsupported by aught beside its native strength. Religion is no less the companion of liberty in all its battles and its triumphs; the cradle of its infancy, and the divine source of its claims. The safe-guard of morality is religion, and morality is the best security of law as well as the surest pledge of freedom.[1095]

The American Judeo-Christian worldview thus influenced the forming of a nation that protected the religious rights of all men and encouraged true religion.

The Free Exercise Clause is, in fact, a clear endorsement of religion's positive role and value in the nation and society. The Founders also likely supported the "free exercise" of religion because it encouraged religion and morality that were so important in a free republic. On Americans' value of religion in society, Tocqueville reports,

> Religion in America takes no direct part in the government of society, but it must nevertheless be regarded as the foremost of the political institutions of that country; for if it does not impart a taste for freedom, it facilitates the use of free institutions. Indeed, it is in this same point of view that the inhabitants of the United States themselves look upon religious belief. I do not know whether all Americans have a sincere faith in their religion; for who can search the human heart? but I am certain that they hold it to be indispensable to the maintenance of republican institutions. This opinion is not peculiar to a class of citizens or to a party, but it belongs to the whole nation and to every rank of society.[1096]

1 Reichley affirms the Founders' endorsement of religion in the nation for its moral value to society: "The
2 founder's belief in the wisdom of placing civil society within a framework of religious values formed part of
3 their reason for enacting the free exercise clause. The First Amendment is no more neutral on the general value
4 of religion than it is on the general value of the free exchange of ideas or an independent press."[1097] "The first
5 Amendment was written to secure the individual right to worship according to one's conscience," explains John
6 Fea. "It was not meant as a means of protecting government from the religious beliefs of its citizens."[1098]

7

8   Because the Bill of Rights, when it was written and added to the Constitution, applied only to the
9 Federal Government, not to state or local governments, the Religion Clause of the First Amendment limited
10 only federal—but not state—government involvement in religion. It did not address the relationship between
11 church and government at the state level. It was, expresses Waldman, "a grand declaration that the *federal
12 government* couldn't support or regulate religion—but it was also a grand declaration that the *states absolutely
13 could*."[1099] Each state could address religion as it chose. The Tenth Amendment of the Bill of Rights affirmed
14 this point with its enumerated powers by stating that "The powers not delegated to the United States by the
15 Constitution, nor prohibited by it to the States, are reserved to the States respectively, or to the people." Voting
16 taxpayers in various states could, if they chose, establish an official state church and create religious laws or
17 taxes in their state. (Many states did, in fact, have partial and/or tolerant establishments for a time if no longer
18 full, strict establishments.) Jefferson affirmed this point in a letter and in his second Presidential Inaugural
19 Address.[1100] To be sure, some Founders were concerned that the states, controlled by powerful interest groups,
20 would abuse their rights and discard civil and religious freedom. To Madison, one of the greatest threats to
21 religious freedom was tyrannical state legislatures in which the majority imposed its will on the minority.[1101]
22 Nevertheless, the limit of the Bill or Rights and the Religion Clause to the federal government enabled the
23 Constitution to gain widespread support even though no consensus existed at the time about church-government
24 establishments at the state level. The Constitution along with the added Bill of Rights was ratified in 1789 and
25 went into effect in 1791, protecting religious freedom.

26

27 **8.13 No Religious Tests for Holding Federal Public Office**

28

29   In keeping with the First Amendment's No Establishment Clause, the U. S. Constitution prohibited
30 religious tests as a qualification for federal public officers, thus separating a candidate's religious belief from
31 his ability to run for and serve in public office. A person could not be excluded from holding national office
32 based solely upon his or her religious convictions. Article 6 in the Constitution states accordingly, "[N]o
33 religious test shall ever be required as a qualification to any office or public trust under the United States."
34 Article 6 applied only to the federal government. The states could maintain religious tests for state public
35 officials and candidates as the people chose. Article 6 departed from the traditional practice in the colonies.
36 For most colonies, historically and at that time, had religious qualifications for state public officials to hold
37 public office, save for Virginia's recent removal of such requirements. But since regulation of religion was an
38 issue only for the states, the federal government had no authority to examine or judge the religious beliefs of
39 any national public officer or candidate. A person of any belief or denomination could potentially hold office.
40 The voters, not the federal government, would decide who they wanted to represent them. While many
41 Americans opposed Article 6, fearing that omitting national religious tests would allow unvirtuous or irreligious
42 men to take over, religious pluralism and diversity made such tests impractical and divisive on the national
43 level. Thus Article 6 reflected the pluralistic reality of the new nation. Yet the article mostly reasserted the
44 Founder's belief that religious laws were state, not federal, matters. The Constitution, however, still required
45 public servants to take an oath of office, typically with a hand placed on the Bible as practiced by most public
46 representatives.

47

8.14 Ratification of the Constitution: Popular Sovereignty, Consent of the Governed, and Civil Covenant or Social Contract

The American Founders' act of submitting the Constitution to the states for ratification—approval and adoption—by the people was a significant event for the nation. It put into practice the American principles of popular sovereignty and consent of the governed. This principle reflected Locke's thinking that man-made laws of a nation require "the consent of the society, over whom nobody can have a power to make laws but by their own consent and by authority received from them…."[1102]

Hamilton raises the issue of the people's consent to approve the nation's form of government and laws in Federalist Paper 1, stating, "It has been frequently remarked that it seems to have been reserved to the people of this country, by their conduct and example, to decide the important question, whether societies of men are really capable or not of establishing good government from reflection and choice, or whether they are forever destined to depend, for their political constitutions, on accident and force."[1103] In Federalist Paper 22, Hamilton affirms the principle of consent as the authorization for the Constitution: "The fabric of American empire ought to rest on the solid basis of THE CONSENT OF THE PEOPLE. The streams of national power ought to flow immediately from that pure, original fountain of all legitimate authority."[1104] American Founder James Wilson hailed the people's ratification of the Constitution as an unprecedented accomplishment: "A people free and enlightened, establishing and ratifying a system of government, which they have previously considered, examined, and approved! This is the spectacle, which we are assembled to celebrate; and it is the most dignified one that has yet appeared on our globe."[1105] The Constitution applies consent in being a body of laws created by the people's chosen representatives, acting for the people, and as a founding document agreed on and voted for by the people. The Constitution itself, like the Declaration, acknowledges the consent of the people. It begins, "We the People of the United States…do ordain and establish this Constitution…."

By the people's consent, the Constitution with the Declaration functioned as a civil covenant or social contract among the people of the nation. As God made a covenant with the Israelites that they would be His people and follow His laws, so did Americans compact or covenant together as a nation under the principles and laws of the Declaration and Constitution.

The U. S. Constitution was modeled after the state constitutions which came from the Puritan colonial covenants and constitutions. Most state constitutions were compacts or agreements that created and defined a people and set up state government and laws.[1106] The state constitutions reflected, says Lutz, "a direct link with religious covenants traced through the compacts written by colonists" in the 1600s. The U. S. Constitution was also derived from the 1600s covenant-based colonial British charters.[1107] Indeed, the state and national constitutions of the United States were, affirms Elazar, "perhaps the greatest products of the American covenant tradition."[1108]

While the Declaration created a people and society with a certain identity and values, the Constitution created the nation's framework of government and laws upon which the people covenanted or agreed.[1109] Elazar explains the dynamics of creating a new people and nation and then a framework of laws by covenant and constitution: "Normally, a covenant precedes a constitution and creates the people or civil society which then proceeds to adopt a constitution of government for itself. Thus, a constitution involves the implementation of a prior covenant—an effectuation or translation of a prior covenant into an actual frame or structure of government."[1110]

The voluntary agreement among the American people to form a nation and then a government framework of laws was understood in more secular terms as a social contract. Drawing from Bible-based covenants and historical Christian political writings, Locke articulates in his *Second Treatise of Civil Government* such an agreement in his social contract theory. In Locke's theory, all citizens willingly agree to give up just enough of their natural rights in order to form a nation and a civil government for their preservation, prosperity, and security. In the spirit of Pufendorf's two covenants to found a society, Locke also recognizes two contracts—the first among the people unanimously to create a people and nation, the second among the people to create a government and laws by the action and consent of the majority.[1111] Locke states,

> When any number of men have so consented to make one community or government, they are thereby presently incorporated, and make one body politic, wherein the majority have a right to act and conclude the rest.
>
> 96. ... And therefore we see that in assemblies empowered to act by positive laws were no number is set by that positive law which empowers them, the act of the majority passes for the act of the whole, and of course determines as having, by the law of Nature and reason, the power of the whole.
>
> 97. And thus every man, by consenting with others to make one body politic under one government, puts himself under an obligation to every one of that society to submit to the determination of the majority....[1112]

Locke points out two agreements by the people's consent—one to form a people into a political body and another to submit to the will of the majority and the civil government and laws to which it agrees. These two contracts indicate that government is made by and serves the people. Lutz expresses,

> The important point to remember here is that Americans were quite aware that one did not create government in a vacuum. Government is instituted by a people in order to reach collective decisions, and before you can have a government you must have a people. The distinction is a logical, not a temporal one. Both compacts can be created at the same time, but the distinction is a powerful reminder that government is the servant of the people. More precisely, it *is* the people, but the people acting in a certain mode or a certain capacity.[1113]

American Founder John Jay applies Locke's thinking with regard to the Constitution, describing the Constitution as a social contract in Federalist Paper 2:

> Nothing is more certain than the indispensable necessity of government; and it is equally undeniable that whenever and however it is instituted, the people must cede to it some of their natural rights, in order to vest it with requisite powers. It is well worthy of consideration, therefore, whether it would conduce more to the interest of the people of America that they should, to all general purposes, be one nation, under one federal government, than that they should divide themselves into separate confederacies....[1114]

The purpose of the contract, Jay reiterates, is for the people's benefit and preservation of rights: "...[T]he prosperity of America depended on its Union. To preserve and perpetuate it was the great object of the people in forming that convention, and it is also the great object of the plan which the convention has advised them to adopt."[1115]

Covenants influenced not only the nation's founding documents but also many aspects of American life and culture in the new nation, just as in the early colonies. Covenants and contracts were a part of human relationships, cities and towns, churches, business and civic organizations, and various associations.

8.15 The Founders Recognize God's Role in the Adoption of the Constitution

The adoption of the U. S. Constitution and the formation of the new nation unlike any in history and approved by the people was, to the Founders, a miraculous accomplishment. That the states overcame so many differences was, they thought, the work of God. Madison proclaims in Federalist Paper 37 that the success of the Constitution is due to God's assistance:

The real wonder is that so many difficulties should have been surmounted, and surmounted with a unanimity almost as unprecedented as it must have been unexpected. ... It is impossible for the man of pious reflection not to perceive in it a finger of that Almighty hand which has been so frequently and signally extended to our relief in the critical stages of the revolution.[1116]

Franklin was convinced that God was involved in such an important event that would positively affect millions of people throughout history. Alluding to Acts 17:26-28, he expresses,

> ...I have so much faith in the general government of the world by Providence, that I can hardly conceive a transaction of such momentous importance to the welfare of millions now existing, and to exist in the posterity of a great nation, should be suffered to pass without being in some degree influenced, guided, and governed by that omnipotent, omnipresent, and beneficent Ruler, in whom all inferior spirits live, and move, and have their being.[1117]

Rush similarly expresses God's role in the great formation of the New Republic:

> I do not believe that the Constitution was the offspring of [divine] inspiration, but I am perfectly satisfied, that the union of the states, in its *form* and *adoption*, is as much the work of divine providence, as any of the miracles recorded in the Old and New Testament were the effects of a divine power. 'Tis done! We have become a nation.[1118]

Rush even seems to make a Biblical allusion to John 19:30 in the manner of his expression "tis' done!" In John 19:30, the Apostle John recounts the final words of Jesus Christ on the cross: "It is finished!"

> At the procession celebrating the ratification of the Constitution, clergy of different sects and religions approved the Constitution and its religious freedom, coming together in unity to support the new nation. Rush observes this unity among religious groups and sects:

> The clergy formed a very agreeable part of the procession—They manifested, by their attendance, their sense of the connexion between religion and good government. They amounted to seventeen in number. Four or five of them marched arm in arm with each other, to exemplify the Union. Pains were taken to connect ministers of the most dissimilar religious principles together, thereby to show the influence of a free government in promoting Christian charity. The Rabbi of the Jews, locked in the arms of two ministers of the gospel, was a most delightful sight. There could not have been a more happy emblem contrived, of that section of the new constitution, which opens all its power and offices alike, not only to every sect of Christians, but to worthy men of every religion.[1119]

The coming together of Americans of differing religious beliefs and denominations was a significant achievement for the nation. The form of government and civil laws framed and implemented by the Constitution created a nation of civil and religious liberty never before realized.

8.16 The Founders Identify America with Ancient Israel

The early Americans and the Founders compared themselves, like the Puritans, with the Israelites. As the early Puritans identified with Israel in their coming to the Promised Land of America, founding-era Americans similarly compared themselves with the Israelites. They compared America's revolution and Constitution to the Biblical Israelites' Exodus from bondage in Egypt and receiving of a covenant and law at Mount Sinai, representing freedom and law respectively. Like the Israelites, God had freed Americans from bondage and given them a new nation with a written covenant and law. Bruce Feiler observes, "One reason the Puritans proved so influential in American history is that they were the first to sear these twin pillars into

American life—freedom and law, Exodus and Sinai. A century and a half later, these parallel ideas would be entrenched in the defining events of American history, the liberation of the Revolution followed by the constriction of the Constitution."[1120] It was in this same identification with the Israelites that three of the five committee drafters of the Declaration—Benjamin Franklin, John Adams, and Thomas Jefferson—originally proposed in 1776 designs for the Great Seal of the United States that illustrated the Exodus of Moses and the Israelites from Egypt.[1121] Franklin proposes,

> Moses [in the Dress of High Priest] standing on the Shore, and extending his Hand over the Sea, thereby causing the same to overwhelm Pharaoh who is sitting in an open Chariot, a Crown on his Head and Sword in his Hand. Rays from a Pillar of Fire in the Clouds reaching to Moses, [expressing] to express that he acts by [the] Command of the Deity.

Franklin also proposes the American Revolution's motto "Rebellion to Tyrants is Obedience to God." Jefferson notes a version of Franklin's suggestion,

> Pharoah sitting in an open chariot, a crown on his head and a sword in his hand passing thro' the divided waters of the Red sea in pursuit of the Israelites: rays from a pillar of fire in the cloud, expressive of the divine presence, [reach] and command, reaching to Moses who stands on the shore and, extending his hand over the sea, causes it to over whelm Pharoah.

Jefferson, John Adams affirms in a letter, likewise proposes, "The children of Israel in the wilderness, led by a cloud by day, and a pillar of fire by night...."[1122]

The Americans identified with the Israelites in their forming of a new nation with a Declaration, Constitution, and Bill of Rights—with these founding documents acting as a covenantal civil law for Americans just as the Biblical commandments and Jewish laws are a covenantal moral and civil law for the Israelites. Rush makes such a comparison between Israel and the United States and the principles of freedom and law, as indicated in Pennsylvania's ratification debate, in his seeing in the Constitution that "the hand of God was employed in this work, as that God had divided the Red Sea to give a passage to the children of Israel, or had fulminated the ten commandments from Mount Sinai."[1123] President Washington also alludes to this comparison, expressing in a letter to a Hebrew Congregation in Savannah,

> May the same wonder-working Deity, who long since delivered the Hebrews from their Egyptian oppressors, planted them in a promised land, *whose providential agency has lately been conspicuous in establishing these United States as an independent nation*, still continue to water them with the dews of heaven and make the inhabitants of every denomination participate in the temporal and spiritual blessings of that people whose God is Jehovah.[1124]

Jefferson also saw parallels between Israel and the destiny of America. In his second presidential Inaugural Address in 1805, he states, "I shall need, too, the favor of that Being in whose hands we are; who led our fathers, as Israel of old, from their native land, and planted them in a country flowing with all the necessaries and comforts of life; who has covered our infancy with his providence, and our riper years with his wisdom and power...."[1125] The new nation with its freedom and law was, to founding-era Americans, a reflection of the forming of the nation of Israel.

8.17 National Encouragement of Bible Education and the Northwest Ordinance of 1787

Founding-era Americans, like the Puritans, strongly encouraged education and the teaching of the Bible in schools. The Founders knew the importance of education in a free republic. Schools and education were, they thought, an effective means to encourage religion and morality among the people. Schools had been originally started by the Puritans to teach children to read and learn the Bible. The moral teachings of the Bible and the Christian religion had always been considered part of a complete education, and many early colonies supported this education. Thus when Americans discussed the teaching of religion and morality, they were usually referring to the Bible and its Judeo-Christian moral teachings. Founding-era Americans similarly supported and encouraged such teaching of religion and morality in schools. John Adams, for example, writes, "…[L]iberty cannot be preserved without a general knowledge among the people, who have a right, from the frame of their nature, to knowledge, as their great Creator, who does nothing in vain, has given them understandings, and a desire to know…."[1126]

Education of the Bible has social benefits, both Locke and the American Founders believed, in promoting a virtuous, peaceful, secure society and in preventing and reducing lawlessness, crimes, and expansion of penal systems. Even those who did not typically favor religious education saw its social value. In a moral nation, they knew, government could regulate and restrain less. Locke supports religious education for its moral, social value, stating in his 1690 *Some Thoughts Concerning Education*,

> I wish, that those, who complain of the great Decay of Christian Piety and Virtue every where, and of Learning and acquired Improvements in the Gentry of this Generation, would consider how to retrieve them in the next. This I am sure, That if the Foundation of it be not laid in the Education and Principling of the Youth, all other Endeavours will be in vain.[1127]

Rush, a strong proponent of public education for youth, supported the teaching of the Bible in schools, noting its moral importance. He states, "By withholding the knowledge of this doctrine [of the Bible and the Law of Love] from children, we deprive ourselves of the best means of awakening moral sensibility in their minds" and "Above all, let both sexes be carefully instructed in the principles and obligations of the Christian religion. This is the most essential part of education."[1128] Rush affirmed the civic and social benefits of teaching religion, namely Christianity, in schools. He considers,

> In contemplating the political institutions of the United States, I lament, that we waste so much time and money in punishing crimes, and take so little pains to prevent them. We profess to be republicans, and yet we neglect the only means of establishing and perpetuating our republican forms of government, that is, the universal education of our youth in the principles of christianity, by means of the bible; for this divine book, above all others, favours that equality among mankind, that respect for just laws, and all those sober and frugal virtues, which constitute the soul of republicanism.[1129]

In addressing the Delaware Indian Chiefs in a 1779 speech, President Washington also encouraged the learning of the Bible, stating, "My ears hear with pleasure the other matters you [Delaware chiefs] mention. Congress will be glad to [hear] them too. You…wish to learn our…ways of life, and above all the Religion of Jesus Christ. [T]hese will make you a greater and happier people than you are. Congress will do everything they can to assist you in this wise intention…."[1130]

Constitution signer Gouverneur Morris notes in 1791 the necessity of religion in society through education: "Religion is the only solid basis of good morals; therefore education should teach the precepts of religion, and the duties of man toward God."[1131]

Bible education is important, early Americans thought, to prepare citizens for their civic responsibilities and to perpetuate the American republic—particularly since the rights and laws of the United States were based on the Laws of Nature and Nature's God and on a Judeo-Christian worldview and thus largely on the Bible. Without knowledge and practice of the Bible and its principles, citizens could not govern themselves or their country wisely or virtuously. The Founders intended for education, religion, and morality to work together to guarantee good government and liberty. They saw the Bible as essential to education and lamented what would happen if it was neglected.

Samuel Adams notes in a 1790 letter to John Adams the importance of Christian education to virtue and citizenship:

> Let Divines, and Philosophers, Statesmen and Patriots unite their endeavours to renovate the Age, by impressing the Minds of Men with the importance of educating their *little boys*, and *girls*—of inculcating in the Minds of youth the fear, and Love of the Deity, and universal Phylanthropy; and in subordination to these great principles, the Love of their Country—of instructing them in the Art of *self* government, without which they never can act a wise part in the Government of Societys great, or small—in short of leading them in the Study, and practice of the exalted Virtues of the Christian system....[1132]

During the ratification of the U. S. Constitution, many Americans wanted the new government to support and facilitate Christian morals and values. One Massachusetts delegate Charles Turner, like many, believed the new constitution would not succeed without Christian morals, "that without the prevalence of *Christian piety, and morals*, the best republican Constitution can never save us from slavery and ruin." (221) Turner thus urged Congress to adopt a bill to promote Bible and moral education. He stresses the importance of education to Christian morality—to the development of the moral "law unto themselves" of Romans 2:14-15— among the people and thus to republican government:

> The world of mankind have always in general, been enslaved and miserable, and always will be until there is a greater prevalence of Christian moral principles; nor have I an expectation of this, in any *great* degree, unless some superiour mode of *education* shall be adopted. It is EDUCATION which almost entirely forms the character, the freedom or slavery, the happiness or misery of the world. And if this Constitution shall be adopted, I hope the Continental Legislature will have the *singular honour*, the *indelible glory*, of making it one of their *first* acts, in their *first* session, most *earnestly* to recommend to the several States in the Union, the institution of such means of education, as shall be *adequate* to the *divine, patriotick purpose* of training up the children and youth at large, in that solid learning, and in those pious and moral principles, which are the *support*, the *life* and SOUL of the republican government and liberty, of which a free Constitution is the body; for as the body without the spirit is dead, so a free form of government without the *animating* principles of piety and virtue, is dead also, being alone. May *religion*, with sanctity of morals prevail and *increase*, that the patriotic civilian and ruler may have the *sublime, parental* satisfaction of *eagerly* embracing every opportunity of mitigating the rigours of government, in proportion to that increase of morality which may render the people more capable of being *a law to themselves*. How *much* more blessed THIS, than to be employed in fabricating Constitutions of an higher tone in obedience to necessity, arising from an increase of turbulent vice and injustice in society. I believe your Excellency's patience will not be further exercised, by hearing the sound of my voice on the occasion, when I have said; may the *United States of America* live before GOD! May they be enlightened, pious, virtuous, free and happy *to all generations*![1133]

Constitution signer, statesman, lawyer, educator Abraham Baldwin affirms the need for religion and education in society, asserting,

> [Free society and government] can only be happy when the public principles and opinions are properly directed and their manners regulated. This is an influence beyond the stretch of laws and punishments, and can be claimed only by religion and education. It should, therefore, be among the first objects of those who wish well to the national prosperity to encourage and support the principles of religion and morality...that by instruction, they [the youth] may be moulded to the love of virtue and good order.[1134]

Noah Webster, who published an American edition of the Bible in 1833, also observes the need for education in the Bible and morals in a free society:

> In my view, the Christian religion is the *most important and one of the first things* in which *all* children, under a free government, ought to be instructed…. No truth is more evident to my mind, than that the Christian religion must be the basis of any government intended to secure the rights and privileges of a free people.[1135]

Because the American Founders so highly valued education and the teaching of the Bible to young people, they formed a law encouraging education for the teaching of religion and morality in schools. During the same period that the Continental Congress adopted the Constitution, Bill of Rights, and First Amendment, it also adopted a law to encourage education for the teaching of religion and morality in schools. This law was known as the Northwest Ordinance of 1787. For the American Founders and early Americans, like the Puritans, highly valued education and the teaching of the Bible to young people. After the Revolutionary War, when the United States acquired new western territory, the Continental Congress was concerned about immorality and corruption in the new territories and stressed the importance of teaching the Bible and religion in these regions. It passed the Northwest Ordinance to endorse education for religious and moral purposes. The ordinance defined the criteria for how western territories would be admitted as states to the union and required that all new states build schools. The Northwest Ordinance was reapproved in 1789 by the first U. S. Congress under President Washington. Article III of the ordinance stated:

> Religion, Morality and knowledge being necessary to good government and the happiness of mankind, Schools and the means of education shall forever be encouraged.[1136]

Apparently, since the same Congress that adopted the Northwest Ordinance also adopted the First Amendment, Congress did not view government encouragement of religion as a violation of the First Amendment's No Establishment Clause. The No Establishment Clause clearly permitted the national government's encouragement of religion and religious education in the nation. "It is hardly credible that Congress would call on a territorial government set up under its authority 'to promote religious and moral education,'" says Reichley, "if it had intended through the First Amendment to forbid all cooperation between the federal government and the churches."[1137] The Founders naturally identified education with the teaching of the Bible, says Reichley, "almost as a matter of course."

In the 1700s, most states encouraged Bible education, though only some financially supported it. Many state constitutions cited the Northwest Ordinance's encouragement of religion and morality through education. Most Americans and public officials supported such laws that encouraged Bible education in a non-sectarian, non-established, non-coercive way. They believed it was the duty of national government to encourage the teaching of the Bible as long as it was done in a non-sectarian way and without use of public funds.[1138] The American view of the connection between education and the Bible, say some scholars, was probably one reason why the Founders did not originally apply the First Amendment and its disestablishment to the states.[1139] The states, at that time, could publicly support religion and education.

Also helping to address the need for Bible education in the nation and society, many Americans and localities formed Bible societies to print, distribute, circulate, and make freely accessible the Bible in all languages in America and worldwide. In the early 1800s, for example, the first Bible societies were formed in Philadelphia, Connecticut, Massachusetts, Baltimore, and Maryland. Over 100 societies quickly sprung up shortly after. In 1816, the American Bible society was founded in New York City. Many notable American leaders and Founders served in leadership posts in these societies. American Founder James McHenry led the Baltimore Bible Society. Former Continental Congress president Elias Boudinot, Declaration signer Benjamin Harrison, Federalist Paper author and statesman John Jay, 6th U. S. President John Quincy Adams, American anthem writer Francis Scott Key, and others served in important leadership roles with the American Bible Society which still operates today.

8.18 The Religion Clause and Thomas Jefferson's "Wall of Separation" Between Church and Federal Government

Following the adoption of the Constitution and Bill of Rights, the Danbury, Connecticut, Baptist Association wrote a letter to third U. S. President Thomas Jefferson on October 7, 1801, expressing their concern for the security of their religious freedom as a natural right. At the time, Connecticut still had a state church establishment which they disliked. They sought Jefferson's reassurance and support for religious freedom as a natural right in the nation, hoping such views would impact the states. The letter states,

> Our Sentiments are uniformly on the side of Religious Liberty—That Religion is at all times and places a matter between God and Individuals - That no man ought to suffer in Name, person or effects on account of his religious Opinions - That the legitimate Power of civil Government extends no further than to punish the man who works *ill to his neighbour*. But Sir our constitution of government is not specific. Our ancient charter, together with the Laws made coincident therewith, were adopted as the Basis of our government at the time of our revolution; and such had been our Laws & usages, & such still are; that Religion is consider,d as the first object of Legislation; & therefore what religious privileges we enjoy (as a minor part of the State) we enjoy as favors granted, and not as inalienable rights: and these favors we receive at the expense of such degrading acknowledgements as are inconsistent with the rights of freemen. It is not to be wondered at therefore; if those, who seek after power & gain under the pretense of *government & Religion* should reproach their fellow men—should reproach their chief Magistrate, as an enemy of religion Law & good order because he will not, dare not assume the prerogative of Jehovah and make Laws to govern the Kingdom of Christ.
>
> Sir, we are sensible that the President of the united States, is not the national Legislator, & also sensible that the national government cannot destroy the Laws of each State; but our hopes are strong that the sentiments of our beloved President, which have had such genial affect already, like the radiant beams of the Sun, will shine & prevail through all these States and all the world till Hierarchy and Tyranny be destroyed from the Earth.[1140]

In response to this letter, Jefferson wrote in 1802 what would become a notable letter on religious freedom to the Danbury, Connecticut, Baptists, who had concerns about the First Amendment's Religion Clause. This letter contains Jefferson's well-known metaphor of the "wall of separation of church and state." The Baptists were concerned that the inclusion of the Religion Clause in the First Amendment of the Bill of Rights might suggest that religious freedom was a right granted by the government and therefore alienable or removable by the government. They appealed to Jefferson for assurance of their religious freedom in the nation. In response, Jefferson reassures them in his letter that the federal government has no authority over religion, that religion is under God's authority. He thus portrays a wall between church and state to express religious freedom as a natural right:

> Believing with you that religion is a matter which lies solely between man and his God, that he owes account to none other for his faith or his worship, that the legislative powers of government reach actions only, and not opinions, I contemplate with sovereign reverence that act of the whole American people which declared that their legislature should 'make no law respecting an establishment of religion, or prohibiting the free exercise thereof,' thus building a wall of separation between church and State. Adhering to this expression of the supreme will of the nation in behalf of the rights of conscience, I shall see with sincere satisfaction the progress of those sentiments which tend to restore to man all his natural rights, convinced he has no natural right in opposition to his social duties.[1141]

Religious freedom is, Jefferson reassured, a God-given, natural right that can never be removed or contradicted by any federal law. Disestablishment of religion in the federal government, to Jefferson as to the other Founders, provides a protection against religious oppression. Jefferson reiterates his recognition of the distinct jurisdictions between the church and the federal government.

Jefferson used the "wall of separation" metaphor in this context to illustrate the protection of the natural rights of conscience and religious freedom from oppressions by civil government. Jefferson used the "wall of separation" phrase in a similar manner as that of early Puritan dissenter and founder of Rhode Island Roger Williams in the 1600s. Alluding to Isaiah 5:3-6 and the Israelite's Exodus, Williams had stated,

> When they [the church of the Jews and the Christians] have opened a gap in the hedge, or wall of separation, between the garden of the church and the wilderness of the world, God hath ever broke down the wall itself, removed the candlestick, &c. and made his garden a wilderness, as at this day. And that therefore if he will ever please to restore his garden and paradise again, it must of necessity be walled in peculiarly unto himself from the world, and that all shall be saved out of the world are to be transplanted out of the wilderness of the world, and added unto his church or garden.[1142]

Jefferson likely adopted this "wall of separation" metaphor because he wanted to reassure the Baptists that he was a friend of religion and of religious freedom. He thus expresses support for religion's freedom from intrusion and regulation by the federal government in accordance with the First Amendment.

8.19 The Civil War Amendments: 13th Amendment Abolishes Slavery, 14th Amendment Applies the First Amendment to the States

With the American Civil War of 1861-1865, the nation would finally address the moral issue of slavery. Following the war, three constitutional amendments were passed. The 13th Amendment of 1865 abolished slavery in the United States. With this law, the nation thus fully realized the Bible-inspired principles of freedom, rights, and equality in the Declaration of Independence and a great moral victory. When the 13th Amendment was passed, however, some protesters vowed to withhold citizenship rights from former slaves in their states. Congress thus created the 14th Amendment in 1868, extending the Bill of Rights to the states, to insure that freed slaves would enjoy all the individual, civil rights of their state and nation. Thus while the Bill of Rights originally applied only to the federal government, the 14th Amendment applied the Bill of Rights to the state governments after the Civil War. Reflecting Locke's presentation of the rights of man—life, liberty, and property—the 14th Amendment states,

> All persons born or naturalized in the United States, and subject to the jurisdiction thereof, are citizens of the United States and of the State wherein they reside. No State shall make or enforce any law which shall abridge the privileges or immunities of citizens of the United States; nor shall any State deprive any person of life, liberty, or property, without due process of law; nor deny to any person within its jurisdiction the equal protection of the laws.

The 15th Amendment in 1870 gave freed slaves the right to vote and to participate in state political affairs. These Civil War amendments limited states' rights and powers in that states could not deny citizens their rights without equal protection and due process of law.

As a result of the 14th Amendment applying the Bill of Rights to the states, the First Amendment and its Religion Clause were also applied to the states, not just the federal government.[1143] State power over religion was thus also limited. While previously states could establish official churches and regulate religious worship if the people chose, the 14th Amendment made such church-government establishments unconstitutional at the state level. The 14th Amendment led thirty-three states between 1877 and 1913 to amend their constitutions and

1   prohibit financial aid to church-operated schools. Despite disestablishment in the states, many states, though
2   not required by law, continued Bible reading and prayer in schools.
3
4   The application of the First Amendment and its Religion Clause to the states raised difficult questions
5   regarding issues of church and government at the state and local levels. Reichley illustrates the challenges and
6   issues that arose on the state and local levels:
7
8   Did prohibition of 'establishment' make traditional practices of prayer and Bible reading in the public
9   schools unconstitutional? Had state aid to religious education been taken out of the hands of the states
10 altogether and placed under the interdict of the federal Constitution? Did exemption of church property
11 from taxation, provided for in all the states, represent a form of 'establishment'?   What of such
12 ministerial relationships as the appointment of chaplains by state legislatures? Were laws prohibiting
13 some kinds of commercial activities on Christian days of worship unconstitutional?[1144]
14
15 Such were the issues that the people and governments faced at state and local levels which were not
16 originally addressed by the First Amendment's Religion Clause or the American Founders.   Whether the
17 Founders who wrote and approved the Bill of Rights would have approved of the Religion Clause's application
18 to the states is, say historians, a matter of debate. In such a context, says Waldman, "the political dynamic
19 would have been different."[1145]
20
21 **8.20 Conclusion: A Nation Applying Bible-Based Principles**
22
23 The drafting and adoption of the United States Constitution created a New Republic, the United States
24 of America.   The Constitution, along with the Declaration, completed the nation's compact among the
25 American people to form a new nation and government under God. This compact recognized and protected the
26 natural, God-given civil and religious liberties of man to an extent previously unrealized in human history and
27 civilization. It upheld God as Creator and Supreme Judge, God's moral law, the dignity and equality of man,
28 the God-given natural rights of man, popular sovereignty, consent of the governed, limited and just government
29 with separation of powers, Rule of Law, social contracts and covenants, the expectation of a virtuous citizenry,
30 and the importance of religion in society.   The Constitution proved more successful and enduring than any other
31 written charter or constitution in history and the world. Today, over 200 years later, it still endures.
32
33 Before the founding of the United States of America, all nations in the world were under various forms
34 of Ruler's Law or absolute rule and oppression. But from the early 1600s, Americans aspired to something
35 different and, in the process, changed the course of history. In 1776, Americans founded the first nation that
36 implemented on a large scale self-government or government by its people. The roots of this new nation did not
37 grow overnight. The founding of this new nation was the culmination of a process over time of the study and
38 practice of Bible-based and moral concepts of life and governance in newly created colonies. It was the result
39 of Americans' goal and hope to form a civil state and society where their God-given rights were upheld and
40 their godly purposes and callings in life could be realized. Early Americans looked to the Bible and Bible-
41 based thinkers for direction and inspiration on how to form a civil state that more closely reflected the godly,
42 moral principles of the Bible and the hope within them. The Bible influenced Americans' understanding of
43 God, man, and life upon which they based their civil institutions and society.   Tocqueville observes the
44 influence of Bible-based principles in the United States:
45
46 In the United States, Christian sects are infinitely diversified and perpetually modified; but Christianity
47 itself is an established and irresistible fact, which no one undertakes either to attack or to defend. The
48 Americans, having admitted the principal doctrines of the Christian religion without inquiry, are obliged
49 to accept in like manner a great number of moral truths originating in it and connected with it.[1146]

1   Americans studied, learned, and believed that freedom, equality, and human rights are unalienable gifts from a
2   Creator God to all human beings. These rights cannot be granted or removed by an earthly ruler or another
3   person. They knew that without such a God-oriented worldview, men are at the mercy of other men, and rights
4   could be given or taken away by a man-made law or by whoever had the most power. In many ways, their work
5   was a process of trial and error and was not perfect, but it led them toward the formation of a new nation that
6   was deeply rooted in Bible-based thought, principles, and values. The influence of the Bible on the American
7   vision led to the creation of a new republic of exceptional moral fortitude.

9   Many early Americans, including those of the late 1700s and 1800s, exhorted their fellow Americans
10   and posterity to honor God and to uphold and abide by the Bible and its principles as the necessary foundation
11   of America's constitutional republic. It is impossible, they believed, to rightly govern without them.

13   For example, after taking the oath of office as first president of the United States on April 30, 1789,
14   Washington, in his Inaugural Address, gives such an exhortation to Congress and the people. He acknowledged
15   the providential workings of God in the formation of the new nation and recognizes the need for God's moral
16   law in the governance of the nation. Admonishing Congress and the American people on these points, he
17   expresses,

19   No people can be bound to acknowledge and adore the invisible Hand which conducts the affairs of
20   men, more than the people of the United States. Every step by which they have advanced to the
21   character of an independent nation seems to have been distinguished by some token of providential
22   agency; and in the important revolution just accomplished in the system of their united government....
23   ...[T]here is no truth more thoroughly established than that there exists in the economy and
24   course of nature an indissoluble union between virtue and happiness, between duty and advantage,
25   between the genuine maxims of an honest and magnanimous policy and the solid rewards of public
26   prosperity and felicity; since we ought to be no less persuaded that the propitious smiles of Heaven can
27   never be expected on a nation that disregards the eternal rules of order and right which Heaven has
28   ordained....[1147]

30   John Adams affirms the Bible-inspired principles of the nation and their eternal endurance in a 1813
31   letter to Jefferson:

33   The *general principles* on which the fathers achieved independence were...the general principles of
34   Christianity...and English and American liberty.... Now I will avow, that I then believed, and now
35   believe that those general principles of Christianity are as eternal and immutable as the existence and
36   attributes of God; and that those principles of liberty are as unalterable as human nature.... I could,
37   therefore safely say, consistently with all my then and present information, that I believed they would
38   never make discoveries in contradiction to these *general principles*.[1148]

40   John Quincy Adams exhorts his son in 1811—much like Elisha Williams had exhorted those in 1744—
41   to read the Bible, recognizing it as the founding source of the new nation: "Let us then search the Scriptures....
42   The Bible contains the revelation of the will of God; it contains the history of the creation, of the world and of
43   mankind; and afterwards the history of one peculiar nation, certainly the most extraordinary nation that has ever
44   appeared upon the earth."[1149]

46   In an address to the New York historical society in 1852, Secretary of State, Congressman, and
47   Constitution scholar Daniel Webster similarly observes the need to abide by Biblical, moral principles for
48   continued success in the republic:

...[I]f we and our posterity shall be true to the Christian religion, if we and they shall live always in the fear of God, and shall respect His commandments, if we and they shall maintain just moral sentiments and such conscientious convictions of duty as shall control the heart and life, we may have the highest hopes of the future fortunes of our country; and if we maintain those institutions of government and that political union...it will go on prospering and to prosper. But if we and our posterity reject religious instruction and authority, violate the rules of eternal justice, trifle with the injunctions of morality, and recklessly destroy the political constitution which holds us together, no man can tell how sudden a catastrophe may overwhelm us that shall bury all our glory in profound obscurity.[1150]

Just as the Puritans sought a "city on a hill," early Americans like Washington hoped that the United States, with its unprecedented civil and religious freedoms, would be an example and model to the world. In his drafting notes for his presidential Inaugural Address, Washington muses on the hope that the new nation would inspire greater freedom and rights for mankind throughout the world:

Though I shall not survive to perceive with these bodily senses, but a small portion of the blessed effects which our Revolution will occasion in the rest of the world; yet I enjoy the progress of human society & human happiness in anticipation. I rejoice in a belief that intellectual light will spring up in the dark corners of the earth; that freedom of enquiry will produce liberality of conduct; that mankind will reverse the absurd position *that the many* were made for *the few*; and that they will not continue as slaves in one part of the globe, when they can become freemen in another.[1151]

America's Bible-based ethic continued to impact ideas and events of the 1800s. Because of the nation's founding, providence and progress became themes of the 1800s. The Second Great Awakening, a second evangelical revival in America from the late 1700s to the early 1800s, led many to convert to Christianity and to join evangelical churches. Extending the spirit of democratization and humanitarianism, the revival energized reform movements to address social evils. In the Civil War of the mid-1800s, Americans wrestled with the moral issue of slavery and the practical application of the idea that all men are created equal and possess God-given rights. During the war, in 1863, second U. S. President Abraham Lincoln delivered his Gettysburg Address which recognized the equality of men, popular sovereignty, and the founding of the nation under God. He states,

Four score and seven years ago our fathers brought forth on this continent, a new nation, conceived in Liberty, and dedicated to the proposition that all men are created equal. ... ...[W]e here highly resolve that these dead shall not have died in vain—that this nation, under God, shall have a new birth of freedom—and that government of the people, by the people, and for the people, shall not perish from the earth.[1152]

The first line of Lincoln's address rung reminiscent of a 1561 Reformation-era hymnal of Bible psalms, titled *Four Score and Seven Psalmes of David in English Metre*.[1153] Ultimately, slaves gained their freedom and constitutional rights in America. Also during this time, America's free marketplace of ideas promoted the rise of consumer capitalism.

Since America's founding, Americans in many ways have realized Bible-based concepts of freedom, equality, and human rights to a degree never before experienced on earth. Americans of every belief have held that freedom, equality, and human rights are unalterable, unalienable states of human existence granted to every human being—not just in America but in the entire world—by a higher source of Moral Truth or a Creator God. They have applied these rights to all races and ethnicities. They have also applied them to people of every religious belief. Through history, Americans have continually learned and sought to honor the idea in the Declaration: "We hold these truths to be self-evident, that all men are created equal, that they are endowed by

their Creator with certain unalienable Rights, that among these are Life, Liberty, and the Pursuit of Happiness."
Indeed, the American idea has uplifted millions of people and given them the opportunity to better their lives.

The endurance of the United States of America and its founding documents for over 200 years attests to the wisdom of the American ethic. However, the future perpetuation and practice of this ethic was never assumed or taken for granted by early Americans. Early Americans recognized that such an ethic cannot be preserved—and will not endure in practice—unless it is taught, learned, and valued by each generation. As Will and Ariel Durant observe, "Civilization is not inherited; it has to be learned and earned by each generation anew; if the transmission should be interrupted for one century, civilization would die, and we should be savages again."[1154] The early Americans seemed to know this. They were vigilant to study, defend, teach, and promote America's founding ethic. They knew that it was essential to their freedoms, rights, and society. They understood that, at its core, the sustenance and glory of America was and would always be rooted in its honor of, devotion to, and love for God the Creator and the eternal principles of the Bible.

Signers of the United States Constitution

1
2
3 The 55 delegates who attended the Constitutional Convention held a strong commitment to Bible-based
4 principles and values. They were also educated and experienced. 36 had been members of the Continental
5 Congress. 20 had been Governors. 20 were U. S. Senators. 13 were U. S. Representatives. 8 were U. S.
6 Judges. 2 had been President. 1 had been Vice-President. Several were diplomats or cabinet members.
7 About 60% were lawyers. 40 delegates signed the Constitution.
8

President and Deputy
George Washington

Connecticut
William Samuel Johnson
Roger Sherman

Delaware
Richard Bassett
Gunning Bedford Jr.
Jacob Broom
John Dickinson
George Read

Georgia
Abraham Baldwin
William Few

Maryland
Daniel Carroll
Dan of St. Thomas Jenifer
James McHenry

Massachusetts
Nathaniel Gorman
Rufus King

New Hampshire
Nicholas Gilman
John Langdon

New Jersey
David Brearley
Jonathan Dayton
William Livingston
William Paterson

New York
Alexander Hamilton

North Carolina
William Blount
Richard Dobbs Spaight
Hugh Williamson

Secretary
Attest William Jackson

Pennsylvania
George Clymer
Thomas Fitzsimons
Benjamin Franklin
Jared Ingersoll
Thomas Mifflin
Gouverneur Morris
Robert Morris
James Wilson

South Carolina
Pierce Butler
Charles Cotesworth
   Pinckney
Charles Pinckney
John Rutledge

Virginia
John Blair
 James Madison Jr.

Preamble of the U. S. Constitution

WE THE PEOPLE of the United States, in Order to form a more perfect Union, establish Justice, insure domestic Tranquility, provide for the common defense, promote the general Welfare, and secure the Blessings of Liberty to ourselves and our Posterity, do ordain and establish this Constitution for the United States of America.

The Bill of Rights
Amendments To The Constitution of the United States of America

AMENDMENT I. Congress shall make no law respecting an establishment of religion, or prohibiting the free exercise thereof; or abridging the freedom of speech, or of the press; or the right of the people peaceably to assemble, and to petition the Government for a redress of grievances.

AMENDMENT II. A well regulated Militia, being necessary to the security of a free State, the right of the people to keep and bear Arms shall not be infringed.

AMENDMENT III. No Soldier shall, in time of peace be quartered in any house, without the consent of the Owner, nor in time of war, but in a manner to be prescribed by law.

AMENDMENT IV. The right of the people to be secure in their persons, houses, papers, and effects, against unreasonable searches and seizures, shall not be violated, and no Warrants shall issue, but upon probable cause, supported by Oath or affirmation, and particularly describing the place to be searched, and the persons or things to be seized.

AMENDMENT V. No person shall be held to answer for a capital, or otherwise infamous crime, unless on a presentment or indictment of a Grand Jury, except in cases arising in the land or naval forces, or in the Militia, when in actual service in time of War or public danger; nor shall any person be subject for the same offence to be twice put in jeopardy of life or limb; nor shall be compelled in any criminal case to be a witness against himself, nor be deprived of life, liberty, or property, without due process of law; nor shall private property be taken for public use, without just compensation.

AMENDMENT VI. In all criminal prosecutions, the accused shall enjoy the right to a speedy and public trial, by an impartial jury of the State and district wherein the crime shall have been committed, which district shall have been previously ascertained by law, and to be informed of the nature and cause of the accusation; to be confronted with the witnesses against him; to have compulsory process for obtaining witnesses in his favor, and to have the Assistance of Counsel for his defence.

AMENDMENT VII. In Suits at common law, where the value in controversy shall exceed twenty dollars, the right of trial by jury shall be preserved, and no fact tried by a jury, shall be otherwise re-examined in any Court of the United States, than according to the rules of the common law.

AMENDMENT VIII. Excessive bail shall not be required, nor excessive fines imposed, nor cruel and unusual punishments inflicted.

AMENDMENT IX. The enumeration in the Constitution, of certain rights, shall not be construed to deny or disparage others retained by the people.

AMENDMENT X. The powers not delegated to the United States by the Constitution, nor prohibited by it to the States, are reserved to the States respectively, or to the people.

Preamble Excerpts of 47 State Constitutions
with Adoption Dates

Alabama 1901

The people of the State of Alabama, in order to establish justice, insure domestic tranquility and secure the blessings of liberty to ourselves and our posterity, invoking the favor and guidance of Almighty God, do ordain and establish the following Constitution and form of government for the State of Alabama.

Arizona 1912

We, the people of the State of Arizona, grateful to Almighty God for our liberties, do ordain this Constitution.

Arkansas 1874

We, the people of the State of Arkansas, grateful to Almighty God for the privilege of choosing our own form of government, for our civil and religious liberty, and desiring to perpetuate its blessings and secure the same to ourselves and posterity, do ordain and establish this Constitution.

California 1879

We, order to secure the people of the State of California, grateful to Almighty God for our freedom, in and perpetuate its blessings, do establish this Constitution.

Colorado 1876

We, the people of Colorado, with profound reverence for the Supreme Ruler of the Universe, in order to form a more independent and perfect government; establish justice; insure tranquility; provide for the common defense; promote the general welfare and secure the blessings of liberty to ourselves and our posterity; do ordain and establish this Constitution for the "State of Colorado."

Connecticut 1818

The people of Connecticut acknowledging with gratitude, the good having permitted them to enjoy a free government, do in order more effectually to define, secure, and perpetuate the liberties, rights and privileges which they have derived from their ancestors, hereby, after a careful providence of God, in consideration and revision, ordain and establish the following Constitution and form of civil government.

Delaware 1897

Through Divine goodness, all men have by nature the rights of worshipping and serving their Creator according to the dictates of their consciences, of enjoying and defending life and liberty, of acquiring and protecting reputation and property, and in general of obtaining objects suitable to their condition, without injury by one to another; and as these rights are essential to their welfare, for the due exercise thereof, power is inherent in them; and therefore all just authority in the institutions of political society is derived from the people and established with their consent, to advance their happiness; and may for this end, as circumstances require, from time to time alter their constitution of government.

Florida 1887

We, the people of the State of Florida, grateful to Almighty God for our constitutional liberty, in order to secure its blessings and to form a more perfect government, insuring domestic tranquility, maintaining public order, and guaranteeing equal civil ad political rights to all, do ordain and establish this Constitution.

Georgia 1887

To Perpetuate the principles of free government, insure justice to all, preserve peace, promote the interest and happiness to the citizen, and transmit to posterity the enjoyment of liberty, we, the people of Georgia, relying upon the protection and guidance of Almighty God, do ordain and establish this Constitution.

Idaho 1890

We, the people of the State of Idaho, grateful to Almighty God for our freedom, to secure its blessings and promote our common welfare, do establish this Constitution.

Illinois 1870

We, the people of the State of Illinois-grateful to Almighty God for the civil, political and religious liberty which He hath so long permitted us to enjoy, and looking to Him for a blessing upon our endeavors to secure and transmit the same unimpaired to succeeding generations-in order to form a more perfect government, establish justice, insure domestic, tranquility, provide for the common defense, promote the general welfare, and secure the blessing of liberty to ourselves and our posterity, do ordain and establish this Constitution for the State of Illinois.

Indiana 1851

To the end that justice be established, public order maintained, and liberty perpetuated: We, the people of the State of Indiana, grateful to Almighty God for the free exercise of the right to choose our own form of government, do ordain this Constitution.

Iowa 1857

We, the people of the State of Iowa, grateful to the Supreme Being for the blessings hitherto enjoyed, and feeling our dependence on Him for a continuation of those blessings, do ordain and establish a free and independent government, by the name of the State of Iowa, the boundaries whereof shall be as follows:

Kansas 1863

We, the people of Kansas, grateful to Almighty God for our civil and religious privileges, in order to insure the full enjoyment of our rights as American citizens, do ordain and establish this Constitution of the State of Kansas, do ordain and establish this Constitution of the State of Kansas, with the following boundaries, to wit: Beginning at a point on the western boundary of the State of Missouri, where the thirty-seventh parallel of north latitude crosses the same; thence running west on said parallel to the twenty-fifth meridian of longitude west from Washington; thence north on said meridian to the fortieth parallel of north latitude; thence east on said meridian to the fortieth parallel of north latitude; thence east on said parallel to the western boundary of the State of Missouri, thence south with the western boundary of said state to the place of beginning.

Kentucky 1891

We, the people of the Commonwealth of Kentucky, grateful to Almighty God for the civil, political and religious liberties we enjoy, and invoking the continuance of these blessings, do ordain and establish this constitution.

Louisiana 1921

We, the people of the State of Louisiana, grateful to Almighty God for the civil, political and religious liberties we enjoy, and desiring to secure the continuance of these blessings, do ordain and establish this Constitution.

Maine 1820 and 1876

We, the people of Maine, in order to establish justice, insure tranquility, provide for our mutual defense, promote our common welfare, and secure to ourselves and our posterity the blessings of liberty, acknowledging with grateful hearts the goodness of the Sovereign Ruler of the Universe in affording us an opportunity, so favorable to the design; and imploring His aid and direction in its accomplishment, do agree to form ourselves into a free and independent state, by the style and title of the State of Maine, and do ordain and establish the following Constitution for the government of the same.

Maryland 1867

We, the people of the State of Maryland, grateful to Almighty God for our civil and religious liberty, and taking in to our serious consideration the best means of establishing a good Constitution in this State for the sure foundation and more permanent security thereof, declare:

Massachusetts 1790

We, therefore, the people of Massachusetts, acknowledging, with grateful hearts, the goodness of the great Legislator of the universe, in affording us, in the course of His providence, an opportunity, deliberately and peaceably, without fraud, violence, or surprise, of entering into an original, explicit, and solemn compact with each other, and for forming a new Constitution of civil government, for ourselves and posterity; and devoutly imploring His direction in so interesting a design, do agree upon, ordain, and establish the following Declaration of Rights, and Frame of Government, as the Constitution of the Commonwealth of Massachusetts.

Michigan 1909

We, the people of the State of Michigan, grateful to Almighty God for the blessings of freedom, and earnestly desiring to secure these blessings undiminished to ourselves and our posterity, do ordain and establish this Constitution.

Minnesota 1857

We, the people of the State of Minnesota, grateful to God for our civil and religious liberty and desiring to perpetuate its blessings and secure the same to ourselves and our posterity, do ordain and establish this Constitution.

Mississippi 1890

We, the people of Mississippi in convention assembled, grateful to Almighty God, and invoking his blessing on our work, do ordain and establish this Constitution.

Missouri 1945

We, the people of Missouri, with profound reverence for the Supreme Ruler of the Universe, and grateful for His goodness, do establish this Constitution for the better government of the State.

Montana 1889

We, the people of Montana, grateful to Almighty God for the blessings of liberty, in order to secure the advantages of a State government, do in accordance with the provisions of the enabling act of Congress, approve the twenty-second of February A. D. 1889, order and establish this Constitution.

Nebraska 1875

We, the people, grateful to Almighty God for our freedom, do ordain and establish the following declaration of rights and frame of government as the Constitution of the State of Nebraska.

Nevada 1864

We, the people of the State of Nevada, grateful to Almighty God for our freedom, in order to secure its blessings, insure domestic tranquility, and forme a more perfect government, do establish this Constitution.

New Hampshire 1784

Every individual has a natural and unalienable right to worship God according to the dictates of his own conscience, and reason * * * morality and piety, rightly grounded on evangelical principles, will give the best and greatest security to government, and will lay, in the hearts of men, the strongest obligations to due subjection; and the knowledge of these is most likely to be propagated through society by the institution of the public worship of the Deity.

New Jersey 1947

We, the people of the State of New Jersey, grateful to Almighty God for the civil and religious liberty which He hath so long permitted us to enjoy, and looking to Him for a blessing upon our endeavors to secure and transmit the same unimpaired to succeeding generations, do ordain and establish this Constitution.

New Mexico 1912

We, the people of New Mexico, grateful to Almighty God for the blessings of liberty, in order to secure the advantages of a State government, do ordain and establish this Constitution.

New York 1895

We, the people of the State of New York, grateful to Almighty God for our freedom, in order to secure its blessings, do establish this Constitution.

North Carolina 1876

We, the people of the State of North Carolina, grateful to Almighty God, the Sovereign Ruler of Nations, for the preservation of the American Union and the existence of our civil, political and religious liberties, and acknowledging our dependence upon Him for the continuance of these blessings to us and our posterity, do, for the more certain security thereof and for the better government of this State, ordain and establish this Constitution.

North Dakota 1889

We, the people of North Dakota, grateful to Almighty God for the blessings of civil and religious liberty, do ordain and establish this Constitution.

Ohio 1851

We, the people of the State of Ohio, grateful to Almighty God for our freedom, to secure its blessings and promote our common welfare, do establish this Constitution.

Oklahoma 1907

Invoking the guidance of Almighty God, in order to secure and perpetuate the blessing of liberty; to secure just and rightful government; to promote our mutual welfare and happiness, we the people of the State of Oklahoma, do ordain and establish this Constitution.

Oregon 1859

We, the people of the State of Oregon, to the end that justice be established, order maintained, and liberty perpetuated, do ordain this Constitution.

Pennsylvania 1874

We, the people of the Commonwealth of Pennsylvania, grateful to Almighty God for the blessings of civil and religious liberty, and humbly invoking His guidance, do ordain and establish this Constitution.

Rhode Island 1843

We, the people of the State of Rhode Island and Providence Plantations, grateful to Almighty God for the civil and religious liberty which He hath so long permitted us to enjoy, and looking to Him for a blessing upon our endeavors to secure and transmit the same unimpaired to succeeding generations do ordain and establish this Constitution of Government.

South Carolina 1895

We, the people of the State of South Carolina, in convention assembled, grateful to God for our liberties, do ordain and establish this Constitution for the preservation and perpetuation of the same.

South Dakota 1889

We, the people of South Dakota, grateful to Almighty God for our civil and religious liberties, in order to form a more perfect and independent government, establish justice, insure tranquillity, provide for the common defense, promote the general welfare and preserve to ourselves and to our posterity the blessings of liberty, do ordain and establish this Constitution for the State of South Dakota.

Tennessee 1870

That all men have a natural and indefeasible right to worship Almighty God according to the dictates of their own conscience; that no man can of right, be compelled to attend, erect, or support any place of worship, or to maintain any minister against his consent; that no human authority can, in any case whatever, control or interfere with the rights of conscience; and that no preference shall ever be given, by law, to any religious establishment or mode of worship.

Texas 1876

Humbly invoking the blessings of Almighty God, the people of the State of Texas, do ordain and establish this Constitution.

Utah 1895

Grateful to Almighty God for life and liberty, we the people of Utah, in order to secure and perpetuate the principles of free government, do ordain and establish this Constitution.

Vermont 1793

That all men have a natural and unalienable right, to worship Almighty God, according to the dictates of their own consciences and understandings, as in their opinion shall be regulated by the word of God: and that no man ought to or of right can be compelled to attend any religious worship, or erect or support any place of worship, or maintain any minister, contrary to the dictates of his conscience, nor can any man be justly deprived or abridged of any civil right as a citizen, on account of his religious sentiments, or peculiar mode of religious worship; and that no authority can, or ought to be vested in, or assumed by, any power whatever, that shall in any case interfere with, or in any manner control the rights of conscience, in the free exercise of religious worship. Nevertheless, every sect or denomination of christians ought to observe the Sabbath or Lord's day, and keep up some sort of religious worship, which to them shall be seem most agreeable to the revealed will of God.

Virginia 1902

That religion or the duty which we owe to our Creator, and the manner of discharging it, can be directed only by reason and conviction, not by force or violence; and, therefore, all men are equally entitled to the free exercise of religion, according to the dictates of conscience; and that it is the mutual duty of all to practice Christian forbearance, love and charity towards each other.

Washington 1889

We, the people of the State of Washington, grateful to Almighty God for our freedom, in order to secure its blessings, form a more perfect government, insure domestic tranquility and promote the general welfare, do establish this Constitution.

Wyoming 1889

We, the people of the State of Wyoming, grateful to God for our civil, political and religious liberties, and desiring to secure them to ourselves and perpetuate them to our posterity, do ordain and establish this Constitution.

THE GREAT SEAL OF THE UNITED STATES OF AMERICA

Design Began 1776 – Design Completed 1782

OBVERSE

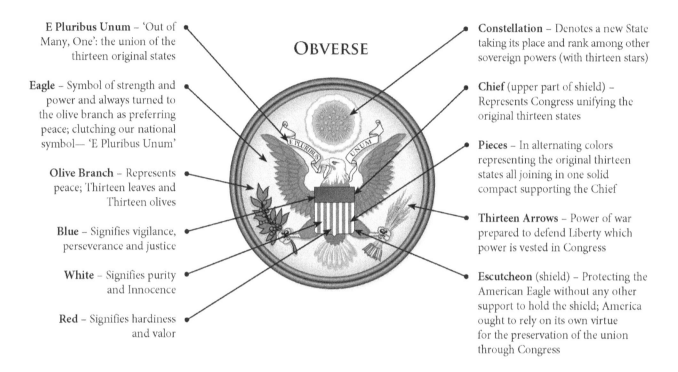

E Pluribus Unum – 'Out of Many, One': the union of the thirteen original states

Eagle – Symbol of strength and power and always turned to the olive branch as preferring peace; clutching our national symbol— 'E Pluribus Unum'

Olive Branch – Represents peace; Thirteen leaves and Thirteen olives

Blue – Signifies vigilance, perseverance and justice

White – Signifies purity and Innocence

Red – Signifies hardiness and valor

Constellation – Denotes a new State taking its place and rank among other sovereign powers (with thirteen stars)

Chief (upper part of shield) – Represents Congress unifying the original thirteen states

Pieces – In alternating colors representing the original thirteen states all joining in one solid compact supporting the Chief

Thirteen Arrows – Power of war prepared to defend Liberty which power is vested in Congress

Escutcheon (shield) – Protecting the American Eagle without any other support to hold the shield; America ought to rely on its own virtue for the preservation of the union through Congress

REVERSE

(Often referred to as the Spiritual side of the Shield)

The Eye of Providence – Alludes to the many signal interpositions of God in favor of the American cause

Annuit Coeptis – 'He' (God) has favored our undertakings

Thirteen layers of an unfinished pyramid representing the thirteen original colonies building a new nation based on new ideas and concepts of self-government never before attempted

Glory – The light of God, the Providence shining on a new nation based on God-given unalienable rights

Pyramid – Symbol of strength and duration

1776 – The year of America's birth

Novus Ordo Seclorum – 'New order of the Ages': symbol of a new nation built on the concept of permanent, unalienable (God-given) rights for all versus vested, man-made and non-permanent rights

THE GREAT SEAL OF THE UNITED STATES OF AMERICA

"Symbolically, the Seal reflects the beliefs and values that the Founding Fathers attached to the new nation and wished to pass on to their descendants."

- U.S. Department of State, Bureau of Public Affairs

CHARLES THOMSON'S "REMARKS AND EXPLANATION," ADOPTED BY THE CONTINENTAL CONGRESS, JUNE 20, 1782.

"The Escutcheon is composed of the chief [upper part of shield] & pale [perpendicular band], the two most honorable ordinaries [figures of heraldry]. The Pieces, paly [alternating pales], represent the several states all joined in one solid compact entire, supporting a Chief, which unites the whole & represents Congress. The Motto alludes to this union. The pales in the arms are kept closely united by the Chief and the Chief depends on that union & the strength resulting from it for its support, to denote the Confederacy of the United States of America & preservation of their union through Congress.

"The colours of the pales are those used in the flag of the United States of America; White signifies purity and innocence, Red, hardiness & valour, and Blue, the colour of the Chief, signifies vigilance, perseverance & justice. The Olive branch and arrows denote the power of peace & war which is exclusively vested in Congress. The Constellation denotes a new State taking its place and rank among other sovereign powers. The Escutcheon is born on the breast of an American Eagle without any other supporters [figures represented as holding up the shield] to denote that the United States of America ought to rely on their own Virtue.

"Reverse. The Pyramid signifies Strength and Duration: The Eye over it & the Motto allude to the many signal interpositions of providence in favour of the American cause. The date underneath is that of the Declaration of Independence and the words under it signify the beginning of the New American Era, which commences from that date."

USES OF THE GREAT SEAL

The Great Seal is used to guarantee the authenticity of a U. S. document. It is used to seal documents several thousand times a year. Custody of the Seal is assigned to the U. S. Department of State with the master die produced by the U. S. Bureau of Engraving. The Seal can only be affixed to a document by an office of the Secretary of State.

HISTORY OF THE GREAT SEAL

It is extremely significant that the responsibility of the design of the Great Seal was first given in 1776 to Thomas Jefferson, Benjamin Franklin and John Adams, the primary author and contributors of the writing of the Declaration of American Independence. Artist Pierre Eugene du Simitiere assisted with his knowledge of shields and coats of arms.

A second committee of James Lovell, John Morin Scott and William Churchill Houston worked on the design with consultant Francis Hopkinson.

A third committee of John Rutledge, Arthur Middleton, Elias Boudinot and William Barton worked on the design with Charles Thomson, Secretary of Congress, considering all previous recommendations. Congress adopted the design on June 20, 1782, six years after the design began.

Review: Checking Out the History

Discuss questions in subgroups or whole group. As an option, the group may come up with main ideas or insights from each question. Responses may be shared and discussed in the whole group.

1. What were the main arguments for the elimination of church-state establishments in the states?

2. What was the significance of Virginia's state constitution to the U. S. Constitution on the issue of religion?

3. Why/How are the Declaration's Laws of Nature and Nature's God significant to the Constitution?

4. Explain the principle of Rule of Law and Constitutional Government. Where/How were they applied in the Bible and Constitution?

5. Explain separation of powers and the checks and balances system. How/In what way was the principle of separation of powers influenced by the Bible, a Bible-based worldview?

6. Where/how was the principle of representative self-government or republicanism applied in the Bible and Constitution?

7. Why did a republic require a virtuous citizenry?

8. Explain the role and importance of the Bible and Christianity in a republic.

9. Why did many of the Founders and states insist on adding a Bill of Rights to the Constitution before ratifying it?

10. Explain the principle of the value of the individual and its Bible-based origins.

11. Explain the meaning of the First Amendment's Religion Clause—including the "No Establishment" Clause and the "Free Exercise of Religion" Clause.

12. Where/how was the principle of consent of the governed applied in the Bible and Constitution?

13. How was the Constitution as a civil covenant like the Israelite's Biblical covenant? Like the Puritan covenants?

14. What was the meaning and significance of the Northwest Ordinance?

15. What was the meaning and significance of the 13th Amendment? The 14th Amendment?

16. What basic Bible-based or Judeo-Christian principles are evident and important in this part of America's heritage?

1 **Activity 1: The Constitution's Application of Bible-Based Ideas, Stated and Implied**
2
3 Consider the philosophies and beliefs that influenced founding-era Americans and affected the development of
4 the U. S. Constitution. Based on what you've read in this and previous chapters, think about whether and how
5 the following philosophical concepts are **stated, implied, reflected, defended,** or **applied** in the Declaration,
6 Federalist Papers, or Constitution. Check appropriate column(s). Jot notes as needed on this or a separate page.
7
8

Philosophical Views and Rights	Declaration of Independence	Federalist Papers	US Constitution or Bill of Rights
God is Creator and Supreme Judge.			
All humans possess certain God-given, unalienable rights.			
Humans have a natural right to religious freedom or the free exercise of religion.			
Humans are inherently sinful and corruptible, needing restraints when in power.			
The moral Law of Nature/Nations and Nature's God is the standard of all human law.			
Everyone is subject to Rule of Law in a constitutional government.			
In a republic, government is administered by elected or appointed representatives.			
Legitimate civil authority or politcial power in a republic is derived from the people.			
Humans are capable of being moral and virtuous.			
Republican self-government requires a virtuous people in order to function properly.			
People are responsible for abiding by civil laws.			
God or Divine Providence intervenes in human affairs.			

9
10

1 **Activity 2: American Principles and Values in the Bible**
2
3 Based on what you have learned in *Miracle of America*, define and/or describe each principle/value in your own
4 words. Next, referring to all chapters in *Miracle of America*, identify Bible verses (if any) <u>cited</u> or <u>alluded</u> to in
5 historical documents and readings, by philosophers, and/or by early Americans influential to American thought
6 and the founding of the United States of America. Use additional sheets and make notes as needed.
7

American Principle	Definition or Description in your own words	Bible Reference and Source
Creator God / Nature's God		
God as Supreme Ruler / Judge		
God as Divine Providence		
Mankind in God's Image / Human Dignity		
Equality		

Law of Nature		
God's Moral Law		
God's Moral Law Over Human Law		
Rule of Law / Constitutions		
Popular Sovereignty / Consent of the Governed		
Covenant / Social Contract and Consent of the Governed		

Representative Self-Government / Republic		
God-Given Unalienable Rights		
Freedom vs. Slavery		
Religious Freedom		
Disestablished Church and Civil Government		
New Testament Grace and Spiritual Law vs. Old Testament Literal Religious Law		

Sinfulness of Man / Limited Government / Separation of Powers		
Role of Civil Government		
Submission to Authority		
Right to Resist Tyranny		
Perseverance in Adversity		
Thanksgiving		
Happiness		

Work Ethic / Industry		
Integrity / Moral Character of the People & Public Officials		

1

Call to Action

Each person will reflect on and write his/her responses to the questions below. Responses may then be shared and discussed in the group.

1. What action have you taken in your life and in the lives of other citizens to support the United States' representative form of self-government?

_____

_____

_____

_____

2. What action have you taken recently to bring discussions of the Bible to society, the public square, and citizens?

_____

_____

_____

_____

3. What action have you taken recently to communicate with representatives your views and positions on moral, ethical, and/or religious issues?

_____

_____

_____

_____

4. What actions have you taken to educate others in your community or church about the Bible-inspired foundation of our nation's government? About their religious freedoms and the role of government in protecting those freedoms?

_____

_____

_____

_____

5. List three things you can do over the next year to share, apply, or act on your understanding of "The Miracle of America."

_____

_____

_____

_____

6. Develop a personal plan of action to demonstrate basic principles of the Bible in your civic life.

_____

_____

_____

_____

Bibliography

Abington v. Schempp, 374 U.S. 203, 255(1963).

Acts and Orders of the General Court of Election, 19-21 May 1647. In *America's Founding Charters: Primary Documents of Colonial and Revolutionary Era Governance*. Vol. 1. Edited by Jon L. Wakelyn, 148-151. Westport, CT: Greenwood Publishing Group, 2006.

Adams, John. *A Defense of the Constitutions of Government of the United States of America, 1778*, Vol. 3 cont. In *The Works of John Adams, Second President of the United States*, Vol. 6, edited by Charles F. Adams, 1-222. Boston, MA: Charles C. Little and James Brown, 1851.

Adams, John. Footnote in *Discourses on Davila; A Series of Papers on Political History*. In *The Works of John Adams, Second President of the United States*, Vol. 6, edited by Charles F. Adams, 223-404. Boston: Charles C. Little and James Brown, 1851.

Adams, John. *A Dissertation on the Canon and the Feudal Law*, 1765. In *The Works of John Adams, Second President of the United States*. Vol. 3. Edited by Charles F. Adams, 447-464. Boston, MA: Charles C. Little and James Brown, 1851.

Adams, John. Inaugural Address, 4 March 1797. In *The Addresses and Messages of the Presidents of the United States*, 4th ed., 67-70. New York: Edward Walker, 1843.

Adams, John. John Adams to Abigail Adams, Philadelphia, 16 September 1774. In *Familiar Letters of John Adams and His Wife Abigail Adams During the Revolution*, edited by Charles F. Adams, 37-38. New York: Hurd and Houghton, 1876.

Adams, John. John Adams to Abigail Adams, 17 June 1775. In *Letters of John Adams Addressed to His Wife*, Vol. 1, edited by Charles F. Adams, 44-46. Boston: Charles C. Little and James Brown, 1841.

Adams, John. John Adams to F. A. Vanderkemp, 16 February 1809. In *The Works of John Adams, Second President of the United States*, Vol. 9, edited by Charles F. Adams, 608-610. Boston, MA: Little, Brown, & Co., 1854.

Adams, John. John Adams to Hezekiah Niles, Quincy, 13 February 1818. In The Works of John Adams, Second President of the United States, Vol. 10, edited by Charles F. Adams, 282-292. Boston: Little, Brown, & Co., 1856.

Adams, John. John Adams to Dr. J. Morse, Quincy, 5 December 1815. In *The Works of John Adams, Second President of the United States*, Vol. 10, edited by Charles F. Adams, 188-191. Boston: Little, Brown, and Co., 1856.

Adams, John. John Adams to F. C. Schaeffer, 25 November 1821. In James H. Hutson, *The Founders on Religion: A Book of Quotations*, 15-16. Princeton, NJ: Princeton U Press, 2005.

Adams, John. John Adams to Mrs. Adams, Philadelphia, 3 July 1776. In *The Works of John Adams, Second President of the United States*, Vol. 9, edited by Charles F. Adams, 417-420. Boston, MA: Little, Brown, & Co., 1854.

Adams, John. John Adams to the Officers of the First Brigade of the Third Division of the Militia of Massachusetts, 11 October 1798. In *The Works of John Adams, Second President of the United States*, Vol. 9, edited by Charles F. Adams, 228-229. Boston, Little, Brown, & Co., 1854.

Adams, John. John Adams to Thomas Jefferson, Quincy, 28 June 1813. In *The Works of John Adams, Second President of the United States*, Vol. 10, edited by Charles F. Adams, 43-46. Boston, MA: Little, Brown, & Co., 1856.

Adams, John. John Adams to Thomas Jefferson, Quincy, 17 September 1823. In *The Works of John Adams, Second President of the United States*, Vol. 10, edited by Charles F. Adams, 410-411. Boston: Little, Brown, & Co., 1856.

Adams, John. John Adams to Timothy Pickering, 6 August 1822. In *The Works of John Adams, Second President of the United States*, Vol. 2, edited by Charles F. Adams, 512-414. Boston: Little, Brown, & Co., 1865.

Adams, John. John Adams to William Tudor, Quincy, 5 April 1818. In *The Works of John Adams, Second President of the United States*, Vol. 10, edited by Charles F. Adams, 298-312. Boston, MA: Little, Brown, & Co., 1856.

Adams, John. John Adams to Zabdiel Adams, Philadelphia, 21 June 1776. In *The Works of John Adams, Second President of the United States*, Vol. 9, edited by Charles F. Adams, 399-401. Boston, MA: Little, Brown, & Co., 1854.

Adams, John. Notes of a Debate in the Senate of the United States, 24 August 1796. In *The Works of John Adams, Second President of the United States*, Vol. 3, edited by Charles F. Adams, 407-424. Boston: Charles C. Little and James Brown, 1851.

Adams, John Quincy. John Quincy Adams to George W. Adams (his son), Letter 5, St. Petersburg, 10 January 1813. In *Letters of John Quincy Adams To His Son On the Bible and Its Teachings*, 59-71. Auburn, NY: Derby, Miller, & Co., 1848.

Adams, John Quincy. John Quincy Adams to G. W. Adams (his son), Letter 6, St. Petersburg, 10 January 1813. In *Letters of Mrs. Adams, The Wife of John Adams*, 4th ed., edited by Charles F. Adams, 448-452. Boston, MA: Wilkins, Carter, & Co., 1848.

Adams, John Quincy. John Quincy Adams to G. W. Adams (his son), Letter 1, St. Petersburg, 1 and 8 September 1811. In *Letters of John Quincy Adams To His Son On the Bible and Its Teachings*, 9-21. Auburn, NY: Derby, Miller, & Co., 1848.

Adams, John Quincy. John Quincy Adams to George W. Adams (his son), St. Petersburg, 1 and 8 September 1811. In *Writings of John Quincy Adams, 1811-1813*, Vol. 4, edited by Worthington C. Ford, 211-217. New York: Macmillan, 1914.

Adams, John Quincy. "The Nation's Birth-Day," Address at Washington, 4 July 1821. *Niles' Weekly Register*, 20, no. 21, Mar-Sept (1821): 324-332.

Adams, John Quincy. *An Oration Delivered Before the Inhabitants of the Town of Newburyport, 61st Anniversary of the Declaration of Independence*, 4 July 1837. Newburyport, MA: Printed by Morss & Brewster, 1837.

Adams, Samuel. *An Oration Delivered at the State-House, in Philadelphia, To A Very Numerous Audience*, 1 August 1776. Philadelphia, PA: Printed for J. Johnson, 1776.

Adams, Samuel. *Report on the Rights of Colonists*, 20 November 1772. In *American Patriotism: Speeches, Letters, and Other Papers Which Illustrate the Foundation, the Development, the Preservation of the United States of America*, compiled by Selim H. Peabody, 32-37. New York: American Book Exchange, 1880.

Adams, Samuel. "A State of the Rights of Colonists," 1772. In *Tracts of the American Revolution, 1763-1776*, edited by Merrill Jensen, 233-255. Indianapolis, IN: Bobbs-Merrill Co., 1967.

Adams, Samuel. Samuel Adams to John Adams, Boston, 4 October 1790. In *The Writings of Samuel Adams, 1778-1802*, Vol. 4, edited by Harry A. Cushing, 340-344. New York: G. P. Putnam's Sons, 1908.

Adams, Samuel. Samuel Adams to John Winthrop, Philadelphia, 21 December 1778. In *The Writings of Samuel Adams: 1778-1802*, Vol. 4, edited by Harry A. Cushing, 101-104. New York: G. P. Putnam's Sons, 1908.

Adams, Samuel. Samuel Adams to the Legislature of Massachusetts, 17 January 1794. In *The Writings of Samuel Adams: 1778-1802*, Vol. 4, edited by Harry A. Cushing, 353-360. New York: G. P. Putnam's Sons, 1908.

Adams, Samuel. Samuel Adams to Richard Henry Lee, Boston, 14 April 1785. In *The Writings of Samuel Adams: 1778-1802*, Vol. 4, edited by Harry A. Cushing, 314-315. New York: G. P. Putnam's Sons, 1908.

Ahlstrom, Sydney. *Religious History of the American People*. New Haven: Yale U Press, 1972.

Althusius, Johannes. *Politics Methodically Set Forth, and Illustrated With Sacred and Profane Examples*. 3rd ed. Abridged ed. In *The Politics of Johannes Althusius*. Translated and edited by Frederick S. Carney, 1-204. Boston, MA: Beacon Press, 1964.

American Heritage Education Foundation. "History of the Declaration of Independence." *America's Heritage: An Adventure in Liberty*. High School Edition. Houston, TX: American Heritage Education Foundation, Inc., 2007.

Ames, William. *The Marrow of Theology*. Translated by John D. Eusden. Grand Rapids, MI: Baker Books, 1997.

Amos, Gary T. *Defending the Declaration: How the Bible and Christianity Influenced the Writing of the Declaration of Independence*. Brentwood, TN: Wolgemuth & Hyatt, 1989.

Amos, Gary and Richard Gardiner. *Never Before in History: America's Inspired Birth.* Edited by William Dembski. Dallas, TX: Haughton, 1998.

Aquinas, Thomas. *The Summa Theologica of St. Thomas Aquinas.* Pt. 2, no. 1/QQ I-XXVI. Translated by the Fathers of the English Dominican Province. New York: Benziger Brothers, 1911.

Aquinas, Thomas. *The Summa Theologica of St. Thomas Aquinas.* Pt. 2, no. 3/QQ XC-CXIV. Translated by the Fathers of the English Dominican Province. New York: Benziger Brothers, 1915.

Aquinas, Thomas. *The Summa Theologica of St. Thomas Aquinas.* Pt. 2 (First Part), no. 3/QQ XC-CXIV. Translated by the Fathers of the English Dominican Province. London: R. & T. Washbourne, 1915.

Augustine. *The Confessions of St. Augustine, Bishop of Hippo.* Bk. 2. Translated by J. G. Pilkington. Edinburgh, Scotland: T. & T. Clark, 1876.

Babaeva, Olga. *Social Contract Theory in Early Modern France, Germany, Poland, and Russia: A Comparison; A Thesis in History Submitted to the Graduate Faculty of Texas Tech University* (Lubbock, TX: December 1998).

Backus, Isaac. *A Declaration of the Rights, of the Inhabitants of the State of Massachusetts-Bay, in New England,* 1779. In *The Sacred Rights of Conscience: Selected Readings on Religious Liberty and Church-State Relations in the American Founding,* edited by Daniel L. Dreisbach and Mark D. Hall, 276-278. Indianapolis, IN: Liberty Fund, 2009.

Bailyn, Bernard. *The Ideological Origins of the American Revolution.* Enlarged ed. Cambridge, MA: Belknap/Harvard U Press, 1967, 1992.

Bailyn, Bernard. *Pamphlets of the American Revolution, 1750-1776.* Vol. 1. Cambridge, MA: Belknap Press, 1965.

Bailyn, Bernard. "Religion and Revolution: Three Biographical Studies." *Perspectives in American History* 4 (1970): 85-169.

Bancroft, George. *History of the United States of America.* Vol 4. New York: D. Appleton & Co., 1890.

Bancroft, George. *History of the United States of America, From the Discovery of the American Continent.* Boston, MA: Little, Brown, & Co., 1874-78.

Bancroft, George. *History of the United State from Discovery of the American Continent to the Declaration of Independence.* Vol. 6. New ed. London: Routledge, Warne, & Routledge, 1861.

Barnard, Henry. "History of the School Fund of Connecticut." In *Report of the Commissioner of the School Fund to the Legislature of the State of Connecticut,* May 1853, 55-110. Hartford, CT: Printed by Order of the Legislature of Connecticut, 1853.

Barton, David. *The Myth of Separation: What is the Correct Relationship Between Church and State?* Aledo, TX: Wallbuilder Press, 1992.

Barton, David. *Original Intent: The Courts, the Constitution, & Religion.* Aledo, TX: Wallbuilder Press, 1996, 2000.

Baxter, Richard. *A Holy Commonwealth.* Edited by William Lamont. Cambridge: Cambridge U Press, 1994.

Beck, James M. *The Constitution of the United States.* London: Hodder and Stoughton, 1922.

Beck, James M. *The Constitution of the United States.* Whitefish, MT: Kessinger, 2004. First published in 1922.

Becker, Carl. *The Declaration of Independence: A Study in the History of Political Ideas.* New York: Vintage Books/Random House, 1922, 1958, 1970.

Berman, Harold J. "The Christian Sources of General Contract Law." In *Christianity and Law: An Introduction,* edited by John Witte, Jr. and Frank S. Alexander, 125-142. Cambridge, UK: Cambridge U Press, 2008.

Beza, Theodore. *On the Rights of Magistrates: Concerning the Rights of Rulers Over Their Subjects and the Duty of Subjects Towards Their Rulers,* 1574. Translated by Patrick S. Poole. Constitution Society, 1995-2013. http://www.constitution.org/cmt/beza/magistrates.htm.

Blackstone, William. Announcement on the Course of Lectures which led to the *Commentaries on the Laws of England*, 23 June 1753. In William Blackstone, *Commentaries on the Laws of England*. Vol. 1. Edited by William C. Jones, xv. San Francisco, CA: Bancroft-Whitney Co., 1915.

Blackstone, William. *Blackstone's Commentaries, in Five Volumes*. 5 Vols. Edited by George Tucker. Union, NJ: Lawbook Exchange, 1996, 2008.

Boettner, Loraine. *The Reformed Doctrine of Predestination*. Grand Rapids, MI: Eerdmans, 1936.

Bonomi, Patricia U. *Under the Cope of Heaven: Religion, Society, and Politics in Colonial America*. New York: Oxford U Press, 2003.

Bonomi, Patricia U. and Peter R. Eisenstadt. "Church Adherence in the Eighteenth Century British Colonies." *William and Mary Quarterly* 39 (April 1982): 245-286.

Book of the General Laws and Liberties of Massachusetts, 1647. In *America's Founding Charters: Primary Documents of Colonial and Revolutionary Era Governance*, vol. 1, edited by Jon L. Wakelyn, 97-105. Westport, CT: Greenwood Press, 2006.

Boucher, Jonathan. "Discourse X: On the Character of Ahitophel." In *A View of the Causes and Consequences of the American Revolution in Thirteen Discourses*, 402-449. Bedford, MA: Applewood Books, 2009. First published in 1797.

Boucher, Jonathan. "Discourse XI: The Dispute Between the Israelites and the Two Tribes and a Half, Respecting Their Settlement Beyond Jordan." In *A View of the Causes and Consequences of the American Revolution in Thirteen Discourses*, 450-494. Bedford, MA: Applewood Books, 2009. First published in 1797.

Boucher, Jonathan. "Discourse XII: On Civil Liberty; Passive Obedience, and Non-Resistance." In *A View of the Causes and Consequences of the American Revolution in Thirteen Discourses*, 495-560. Bedford, MA: Applewood Books, 2009. First published in 1797.

Bradford, Alden. *Memoir of the Life and Writings of Rev. Jonathan Mayhew, D. D.* Boston, MA: C. C. Little & Co., 1838.

Bradford, William. *Bradford's History of Plymouth Settlement, 1608-1650*. Translated by Harold Paget. New York: E. P. Dutton & Co., 1909, 1920.

Bradford, William. Excerpt From *Of Plymouth Plantation, 1602-1646*, in *The Mayflower Papers: Selected Writings of Colonial New England*, eds. Nathaniel Philbrick and Thomas Philbrick (New York: Penguin Classics, 2007), 14.

Bradford, William. *History of Plymouth Plantation, 1602-1646*. Edited by Charles Deane. Boston, MA: Little, Brown, and Co., 1856.

Bradford, William. *Of Plymouth Plantation-1620-1647: A New Edition: The Complete Text, with Notes and an Introduction*. Translated by Samuel Eliot Morison. New York: Alfred A. Knopf, 1993.

Bradford, William and Edward Winslow. *The Journal of the Pilgrims at Plymouth in New England, in 1620*. 2nd ed. Edited by George B. Cheever. New York: John Wiley, 1849.

Brake, Donald L. *A Visual History of the King James Bible: The Dramtic Story of the World's Best-Known Translation*. Grand Rapids, MI: Baker Books, 2011.

Brewer, David J. *The United States: A Christian Nation*. Philadelphia, PA: John C. Winston Co., 1905.

Brown, Alexander. *The Genesis of the United States*, 2 Vols. New York: Houghton, Mifflin, & Co., 1890.

Brown University. *The Charter of Brown University, Granted 1764*. Providence, RI: H. H. Brown, 1834.

Brutus, Stephanus J. *Vindiciae, Contra Tyrannos: or, Concerning the Legitimate Power of a Prince Over the People, and Of the People Over a Prince*. Edited by George Garnett. Cambridge, UK: Cambridge U Press, 1994.

Bryce, James. *The American Commonwealth: The National Government, The State Governments*, Vol. 1, new ed. New York: Macmillan, 1919.

Bullinger, Heinrich. "A Brief Exposition of the One and Eternal Testament or Covenant of God," 1534. In *Fountainhead of Federalism: Heinrich Bullinger and the Covenantal Tradition*, edited by Charles S. McCoy and J. Wayne Baker, 99-138. Louisville, KY: Westminster/John Knox Press, 1991.

Burlamaqui, Jean-Jacques. *The Principles of Natural Law, in Which the True Systems of Morality and Civil Government Are Established*, 1748, Pt. 2, translated by Thomas Nugent. London: Printed for J. Nourse, 1748.

Bushman, Richard. *From Puritan to Yankee: Character and the Social Order in Connecticut, 1690-1765*. Cambridge, MA: Harvard U Press, 1980.

Butler, Jon, Grant Wacker, and Randall Balmer. *Religion in American Life: A Short History*. New York: Oxford U Press, 2000, 2003.

Butler, Paul T. *What the Bible Says About Civil Government*. Joplin, MO: College Press, 1990.

Calvin, John. *Calvin's Bible Commentaries: Genesis, Part 1*. Translated by John King. Forgotten Books, 2007. First published 1847.

Calvin, John. *Calvin's Bible Commentaries: Matthew, Mark, and Luke, Part 1*. Translated by John King. Forgotten Books, 2007. First published 1847.

Calvin, John. *Calvin's Bible Commentaries: Psalms, Part V*. Translated by John King. Forgotten Books, 2007. First published 1847.

Calvin, John. *Commentaries on the First Book of Moses, Called Genesis*, Vol. 1. Edited by John King. Grand Rapids, MI: Eerdmans, 1948.

Calvin, John. *The Institutes of the Christian Religion*, Vol. 3. Translated by John Allen. Philadelphia, PA: Philip H. Nicklin, 1816.

Calvin, John. *The Institutes of the Christian Religion: A New Translation*, Vol. 1. Translated by Henry Beveridge. Edinburgh, Scotland: Printed for Calvin Translation Society, 1845.

Calvin, John. *The Institutes of the Christian Religion: A New Translation*, Vol. 2. Translated by Henry Beveridge. Edinburgh, Scotland: Printed for Calvin Translation Society, 1845.

Carroll, Charles. Charles Carroll to James McHenry, 4 November 1800. In *The Life and Correspondence of James McHenry*. Edited by Bernard C. Steiner. Cleveland, OH: Burrows Brothers Co., 1907.

Carroll, John. John Carroll to the Editor of *Columbian* Magazine, 1 September 1787. In *Biographical Sketch of the Most Rev. John Carroll: First Archbishop of Baltimore*, edited by John Carroll Brent, 141-144. Baltimore, MD: John Murphy, 1843.

Cambridge Platform of Church Discipline: Adopted in 1648, and the Confession of Faith, Adopted in 1680. Boston, MA: Congregational Board of Publication, 1855.

Campbell, Robert, ed. *Calvin's Case, 1608*. In *Ruling Cases Arranged, Annotated, and Edited*. Vol. 2. Action-Amendment. 575-668. London: Stevens and Sons, 1894.

Cantwell v. Connecticut, 310 U.S. 296 (1940).

Carroll, Charles. Charles Carroll to James McHenry, 4 November 1800. In *The Life and Correspondence of James McHenry*, by Bernard C. Steiner, 473-476. Cleveland, OH: Burrows Brothers Co., 1907.

Charter of Rhode Island and Providence Plantation, July 8, 1663. In *America's Founding Charters: Primary Documents of Colonial and Revolutionary Era Governance*. Vol. 1. Edited by Jon L. Wakelyn, 151-159. Westport, CT: Greenwood Publishing Group, 2006.

Cheever, George B., ed. *The Journal of the Pilgrims at Plymouth in New England, 1620*. 2nd ed., by William Bradford. New York: John Wiley, 1848.

Chisholm v. Georgia, 2 U.S. 419 (1793).

Church of the Holy Trinity v. United States, 143 U.S. 457 (1892).

Cicero, Marcus Tullius. *Treatise on the Republic*. In *The Political Works of Marcus Tullius Cicero*. Vol. 1. Translated by Francis Barham. London: Edmund Spettigue, 1841.

Clinton, William. Excerpt in Introductory Letter of U. S. Secretary of Education Richard Riley, U. S. Department of Education Legal Guidelines on Religious Expression in Public Schools, 1995, 1998. In "Religious Expression in Public Schools," *America's Heritage: An Adventure in Liberty*, High School Edition. Houston, TX: American Heritage Education Foundation, Inc., 2012.

Clinton, William. Excerpt in Introductory Letter of U. S. Secretary of Education Richard Riley, U. S. Department of Education Legal Guidelines on Religious Expression in Public Schools. Washington, DC: U. S. Department of Education, 1995, revised 1998.

Cole, Franklin P. *They Preached Liberty*. Ft. Lauderdale, FL: Coral Ridge Ministries, c1985.

Coley, Richard J. and Andrew Sum. *Fault Lines in Our Democracy: Civic Knowledge, Voting Behavior, and Civic Engagement in the United States*. Princeton, NJ: Educational Testing Service, 2012. <www.ets.org/faultlines> (Feb 2013).

College of William and Mary. Charter of the College of William and Mary, in Virginia. In *The History of the College of William and Mary From Its Foundation, 1660, to 1874*, 3-16. Richmond, VA: J. W. Randolph & English, 1874.

Colony of Pennsylvania, Great Britain, Secretary of Commonwealth. *Frame of Government* Preface. In *Charter to William Penn, and Laws of Province of Pennsylvania, 1682-1700*. Vol. 2. Edited by Staughton George, Benjamin M. Nead, and Thomas McCamant. Harrisburg, PA: Published under John Blair Linn, Sec. of the Commonwealth, 1879.

Columbus, Christopher. "Letter to King Ferdinand of Spain, describing the results of the first voyage." 1493. In Henry Nash Smith, *Virgin Land: The American West as Symbol and Myth: A Synoptic Hypertext*. Edited and formatted by Eric J. Gislason. American Studies Group, U of Virginia. <http://xroads.Virginia.edu/~hyper/hns/garden/Columbus.html> (1950, 1978, 1996).

Commager, Henry Steele. *Documents of American History*. New York: F.S. Crofts & Co., 1943.

Connecticut Secretary of State, *The Fundamental Orders of Connecticut, 1639*. In *State of Connecticut Register and Manual, 1922*, 39-43. Hartford, CT: State of Connecticut, 1922.

Cooper, Samuel. "A Place For My People Israel," 7 April 1776, *New England Historical and Genealogical Register* 132 (1978): 128-129.

Cotton, John. *Abstract of the Laws of New England*. London: Printed for F. Coules and W. Ley at Paules Chain, 1641.

Cotton, John. "Christian Calling," Sermon. In The Puritans: A Sourcebook of Their Writings, Vols. 1 & 2. Edited by Perry Miller and Thomas H. Johnson, 319-327. Mineola, NY: Courier Dover Publications, 2001. First published in 1938 by American Book Company and then in 1963 by Harper & Row.

Cotton, John. John Cotton to William Fiennes, Lord Saye and Sele, 1636. In *Puritan Political Ideas, 1558-1794*, edited by Edmund S. Morgan, 167-173. Indianapolis, IN: Hackett, 2003. First published in 1965 by Bobbs-Merrill.

Cotton, John. "Limitation of Government, 1646." In *Political Thought in the United States: A Documentary History*, edited by Lyman T. Sargent, 36-38. New York: New York U Press, 1997.

Cotton, John. *Practical Commentary or An Exposition With Observations, Reasons and Uses Upon the First Epistle General of John, 1654*. Whitefish, MT: Kessinger Publishing, 2003. First published in 1654.

Cotton, John. "Sermon on God's Promise to His Plantations." In *Masterpieces of Eloquence: Famous Orations of Great World Leaders From Early Greece to the Present Time*, Vol. 4, edited by Mayo W. Hazeltine et al., 1422-1438. New York: P. F. Collier & Son, 1905.

Danbury Baptist Association. Danbury, Connecticut, Baptist Association to Thomas Jefferson, 7 October 1801. In *The Thomas Jefferson Papers*, Series 1, General Correspondence, 1651-1827, American Memory. Washington, DC: Library of Congress, <http://memory.loc.gov/cgi-bin/ampage?collId=mtj1&fileName=mtj1page024.db&recNum=956> (August 2012).

Davenport, Frances G., ed. *European Treaties Bearing on the History of the United States and Its Dependencies to 1648*. Issue 254, Vol. 2. Clark, NJ: Lawbook Exchange, 2004.

DeMar, Gary. *America's Christian History: The Untold Story*. Powder Springs, GA: American Vision, 1993, 1995.

Demos, John. *A Little Commonwealth: Family Life in Plymouth Colony*. New York: Oxford U Press, 1970.

The Doctrines of the New England Churches. In *Essays, Theological and Miscellaneous, Reprinted from the Princeton Review*, 2nd series, edited by Albert B. Dod, 206-235. New York: Wiley and Putnam, 1847.

Dolan, Jay P. *The American Catholic Experience: A History From Colonial Times to the Present*. Notre Dame, IN: U of Notre Dame Press, 1992.

Doyle, John P., ed. *Collected Studies on Francisco Suarez*. Leuven, Belgium: Leuven U Press, 2010.

Dreisbach, Daniel L. "The Bible in the Political Rhetoric of the American Founding." *Politics and Religion* 4, issue 3 (Dec 2011): 401-427. doi: 10.1017/S1755048311000423

Dreisbach, Daniel L. "The Mythical 'Wall of Separation': How a Misused Metaphor Changed Church-State Law, Policy, and Discourse." First Principles Series, no. 6. Washington, DC: The Heritage Foundation, June 23, 2006.

Dreisbach, Daniel L., and Mark D. Hall, eds. *The Sacred Rights of Conscience: Selected Readings on Religious Liberty and Church-State Relations in the American Founding*. Indianapolis, IN: Liberty Fund Press, 2009.

Dunbar, Cynthia N. *One Nation Under God: How the Left is Trying to Erase What Made Us Great*. Oviedo, FL: Onward, 2008.

Duning, Natilee, ed. *The Bible & Public Schools: A First Amendment Guide*. Nashville, TN: First Amendment Center, 1999; New York: Bible Literacy Project, Inc., 1999, 8-9. www.freedomforum.org

Durant, Will and Ariel. *The Lessons of History*. New York: Simon and Schuster, 1968.

Edwards, Jonathan. *Charity and Its Fruits, Or, Christian Love as Manifested in the Heart and Life*. Lecture 11. Edited by Tryon E. W. New York: Robert Carter & Bros., 1856.

Edwards, Jonathan. *Concerning Efficacious Grace*. In *The Works of President Edwards in Four Volumes: A Reprint of the Worcester Edition*, Vol. 2, 547-597. New York: Leavitt & Allen, 1858.

Edwards, Jonathan. *Decrees and Election*. In *The Works of President Edwards: A Reprint of the Worcester Edition*, Vol. 2, 513-546. New York: Leavitt & Allen, 1858.

Edwards, Jonathan. *The End for Which God Created the World*. In *The Works of President Edwards: A Reprint of the Worcester Edition*, Vol. 2, 191-257. New York: Leavitt & Allen, 1858.

Edwards, Jonathan. *Freedom of the Will*. In *The Works of President Edwards, A Reprint of the Worcester Edition*, Vol. 2, 1-190. New York: Leavitt & Allen, 1858.

Edwards, Jonathan. *God's Sovereignty*. Sermon 34. In *The Works of President Edwards, A Reprint of the Worcester Edition*, Vol. 4, 548-560. New York: Leavitt & Allen, 1858.

Edwards, Jonathan. *The Great Christian Doctrine of Original Sin Defended*. In *The Works of President Edwards, A Reprint of the Worcester Edition*, Vol. 2, 305-510. New York: Leavitt & Allen, 1858.

Edwards, Jonathan. *A History of the Work of Redemption*. In *The Works of President Edwards: A Reprint of the Worcester Edition*, Vol. 1, 293-516. New York: Leavitt & Allen, 1858.

Edwards, Jonathan. *Miscellaneous Observations on Important Doctrines*. In *The Works of President Edwards, A Reprint of the Worcester Edition*, Vol. 1, 563-642. New York: Leavitt & Allen, 1858.

Edwards, Jonathan. *Narrative of Surprising Conversions*. In *The Works of President Edwards in Four Volumes: A Reprint of the Worcester Edition*, Vol. 3, 231-272. New York: Leavitt & Allen, 1858.

Edwards, Jonathan. *The Nature of True Virtue*. In *The Works of President Edwards, A Reprint of the Worcester Edition*, Vol. 2, 259-304. New York: Leavitt & Allen, 1858.

Edwards, Jonathan. "Notes on the Mind," 1718-1722. In *Benjamin Franklin and Jonathan Edwards: Selections From Their Writings*. Edited by Carl Van Doren. New York: Charles Scribner's Sons, 1920.

Edwards, Jonathan. *The Soul's Immortality and Future Retribution*. Sermon 19. In *The Works of Jonathan Edwards*, Vol. 2 of 2, edited by Tryon Edwards, 302-322. Boston, MA: Doctrinal Tract and Book Society, 1850.

Edwards, Jonathan. *Thoughts on the Revival of Religion in New England, 1740*. In *The Works of President Edwards in Four Volumes: A Reprint of the Worcester Edition*, Vol. 3, 273-425. New York: Leavitt & Allen, 1858.

Edwards, Jonathan. *Treatise Concerning Religious Affections*. In *The Works of President Edwards in Four Volumes: A Reprint of the Worcester Edition*, Vol. 3, vii-228. New York: Leavitt & Allen, 1858.

Edwards, Jonathan. *The Wisdom of God Displayed in the Way of Salvation*. Sermon 5. In *The Works of President Edwards in Four Volumes: A Reprint of the Worcester Edition*, Vol. 4, 133-168. New York: Leavitt & Allen, 1858.

Edwards, Jonathan. *The Works of President Edwards in Four Volumes: A Reprint of the Worcester Edition*. Vol. 1. New York: Leavitt & Allen, 1858.

Edwards, Jonathan. *The Works of President Edwards in Four Volumes: A Reprint of the Worcester Edition*. Vol. 2. New York: Leavitt & Allen, 1858.

Edwards, Jonathan. *The Works of President Edwards in Four Volumes: A Reprint of the Worcester Edition*. Vol. 3. New York: Leavitt & Allen, 1858.

Edwards, Jonathan. *The Works of President Edwards in Four Volumes: A Reprint of the Worcester Edition*. Vol. 4. New York: Leavitt & Allen, 1858.

Elazar, Daniel J. *Covenant & Commonwealth: From Christian Separation Through the Protestant Reformation*. New Brunswick, NJ: Transaction Publishers, 1996.

Elazar, Daniel J. *Covenant and Constitutionalism: The Great Frontier and the Matrix of Federal Democracy*. New Brunswick, NJ: Transaction Publishers, 1998.

Elazar, Daniel J. *Covenant and Polity in Biblical Israel: Biblical Foundations and Jewish Expressions*. New Brunswick, NJ: Transaction Publishers, 1995.

Elazar, Daniel J. "The Political Theory of Covenant: Biblical Origins and Modern Developments." *Covenant, Polity, and Constitutionalism, Publius: The Journal of Federalism* 10, no. 4 (1980): 3-30.

Eliot, Charles W., ed. *American Historical Documents, 1000-1904*. New York: P. F. Collier & Son, 1910.

Eliot, John. *The Christian Commonwealth or, The Civil Policy of the Rising Kingdom of Jesus Christ*. In *Collections of the Massachusetts Historical Society*, Volume IX, edited by Massachusetts Historical Society, 127-164. Boston, MA; Little, Brown, & Co., 1846.

Emerson, William. "Sermon on 2 Chronicles 13:12." In *Diaries and Letters of William Emerson, 1743-1776*. Edited by Amelia F. Emerson. Boston, MA: Privately Printed/Thomas Todd, 1972.

Ertl, Alan W. *The Political Economic Foundation of Democratic Capitalism: From Genesis to Maturation*. Boca Raton, FL: BrownWalker Press, 2007.

Evans, M. Stanton. *The Theme is Freedom: Religion, Politics, and the American Tradition*. Washington, DC: Regnery Publishing, 1994.

Everson v. Board of Education, 330 U.S. 1 (1947).

Fea, John. *Was America Founded As A Christian Nation? A Historical Introduction.* Louisville, KY: Westminster/John Knox Press, 2011.

Federer, William J. *America's God and Country: Encyclopedia of Quotations.* Coppell, TX: FAME Publishing, 1994.

Federer, William J. *America's God and Country: Encyclopedia of Quotations.* St. Louis, MO: Amerisearch, 2000.

Federer, William J. *The Ten Commandments & Their Influence on American Law: A Study in History.* St. Louis, MO: Amerisearch, 2003.

Feiler, Bruce. *America's Prophet: Moses and the American Story.* New York: William Morrow, 2009.

Felt, Joseph B. *The Ecclesiastical History of New England*, Vol. 2. Boston, MA: Congregational Library Association, 1862.

Filmer, Robert. *Patriarcha*, 1680. In John Locke, *Two Treatises on Civil Government*, 11-73. London: George Routledge and Sons, 1884.

Finke, Roger and Rodney Stark. *The Churching of America, 1776-1990: Winners and Losers in Our Religious Economy.* New Brunswick, NJ: Rutgers U Press, 1992.

First Charter of Virginia, April 10, 1606. In *American Historical Documents, 1000-1904*, edited by Charles W. Eliot, 51. New York: P. F. Collier & Son, 1910.

Fitzpatrick, Martin. "Toleration and the Enlightenment Movement." In *Toleration in Enlightenment Europe*, edited by Ole Peter Grell and Roy Porter, 23-68. Cambridge, UK: Cambridge U Press, 2000.

Fonte, Richard W., Peter W. Wood, and Ashley Thorne. *Recasting History: Are Race, Class, and Gender Dominating American History? A Study of U. S. History Courses at the University of Texas and Texas A&M University.* Princeton, NJ: National Association of Scholars, 2013. <http://www.nas.org> <http://www.nas.org/articles/recasting_history_are_race_class_and_gender_dominating_american_history> (Sept 2013).

Ford, Worthington C., ed. *The Writings of George Washington.* Vol. 3/1775-1776. New York: G. P. Putnam's Sons, 1889.

Ford, Worthington C., ed. *The Writings of George Washington: 1776.* Vol. 4. New York: G. P. Putnam's Sons, 1889.

Fornieri, Joseph R. *Abraham Lincoln's Political Faith.* DeKalb, IL: Northern Illinois U Press, 2005.

Frame of Government of Pennsylvania with Laws Agreed Upon in England, May 5, 1682. In *America's Founding Charters: Primary Documents of Colonial and Revolutionary Era Governance.* Vol. 1. Edited by Jon L. Wakelyn, 256-265. Westport, CT: Greenwood Publishing Group, 2006.

Franklin, Benjamin. *Autobiography of Benjamin Franklin.* Edited by John Bigelow. Philadelphia, PA: J. B. Lippincott & Co., 1869.

Franklin, Benjamin. Benjamin Franklin to Dr. Richard Price, Passy, 9 October 1780. In *The Life and Writings of Benjamin Franklin in Two Volumes*, Vol. 1, edited by William Temple Franklin and William Duane, 366-367. Philadelphia, PA: M'Carty & Davis, 1834.

Franklin, Benjamin. Benjamin Franklin to Messrs. Les Abbés Chalut and Arnaud, Philadelphia, 17 April 1787. In *The Works of Benjamin Franklin in Philosophy, Politics, and Morals*, 1753-1790, Vol. 6, edited by William T. Franklin, 199. Philadelphia, PA: William Duane, 1817.

Franklin, Benjamin. "A Comparison of the Conduct of the Ancient Jews and of the Anti-Federalists in the United States of America." In *The Works of Benjamin Franklin*, Vol. 5, edited by Jared Sparks, 158-162. New York: Hilliard, Gray, and Co., 1837.

Franklin, Benjamin. *The Way to Wealth.* New York: New York Association for Improving the Condition of the Poor, 1848.

Franciscan Province of the Most Holy Name of Jesus. *The 1959 National Catholic Almanac, 55th Yr.* Paterson, NJ: St. Anthony's Guild, 1959.

Frazer, Gregg L. *The Religious Beliefs of America's Founders: Reason, Revelation, and Revolution.* Lawrence, KS: U Press of Kansas, 2012.

Frothingham, Richard. *The Rise of the Republic of the United States*. Boston, MA: Little, Brown, & Co, 1872.

Fundamental Constitutions of the Carolinas, March 1, 1669. In *America's Founding Charters: Primary Documents of Colonial and Revolutionary Era Governance*. Vol. 1. Edited by Jon L. Wakelyn, 222-233. Westport, CT: Greenwood Publishing Group, 2006.

Fuson, Robert H., trans. *The Log of Christopher Columbus, 1492*. Camden, ME: International Marine, 1987.

General Assembly of Massachusetts. Resolutions of the House of Representatives of Massachusetts, 29 October 1765. In *The Writings of Samuel Adams, 1764-1769*, Vol. 1, edited by Harry A. Cushing, 23-26. New York: G. P. Putnam's Sons, 1904.

General Assembly of Virginia. Virginia Declaration of Rights, 12 June 1776. In *Documents of American Democracy: A Collection of Essential Works*, edited by Roger L. Kemp, 52-54. Jeffrseon, NC: McFarland & Co., 2010.

General Assembly of Virginia. Virginia Declaration of Rights, 12 June 1776. In *The Revised Code of the Laws of Virginia, Being a Collection of All Such Acts of the General Assembly*, Vol. 1, 31-32. Richmond, VA: Printed by Thomas Ritchie, 1819.

George, Robert P. *The Clash of Orthodoxies: Law, Religion, and Morality in Crisis*. Wilmington, DE: ISI Books, 2001.

George, Robert P. *In Defense of Natural Law*. New York: Oxford U Press, 1999.

George, Robert P. "Freedom and Its Counterfeit," *Imprimis* 32-34 (August 2003).

Gibbs, David C. Jr. *One Nation Under God: Ten Things Every Christian Should Know*. Seminole, FL: Christian Law Association, 2005.

Grell, Ole Peter and Roy Porter, eds. *Toleration in Enlightenment Europe*. Cambridge, UK: Cambridge U Press, 2000.

Hakluyt, Richard. *A Discourse Concerning Western Planting*. Edited by Charles Deane. Cambridge, MA: John Wilson & Son, 1877.

Hall, David D. *A Reforming People: Puritanism and the Transformation of Public Life in New England*. New York, NY: Alfred A. Knopf, 2011.

Hall, David W. *The Genevan Reformation and the American Founding*. Lanham, MD: Lexington Books, 2005.

Hall, Mark D. *Roger Sherman and the Creation of the American Republic*. New York: Oxford U Press, 2013.

Hall, Mark D. "Vindiciae, Contra Tyrannos: The Influence of the Reformed Tradition on the American Founding" (Washington, DC, 2010). American Political Science Association 2010 Annual Meeting Paper. Available at SSRN: http://ssrn.com/abstract=1644085.

Hall, Verna M., comp. *The Christian History of the American Revolution*. San Francisco, CA: Foundation for American Christian Education, 1976.

Hall, Verna M., comp. *The Christian History of the Constitution of the United States*. American Revolution Bicentennial Edition. San Francisco, CA: Foundation for American Christian Education, 1966.

Hamburger, Philip. *Separation of Church and State*. Cambridge, MA: Harvard U Press, 2002.

Hamilton, Alexander. "The Farmer Refuted," 5 February 1775. In *The Works of Alexander Hamilton; Comprising His Correspondence, and His Political and Official Writings*. Vol. 2. Edited by John C. Hamilton, 37-126. New York: John F. Trow for Library of Congress, 1850.

Hamilton, Alexander. Federalist Paper #1. In *The Federalist Papers*, edited by Clinton Rossiter, 33-37. New York: Mentor Penguin, 1961.

Hamilton, Alexander. Federalist Paper #15. In *The Federalist Papers*, edited by Clinton Rossiter, 105-113. New York: Mentor Penguin, 1961.

Hamilton, Alexander, Federalist Paper #22. In *The Federalist Papers*, edited by Clinton Rossiter, 143-152. New York: Mentor Penguin, 1961.

Hamilton, Alexander. Federalist Paper #76. In *The Federalist Papers*, edited by Clinton Rossiter, 454-459. New York: Mentor Penguin, 1961.

Hamilton, Alexander. Federalist Paper #78. In *The Federalist Papers*, edited by Clinton Rossiter, 464-472. New York: Mentor Penguin, 1961.

Hampton Court Conference, 14 January 1604. In *A Complete Collection of State Trials and Proceedings for High Treason and Other Crimes and Misdemeanors, 1783*, vol. 2/1603-1627, compiled by T. B. Howell, 69-92. London: Printed by T. C. Hansard, 1816.

Hancock, John. Inaugural Address of John Hancock as Governor of Massachusetts, 1780. In *John Hancock: His Book*, edited by Abram E. Brown, 267-270. Boston, MA: Lee and Shepard, 1898.

Hart, Benjamin. *Faith & Freedom: The Christian Roots of American Liberty*. Christian Defense Fund, 1997.

Haynes, Charles C. *Religion in American History: What to Teach and How*. Alexandria, VA: Association for Supervision and Curriculum Development, 1990.

Haynes, Charles C. and Oliver Thomas. "Religious Expression in Public Schools: United States Department of Education Guidelines." In *Finding Common Ground: A Guide to Religious Liberty in Public Schools*, 125-132. Nashville, TN: First Amendment Center, 2002.

Haynes, Charles C. and Oliver Thomas. "Religion in the Public School Curriculum: Questions and Answers." In *Finding Common Ground: A Guide to Religious Liberty in Public Schools*, 87-102. Nashville, TN: First Amendment Center, 2002. www.firstamendmentcenter.org.

Heimert, Alan. *Religion and the American Mind: From the Great Awakening to the Revolution*. Cambridge, MA: Harvard U Press, 1966.

Henry, William W. *Patrick Henry: Life, Correspondence and Speeches*, Vol. 1. New York: Charles Scribner's Sons, 1891.

Higginson, John. Excerpts from "The Cause of God and His People in New England," 1663. In *The Ecclesiastical History of New England*, Vol. 2, by Joseph B. Felt, 303-4. Boston, MA: Congregational Library Association, 1862.

Hobbes, Thomas. *Leviathan, or The Matter, Form and Power of A Commonwealth, Ecclesiastical and Civil*. 2nd ed. Edited by Henry Morley. London: George Routledge and Sons, 1886.

Holbrook, Clyde A. "Crime and Sin in Puritan Massachusetts." In *Crimes, Values, and Religion*, edited by James M. Day and William S. Laufer, 1-22. Westport, CT: Ablex Publishing, 1987.

Holifield, E. Brooks. "Edwards as Theologian." In *The Cambridge Companion to Jonathan Edwards*, edited by Stephen J. Stein, 144-161. New York: Cambridge U Press, 2007.

Hooker, Richard. *The Laws of Ecclesiastical Polity*. Bk. 1. London: George Routledge and Sons, 1888.

Hooker, Thomas. *A Letter From Rev. Thomas Hooker of Hartford In Answer to the Complaints of Gov. Winthrop of Massachusetts Against Connecticut*. Hartford, CT: Connecticut Historical Society, 1859.

Hooker, Thomas. Sermon Before the Connecticut General Court in Hartford, May 31, 1638. In *The Puritan Tradition in America, 1620-1730*, Revised ed., edited by Alden T. Vaughan, 82-91. Hanover, NH: U Press of New England, 1997.

Hooker, Thomas. *A Survey of the Summe of Church-Discipline*. London: Printed by A. M. for John Bellamy, 1648.

Hooker, Thomas. Thomas Hooker to John Winthrop, Fall, 1638. In *Collections of the Connecticut Historical Society*, Vol. 1, 1-18. Hartford, CT: Published for the Society, 1860.

Hopkins, Samuel. *Slavery of the Africans*. In *The Works of Samuel Hopkins*. Vol. 2. Edited by Sewall Harding. Boston, MA: Doctrinal Tract and Book Society, 1852.

Hull, Augustus L. *A Historical Sketch of the University of Georgia.* Atlanta, GA: Foote & Davies Co., 1894.

Hutcheson, Francis. *A Short Introduction to Moral Philosophy: In Three Parts, Containing the Elements of Ethicks and the Law of Nature*, Bk. 2. Dublin: Printed by William McKenzie, 1787.

Hutcheson, Francis. *A System of Moral Philosophy in Three Books*, Vol. 1, Bk. 1, edited by William Leechman. London: Published by His Son Francis Hutcheson, 1755.

Hutson, James H. *Forgotten Features of the Founding: The Recovery of Religious Themes in the Early American Republic.* Lanham, MD: Lexington Books, 2003.

Hutson, James H. *The Founders on Religion: A Book of Quotations.* Princeton, NJ: Princeton U Press, 2005.

Hutson, James H. *Religion and the Founding of the American Republic.* Washington, DC: Library of Congress, 1998.

Intercollegiate Studies Institute. *The Coming Crisis in Citizenship: Higher Education's Failure to Teach America's Heritage and Institutions.* Wilmington, DE: Intercollegiate Studies Institute, 2006. <www.americancivicliteracy.org/2006/introduction.html> <www.americancivicliteracy.org/2006/summary.html> (Feb 2013).

Intercollegiate Studies Institute. *Failing Our Students, Failing America: Holding Colleges Accountable for Teaching America's History and Institutions.* Wilmington, DE: Intercollegiate Studies Institute, 2007. <http://www.americancivicliteracy.org/2007/summary_summary.html> (Feb 2013).

Intercollegiate Studies Institute. *Our Fading Heritage: Americans Fail A Basic Test on Their History and Institutions.* Wilmington, DE: Intercollegiate Studies Institute, 2008. <http://www.americancivicliteracy.org/2008/summary_summary.html> (Feb 2013).

Isaac, Rhys. *The Transformation of Virginia, 1740-1790.* Chapel Hill, NC: Published for the Institute of Early American History and Culture, Williamsburg, VA, by U of North Carolina Press, 1982.

James I. Instructions for the Government of Virginia, 1606. In William Stith, *The History of the First Discovery and Settlement of Virginia*, bk. 2, 37-41. New York: Reprinted for Joseph Sabin, 1865.

"Jamestown: Where America Became a Christian Nation." Christian Law Association. <www.christianlaw.org> (April 2007).

Jane, Cecil, trans. *The Journal of Christopher Columbus, 1493.* New York: Bramhall House, 1960.

Jay, John. Federalist Paper #2. In *The Federalist Papers*, edited by Clinton Rossiter, 37-41. New York: Mentor Penguin, 1961.

Jefferson, Thomas. "Appendix to the Memoir." In *Memoir, Correspondence, and Miscellanies, From the Papers of Thomas Jefferson*, Vol. 1, 2nd ed., edited by Thomas J. Randolph, 92-146. Boston: Gray and Bowen, 1830.

Jefferson, Thomas. *An Act for Establishing Religious Freedom, 1786.* In Thomas Jefferson, *Notes on the State of Virginia, 1785*, 8th ed., 326-328. Boston, MA: Printed by David Carlisle, 1801.

Jefferson, Thomas. Excerpt on Truth From a Bill for Establishing Religious Freedom, 1779. *The Life and Writings of Thomas Jefferson*, edited by Samuel E. Forman, 413. Indianapolis, IN: Bowen-Merrill, 1900.

Jefferson, Thomas. Excerpt on Church and State From Notes on Virginia, 1782, 1785. *The Life and Writings of Thomas Jefferson*, edited by Samuel E. Forman, 154. Indianapolis, IN: Bowen-Merrill, 1900.

Jefferson, Thomas. Inaugural Address, 4 March 1801. In *The Addresses and Messages of the Presidents of the United States, From 1789 to 1839*, 89-92. New York: McLean & Taylor, 1839.

Jefferson, Thomas. Inaugural Speech of President Jefferson, 4 March 1805. In *American State Papers: Documents, Legislative and Executive of the Congress of the United States, 1st-13th Congress, March 3, 1780 - March 3, 1815*, Class 1, Vol. 1, 64-66. Washington, DC: Gales and Seaton, 1832.

Jefferson, Thomas. Second Inaugural Address, 4 March 1805. In *The Addresses and Messages of the Presidents of the United States, 1789-1846*, Vol. 1, compiled by Edwin Williams, 173-176. New York: Edward Walker, 1849.

Jefferson, Thomas. *The Life and Writings of Thomas Jefferson*. Edited by Samuel E. Forman. Indianapolis, IN: Bowen-Merrill Co., 1900.

Jefferson, Thomas. *Notes on Religion*, October 1776. In *The Works of Thomas Jefferson in Twelve Volumes*, Vol. 2, Federal ed., edited by Paul L. Ford, 252-268. New York: G. P. Putnam's Sons, 1904.

Jefferson, Thomas. *Notes on the State of Virginia, 1785*. 8th ed. Boston, MA: Printed by David Carlisle, 1801.

Jefferson, Thomas. *Notes on Virginia, 1785*. In *The Writings of Thomas Jefferson*, Vol. 8, Bk. 4, edited by Henry A. Washington, 247-428. Philadelphia, PA: J. B. Lippincott & Co., 1864.

Jefferson, Thomas. Resolutions Relative to the Alien and Sedition Laws, 1798. In *The Writings of Thomas Jefferson*, Vol. 17, Definitive ed., edited by Albert E. Bergh, 379-391. Washington, DC: Thomas Jefferson Memorial Association, 1907.

Jefferson, Thomas. Thomas Jefferson to Rev. A. Millar, Washington, 23 January 1808. In *Memoirs, Correspondence and Private Papers of Thomas Jefferson, Late President of the United States*, Vol. 4, edited by Thomas J. Randolph, 106-107. London: Henry Colburn and Richard Bentley, 1829.

Jefferson, Thomas. Thomas Jefferson to Benjamin Rush, 21 April 1803. In *The Writings of Thomas Jefferson*, Vol. 4, edited by Henry A. Washington, 479-483. New York: Derby & Jackson, 1859.

Jefferson, Thomas. Thomas Jefferson to Colonel Yancey, Monticello, 6 January 1816. In *The Writings of Thomas Jefferson*, Vol. 6, ed. Henry A. Washington, 514-517. New York: Riker, Thorne, &. Co., 1854.

Jefferson, Thomas. Thomas Jefferson to the Danbury Baptist Association in Connecticut, 1 January 1802. In *The Writings of Thomas Jefferson*, edited by Henry A. Washington, 113-114. New York: Derby & Jackson, 1859.

Jefferson, Thomas. Thomas Jefferson to David Barrow, Monticello, 1 May 1815. In *The Writings of Thomas Jefferson*, Vol. 13-14, Definitive ed., edited by Albert E. Bergh, 296-297. Washington, DC: Thomas Jefferson Memorial Association, 1907.

Jefferson, Thomas. Thomas Jefferson to Henry Lee, Monticello, 8 May 1825. In *The Writings of Thomas Jefferson*, Vol. 15, Definitive ed., edited by Albert E. Bergh, 117-119. Washington, DC: Thomas Jefferson Memorial Association, 1907.

Jefferson, Thomas. Thomas Jefferson to Henry Lee, Monticello, 8 May 1825. In *The Writings of Thomas Jefferson*, Vol. 71, edited by H. A. Washington, 407. Washington, DC: Taylor & Maury, 1854.

Jefferson, Thomas. Thomas Jefferson to James Fishback, 27 September 1809. In *The Writings of Thomas Jefferson*, Vol. 12, edited by Albert E. Bergh, 314-316. Washington, DC: Thomas Jefferson Memorial Association, 1904.

Jefferson, Thomas. Thomas Jefferson to James Madison, Monticello, 17 February 1826. In *Memoir, Correspondence, and Miscellanies: From the Papers of Thomas Jefferson*, Vol. 4, edited by Thomas J. Randolph, 426-428. Charlottesville, VA: F. Carr & Co, 1829.

Jefferson, Thomas. Thomas Jefferson to James Smith, Monticello, 8 December 1822. In *Memoir, Correspondence, and Miscellanies From the Papers of Thomas Jefferson*, Vol. 4, edited by Thomas J. Randolph, 360-361. Charlottesville, VA: F. Carr & Co., 1829.

Jefferson, Thomas. Thomas Jefferson to John Norvell, Washington, 11 June 1807. In *The Writings of Thomas Jefferson*, Vol. 11, edited by Albert E. Bergh, 222-226. Washington, DC: Thomas Jefferson Memorial Association, 1905.

Jefferson, Thomas. Thomas Jefferson to Moses Robinson, Washington, 23 March 1801. In *The Writings of Thomas Jefferson: Correspondence*, Vol. 4, edited by Henry A. Washington, 379-380. New York: Derby & Jackson, 1859.

Jefferson, Thomas. Thomas Jefferson to Roger Weightman, Monticello, 24 June 1826. In *Memoir, Correspondence, and Miscellanies: From the Papers of Thomas Jefferson*, edited by Thomas J. Randolph. Charlottesville, VA: F. Carr & Co., 1829.

Jefferson, Thomas. Thomas Jefferson to Thomas Law, 13 June 1814. In *The Writings of Thomas Jefferson*, Vol. 6, edited by Henry A. Washington, 348-351. New York: Derby & Jackson, 1859.

Jefferson, Thomas. Thomas Jefferson to Mr. Thomas Mann Randolph, New York, 30 May 1790. In *The Writings of Thomas Jefferson*, Vol. 7, edited by Albert E. Bergh, 29-33. Washington, DC: Thomas Jefferson Memorial Association, 1907.

Jefferson, Thomas. Thomas Jefferson to William Canby, Monticello, 18 September 1813. In *The Writings of Thomas Jefferson*, Vol. 6, edited by Henry A. Washington, 210-211. Washington, DC: Taylor & Maury, 1854.

Johnson, Paul. *A History of the American People*. New York: HarperCollins, 1997.

Johnson, Stephen. *Some Important Observations, Occasioned By, and Adapted To, the Publick Fast, Ordered by Authority*, 18 December 1765. Newport, RI: Samuel Hall, 1766.

Johnson, William J. *George Washington, The Christian*. New York: Abingdon Press, 1919.

Jones, Charles E. Excerpts of Bill for the Establishment of the University of Georgia, 1785. In *Education in Georgia*, No. 5, 42-43. Washington, DC: Government Printing Office, 1889.

Jones, David. *Defensive War in A Just Cause Sinless*. Philadelphia, PA: Henry Miller, 1775.

Jones, William. *An Address to the British Government on a Subject of Present Concern, 1776*. In *The Theological and Miscellaneous Works of the late Rev. William Jones, in Six Volumes*, New ed., vol. 6, ed. William Stevens, 268-274. London: Printed for C. and J. Rivington, 1826.

Keane, John. *The Life and Death of Democracy*. New York: W. W. Norton & Co., 2009.

Kemp, Roger L., ed. *Documents of American Democracy: A Collection of Essential Works*. Jefferson, NC: McFarland & Co., 2010.

Kidd, Thomas S. *God of Liberty: A Religious History of the American Revolution*. New York: Basic Books, 2010.

Kirk, Russell. *The American Cause*. Edited by Gleaves Whitney. Wilmington, DE: Intercollegiate Studies Institute, 2002.

Kirk, Russell. *The Roots of American Order*. Washington DC: Regnery Gateway, 1991.

Klosko, George, ed. *The Oxford Handbook of the History of Political Philosophy*. Oxford: Oxford U Press, 2011.

Ladd, George T., ed. *The Principles of Church Polity: An Analysis of Modern Congregationalism and Applied to Certain Important Practical Questions in the Government of Christian Churches*. New York: Charles Scribner's Sons, 1882.

Lambert, Frank. *The Founding Fathers and the Place of Religion in America*. Princeton, NJ: Princeton U Press, 2003.

Langdon, Samuel. *Government Corrupted by Vice, and Recovered by Righteousness, A Sermon Preached Before the Honorable Congress of the Colony of Massachusetts Bay*, 31 May 1775. Watertown, MA: Printed and sold by Benjamin Edes, 1775.

Laski, Harold J. Historical Introduction of *A Defense of Liberty Against Tyrants*. In Junius Brutus, *A Defense of Liberty Against Tyrants*. Edited by Harold J. Laski. New York: Burt Franklin, 1972, 4.

Laughead, George, and Lynn H. Nelson, eds. "Note on Charter of Massachusetts Bay, 1629." *AMDOCS: Documents for the Study of American History, WWW Virtual Library*. <http://www.vlib.us/amdocs/texts/massbay_note.html> (2005-2010) (April 2012).

Lee, Richard G. *The American Patriot's Bible: The Word of God and the Shaping of America*. Nashville, TN: Thomas Nelson, 2009.

Lee, Richard H. Richard Henry Lee to Colonel Martin Pickett, Chantilly, 5 March 1786. In *Memoir of the Life of Richard Henry Lee and His Correspondence*, Vol. 1, by grandson Richard H. Lee, 70-71. Philadelphia, PA: Carey and Lea, 1825.

Lee, Sang Hyun. "God's Relation to the World." In *The Princeton Companion to Jonathan Edwards*, edited by Sang Hyun Lee, 59-71. Princeton, NJ: Princeton U Press, 2005.

Lessnoff, Michael H., ed. *Social Contract Theory: Readings in Social and Political Theory*. New York: New York U Press, 1990.

Lessnoff, Michael H. *Social Contract: Issues in Political Theory*. Atlantic Highlands, NJ: Humanities Press International, 1986.

Lewis, Jon E. *A Documentary History of Human Rights: A Record of Events, Documents, and Speeches That Shaped Our World*. New York: Carroll & Graf, 2003.

Lillback, Peter A. *George Washington's Sacred Fire*. Bryn Mawr, PA: Providence Forum Press, 2006.

Lincoln, Abraham. Address at Gettysburg, 19 November 1863. In *The Writings of Abraham Lincoln*, Vol 7/1863-1865, edited by Arthur B. Lapsley, 20-21. New York: G. P. Putnam's Sons, 1906.

Lincoln, Abraham. Address in Independence Hall, Philadelphia, 22 February 1861. In *Abraham Lincoln: Complete Works, Comprising His Speeches, Letters, State Papers, and Miscellaneous Writings*, Vol. 1, edited by John G. Nicolay and John Hay, 690-691. New York: Century Co., 1907.

Lincoln, Abraham. His Proclamation for a Day of Thanksgiving, 3 October 1863. In *Speeches and Letters of Abraham Lincoln, 1832-1865*, Vol. 14721 of Project Gutenberg, unpaged. Mundus Publishing, 2007.

Lincoln, Abraham. Proclamation for Thanksgiving, 3 October 1863. In *State Papers, 1861-1865*, in *Life and Works of Abraham Lincoln*, vol. 7, edited by Marion M. Miller, 159-161. New York: Current Literature Publishing Co., 1907.

Locke, John. *An Essay Concerning Human Understanding*. 27th ed. London: Printed for T. Tegg and Son, 1836.

Locke, John. *Essays on the Law of Nature*. Leyden: Oxford Clarendon Press, 1954.

Locke, John. John Locke to Rev. Edward Stillingfleet, Lord Bishop of Worcester, Oates, 7 January 1696-7. In *The Works of John Locke in Ten Volumes*, Vol. 4., 11th ed., edited by T. Davison, 1-96. London: Printed for W. Otridge and Son et al., 1812.

Locke, John. *A Letter Concerning Toleration, 1689*. In *The Works of John Locke in Nine Volumes*. Vol. 5. 12th ed., 5-58. London: Printed for C. and J. Rivington et al., 1824.

Locke, John. *Paraphrase and Notes on the Epistles of St. Paul to the Galatians, I and II Corinthians, Romans, and Ephesians*. In *The Works of John Locke in Nine Volumes*. Vol. 7. 12th ed. London: Printed for C. and J. Rivington et al., 1824.

Locke, John. *The Reasonableness of Christianity, As Delivered in the Scriptures*. 2nd ed. London: Printed for Awnsham and John Churchill, 1696.

Locke, John. *A Second Letter Concerning Toleration, 1690*. In *The Works of John Locke in Nine Volumes*. Vol. 5, 12th ed., 59-138. London: Printed for C. and J. Rivington et al., 1824.

Locke, John. *First Treatise of Civil Government, 1690*, in *Two Treatises on Government*, Bk. 1, 1-190. London: George Routledge and Sons, 1884.

Locke, John. *Second Treatise of Civil Government, 1690*, in *Two Treatises on Government*, Bk. 2, 191-318. London: George Routledge and Sons, 1884.

Locke, John. *Second Treatise of Civil Government*, 1690, in *Two Treatises on Government, 2 Books*, Bk. 2, 187-401. London: Printed for R. Butler, W. Reid, W. Sharpe, and John Bumpus, 1821.

Locke, John. *A Second Vindication of the Reasonableness of Christianity*. In *The Works of John Locke*, Vol. 2., 3rd ed. corrected, 555-671. London: Printed for Arthur Bettesworth, John Pemberton, and Edward Symon, 1727.

Locke, John. *Some Thoughts Concerning Education, 1690*. In *The Works of John Locke*, Vol. 3, 1-98. London: Printed for Arthur Bettesworth, John Pemberton, and Edward Symon, 1727.

Locke, John. *A Third Letter for Toleration, 1692*. In *The Works of John Locke in Nine Volumes*. Vol. 5, 12th ed., 139-546. London: Printed for C. and J. Rivington et al., 1824.

Locke, John. *Two Treatises on Government*. Bk. 1, 1-190. London: George Routledge and Sons, 1884.

Locke, John. *Two Treatises on Government*. Bk. 2, 191-318. London: George Routledge and Sons, 1884.

Locke, John. *Two Treatises on Government*. 2 Bks. London: Printed for R. Butler, W. Reid, W. Sharpe, and John Bumpus, 1821.

Logan, Walter S. *Thomas Hooker: The First American Democrat: An Address*. New York: New York Society of the Order of the Founders and Patriots of America, 1904.

Luther, Martin. *An Appeal to the Ruling Class of German Nationality as to the Amelioration of the State of Christendom, 1520*. In *Martin Luther: Selections From His Writings*, edited by John Dillenberger, 403-485. New York: Anchor Books/Doubleday, 1961.

Luther, Martin. *Commentary on St. Paul's Epistle to the Galatians, 1531*. In *Martin Luther: Selections From His Writings*, ed. John Dillenberger, 99-165. New York: Doubleday, 1961.

Luther, Martin. *The Ninety-Five Theses, 1517*. In *Martin Luther: Selections From His Writings*, edited by John Dillenberger, 489-500. New York: Anchor Books/Doubleday, 1961.

Luther, Martin. *Pagan Servitude of the Church, 1520*. In *Martin Luther: Selections From His Writings*, edited by John Dillenberger, 249-359. New York: Anchor Books/Doubleday, 1961.

Luther, Martin. Second Sermon of The Eight Wittenberg Sermons, 1522. In *Works of Martin Luther, with Introductions and Notes*, Vol. 2, edited by Henry E. Jacobs and Adolph Spaeth, 385-425. Philadelphia, PA: A. J. Holman Co., 1915.

Luther, Martin. *Secular Authority: To What Extent It Should Be Obeyed, 1523*. In *Martin Luther: Selections From His Writings*, edited by John Dillenberger, 363-402. New York: Anchor Books/Doubleday, 1961.

Lutz, Donald S. "From Covenant to Constitution in American Political Thought." *Covenant, Polity, and Constitutionalism: Publius: The Journal of Federalism* 10, no. 4 (1980): 101-134.

Lutz, Donald S. *The Origins of American Constitutionalism*. Baton Rouge, LA: Louisiana State U Press, 1988.

Lutz, Donald S. "The Relative Influence of European Writers on Late Eighteenth-Century American Political Thought." *American Political Science Review* 78, no. 1 (Mar 1984): 189-197.

Lutz, Donald S. and Jack Warren. *The Religion Tradition and the Origins of American Constitutionalism*. Providence, RI: John Carter Brown Library, 1987.

The Lynde and Harry Bradley Foundation. *E Pluribus Unum: The Bradley Project on America's National Identity*. Milwaukee, WI: Lynde and Harry Bradley Foundation, 2008. <www.bradleyproject.org> (Feb 2013).

MacDonald, William, ed. *Documentary Source Book of American History, 1606-1913*. New York: Macmillan, 1920.

Madison, James. Federalist Paper #10. In *The Federalist Papers*, edited by Clinton Rossiter, 77-84. New York: Mentor Penguin, 1961.

Madison, James. Federalist Paper #14. In *The Federalist Papers*, edited by Clinton Rossiter, 99-105. New York: Mentor Penguin, 1961.

Madison, James. Federalist Paper #37. In *The Federalist Papers*, edited by Clinton Rossiter, 224-231. New York: Mentor Penguin, 1961.

Madison, James. Federalist Paper #39. In *The Federalist Papers*, edited by Clinton Rossiter, 240-246. New York: Mentor Penguin, 1961.

Madison, James. Federalist Paper #47. In *The Federalist Papers*, edited by Clinton Rossiter, 300-308. New York: Mentor Penguin, 1961.

Madison, James. Federalist Paper #51. In *The Federalist Papers*, edited by Clinton Rossiter, 320-325. New York: Mentor Penguin, 1961.

Madison, James. Federalist Paper #55. In *The Federalist Papers*, edited by Clinton Rossiter, 341-346. New York: Mentor Penguin, 1961.

Madison, James. Federalist Paper #57. In *The Federalist Papers*, edited by Clinton Rossiter, 350-356. New York: Mentor Penguin, 1961.

Madison, James. James Madison to Edward Everett, 19 March 1823. In *Letters and Other Writings of James Madison: 1816-1828*, Vol. 3, 305-309. Philadelphia, PA: J. B. Lippincott & Co., 1865.

Madison, James. James Madison to Edward Livingston, Montpelier, 10 July 1822. In *Letters and Other Writings of James Madison: 1816-1828*, Vol. 3, 273-276. Philadelphia, PA: J. B. Lippincott & Co., 1865.

Madison, James. James Madison to Frederick Beasley, Montpellier, 20 November 1825. In *The Writings of James Madison*, Vol. 9/1819-1836, edited by Gaillard Hunt, 229-231. New York: G. P. Putnam's Sons, 1910.

Madison, James. James Madison to George Thomson, 30 June 1825. In *Letters and Other Writings of James Madison: 1816-1828*, Vol. 3, 490-492. Philadelphia, PA: J. B. Lippincott & Co., 1865.

Madison, James. *Memorial and Remonstrance Against Religious Assessments, 1785.* In *The Writings of James Madison: 1783-1787*, Vol. 2, edited by Gaillard Hunt, 183-191. New York: G. P. Putnam's Sons, 1901.

Madison, James. Prayer and Thanksgiving Proclamation, 23 July 1813. In *A Compilation of the Messages and Papers of the Presidents, 1789-1897*, Vol. 1, edited by James D. Richardson, 532-533. Washington, DC: Government Printing Office, 1896.

Madison, James. "Property," from the *The National Gazette*, 29 March 1792. In *The Writings of James Madison*, Vol. 6/1790-1802, edited by Gaillard Hunt, 101-103. New York: G. P. Putnam's Sons, 1906.

Madison, James. Speech on the Power of Judiciary at the Virginia Ratifying Convention, 20 June 1788. In *The Writings of James Madison*, Vol. 5/1787-1790, edited by Gaillard Hunt, 216-225. New York: G. P. Putnam's Sons, 1904.

Madison, James. *The Writings of James Madison*. Vol. 3/1787: The Journal of the Continental Convention. Edited by Gaillard Hunt. New York: G. P. Putnam's Sons, 1902.

Manion, Clarence. *The Key to Peace: A Formula for the Perpetuation of Real Americanism*. Chicago, IL: Heritage Foundation, 1950.

Mann, Horace. Ninth Annual Report on Education for 1845. In Horace Mann, *Life and Works of Horace Mann*, Vol. 4/Annual Reports of the Secretary of the Board of Education of Massachusetts for the Years 1845-1848, 1-104. Boston, MA: Lee and Shepard Publishers, 1891.

Marshall, John. *John Locke, Toleration and Early Enlightenment Culture*. Cambridge, UK: Cambridge U Press, 2006.

Marshall, Peter, and David Manuel. *The Light and the Glory*. Grand Rapids, MI: Revell, 1977.

Maryland Toleration Act, April, 1649. In *Documentary Source Book of American History, 1606-1913*. Edited by William MacDonald, 53-55. New York: Macmillan, 1920.

Mason, George. George Mason to Patrick Henry, Fairfax County, Gunston Hall, 6 May 1783. In *The Life of George Mason, 1725-1792*, Vol. 11, by Kate Mason Rowland, 44-47. New York: G. P. Putnam's Sons, 1892.

Mather, Cotton. *Essays to Do Good: Addressed To All Christians Whether in Public or Private Capacities*. Edited by George Burder. London: Printed for Williams and Son, 1816.

Mather, Cotton. *Magnalia Christi Americana or, The Ecclesiastical History of New England, 1620-1698*. Vol. 1. Bedford, MA: Applewood Books, 2009. First published 1820 by Silas Andrus.

Mather, Cotton. *Magnalia Christi Americana or, The Ecclesiastical History of New England, 1620-1698*. Vol. 2. Bedford, MA: Applewood Books, 2009. First published 1820 by Silas Andrus.

Massachusetts General Court. *Massachusetts Body of Liberties, 1641.* In *American Historical Documents, 1000-1904*, edited by Charles W. Eliot, 70-89. New York: P. F. Collier & Son, 1910.

Mayhew, Jonathan. *A Discourse Concerning Unlimited Submission and Non-Resistance to the Higher Powers, Boston, 1750*. In *The Pulpit of the American Revolution: or, The Political Sermons of the Period of 1776*. 2nd ed. Edited by John W. Thornton, 39-104. Boston, MA: D. Lothrop & Co., 1876.

Mayhew, Jonathan. *From "The Snare Broken," A Thanksgiving Discourse Preached at the Desire of the West Church in Boston, Occasioned by the Repeal of the Stamp Act*, 23 May 1766. In *Cyclopaedia of American Literature, in Two Volumes*, Vol. 1, edited by Evert A. Duyckinck and George L. Duyckinck, 145-146. New York: Charles Scribner, 1856.

Mayhew, Jonathan. "The Right of Revolution," 1750. In *Puritan Political Ideas, 1558-1794*. Edited by Edmund S. Morgan, 304-330. Indianapolis, IN: Hackett Publishing, 2003. First published in 1965.

McCoy, Charles S. and J. Wayne Baker. *Fountainhead of Federalism: Heinrich Bullinger and the Covenantal Tradition*. Louisville, KY: Westminster/John Knox Press, 1991.

McElroy, John H. *American Beliefs: What Keeps A Big Country and A Diverse People United*. Chicago, IL: Ivan R. Dee, 1999.

McMaster, John B. and Frederick D. Stone, eds. *Pennsylvania and the Federal Constitution, 1787-1788*. Philadelphia, PA: Historical Society of Pennsylvania, 1888.

Meacham, Jon. *American Gospel*. New York: Random House, 2006.

Miller, Perry. *Nature's Nation*. Cambridge, MA: Belknap Press/Harvard U Press, 1967.

Miller, Perry. 1948. The Religious Impulse in the Founding of Virginia: Religion and Society in the Early Literature. *William and Mary Quarterly*, 3rd Series, Vol. 5, No 4. (October 1948): 493. Quoted in Lambert 2003, 46.

Milton, John. *A Defense of the People of England in Answer to Salmsius's Defense of the King*. In *The Works of John Milton, Historical, Political, and Miscellaneous*. Vol. 1. Edited by Thomas Birch, 489-598. London: Printed for A. Millar, 1753.

Missouri Bar Association, Proceedings, *Report of the Tenth Annual Meeting of the Missouri Bar Association*, 24-26 June 1890. Saint Louis, MO: Continental Printing Co., 1891.

Moehlman, Conrad Henry, comp. *The American Constitutions and Religion: Religious References in the Charters of the Thirteen Colonies and the Constitutions of the Forty-Eight States*. Clark, NJ: Lawbook Exchange, 2007.

Montesquieu, Charles Louis Secondat de. *The Spirit of Laws*, 1748. Vol. 1. Revised ed. Translated by Thomas Nugent. Edited by Jean Le Rond D'Alembert. London: Colonial Press, 1900.

Montesquieu, Charles Louis Secondat de. *The Spirit of Laws, in Two Volumes*, 1748. Vol. 2. New ed. Translated by Thomas Nugent. Edited by J. V. Prichard. London: George Bell & Sons, 1892.

Moon, Reuben O. Speech of Honorable Reuben O. Moon on Revision of the Laws—The Judiciary, 7 December 1910. *Senate Documents*, 62nd U. S. Congress, April 4 – August 22, 1911, Vol, 27, no. 23, 1-21. Washington, DC: Government Printing Office, 1911.

Morely, Felix M. *The Power in the People*. New York: D. Van Nostrand, Co., 1949.

Morgan, Edmund S. *The Puritan Dilemma: The Story of John Winthrop*. Boston, MA: Little, Brown, & Co., 1958.

Morgan, Edmund S. *The Puritan Family: Religion and Domestic Relations in Seventeenth-Century New England*. New York: Harper & Row, 1966.

Morgan, Edmund S., ed. *Puritan Political Ideas, 1558-1794*. Indianapolis, IN: Hackett, 1965.

Morrison, Jeffry H. *John Witherspoon and the Founding of the American Republic*. Notre Dame: U of Notre Dame, 2005.

Morison, Samuel Eliot, ed. *Sources & Documents Illustrating the American Revolution, 1764-1788*. 2nd ed. London/New York: Oxford U Press, 1929, 1965.

Morris, Benjamin F. *The Christian Life and Character of the Civil Institutions of the United States*. Oxford: Benediction Classics, 2010. First published 1864 by George W. Childs.

Morris, Gouverneur. Notes on the Form of a Constitution for France, c1791. In *The Life of Gouverneur Morris*, Vol. 3, edited by Jared Sparks, 479-500. Boston, MA: Gray & Bowen, 1832.

Morton, Nathaniel. *New-England's Memorial or, A Brief Relation of the Most Memorable and Remarkable Passages of the Providence of God, Manifested to the Planters of New-England in America.* 6th ed. 1669. Reprint, Boston, MA: Congregational Board of Publication, 1855.

Morse, Jedidiah. *Annals of the American Revolution.* Hartford, CT: 1824.

Morse, Jedidiah. *A Sermon Exhibiting the Present Dangers, and Consequent Duties of the Citizens of the United States of America,* Charlestown, 25 April 1799. Charlestown, MA: Published at the Request of the Hearers, 1799.

Murdock v. Pennsylvania, 319 U.S. 105 (1943).

Muzzey, David Saville. *An American History.* Boston, MA: Ginn and Company, 1911.

National Association of Scholars. *Recasting History: Are Race, Class, and Gender Dominating American History? A Study of U. S. History Courses at the University of Texas and Texas A&M University.* Princeton, NJ: National Association of Scholars, 2013. <http://www.nas.org> <http://www.nas.org/articles/recasting_history_are_race_class_and_gender_dominating_american_history> (Sept 2013).

National Association of Scholars. *The Vanishing West: 1964-2010: The Disappearance of Western Civilization From the American Undergraduate Curriculum.* Princeton, NJ: National Association of Scholars, 2011. <http://www.nas.org> <http://www.nas.org/articles/The_Vanishing_West_1964-2010> (Sept 2013).

National Council for the Social Studies. "Study About Religions in the Social Studies Curriculum: A Position Statement of the National Council for the Social Studies." Silver Spring, MD: National Council for the Social Studies, 1984, 1998, www.socialstudies.org.

New England's First Fruits: With Diverse Other Special Matters Concerning That Country. New York: Reprinted for Joseph Sabin, 1865. First published in London, 1643.

Newcombe, Jerry. *The Book That Made America: How the Bible Formed Our Nation.* Ventura, CA: Nordskog Publishing, 2009.

Niebuhr, H. Richard. *The Kingdom of God in America.* Middleton, CT: Wesleyan U Press, 1988.

Noll, Mark A. *America's God: From Jonathan Edwards to Abraham Lincoln.* New York: Oxford U Press, 2002.

Noll, Mark A. *A History of Christianity in the United States and Canada.* Grand Rapids, MI: Eerdmans, 1992.

Noll, Mark A., Nathan O. Hatch, and George M. Marsden. *The Search for Christian America.* Colorado Springs, CO: Helmers & Howard, 1989.

Northwest Ordinance, An Ordinance for the Government of the Territory of the United States North-West of the River Ohio, 13 July 1787. In Emlin McClain, *Constitutional Law in the United States*, 398-404. Longmans, Green, & Co., 1907.

Novak, Michael. *On Two Wings: Humble Faith and Common Sense at the American Founding.* San Francisco, CA: Encounter Books, 2002.

Novak, Michael, and Jana Novak. *Washington's God: Religion, Liberty, and the Father of Our Country.* New York: Basic Books, Perseus Books, 2006.

Olevian, Gaspar. "Method and Arrangement or Subject of the Whole Work, From An Epitome of the Institutions." In John Calvin, *The Institutes of the Christian Religion: A New Translation*, Vol. 1, translated by Henry Beveridge (Edinburgh: Printed for Calvin Translation Society, 1845.

An Ordinance for the Government of the Territory of the United States North West of the River Ohio, 13 July 1787. In *Journals of the Continental Congress, 1774-1789*, Vol. 32, edited by Roscoe R. Hill, 340. Washington, DC: Government Printing Office, 1936.

Otis, James. *The Rights of the British Colonists Asserted and Proved,* Boston, 1764. In *Pamphlets of the American Revolution, 1750-1776*, Vol. 1, edited by Bernard Bailyn, 408-470. Cambridge, MA: Belknap Press, 1965.

Paine, Thomas. *Common Sense*, 1776. In *Tracts of the American Revolution, 1763-1776*. Edited by Merrill Jensen. Indianapolis, IN: Bobbs-Merrill Co., 1966.

Patrick, John J. and Gerald P. Long. *Constitutional Debates on Freedom of Religion: A Documentary History*. Westport, CT: Greenwood Press, 1999.

Penn, William. "The Great Case of Liberty of Conscience Once More Briefly Debated and Defended by the Authority of Reason, Scripture, and Antiquity," 1671. In *The Select Works of William Penn*, 3rd ed., edited by John Fothergill, i-viii, 9-51. London: Printed by James Phillips, 1782.

Perry, William S. *The History of the American Episcopal Church, 1587-1883, in Two Volumes*. Vol. 1/1587-1783. Boston, MA: James R. Osgood and Co., 1885.

Philbrick, Nathaniel, and Thomas Philbrick, eds. *The Mayflower Papers: Selected Writings of Colonial New England*. New York: Penguin Classics, 2007.

Pinckney, Charles. Speech, Wednesday, 14 May 1788. In South Carolina General Assembly, *Debates Which Arose in the House of Representatives of South Carolina, on the Constitution Framed for the United States, by a Convention of Delegates Assembled at Philadelphia*, 61-73. Charleston, SC: Printed by A. E. Miller, 1831.

Ponet, John. *A Short Treatise on Political Power, and of the True Obedience Which Subjects Owe to Our Kings and Other Civil Governors, with an Exhortation to All True and Natural English men, 1556*, ed. Patrick S. Poole, Edited for the Modern Reader, Constitution Society, edited by Jon Roland, 1995-2012. <http://www.constitution.org/cmt/ponet/polpower.htm> (April 2012).

Price, David A. *Love and Hate in Jamestown: John Smith, Pocahontas, and the Start of a New Nation*. New York: Random House, 2003, 2005.

Pufendorf, Samuel. *Of the Law of Nature and Nations, Eight Books*, 1703. 2nd ed. English ed. Edited by Jean Barbeyrac. Translated by Basil Kennett. Oxford: Printed by L. Lichfield for A. and J. Churchil, 1710.

Pufendorf, Samuel. *The Whole Duty of Man According to the Law of Nature*. 4th ed. English ed. Edited by Jean Barbeyrac. Translated by Andrew Tooke. London: Printed for B. Tooke and J. Hooke, 1716.

Ramsay, David. "Prelude to the American Revolution, 1765 to 1775." In *The Christian History of the American Revolution*, compiled by Verna M. Hall, 427-506. San Francisco, CA: Foundation for American Christian Education, 1975.

Ramsey, David. *History of the United States, From Their First Settlement as English Colonies in 1607 to the Year 1808, in Three Volumes*. Vol. 3. 2nd ed. Philadelphia, PA: M. Carey and Son, 1818.

Rauchet, Edward A. *American Vision and Values: A Companion to the Kirkpatrick Signature Series*. Bellevue, NE: Bellevue University Press, 2008.

Reichley, A. James. *Religion in American Public Life*. Washington, DC: Brookings Institution, 1985.

Reid, Thomas. "Lecture VII: Of Reasoning." In *Essays on the Powers of the Human Mind*. Vol. 2. 415-448. Edinburgh: Printed for Bell & Bradfute, 1812.

Ricketts, Glenn, Peter W. Wood, Stephen H. Balch, and Ashley Thorne. *The Vanishing West: 1964-2010: The Disappearance of Western Civilization From the American Undergraduate Curriculum*. Princeton, NJ: National Association of Scholars, 2011. <http://www.nas.org> <http://www.nas.org/articles/The_Vanishing_West_1964-2010> (Sept 2013).

Rider, Jeff. *God's Scribe: The Historiographical Art of Galbert of Bruges*. Washington, DC: Catholic University of America Press, 2001.

Robbins, Caroline. "Algernon Sidney's Discourses Concerning Government: Textbook of Revolution." *William and Mary Quarterly*, 3rd series, 4 (1947): 266-296.

Robinson, Daniel N. "James Wilson and Natural Rights Constitutionalism: The Influence of the Scottish Enlightenment." *Natural Law, Natural Rights, and American Constitutionalism Online Resource* (2012), Witherspoon Institute <http://www.nlnrac.org/american/scottish-enlightenment> (April 2012).

Robinson, John. John Robinson to the Pilgrims, 1620. In *History of Plymouth Plantation, 1620-1647*, by William Bradford, edited by Charles Deane, 64-67. Boston, MA: Little, Brown, & Co., 1856.

Robinson, John, and John Ashton. *The Works of John Robinson: Pastor of the Pilgrim Fathers*. Vol 1. London: John Snow, 1851.

Robinson, John, and John Ashton. *A Justification of Separation From the Church of England Against Mr. Richard Bernard His Invective, 1610*. In *The Works of John Robinson*, Vol. 2, edited by Robert Ashton. London: John Snow, 1851.

Rogal, Samuel J. *A General Introduction to Hymnody and Congregational Song*. Metuchen, NJ: Scarecrow Press, 1991.

Roland, Jon. *Introduction to Samuel Rutherford's Lex Rex*. Constitution Society, ed. Jon Roland, 1994-2012. <http://www.constitution.org/sr/intro_jr.htm> (April 2012).

Roland, Jon, ed. *Primary Source Documents Pertaining to Early American History, 500 BC-1800 AD*. Constitution Society, ed. Jon Roland, 1994-2012. <http://www.constitution.org/primarysources/primarysources.html> (accessed April 2012).

Rossiter, Clinton, ed. *The Federalist Papers*. New York: Mentor Penguin Books, 1961.

Rush, Benjamin. Benjamin Rush to Citizens of Philadelphia, "A Plan for Free Schools," 28 March 1787. In *Letters of Benjamin Rush, 1761-1792*, Vol. 1, by Benjamin Rush, 414. Princeton, NJ: Princeton U Press for American Philosophical Society, 1951.

Rush, Benjamin. Benjamin Rush to Elias Boudinot?, Observations on the Federal Procession in Philadelphia, 9 July 1788. In *Letters of Benjamin Rush, 1761-1792*, vol. 1, edited by Lyman H. Butterfield, 470-476. Princeton NJ: Princeton U Press for American Philsophical Society, 1951.

Rush, Benjamin. Benjamin Rush to Rev. Jeremy Belknap, "A Defense of the Use of the Bible in Schools," Philadelphia, 10 March 1791. In Benjamin Rush, *Essays, Literary, Moral and Philosophical*, 2nd ed., 93-113. Philadelphia, PA: Printed by Thomas and William Bradford, 1806.

Rush, Benjamin. Benjamin Rush to Thomas Jefferson, 22 August 1800. In *Letters of Benjamin Rush, 1793-1813*, Vol. 2, edited by Lyman H. Butterfield, 820-821. Princeton: Princeton U Press for American Philosophical Society, 1951.

Rush, Benjamin. "Observation on the Federal Procession of the Fourth of July, 1788, in the City of Philadelphia, in a Letter From a Gentleman in This City to His Friend in a Neighboring State." In *A Brief History of the Revolution*, by Sarah Alcock, 104-110. Philadelphia, PA: Published by Sarah Alcock, 1843.

Rush, Benjamin. "Observations on the Fourth of July Procession in Philadelphia," Philadelphia, July 1788. In *Documentary History of the Ratification of the Constitution*, Vol. 18, edited by John P. Kaminski, Richard Leffler, and Gaspare J. Saladino, 266. Madison, WI: State Historical Society of Wisconsin, 1976.

Rush, Benjamin. *Observations Upon the Present Government in Pennsylvania: In Fours Letters to the People of Pennsylvania*. Philadelphia, PA: Printed by Styner and Cist, 1777.

Rush, Benjamin. *Of the Mode of Education Proper in a Republic*. In *Essays, Literary, Moral and Philosophical*, 2nd ed., 6-20. Philadelphia, PA: Printed by Thomas and William Bradford, 1806.

Rush, Benjamin. *The Road to Fulfillment*. New York: Harper & Brothers, 1942.

Rutherford, Samuel. *Lex Rex, or The Law and the Prince; A Dispute For the Just Prerogative of King and People*. Edinburgh, Scotland: Robert Ogle and Oliver & Boyd, 1843.

Rutledge, John. John Rutledge to his brother, Charleston, 30 July 1769. In John B. O'Neall, *Biographical Sketches of the Bench and Bar of South Carolina*, 2 Vols., Vol. 2, 120-127. Charleston, SC: S. G. Courtenay & Co., 1859.

Sandoz, Ellis, ed. *Political Sermons of the Founding Era: 1730-1805*. 2 Vols. 2nd ed. Indianapolis, IN: Liberty Fund, 1998.

Sandoz, Ellis. *Republicanism, Religion, and the Soul of America*. Columbia, MO: U of Missouri Press, 2006.

Schaeffer, Francis A. *A Christian Manifesto*. Westchester, IL: Crossway Books, 1981.

Scott, E. H., ed. *Journal of the Constitutional Convention*. New York: Scott Foresman, 1893. First published 1840.

Seabury, Samuel. *Samuel Seabury's Ungathered Imprints: Historical Perspectives of the Early National Years*. Edited by Kenneth W. Cameron. Hartford, CT: Transcendental Books, 1978.

Seabury, William J. *Memoir of Bishop Seabury*. New York: Edwin S. Gorham, 1908.

Seaton, Alexander A. *The Theory of Toleration Under the Later Stuarts*. Cambridge, MA: University Press, 1911.

Seiler, William. "The Anglican Parish in Virginia." In *Seventeenth-Century America: Essays in Colonial History*, edited by James Morton Smith, 122. Chapel Hill, NC: U of North Carolina, 1959.

Sidney, Algernon. *Discourses Concerning Government, to which are added, Memoirs of His Life*, 1698. 3rd ed. London: Printed for A. Millar, 1751.

Skousen, W. Cleon. *The Making of America: The Substance and Meaning of the Constitution*. Washington, DC: National Center for Constitutional Studies, 1985.

Slater, Rosalie J. *Teaching and Learning America's Christian History: The Principle Approach*. San Francisco, CA: Foundation for American Christian Education, 1965.

Smith, James Morton, ed. *Seventeenth-Century America: Essays in Colonial History*. Chapel Hill, NC: U of North Carolina, 1959.

Smith, John. *The General History of Virginia, New England, 1606-1624*. Book 3. In *Captain J. Smith's Works, 1608-1631*, No. 16, edited by Edward Arber, 384-488 (entire work 273-784). Birmingham, England, English Scholar's Library, 1884.

Smith, John. *The General History of Virginia, New England, 1606-1624*. Book 6. In *Captain J. Smith's Works, 1608-1631*, No. 16, edited by Edward Arber, 692-783 (entire work 273-784). Birmingham, England, English Scholar's Library, 1884.

Smith, John. *Captain J. Smith's Works, 1608-1631*. No. 16. Edited by Edward Arber. Birmingham, England: English Scholar's Library, 1884.

Smith, John E. "Christian Virtue and Common Morality." In *The Princeton Companion to Jonathan Edwards*, edited by San Hyun Lee, 147-166. Princeton, NJ: Princeton U Press, 2005.

Sparks, Jared, ed. *The Writings of George Washington*. Vol. 3. Boston: Russell, Odiorne, and Metcalf and Hilliard, Gray, and Co., 1834.

Sparks, Jared, ed. *The Writings of George Washington*. Vol. 12. New York: Harper & Brothers, 1848.

Sparks, Jared, ed. *The Writings of George Washington*. Vol. 12. New York: Harper & Row, 1848.

Steiner, Bernard C. *One Hundred and Ten Years of Bible Society Work in Maryland, 1810-1920*. Baltimore, MD: Maryland Bible Society, 1921.

Sternhold, Thomas, and John Hopkins. *Four Score and Seven Psalmes of David in English Metre*. Geneva, Switzerland, 1561.

Stith, William. *The History of the First Discovery and Settlement of Virginia*. New York: Reprinted for Joseph Sabin, 1865.

Stout, Harry S. *The New England Soul: Preaching and Religious Culture in Colonial New England*. New York: Oxford U Press, 1986.

Stone, Andrew L. *A Sermon Delivered Before the Executive and Legislative Departments of the Government of Massachusetts at the Annual Election*, 4 January 1865. Boston, MA: Wright & Potter, 1865.

Story, Joseph. *Commentaries of the Constitution of the United States*. Vol. 3. Boston, MA: Hilliard, Gray, & Co., 1833.

Story, Joseph. *The Constitutional Class Book: Being A Brief Exposition of the Constitution of the United States*. Boston, MA: Hilliard, Gray, & Co., 1834.

Story, Joseph. *A Discourse Pronounced Upon the Inauguration of the Author, as Dane Professor of Law in Harvard University*, 25 August 1829. Boston, MA: Hilliard, Gray, Little, and Wilkins, 1829.

Suarez, Francisco. *Selections From Three Works of Francisco Suarez, S. J.: The Translations*. Vol. 2. Translated by Gwladys L. Williams. Edited by Henry Davis. Oxford: Clarendon Press, 1944.

Supreme Judicial Court of Massachusetts. *Review of the Brookfield Case*. In *The Spirit of the Pilgrims*. Vol 5. Boston: Pierce & Parker, 1832.

Thornton, John W. *The Pulpit of the American Revolution*. Boston, MA: D. Lothrop & Co., 1876.

Thorpe, F. N., ed. *Federal and State Constitutions*. Vol. 2. Washington, DC: U. S. Government Printing Office, 1909.

Toqueville, Alexis de. *Democracy in America, 1831-1832*, Vol. 1, 2nd American ed. Translated by Henry Reeve. New York: George Adlard, 1838.

Toqueville, Alexis de. *Democracy in America, 1831-1832*. Edited by Richard D. Heffner. New York: Penguin Books, 1956, 1984.

Trinterud, Leonard J. "The Origins of Puritanism." *Church History* 20, no. 1 (Mar., 1951): 37-57.

Tucker, George, ed. *Blackstone's Commentaries*. Union, NJ: Lawbook Exchange, 1996.

Turner, Charles. Speech in the Massachusetts Ratifying Convention, 6 February 1788. In *The Complete Anti-Federalist, An Electronic Version of the Four Volumes*, Vol. 4, edited by Herbert J. Storing, 217-222. Chicago, IL: U of Chicago Press, 1981.

U. S. Constitutional Convention. *The Records of the Federal Convention of 1787*. Vol. 2. Edited by Max Farrand. New Haven, CT: Yale U Press, 1911.

U. S. Continental Congress. An Address of the Congress to the Inhabitants of the United States of America, 8 May 1778. In U. S. Library of Congress, *Journals of the Continental Congress, 1774-1789*, Vol. 11/May 2-Sept 1, 1778, edited by Worthington C. Ford, 474-483. Washington, DC: Government Printing Office, 1908.

U. S. Continental Congress. Articles of War, 20 September 1776. In U. S. Library of Congress, *Journals of the Continental Congress, 1774-1789*, Vol. 5/June 5-Oct 8, 1776, edited by Worthington C. Ford, 788-808. Washington, DC: Government Printing Office, 1906.

U. S. Continental Congress. Congressional Resolution, Monday, 12 June 1775. In U. S. Library of Congress, *Journals of the Continental Congress, 1774-1789*, Vol. 2/May 10-Sept 20, 1775, edited by Worthington C. Ford, 87-88. Washington, DC: Government Printing Office, 1905.

U. S. Continental Congress. Congressional Resolution, Saturday, 16 March 1776. In U. S. Library of Congress, *Journals of the Continental Congress, 1774-1789*, Vol. 4/Jan 1-Jun 4, 1776, edited by Worthington C. Ford, 207-210. Washington, DC: Government Printing Office, 1906.

U. S. Continental Congress. Congressional Resolution, 20 August 1776. In U. S. Library of Congress, *Journals of the Continental Congress, 1774-1789*, Vol. 5/Jun 5-Oct 8, 1776, edited by Worthington C. Ford, 672-692. Washington, DC: Government Printing Office, 1906.

U. S. Continental Congress. Congressional Resolution, 7 March 1778. In U. S. Library of Congress, *Journals of Congress*, Vol. 4/Jan 1778-Jan 1779. 136-140. Philadelphia: U. S. Library of Congress, Printed by David C. Claypoole.

U. S. Continental Congress. Congressional Resolution, November 17, 1778. In U. S. Library of Congress, *Journals of Congress*, Vol. 4/ Jan 1778-Jan 1779. 659-662. Philadelphia, PA: U. S. Library of Congress, Printed by David C. Claypoole.

U. S. Continental Congress. Congressional Resolution, November 17, 1778. In U. S. Library of Congress, *Journals of the Continental Congress, 1774-1789*, Vol. 12/Sept 2-Dec 31, 1778, edited by Worthington C. Ford, 1137-1140. Washington, DC: Government Printing Office, 1908.

U. S. Continental Congress. Congressional Resolution, March 20, 1779. In U. S. Library of Congress, *Journals of the Continental Congress, 1774-1789*, Vol. 13/Jan 1-Apr 22, 1779, edited by Worthington C. Ford, 342-344. Washington, DC: Government Printing Office, 1909.

U. S. Continental Congress. Congressional Resolution, Treasury Office, 16 March 1781. In U. S. Library of Congress, *Journals of the Continental Congress, 1774-1789*, Vol. 19/Jan 1-April 23, 1781, edited by Gaillard Hunt, 283-286. Washington, DC: Government Printing Office, 1912.

U. S. Continental Congress. Congressional Resolution, 20 March 1781. In *Journals of the Continental Congress, 1774-1789*, Vol. 19/Jan 1-Apr 23, 1781, edited by Gaillard Hunt, 283-289. Washington, DC: Government Printing Office, 1912.

U. S. Continental Congress. Congressional Resolution, Thursday, Sept 27, 1781. In U. S. Library of Congress, *Journals of the Continental Congress, 1774-1789*, Vol. 21/July 23-Dec 31, 1781, edited by Gaillard Hunt, 1015-1019. Washington, DC: Government Printing Office, 1912.

U. S. Continental Congress. Congressional Resolution, 19 March 1782. In U. S. Library of Congress, *Journals of the American Congress, From 1774 to 1788, in Four Volumes*, Vol. 3/Aug 1, 1778-Mar 30, 1782. 735-737. Washington, DC: Printed and Published by Way and Gideon, 1823.

U. S. Continental Congress. Declaration on Taking Arms, 6 July 1775. In U. S. Library of Congress, *Journals of the Continental Congress, 1774-1789*, Vol. 2/May 10-Sept 20, 1775, edited by Worthington C. Ford, 128-157. Washington, DC: Government Printing Office, 1905.

U. S. Continental Congress. Definitive Treaty of Peace Between the United States of America and His Brittanic Majesty, 3 September 1783. In *The Public Statutes at Large of the United States of America, From the Organization of Government in 1789 to Mar 3, 1845*, Vol. 8, edited by Richard Peters, 80-83. Boston: Charles C. Little and James Brown, 1848.

U. S. Continental Congress. A Manifesto, 27 September 1781/30 October 1778. In U. S. Library of Congress, *Journals of the Continental Congress*, Vol. 4/Jan 1778-Jan 1779. 628-630. Philadelphia, PA: U. S. Library of Congress, Printed by David C. Claypoole.

U. S. Continental Congress. An Ordinance for the Government of the Territory of the United States North West of the River Ohio, 13 July 1787. In *Journals of the Continental Congress, 1774-1789*, Vol. 32, edited by Roscoe R. Hill, 340. Washington, DC: Government Printing Office, 1936.

U. S. Continental Congress. *Rules for the Regulation of the Navy of the Colonies of North-America*, 28 November 1775. Washington, DC: Naval Historical Foundation, 1994. First published in 1775 by William and Thomas Bradford.

U. S. Continental Congress. Thanksgiving Day Proclamation, 1 November 1777. In Jedidiah Morse, *Annals of the American Revolution*. Hartford, CT: 1824.

U. S. Continental Congress. Thanksgiving Day Proclamation, 1 November 1777. In U. S. Library of Congress, *Journals of the Continental Congress, 1774-1789*, Vol. 9/Oct 3-Dec 31, 1777, edited by Worthington C. Ford, 854-856. Washington, DC: Government Printing Office, 1907.

U. S. Continental Congress. Thanksgiving Day Proclamation, 20 October 1779. In *Journals of the American Congress, From 1774 to 1788, in Four Volumes*, Vol. 3/Aug 1, 1778-Mar 30, 1782. 377-378. Washington, DC: Printed and Published by Way and Gideon, 1823.

U. S. Department of Education. Legal Guidelines on Religious Expression in Public Schools, 1995, 1998. In "Religious Expression in Public Schools," *America's Heritage: An Adventure in Liberty*, High School Edition, 167-184. Houston, TX: American Heritage Education Foundation, 2012.

U. S. Department of State. "The Great Seal of the United States." Bureau of Public Affairs, 2003. <http://www.state.gov/documents/organization/27807.pdf> (April 2012).

U. S. Department of State. *Treaties and Conventions Concluded Between the United States of America and Other Powers, Since July 4, 1776*. Washington, DC: Government Printing Office, 1871.

U. S. Department of State. Treaty of Peace and Friendship Between the United States of America and the Bey and Subjects of Tripoli, of Barbary, Concluded November 4, 1796. In U. S. Department of State, *Treaties and Conventions Concluded Between the United States of America and Other Powers, Since July 4, 1776*. 837-840. Washington, DC: Government Printing Office, 1871.

U. S. Library of Congress. *Journals of the Continental Congress, 1774-1789*, Vol. 5/1776. Washington, DC: Government Printing Office, 1906.

University of Georgia Charter, 27 January 1785. In Augustus L. Hull, *A Historical Sketch of the University of Georgia*, 4-9. Atlanta, GA: Foote & Davies Co., 1894.

University of Virginia Board of Visitors. Transcript of the Minutes of the Board of Visitors of the University of Virginia, during the Rectorship of Thomas Jefferson, 4 March 1825. In *The Works of Thomas Jefferson*, Vol. 19, edited by Albert E. Bergh, 459-462. Washington, DC: Thomas Jefferson Memorial Association, 1907.

Vaughan, Alden T., ed. The Puritan Tradition in America, 1620-1730. Hanover, NH: U Press of New England, 1997.

Virginia Citizens, *Petition Against The Religious Assessment Bill to the Virginia General Assembly*, 2 November 1784. In *The Sacred Rights of Conscience: Selected Readings on Religious Liberty and Church-State Relations in the American Founding*, edited by Daniel L. Dreisbach and Mark D. Hall, 307-308. Indianapolis, IN: Liberty Fund, 2009.

Virginia Declaration of Rights, 1776. In *Documents of American Democracy: A Collection of Essential Works*, edited by Roger L. Kemp, 52-54. Jefferson, NC: McFarland & Co., 2010.

Virginia Gazette, 31 October 1745.

Virginia Statute for Religious Freedom, 1786. In *A History of Us: Sourcebook and Index: Documents That Shaped the American Nation*, Vol. 11, edited by Steven Mintz, 56-58. New York: Oxford U Press, 2002.

Wakelyn, Jon L., ed. *America's Founding Charters: Primary Documents of Colonial and Revolutionary Era Governance*. Vol. 1. Westport, CT: Greenwood Publishing Group, 2006.

Waldman, Steven. *Founding Faith: Providence, Politics, and the Birth of Religious Freedom in America*. New York: Random House, 2008.

Wallbuilders. *Spirit of the American Revolution*. DVD. Directed by David Barton. Aledo, TX: Wallbuilders, 2007.

Ward, Nathaniel. *The Simple Cobler of Aggawam in America*. Edited by David Pulsifer. Boston: James Munroe and Co., 1843.

Washington, George. Farewell Address, 17 September 1796. In *The Addresses and Messages of the Presidents of the United States, 1789-1846*, Vol. 1, compiled by Edwin Williams, 69-78. New York: Edward Walker, 1846.

Washington, George. Farewell Address to the People of the United States, 17 September 1796. In *The Writings of George Washington, 1794-1798*, Vol. 13, edited by Worthington C. Ford, 275-325. New York: G. P. Putnam's Sons, 1892.

Washington, George. Fragments of the Discarded Inaugural Address, April 1789. In *George Washington: A Collection*, edited by W. B. Allen, 453-457. Indianapolis, IN: Liberty Fund, 1988.

Washington, George. General Order, Orderly Book, 4 July 1775. In *The Writings of George Washington*, Vol. 3, edited by Jared Sparks. Boston: Russell, Odiorne, and Metcalf and Hilliard, Gray, and Co., 1834.

Washington, George. General Order, Orderly Book, 4 July 1775. In *The Writings of George Washington*, Vol. 3, edited by Worthington C. Ford. New York: G. P. Putnam's Sons, 1889.

Washington, George. General Order, Orderly Book, 27 February 1776. In *The Writings of George Washington*, Vol. 3/1775-1776, edited by Worthington C. Ford. New York: G. P. Putnam's Sons, 1889.

Washington, George. General Order, Orderly Book, Headquarters, Valley Forge, 2 May 1778. In *Revolutionary Orders of General Washington, Issued During the Years 1778, '80, '81, & '82*, edited by Henry Whiting, 74-75 (#50). New York: Wiley and Putnam, 1844.

Washington, George. George Washington to Brigadier-General Nelson, Camp at White Plains, Virginia, 20 August 1778. In *The Writings of George Washington*, Vol. 6, Pt. 2 cont., edited by Jared Sparks, 34-37. Boston: Russell, Odiorne, and Metcalf, 1834.

Washington, George. George Washington to the Delaware Chiefs, Middle Brook, 12 May 1779, Transcript of Speech, 1H78-80. In *Frontier Advance on the Upper Ohio, 1778-1779*, Draper Vol. 4, Collections Vol. 23, edited by Louise P. Kellogg, 322-324. Madison, WI: Wisconsin Historical Society, 1916.

Washington, George. George Washington to Hebrew Congregation of the City of Savannah, May 1790. In *Publications of the American Jewish Historical Society*, No. 3, 89-90. New York: American Jewish Historical Society, 1895.

Washington, George. George Washington to Hebrew Congregation in Newport, Rhode Island, 1790. In *Publications of the American Jewish Historical Society*, No. 3, 91-92. New York: American Jewish Historical Society, 1895.

Washington, George. George Washington to Rev. Israel Evans, Valley Forge, 13 March 1778. In *The Writings of George Washington*, Vol. 5, edited by Jared Sparks, 275-276. Boston: Russell, Odiorne, and Metcalf, and Hilliard, Gray, and Co., 1834.

Washington, George. George Washington to Lund Washington, Headquarters Middlebrook, 29 May 1779. In *Proceedings of the Massachusetts Historical Society, 1871-1873*. 56. Boston: Published by the Massachusetts Historical Society, 1873.

Washington, George. Inaugural Address, 30 April 1789. In *The Addresses and Messages of the Presidents of the United States, 1789-1846, in Two Volumes*, Vol. 1, compiled by Edwin Williams, 31-35. New York: Edward Walker, 1846.

Washington, George. Thanksgiving Day Proclamation, 25 September 1789. In *Proclamations for Thanksgiving*, edited by Franklin B. Hough, 30-32. Albany, NY: Munsell & Rowland for U. S. Continental Congress and Pres. Washington, 1858.

Washington, George. Unused Notes for the First Inaugural Address, April 1789. In Michael Novak and Jana Novak, *Washington's God: Religion, Liberty, and the Father of Our Country*, 235-236. New York: Basic Books, 2006.

Webster, Daniel. "The Dignity and Importance of History," An Address Delivered Before the New York Historical Society," New York, 23 February 1852. In *The Writings and Speeches of Daniel Webster*, Vol. 1/Vol. 13, edited by Edward Everett, 463-497. Boston, MA: Little, Brown, & Co., 1903.

Webster, Daniel. "Pilgrim Festival at New York in 1850." In *The Works of Daniel Webster*, Vol. 2. 20th ed. Boston: Little, Brown, and Co., 1890.

Webster, Daniel. *The Works of Daniel Webster*. Vol 2. 20th ed. Boston: Little, Brown, and Co., 1890.

Webster, Noah. *History of the United States*. New Haven, CT: Durrie & Peck, 1832.

Webster, Noah. *Noah Webster's First Edition of An American Dictionary of the English Language*, 1828. San Francisco, CA: Foundation for American Christian Education, 1967, 1995, 1998. First printed in 1828.

Webster, Noah. Noah Webster to A Young Gentleman Commencing His Education, Letter 1. In Noah Webster, *Letters to A Young Gentleman Commencing His Education*, 5-20. New Haven, CT: Howe & Spalding, 1823.

Webster, Noah. Noah Webster to David McClure, New Haven, 25 October 1836. In Noah Webster, *A Collection of Papers on Political, Literary, and Moral Subjects*, 291-294. New York: Webster & Clark, 1843.

Wells, H. G. *The Outline of History: Being a Plain History of Life and Mankind*. Vol II. Garden City, NY: Garden City Books, 1940, 1949.

Wells, William V., ed. *The Life and Public Service of Samuel Adams*, Vol. 1. Boston, MA: Little, Brown, & Co., 1865.

West, Delno C. & August Kling, trans. *The Libro de las Profecias of Christopher Columbus*, en face ed., 1492. Gainesville, FL: U of Florida, 1991.

Westminster General Assembly. *The Confession of Faith, the Larger and Shorter Catechisms*, 1647. Printed by W. Duncan, 1768.

Wheatley, Phillis. *An Elegiac Poem on the Death of the Celebrated Divine, and Eminent Servant of Jesus Christ, the Reverend and Learned Mr. George Whitefield, 1770*. In Ebenezer Pemberton, *Heaven the Residence of Saints, A Sermon Occasioned by the Sudden and Much Lamented Death of the Rev. George Whitefield, Boston, 11 October 1770*, 29-31. Boston, MA: Reprinted for E. and C. Dilly, 1771.

Willard, Samuel. "The Character of a Good Ruler," 1694. In *The Puritans: A Sourcebook of Their Writings, Two Volumes Bound As One*, edited by Perry Miller and Thomas H. Johnson, 250-255. Mineola, NY: Dover, 2001. First published in 1963 by Harper & Row.

Williams, Elisha. "The Essential Rights and Liberties of Protestants, A Seasonable Plea for Liberty of Conscience and the Right of private Judgment in matters of Religion, without any control from Human Authority." In *The Christian History of the American Revolution*, compiled by Verna M. Hall, 183-189. San Francisco, CA: Foundation for American Christian Education, 1976.

Williams, Roger. *The Bloody Tenent Yet More Bloody: Selections From the Works of Roger Williams*. Edited by James Calvin Davis. Cambridge, MA: Harvard U Press, 2008.

Williams, Roger. *The Bloudy Tenent of Persecution For Cause of Conscience Discussed: and Mr. Cotton's Letter Examined and Answered, 1644*. Edited by Edward B. Underhill. London: Printed for the Hanserd Knollys Society by J. Haddon, 1848.

Williams, Roger. "Mr. Cotton's Letter Examined and Answered," London, 1644. In *The Bloudy Tenent of Persecution for Cause of Conscience Discussed and Mr. Cotton's Letter Examined and Answered*, edited by Edward B. Underhill, 435. London: Printed for the Hanserd Knollys Society by J. Haddon, 1848.

Wills, Garry. *Inventing America: Jefferson's Declaration of Independence*. New York: Vintage Books, 1978.

Wilson, James. Lectures on Law, Part 1, 1790-1791. In *The Works of the Honourable James Wilson*, Vol. 1, edited by Bird Wilson. Philadelphia, PA: Lorenzo Press, Printed for Bronson and Chauncey, 1804.

Wilson, James. Oration at the Procession Formed at Philadelphia to Celebrate the Adoption of the Constitution of the United States, Philadelphia, 4 July 1788. In *The Works of the Honourable James Wilson*, Vol. 3, edited by Bird Wilson, 299-311. Philadelphia, PA: Printed for Bronson and Chauncey, 1804.

Wilson, James. Consideration on the Nature and Extent of the Legislative Authority of the British Parliament, 1774. In *The Works of the Honourable James Wilson*, Vol. 3, edited by Bird Wilson, 199-246. Philadelphia, PA: Printed for Bronson and Chauncey at Lorenzo Press, 1804.

Wilson, John R. *Church and State in American History: Studies in History and Politics*. Lexington, MA: DC Heath and Co., 1965.

Winslow, Edward. *Hypocrisie Unmasked*. 1646. Reprint, Bedford, MA: Applewood Books, 2009.

Winthrop, John. *The History of New England From 1630 to 1649*, vol. 2, edited by James Savage. Boston, MA: 1826, 229.

Winthrop, John. *The History of New England From 1630 to 1649*. Vol. 2. Boston, MA: Little, Brown, & Co., 1853.

Winthrop, John. John Winthrop to____, Boston (8) 14, 1642. In *Life and Letters of John Winthrop, 1620-1649*, Vol. 2, 2nd ed., edited by Robert C. Winthrop, 277-279. Boston, MA: Little, Brown, and Co., 1869.

Winthrop, John. *A Model of Christian Charity, 1630*. In *Puritan Political Ideas, 1558-1794*, edited by Edmund S. Morgan, 75-93. Indianapolis, IN: Hackett Publishing, 2003. First printed 1965 by Bobbs-Merrill.

Winthrop, John. "Reasons to Be Considered for Justifying the Undertakers of the Intended Plantation in New England, 1629." In *Envisioning America: English Plans For the Colonization of North America, 1580-1640*, edited by Peter C. Mancall, 133-136. Boston, MA; Bedford Books, 1995.

Winthrop, John. "A Replye to the Answ: Made to the Discourse About the Neg: Vote." In *Life and Letters of John Winthrop, 1630-1649*, Vol. 2, 2nd ed., edited by Robert C. Winthrop, 427-437. Boston, MA: Little, Brown, and CO., 1869.

Wise, John. "John Wise on the Principles of Government, 1717." In *Puritan Political Ideas, 1558-1794*, edited by Edmund S. Morgan, 251-266. Indianapolis, IN: Hackett Publishing, 2003.

Witherspoon, John. "The Dominion of Providence Over the Passions of Men," 17 May 1776. In *The Works of John Witherspoon, in Three Volumes,* Vol. 2, edited by John Rodgers, 407-436. Philadelphia, PA: William W. Woodward, 1800).

Witherspoon, John. Lectures on Divinity. In *The Works of John Witherspoon*, Vol. 8, 9-162. Edinburgh, Scotland: Printed for Ogles, Duncan, Cochran, and Johnston, 1815.

Witherspoon, John. "The Yoke of Christ." In *The Works of John Witherspoon, in Four Volumes*, Vol. 2, 2nd ed., edited by John Rodgers, 289-302. Philadelphia, PA: William W. Woodward, 1802.

Witte, John, Jr. *God's Joust, God's Justice: Law and Religion in the Western Tradition.* Grand Rapids, MI: Eerdmans, 2006.

Witte, John, Jr. *The Reformation of Rights: Law, Religion, and Human Rights in Early Modern Calvinism.* Cambridge, UK: Cambridge U Press, 2007.

Witte, John, Jr., and Frank S. Alexander, eds. *Christianity and Law: An Introduction.* Cambridge, UK: Cambridge U Press, 2008.

Wood, Gordon S. *The Creation of the American Republic 1776-1787.* New York: W. W. Norton., U of North Carolina Press, 1969, 1972, 1993.

Zuckert, Michael. *The Natural Rights Republic.* Notre Dame: U of Notre Dame Press, 1996.

Endnotes

Opening and Introduction

[1] Thomas Jefferson, *Notes on the State of Virginia, 1785*, 8th ed. (Boston, MA: Printed by David Carlisle, 1801), 241; Thomas Jefferson, *Notes on Virginia, 1785*, in *The Writings of Thomas Jefferson*, vol. 8, ed. Henry A. Washington (Philadelphia, PA: J. B. Lippincott & Co., 1864), bk. 4, 404.

[2] Thomas Jefferson, *An Act for Establishing Religious Freedom*, 1786, in Thomas Jefferson, *Notes on the State of Virginia, 1785*, 8th ed. (Boston, MA: Printed by David Carlisle, 1801), 326-328.

[3] Benjamin Rush to Elias Boudinot?, Observations on the Federal Procession in Philadelphia, July 9, 1788, in *Letters of Benjamin Rush, 1761-1792*, vol. 1, ed. Lyman H. Butterfield (Princeton, NJ: Princeton U Press for American Philosophical Society, 1951), 475. See also Benjamin Rush, "Observation on the Federal Procession of the Fourth of July, 1788, in the City of Philadelphia, in a Letter From a Gentleman in This City to His Friend in a Neighboring State," July 4, 1778, in *A Brief History of the Revolution*, by Sarah Alcock (Philadelphia, PA: Published by Sarah Alcock, 1843), 109-110.

[4] John Quincy Adams to George W. Adams, St. Petersburg, 1 and 8 September 1811, in *Writings of John Quincy Adams, 1811-1813*, vol. 4, ed.Worthingon C. Ford (New York: Macmillan Co., 1914), 216-17.

[5] Daniel Webster, "The Dignity and Importance of History, An Address Delivered Before the New York Historical Society," New York, 23 February 1852, in *The Writings and Speeches of Daniel Webster*, vol. 1/vol. 13, ed. Edward Everett (Boston, MA: Little, Brown, & Co., 1903), 492-493.

[6] James Madison to George Thomson, 30 June 1825, in *Letters and Other Writings of James Madison: 1816-1828*, vol. 3 (Philadelphia, PA: J. B. Lippincott & Co., 1865), 492.

[7] Thomas Jefferson to Colonel Yancey, Monticello, 6 January 1816, in *The Writings of Thomas Jefferson*, vol. 6, ed. H. A. Washington (New York: Riker, Thorne, &. Co., 1854), 517.

[8] Intercollegiate Studies Institute, *The Coming Crisis in Citizenship: Higher Education's Failure to Teach America's History and Institutions* (Wilmington, DE: Intercollegiate Studies Institute, 2006), <http://www.americancivicliteracy.org/2006/introduction.html> <http://www.americancivicliteracy.org/2006/summary.html> (Feb 2013); Intercollegiate Studies Institute, *Failing Our Students, Failing America: Holding Colleges Accountable for Teaching America's History and Institutions* (Wilmington, DE: Intercollegiate Studies Institute, 2007), <http://www.americancivicliteracy.org/2007/summary_summary.html> (Feb 2013); Intercollegiate Studies Institute, *Our Fading Heritage: Americans Fail A Basic Test on Their History and Institutions* (Wilmington, DE: Intercollegiate Studies Institute, 2008), <http://www.americancivicliteracy.org/2008/summary_summary.html> (Feb 2013). See www.americancivicliteracy.org.

[9] The Lynde and Harry Bradley Foundation, *E Pluribus Unum: The Bradley Project on America's National Identity* (Milwaukee, WI: Lynde and Harry Bradley Foundation, 2008), <http://www.bradleyproject.org> (Feb 2013). See www.bradleyproject.org.

[10] Glenn Ricketts, Peter W. Wood, Stephen H. Balch, and Ashley Thorne, *The Vanishing West: 1964-2010: The Disappearance of Western Civilization From the American Undergraduate Curriculum* (Princeton, NJ: National Association of Scholars, 2011), <http://www.nas.org> <http://www.nas.org/articles/The_Vanishing_West_1964-2010> (Sept 2013); Richard W. Fonte, Peter W. Wood, and Ashley Thorne, *Recasting History: Are Race, Class, and Gender Dominating American History? A Study of U. S. History Courses at the University of Texas and Texas A&M University* (Princeton, NJ: National Association of Scholars, 2013), <http://www.nas.org> <http://www.nas.org/articles/recasting_history_are_race_class_and_gender_dominating_american_history> (Sept 2013). See www.nas.org.

[11] Richard J. Coley and Andrew Sum, *Fault Lines in Our Democracy: Civic Knowledge, Voting Behavior, and Civic Engagement in the United States* (Princeton, NJ: Educational Testing Service, 2012), <http://www.ets.org/faultlines> (Feb 2013). See www.ets.org/faultlines.

[12] John Adams, *A Dissertation on the Canon and Feudal Law*, 1765, in *The Works of John Adams, Second President of the United States*, ed. Charles F. Adams, vol. 3 (Boston: Little, Brown, & Co., 1851), 456.

[13] Horace Mann, Ninth Annual Report on Education for 1845, in Horace Mann, *Life and Works of Horace Mann*, vol. 4: Annual Reports of the Secretary of the Board of Education of Massachusetts for the Years 1845-1848 (Boston, MA: Lee and Shepard Publishers, 1891), 4.

[14] William Clinton, Excerpt in Introductory Letter of U. S. Secretary of Education Richard Riley, U. S. Department of Education Legal Guidelines on Religious Expression in Public Schools, 1995, 1998, in "Religious Expression in Public Schools," *America's Heritage: An Adventure in Liberty*, High School Edition (Houston, TX: American Heritage Education Foundation, Inc., 2012), 171; William Clinton, Excerpt in Introductory Letter of U. S. Secretary of Education Richard Riley, U. S. Department of Education Legal Guidelines on Religious Expression in Public Schools (Washington, DC: U. S. Department of Education, 1995, revised 1998), <http://www.ed.gov>.

[15] U. S. Department of Education, Legal Guidelines on Religious Expression in Public Schools, 1995, 1998, in "Religious Expression in Public Schools," *America's Heritage: An Adventure in Liberty*, High School Edition (Houston, TX: American Heritage Education Foundation, Inc., 2012), 176. See also Charles C. Haynes and Oliver Thomas, "Religious Expression in Public Schools: United States Department of Education Guidelines," in *Finding Common Ground: A Guide to Religious Liberty in Public Schools* (Nashville, TN: First Amendment Center, 2002), 128.

[16] U. S. Department of Education, Legal Guidelines on Religious Expression in Public Schools, *America's Heritage*, 176. See also Haynes and Thomas, "Religious Expression in Public Schools," *Finding Common Ground*, 129.

[17] U. S. Department of Education, Legal Guidelines on Religious Expression in Public Schools, *America's Heritage*, 176. See also Haynes and Thomas, "Religious Expression in Public Schools," *Finding Common Ground*, 128.

[18] *Abington v. Schempp, 374 U.S. 203, 255 (1963).*

[19] *Abington v. Schempp, 374 U.S. 203, 255 (1963).*

[20] National Council for the Social Studies, "Study About Religions in the Social Studies Curriculum: A Position Statement of the National Council for the Social Studies" (Silver Spring, MD: National Council for the Social Studies, 1984, 1998), <http://www.socialstudies.org>.

[21] Charles C. Haynes and Oliver Thomas, "Religion in the Public School Curriculum: Questions and Answers," in *Finding Common Ground: A Guide to Religious Liberty in Public Schools* (Nashville, TN: First Amendment Center, 2002), 90. <http://www.firstamendmentcenter.org>.

[22] Natilee Duning, ed., *The Bible & Public Schools: A First Amendment Guide* (Nashville, TN: First Amendment Center; New York: The Bible Literacy Project, Inc., 1999), 8-9. <http://www.freedomforum.org>.

Chapter 1: The Roots of Popular Sovereignty

[23] See Theodore Beza, *On the Rights of Magistrates: Concerning the Rights of Rulers Over Their Subjects and the Duty of Subjects Towards Their Rulers*, 1574, trans. Patrick S. Poole (Constitution Society, 1995-2013). <http://www.constitution.org/cmt/beza/magistrates.htm> (accessed April 2013).

[24] Martin Luther, *The Ninety-Five Theses, 1517*, in *Martin Luther: Selections From His Writings*, ed. John Dillenberger (New York: Anchor Books/Doubleday, 1961), 489-500. This work is also titled *A Disputation of Doctor Martin Luther on the Power and Efficacy of Indulgences*. Luther's criticisms of the church were reminiscent of those made by John Wycliffe of England in the 1300s and John Huss of Bohemia in the 1400s. Wycliffe played a significant role in the translation of the first complete Bible into English in the late 1300s.

[25] Cotton Mather, *Magnalia Christi Americana or, The Ecclesiastical History of New England, 1620-1698*, vol. 1 (1820; repr., Bedford, MA: Applewood Books, 2009), 250.

[26] John Witte, Jr., *The Reformation of Rights: Law, Religion, and Human Rights in Early Modern Calvinism* (Cambridge, UK, 2007), 77-80.

[27] Gary Amos and Richard Gardiner, *Never Before In History: America's Inspired Birth* (Dallas, TX: Haughton, 1998), 11.

[28] John Ponet, *A Short Treatise on Political Power, and of the true obedience which subjects owe to our kings and other civil governors, with an Exhortation to all true and natural English men*, 1556, ed. Patrick S. Poole, Edited for the Modern Reader (Constitution Society, 1995-2012) <http://www.constitution.org/cmt/ponet/polpower.htm> (accessed April 2012).

[29] John Adams, *A Defense of the Constitutions of Government of the United States of America, 1778*, vol. 3, in *The Works of John Adams, Second President of the United States*, vol. 6, ed. Charles F. Adams (Boston: Charles C. Little and James Brown, 1851), 3-4.

[30] See Witte, *Reformation of Rights*, 135-137, and Beza, *On the Rights of Magistrates*, 12-14. Beza and then *Vindiciae* also argued against religious persecution.

[31] See Gary T. Amos, *Defending the Declaration: How the Bible and Christianity Influenced the Writing of the Declaration of Independence* (Brentwood, TN: Wolgemuth & Hyatt, 1989), 138-139; See Jon Roland, ed., *Primary Source Documents Pertaining to Early American History, 500 BC-1800 AD*, Constitution Society, 2000-2011 <http://www.constitution.org/primarysources/primarysources.html>.

[32] John Adams, *Defense of the Constitutions of Government*, 3-4.

[33] Francis A. Schaeffer, *A Christian Manifesto* (Westchester, IL: Crossway Books, 1981), 32, 99-100. See also Gary Amos and Richard Gardiner, *Never Before in History: America's Inspired Birth*, ed. William Dembski (Dallas, TX: Haughton, 1998), 23. See also Jon Roland, *Introduction to Samuel Rutherford's Lex, Rex*, Constitution Society (1995-2012), <http://www.constitution.org/sr/intro_jr.htm> (accessed September 2013).

[34] Amos, *Defending the Declaration*, 140.

[35] Catholic sources that influenced *Lex Rex* included Thomas Aquinas and Jesuit priest Francisco Suarez.

[36] Jon Roland, ed., *Primary Source Documents Pertaining to Early American History, 500 BC-1800 AD*, Constitution Society, 2000-2011 <http://www.constitution.org/primarysources/primarysources.html>.

[37] Amos and Gardiner, *Never Before in History*, 23.

[38] Schaeffer, *Christian Manifesto*, 32, 99-100, 105; Amos, *Defending the Declaration*, 62-64.

[39] Amos and Gardiner, *Never Before in History*, 25-26.

[40] Other translators and scholars who also contributed to the Geneva Bible included Anthony Gilby, Thomas Sampson, Christopher Goodman, and William Cole. Calvin's brother-in-law William Whittingham coordinated the translation.

[41] See Donald L. Brake, *A Visual History of the King James Bible: The Dramatic Story of the World's Best-Known Translation* (Grand Rapids, MI: Baker Books, 2011).

42   Robert Filmer, *Patriarcha*, 1680, in *Two Treatises on Civil Government*, John Locke (London: George Routledge and Sons, 1884), 14. Bellarmine was cited by Sir Robert Filmer, the theologian of King James 1 of England, who in his *Patriarcha* supported the Divine Right of Kings. Filmer was refuting Bellarmine. Locke would later refute Filmer's argument and support the position of Bellarmine. See also Bellarmine, *De Laicis* or *The Treatise on Civil Government*, bk. 3, ch. 4, 6, 7. *De Laicis* appears in Bellarmine's main work *De Controversiis* or *Disputations and Controversies regarding the Catholic Faith against the Heretics of the Present Day*, 1581, 1582, 1593. Bellarmine states, "Secular or civil power…is in the people, unless they bestow it on a prince. This power is immediately in the whole multitude…for this power is in the divine law [the Bible, brackets mine], but the divine law hath given this power to no particular man—if the positive law be taken away, there is left no reason why amongst a multitude (who are equal) one rather than another should bear rule over the rest. Power is given by the multitude to one man, or to more by the same law of nature…. It depends upon the consent of the multitude to ordain over themselves a king, or consul, or other magistrates…." Bellarmine also stated on popular sovereignty: "It depends upon the consent of the multitude to constitute over itself a king, consul, or other magistrate. This power is, indeed, from God, but vested in a particular ruler by the counsel and election of men." (*De Laicis*, ch. 6, notes 4 and 5). "The people themselves immediately and directly hold the political power." (*De Clericis*, ch. 7) Bellarmine states of equality of humans with regard to freedom: "All men are equal, not in wisdom or grace, but in the essence and nature of mankind." (*De Laicis*, ch. 7). "There is no reason why among equals one should rule rather than another." "Let rulers remember that they preside over men who are of the same nature as they themselves." (*De Officus Princ*, ch. 22). "Political right is immediately from God and necessarily inherent in the nature of man." (*De Laicis*, ch. 6, note 1) "For legitimate reasons the people can change the government to an aristocracy or a democracy or vice versa." (*De Laicis*, ch. 6) "The people never transfers its powers to a king so completely but that it reserves to itself the right of receiving back this power." (*Recognitio de Laicis*, ch. 6). Thomas Aquinas also asserted such equality of humans in freedom: "Nature made all men equal in liberty, though not in their natural perfections." (II Sent., d. xliv, q. 1, a. 3, ad 1) Bellarmine further acknowledged that the Pope could possibly err in some cases or fall into heresy. A heretical Pope, he acknowledged, should be deposed.

43   See John P. Doyle, ed., *Collected Studies on Francisco Suarez* (Leuven, Belgium: Leuven U Press, 2010), 264, notes 48-52. See also *De Legibus* III, ch. 2, note 3.

44   Filmer, *Patriarcha*, 24. Filmer was refuting Suarez. Locke would later refute Filmer and support the position of Bellarmine and Suarez. In his *De Legibus* III (vol. 5, ch. 2, note 3, p179-180), Suarez asserts that in Genesis power is not conferred on any one man, not even on Adam. See Suarez's *Tractatus De Legibus* or *Tract On Laws*, 1612. See also Suarez's *De Defensione Fidei*, 1613. Suarez states, "By right of creation…Adam had only economical power, but not political. He had a power over his wife, and a fatherly power over his sons…. … But political power did not begin until families began to be gathered together into one perfect community; …as the community did not begin by the creation of Adam, nor by his will alone, but of all them which did agree in this community, so we cannot say that Adam naturally had political primacy in that community; …because by the force of the law of Nature alone it is not due unto any progenitor to be also king of his posterity. And…we cannot say, God…gave him this power, for there is no revelation of this, nor testimony of Scripture."

45   Martin Luther, *An Appeal to the Ruling Class of German Nationality as to the Amelioration of the State of Christendom*, 1520, in *Martin Luther: Selections From His Writings*, ed. John Dillenberger (New York: Anchor Books/Doubleday, 1961), 408.

46   Luther, *Appeal to the Ruling Class*, 414.

47   Luther, *Appeal to the Ruling Class*, 409-410. Luther states, pp. 408-410, "The fact is that our baptism consecrates us all without exception, and makes us all priests. As St. Peter says, I Pet. 2 [:9 brackets editor's], 'You are a royal priesthood and a realm of priests,' and Revelation, 'Thou hast made us priests and kings by Thy blood' [Rev. 5:9 f.]….

When a bishop consecrates, he simply acts on behalf of the entire congregation, all of whom have the same authority. They may select one of their number and command him to exercise this authority on behalf of the others. It would be similar if ten brothers, king's sons and equal heirs, were to choose one of themselves to rule the kingdom for them. All would be kings and of equal authority, although one was appointed to rule. To put it more plainly, suppose a small group of earnest Christian laymen were taken prisoner and settled in the middle of a desert without any episcopally ordained priest among them; and they then agreed to choose one of themselves…; that man would be as truly a priest as if he had been ordained by all the bishops and the popes. … [I]n former days, Christians used to choose their bishops and priests from their own members….

Hence we deduce that there is, at bottom, really no other difference between laymen, priests, princes, bishops, or, in Romanist terminology, between religious and secular, than that of office or occupation, and not that of Christian status. All have spiritual status, and all are truly priests, bishops, and popes. But Christians do not all follow the same occupation. Similarly, priests and monks do not all work at the same task. This is supported by Romans 12 [:4f] and I Corinthians 12 [:12f.], and by I Peter 2 [:9], as I showed above. In these passages, St. Paul and St. Peter say that we are all one body, and belong to Jesus Christ who is the head, and we are all members of one another. Christ has not two bodies, nor two kinds of bodies, one secular and the other religious. He has one head and one body.

Therefore those now called 'the religious', i.e., priests, bishops, and popes, possess no further or greater dignity than other Christians, except that their duty is to expound the word of God and administer the sacraments—that being their office. In the same way, the secular authorities 'hold the sword and the rod', their function being to punish evil-doers and protect the law-abiding. A shoemaker, a smith, a farmer, each has his manual occupation and work; and yet, at the same time, all are eligible to act as priests and bishops. Every one of them in his occupation or handicraft ought to be useful to his fellows, and serve them in such a way that the various trades are all directed to the best advantage of the community, and promote the well-being of body and soul, just as all the organs of the body serve each other."

[48] Luther, *Appeal to the Ruling Class*, 409-410.

[49] John Calvin, *Institutes of the Christian Religion*, vol. 3, trans. John Allen (Philadelphia, PA: Philip H. Nicklin, 1816), 112-113.

[50] Calvin, *Institutes*, vol. 3, 112-113. Calvin states, "…[W]e can obtain no better decision of this point than from the scripture itself, if we compare all the places where it shews what office and power Peter held among the apostles, how he conducted himself, and in what manner he was received by them. On an examination of the whole, we shall only find that he was one of the twelve, equal to the rest, their companion, not their master. He proposes to the assembly, indeed, if there be any thing to be done, and delivers his opinion on what is necessary to be done; but he hears the observations of others, and not only gives them the opportunity of speaking their sentiments, but leaves them to decide, and when they have determined, he follows and obeys. (Acts 15:6-29, scripture references are footnoted in text) When he writes to pastors, he does not command them with authority like a superior; but makes them his colleagues, and exhorts them with a courteousness which is usual among equals. (1 Peter 5:1) When he is accused for having associated with the gentiles…yet he answers it and vindicates himself. (Acts 11:2 &c) Commanded by his colleagues to go with John to Samaria, he refuses not. (Acts 8:14-15) The apostles, by sending him, declared that they did not consider him as their superior. By his compliance and execution of the commission entrusted to him, he confessed that he was a colleague to them, but had no authority over them. If none of these facts had remained upon record, yet the Epistle to the Galatians might alone easily remove every doubt; where Paul devotes nearly two whole chapters to the sole purpose of shewing that he was equal to Peter in the dignity of the apostleship. Hence he related that he went to Peter, not to profess subjection to him, but to testify to all the harmony of their doctrine: and that Peter required no such thing as submission, but gave him the right-hand of fellowship, that they might labour together in the vineyard of the Lord: that no less grace had been conferred upon him among the gentiles, than upon Peter among the Jews: and lastly, that when Peter acted with some degree of unfaithfulness, he was reproved by him, and stood corrected by the reproof. (Galatians 1, 2) All these things fully prove, either that there was an equality between Paul and Peter, or at least that Peter had no more power over the rest than they had over him. And this, as I have already observed, is the professed object of Paul; to prevent his being considered as inferior in his apostolic character to Peter or John, who were his colleagues, not his masters."

[51] H. Richard Niebuhr, *The Kingdom of God in America* (Middletown, CT: Weslayan U Press, 1988), 23-24.

[52] Stephanus J. Brutus, *Vindiciae, Contra Tyrannos, or Concerning the Legitimate Power of a Prince Over the People, and of the People Over a Prince*, ed. George Garnett (Cambridge, UK: Cambridge U Press, 1994, 2003), 68. Brutus states, "Several ages before the people of Israel petitioned God for a king, God had already sanctioned the law of the kingdom which is found in Deuteronomy ch. XVII: 'When', says Moses, 'you have come to that land which the Lord your God has given you in possession, and when you have dwelt there, you will say: "Let me constitute a king over myself, like the other nations round about." Then you will constitute that king, whom your Lord will have elected from the midst of your bretheren, etc.' Here you see the king's election attributed to God, and his constitution to the people."

[53] Brutus, *Vindiciae*, 68-69. Brutus states, "Partly because they [the people of Israel, brackets mine] were disgusted with Samuel's sons, who judged unjustly, and partly because they believed that their wars would be better conducted, they asked Samuel for a king [1 Samuel 8:4-5, verses footnoted by editor]. When consulted by Samuel, God revealed that He had elected Saul to rule the people [1 Samuel 9:16]. And so Samuel anointed Saul [1 Samuel 10:1]: for all these procedures pertained to the election of a king made at the request of the people.

And perhaps it might have seemed sufficient, if Samuel had presented the king elected by God to the people and admonished it to obey him. Nevertheless, in order that the king should know himself to be constituted by the people, Samuel appointed an assembly [*comitia*, brackets editor's] to meet at Mizpeh; there, as if the matter were still wholly unopened and unsettled—as if, I say the election of Saul had not yet been established—the lot was drawn. Out of the tribes, it fell on the tribe of Benjamin; out of the families, it fell on the family of Matri; and from that family, upon Saul, the same whom God had elected. Then finally, with the acclamation of the whole people, Saul was said to be nominated king [1 Samuel 10:17-24]. … Saul was confirmed as king in the presence of the Lord by all together [*universi*] at Gilgal, despite the dissent of a few of the people [1 Samuel 11:14-15, 1 Samuel 10:27]. Here you see the one whom God Himself had elected, and who had been marked off from the rest by lot, constituted king by the votes of the people."

[54] Brutus, *Vindiciae*, 68. Brutus states, "We have demonstrated…that God institutes kings, gives kingdoms to them, and elects them. We now say that the people constitute kings, confers kingdoms, and approves the election by its vote [*suffragio*, italicized Latin word editor's]. Indeed, God willed that it should be done this way, so that whatever authority and power they have, should be received from the people after Him; and that thus they would apply all their care, thought, and effort to the welfare of the people [*utilitas populi*]."

[55] Samuel Rutherford, *Lex Rex, or the Law and the Prince; A Dispute for the Just Prerogative of King and People* (Edinburgh, Scotland: Robert Ogle and Oliver & Boyd, 1843), 7-8. Rutherford also cites, like *Vindiciae*, 1 Samuel 10:21 in which Saul is chosen from among the tribes of Israel, 1 Samuel 11:14-15 in which "'all the people went to Gilgal, and there they made Saul king before the Lord,'" and 1 Samuel 12:1 in which the prophet Samuel, heeding the people's voice, declares Saul as king.

[56] Rutherford, *Lex Rex*, 143. See 2 Chronicles 22:10-11, 23:11-15 and 2 Kings 11:17-20. Rutherford states, "If the estates [ie. the people, brackets mine] of a kingdom give the power to a king, it is their own power in the fountain; and if they give it for their

own good, they have power to judge when it is used against themselves, and for their evil, and so power to limit and resist the power that they gave. Now, that they may take away this power, is clear in Athaliah's case."

57 Rutherford, *Lex Rex*, 6, 7.

58 Rutherford, *Lex Rex*, 8.

59 Rutherford, *Lex Rex*, 80. Rutherford states, "The Scripture saith plainly, as we heard before, the people made kings; and if they do, as other second causes produce their effects, it is all one that God, as the principal cause, maketh kings…. God, by that same action that the people createth a king, doth also, by them, as by his instruments, create a king…. … The people can, and doth, limit and bind royal power in elected kings, therefore they have in them royal power to give to the king."

60 Rutherford, *Lex Rex*, 7. Rutherford states, "This is what we say, God by the people, by Nathan the prophet, and by the servants of David and the states crying 'God save king Solomon!' made Solomon king; and here is a real action of the people. God is the first agent in all acts of the creature. Where a people maketh choice of a man to be their king, the states do no other thing, under God, but create this man rather than another; and we cannot here find two actions, one of God, another of the people; but in one and the same action, God, by the people's free suffrages and voices, createth such a man king, passing by many thousands; and the people are not passive in the action, because by the authoritative choice of the states the man is made of a private man and no king, a public person and a crowned king."

61 Donald S. Lutz, "From Covenant to Constitution in American Political Thought," in *Covenant, Polity, and Constitutionalism: Publius: The Journal of Federalism* 10, no. 4 (1980): 109-110.

Chapter 2: The Pilgrims, the Mayflower Compact, and the First Thanksgiving in America

62 First Charter of Virginia, April 10, 1606, in *American Historical Documents, 1000-1904*, ed. Charles W. Eliot (New York: P. F. Collier & Son, 1910), 51.

63 James I, Instructions for the Government of Virginia, 1606, in William Stith, *The History of the First Discovery and Settlement of Virginia*, bk. 2 (New York: Reprinted for Joseph Sabin, 1865), 37. The king directed the Virginia Company to see that the "true Word and Service of God be preached, planted, and used…according to the Rites and Doctrine of the Church of England."

64 Hampton Court Conference, 14 January 1604, in T. B. Howell, comp., *A Complete Collection of State Trials and Proceedings for High Treason and Other Crimes and Misdemeanors, 1783*, vol. 2/1603-1627 (London: Printed by T. C. Hansard, 1816), 86.

65 Alexis de Tocqueville, *Democracy in America, 1831-1832*, ed. Richard D. Heffner (New York: Penguin Books, 1956, 1984), 43.

66 William Bradford, *Bradford's History of Plymouth Settlement, 1608-1650*, modern trans. Harold Paget (New York: E . P. Dutton & Co., 1909, 1920), 21, 321.

67 Bradford, *Bradford's History of Plymouth Settlement*, xix.

68 Gaspar Olevian, "Method and Arrangement or Subject of the Whole Work, From *An Epitome of the Institutions*," in John Calvin, *The Institutes of the Christian Religion: A New Translation*, vol. 1, trans. Henry Beveridge (Edinburgh: Printed for Calvin Translation Society, 1845), 34.

69 John Calvin, *The Institutes of the Christian Religion: A New Translation*, vol. 1, bk. 1, trans. Henry Beveridge (Edinburgh: Printed for Calvin Translation Society, 1845), 85, 116, 189.

70 See Amos, *Defending the Declaration*, 165-6.

71 William Ames, *The Marrow of Theology*, trans. John D. Eusden (Grand Rapids, MI: Baker Books, 1997), 107. Calvin had stated of God's providence in his *Institutes of the Christian Religion*, vol. 1, bk. 1, p242: "…(W)e hold that God is the disposer and ruler of all things,--that from the remotest eternity, according to his own wisdom, he decreed what he was to do, and now by his power executes what he decreed. Hence we maintain, that by his providence, not heaven and earth and inanimate creatures only, but also the counsels and wills of men are so governed as to move exactly in the course which he has destined."

72 Ames cites Psalm 145:15, 16; Proverbs 16:9, 33; and Exodus 21:13. Ames cites Deuteronomy 8:3 and Isaiah 28:26. Providence, Ames says, can be ordinary or extraordinary. God sometimes uses unlikely means in order to make His provision more obvious, and He sometimes makes the most suitable means ineffective. Ames cites 1 Samuel 14:6; 1 Corinthians 1:27, 28; Amos 9:5; 2 Chronicles 24:24; Psalms 33:16, 127:1, 2; and Hosea 4:10.

73 Ames cites Psalm 104:19, 20, 29; Acts 17:28; Hebrews 1:3; and Nehemiah 9:6 on God's conservation of creation. Ames cites Psalm 29:10; Genesis 50:20; Job 38:12, 26; Job 5:7, 1:12, 2:6, 38:10; Proverbs 6:6, 30:24-28; Jeremiah 8:7; Psalm 103:21 and 148:8; Isaiah 55:10; 2 Samuel 16:10; and Ezekiel 21:21, 22 on God's governing over His creatures and creation.

74 1 Timothy 6:15: "…He who is the blessed and only Potentate, the King of kings and Lord of lords,…" Revelation 17:14: "for He is Lord of Lords and Kings of kings…" Revelation 19:16: "And He has on His robe and on His thigh a name written: KING OF KINGS AND LORD OF LORDS."

75 Brutus, *Vindiciae*, 19-20. Brutus asserts, "That opinion of Almighty God always remains: 'I will not give my name to another'; I will not transfer my glory to another [Isaiah 48:11, verses footnoted by editor]: that is, I will not hand that power [*potentia*, italicized terms editor's] to anyone, but will always take the highest right [*summum ius*] upon myself. God never divests Himself of His power and authority. He holds a scepter in one hand to restrain raging kings and crush defiant ones, and in the other a pair of scales in order to weigh those who distribute right inequitably [Psalm 2:9, Wisdom 6:4-6]. No more certain insignia of supreme command could be given."

[76] Brutus, *Vindiciae*, 16. See Wisdom 6:4-7, Proverbs 8:15, and Job 12:18-25. Brutus states, "...the Holy Scriptures teach that God rules by His own authority, but kings as if by sufferance of another [*precario*, italicized terms editor's]: God by Himself, and kings through God: that God exercises his own jurisdiction, but kings only a delegated one. It follows, therefore, from Wisdom ch. 6, Proverbs ch. 8, and Job ch. 12 etc., that God's jurisdiction is immeasurable, whilst that of kings is measured; that God's sway [*potentia*] is infinite, whilst that of kings is limited; that the kingdom of God is not circumscribed by any frontiers [*limites*], whilst on the contrary those of kings are restricted to specific regions and bounded by certain boundaries [*cancelli*]."

[77] Niebuhr, *Kingdom of God*, 51, 56.

[78] Richard Baxter, *A Holy Commonwealth*, Thesis 24, 1659, ed. William Lamont (Cambridge: Cambridge U Press, 1994), 56.

[79] Richard Baxter, *A Holy Commonwealth*, Thesis 28, 1659, ed. William Lamont (Cambridge: Cambridge U Press, 1994), 58.

[80] John Robinson and John Ashton, *The Works of John Robinson: Pastor of the Pilgrim Fathers*, vol. 1 (London: John Snow, 1851), 311; John Robinson, *A Justification of Separation From the Church of England Against Mr. Richard Bernard His Invective, 1610*, in *The Works of John Robinson*, vol. 2, ed. Robert Ashton (London: John Snow, 1851), 40.

[81] Thomas Hooker, *A Survey of the Summe of Church-Discipline* (London: Printed by A. M. for John Bellamy, 1648), 16. Isaiah 33:22 states, "For the Lord is our Judge, The Lord is our Lawgiver, The Lord is our King; He will save us." This verse is cited in Hooker's *Survey of the Summe of Church Discipline* in 1648 and Cotton's *Abstract of the Laws of New England* in 1641. See also Niebuhr, *Kingdom of God*, 53.

[82] John Higginson, Excerpts from "The Cause of God and His People in New England," 1663, in *The Ecclesiastical History of New England*, vol. 2, Joseph B. Felt (Boston, MA: Congregational Library Association, 1862), 303-304; John Cotton, *Practical Commentary Or An Exposition With Observations, Reasons and Uses Upon the First Epistle General of John, 1654* (1654; repr. Whitefish, MT: Kessinger Publishing, 2003), 394. Referencing 1 Kings 8:57-59, Puritan Rev. John Higginson of Salem also later preached on Christ's sole headship in the church: "...[T]he knee of Magistracie is to bow at the name of Jesus. ... Reformation of Religion according to God's Word; that Christ alone might be acknowledged by us as the only head, Lord, and Law-giver in his Church; that his written word might be acknowledged as the onely Rule; that onely and all his institutions might be observed and enjoyed by us, and that with puritie and libertie, with peace and power." 1 Kings 8:57-59: "May the Lord our God be with us, as He was with our fathers. May He not leave us nor forsake us, that He may incline our hearts to Himself, to walk in all His ways, and to keep His commandments and His statutes and His judgments, which He commanded our fathers. And may these words of mine, with which I have made supplication before the Lord, be near the Lord our God day and night, that He may maintain the cause of His servant and the cause of His people Israel, as each day may require...." Puritan minister Rev. John Cotton of Massachusetts similarly asserted Christ as governor based on Acts 5:31 and Isaiah 9:6. Cotton writes, "If we have Christ for our Saviour, we must have him for our Prince, Act. 5.31. that is, we must resigne up our selves, and submit our selves to him. Isa. 9.6. *Unto us a Son is born, to us a childe is given*. And why, how shall I know whether the Son be given me? Why, *the government is upon his shoulders.*" Acts 5:31 states, "Him God has exalted to His right hand *to be* Prince and Savior...." Isaiah 9:6 states, "...And the Government will be upon His shoulder."

[83] Paul Johnson, *A History of the American People* (New York: HarperCollins, 1997), 28.

[84] William Bradford, *Of Plymouth Plantation, 1602-1646*, excerpt in *The Mayflower Papers: Selected Writings of Colonial New England*, eds. Nathanial Philbrick and Thomas Philbrick (New York: Penguin Classics, 2007), 14.

[85] Tocqueville, *Democracy in America*, ed. Richard D. Heffner, 42-43.

[86] Niebuhr, *Kingdom of God*, 51, 56.

[87] Tocqueville, *Democracy in America*, ed. Richard Heffner, 44.

[88] Daniel J. Elazar, "The Political Theory of Covenant: Biblical Origins and Modern Developments," *Covenant, Polity, and Constitutionalism, Publius: The Journal of Federalism* 10, no. 4 (1980): 6, 26, 27.

[89] Elazar, "Political Theory of Covenant," 11.

[90] Elazar, "Political Theory of Covenant," 11.

[91] See Elazar, "Political Theory of Covenant," 13-14.

[92] Charles S. McCoy and J. Wayne Baker, *Fountainhead of Federalism: Heinrich Bullinger and the Covenantal Tradition* (Louisville, KY: Westminster/John Knox Press, 1991), 12-13, 25, 37, 61, 90, 52, 56, 73. See also Heinrich Bullinger, "A Brief Exposition of the One and Eternal Testament or Covenant of God," 1534, in *Fountainhead of Federalism: Heinrich Bullinger and the Covenantal Tradition*, Charles S. McCoy and J. Wayne Baker (Louisville, KY: Westminster/John Knox Press, 1991), 103, 107. The Bullinger excerpt is taken from Bullinger's 1534 treatise, *The One and Eternal Testament or Covenant of God*.

[93] McCoy and Baker, *Fountainhead*, 24-26, 40.

[94] Westminster General Assembly, *The Confession of Faith, the Larger and Shorter Catechisms, 1647* (Printed by W. Duncan, 1768), 103-104, 106.

[95] Genesis 17:2, 4, 7-11 tells of this covenant in which God says to Abraham, "I will make My covenant between Me and you, and will multiply you exceedingly. ... As for Me, behold, My covenant is with you, and you shall be a father of many nations. ... And I will establish My covenant between Me and you and your descendants after you. Also I give to you and your descendants after you the land in which you are a stranger, all the land of Canaan, as an everlasting possession; and I will be their God. ... As for you, you shall keep My covenant, you and your descendants after you throughout their generations. This is My covenant which you shall keep, between Me and you and your descendants after you: Every male child among you shall be circumcised...and it shall be a sign of the covenant between Me and you."

[96] Genesis 22:15-18 states, "Then the Angel of the LORD called to Abraham a second time out of heaven, and said: "By Myself I have sworn, says the LORD, because you have done this thing, and have not withheld your son, your only *son*—blessing I will bless you, and multiplying I will multiply your descendants as the stars of the heaven and as the sand which *is* on the seashore; and your descendants shall possess the gate of their enemies. In your seed all the nations of the earth shall be blessed, because you have obeyed My voice."

[97] Exodus 20:1-17 states, "And God spoke all these words, saying: 'I *am* the LORD your God, who brought you out of the land of Egypt, out of the house of bondage. You shall have no other gods before Me. You shall not make for yourself a carved image—any likeness *of anything* that *is* in heaven above, or that *is* in the earth beneath, or that *is* in the water under the earth; you shall not bow down to them nor serve them. For I, the LORD your God, *am* a jealous God, visiting the iniquity of the fathers upon the children to the third and fourth *generations* of those who hate Me, but showing mercy to thousands, to those who love Me and keep My commandments. You shall not take the name of the LORD your God in vain, for the LORD will not hold *him* guiltless who takes His name in vain. Remember the Sabbath day, to keep it holy. Six days you shall labor and do all your work, but the seventh day *is* the Sabbath of the LORD your God. *In it* you shall do no work: you, nor your son, nor your daughter, nor your male servant, nor your female servant, nor your cattle, nor your stranger who *is* within your gates. For *in* six days the LORD made the heavens and the earth, the sea, and all that *is* in them, and rested the seventh day. Therefore the LORD blessed the Sabbath day and hallowed it. Honor your father and your mother, that your days may be long upon the land which the LORD your God is giving you. You shall not murder. You shall not commit adultery. You shall not steal. You shall not bear false witness against your neighbor. You shall not covet your neighbor's house; you shall not covet your neighbor's wife, nor his male servant, nor his female servant, nor his ox, nor his donkey, nor anything that *is* your neighbor's.'"

[98] The Ten Commandments in Exodus 20:1-17: "And God spoke all these words, saying: 'I *am* the LORD your God, who brought you out of the land of Egypt, out of the house of bondage. You shall have no other gods before Me. You shall not make for yourself a carved image—any likeness *of anything* that *is* in heaven above, or that *is* in the earth beneath, or that *is* in the water under the earth; you shall not bow down to them nor serve them. For I, the LORD your God, *am* a jealous God, visiting the iniquity of the fathers upon the children to the third and fourth *generations* of those who hate Me, but showing mercy to thousands, to those who love Me and keep My commandments. You shall not take the name of the LORD your God in vain, for the LORD will not hold *him* guiltless who takes His name in vain. Remember the Sabbath day, to keep it holy. Six days you shall labor and do all your work, but the seventh day *is* the Sabbath of the LORD your God. *In it* you shall do no work: you, nor your son, nor your daughter, nor your male servant, nor your female servant, nor your cattle, nor your stranger who *is* within your gates. For *in* six days the LORD made the heavens and the earth, the sea, and all that *is* in them, and rested the seventh day. Therefore the LORD blessed the Sabbath day and hallowed it. Honor your father and your mother, that your days may be long upon the land which the LORD your God is giving you. You shall not murder. You shall not commit adultery. You shall not steal. You shall not bear false witness against your neighbor. You shall not covet your neighbor's house; you shall not covet your neighbor's wife, nor his male servant, nor his female servant, nor his ox, nor his donkey, nor anything that *is* your neighbor's."

[99] For the full text of these covenants, see Exodus 20:1-17 and 34:10-28.

[100] Jeremiah 31:31-34 states, "Behold, the days are coming, says the LORD, when I will make a new covenant with the house of Israel and with the house of Judah— not according to the covenant that I made with their fathers in the day *that* I took them by the hand to lead them out of the land of Egypt, My covenant which they broke, though I was a husband to them, says the LORD. But this *is* the covenant that I will make with the house of Israel after those days, says the LORD: I will put My law in their minds, and write it on their hearts; and I will be their God, and they shall be My people. No more shall every man teach his neighbor, and every man his brother, saying, 'Know the LORD,' for they all shall know Me, from the least of them to the greatest of them, says the LORD. For I will forgive their iniquity, and their sin I will remember no more."

[101] See also Mark 14:24, Luke 22:20, 1 Corinthians 11:25, and Hebrews 12:24.

[102] See also 2 Corinthians 3:5-6 which states, "Not that we are sufficient of ourselves to think of anything as *being* from ourselves, but our sufficiency *is* from God, who also made us sufficient as ministers of the new covenant, not of the letter but of the Spirit; for the letter kills, but the Spirit gives life."

[103] Elazar, "Political Theory of Covenant," 26.

[104] Elazar, "Political Theory of Covenant," 26.

[105] Elazar, "Political Theory of Covenant," 24.

[106] Daniel J. Elazar, *Covenant & Commonwealth: From Christian Separation Through the Protestant Reformation* (New Brunswick, NJ: Transaction Publishers, 1996), 165; Leonard J. Trinterud, "The Origins of Puritanism," *Church History* 20, no. 1 (Mar., 1951): 41; Elazar, "Political Theory of Covenant," 20. See Bullinger's 1525 Isaiah commentaries.

[107] Heinrich Bullinger, "A Brief Exposition of the One and Eternal Testament or Covenant of God," 1534, in *Fountainhead of Federalism: Heinrich Bullinger and the Covenantal Tradition*, Charles S. McCoy and J. Wayne Baker (Louisville, KY: Westminster/John Knox Press, 1991), 103, 107. In Covenant Theology, particular individuals typically represent and act for entire human groups or communities. Adam, for example, represents all mankind in his creation and fall. Jesus Christ likewise represents all mankind in His life and sonship with God.

[108] Elazar, "Political Theory of Covenant," 5, 8-9.

[109] McCoy and Baker, *Fountainhead*, 52-53.

[110] Theodore Beza, *The Right of Magistrates Over Their Subjects, 1572* (Constitution Society, 1995-2013), http://www.constitution.org/cmt/beza/magistrates.htm. See Question 6, A Restatement of the Sixth Question, para. 16.

[111] Beza, *Right of Magistrates.* http://www.constitution.org/cmt/beza/magistrates.htm. See Question 6, A Restatement of the Sixth Question, Epilogue and Conclusion, I, para. 1.

[112] Brutus, *Vindiciae*, 21.

[113] See Witte, *Reformation of Rights*, 135-137, and Beza, *On the Rights of Magistrates*, 12-14. Beza and then *Vindiciae* also argued against religious persecution. Brutus, *Vindiciae*, 22-23, 41. Vindiciae notes, for example, the terms of Israel's covenant with God based on Deuteronomy 27, 29, 30, and 31 and Joshua 5 and 24. If the Israelites honored God and His law they prospered. If they broke His law, they could be scattered or destroyed. The tract also stresses the need for a *free* people to enter covenants. It poses, "For why might we insist that the consent of the whole people is required, that Israel or Judah is bound to the observance of divine law, and that it should solemnly promise that it would forever be the people of God, unless we equally maintain that authority or capacity is conceded to it both to free itself from perjury and the church from devastation? For what would be the purpose of the covenant with the people to the effect that it should be the people of God, if it allowed itself to be seduced by kings in favour of foreign Gods, or if it were bound to do so? For how might God be worshipped in pure fashion, if the people is in the position of a slave [*servi loco*, brackets editor's], with whom there can be no obligation? If, in short, it were not lawful to give the people the capacity to fulfil what it had promised, God would surely not have sealed a covenant with one who had neither the right to promise nor to fulfil what had been promised? Is it not much more likely that in sealing a covenant with the people and stipulating what should be done, He wanted to show plainly that the people had the right to promise this, to fulfil it, and to take responsibility for fulfilling it?"

[114] Brutus, *Vindiciae*, 21-50.

[115] George Klosko, ed., *The Oxford Handbook of the History of Political Philosophy* (Oxford, UK: Oxford U Press, 2011), 579-581.

[116] See Francisco Suarez, *Selections From Three Works of Francisco Suarez, S. J.: The Translations*, vol. 2, trans. Gwladys L. Williams, ed. Henry Davis (Oxford: Clarendon Press, 1944).

[117] See Rutherford, *Lex Rex*, Question XIV, 54-61.

[118] Johannes Althusius, *Politics Methodically Set Forth, and Illustated With Sacred and Profane Examples*, 3rd ed., abridged, in *The Politics of Johannes Althusius*, trans. Frederick S. Carney (Boston, MA: Beacon Press, 1964; Constitution Society, 1995-2013), http://www.constitution.org/alth/alth.htm; McCoy and Baker, *Fountainhead*, 46.

[119] Klosko, *Oxford Handbook*, 578.

[120] McCoy and Baker, *Fountainhead*, 55-6; Althusius, *Politics*, ch. 1, 1-2.

[121] Althusius, *Politics*, ch. 1, 26-27; McCoy and Baker, *Fountainhead*, 56.

[122] McCoy and Baker, *Fountainhead*, 53-54. See also Michael H. Lessnoff, ed., *Social Contract Theory: Readings in Social and Political Theory* (New York: New York U Press, 1990) or Michael H. Lessnoff, *Social Contract: Issues in Political Theory* (Atlantic Highlands, NJ: Humanities Press International, 1986).

[123] Elazar, "Political Theory of Covenant," 20; McCoy and Baker, *Fountainhead*, 50; Althusius, *Politics*, 117.

[124] McCoy and Baker, *Fountainhead*, 21; Elazar, *Covenant & Commonwealth*, 165.

[125] See Witte, *Reformation of Rights*, 135-137, and Beza, *On the Rights of Magistrates*, 12-14. Beza and then *Vindiciae* also argued against religious persecution.

[126] See Edward Winslow, *Hypocrisie Unmasked* (1646; repr., Bedford, MA: Applewood Books, 2009), 97. Before the Pilgrims set sail for America, their pastor Rev. John Robinson reminded them to keep their religious covenants. They had promised to walk according to the Bible and in peaceful fellowship with one another. Keeping their covenants with God, they believed, insured the favor and blessings of God. Pilgrim voyager Edward Winslow recounted Robinson's message: "Here also he put us in mind of our Church-Covenant…whereby wee promise and covenant with God and one with another, to receive whatsoever light or truth shall be made known to us from his written Word…."

[127] See Elazar, "Political Theory of Covenant," 11, 22-23; Lutz, "From Covenant to Constitution," 107-110, 117.

[128] Daniel Webster, "Pilgrim Festival at New York in 1850," in *The Works of Daniel Webster*, vol. 2, 20th ed. (Boston: Little, Brown, and Co., 1890), 522.

[129] Elazar, "Political Theory of Covenant," 22-23.

[130] See Lutz, "From Covenant to Constitution," 125; Elazar, "Political Theory of Covenant," 5, 8-9; Amos, *Defending the Declaration*, 128-129.

[131] Johnson, *History of the American People*, 30.

[132] Benjamin F. Morris, *The Christian Life and Character of the Civil Institutions of the United States* (1864; repr. Oxford: Benediction Classics, 2010), 51-54.

[133] George B. Cheever, ed., *The Journal of the Pilgrims at Plymouth in New England, 1620*, 2nd ed., by William Bradford (New York: John Wiley, 1848), 337. See also David Gibbs, Jr., *One Nation Under God: Ten Things Every Christian Should Know* (Seminole, FL: Christian Law Association, 2005), 32-33, 36.

[134] Luther, *Appeal to the Ruling Class*, 415. Luther argues, "…if the pope acts contrary to Scripture, we ourselves are bound to abide by Scripture. We must punish him and constrain him, according to the passage, "If thy brother sin against thee, go and tell him between thee and him alone; but if he hear thee not, take with thee one or two more; and if he hear them not, tell it to the church; and if he hear not the church, let him be unto thee as a Gentile" [Matt. 18:15-17, bracket editor's]. This passage commands each

member to exercise concern for his fellow; much more is it our duty when the wrongdoer is one who rules over us all alike, and who causes much harm and offence to the rest by his conduct. And if I am to lay a charge against him before the church, then I must call it together."

135 Luther, *Appeal to the Ruling Class*, 416. Luther states, "…if the pope acts contrary to Scripture, we ourselves are bound to abide by Scripture. We must punish him and constrain him, according to the passage, "If thy brother sin against thee, go and tell him between thee and him alone; but if he hear thee not, take with thee one or two more; and if he hear them not, tell it to the church; and if he hear not the church, let him be unto thee as a Gentile" [Matt. 18:15-17]. This passage commands each member to exercise concern for his fellow; much more is it our duty when the wrongdoer is one who rules over us all alike, and who causes much harm and offence to the rest by his conduct. And if I am to lay a charge against him before the church, then I must call it together.
Romanists have no Scriptural basis for their contention that the pope alone has the right to summon or sanction a council. …
… No one in Christendom has authority to do evil, or to forbid evil from being resisted. The church has no authority except to promote the greater good. Hence, if the pope should exercise his authority to prevent a free council, and so hinder the reform of the church, we ought to pay no regard to him and his authority. … …for this authority of his would be presumptuous and empty. He does not possess it, and he would fall an easy victim to a passage of Scripture; for Paul says to the Corinthians, "For God gave us authority, not to cast down Christendom, but to build it up" [II Cor. 10:8]. Who would pretend to ignore this text? Only the power of the devil and the Antichrist attempting to arrest whatever serves the reform of Christendom. Wherefore, we must resist that power with life and limb, and might and main." 2 Corinthians 10:8 Paul says to church, "For even if I should boast somewhat more about our authority, which the Lord gave us for edification and not for your destruction, I shall not be ashamed…."

136 Bradford, *Bradford's History of Plymouth Settlement,* trans. Harold Paget, 55-56. In Deuteronomy 1:13 Moses speaks to thepeople, "'Choose wise, understanding, and knowledgeable men from among your tribes, and I will make them heads over you.'" Romans 13:1-5 states, "Let every soul be subject to the governing authorities. For there is no authority except from God, and the authorities that exist are appointed by God. … For he is God's minister to you for good."

137 Cheever, ed., *Journal of the Pilgrims*, 337.

138 William Bradford and Edward Winslow, *Mourt's Relation: A Journal of the Pilgrims at Plymouth, 1622*, ed. Dwight B. Heath (1622; Bedford, MA: Applewood Books, 1963), 81-82.

139 Bradford, *Bradford's History of Plymouth Settlement*, trans. Harold Paget, 115-116.

140 John Masefield, ed., *Chronicles of the Pilgrim Fathers*, Vol. 480. (1910; repr., London: J. M. Dent, 1920), 335. See also pp. 334-336; William Bradford and Edward Winslow, *Journal of the Pilgrims at Plymouth in New England, in 1620*, 2nd edition, ed. George B. Cheever (1622; New York: John Wiley, 1849), 284.

141 Masefield, ed., *Chronicles of the Pilgrim Fathers*, 337; Bradford and Winslow, *Journal of the Pilgrims*, ed. Cheever, 286.

142 George E. Bowman, ed. *The Mayflower Descendant: A Quarterly Magazine of Pilgrim Genealogy and History*. Vol. 7. No. 3. Whole No. 27. (Boston, MA: Massachusetts Society of Mayflower Descendants, July 1905), 152; Evert A. and George L. Duyckinck, eds., *Cyclopaedia of American Literature*. Vol 1. (New York: Charles Scribner, 1855), 30-31.

143 Bradford, *Bradford's History of Plymouth Settlement*, trans. Harold Paget, 226.

144 Nathaniel Morton, *New-England's Memorial or, A Brief Relation of the Most Memorable and Remarkable Passages of the Providence of God, Manifested to the Planters of New-England in America*, 6th ed. (1669; repr., Boston, MA: Congregational Board of Publication, 1855), 24-26.

Chapter 3: The Puritans Create Bible Commonwealths in Early America

145 George Laughead and Lynn H. Nelson, eds., "Note on Charter of Massachusetts Bay, 1629," in *AMDOCS: Documents for the Study of American History*, *WWW Virtual Library*, <http://www.vlib.us/amdocs/texts/massbay_note.html> (2005-2010).

146 John Winthrop, "Reasons to Be Considered for Justifying the Undertakers of the Intended Plantation in New England, 1629," in *Envisioning America: English plans for the colonization of North America, 1580-1640*, ed. Peter C. Mancall (Boston, MA: Bedford Books, 1995), 135. In laying out the reasons for coming to America, Winthrop stated, "…[G]od hath provided this place [America] to be a refuge for many whom he meanes to save out of the generall callamitie, and seeinge the Church hath no place lefte to flie into but the wildernesse what better worke cann there be, then to goe before & provide Tabernacles, and food for her…."

147 Winthrop, "Reasons to Be Considered," 133-136. See also Cotton Mather, *Magnalia*, 44. See also John Cotton, "Sermon on God's Promise to His Plantations" in *Masterpieces of Eloquence: Famous Orations of Great World Leaders From Early Greece to the Present Time*, Volume 4, ed. Mayo W. Hazeltine et al. (New York: P. F. Collier & Son, 1905), 1437. Regarding the Puritans' intent to spread the Gospel to the natives, Pastor Rev. Cotton Mather stated of their colony in his *Magnalia* that "as for *one* of these English plantations, this [planting of the Gospel] was not only a *main end*, but the *sole end* upon which it was erected.'" The Puritans, however, were not as successful in this goal as in the others. Like some explorers before them, they often engaged in conflict with the natives. Still, the Puritans believed God would provide space for them to settle and aimed to convert the natives in a humane manner. Pastor Rev. John Cotton instructed the Puritans in his "Sermon on God's Promise,"

"...[O]ffend not the poor natives, but, as you partake of their land, so make them partakers of your precious faith; as you reap their temporals, so feed them with your spirituals: win them to the love of Christ, for whom Christ died."

[148] John Winthrop, *A Model of Christian Charity (1630)*, in *Puritan Political Ideas, 1558-1794*, ed. Edmund S. Morgan (1965; repr., Indianapolis, IN: Hackett Publishing, 2003), 90. Winthrop states, "The end is to improve our lives to doe [do] more service to the Lord the comforte [comfort] and encrease [increase] of the body of christe [Christ] whereof wee [wherefore we] are members that our selves and posterity may be the better preserved from the Common corrupcions [corruptions] of this evill [evil] world to serve the Lord and worke [work] out our Salvation under the power and purity of his [God's] holy Ordinances."

[149] Winthrop, "Reasons to Be Considered," 133. See also Winthrop, *Model of Christian Charity*, 90. In his *Model* sermon, Winthrop stated, "...[I]t is by a mutuall consent through a speciall overruleing providence, and a more then an ordinary approbation of the Churches of Christ to seeke out a place of Cohabitation and Consorteshipp under a due forme of Government both civill and ecclesiasticall."

[150] Winthrop, *Model of Christian Charity*, 90, 92.

[151] Clyde A. Holbrook, "Crime and Sin in Puritan Massachusetts" in *Crimes, Values, and Religion*, eds. James M. Day and William S. Laufer (Westport, CT: Ablex/Greenwood Publishers, 1987), 2-3.

[152] Winthrop, *Model of Christian Charity*, 92, 93.

[153] Winthrop, *Model of Christian Charity*, 92-93.

[154] See Cotton, "Sermon on God's Promise," 1422, 1424. Like the Pilgrims, the Puritans compared their move to America with the Israelites' Biblical exodus from Egypt and arrival in the Promised Land of Canaan. In his sermon, Rev. Cotton spoke of God's arrangement of a place for them as He had appointed a place for Israel, citing 2 Samuel 7:10: "'Moreover I will appoint a place for my people Israel, and I will plant them, that they may dwell in a place of their own, and move no more.'" Citing Ezekiel 20:6, Rev. Cotton asserted that God was leading the Puritans to America as He had led Israel to Canaan, having "brought them into a land that he had espied for them." Ezekiel 20:6 states, "On that day I [God] raised My hand in an oath to them [Israel], to bring them out of the land of Egypt into a land that I had searched out for them, 'flowing with milk and honey,' the glory of all lands."

[155] Elazar, "Political Theory of Covenant," 23-24.

[156] In Matthew 5:44 Jesus tells his disciples to love others, even their enemies: "But I say to you, love your enemies, bless those who curse you, do good to those who hate you, and pray for those who spitefully use you and persecute you...." In Matthew 7:12, Jesus further tells his disciples to treat all others as they wish to be treated: "Whatever you want men to do to you, do also to them, for this is the Law and the Prophets."

[157] Winthrop, *Model of Christian Charity*, 92-93.

[158] Winthrop, *Model of Christian Charity*, 91-92.

[159] Winthrop, *Model of Christian Charity*, 90.

[160] Winthrop, *Model of Christian Charity*, 90. Winthrop states, "for the work wee have in hand, it is by a mutuall consent through a speciall overruleing providence, and a more then an ordinary approbation of the Churches of Christ to seeke out a place of Cohabitation and Consorteshipp under a due forme of Government both civill and ecclesiasticall. In such cases as this the care of the publique [public] must oversway all private respects, by which not onely [only] conscience, but meare Civill policy doth binde us; for it is a true rule that perticuler [particular] estates cannot subsist in the ruine of the publique."

[161] Elazar, "Political Theory of Covenant," 25.

[162] See Winthrop, *Model of Christian Charity*, 92, 93. Winthrop warned in his *Model* sermon against breaking God's covenant: "...[I]f we shall neglect the observacion of these Articles...the Lord will surely breake out in wrathe against us be revenged of such a perjured people and make us knowe the price of the breache of such a Covenant" and "...[I]f wee shall deale falsely with our god in this worke...and soe cause him to withdrawe his present help from us, wee shall...cause theire [God's servants'] prayers to be turned into Cursses upon us till we be consumed out of the good land whether wee are goeing.... ...[I]f our heartes shall turne away soe that wee will not obey, but shall be seduced and worshipp other Gods our pleasures, and proffitts, and serve them; ...wee shall surely perishe out of the good Land whether wee passe over this vast Sea to possesse it."

[163] Elazar, "Political Theory of Covenant," 24.

[164] Thomas Hooker, Sermon before the Connecticut General Court in Hartford, May 31, 1638, in *The Puritan Tradition in America, 1620-1730*, Revised ed., ed. Alden T. Vaughan (Hanover, NH: U Press of New England, 1997), 83.

[165] See Walter Seth Logan's *Thomas Hooker: The First American Democrat*.

[166] Romans 5:12 states, "...[T]hrough one man [Adam] sin entered the world, and death through sin, and thus death spread to all men, because all sinned...."

[167] John Calvin, *Calvin's Bible Commentaries: Genesis, pt. 1*, 1563, trans. John King (Forgotten Books, 2007), 90.

[168] Martin Luther, *Commentary on St. Paul's Epistle to the Galatians, 1531*, in *Martin Luther: Selections From His Writings*, ed. John Dillenberger (New York: Doubleday, 1961), 139.

[169] Winthrop, *Model of Christian Charity*, 86.

[170] John Winthrop, *The History of New England From 1630 to 1649*, vol. 2, ed. James Savage (Boston, MA: 1826), 229.

[171] Mather, *Magnalia*, vol. 1, 427. This book, written in 1702 by Mathew, means in Latin "The Glorious Works of Christ in America." It is subtitled "The Ecclesiastical History of New England."

[172] Winthrop, *History of New England*, ed. James Savage, 229.

[173] Luther, *Secular Authority*, Section I, 366. Luther states, "We must firmly establish secular law and the sword, that no one may doubt that it is in the world by God's will and ordinance. The passages which establish this are the following: Romans 13 [:1f.], 'Let every soul be subject to power and authority, for there is no power but from God. The power that

is everywhere is ordained of God. He then who resists the power resists God's ordinance. But he who resists God's ordinance shall bring himself under condemnation.' Likewise, I Peter 2 [:13-14], 'Be subject to every kind of human ordinance, whether to the king as supreme, or to the governors, as to those sent of Him for the punishing of the evil and for the reward of the good.'"

[174] Luther, *Commentary on Galatians*, 139-140.

[175] Calvin, *Institutes*, vol. 3, bk. 4, 537. See also pp. 515-519. Calvin states, "'the minister of God to us for good;' we understand from this, that he [the civil officer] is divinely appointed in order that we may be defended by his power and protection against the malice and injuries of wicked men, and may lead peaceable and secure lives. But if it be in vain that he is given to us by the Lord for our protection, unless it be lawful for us to avail ourselves of such an advantage, it clearly follows that we may appeal to him, and apply for his aid, without any violation of piety."

[176] Luther, *Appeal to the Ruling Class*, 410-412, 480. Luther states, "…I maintain, that since the secular authorities are ordained by God to punish evil-doers and to protect the law-abiding, so we ought to leave them free to do their work without let or hindrance everywhere in Christian countries, and without partiality, whether for pope, bishops, pastors, monks, nuns, or anyone else. …
…[W]hat is the purpose of Romanist writers who make laws by which they exempt themselves from the secular Christian authorities? It is simply that they may do evil unpunished, and fulfil what St. Peter said, 'There shall arise false teachers among you, moving among you with false and imaginary sayings, selling you a bad bargain [2 Peter 2:1].'

Hence secular Christian authorities should exercise their office freely and unhindered and without fear, whether it be pope, bishop, or priest with whom they are dealing; if a man is guilty let him pay the penalty. What canon law says to the contrary is Romish presumptuousness and pure invention. For this is what St. Paul says to all Christians, 'Let every soul (I hold that includes the pope's) be subject to the higher powers, for they bear not the sword in vain. They serve God alone, punishing the evil and praising the good' [Rom. 13:1-4]. And St. Peter [I Pet. 2:13, 15], 'Be subject unto every ordinance of man for God's sake, whose will is that it should be so.' …

… The reason is that the social corpus of Christendom includes secular government as one of its component functions. … That is why guilty priests, before being handed over to the secular arm, are previously deprived of the dignities of their office. This would not be right unless the secular 'sword' already possessed authority over them by divine ordinance. Moreover, it is intolerable that in canon law, the freedom, person, and goods of the clergy should be given this exemption, as if laymen were not exactly as spiritual, and as good Christians, as they, or did not equally belong to the church. Why would your person, life, possessions, and honour be exempt, whereas mine are not, although we are equally Christian, with the same baptism, guilt, and spirit and all else? If a priest is killed, a country is placed under interdict; why not also if a farmer is killed? Whence comes such a great difference between two men equally Christians? Simply from human law and fabrications. …

There is no longer any defense against punishment where sin exists. St. Gregory himself wrote that, while we are all equal, guilt makes one man subject to others. All this shows plainly how the Romanists deal with Christian people, robbing them of their freedom without any warrant from Scripture, but by sheer wantonness. But God and the apostles made them subject to the secular 'sword.'"

[177] See John Eliot, *The Christian Commonwealth or, The Civil Policy of The Rising Kingdom of Jesus Christ* in *Collections of the Massachusetts Historical Society*, vol. 9, 3rd series (Boston, MA: Little, Brown, & Co., 1846), 134. Puritan John Eliot expressed, "There is undoubtedly a forme of Civil Government instituted by God himself in the holy Scriptures; whereby any Nation may enjoy all the ends and effects of Government in the best manner; were they but perswaded to make trial of it. We should derogate from the sufficiency and perfection of the Scriptures, if we should deny it."

[178] Benjamin Hart, *Faith & Freedom: The Christian Roots of American Liberty* (Christian Defense Fund, 1997), 103, 106-107.

[179] Connecticut Secretary of State, The Fundamental Orders of Connecticut, 1639, in *State of Connecticut Register and Manuel, 1922* (Hartford, CT: State of Connecticut, 1922), 39.

[180] Niebuhr, *Kingdom of God*, 77.

[181] John Cotton, "Limitation of Government," 1646, in *Political Thought in the United States: A Documentary History*, ed. Lyman T. Sargent (New York: New York U Press, 1997), 36-8. The original source of the sermon is John Cotton, *An Exposition Upon the Thirteenth Chapter of the Revelation* (London: Printed for Livewel Chapman), 1655. In Jeremiah 3:5, God says to the people of Israel, "Behold, you have spoken and done evil things, As you were able." This sermon was published in 1655.

[182] John Winthrop, "A Replye to the Answ: Made to the Discourse About the Neg. Vote," in *Life and Letters of John Winthrop*, 1630-1649, vol. 2, 2nd ed., ed. Robert C. Winthrop (Boston: Little, Brown, & Co., 1869), 430.

[183] Calvin, *Institutes*, vol. 3, bk. 4, ch. 20, 520-521. In Isaiah 49:22-23 God says to the people of Israel, "'Behold, I will lift My hand in an oath to the nations, And set up My standard for the peoples; They shall bring your sons in *their* arms, And your daughters shall be carried on *their* shoulders; Kings shall be your foster fathers, And their queens your nursing mothers….'" In 1 Timothy 2:1-2 the Apostle Paul says to the disciple Timothy, "Therefore I exhort first of all that supplications, prayers, intercessions, *and* giving of thanks be made for all men, for kings and all who are in authority, that we may lead a quiet and peaceable life in all godliness and reverence."

[184] Luther, *Appeal to the Ruling Class*, 422.

[185] The Ten Commandments in Exodus 20:1-17: "And God spoke all these words, saying: 'I *am* the LORD your God, who brought you out of the land of Egypt, out of the house of bondage. You shall have no other gods before Me. You shall not make for yourself a carved image—any likeness *of anything* that *is* in heaven above, or that *is* in the earth beneath, or that *is* in the water under the earth; you shall not bow down to them nor serve them. For I, the LORD your God, *am* a jealous God, visiting the iniquity of the fathers upon the children to the third and fourth *generations* of those who hate Me, but showing mercy to

thousands, to those who love Me and keep My commandments. You shall not take the name of the LORD your God in vain, for the LORD will not hold *him* guiltless who takes His name in vain. Remember the Sabbath day, to keep it holy. Six days you shall labor and do all your work, but the seventh day *is* the Sabbath of the LORD your God. *In it* you shall do no work: you, nor your son, nor your daughter, nor your male servant, nor your female servant, nor your cattle, nor your stranger who *is* within your gates. For *in* six days the LORD made the heavens and the earth, the sea, and all that *is* in them, and rested the seventh day. Therefore the LORD blessed the Sabbath day and hallowed it. Honor your father and your mother, that your days may be long upon the land which the LORD your God is giving you. You shall not murder. You shall not commit adultery. You shall not steal. You shall not bear false witness against your neighbor. You shall not covet your neighbor's house; you shall not covet your neighbor's wife, nor his male servant, nor his female servant, nor his ox, nor his donkey, nor anything that *is* your neighbor's."

[186] Calvin, *Institutes*, vol. 3, bk. 4, ch. 20, sect. 15, 534. Calvin writes, "The moral law, therefore, with which I shall begin, being comprised in two leading articles, of which one simply commands us to worship God with pure faith and piety, and the other enjoins us to embrace men with sincere love; this law, I say, is the true and eternal rule of righteousness, prescribed to men of all ages and nations, who wish to conform their lives to the will of God. For this is his eternal and immutable will, that he himself be worshipped by us all, and that we mutually love one another."

[187] Andrew L. Stone, *A Sermon Delivered Before the Executive and Legislative Departments of the Government of Massachusetts at the Annual Election,* 4 January 1865 (Boston, MA: Wright & Potter, 1865), 18.

[188] Book of the General Laws and Liberties of Massachusetts, 1647, in *America's Founding Charters: Primary Documents of Colonial and Revolutionary Era Governance*, vol. 1, ed. Jon L. Wakelyn (Westport, CT: Greenwood Press, 2006), 97-98.

[189] Rule of Law is supported in verses like Leviticus 24:22, Deuteronomy 1:17, 17:10-11, Proverbs 24:23, and John 7:24. Leviticus 24:22 states, "You shall have the same law for the stranger and for one from your own country; for I *am* the LORD your God.'" Deuteronomy 1:17 states, "'You shall not show partiality in judgment; you shall hear the small as well as the great; you shall not be afraid in any man's presence, for the judgment *is* God's. The case that is too hard for you, bring to me, and I will hear it.'" Proverbs 24:23 states, "These *things* also *belong* to the wise: *It is* not good to show partiality in judgment."

[190] Calvin, *Institutes*, vol. 1, 471.

[191] Calvin, *Institutes*, vol. 3, bk. 4, 534-535. Some Bible verses relating to equity include Deuteronomy 1:17, Psalm 98:9, Psalm 99:4, Acts 10:34-35, and Romans 2:9-11.

[192] Calvin, *Institutes*, vol. 3, bk. 4, ch. 20, sect. 16, 535.

[193] Thomas Hooker to John Winthrop, Fall 1638, in *Collections of the Connecticut Historical Society*, vol. 1 (Hartford, CT: Published for the Society, 1860), 11. Deuteronomy 17:10-11 states, "You shall do according to the sentence which they pronounce upon you in that place which the LORD chooses. And you shall be careful to do according to all that they order you. 11 According to the sentence of the law in which they instruct you, according to the judgment which they tell you, you shall do; you shall not turn aside *to* the right hand or *to* the left from the sentence which they pronounce upon you." Acts 5:26-32 states, "Then the captain went with the officers and brought them without violence, for they feared the people, lest they should be stoned. And when they had brought them, they set *them* before the council. And the high priest asked them, saying, 'Did we not strictly command you not to teach in this name? And look, you have filled Jerusalem with your doctrine, and intend to bring this Man's blood on us!' But Peter and the *other* apostles answered and said: 'We ought to obey God rather than men. The God of our fathers raised up Jesus whom you murdered by hanging on a tree. Him God has exalted to His right hand *to be* Prince and Savior, to give repentance to Israel and forgiveness of sins. And we are His witnesses to these things, and *so* also *is* the Holy Spirit whom God has given to those who obey Him.'" Acts 4:18-20 states: "And when they [high priests] called them [Apostles Peter and John], they charged them no to utter anything at all nor teached based upon the name of Jesus. But Peter and John answered and said to them, Whether it is right in the sight of God to listen to you rather than to God, you judge; For we cannot but speak the things which we have seen and heard."

[194] Niebuhr, *Kingdom of God*, 59.

[195] Sections 39 and 40 of the Magna Carta asserted Due Process of Law, stating, "No free men shall be taken or imprisoned or disseised or exiled or in any way destroyed, nor will we go upon him nor send upon him, except by lawful judgment of his peers or by the law of the land. To no one will we sell, to no one will we refuse or delay, right or justice." The Magna Carta (The Great Charter), *Constitution Society*, ed. Jon Roland <http://www.constitution.org/eng/magnacar.htm> (1994-2010) (accessed April 2012).

[196] Johnson, *History of the American People*, 44.

[197] David C. Gibbs, Jr., *One Nation Under God: Ten Things Every Christian Should Know* (Seminole, FL: Christian Law Association, 2005), 40, 41.

[198] Connecticut Secretary of State, The Fundamental Orders of Connecticut, 1639, in *State of Connecticut Register and Manuel, 1922* (Hartford, CT: State of Connecticut, 1922), 39.

[199] Massachusetts General Court, Massachusetts Body of Liberties, 1641, in *American Historical Documents: 1000-1904*, vol. 43, ed. Charles W. Eliot (New York: P. F. Collier & Son), 70.

[200] Thomas Hooker, Sermon before the Connecticut General Court in Hartford, May 31, 1638, in *The Puritan Tradition in America, 1620-1730*, Revised ed., ed. Alden T. Vaughan (Hanover, NH: U Press of New England, 1997), 83.

[201] Martin Luther, *Pagan Servitude of the Church*, 1520, in *Martin Luther: Selections From His Writings*, ed. John Dillenberger (New York: Anchor Books/Doubleday, 1961), 320; Luther, *Commentary on Galatians*, 152; Luther, *Ninety-Five Theses*, 496.

[202] Luther, *Appeal to the Ruling Class*, 413.

[203] Hooker, *Summe of Church-Discipline*, 214-216. Hooker states, "Key, being an ensigne of power: by *keyes* in the plural *all* delegated power for the ordering of the affaires of the Church, is here understood, as the use of the keyes expressed in the words doth fully evidence. For all power that the Lord Christ hath betrusted his Church withal, aimes at this end, to open and shut, *binde and loose.* … These *keyes* and power must be given to a *single society* (as Mr. *Rutherford* is wont to speak) i. e. to a *sort or condition* of men under some *speciall* relation. *To thee* as a single society, not to them. … This *single society* under such a relation and respect, *share* alike in equality of this power promised to them, the reason is this: Those which have the same commission share alike in the same and equall power, because the power they do possesse and partake of issues only from their commission, but there is but one and the same commission given to all: *I will give to thee* &c. … This *single* society here related unto, *cannot* be the *condition of Rulers*: because to the persons here intended *all* power is given. But *all* power is not given to *the Rulers* firstly. For there is a power before the power of Rulers, to wit power of election, and so admission into their places. And that both these acts imply a power, is thus made plain. An office is a *key*, and consequently comes under the *power of the keyes*: and to give that key implies a *power*. 2. If excommunication argues a power, then also admission doth the like, in that there is a parity of reason on both sides: one gives that, which another takes away. … Hence it followes undeniably, These keys, and the power signified by them, must be given to such who have some of this power *firstly*, and *formally*, and *originally*, and *virtually* can give the rest of the power, which so given, may be fully exercised in all the acts of binding and loosing, according to all the necessities of the Church and intendment of our Saviour Christ. And this may readily be accomplished and easily apprehended to be done by a Church of beleevers: They can admit, elect; this *formally* belongs to them: and officers being elected by them, the whole government of the Church, will then go on in all the operations thereof, and be fit to attain the ends, attended by our Saviour."

[204] Hooker, *Summe of Church-Discipline*, 189-190. Hooker writes, "*No man by nature hath Ecclesiasticall power over another….* As nature gives not this power, so a Civil Ruler should not impose it. … If then nature gives not this: nor Civil authority imposeth this: it comes not by constraint; therefore it must come by mutual and free consent. …From all which premises, the inference is undeniable, so far, as by free consent their [the people's, brackets mine] combination [or covenant] goes, so farre, and no further, the power they have one over another reacheth: because this is the foundation, upon which it is built; and the root upon which it growes…."

[205] Hooker, *Summe of Church-Discipline*, 368-371. Hooker states, "…*[T]here is a communicating of power* by Voluntary Subjection when, though there be *no Office-power, formaliter* [sic] in the people, yet they be willingly yeelding themselves to be ruled by another, desiring and calling of him to take that rule; he accepting of what they yeeld, possessing that right which they put upon him by free consent; *hence ariseth this Relation and authority of Office-rule.* The reason; *Those in whose choice it is whether any shall rule over them or no; from their voluntary subjection it is, that the party chosen hath right, and stands possessed of rule and authority over them.*"

[206] Hooker, *Summe of Church-Discipline*, 368-371. Hooker states, "…[T]here is *an act of power put forth in election.* That which causally gives essense and Office-power, that puts forth an act of power, *Ergo.* … *Election* in the *concrete* (as we call it) implies two things; 1. The *choice* on the peoples part: 2. The *acceptation* of the call on his [the pastor's] part. True, *consenting* argues no power; but *their giving of him authority* over them, their calling and by willing *subjection*, delivering up themselves to be ruled by him in Christ, *is an act of Power.* … Hence the *power* that the *Pastor* hath, extends no *larger* nor further then *his own* people; he hath no more then what they give, no more but this: for their subjection is onely [only] from themselves."

[207] Hooker, Sermon before the Connecticut General Court, 83.

[208] Franciscan Province of the Most Holy Name of Jesus, *The 1959 National Catholic Almanac, 55th yr* (Paterson, NJ: St. Anthony's Guild, 1959), 370. See also Thomas Aquinas, *De Rege et Regno*, bk. 1, ch. 6.

[209] Deuteronomy 1:9-18: "And I [Moses] spoke to you [Israel] at that time, saying: 'I alone am not able to bear you. The LORD your God has multiplied you, and here you *are* today, as the stars of heaven in multitude. May the LORD God of your fathers make you a thousand times more numerous than you are, and bless you as He has promised you! How can I alone bear your problems and your burdens and your complaints? Choose wise, understanding, and knowledgeable men from among your tribes, and I will make them heads over you.' And you answered me and said, 'The thing which you have told *us* to do *is* good.' So I took the heads of your tribes, wise and knowledgeable men, and made them heads over you, leaders of thousands, leaders of hundreds, leaders of fifties, leaders of tens, and officers for your tribes.

"Then I commanded your judges at that time, saying, 'Hear *the cases* between your brethren, and judge righteously between a man and his brother or the stranger who is with him. You shall not show partiality in judgment; you shall hear the small as well as the great; you shall not be afraid in any man's presence, for the judgment *is* God's. The case that is too hard for you, bring to me, and I will hear it.' And I commanded you at that time all the things which you should do."

[210] 2 Chronicles 19:4-11 states, "So Jehoshaphat dwelt at Jerusalem; and he went out again among the people from Beersheba to the mountains of Ephraim, and brought them back to the LORD God of their fathers. Then he set judges in the land throughout all the fortified cities of Judah, city by city, and said to the judges, 'Take heed to what you are doing, for you do not judge for man but for the LORD, who *is* with you in the judgment. Now therefore, let the fear of the LORD be upon you; take care and do *it,* for *there is* no iniquity with the LORD our God, no partiality, nor taking of bribes.' Moreover in Jerusalem, for the judgment of the LORD and for controversies, Jehoshaphat appointed some of the Levites and priests, and some of the chief fathers of Israel, when they returned to Jerusalem. And he commanded them, saying, 'Thus you shall act in the fear of the LORD, faithfully and with a loyal heart: Whatever case comes to you from your brethren who dwell in their cities, whether of bloodshed or offenses against law or commandment, against statutes or ordinances, you shall warn them, lest they trespass against the LORD and wrath come upon you and your brethren. Do this, and you will not be guilty. And take notice: Amariah the chief priest *is* over you in all matters of the

LORD; and Zebadiah the son of Ishmael, the ruler of the house of Judah, for all the king's matters; also the Levites *will be* officials before you. Behave courageously, and the LORD will be with the good.'"

[211] Deuteronomy 17:8-11 states, "If a matter arises which is too hard for you to judge, between degrees of guilt for bloodshed, between one judgment or another, or between one punishment or another, matters of controversy within your gates, then you shall arise and go up to the place which the LORD your God chooses. And you shall come to the priests, the Levites, and to the judge *there* in those days, and inquire *of them;* they shall pronounce upon you the sentence of judgment. You shall do according to the sentence which they pronounce upon you in that place which the LORD chooses. And you shall be careful to do according to all that they order you. According to the sentence of the law in which they instruct you, according to the judgment which they tell you, you shall do; you shall not turn aside *to* the right hand or *to* the left from the sentence which they pronounce upon you."

[212] Brutus, *Vindiciae*, 78-79. Brutus states, "But from the time when kings began to extend their frontier…, and the whole people could not assemble in one place without confusion, officers in the kingdom were instituted to protect, ordinarily, the rights of the people—but with the proviso that if the occasion for it should arise, either the whole people or at least some sort of epitome of it might be convoked extraordinarily. …

We see this to have been the arrangement…in the Israelite kingdom, which, in the judgement of almost all political thinkers, was the best constituted. The king had his butlers, his serving men, his chamberlains, and his mayors of the palace or stewards, who looked after his household. And the kingdom had its officers, seventy-one elders and the leaders elected by individual tribes, to take care of the commonwealth in time of peace or war; and then its magistrates in individual towns, each to protect the cities of the kingdom, as the former did the whole kingdom [Numbers 11:16, Exodus 24:1, verses footnoted by editor]. If the gravest matters had to be deliberated upon, these officers convened, and nothing which pertained to the highest affairs of the commonwealth…could be determined without their being consulted. Thus David convoked them when he wanted Solomon to be invested with the kingdom, when he wanted the constitution [Politia] which he had restored to be examined and approved, when the Ark was to be moved, and so on [1 Chronicles 29:1, 2 Samuel 5:3, 1 Chronicles 11:3, 1 Chronicles 13:1-5]. Because they represent the whole people, the whole people was then said to have been assembled.

[213] Hooker, Sermon before the Connecticut General Court, 83.

[214] John Cotton, *Abstract of Laws of New England, 1641* (London: Printed for F. Coules and W. Ley at Paules Chain, 1641), 3.

[215] Hooker, Thomas Hooker to John Winthrop, Fall 1638, 12.

[216] Hooker, Sermon before the Connecticut General Court, 83.

[217] Exodus 18:21: "'Moreover you shall select from all the people able men, such as fear God, men of truth, hating covetousness; and place *such* over them *to be* rulers of thousands, rulers of hundreds, rulers of fifties, and rulers of tens.'"

[218] John Cotton to William Fiennes, Lord Saye and Sele, 1636, in *Puritan Political Ideas, 1558-1794*, ed. Edmund S. Morgan (1965; repr., Indianapolis, IN: Hackett, 2003), 170; Cotton, *Abstract of Laws of New England*, 3.

[219] Samuel Willard, "The Character of a Good Ruler," 1694, in *The Puritans: A Sourcebook of Their Writings*, 2 vols., eds. Perry Miller and Thomas H. Johnson (1963; repr., Mineola, NY: Dover, 2001), 251-253. Deuteronomy 1:17: "'You shall not show partiality in judgment; you shall hear the small as well as the great; you shall not be afraid in any man's presence, for the judgment *is* God's. The case that is too hard for you, bring to me, and I will hear it.'" Deuteronomy 16:19: "'You shall not pervert justice; you shall not show partiality, nor take a bribe, for a bribe blinds the eyes of the wise and twists the words of the righteous.'" Deuteronomy 17:18-19: "'Also it shall be, when he sits on the throne of his kingdom, that he shall write for himself a copy of this law in a book, from *the one* before the priests, the Levites. [19] And it shall be with him, and he shall read it all the days of his life, that he may learn to fear the LORD his God and be careful to observe all the words of this law and these statutes,….'" Psalms 75:10: "'All the horns of the wicked I will also cut off, *But* the horns of the righteous shall be exalted.'"

[220] Roger Williams, *The Bloudy Tenent of Persecution for the Cause of Conscience Discussed: and Mr. Cotton's Letter Examined and Answered, 1644*, ed. Edward B. Underhill (London: Printed for Hanserd Knollys Society by J. Haddon, 1848), 341-342. 1 Peter 1:15 states, "…but as He who called you *is* holy, you also be holy in all *your* conduct…." Williams states, "…Christianity teaches all these to act in their several callings, to a higher ultimate end, from higher principles, in a more heavenly and spiritual manner, &c. … A Christian pilot…acts from a root of the fear of God and love of mankind in his whole course. …[H]is aim is more to glorify God, than to gain his pay, or make his voyage. …[H]e walks heavenly with men and God, in a constant observation of God's hand in storms, calms, &c. So that the thread of navigation being equally spun by a believing or unbelieving pilot, yet is it drawn over with the gold of godliness and Christianity by a Christian Pilot, while he is holy in all manner of Christianity, 1 Peter 1:15."

[221] Hooker, *Summe of Church-Discipline*, 328. Hooker writes, "But the Lord Christ, as a King of infinite mercy as well as wisdome, he provides for the outward good and comfort of all his houshold and subjects, in regard of their estates, that they may be maintained, and their health also, and so their lives preserved in a prosperous condition, and to this end he hath appointed Officers…. … *The name Deacon* in our English comes from the originall Greek word, which…signifies as much as to administer, and implies any kind of administration, whether Civill or Ecclesiasticall. Matt. 22.13. *Then said the King unto his Servants*; the word is…used also to express the administratio of the civil Magistrate, *Rom.*13.4. when their administratios are considered as under God, being his servants, *he is the Minister of God to thee for good….*"

[222] John Winthrop to___, Boston, (8) 14, 1642, in *Life and Letters of John Winthrop*, 1630-1649, vol. 2, 2nd ed., ed. Robert C. Winthrop (Boston: Little, Brown, and Co., 1869), 279.

[223] Hart, *Faith & Freedom*, 98.

[224] Luther, *Appeal to the Ruling Class*, 412-415. Luther states, "The Romanists profess to be the only interpreter of Scripture, even though they never learn anything contained in it their lives long. They claim authority for themselves alone, juggle with words shamelessly before our eyes, saying that the pope cannot err as to the faith, whether he be bad or good; although they cannot

quote a single letter of Scripture to support their claim. Thus it comes about that so many heretical, unchristian, and even unnatural laws are contained in the canon [church] law—matters of which there is no need for discussion at the present juncture. Just because the Romanists profess to believe that the Holy Spirit has not abandoned them, no matter if they are as ignorant and bad as they could be, they presume to assert whatever they please. In such a case, what is the need or the value of Holy Scripture? Let it be burned, and let us be content with the ignorant gentlemen at Rome... ... But lest we fight them with mere words, let us adduce Scripture. St. Paul says, I Corinthians 14 [:30], "If something superior be revealed to any one sitting there and listening to another speaking God's word, the first speaker must be silent and give place." What would be the virtue of this commandment if only the speaker, or the person in the highest position, were to be believed? Christ Himself says, John 6 [:45], "that all Christians shall be taught by God." ... Has not the pope made many errors? Who could enlighten Christian people if the pope erred, unless someone else, who had the support of Scripture, were more to be believed than he?

Therefore it is a wicked, base invention, for which they cannot adduce a tittle of evidence in support, to aver that it is the function of the pope alone to interpret Scripture, or to confirm any particular interpretation. And if they claim that St. Peter received authority when he was given the keys [Matthew 16:-18-20]—well, it is plain enough that the keys were not given to St. Peter only, but to the whole Christian community. ... ...Christ did not pray for Peter only, but for all apostles and Christians. As He said in John 17 [:9, 20], "Father, I pray for those whom Thou hast given me, and not only them, but for all those who believe on me through their word." Surely these words are plain enough.

Think it over for yourself. You must acknowledge that there are good Christians among us who have the true faith, spirit, understanding, word, and mind of Christ. Why ever should one reject their opinion and judgment, and accept those of the pope, who has neither that faith nor that spirit? That would be to repudiate the whole faith and the Christian church itself. Moreoever, it can never be the pope alone who is in the right, if the creedis correct in the article, "I believe in one, holy, Christian church"; or should the confession take the form: "I believe in the pope of Rome?" ...

In addition, as I have already said, each and all of us are priests because we all have the one faith, the one gospel, one and the same sacrament; why then should we not be entitled to taste or test, and to judge what is right or wrong in the faith? How otherwise does St. Paul's dictum stand, I Corinthians 2 [:15], "He that is spiritual judges all things and is judged by none," and II Corinthians 4 [:13], "We all have the one spirit of faith"? Why then should we not distinguish what accords or does not accord with the faith quite as well as an unbelieving pope? These and many other passages should give us courage and set us free. We ought not to allow the spirit of liberty—to use St. Paul's term—to be frightened away by pronouncements confabricated by the popes. We ought to march boldly forward, and test everything the Romanists do or leave undone. We ought to apply that understanding of the Scriptures which we possess as believers, and constrain the Romanists to follow, not their own interpretation, but that which is in fact the better. ... ...St. Paul upbraided St. Peter as a wrongdoer [Gal. 2:11]. Hence it is the duty of every Christian to accept the implications of the faith, understand and defend it, and denounce everything false.[224]

[225] Luther, *Appeal to the Ruling Class*, 475.

[226] Hart, *Faith & Freedom*, 112-113.

[227] *New England's First Fruits: With Diverse Other Special Matters Concerning That Country* (London, 1643; repr., New York: Reprinted for Joseph Sabin, 1865), 26.

[228] *The Doctrines of the New England Churches* in *Essays, Theological and Miscellaneous, Reprinted from the Princeton Review*, 2nd series, ed. Albert B. Dod (New York: Wiley and Putnam, 1847), 211. See also Morris, *Christian Life and Character*, 78.

[229] College of William and Mary, Charter of the College of William and Mary, in Virginia, in *The History of the College of William and Mary From Its Foundation, 1660, to 1874* (Richmond, VA: J. W. Randolph & English, 1874), 3.

[230] Johnson, *History of the American People*, 40.

[231] Hart, *Faith & Freedom*, 111.

[232] John Smith, *The General History of Virginia, New England, 1606-1624*, bk. 3, in *Captain J. Smith's Works, 1608-1631*, no. 16, ed. Edward Arber (Birmingham, England: English Scholar's Library, 1884), 466.

[233] Luther, *Appeal to the Ruling Class*, 461.

[234] John Smith, *The General History of Virginia, New England, 1606-1624*, bk. 6, in *Captain J. Smith's Works, 1608-1631*, no. 16, ed. Edward Arber (Birmingham, England: English Scholar's Library, 1884), 710.

[235] Smith, *General History of Virginia*, bk. 6, 772.

[236] John Cotton, "Christian Calling," in *The Puritans: A Sourcebook of Their Writings*, 2 vols., eds. Perry Miller and Thomas H. Johnson (1963; repr., Mineola, NY: Dover, 2001), 320. In 1 Timothy 1:12, the Apostle Paul says to the disciple Timothy, "I thank Christ Jesus our Lord who has enabled me...." In 1 Corinthians 7:19-20, Paul says to the church, "Let each one remain in the same calling in which he was called."

[237] Benjamin Franklin, *The Way To Wealth* (New York: New York Association for Improving the Condition of the Poor, 1848), 2, 3.

[238] Franklin, *Way to Wealth*, 1.

[239] Franklin, *Way to Wealth*, 3.

[240] Franklin, *Way to Wealth*, 2.

[241] John Calvin, *Calvin's Bible Commentaries: Psalms, pt. 5*, trans. John King (Forgotten Books, 2007), 84.

[242] Franklin, *Way to Wealth*, 7.

[243] Franklin, *Way to Wealth*, 10.

[244] Franklin, *Way to Wealth*, 7, 2.

[245] Mark A. Noll, *A History of Christianity in the United States and Canada* (Grand Rapids, MI: Eerdmans, 1992), 51.

[246] Steven Waldman, *Founding Faith: Providence, Politics, and the Birth of Religious Freedom in America* (New York: Random

House, 2008), 8; Mark A. Noll, Nathan O. Hatch, and George M. Marsden, *The Search for Christian America* (Colorado Springs, CO: Helmers & Howard, 1989), 30. See also Sydney Ahlstrom, *Religious History of the American People* (New Haven, Yale U Press, 1972), 1090. See also Alan W. Ertl, *The Political Economic Foundation of Democratic Capitalism: From Genesis to Maturation* (Boca Raton, FL: BrownWalker Press/Universal Publishers, 2007, 92-93. The American attitude toward work, says author Alan Ertl, would influence the idea, growth, and development of western capitalism in a free market.

[247] Nathaniel Ward, *The Simple Cobler of Aggawam in America*, ed. David Pulsifer (Boston: James Munroe and Co., 1843), 3.

[248] See Mark A. Noll, Nathan O. Hatch, and George M. Marsden, *The Search for Christian America* (Colorado Springs, CO: Helmers & Howard, 1989), 34-35.

[249] Niebuhr, *Kingdom of God*, 61-62.

[250] Johnson, *History of the American People*, 42, 45.

[251] Mark A. Noll, Nathan O. Hatch, and George M. Marsden, *The Search for Christian America* (Colorado Springs, CO: Helmers & Howard, 1989), 32; Frank Lambert, *The Founding Fathers and the Place of Religion in America* (Princeton, NJ: Princeton U Press, 2003), 77.

[252] Holbrook, "Crime and Sin in Puritan Massachusetts," 2-3.

[253] Noll, *History of Christianity*, 40.

[254] Noll, Hatch, and Marsden, *Search for Christian America*, 30. See Sydney Ahlstrom, *Religious History of the American People*, 1090.

[255] Connecticut Secretary of State, *The Fundamental Orders of Connecticut, 1639*, in *State of Connecticut Register and Manual, 1922* (Hartford, CT: State of Connecticut, 1922), 39.

[256] Connecticut Secretary of State, *Fundamental Orders of Connecticut*, 40.

[257] Massachusetts General Court, *Massachusetts Body of Liberties, 1641*, in *American Historical Documents, 1000-1904*, ed. Charles. W. Eliot (New York: P. F. Collier & Son, 1910), 70. I have translated this excerpt into modern English.

Chapter 4: Freedom of Conscience and Religious Tolerance in Early America

[258] Amos and Gardiner, *Never Before in History*, 7, 12.

[259] John Calvin, *The Institutes of the Christian Religion, A New Translation*, vol. 2, trans. Henry Beveridge (Edinburgh, Scotland: Printed for Calvin Translation Society), 1845, bk. 3, ch. 19, sect. 15, 442-443.

[260] Roger Williams, *The Bloudy Tenent of Persecution for the Cause of Conscience Discussed: and Mr. Cotton's Letter Examined and Answered, 1644*, ed. Edward B. Underhill (London: Printed for Hanserd Knollys Society by J. Haddon, 1848), 154, 316.

[261] Philip Hamburger, *Separation of Church and State* (Cambridge, MA: Harvard U Press, 2002), 52.

[262] Westminster General Assembly, *Confession of Faith*, ch. 20, 111-112. The Westminster Confession footnotes the following verses, and they appear worded here as cited in the Confession. James 4:12: "There is one law-giver; who is able to save, and to destroy: who art thou that judgest another? Romans 14:4: "Who art thou that judgest another man's servant? to his own master he standeth or falleth: Yea, he shall be holden up: for God is able to make him stand." Acts 4:19: "But Peter and John answered and said unto them, Whether it be right in the sight of God to hearken unto you, more than unto God, judge ye. Acts 5:29: "Then Peter and the other apostles answered and said, We ought to obey God rather than men." 1 Corinthians 7:23: "Ye are bought with a price, be not ye the servants of men." Matthew 23:8-10: "But be not ye called Rabbi, for one is your Master, even Christ, and all ye are brethren. And call no man your Father upon the earth: for one is your Father, who is in heaven. Neither be ye called masters; for one is your Master, even Christ. 2 Corinthians 1:24: "Not for that we have dominion over your faith, but are helpers of your joy: for by faith ye stand." Matthew 15:9: "But in vain they do worship me, teaching for doctrines the commandments of men."

[263] William Penn, *The Great Case of Liberty of Conscience Once More Briefly Debated and Defended by the Authority of Reason, Scripture, and Antiquity, 1671*, in *The Select Works of William Penn in Five Volumes*, vol. 3, 3rd ed., ed. John Fothergill (London: Printed by James Phillips, 1782), viii, 10, 11, 45.

[264] Penn, *Liberty of Conscience*, 45-46.

[265] Alexander A. Seaton, *The Theory of Toleration Under the Later Stuarts* (Cambridge, MA: University Press, 1911), 172.

[266] Penn, *Liberty of Conscience*, vi, 11.

[267] Amos and Gardiner, *Never Before in History*, 48.

[268] Williams, *Bloudy Tenent*, 34.

[269] Williams, *Bloudy Tenent*, 303.

[270] Williams, *Bloudy Tenent*, 305-307. He based this view on other verses as well including Isaiah 9, Daniel 7, and Micah 4 as compared with Luke 1:32, Matthew 18, Mark 13:34, Acts 2:30, and 1 Corinthians 5.

[271] Williams, *Bloudy Tenent*, 309.

[272] Calvin, *Institutes*, vol. 1, bk. 2, 533-534. See also Chapter 11 of vol. 1, bk. 1 of *Institutes*. Calvin explains, "I proceed to the third distinction, which is thus expressed by Jeremiah: "Behold, the days come, saith the Lord, that I will make a new covenant with the house of Israel, and with the house of Judah; not according to the covenant that I made with their fathers, in the day that I took them by the hand, to bring them out of the land of Egypt; (which my covenant they brake, although I was an husband unto them, saith the Lord;) but this shall be the covenant that I will make with the house of Israel; After whose days, saith the Lord, I will put my law in their inward parts, and write it in their hearts; and will be a their God, and they shall be my people. And they shall teach no more every man his neighbour, and every man his brother, saying, Know the Lord: for they shall all know me,

from the least of them unto the greatest of them," (Jer. xxxi. 31-34.) From these words, the Apostle [Paul] took occasion to institute a comparison between the Law and the Gospel, calling the one a doctrine of the letter, the other a doctrine of the spirit; describing the one as formed on tables of stone, the other on tables of the heart; the one the preaching of death, the other of life; the one of condemnation, the other of justification; the one made void, the other permanent, (2 Cor. iii. 5, 6.) ... All which is attributed to it [the law] is, that it commands what is right, prohibits crimes, holds forth rewards to the cultivators of righteousness, and threatens transgressors with punishment, while at the same time it neither changes nor amends that depravity of heart which is naturally inherent in all.

    8. Let us now explain the Apostle's contrast step by step. The Old Testament is literal, because promulgated without the efficacy of the Spirit: the New spiritual, because the Lord has engraven it on the heart. ... The Old is deadly, because it can do nothing but involve the whole human race in a curse; the New is the instrument of life, because those who are freed from the curse it restores to favour with God. The former is the ministry of condemnation, because it charges the whole sons of Adam with transgression; the latter the ministry of righteousness, because it unfolds the mercy of God, by which we are justified

[273] John Locke, *A Letter Concerning Toleration*, 1689, in *The Works of John Locke in Nine Volumes*, vol. 5, 12th ed. (London: Printed for C. and J. Rivington et al., 1824), 37.

[274] Calvin, *Institutes*, vol. 3, bk. 4, ch. 10, sect. 8, 195-196. Calvin asserted, "...if God is the sole legislator [of conscience, brackets mine], it is not lawful for men to assume this honour to themselves; we ought also to bear in mind the two reasons which we have stated, why God asserts this exclusively to himself. The first is, that his will may be received as the perfect rule of all righteousness and holiness, and so that an acquaintance with it may be all the knowledge necessary to a good life. The second is, that with respect to the mode of worshipping him aright, he [God] may exercise the sole empire over our souls, to whom we are under the strongest obligation to obey his authority and await his commands. When these two reasons are kept in view, it will be easy to judge what constitutions of men are contrary to the word of God. ... Let us remember therefore, that all human laws are to be weighed in this balance, if we would have a certain and infallible test."

[275] Luther, *Secular Authority*, 387-388, 390-391. Luther states, "Christ Himself made this nice distinction and summed it all up briefly when He said, "Give unto Caesar the things that are Caesar's, and unto God the things that are God's" [Matt. 22:21]. If, then, imperial power extended to God's kingdom and power, and were not something by itself, He would not thus have made it a separate thing. For, as was said, the soul is not under Caesar's power; he can neither teach nor guide it, neither kill it nor make it alive, neither bind it nor loose it, neither judge it nor condemn it, neither hold it nor release it, which he must do had he power to command it and impose laws upon it; but over life, goods and honor he indeed has this right, for such things are under his authority.

    David, too, stated this long ago in one of his short sayings when he says in Psalm 115 [:16], "The heavens hath he given to the Lord of heaven; but the earth hath he given to the children of men." That is, over what is on earth and belongs to the temporal, earthly kingdom, man has authority from God, but that which belongs to the heavenly eternal kingdom is entirely under the heavenly Lord. Nor does Moses forget this when he says in Genesis 1 [:26], "God said, Let us make man to rule over the beasts of the earth, over the fish in the waters, over the birds in the air." There only external rule is ascribed to men. And, in short, this is the meaning, as St. Peter says, Acts 5 [:29], "We must obey God rather than men." Thereby he clearly sets a limit to worldly government. ...

    Nevertheless such a world as this deserves such princes, none of whom do their duty. ... ...[T]hey [secular and religious authorities] turn things topsy-turvy, and rule souls with iron and the body with bans, so that worldly princes rule in a spiritual, and spiritual princes in a worldly way. What else does the devil have to do on earth than thus to play the fool and hold carnival with his folk?"

[276] Luther, *Appeal to the Ruling Class*, 434-435. Luther says, "It should be decreed that no secular matter is to be referred to Rome [Roman Catholic Church]. All such issues should be left to the secular arm .... [T]he...judges in the ecclesiastical courts...ought to be concerned only with matters of faith and good morals; whereas money, property, life, and honour should be left for the secular judges to deal with."

[277] Ponet, *Short Treatise*, ch. 4, para. 7.

[278] Brutus, *Vindiciae*, 27-28. "Man is made up of body and soul: God formed the body and also infused the soul. Therefore He alone could use both of them with absolute right. But if He freely granted to kings that they might use the bodies and goods of their subjects only for the subjects' preservation, they ought clearly to remember that the use was conceded, not the abuse. For above all, they have nothing which they may requisition [*imperent*] from the soul under the title of tribute, who themselves are bound to profess their own souls as liable to pay tribute to God. The king takes tribute or dues [census] from the body and from those things which are acquired or cultivated by the agency of the body; and God from the soul in particular, which actually exercises its functions through the body. To the former type of tribute belong renders in kind, money payments, and other dues both real and personal; to the latter, sacrifices, congregations, and divine worship both private and public. These two tributes are so different and distinct that neither impedes the other; the fisc of God deprives Caesar's fisc of nothing, but each one keeps its rights. In short, anyone who confuses these mixes up heaven and earth and wants to reduce everything to primordial Chaos. David drew an excellent distinction between them, when he designated some officials for divine affairs, others for those of the king [1 Chronicles 26:26-30]. Jehoshaphat did the same when he appointed some to the judgement of Jehovah and others to the lawsuits of the king—that is, some who upheld the worship of God, and others the rights of the king [2 Chronicles 19:5-6, 11]. But if a king claims for himself both types of tribute—as if he were trying to reach and scale the heavens after the manner of Giants—he is guilty of attempting to seize the [heavenly] kingdom; and just like a vassal who usurps regalian rights, he forfeits his fief and is most widely deprived of it. This is all more fair because there is some proportion between a vassal and a superior

lord, but there can be none between a king and God, between some simple man and the Almighty. For whenever some prince insolently says: 'I shall scale heaven, I shall exalt my throne above God's stars, and shall be like the highest mountain'; God replies: 'But I, on the contrary, shall elevate Myself, and shall rise up against you, and shall obliterate your name to the last of your descendants. And your schemes shall fade away, because what I have once decreed cannot be altered or fall into abeyance' [Isaiah 14:13-14, 22]. The Lord said to Pharoah: 'Release My people, so that it may serve Me and perform sacrifices to Me' [Exodus 5]. But because he was bloated with pride, and answered that he did not recognize this God, he plunged headlong to ruin [Exodus 8, 9, 10, 11]. Nebuchadnezzar wanted his statue to be worshipped and divine honours to be paid to him [Daniel 3, 5]. God immediately checked the unbridled audacity of the wretched little man. He who wanted to appear a God ceased to be a man, and strayed through wild, deserted places like an ass 'until', says Daniel, 'he acknowledged the God of Israel to be supreme Lord of all'. His son Belshazzar, for the sake of his own drunkenness, abused the sacred vessels of the temple, which were dedicated to divine worship [Daniel 5:23]. So, because he did not render glory to God, in Whose hand were his soul and all his ways, his kingdom was destroyed and he was slain the same night [Daniel 5:30-31].

[279] Luther, *Secular Authority*, 382-387.

[280] Luther, *Secular Authority*, 387-388, 390-391. Luther writes, "If then your prince or temporal lord commands you to hold with the pope, to believe this or that, or commands you to give up certain books, you should say, It does not befit Lucifer to sit by the side of God. Dear [civil, bracket mine] Lord, I owe you obedience with life and goods; command me within the limits of your power on earth, and I will obey. But if you command me to believe, and to put away books, I will not obey; for in this case you are a tyrant and overreach yourself, and command where you have neither right now power, etc."

[281] Ponet, *Short Treatise*, ch. 4, para. 10, 31; Williams, *Bloudy Tenent*, 49. Williams also cites Corinthians 7:23 and Colossians 2:18 on this point.

[282] Calvin, *Institutes*, vol. 3, bk. 4, ch. 20, sect. 32, 551.

[283] Calvin, *Institutes*, vol. 3, bk. 4, ch. 10, sect. 8, 196. Calvin explains, "In the Epistle of the Colossians, he [the Apostle Paul], contends that the doctrine of the true worship of God is not to be sought from men, because the Lord hath faithfully and fully instructed us how we ought to worship him. To prove this, in the first chapter he states that all the wisdom by which the man of God is made perfect in Christ, is contained in the gospel. In the beginning of the second chapter, he declares that "in Christ are hid all the treasures of wisdom and knowledge;" from which he concludes that the faithful should "beware lest any man spoil them through philosophy and vain deceit, after the tradition of men." At the end of the chapter he still more confidently condemns all "will worship;" [Colossians 1:27, 28; 2:3, 8, 23] this includes all those services which men either invent for themselves or receive from others, together with any of the precepts by which they presume to regulate the worship of God. ... The passages in the Epistle to the Galatians, in which he argues that chains ought not to be imposed on consciences, which are subject to the government of God alone, are too plain to be mistaken; especially in the fifth chapter. [Galatians 5:1-18]."

[284] Calvin, *Institutes*, vol. 3, bk. 4, ch. 10., sect. 8, 196. Calvin states, "In the Epistle of the Colossians, he [the Apostle Paul], contends that the doctrine of the true worship of God is not to be sought from men, because the Lord hath faithfully and fully instructed us how we ought to worship him. To prove this, in the first chapter he states that all the wisdom by which the man of God is made perfect in Christ, is contained in the gospel [Colossians 1:27-28]. In the beginning of the second chapter, he declares that "in Christ are hid all the treasures of wisdom and knowledge [Colossians 2:3];" from which he concludes that the faithful should "beware lest any man spoil them through philosophy and vain deceit, after the tradition of men [Colossians 2:8]." At the end of the chapter he still more confidently condemns all "will worship;" [Colossians 2:23] this includes all those services which men either invent for themselves or receive from others, together with any of the precepts by which they presume to regulate the worship of God. ... The passages in the Epistle to the Galatians, in which he argues that chains ought not to be imposed on consciences, which are subject to the government of God alone, are too plain to be mistaken; especially in the fifth chapter [Galatians 5:1-18]."

[285] Williams, *Bloudy Tenent*, 49-50. Williams explains, "...God's people, since the coming of the King of Israel, the Lord Jesus, have openly and constantly professed, that no civil magistrate, no king, nor Caesar, have any power over the souls or consciences of their subjects, in the matters of God and the crown of Jesus; but the civil magistrates themselves, yea, kings and Caesars, are bound to subject their own souls to the ministry and church, the power and government of this Lord Jesus, the King of kings." In Psalm 2:9, God says of the Messiah among the nations, ""You shall break them with a rod of iron; You shall dash them to pieces like a potter's vessel."" In Acts 2:36 the Apostle Peter says to the people, "'[L]et all the house of Israel know assuredly that God has made this Jesus, whom you crucified, both Lord and Christ.'"

[286] Penn, *Liberty of Conscience*, 12.

[287] Penn, *Liberty of Conscience*, 12.

[288] Penn, *Liberty of Conscience*, 13.

[289] Bible verses that address God as judge of man's conscience include Romans 14:12-13, Matthew 25:31-32, and Acts 10:42.

[290] Penn, *Liberty of Conscience*, 13.

[291] Williams, *Bloudy Tenent*, 38, 46, 240.

[292] Williams, *Bloudy Tenent*, 49.

[293] Williams, *Bloudy Tenent*, 305-6.

[294] Williams, *Bloudy Tenent*, 1, 35.

[295] Williams, *Bloudy Tenent*, 103; Penn, *Liberty of Conscience*, 16-17.

[296] Williams, *Bloudy Tenent*, 103.

[297] Williams, *Bloudy Tenent*, 364.

[298] Penn, *Liberty of Conscience*, 16-18.

[299] John Locke, *A Second Letter Concerning Toleration*, 1690, in *The Works of John Locke in Nine Volumes*, vol. 5, 12th ed. (London: Printed for C. and J. Rivington, et al., 1824), 77.

[300] John Locke, *Paraphrase and Notes on the Epistles of St. Paul to the Galatians, I and II Corinthians, Romans, and Ephesians* in *The Works of John Locke in Nine Volumes*, vol. 7, 12th ed. (London: Printed for C. and J. Rivington, et al., 1824), 171-173.

[301] Locke, *Letter Concerning Toleration*, 1689, 8, 6.

[302] John Locke, *A Third Letter for Toleration*, 1692, in *The Works of John Locke in Nine Volumes*, vol. 5, 12th ed. (London: Printed for C. and J. Rivington, et al., 1824), 544-545.

[303] Williams, *Bloudy Tenent*, 117-120.

[304] Luther, *Secular Authority*, 389, 392. Citing 2 Corinthians 10:4-5, Luther asserts on this point that spiritual warfare must be fought with the Word of God, not with the iron sword and physical punishments: "Heresy can never be prevented by force. That must be taken hold of in a different way, and must be opposed and dealt with otherwise than with the sword. Here God's Word must strive; if that does not accomplish the end it will remain unaccomplished through secular power, though it fill the world with blood. Heresy is a spiritual matter, which no iron can strike, no fire burn, no water drown. God's Word alone avails here, as Paul says, II Corinthians 10 [:4 f.], "Our weapons are not carnal, but mighty through God to destroy every counsel and high thing that exalteth himself against the knowledge of God, and to bring into captivity every thought to the obedience of Christ. …
… Faith, however, can come through no word of man, but only through the Word of God, as Paul says in Romans 10 [:17], "Faith cometh by hearing, and hearing by the Word of God."

[305] Williams, *Bloudy Tenent*, 303-4.

[306] Williams, *Bloudy Tenent*, 34.

[307] Martin Luther, Second Sermon of The Eight Wittenberg Sermons, 1522, in *Works of Martin Luther, with Introductions and Notes*, vol. 2, eds. Henry E. Jacobs and Adolph Spaeth (Philadelphia, PA: A. J. Holman Co., 1915), 399.

[308] Williams *Bloudy Tenent*, 48.

[309] Luther, *Appeal to the Ruling Class*, 467.

[310] Penn, *Liberty of Conscience*, 18-19.

[311] Penn, *Liberty of Conscience*, 19-20.

[312] Penn, *Liberty of Conscience*, 11, 25-6.

[313] Luther, *Secular Authority*, 385.

[314] Williams, *Bloudy Tenent*, 107.

[315] Penn, *Liberty of Conscience*, 21-22. See also pp. v and vii in Penn.

[316] Penn, *Liberty of Conscience*, 20.

[317] Locke, *Second Letter Concerning Toleration*, 63-64.

[318] Penn, *Liberty of Conscience*, 20-21.

[319] Penn, *Liberty of Conscience*, 20.

[320] Penn, *Liberty of Conscience*, 22. Luther, *Secular Authority*, 385. Luther similarly states, "…Every man is responsible for his own faith, and he must see to it for himself that he believes rightly. As little as another can go to hell or heaven for me, so little can he believe or disbelieve for me; and as little as he can open or shut heaven or hell for me, so little can he drive me to faith or unbelief. Since, then, belief or unbelief is a matter of every one's conscience, and since this is no lessening of the secular power, the latter should be content and attend to its own affairs and permit men to believe one thing or another, as they are able and willing, and constrain no one by force. For faith is a free work, to which no one can be forced. Nay, it is a divine work, done in the Spirit, certainly not a matter which outward authority should compel or create. Hence arises the well-known saying, found also in Augustine, 'No one can or ought to be constrained to believe.'"

[321] Penn, *Liberty of Conscience*, 21.

[322] Penn, *Liberty of Conscience*, 21-22. See also pp. v and vii in Penn.

[323] Locke, *Letter Concerning Toleration*, 1689, 11.

[324] Penn, *Liberty of Conscience*, 23.

[325] Penn, *Liberty of Conscience*, 24-26.

[326] Penn, *Liberty of Conscience*, 26.

[327] Penn, *Liberty of Conscience*, 32.

[328] Penn, *Liberty of Conscience*, 27-29.

[329] Williams, *Bloudy Tenent*, 34.

[330] Penn, *Liberty of Conscience*, 32.

[331] Williams, *Bloudy Tenent*, 46.

[332] Williams, *Bloudy Tenent*, 50-51. Williams cites upheavals in Acts 14:4, Acts 19:29, 40, and Acts 21: 30, 31.

[333] Williams, *Bloudy Tenent*, 34. He also refers to Genesis 10:8-9.

[334] Hamburger, *Separation*, 21.

[335] Hamburger, *Separation*, 22, 24.

[336] Hamburger, *Separation*, 29-30.

[337] Hamburger, *Separation*, 31.

[338] Hamburger, *Separation*, 29-31.

[339] Hamburger, *Separation*, 38.

[340] Hamburger, *Separation*, 44, 45.

[341] Roger Williams, "Mr. Cotton's Letter Examined and Answered," London, 1644, in *The Bloudy Tenent of Persecution For Cause of Conscience Discussed and Mr. Cotton's Letter Examined and Answered*, ed. Edward B. Underhill (London: Printed for Hanserd Knollys Society, 1848), 435.

[342] Williams, *Bloudy Tenent*, 201.

[343] Roger Williams, *The Bloody Tenent Yet More Bloody* in *On Religious Liberty: Selections From the Works of Roger Williams*, ed. James Calvin Davis (Cambridge, MA: Harvard U Press, 2008), 217.

[344] Frank Lambert, *The Founding Fathers and the Place of Religion in America* (Princeton, NJ: Princeton U Press, 2003), 89.

[345] Williams, *Bloudy Tenent*, 99.

[346] Williams, *Bloudy Tenent*, 100.

[347] Locke, *Letter Concerning Toleration*, 10-11.

[348] Locke, *Letter Concerning Toleration*, 12.

[349] Williams, *Bloudy Tenent*, 80, 149; Penn, *Liberty of Conscience*, 16.

[350] Williams, *Bloudy Tenent*, 82.

[351] Locke, *Letter Concerning Toleration*, 37.

[352] Hamburger, *Separation*, 23-24, 34.

[353] Williams, *Bloudy Tenent*, xxv.

[354] Charter of Rhode Island and Providence Plantation, July 8, 1663, in *America's Founding Charters: Primary Documents of Colonial and Revolutionary Era Governance*, vol. 1, ed. Jon L. Wakelyn (Westport, CT: Greenwood Publishing Group, 2006), 152-153.

[355] Acts and Orders of the General Court of Election, May 19-21, 1647, in *America's Founding Charters: Primary Documents of Colonial and Revolutionary Era Governance*, vol. 1, ed. Jon L. Wakelyn (Westport, CT: Greenwood Publishing Group, 2006), 150.

[356] Johnson, *History of the American People*, 50.

[357] Noll, *History of Christianity*, 28.

[358] Maryland Toleration Act, April, 1649, in *Documentary Source Book of American History, 1606-1913*, ed. William MacDonald (New York: Macmillan, 1920), 54.

[359] Fundamental Constitutions of the Carolinas, March 1, 1669, in *America's Founding Charters: Primary Documents of Colonial and Revolutionary Era Governance*, vol. 1, ed. Jon L. Wakelyn (Westport, CT: Greenwood Publishing Group, 2006), 232.

[360] Lambert, *Founding Fathers*, 122.

[361] Noll, *History of Christianity*, 66.

[362] Frame of Government of Pennyslvania with Laws Agreed Upon in England, May 5, 1682, in *America's Founding Charters: Primary Documents of Colonial and Revolutionary Era Governance*, vol. 1, ed. Jon L. Wakelyn (Westport, CT: Greenwood Publishing Group, 2006), 257.

[363] Lambert, *Founding Fathers*, 100-101.

[364] Gibbs, *One Nation Under God*, 58.

[365] Frame of Government of Pennsylvania with Laws Agreed Upon in England, 1682, ed. Wakelyn, 257-258.

[366] Frame of Government of Pennsylvania with Laws Agreed Upon in England, 1682, ed. Wakelyn, 258.

[367] Lambert, *Founding Fathers*, 115-116, 119.

[368] Lambert, *Founding Fathers*, 122.

[369] John J. Patrick and Gerald P. Long, *Constitutional Debates on Freedom of Religion: A Documentary History* (Westport, CT: Greenwood Press, 1999), 19-20.

[370] Lambert, *Founding Fathers*, 129.

[371] Jon Meacham, *American Gospel* (New York: Random House, 2006), 56.

Chapter 5: The Great Awakening, An Evangelical Revival in the American Colonies

[372] Niebuhr, *Kingdom of God*, 100. Niebuhr cites *Letters of Crevecoeur*.

[373] Lambert, *Founding Fathers,* 129.

[374] Niebuhr, *Kingdom of God*, 99-100.

[375] Noll, Hatch, and Marsden, *Search for Christian America*, 50-52.

[376] Johnson, *History of the American People*, 110.

[377] Jon Butler, Grant Wacker, and Randall Balmer, *Religion in American Life: A Short History* (New York: Oxford U Press, 2000, 2003), 131.

[378] Johnson, *History of the American People*, 110.

[379] Noll, Hatch, and Marsden, *Search for Christian America*, 52.

[380] Niebuhr, *Kingdom of God*, 99.

[381] Niebuhr, *Kingdom of God*, 99, 101-4.

[382] Gibbs, *One Nation Under God*, 87.

[383] Johnson, *History of the American People*, 111.

[384] Johnson, *History of the American People*, 112.

385 Noll, *History of Christianity*, 91.

386 Noll, *History of Christianity*, 91.

387 Noll, *History of Christianity*, 95.

388 Benjamin Franklin, *Autobiography of Benjamin Franklin*, ed. John Bigelow (Philadelphia, PA: J. B. Lippincott & Co., 1869), 253.

389 Butler, Wacker, and Balmer, *Religion in American Life*, 128-129.

390 Noll, *History of Christianity*, 92-93.

391 Lambert, *Founding Fathers*, 124.

392 Noll, *History of Christianity*, 105.

393 Noll, *History of Christianity*, 93.

394 Noll, *History of Christianity*, 112.

395 Gibbs, *One Nation Under God*, 88.

396 Rosalie J. Slater, *Teaching and Learning America's Constitutional History: The Principle Approach* (San Francisco, CA: Foundation for American Christian Education, 1965), 190, 245.

397 Calvin, *Bible Commentaries: Genesis,* 47.

398 Calvin, *Institutes*, vol. 1, bk. 1, 66-71. Calvin states, "[A]ll men acknowledge that the human body bears on its face such proofs of ingenious contrivance as are sufficient to proclaim the admirable wisdom of its Maker. Hence certain philosophers have not improperly called man a microcosm, (miniature world,) as being a rare specimen of divine power, wisdom, and goodness, and containing within himself wonders sufficient to occupy our minds, if we are willing so to employ them."

399 Calvin, *Institutes*, vol. 1, bk. 1, 66-71. Calvin cites Psalms 104:2, Psalms 8:2, 4, Hebrews 11:3, and Acts 17:27-28.

400 Jonathan Edwards, *Miscellaneous Observations on Important Doctrines*, in *The Works of President Edwards, A Reprint of the Worcester Edition*, vol. 1 (New York: Leavitt & Allen, 1858), 566.

401 Edwards, *Miscellaneous Observations*, 566.

402 Jonathan Edwards, *The Nature of True Virtue*, in *The Works of President Edwards in Four Volumes: A Reprint of the Worcester Edition*, vol. 2 (New York: Leavitt & Allen, 1858), 287-9, 303; Jonathan Edwards, *The Great Christian Doctrine of Original Sin Defended*, in *The Works of President Edwards in Four Volumes: A Reprint of the Worcester Edition*, vol. 2 (New York: Leavitt & Allen, 1858), 329.

403 Jonathan Edwards, *Freedom of the Will*, in *The Works of President Edwards in Four Volumes: A Reprint of the Worcester Edition*, vol. 2 (New York: Leavitt & Allen, 1858), 19-20. Edwards writes, "The essential qualities of a moral Agent are in God, in the greatest possible perfection; such as understanding, to perceive the difference between moral good and evil; a capacity of discerning that moral worthiness and demerit, by which some things are praiseworthy, others deserving of blame and punishment; and also a capacity of choice, and choice guided by understanding, and a power of acting according to his choice or pleasure, and being capable of doing those things which are in the highest sense praiseworthy. And herein does very much consist that image of God wherein he made man, (which we read of Gen. i. 26 27, and chapter ix. 6) by which God distinguishes man from the beasts, viz., in those faculties and principles of nature, whereby He is capable of moral Agency. Herein very much consists the natural image of God; as his spiritual and moral image, wherein man was made at first, consisted in that moral excellency, that he was endowed with."

404 Edwards, *Nature of True Virtue*, 289.

405 Calvin, *Bible Commentaries: Genesis,* 63. See also John Calvin, *Commentaries on the First Book of Moses, Called Genesis*, vol. 1, ed. John King (Grand Rapids, MI: Eerdmans, 1948), 112. Calvin states in his *Bible Commentaries*, "Three gradations, indeed are to be noted in the creation of man; that his dead body was formed out of the dust of the earth; that it was endued with a soul, whence it should receive vital motion; and that on this soul God engraved his own image, to which immortality is annexed."

406 Calvin, *Institutes*, vol 1, bk. 1, 66-71. Calvin states, "...[T]hey [men] have in their own persons a factory where innumerable operations of God are carried on, and a magazine stored with treasures of inestimable value.... Whether they will or not, they cannot but know that these are proofs of his Godhead.... ... The swift and versatile movements of the soul in glancing from heaven to earth, connecting the future with the past, retaining the remembrance of former years, nay, forming creations of its own—its skill, moreover, in making astonishing discoveries, and inventing so many wonderful arts, are sure indications of the agency of God in man. ... What shall we say but that man bears about with him a stamp of immortality which can never be effaced?"

407 John Calvin, *Commentaries on the First Book of Moses, Called Genesis*, vol. 1, ed. John King (Grand Rapids, MI: Eerdmans, 1948), 111.

408 Jonathan Edwards, *The Soul's Immortality and Future Retribution*, Sermon 19, in *The Works of Jonathan Edwards*, vol. 2, ed. Tryon Edwards (Boston: Doctrinal Tract and Book Society, 1850), 308-314.

409 Edwards, *Soul's Immortality,* 321-322.

410 Jonathan Edwards, *The Wisdom of God Displayed in the Way of Salvation*, Sermon 5, in *The Works of President Edwards in Four Volumes: A Reprint of the Worcester Edition*, vol. 4 (New York: Leavitt & Allen, 1858), 139.

411 Edwards, *Wisdom of God,* 140.

412 Edwards, *Wisdom of God,* 140.

413 Edwards, *Wisdom of God,* 140-142.

414 Edwards, *Wisdom of God,* 142-146.

415 John Calvin, *Calvin's Bible Commentaries: Matthew, Mark, and Luke, Pt. 1*, trans. John King (Forgotten Books, 2007), 436-437.

Calvin states, "Christ takes a general view of the providence of God as extending to all creatures, and thus argues from the greater to the less, that we are upheld by his special protection. There is hardly any thing of less value than sparrows, (for two were then sold for a farthing, or, as Luke states it, five for two farthings,) and yet God has his eye upon them to protect them, so that nothing happens to them by chance. Would He who is careful about the sparrows disregard the life of men?" Of the Biblical principle that a human life and soul are of great worth to God, Calvin concludes, "This [principle] is true in general of all men, for the sparrows were created for their advantage.... Now the rank which belongs to men arises solely from the undeserved kindness of God."

[416] Thomas Hooker, *Summe of Church-Discipline*, 224. Hooker states, "...[T]he Lord never sets up Churches or Officers, gives power to them, and requires the execution of power from them, but...the Lord looks at the *particular* in the *generall* & the generall as *determined* in *the particular*: The *Reason* is, because the *exist[ence]* and *working* of Churches and Officers is *only* to be seen, as it...appears, & is expressed in the *individuals*. As when God makes...*Officer* by election, erects a *Church*, it's a *particular Church* and *individuall Officer*; therefore the individuall *there* first exists, and the *generall* in the *individuall*. Hence lastly upon the same ground, and for the same reason as the general is divided into his particulars, so the *generals [are] preserved in them. All visible members exist in particular congregations, and are perfected by Ordinances therein.*"

[417] Franklin, *Way To Wealth*, 10.

[418] Calvin *Institutes*, vol. 1, bk. 2, 487. Calvin had asserted the equal standing and value of men before God and thus the Biblical requirement that men are to have charity or love toward all mankind. He states, "...[T]he condition of humanity requires that there be more duties in common between those who are more nearly connected by the ties of relationship, or friendship, or neighborhood. And this is done without any offence to God, by whose providence we are in a manner impelled to do it. But I say that the whole human race, without exception, are to be embraced with one feeling of charity: that here there is no distinction of Greek or Barbarian, worthy or unworthy, friend or foe, since all are to be viewed not in themselves, but in God. If we turn aside from this view, there is no wonder that we entangle ourselves in error. Wherefore, if we would hold the true course in love, our first step must be to turn our eyes not to man, the sight of whom might oftener produce hatred than love, but to God, who requires that the love which we bear to him be diffused among all mankind, so that our fundamental principle must ever be, Let a man be what he may, he is still to be loved, because God is loved."

[419] Jonathan Edwards, *The Great Christian Doctrine of Original Sin Defended*, in *The Works of President Edwards in Four Volumes: A Reprint of the Worcester Edition*, vol. 2 (New York: Leavitt & Allen, 1858), 492.

[420] Jonathan Edwards, *Treatise Concerning Religious Affections*, in *The Works of President Edwards in Four Volumes: A Reprint of the Worcester Edition*, vol. 3 (New York: Leavitt & Allen, 1858), 156.

[421] Jonathan Edwards, *God's Sovereignty*, Sermon 34, in *The Works of President Edwards in Four Volumes: A Reprint of the Worcester Edition*, vol. 4 (New York: Leavitt & Allen, 1858), 550-1, 553, 555-9; Edwards, *Nature of True Virtue*, 266-271, 281.

[422] Jonathan Edwards, *Narrative of Surprising Conversions*, in *The Works of President Edwards in Four Volumes: A Reprint of the Worcester Edition*, vol. 3 (New York: Leavitt & Allen, 1858), 238.

[423] Jonathan Edwards, *Thoughts on the Revival of Religion in New England*, 1740, in *The Works of President Edwards in Four Volumes: A Reprint of the Worcester Edition*, vol. 3 (New York: Leavitt & Allen, 1858), 333.

[424] Jonathan Edwards, *Concerning Efficacious Grace*, in *The Works of President Edwards in Four Volumes: A Reprint of the Worcester Edition*, vol. 2 (New York: Leavitt & Allen, 1858), 586.

[425] Edwards, *Concerning Efficacious Grace*, 586-588. Edwards cites Romans 3:27, 9:14-27, 11:4-7, 17-18, 35-36, and Ephesians 2:9.

[426] Edwards, *Concerning Efficacious Grace*, 587-8.

[427] Edwards, *Doctrine of Original Sin*, 469, 417.

[428] Edwards, *Doctrine of Original Sin*, 467.

[429] Lambert, *Founding Fathers*, 145.

[430] Edwards, *Concerning Religious Affections*, 10. Edwards also cites 1 Timothy 1:5, Galatians 5:14, Romans 13:8,10, 1 Corinthians 13:13, Psalms 33:18, Romans 12:11, James 2:8, Deuteronomy 10:12, 6:6, 30:6, Luke 24:32, 2 Timothy 1:7, 1 John 5:1, and 1 Corinthians 2:9.

[431] Edwards, *Religious Affections*, 6. See also 2-3, 5-6, 16-20.

[432] Edwards also cites Ephesians 4:11-12.

[433] Edwards, *Religious Affections*, 15-16, 20-21.

[434] Niebuhr, *Kingdom of God*, 113.

[435] John Locke, *Second Treatise of Civil Government, 1690*, in *Two Treatises on Government*, bk. 2 (London: George Routledge and Sons, 1884), 193. See also Richard Hooker, *The Laws of Ecclesiastical Polity, Books 1-4, 1593*, bk. 1 (London: George Routledge and Sons, 1888), 84-85.

[436] See Luther, *Secular Authority*, 400-401. See also Calvin, *Institutes*, vol. 1, bk. 2, 439-440, 483-4. As a Calvinist and Congregationalist, Edwards was influenced in the Law of Love by reformed Christian thinkers. Reformer Martin Luther, as mentioned, had recognized the Law of Love among men in his *Secular Authority*: "No more definite law can be found on this subject than the law of love. ... For nature, like love, teaches that I should do as I would be done by [Matt. 7:12; also Luke 6:31]." In his *Institutes*, reformer John Calvin further examined God's commandments of love. Calvin affirmed the sum of God's law in the two Great Commandments of Matthew 22:37-40 and Luke 10:27: "God thus divided his Law into two parts, containing a complete rule of righteousness, that he might assign the first place to the duties of religion which relate especially to His worship, and the second to the duties of charity which have respect to man. ... Hence, as related by the Evangelists, (Matth.

xxii. 37; Luke x. 27,) our Saviour summed up the whole Law in two heads, viz., to love the Lord with all our heart, with all our soul, and with all our strength, and our neighbor as ourselves. You see how, of the two parts under which he comprehends the whole Law, he devotes the one to God, and assigns the other to mankind." Citing Deuteronomy 10:12-13, 6:5, 11:13, and 1 Timothy 1:5, Calvin further explains that to follow these two laws would fulfill all righteousness of God and would become the expression of God in one's life: "It will not now be difficult to ascertain the general end contemplated by the whole law, viz., the fulfillment of righteousness, that man may form his life on the model of divine purity. For therein God has so delineated his own character, that any one exhibiting in action what is commanded, would in some measure exhibit a living image of God. Wherefore Moses, when he wished to fix a summary of the whole in memory of the Israelites, thus addressed them, 'And now, Israel, what doth the Lord thy God require of thee, but to fear the Lord thy God, to walk in all his ways, and to love him, and to serve the Lord thy God with all thy heart, and with all thy soul, to keep the commandments of the Lord and his statutes which I command thee this day for thy Good?' (Deut.x. 12, 13.) And he ceased not to reiterate the same thing, whenever he had occasion to mention the end of the Law. To this doctrine of Law pays so much regard, that it connects man, by holiness of life, with his God; and, as Moses elsewhere expresses it, (Deut. vi. 5;xi. 13,) and makes him cleave to him. Moreover, this holiness of life is comprehended under the two heads above mentioned. 'Thou shalt love the Lord thy God with all thy heart, and with all thy soul, and with all thy mind, and with all thy strength, and thy neighbor as thyself.' First, our mind must be completely filled with love to God, and then this love must forthwith flow out toward our neighbor. This the Apostle shows when he says, 'The end of the commandment is charity out of a pure heart, and a good conscience, and of faith unfeigned,' (1 Tim. i. 5.)." Calvin also cites Matthew 7:12 which states, "All things whatsoever ye would that man should do to you, do ye even so to them: for this is the law and the prophets." The two Biblical commandments of love were, Calvin affirmed, the fulfillment of God's laws and righteousness and the expression of God in one's life.

[437] Edwards, *Religious Affections*, 8-9, 11.

[438] Edwards, *Religious Affections*, 10.

[439] Jonathan Edwards, "Notes on the Mind," 1718-1722, in *Benjamin Franklin and Jonathan Edwards: Selections from their Writings*, ed. Carl Van Doren (New York: Charles Scribner's Sons, 1920), 216-217.

[440] Niebuhr, *Kingdom of God*, 113.

[441] Jonathan Edwards, *Charity and Its Fruits, Or, Christian Love as Manifested in the Heart and Life*, Lecture 11, ed. Tryon E. W. (New York: Robert Carter & Bros., 1856), 337-338.

[442] Edwards, *Nature of True Virtue*, 271.

[443] Mark D. Hall, *Roger Sherman and the Creation of the American Republic* (New York: Oxford U Press, 2013), 22.

[444] This work is also known as "A Seasonable Plea for the Liberty of Conscience and the Right of Private Judgment in Matters of Religion Without any Control from Human Authority."

[445] Elisha Williams, *The Essential Rights and Liberties of Protestants*, 1744, in *The Christian History of the American Revolution*, comp. Verna M. Hall (San Francisco, CA: Foundation for American Christian Education, 1976), 186-187.

[446] Williams, *Essential Rights and Liberties*, 189.

[447] Williams, *Essential Rights and Liberties*, 188, 189.

[448] Edwards, *Miscellaneous Observations*, vol. 1, 571.

[449] Edwards, *Concerning Efficacious Grace*, 547-8.

[450] Jonathan Edwards, *A History of the Work of Redemption*, in *The Works of President Edwards: A Reprint of the Worcester Edition*, vol. 1 (New York: Leavitt & Allen, 1858), 387; Jonathan Edwards, *Decrees and Election*, in *The Works of President Edwards: A Reprint of the Worcester Edition*, vol. 2 (New York: Leavitt & Allen, 1858), 517; Edwards, *Miscellaneous Observations*, 624, 633-635.

[451] Jonathan Edwards, *The End for Which God Created the World*, in *The Works of President Edwards: A Reprint of the Worcester Edition*, vol. 2 (New York: Leavitt & Allen, 1858), 249.

[452] Edwards, *Work of Redemption*, 402.

[453] Edwards, *Doctrine of Original Sin*, 337.

[454] Edwards, *End for Which God Created the World*, 244.

[455] Edwards footnotes on this issue Ephesians 1:20-23, John 17:2, Matthew 11:27, Matthew 28:18-19, and John 3:35.

[456] Edwards, *Miscellaneous Observations*, vol. 1, 566.

[457] Edwards, *Miscellaneous Observations*, vol. 1, 565-9, 586-7; Edwards, *Freedom of the Will*, 144-145.

[458] Edwards, *Miscellaneous Observations*, vol. 1, 568-570.

[459] Edwards, *Miscellaneous Observations*, vol. 1, 569-570.

[460] Edwards, *Miscellaneous Observations*, vol. 1, 569-571, 587.

[461] Edwards, *Miscellaneous Observations*, vol. 1, 571.

[462] Edwards, *Miscellaneous Observations*, vol. 1, 572, 574-5.

[463] Edwards, *Miscellaneous Observations*, vol. 1, 577. Edwards cites Ecclesiastes 5:8 and 3:16-17.

[464] Edwards, *End for Which God Created the World*, in *Works*, vol. 2, 235.

[465] Edwards, *Miscellaneous Observations*, 571-2.

[466] Edwards, *Miscellaneous Observations*, 575-6.

[467] Butler, Wacker, and Balmer, *Religion in American Life*, 131-2; Johnson, *History of the American People*, 115.

[468] Johnson, *History of the American People*, 115.

[469] Lambert, *Founding Fathers*, 208.

[470] Richard Bushman, *From Puritan to Yankee: Character and the Social Order in Connecticut, 1690-1765* (Cambridge, MA: Harvard U Press, 1980), 231.

[471] Lambert, *Founding Fathers*, 123-5, 129, 157-8.

[472] Noll, *History of Christianity*, 83.

[473] Johnson, *History of the American People*, 109; Noll, *History of Christianity*, 98-99.

[474] Noll, *History of Christianity*, 86.

[475] Noll, Hatch, and Marsden, *Search for Christian America*, 52; Noll, *History of Christianity*, 110.

[476] Johnson, *History of the American People*, 116.

[477] Lambert, *Founding Fathers*, 135, 142, 148, 157-8, 208.

[478] Lambert, *Founding Fathers*, 128-129.

[479] Lambert, *Founding Fathers*, 145.

[480] Waldman, *Founding Faith*, 31.

[481] Brown University, *The Charter of Brown University, Granted 1764* (Providence, RI: H. H. Brown, 1834), 12.

[482] Niebhur, *Kingdom of God*, 123.

[483] Butler, Wacker, and Balmer, *Religion in American Life*, 133-137.

[484] Niebuhr, *Kingdom of God*, 121.

[485] Noll, *History of Christianity*, 110.

[486] Gibbs, *One Nation*, 90; Noll, Hatch, and Marsden, *Search for Christian America*, 55.

[487] Noll, Hatch, and Marsden, *Search for Christian America*, 54.

[488] Ellis Sandoz, *Republicanism, Religion, and the Soul of America* (Columbia, MO: U of Missouri, 2006), 17.

[489] Johnson, *History of the American People*, 116

[490] Niebuhr, *Kingdom of God*, 126.

[491] Noll, Hatch, and Marsden, *Search for Christian America*, 65; Johnson, *History of the American People*, 116; Lambert, *Founding Fathers*, 155; Niebuhr, *Kingdom of God*, 123-124.

[492] Niebuhr, *Kingdom of God*, 124.

[493] Noll, Hatch, and Marsden, *Search for Christian America*, 49.

[494] Noll, Hatch, and Marsden, *Search for Christian America*, 55.

[495] Noll, Hatch, and Marsden, *Search for Christian America*, 49.

[496] Noll, Hatch, and Marsden, *Search for Christian America*, 54.

[497] Waldman, *Founding Faith*, 31.

[498] Noll, Hatch, and Marsden, *Search for Christian America*, 48.

[499] Alan Heimert, *Religion and the American Mind: From the Great Awakening to the Revolution* (Cambridge, MA: Harvard U Press, 1966); Noll, Hatch, and Marsden, *Search for Christian America*, 49.

[500] Johnson, *History of Christianity*, 117, 116.

[501] Noll, Hatch, and Marsden, *Search for Christian America*, 60-1.

[502] Noll, Hatch, and Marsden, *Search for Christian America*, 61.

[503] *Virginia Gazette*, October 31, 1745; Rhys Isaac, *The Transformation of Virginia, 1740-1790* (Chapel Hill, NC: Published for Institute of Early American History and Culture, Williamsburg, VA, by U of North Carolina Press, 1982), 150.

[504] Noll, *History of Christianity*, 90.

[505] Lambert, *Founding Fathers*, 128-129.

[506] Noll, *History of Christianity*, 111.

[507] Waldman, *Founding Faith*, 27.

[508] Gibbs, *One Nation*, 87; Lambert, *Founding Fathers*, 128.

[509] Phillis Wheatley, *An Elegiac Poem on the Death of the Celebrated Divine, and Eminent Servant of Jesus Christ, the Reverend and Learned Mr. George Whitefield, 1770*, in Ebenezer Pemberton, *Heaven the Residence of Saints, A Sermon Occasioned by the Sudden and Much Lamented Death of the Rev. George Whitefield*, Boston, 11 October 1770 (Boston, MA: Reprinted for E. and C. Dilly, 1771), 29-31.

Chapter 6: The Bible-Centered Debate on Revolution

[510] The Navigation, Stamp, Sugar, and Coercive or Intolerable Acts, for example, were protested by the American colonists.

[511] See the Boston Port Act of 1774 and the Massachusetts Bay Regulating Act of 1774.

[512] Butler, Wacker, and Balmer, *Religion in American Life*, 144.

[513] Harry S. Stout, *The New England Soul: Preaching and Religious Culture in Colonial New England* (New York: Oxford U Press, 1986), 264. See also Bernard Bailyn, *Religion and Revolution: Three Biographical Studies* in *Perspectives in American History*, vol. 4 (1970), 144-48, 155, 163-164.

[514] George Bancroft, *History of the United States from the Discovery of the American Continent to the Declaration of Independence*, vol. 6, new ed. (London: Routledge, Warne, & Routledge, 1861), 55.

[515] Donald S. Lutz, *The Origins of American Constitutionalism* (Baton Rouge, LA: Louisiana State U Press, 1988), 140-143. See Tables 1 and 3 in Lutz.

[516] Lutz, *Origins*, 140-143. Other frequently cited books of the Bible, says Lutz, were Psalms, Proverbs, Jeremiah, Chronicles, and

Judges. Popular sections of the books mentioned include, says Lutz, Deuteronomy 1 (13-17), 4 (20, 23, 29-40), 5, 8, 9, 10, 27, and 31; Exodus 24 (3-8) and 25; Leviticus 24; 1 Samuel 3 (11) and 20; 2 Samuel 7; 1 Kings 8 (22-66); 2 Kings 23 (1-3); and Joshua 4 and 5.

[517] Lutz, *Origins*, 142.

[518] Daniel L. Dreisbach, "The Bible in the Political Rhetoric of the American Founding," *Politics and Religion* 4, issue 3 (2011): 3. DOI: 10.1017/S1755048311000423

[519] Dreisbach, "Bible in the Political Rhetoric," 5.

[520] Dreisbach, "Bible in the Political Rhetoric," 5.

[521] Dreisbach, "Bible in the Political Rhetoric," 19-20.

[522] Dreisbach, "Bible in the Political Rhetoric," 4-5.

[523] Dreisbach, "Bible in the Political Rhetoric," 2, 5, 12, 20.

[524] Dreisbach, "Bible in the Political Rhetoric," 12-14.

[525] Dreisbach, "Bible in the Political Rhetoric," 14-15, 17-18.

[526] Joseph R. Fornieri, *Abraham Lincoln's Political Faith* (DeKalb, IL: Northern Illinois U Press, 2005), 37, 41-42, 43; Dreisbach, "Bible in the Political Rhetoric," 12, 14.

[527] Mark D. Hall, "Vindiciae, Contra Tyrannos: The Influence of the Reformed Tradition on the American Founding" (American Political Science Association 2010 Annual Meeting Paper, Washington, DC, 2010), 25-28. Available at SSRN: http://ssrn.com/abstract=1644085; Hall, *Roger Sherman*, 27-29. See also James H. Hutson, "The Christian Nation Question," in James H. Hutson, *Forgotten Features of the Founding: The Recovery of Religious Themes in the Early American Republic* (Lanham, MD: Lexington Books, 2003), 111-32; Patricia U. Bonomi and Peter R. Eisenstadt, "Church Adherence in the Eighteenth Century British Colonies," *William and Mary Quarterly*, 39 (April 1982), 275; Roger Finke and Rodney Stark, *The Churching of America, 1776-1990: Winners and Losers in Our Religious Economy* (New Brunswick, NJ: Rutgers U Press, 1992), 29.

[528] Hall, *Roger Sherman*, 27-29.

[529] Hall, *Roger Sherman*, x, 9, 22; Hall, "Vindiciae," 36.

[530] Sandoz, *Republicanism*, 78.

[531] Harold J. Laski, Historical Introduction, in Junius Brutus, *A Defense of Liberty Against Tyrants*, ed. Harold J. Laski (New York: Burt Franklin, 1972), 4.

[532] William Jones, *An Address to the British Government on a Subject of Present Concern, 1776*, in *The Theological and Miscellaneous Works of the late Rev. William Jones, in Six Volumes*, new ed., vol. 6, ed. William Stevens (London: Printed for C. and J. Rivington, 1826), 269.

[533] William Stevens Perry, *The History of the American Episcopal Church, 1587-1883, in Two Volumes*, vol. 1/1587-1783 (Boston, MA: James R. Osgood and Co., 1885), 451. This quote is taken from an excerpt of a letter of a loyalist in New York. This source indicates that the quote is taken from Extracts of a letter from a gentleman in New York, to his correspondence in London, May 31, 1774, as cited in *American Archives*, Series 4, Vol. 1, 300-301.

[534] John Adams, John Adams to F. C. Schaeffer, 25 November 1821, in James H. Hutson, *The Founders on Religion: A Book of Quotations* (Princeton, NJ: Princeton U Press, 2005), 15-16. See also Adams' Papers (microfilm), reel 124, Library of Congress.

[535] Amos, *Defending the Declaration*, 150, 127.

[536] Calvin, *Institutes*, vol. 3, bk. 4, ch. 20, sect. 23, 542.

[537] Jonathan Boucher, "Discourse X: On the Character of Ahitophel," in *A View of the Causes and Consequences of the American Revolution in Thirteen Discourses* (1797; repr., Bedford, MA: Applewood Books, 2009), 423.

[538] Jonathan Boucher, "Discourse XI: The Dispute Between the Israelites and the Two Tribes and a Half, Respecting Their Settlement Beyond Jordan," in *A View of the Causes and Consequences of the American Revolution in Thirteen Discourses* (1797; repr., Bedford, MA: Applewood Books, 2009), 485-486.

[539] Jonathan Boucher, "Discourse XII: On Civil Liberty; Passive Obedience, and Non-Resistance," in *A View of the Causes and Consequences of the American Revolution in Thirteen Discourses* (1797; repr., Bedford, MA: Applewood Books, 2009), 560.

[540] Samuel Seabury, *St. Peter's Exhortation to Fear God and Honor the King* (New York: H. Gaine, 1777), 5-6, quoted in John Fea, *Was America Founded as a Christian Nation?* (Louisville, KY: Westminster/John Knox Press, 2011), 116.

[541] Samuel Seabury, *St. Peter's Exhortation to Fear God and Honor the King*, 5-6, 12, quoted in Fea, *Was America Founded*, 116.

[542] Charles Inglis, *The Duty of Honouring the King, Explained and Recommended*, January 30, 1780 (New York: Hugh Gaine, 1780), 10, quoted in John Fea, *Was America Founded as a Christian Nation?* (Louisville, KY: Westminster/John Knox Press, 2011), 116.

[543] Charles Inglis, *Duty of Honouring the King*, 11, quoted in Fea, *Was America Founded*, 116.

[544] Hall, "Vindiciae," 37.

[545] John Adams to William Tudor, Quincy, 5 April, 1818, in John Adams, *The Works of John Adams, Second President of the United States*, vol. 10, ed. Charles F. Adams (Boston: Little, Brown, and Co., 1856), 301. Other notable colonial writings on resistance to British taxes included John Dickinson's 1768 *Letters From a Farmer in Pennsylvania*.

[546] Amos and Gardiner, *Never Before in History*, 113-114.

[547] John W. Thornton, ed., *The Pulpit of the American Revolution: Or, The Political Sermons of the Period of 1776*, 2nd ed. (Boston, MA: D. Lothrop & Co., 1876), 43.

[548] Jonathan Mayhew, *A Discourse Concerning Unlimited Submission and Non-Resistance to the Higher Powers*, Boston 1750, in

The Pulpit of the American Revolution: or, The Political Sermons of the Period of 1776 , 2nd ed., ed. John W. Thornton (Boston, MA: D. Lothrop & Co., 1876), 79.

549 Mayhew, *Discourse Concerning Unlimited Submission*, 73. In 2 Corinthians 12:7 Paul expresses, "And lest I should be exalted above measure by the abundance of the revelations, a thorn in the flesh was given to me, a messenger of Satan to buffet me, lest I be exalted above measure."

550 Mayhew, *Discourse Concerning Unlimited Submission*, 73-74.

551 Mayhew, *Discourse Concerning Unlimited Submission*, 78.

552 Mayhew, *Discourse Concerning Unlimited Submission*, 78-79. Such Biblical arguments for resistance to tyranny by Mayhew reflected Rev. Samuel Rutherford's 1644 *Lex Rex*, Ogle and Oliver & Boyd, 1843, 141-143. In *Lex Rex*, Rutherford cites additional Bible verses to support this argument. He states, "Arg. 1.—That power which is obliged to command and rule justly and religiously for the good of the subjects, and is only set over the people on these conditions, and not absolutely, cannot tied the people to subjection without resistance, when the power is abused to the destruction of laws, religion, and the subjects. But all power of the law is thus obliged, [Rutherford here cites Romans 13:4, Deuteronomy 17:18-20, 2 Chronicles 19:6, Psalm 132:11-12, 89:30-31, 2 Samuel 7:12, Jeremiah 17:24-25], and hath, and may be, abused by kings, to the destruction of laws, religion, and subjects. The proposition is clear. 1. For the powers that tie us to subjection only are of God. 2. Because to resist them, is to resist the ordinance of God. 3. Because they are not a terror to good works, but to evil. 4. Because they are God's ministers for our good, but abused powers are not of God, but of men, or not ordinances of God; they are a terror to good works, not to evil; they are not God's ministers for our good.

Arg. 2.—That power which is contrary to law, and is evil and tyrannical, can tie none to subjection, but is a mere tyrannical power and unlawful; and if it tie not to subjection, it may lawfully be resisted. ... Obligation to suffer of wicked men falleth under no commandment of God, except in our Saviour. A passion, as such, is not formally commanded, I mean a physical passion, such as to be killed, God hath not said to me in any moral law, Be thou killed, tortured, beheaded; but only, Be thou patient, if God deliver thee to wicked men's hands, to suffer these things. ...

Arg. 4.—That which is given as a blessing, and a favour, and a screen, between the people's liberty and their bondage, cannot be a given of God as a bondage and slavery to the people. But the power of king is given as a blessing and favour God to defend the poor and needy, to preserve both tables of the law, and to keep the people in their liberties from oppressing and treading one upon another. ...

Arg. 6.—If the estates of a kingdom give the power to a king, it is their own power in the fountain; and if they give it for their own good, they have power to judge when it is used against themselves, and for their evil, and so power to limit and resist the power that they gave. Now that they may take away this power, is clear in Athaliah's case [Rutherford alludes to 2 Chronicles 22 and 23]."

553 Stephen Johnson, *Some Important Observations, Occasioned By, and Adapted To, the Publick Fast, Ordered by Authority, 18 December 1765* (Newport, RI: Samuel Hall, 1766), 5-9, 20, 52. See Bernard Bailyn, *Ideological Origins of the American Revolution*, enlarged ed. (Cambridge, MA: Belknap/Harvard U Press, 1967, 1992), 238.

554 Samuel Cooper, *A Place for My People Israel, 7 April 1776, New England Historical and Genealogical Register* 132 (1978): 128-129. Other ministers also addressed these themes and justifications.

555 Luther, *Appeal to the Ruling Class*, 468.

556 Bernard Bailyn, *Pamphlets of the American Revolution, 1750-1776*, vol. 1 (Cambridge, MA: Belknap Press, 1965), 144-150.

557 Samuel Cooke, A Sermon Preached at Cambridge, 30 May 1770 (Boston, 1770), 41-42, quoted in Bernard Bailyn, *Ideological Origins of the American Revolution*, enlarged ed. (Cambridge, MA: Belknap/Harvard U Press, 1967, 1992), 239.

558 Benjamin Rush, "On Slave Keeping," 1773, in *The Selected Writings of Benjamin* Rush (New York, 1947), 17, quoted in Bernard Bailyn, *Ideological Origins of the American Revolution*, enlarged ed. (Cambridge, MA: Belknap/Harvard U Press, 1967, 1992), 239.

559 John Allen, *An Oration on the Beauties of Liberty, or The Essential Rights of the Americans,* 1772, quoted in Bernard Bailyn, *Ideological Origins of the American Revolution*, enlarged ed. (Cambridge, MA: Belknap/Harvard U Press, 1967, 1992), 240-241.

560 Levi Hart, *Liberty Described and Recommended* (Hartford, CT: 1775), v, 9 ff., 15, 16, 20-23, quoted in Bernard Bailyn, *Ideological Origins of the American Revolution*, enlarged ed. (Cambridge, MA: Belknap/Harvard U Press, 1967, 1992), 243.

561 Richard Wells, *A Few Political Reflections* (Philadelphia, PA: 1774), 79-83, quoted in Bernard Bailyn, *Ideological Origins of the American Revolution*, enlarged ed. (Cambridge, MA: Belknap/Harvard U Press, 1967, 1992), 239-241.

562 Samuel Hopkins, *Slavery of the Africans*, in *The Works of Samuel Hopkins*, vol. 2, ed. Sewall Harding (Boston, MA: Doctrinal Tract and Book Society, 1852), 571.

563 Bernard Bailyn, *Ideological Origins of the American Revolution*, enlarged ed. (Cambridge, MA: Belknap/Harvard U Press, 1967, 1992), 246.

564 Niebuhr, *Kingdom of God*, 121.

565 For an overview of the Biblical verses and arguments used to both support and denounce slavery prior to the American Civil War in the 1800s, see Bruce Feiler, *America's Prophet: Moses and the American Story* (New York: William Morrow, 2009), 153-157.

566 John Milton, *A Defense of the People of England* in *The Works of John Milton, Historical, Political, and Miscellaneous*, vol. 1, ed. Thomas Birch (London: Printed for A. Millar, 1753), 513.

567 John Adams, *Dissertation on the Canon and the Feudal Law*, 456.

568 Paine's tract echoed the Biblical arguments of ministers Jonathan Mayhew and Ebenezer Chaplin. In his "Sermon on 2 Samuel

1:18," 25 July 1779, Chaplin preached that Israel had peace and prosperity for four hundred years under the republic of the judges but suffered greatly after asking for and insisting on having a king like all the nations. See Stout, *New England Soul*, 288-289.

[569] Thomas Paine, *Common Sense*, 1776, in *Tracts of the American Revolution, 1763-1776*, ed. Merrill Jensen (Indianapolis, IN: Bobbs-Merrill Co., 1966), 411-412.

[570] Ponet, *Short Treatise*, ch. 5, para. 10.

[571] Rutherford, *Lex Rex*, 74.

[572] Paine, *Common Sense*, 434.

[573] See Stout, *New England Soul*, 280, 304, 307.

[574] Stout, *New England Soul*, 293-5.

[575] Samuel Langdon, *Government Corrupted by Vice, and Recovered by Righteousness, A Sermon Preached Before the Honorable Congress of the Colony of Massachusetts Bay*, May 31, 1775 (Watertown, MA: Printed and sold by Benjamin Edes, 1775), 11-12.

[576] Langdon, *Government Corrupted by Vice*, 26.

[577] Samuel Adams to Richard Henry Lee, Boston, 14 April 1785, in *The Writings of Samuel Adams: 1778-1802*, vol. 4, ed. Harry A. Cushing (New York: G. P. Putnam's Sons, 1908), 314.

[578] Amos, *Defending the Declaration*, 132. See also Michael H. Lessnoff, *Social Contract: Issues in Political Theory* (Atlantic Highlands, NJ: Humanities Press International, 1986), 12, 15-16.

[579] Manegold of Lautenbach, *Liber ad Gebehardum*, 1085, ed. Kuno Francke, 30, 43, 47, 48, in *Monumenta Germaniae Historica, Libelli de Lite Imperatorum et Pontificum*, 3 vols., ed. E. Sackur (Hannover, 1881-1897), 1:365, 385, 391-2; trans. Ewart Lewis, *Medieval Political Ideas*, 2 vols. (New York, 1954), 1:165, and Wilfrid Parsons, "The Medieval Theory of the Tyrant," *Review of Politics* 4 (1942): 136, quoted in Jeff Rider, *God's Scribe: The Historiographical Art of Galbert of Bruges* (Washington, DC: Catholic University of America Press, 2001), 154-5, 305.

[580] Daniel J. Elazar, *Covenant and Polity in Biblical Israel: Biblical Foundations and Jewish Expressions* (New Brunswick, NJ: Transaction Publishers, 1995), 81, 213; Elazar, *Covenant & Commonwealth*, 78-79, 89. In his work, Manegold includes a synopsis of the Bible and closely linked his views with the Bible.

[581] Elazar, *Covenant & Commonwealth*, 79.

[582] Daniel J. Elazar, *Covenant and Constitutionalism: The Great Frontier and the Matrix of Federal Democracy* (New Brunswick, NJ: Transaction Publishers, 1998), 7.

[583] Manegold of Lautenbach, *Liber ad Gebehardum*, 1085, quoted in John Keane, *The Life and Death of Democracy* (New York: W. W. Norton & Co., 2009), 217.

[584] Keane, *Life and Death*, 217.

[585] See Michael Lessnoff, ed., *Social Contract Theory*, 5. See also Michael Lessnoff, *Social Contract: Issues in Political Theory*.

[586] Olga Babaeva, *Social Contract Theory in Early Modern France, Germany, Poland, and Russia: A Comparison; A Thesis in History submitted to the Graduate Faculty of Texas Tech University* (Lubbock, TX: December 1998), 2-3.

[587] Brutus, *Vindiciae*, 21.

[588] Brutus, *Vindiciae*, 22.

[589] Brutus, *Vindiciae*, 21-23, 41, 52.

[590] Brutus, *Vindiciae*, 40-41.

[591] Brutus, *Vindiciae*, 38.

[592] Brutus, *Vindiciae*, 22-23.

[593] Brutus, *Vindiciae*, 41-42.

[594] Brutus, *Vindiciae*, 25-26.

[595] Brutus, *Vindiciae*, 129-131.

[596] Brutus, *Vindiciae*, 130.

[597] Brutus, *Vindiciae*, 130.

[598] Brutus, *Vindiciae*, 30.

[599] Brutus, *Vindiciae*, 131.

[600] Brutus, *Vindiciae*, 21-50.

[601] Althusius, *Politics*, 117.

[602] Elazar, "Political Theory of Covenant," 20; McCoy and Baker, *Fountainhead of Federalism*, 46, 50, 53-56; Klosko, *Oxford Handbook*, 578. See also Althusius's *Politics*; Lessnoff's *Social Contract*;

[603] Judah Champion, *A Brief View of the Distresses, Hardships and Dangers Our Ancestors Encountered* (Hartford, CT: Printed by Green and Watson, 1770), 40, quoted in Harry S. Stout, *New England Soul: Preaching and Religious Culture in Colonial New England* (New York: Oxford U Press, 1986), 274, 376.

[604] Edward Barnard, "Sermon on Psalm 122:1-6," July 24, 1766, Sermons Collection, Folder 4, EI, quoted in Harry S. Stout, *New England Soul: Preaching and Religious Culture in Colonial New England* (New York: Oxford U Press, 1986), 266-267, 375.

[605] Calvin, *Institutes*, vol. 3, bk. 4, ch. 20, sect. 32, 551.

[606] Calvin, *Institutes*, vol. 3, bk. 4, ch. 20, sect. 32, 552.

[607] Ponet *Short Treatise*, ch. 1, para. 11.

[608] Brutus, *Vindiciae*, 30.

[609] Ponet, *Short Treatise*, ch. 3, para. 1.

[610] Brutus, *Vindiciae*, 20.

[611] Luther, *Secular Authority*, 399.

[612] Ponet, *Short Treatise*, ch. 4, para. 14.

[613] Ponet, *Short Treatise*, ch. 4, para. 10, 15, 31.

[614] Ponet, *Short Treatise*, ch. 4, para. 31.

[615] Brutus, *Vindiciae*, 29-30.

[616] Brutus, *Vindiciae*, 31-32.

[617] Brutus, *Vindiciae*, 32.

[618] Brutus, *Vindiciae*, 32-33.

[619] Brutus, *Vindiciae*, 33.

[620] Brutus, *Vindiciae*, 33.

[621] Ponet, *Short Treatise*, ch. 4, para. 34.

[622] Ponet, *Short Treatise*, ch. 4, para. 37.

[623] Mayhew, *Discourse Concerning Unlimited Submission*, 86.

[624] Ponet, *Short Treatise*, ch. 2, para. 12.

[625] Ponet, *Short Treatise*, ch. 4, para. 37.

[626] Ponet, *Short Treatise*, ch. 6, para. 26.

[627] Brutus, *Vindiciae*, 149.

[628] Brutus, *Vindiciae*, 150.

[629] Ponet, *Short Treatise*, ch. 3, para. 3.

[630] Rutherford, *Lex Rex*, 31, 32, 196, 171-2.

[631] Revolutionaries like John Allen cited Judges 5:9 on this point.

[632] William Emerson, "Sermon on 2 Chronicles 13:12," 13 March 1775, in *Diaries and Letters of William Emerson, 1743-1776*, ed. Amelia F. Emerson (Concord, MA: Privately printed, 1972), 61, 66, 69. See also Harry Stout, *New England Soul*, 289-290.

[633] Stout, *New England Soul*, 288-289.

[634] Stout, *New England Soul*, 290.

[635] David Jones, *Defensive war in A Just Cause Sinless* (Philadelphia, PA: Henry Miller, 1775), 4.

[636] Jones, *Defensive War*, 3.

[637] John Carmichael, *A Self-Defensive War Lawful* (Philadelphia, PA: John Dean, 1775), 8-9, 15-17, quoted in John Fea, *Was America Founded As A Christian Nation? A Historical Introduction* (Louisville, KY: Westminster/John Knox Press, 2011), 114.

[638] In a sermon on 2 Chronicles 13:12, Rev. William Emerson, chaplain in the Revolutionary Army, for example, preached, "…[O]ur Military Preparation here for our own Defense is not only excusable but justified in the Eyes of the impartial World: nay, for should we neglect to defend ourselves by military Preparation, we never could answer it to God and to our own Consciences or the rising [generations]." William Emerson, "Sermon on 2 Chronicles 13:12" in *Diaries and Letters of William Emerson, 1743-1776*, ed. Amelia F. Emerson (Boston, MA: Privately printed/Thomas Todd, 1972), 66.

Chapter 7: The Rationale of America's Revolution

[639] William J. Seabury, *Memoir of Bishop Seabury* (New York: Edwin S. Gorham, 1908), 162. The papers of "A Westchester Farmer" were attributed by William Seabury and other scholars to Samuel Seabury.

[640] Samuel Seabury, *Samuel Seabury's Ungathered Imprints: Historical Perspectives of the Early National Years,* ed. Kenneth W. Cameron (Hartford, CT: Transcendental Books, 1978), 70; Alexander Hamilton, "The Farmer Refuted," 5 February 1775, in *The Works of Alexander Hamilton; Comprising His Correspondence, and His Political and Official Writings*, vol. 2, ed. John C. Hamilton (New York: John. F. Trow for Library of Congress, 1850), 62.

[641] Stout, *New England Soul*, 291-292.

[642] Alexander Hamilton, Federalist Paper #1 in *The Federalist Papers*, ed. Clinton Rossiter (New York: Mentor/Penguin Books, 1961), 33.

[643] Michael Novak, *On Two Wings: Humble Faith and Common Sense at the American Founding* (San Francisco, CA: Encounter Books, 2002), 12.

[644] Perry Miller, *Nature's Nation* (Cambridge, MA: Belknap Press/Harvard U Press, 1967), 104.

[645] For more on Theistic Rationalism, see Gregg L. Frazer, *The Religious Beliefs of America's Founders: Reason, Revelation, and Revolution* (Lawrence, KS: U Press of Kansas, 2012), 19-20. Influenced by the Enlightenment, theistic rationalists like Thomas Jefferson and Benjamin Franklin believed truth is understood by reason. Reason is the basis of truth. However, they did acknowledge some divine revelation that complemented and could be understood by reason. They believed in a benevolent Creator who was involved in human affairs and responded to prayer, and they believed serving God involved living a moral life. They also believed in an afterlife with rewards and punishments. While they did not generally believe the supernatural elements of the Bible or that Jesus was the Son of God, they did view the Bible as a great moral book and Jesus as a great moral teacher. They encouraged religion and the reading of the Bible because it increased morality which was necessary in civil society.

[646] Thomas Jefferson to Henry Lee, Monticello, 8 May 1825, in *The Writings of Thomas Jefferson*, definitive ed., ed. Albert E. Bergh, vol. 15 (Washington, DC: Thomas Jefferson Memorial Association, 1907), 118-119.

[647] For support on the divide between the intellectual rationalists and the Christian masses, see Gregg L. Frazer, *Religious Beliefs of*

America's Founders, 20-22. I would offer that many Christians of the 1700s, particularly the orthodox ministers, were well-educated and well-read. See also chapter 6 and the statistics on active church-goers in the founding-generation.

[648] James Wilson, *Lectures on Law, Part 1, 1790-1791*, in *The Works of the Honourable James Wilson*, vol. 1, ed. Bird Wilson (Philadelphia, PA: Lorenzo Press, Printed for Bronson and Chauncey, 1804), 109. See also Jean-Jacques Burlamaqui, *The Principles of Natural Law, in which the True Systems of Morality and Civil Government Are Established, 1748*, pt. 2, trans. Thomas Nugent (London: Printed for J. Nourse, 1748), 83-84. Burlamaqui is quoting Jean Barbeyrac whose discourse and notes are found in Barbeyrac's editions of Samuel von Pufendorf's *Law of Nature and Nations* (book 1, ch. 6), and *Duty of Man and Citizen* (book 1, ch. 2).

[649] Wilson *Lectures on Law*, 111.

[650] Wilson, *Lectures on Law*, 108.

[651] James Madison, James Madison to Frederick Beasley, Montpellier, 20 November 1825, in *The Writings of James Madison*, vol. 9/1819-1836, ed. Gaillard Hunt (New York: G. P. Putnam's Sons, 1910), 230.

[652] See Genesis 1:26-27 and 2:7. See also Rosalie Slater's *Teaching and Learning America's Christian History*, p. 154-55.

[653] Russell Kirk, *American Cause*, ed. Gleaves Whitney (Wilmington, DE: Intercollegiate Studies Institute, 2002), 20, 23.

[654] Kirk, *American Cause*, 24-25.

[655] See Wilson, *Lectures on Law*, 104; Russell Kirk, *The Roots of American Order* (Washington, DC: Regnery Gateway, 1991), 109-112, 369-370; Novak, *Two Wings*, 13, 78.

[656] Marcus Tullius Cicero, *Treatise on the Republic*, in *The Political Works of Marcus Tullius Cicero*, vol. 1, ed. Francis Barham (London: Edmund Spettigue, 1841), 270.

[657] Amos, *Defending the Declaration*, 72.

[658] Thomas Jefferson to James Madison, Monticello, 17 February 1826, in *Memoir, Correspondence, and Miscellanies: From the Papers of Thomas Jefferson*, Vol. 4, ed. Thomas J. Randolph (Charlottesville, VA: F. Carr & Co, 1829), 426.

[659] John Rutledge to his brother, Charleston, 30 July 1769, in John B. O'Neall, *Biographical Sketches of the Bench and Bar of South Carolina*, vol. 2 (Charleston, SC: S. G. Courtenay & Co., 1859), 124.

[660] Sandoz, *Republicanism*, 111.

[661] Sandoz, *Republicanism*, 97.

[662] Sandoz, *Republicanism*, 111.

[663] The canon law of the Catholic church influenced English law and thus also American law. The early canon law helped to develop what is today understood as property law, inheritance law, contract law, constitutional law, and criminal law.

[664] William Blackstone, Announcement on the Course of Lectures which led to the Commentaries on the Laws of England, 23 June 1753, in William Blackstone, *Commentaries on the Laws of England*, vol. 1, ed. William C. Jones (San Francisco, CA: Bancroft-Whitney Co., 1915), xv.

[665] Kirk, *Roots*, 369-370.

[666] William Blackstone, *Blackstone's Commentaries, in Five Volumes*, vol. 1, ed. George Tucker (Union, NJ: Lawbook Exchange, LTD, 1996, 2008), 39-41.

[667] Locke, *Second Treatise*, Routledge, 193-194.

[668] Paul drew from Old Testament scriptures on God's creation laws in the world, says Amos, including Psalm 19, Psalm 78:2-3, Psalm 119:89-91, and the book of Job (Job 8:8-10, 12:3, 13:1, 15:7-10). See Amos, *Defending the Declaration*, 44-46.

[669] Saint Augustine, *The Confessions of St. Augustine, Bishop of Hippo*, bk. 2, trans. J. G. Pilkington (Edinburgh, Scotland: T & T Clark, 1876), 30.

[670] Thomas Aquinas, *The Summa Theologica of St. Thomas Aquinas*, pt. 2, no. 3/QQ XC-CXIV, trans. Fathers of the English Dominican Province (London: R. &. T. Washbourne, 1915), 11, q. 91, a. 2.

[671] Aquinas, *Summa Theologica*, pt. 2, Washbourne, 1915, 52, q. 94, a. 6.

[672] Calvin, *Institutes*, vol. 1, bk. 2, 325.

[673] Ponet, *Short Treatise*, ch. 6, para. 14.

[674] Ames, *Marrow of Theology*, 108-9, 112, 123.

[675] Richard Hooker, *The Laws of Ecclesiastical Polity, Books 1-4, 1593*, bk. 1 (London: George Routledge and Sons, 1888), 86. Richard Hooker further states on page 81, "The general and perpetual voice of men is as the sentence of God himself. For that which all men have at all times learned, Nature herself must needs have taught; and God being the author of Nature, her voice is but his instrument. By her from Him we receive whatsoever in such sort we learn. Infinite duties there are, the goodness whereof is by this rule sufficiently manifested, although we had no other warrant besides to approve them. The Apostle St. Paul having speech concerning the heathen saith of them, 'They are a law unto themselves.' His meaning is, that by force of the light of reason, wherewith God illuminateth every one which cometh into the world, men being enabled to know truth from falsehood, and good from evil, do thereby learn in many things what the will of God is; which will Himself not revealing by any extraordinary means unto them, but by natural discourse attaining the knowledge thereof, seem the makers of those laws which indeed are His, and they but only the finders of them out." Hooker also states on page 87, "Wherefore as touching the law of reason, this was, it seemeth, St. Augustine's judgment, namely, that there are in it some things which stand as principles universally agreed upon, and that out of those principles, which are in themselves evident, the greatest moral duties we owe towards God or man may without any great difficulty be concluded."

[676] Amos, *Defending the Declaration*, 47-8.

[677] Edward Coke, *Coke v. Smith and Another*, Trin. 6 Jac. 1, 7 Coke's, *Reports*, 1, quoted in Gary T. Amos, *Defending the*

Declaration: How the Bible and Christianity Influenced the Writing of the Declaration of Independence (Brentwood, TN: Wolgemuth & Hyatt, 1989), 43, 188; Robert Campbell, ed., *Calvin's Case, 1608*, in *Ruling Cases Arranged, Annotated, and Edited*, vol. 2: Action-Amendment (London: Stevens and Sons, 1894), 598-599.

[678] Samuel von Pufendorf, *Of the Law of Nature and Nations, Eight Books*, English ed., 2nd ed., ed. Jean Barbeyrac, trans. Basil Kennett (Oxford: Printed by L. Lichfield for A. and J. Churchil, 1710), bk. 2, 117-118. Dutch theologian Hugo Grotius and German professor Baron Samuel von Pufendorf were influential in making Natural Law the basis of International Law. Grotius authored the first significant text on international law, *Concerning the Law of War and Peace*, in 1625. (He also wrote *The Truth of the Christian Religion* in 1627.) Pufendorf wrote on the Law of Nature among nations in his *Of the Law of Nature and Nations* in 1703.

[679] Pufendorf, *Law of Nature and Nations*, bk. 2, 107.

[680] John Locke, *The Reasonableness of Christianity, As Delivered in the Scriptures,* 2nd ed. (London: Printed for Awnsham and John Churchil at the Black Swan, 1696), 17-18. See also John Locke's *Essays on the Law of Nature* and *Second Treatise of Civil Government*.

[681] Deuteronomy 6:5: "You shall love the LORD your God with all your heart, with all your soul, and with all your strength." Leviticus 19:18: "…[Y]ou shall love your neighbor as yourself…." Matthew 7:12: "Therefore, whatever you want men to do to you, do also to them, for this is the Law and the Prophets."

[682] Kirk, *American Cause*, 20-21.

[683] Noah Webster to A Young Gentleman Commencing His Education, Letter 1, in *Letters to A Young Gentleman Commencing His Education*, Noah Webster (New Haven, CT: Howe & Spalding, 1823), 7.

[684] Kirk, *Roots*, 11-13, 16-7.

[685] John Adams to F. A. Vanderkemp, 16 February 1809, in *The Works of John Adams, Second President of the United States*, Vol. 9, ed. Charles F. Adams (Boston, MA: Little, Brown, & Co., 1854), 609-10.

[686] Locke, *Reasonableness of Christianity*, 22.

[687] Amos, *Defending the Declaration*, 42-44, 65, 68.

[688] Amos, *Defending the Declaration*, 44-46.

[689] Calvin, *Institutes*, vol. 3, bk. 4, 534.

[690] Calvin, *Institutes*, vol. 3, bk. 4, 534-535.

[691] Calvin, *Institutes*, vol. 1, 430.

[692] On the recognition of Ponet's influence to the American founding, see John Adams, *A Defence of the Constitution of Government of the United States of America*, vol. 3 cont., in *The Works of John Adams, Second President of the United States*, vol. 6, ed. Charles F. Adams (Boston: Charles C. Little and James Brown, 1851), 3-4.

[693] Ponet, *Short Treatise*, ch. 1, para. 3-4.

[694] Winthrop, *Model of Christian Charity*, 77-78.

[695] Westminster General Assembly, *Confession of Faith*, 103-104, 106. The Confession of Faith includes footnoted references to and excerpts of the following verses: a. Genesis 1:26-27, Genesis 2:17, Romans 2:14-15, Romans 10:5, Romans 5:12, 19, Galatians 3:10, 12, Ecclesiastes 7:29, Job 28:8. b. James 1:25, James 2:8-12, Romans 13:8-9, Deuteronomy 5:32, Deuteronomy 10:4, Exodus 34:1. c. Matthew 22:37-40. h. Romans 13:8-10, Ephesians 6:2, 1 John 2:3-4, 7-8. i. James 2:10-11. k. Matthew 5:17-19, James 2:8, Romans 3:31.

[696] Richard Hooker, *Ecclesiastical Polity*, bk. 1, 111.

[697] Locke, *Reasonableness of Christianity*, 17-18.

[698] John Locke, *First Treatise of Civil Government*, in *Two Treatises on Government*, bk. 1 (London: George Routledge and Sons, 1884), 142, 157, 164; Locke, *Second Treatise*, Routledge, 223, 266, 293.

[699] Locke, *Reasonableness of Christianity*, 21-22,

[700] John Locke, *An Essay Concerning Human Understanding*, 27th ed. (London: Printed for T. Tegg and Son, 1836), 251, bk. 2, ch. 28.

[701] Blackstone, *Commentaries*, ed. Tucker, 41. Blackstone's views of the Law of Nature reflected, says Amos, Genesis 1, Hebrews 11, and Romans 1 and 2. Amos, *Defending the Declaration*, 42.

[702] Pufendorf, *Law of Nature and Nations*, bk. 3, 205.

[703] Samuel von Pufendorf, *The Whole Duty of Man According to the Law of Nature*, English ed., 4th ed., ed. Jean Barbeyrac, trans. Andrew Tooke (London: Printed for B. Tooke and J. Hooke, 1716), bk. 1, 65-66.

[704] Pufendorf, *Duty of Man*, bk. 1, 118-119.

[705] Pufendorf, *Duty of Man*, bk. 1, 135.

[706] Pufendorf, *Duty of Man*, bk. 1, 74-75.

[707] Pufendorf, *Duty of Man*, bk. 1, 45-73. See chs. 3 & 4.

[708] Novak, *Two Wings*, 82. See also pp. 81, 90.

[709] John Adams, *Dissertation on the Canon and Feudal Law*, 462-463.

[710] Thomas Aquinas, *The Summa Theologica of St. Thomas Aquinas*, pt. 2, no. 1/QQ I-XXVI, trans. Fathers of the English Dominican Province (New York: Benziger Brothers, 1911), 19-20.

[711] Aquinas, *The Summa Theologica of St. Thomas Aquinas*, pt. 2, no. 3/QQ XC-CXIV, trans. Fathers of the English Dominican Province (New York: Benziger Brothers, 1915), 118, q. 100, a. 3.

[712] Richard Hooker, *Ecclesiastical Polity*, bk. 1, 82, 87. See also John Locke, *Essays on the Law of Nature* (Leyden: Oxford

Clarendon Press, 1954), 36.

[713] Locke, *Essay Concerning Human Understanding*, 453, 455, 457, bk. 4, ch. 7.

[714] Locke, *Essay Concerning Human Understanding*, 476, bk. 4, ch. 10, sec. 7.

[715] Locke, *Essay Concerning Human Understanding*, 458, bk. 4, ch. 7, sec. 11.

[716] Thomas Reid, *Lecture VII: Of Reasoning*, in *Essays on the Powers of the Human Mind*, vol. 2 (Edinburgh, Scotland: Printed for Bell & Bradfute, 1812), 435-437.

[717] Reid, *Of Reasoning*, 431. Reid also states, "The propositions which I think are properly called moral, are those that affirm some moral obligation to be, or not to be incumbent on one or more individual persons. … They are given the creatures of God; their obligation results from the constitution which God has given them, and the circumstances in which he has placed them." (Reid, *Of Reasoning*, 430).

[718] See Amos, *Defending the Declaration*, 99-101. See also Jeffry H. Morrison, *John Witherspoon and the Founding of the American Republic* (Notre Dame: University of Notre Dame Press, 2005).

[719] Daniel N. Robinson, "James Wilson and Natural Rights Constitutionalism: The Influence of the Scottish Enlightenment," *Natural Law, Natural Rights, and American Constitutionalism Online Resource* (2012), Witherspoon Institute, http://www.nlnrac.org/american/scottish-enlightenment (accessed April 2012).

[720] Wilson, *Lectures on Law*, ch. 6, 256-257.

[721] Thomas Jefferson to Henry Lee, Monticello, 8 May 1825, in *The Writings of Thomas Jefferson*, vol. 7, ed. H. A. Washington (Washington, DC: Taylor & Maury, 1854), 407.

[722] Thomas Jefferson to Thomas Law, 13 June 1814, in *The Writings of Thomas Jefferson*, vol. 6, ed. Henry A. Washington (New York: Derby & Jackson, 1859), 348-50.

[723] Thomas Jefferson to James Fishback, 27 September 1809, in *The Writings of Thomas Jefferson*, vol. 12, ed. Albert E. Bergh (Washington, DC: Thomas Jefferson Memorial Association, 1904), 315.

[724] James Otis, *The Rights of the British Colonists Asserted and Proved, Boston 1764*, in *Pamphlets of the American Revolution, 1750-1776*, vol. 1, ed. Bernard Bailyn (Cambridge, MA: Belknap Press, 1965), 426.

[725] Otis, *Rights of the British Colonists*, 454.

[726] General Assembly of Massachusetts, Resolutions of the House of Representatives of Massachusetts, 29 Oct 1765, in *The Writings of Samuel Adams: 1764-1769*, vol. 1, ed. Harry A. Cushing (New York: G. P. Putnam's Sons, 1904), 23-24.

[727] Samuel Adams, *Report on the Rights of the Colonists*, 20 November 1772, in *American Patriotism: Speeches, Letters, and Other Papers Which Illustrate the Foundation, the Development, the Preservation of the United States of America*, comp. Selim H. Peabody (New York: American Book Exchange, 1880), 33.

[728] John Adams to Dr. J. Morse, Quincy, 5 December, 1815, in *The Works of John Adams, Second President of the United States*, vol. 10, ed. Charles F. Adams (Boston: Little, Brown, and Co., 1856), 190.

[729] John Adams to Timothy Pickering, 6 August 1822, in *The Works of John Adams, Second President of the United States*, vol. 2, ed. Charles F. Adams (Boston: Little, Brown, and Co., 1865), 514.

[730] Wilson, *Lectures on Law*, 64. See 12th lecture. Declaration and Constitution signer and lawyer James Wilson's views of the Law of Nature, says scholar Daniel Robinson, made important contributions to constitutional legal thought of the United States. See Robinson, "James Wilson and Natural Rights Constitutionalism," Witherspoon Institute, http://www.nlnrac.org/american/scottish-enlightenment (accessed April 2012).

[731] Samuel Adams to the Legislature of Massachusetts, 17 January 1794, in *The Writings of Samuel Adams: 1778-1802*, vol. 4, ed. Harry A. Cushing (New York: G. P. Putnam's Sons, 1908), 356.

[732] John Adams, Diary, Notes of a Debate in the Senate of the United States, 24 August 1796, in *The Works of John Adams, Second President of the United States*, vol. 3, ed. Charles F. Adams (Boston: Charles C. Little and James Brown, 1851), 423.

[733] John Witherspoon, "The Yoke of Christ," in *The Works of John Witherspoon, in Four Volumes*, vol. 2, 2nd ed., ed. John Rodgers (Philadelphia, PA: William W. Woodward, 1802), 296-297. Witherspoon's sermon refers to Matthew 11:30 which states, "For my yoke is easy, and my burden is light."

[734] Wilson, *Lectures on Law*, 118.

[735] Wilson, *Lectures on Law*, 104, 120.

[736] Wilson, *Lectures on Law*, 120.

[737] Wilson, *Lectures on Law*, 105, 155.

[738] Benjamin Rush to Rev. Jeremy Belknap, "A Defense of the Use of the Bible in Schools," Philadelphia, 10 March 1791, in *Essays, Literary, Moral and Philosophical*, 2nd ed., by Benjamin Rush (Philadelphia, PA: Printed by Thomas and William Bradford, 1806), 105. John 13:34 states: "A new commandment I [Jesus] give to you, that you love one another; as I have loved you, that you also love one another."

[739] Benjamin Rush, *The Road to Fulfillment* (New York: Harper & Brothers, 1942), 15.

[740] Amos, *Defending the Declaration*, 60-61, 68, 74. See Locke's *Reasonableness of Christianity*, ch. 30, sec. 22. See also Morton White, *The Philosophy of the American Revolution* (New York: Oxford U Press, 1978), 157, quoted in Amos, *Defending the Declaration*, 61, 196.

[741] Amos, *Defending the Declaration*, 60.

[742] Kirk, *Roots*, 403.

[743] Calvin, *Institutes*, vol 3., 533-535.

[744] Ponet, *Short Treatise*, ch. 1, para. 2. Acts 17:24-28: "God, who made the world and everything in it, since He is Lord of heaven

and earth, does not dwell in temples made with hands. Nor is He worshiped with men's hands, as though He needed anything, since He gives to all life, breath, and all things. And He has made from one blood every nation of men to dwell on all the face of the earth, and has determined their preappointed times and the boundaries of their dwellings, so that they should seek the Lord, in the hope that they might grope for Him and find Him, though He is not far from each one of us; for in Him we live and move and have our being, as also some of your own poets have said, 'For we are also His offspring.'" Psalms 100:3: "Know that the LORD, He *is* God; *It is* He *who* has made us, and not we ourselves; *We are* His people and the sheep of His pasture." Hebrews 2:10: "For it was fitting for Him, for whom *are* all things and by whom *are* all things, in bringing many sons to glory...." Isaiah 9:6-7: For unto us a Child is born, Unto us a Son is given; And the government will be upon His shoulder. ... Of the increase of *His* government and peace *There will be* no end, Upon the throne of David and over His kingdom, To order it and establish it with judgment and justice From that time forward, even forever."

[745] Charles Louis Secondat Baron de Montesquieu, *The Spirit of Laws, in Two Volumes*, New ed., vol. 2, trans. Thomas Nugent, ed. J. V. Prichard (London: George Bell & Sons, 1892), bk. 24, 111.

[746] Montesquieu, *Spirit of Laws*, vol. 2, bk. 24, 113.

[747] Blackstone, *Commentaries*, ed. Tucker, 42.

[748] Richard Hooker, *Ecclesiastical Polity,* bk. 3, 203.

[749] Locke, *Second Treatise*, Routledge, 262.

[750] Locke, *Second Treatises*, Routledge, 262.

[751] Algernon Sidney, *Discourses Concerning Government, to which are added, Memoirs of his Life*, 1698, 3rd ed. (London: Printed for A. Millar, 1751), 48.

[752] Wilson, *Lectures on Law*, 104-105, 106.

[753] Alexander Hamilton, "The Farmer Refuted," February 5, 1775, in *The Works of Alexander Hamilton; Comprising His Correspondence and His Political and Official Writings*, vol. 2, ed. John C. Hamilton (New York: Joint Library Committee of Congress, Printed by John F. Trow, 1850), 61.

[754] Bernard C. Steiner, *One Hundred and Ten Years of Bible Society Work in Maryland, 1810-1920*, (Baltimore, MD: Maryland Bible Society, 1921), 13-14.

[755] Joseph Story, *A Discourse Pronounced Upon the Inauguration of the Author, as Dane Professor of Law in Harvard University, 25 August 1829* (Boston, MA: Hilliard, Gray, Little, and Wilkins, 1829), 20-21.

[756] John Quincy Adams, "The Nation's Birth-Day," 4 July 1821, Address at Washington, *Niles' Weekly Register, Mar-Sept 1821* (Baltimore) 20, no. 21 (Mar-Sept, 21 July 1821): 331.

[757] See Amos, *Defending the Declaration*, 142-147; Amos and Gardiner, *Never Before in History*, 36-37; Jon Roland, *Introduction to Samuel Rutherford's Lex, Rex*, Constitution Society (1995-2012), <http://www.constitution.org/sr/intro_jr.htm> (accessed April 2012).

[758] Caroline Robbins, "Algernon Sidney's Discourses Concerning Government: Textbook of Revolution," *William and Mary Quarterly*, 1947, 3rd series, 4:266-296.

[759] Lutz, *Origins*, 119.

[760] Novak, *Two Wings*, 81.

[761] Locke, *First Treatise*, 122-3.

[762] Locke, *Second Treatise*, Routledge, 192.

[763] Locke, *Second Treatise*, Routledge, 192-193.

[764] Locke, *Second Treatise*, Routledge, 217.

[765] Sidney, *Discourses*, 16-17.

[766] Benjamin Rush, *Of The Mode of Education Proper in a Republic*, in *Essays, Literary, Moral and Philosophical*, 2nd ed. (Philadelphia, PA: Printed by Thomas and William Bradford, 1806), 8-9.

[767] John Adams, Notes of A Debate in the Senate of the United States, 421.

[768] Wilson, *Lectures on Law*, 309.

[769] Thomas Jefferson to Roger C. Weightman, Monticello, 24 June 1826, in *Memoir, Correspondence, and Miscellanies: From the Papers of Thomas Jefferson*, ed. Thomas J. Randolph (Charlottesville, VA: F. Carr & Co., 1829), 441.

[770] Amos, *Defending the Declaration*, 106-7.

[771] Novak, *Two Wings*, 10-11, 24, 87.

[772] Thomas Jefferson, "Appendix to the Memoir" in *Memoir, Correspondence, and Miscellanies, From the Papers of Thomas Jefferson*, vol. 1, 2nd ed., ed. Thomas J. Randolph (Boston, MA: Gray and Bowen, 1830), 116.

[773] Thomas Jefferson, "Notes on Virginia," in *The Writings of Thomas Jefferson*, vol. 8, ed. Henry A. Washington (Philadelphia, PA: J. B. Lippincott & Co., 1864), bk. 4, 404.

[774] Amos, *Defending the Declaration*, 115-6, 124-5.

[775] Amos, *Defending the Declaration*, 117-119, 122. The Dominicans also viewed man's material property, his goods and estate, though transferable, as a provision from God and a natural aspect of man. In this sense, says Amos, they saw the right to estate property also as unalienable. Though other Catholic orders differed in this view, the Dominican view was endorsed by the Catholic Church and accepted by Calvinists and English common law.

[776] Amos, *Defending the Declaration*, 105, 107-8. See Genesis 1-4 (specifically 2:16-17, 3:1-13, and 4:7). Genesis 4:6-7 states, "So the LORD said to Cain, 'Why are you angry? And why has your countenance fallen? If you do well, will you not be accepted? And if you do not do well, sin lies at the door. And its desire *is* for you, but you should rule over it."

[777] Calvin, *Institutes*, vol. 1, bk. 1, 52-53.

[778] Calvin, *Institutes*, vol. 1, bk. 2, 430-1.

[779] Ponet, *Short Treatise*, ch. 4, para. 11-12.

[780] Ponet, *Short Treatise*, ch. 4, para. 10.

[781] Brutus, *Vindiciae*, 16-17.

[782] Roger Williams, *Bloudy Tenent*, 219. On stewardship, see Luke 12:35-48, Luke 16:1-12, 1 Corinthians 4:1-2, 1 Corinthians 9:17, Colossians 1:25, and 1 Peter 4:10.

[783] Sidney, *Discourses*, ch. 3, 406.

[784] Sidney, *Discourses*, ch. 3, 406.

[785] Sidney, *Discourses*, ch. 1, 24.

[786] Sidney, *Discourses*, ch. 3, 406.

[787] Locke, *Second Treatise*, Routledge, ch. 7, 234 and ch. 9, 256.

[788] Locke, *Second Treatise*, Routledge, ch. 5, 203-216.

[789] Locke, *Second Treatise*, Routledge, ch. 2, 194.

[790] Samuel Adams, "A State of the Rights of Colonists," 1772, in *Tracts of the American Revolution, 1763-1776*, ed. Merrill Jensen (Indianapolis, IN: Bobbs-Merrill Co., 1967), 235-236.

[791] Samuel Adams, "Rights of Colonists," 236.

[792] Samuel Adams, "Rights of Colonists," 238.

[793] Francis Hutcheson, *A System of Moral Philosophy in Three Books*, vol. 1, bk. 1, ed. William Leechman (London: Published by His Son Francis Hutcheson, 1755), 261. See also pp. 309, 288-289. See also Burlamaqui's *Principles of Natural Right*.

[794] Garry Wills, *Inventing America: Jefferson's Declaration of Independence* (New York: Vintage Books, 1978), 237.

[795] Robinson, "James Wilson and Natural Rights Constitutionalism," Witherspoon Institute, <http://www.nlnrac.org/american/scottish-enlightenment> (accessed April 2012).

[796] Wilson, *Lectures on Law*, 308.

[797] *Chisholm v. Georgia*, 2 U.S. 419 (1793). *Natural Law, Natural Rights, and American Constitutionalism Online Resource* (2012), Witherspoon Institute, <http://www.nlnrac.org/american/scottish-enlightenment> (accessed April 2012).

[798] Robinson, "James Wilson and Natural Rights Constitutionalism," Witherspoon Institute, <http://www.nlnrac.org/american/scottish-enlightenment> (accessed April 2012).

[799] Waldman, *Founding Faith*, 92-93.

[800] Amos, *Defending the Declaration*, 112.

[801] Wills, *Inventing America*, 245-247, 251.

[802] Francis Hutcheson, *A Short Introduction to Moral Philosophy: In Three Parts, Containing the Elements of Ethicks and the Law of Nature*, bk. 2 (Dublin: Printed by William McKenzie, 1787), 96.

[803] Amos, *Defending the Declaration*, 120. Matthew 5:1-11 states, "And seeing the multitudes, He went up on a mountain, and when He was seated His disciples came to Him. Then He opened His mouth and taught them, saying: 'Blessed *are* the poor in spirit, For theirs is the kingdom of heaven. Blessed *are* those who mourn, For they shall be comforted. Blessed *are* the meek, For they shall inherit the earth. Blessed *are* those who hunger and thirst for righteousness, For they shall be filled. Blessed *are* the merciful, For they shall obtain mercy. Blessed *are* the pure in heart, For they shall see God. Blessed *are* the peacemakers, For they shall be called sons of God. Blessed *are* those who are persecuted for righteousness' sake, For theirs is the kingdom of heaven. Blessed are you when they revile and persecute you, and say all kinds of evil against you falsely for My sake. Rejoice and be exceedingly glad, for great *is* your reward in heaven, for so they persecuted the prophets who were before you.'"

[804] Jean-Jacques Burlamaqui, *The Principles of Natural Law, in Which the True Systems of Morality and Civil Government Are Established, 1748*, pt. 2, trans. Thomas Nugent (London: Printed for J. Nourse, 1748), ch. 4, 161.

[805] Blackstone, *Commentaries*, ed. Tucker, 40.

[806] Pufendorf, *Law of Nature and Nations*, bk. 2, ch. 3, 117.

[807] Hutcheson, *Short Introduction to Moral Philosophy*, 238.

[808] General Assembly of Virginia, Virginia Declaration of Rights, June 12, 1776, in *Documents of American Democracy: A Collection of Essential Works*, ed. Roger L. Kemp (Jefferson, NC: McFarland & CO., 2010), 53. See also General Assembly of Virginia, Virginia Declaration of Rights, June 12, 1776, in *The Revised Code of the Laws of Virginia, Being a Collection of All Such Acts of the General Assembly*, vol. 1 (Richmond, VA: Printed by Thomas Ritchie, 1819), 31.

[809] Wilson, *Lectures on Law*, 112.

[810] Wilson, *Lectures on Law*, 309.

[811] James Wilson, *Considerations on the Nature and Extent of the Legislative Authority of the British Parliament, 1774*, in *The Works of the Honourable James Wilson*, vol. 3, ed. Bird Wilson (Philadelphia, PA: Printed for Bronson and Chauncey at Lorenzo Press, 1804), 205-207. Wilson notes Burlamaqui's assertion that "The right of sovereignty is that of commanding finally—but in order to procure real felicity; for if this end is not obtained, sovereignty ceases to be a legitimate authority. 2. Burl. 32, 33." Wilson also notes Blackstone's assertion that "The law of nature is superior in obligation to any other. 1. Bl. Com. 41."

[812] Wills, *Inventing America*, 238, 251.

[813] Thomas Jefferson, Inaugural Address, 4 March 1801, in *The Addresses and Messages of the Presidents of the United States, From 1789 to 1839* (New York: McLean & Taylor, 1839), 90.

[814] Kirk, *Roots*, 405.

[815] See Locke, *Second Treatise*, Routledge, ch. 18.

[816] Pufendorf, *Law of Nature and Nations*, bk. 7, ch. 3, 527.

[817] Locke, *Second Treatise*, Routledge, ch. 9, 256.

[818] See Locke, *Second Treatise*, Routledge, chs. 2 and 5.

[819] Locke, *Second Treatise*, Routledge, ch. 5, 203.

[820] Locke, *Second Treatise*, Routledge, ch. 2, 194.

[821] Sidney, *Discourses*, ch. 1, 23.

[822] Sidney, *Discourses,* ch. 1, 38, and ch. 3, 407.

[823] See Locke, *Second Treatise*, Routledge, chs. 18 & 19.

[824] Amos, *Defending the Declaration*, 147.

[825] Locke, *Second Treatise*, Routledge, 309.

[826] See Elazar, "Political Theory of Covenant," 9.

[827] Klosko, *Oxford Handbook*, 575.

[828] Thomas Hobbes, *Leviathan, or The Matter, Form and Power of A Commonwealth, Ecclesiastical and Civil*, 2nd ed., ed. Henry Morley (London: George Routledge and Sons, 1886), 61.

[829] Hobbes, *Leviathan*, 185.

[830] Hobbes, *Leviathan*, 173.

[831] Sidney, *Discourses*, ch. 2, 68.

[832] Sidney, *Discourses*, ch. 2, 79.

[833] Sidney, *Discourses*, ch. 2, 93.

[834] Sidney, *Discourses*, ch. 2, 81.

[835] Sidney, *Discourses*, ch. 3, 329.

[836] Sidney, *Discourses*, ch. 3, 261.

[837] Sidney addressed social contract theory in his *Discourses Concerning Government* of 1689, and Locke did so in his *Second Treatise of Government* of 1690.

[838] Locke, *Second Treatise*, Routledge, 240-241.

[839] Locke, *Second Treatise*, Routledge, 258.

[840] Locke, *Second Treatise*, Routledge, 242. See also Algernon Sidney, *Discourses*, ch. 3, 406-407. Sidney expressed man's right to consent in government: "This necessarily…proves the governor to be their [man's] creature; and the right of disposing the government must be in them, or they who receive it [government authority] can have none." Thomas Hooker, Puritan founder of Connecticut who had a major impact on his colony's constitution, addressed consent of the governed in his *Survey of the Summe of Church Discipline.*

[841] See, for example, Amos, *Defending the Declaration*, 141-142; Hart, *Faith & Freedom*, 78.

[842] Locke, *Second Treatise*, Routledge, 260-261. Locke cites Richard Hooker's *Ecclesiastical Polity*, bk. 1, sect. 10.

[843] Samuel Webster, *The Misery and Duty of an Oppressed and Enslav'd People, Salisbury, MA, 14 July 1774* (Boston, MA: Edes and Gill, 1774), 10, 22, quoted in Bernard Bailyn, *Pamphlets of the American Revolution, 1750-1776*, vol. 1 (Cambridge, MA: Belknap Press, 1965), 111-112; Moses Mather, *America's Appeal to an Impartial World* (Hartford, CT: Ebenezer Watson, 1775), 24, cited in Bernard Bailyn, *Pamphlets of the American Revolution, 1750-1776*, vol. 1 (Cambridge, MA: Belknap Press, 1965), 111-112.

[844] Samuel Adams, "Rights of the Colonists," 235-236.

[845] See, for example, Lutz's *Origins*.

[846] Pufendorf, *Whole Duty of Man*, bk. 2, 293-294.

[847] Lutz, *Origins*, 80, 111.

[848] Elazar, "Political Theory of Covenant," 13.

[849] Elazar, "Political Theory of Covenant," 21.

[850] Elazar, "Political Theory of Covenant," 9.

[851] Elazar, "Political Theory of Covenant," 20.

[852] Amos, *Defending the Declaration*, 150.

[853] Jefferson, Thomas Jefferson to Henry Lee, Monticello, 8 May 1825, Thomas Jefferson Memorial Association, 118-119.

[854] Thomas Jefferson to Mr. Thomas Mann Randolph, New York, 30 May 1790, in *The Writings of Thomas Jefferson*, vol. 7, ed. Albert E. Bergh (Washington, DC: Thomas Jefferson Memorial Association, 1907), 31.

[855] Thomas Jefferson to John Norvell, Washington, 11 June 1807, in *The Writings of Thomas Jefferson*, vol. 11, ed. Albert E. Bergh (Washington, DC: Thomas Jefferson Memorial Association, 1905), 222.

[856] See Alden Bradford, *Memoir of the Life and Writings of Rev. Jonathan Mayhew, D. D.* (Boston: C. C. Little & Co., 1838), 462.

[857] Jonathan Mayhew, *Discourse*, quoted in Alden Bradford, *Memoir of the Life and Writings of Rev. Jonathan Mayhew, D. D.*, pt. 4, (Boston: C. C. Little & Co., 1838), 119-120; Jonathan Mayhew, *From "The Snare Broken," A Thanksgiving Discourse Preached at the Desire of the West Church in Boston, Occasioned by the Repeal of the Stamp Act*, 23 May 1766, in *Cyclopaedia of American Literature, in Two Volumes*, vol. 1, eds. Evert A. Duyckinck and George L. Duyckinck (New York: Charles Scribner, 1856), 146.

[858] Benjamin Rush, *Observations Upon the Present Government in Pennsylvania: In Four Letters to the People of Pennsylvania* (Philadelphia, PA: Printed by Styner and Cist, 1777), 20.

[859] John Adams, *Defence of the Constitutions of Government*, 3-4.

[860] John Adams to Thomas Jefferson, Quincy, 17 September 1823, in *The Works of John Adams, Second President of the United States,* vol. 10, ed. Charles F. Adams (Boston: Little, Brown, and Co. 1856), 410.

[861] University of Virginia Board of Visitors, Transcript of the Minutes of the Board of Visitors of the University of Virginia, during the Rectorship of Thomas Jefferson, Mar. 4, 1825, from *Manuscripts From the University of Virginia Collection*, 360-498, in *The Works of Thomas Jefferson*, vol. 19, ed. Albert E. Bergh (Washington, DC: Thomas Jefferson Memorial Association, 1907), 460–461.

[862] Lutz, *Origins*, 119-120.

[863] Lutz, *Origins*, 114.

[864] Waldman, *Founding Faith*, 88.

[865] John Locke, *Second Treatise of Civil Government*, in *Two Treatises on Government, 2 Books*, bk. 2 (London: Printed for R. Butler, W. Reid, W. Sharpe, and John Bumpus, 1821), 204-205. See also Locke, *Second Treatise*, Routlege, 201. The Routledge version states, "Want of a common judge with authority puts all men in a state of Nature; force without right upon a man's person makes a state of war both where there is, and is not, a common judge. 20. But when the actual force is over, the state of war ceases between those that are in society and are equally on both sides subject to the judge; and, therefore, in such controversies, where the question is put, "Who shall be judge?" it cannot be meant who shall decide the controversy; every one knows what Jephtha here tells us, that "the Lord the Judge" shall judge. Where there is no judge on earth the appeal lies to God in Heaven. That question then cannot mean who shall judge, whether another hath put himself in a state of war with me, and whether I may, as Jephtha did, appeal to Heaven in it? Of that I myself can only be judge in my own conscience, as I will answer it at the great day to the Supreme Judge of all men."

[866] Amos, *Defending the Declaration*, 56.

[867] United States Continental Congress, Declaration on Taking Arms, July 6, 1775, in United States Library of Congress, *Journals of the Continental Congress, 1774-1789*, vol. 2/May 10-Sept 20, 1775, ed. Worthington C. Ford (Washington, DC: Government Printing Office, 1905), 156-157.

[868] United States Continental Congress, An Address of the Congress to the Inhabitants of the United States of America, May 8, 1778, in United States Library of Congress, *Journals of the Continental Congress, 1774-1789*, vol. 11/May 2-Sept 1, 1778, ed. Worthington C. Ford (Washington, DC: Government Printing Office, 1908), 475; United States Continental Congress, A Manifesto, September 27, 1781, A Manifesto, October 30, 1778, in United States Library of Congress, *Journals of the Continental Congress*, vol. 4/Jan 1778-Jan 1779 (Philadelphia, PA: U. S. Library of Congress, Printed by David C. Claypoole), 629. See also United States Continental Congress, Congressional Resolution, Thursday, September 27, 1781, in *Journals of the Continental Congress*, 1774-1789, vol. 21/July 23-Dec 31, 1781, ed. Gaillard Hunt (Washington, DC: Government Printing Office, 1912), 1017.

[869] Jonathan Mayhew, "The Right of Revolution," in *Puritan Political Ideas 1558-1794*, ed. Edmund S. Morgan (1965; repr., Indianapolis, IN: Hackett Publishing, 2003), 330.

[870] Samuel Adams, *An Oration Delivered At the State-House, in Philadelphia, To A Very Numerous Audience,* 1 August 1776 (Philadelphia, PA: Printed for J. Johnson, 1776), 3-4.

[871] John Witherspoon, "The Dominion of Providence Over the Passions of Men," 17 May 1776, in *The Works of John Witherspoon, in Three Volumes,* vol. 2, ed. John Rodgers (Philadelphia, PA: William W. Woodward, 1800), 408, 410.

[872] Thomas Jefferson to David Barrow, Monticello, 1 May 1815, in *The Writings of Thomas Jefferson*, Definitive ed., vol. 13-14, ed. Albert E. Bergh (Washington, DC: Thomas Jefferson Memorial Association, 1907), 297.

[873] United States Continental Congress, Congressional Resolution, Treasury Office, March 16, 1781, in United States Library of Congress, *Journals of the Continental Congress, 1774-1789*, vol. 19/January 1-April 23, 1781, ed. Gaillard Hunt (Washington, DC: Government Printing Office, 1912), 284.

[874] Elazar, "Political Theory of Covenant," 10.

[875] Lutz, *Origins*, 112.

[876] Novak, *Two Wings*, 17.

[877] Lutz, *Origins*, 113, 117.

[878] See Lutz, *Origins*, 123; Johnson, *History of the American People*, 204-205. The Declaration, like the Revolutionary War, was, affirms Johnson, a religious as well as secular act created under God like the compacts of the 1600s.

[879] Johnson, *History of the American People*, 148.

[880] Stout, *New England Soul*, 302.

[881] William W. Henry, *Patrick Henry: Life, Correspondence and Speeches*, vol. 1 (New York: Charles Scribner's Sons, 1891), 222.

[882] Stout, *New England Soul*, 285.

[883] Novak, *Two Wings*, 17-18.

[884] Meacham, *American Gospel*, 75.

[885] John Adams to Abigail Adams, Philadelphia, 16 September 1774, *Familiar Letters of John Adams and His Wife Abigail Adams During the Revolution*, ed. Charles F. Adams (New York: Hurd and Houghton, 1876), 37, 38.

[886] James H. Hutson, *Religion and the Founding of the American Republic* (Washington, DC: Library of Congress, 1998), 53.

[887] United States Continental Congress, Congressional Resolution, Monday, June 12, 1775, in United States Library of Congress, *Journals of the Continental Congress, 1774-1789*, vol. 2/May 10-September 20, 1775, ed. Worthington C. Ford (Washington, DC: Government Printing Office, 1905), 87-88.

[888] United States Continental Congress, Congressional Resolution, Saturday, March 16, 1776, in United States Library of Congress,

Journals of the Continental Congress, 1774-1789, vol. 4/Jan 1-June 4, 1776, ed. Worthington C. Ford (Washington, DC: Government Printing Office, 1906), 208, 209.

[889] United States Continental Congress, Congressional Resolution, November 17, 1778, in United States Library of Congress, *Journals of Congress, Jan 1778-Jan 1779*, vol. 4 (Philadelphia: U. S. Library of Congress, Printed by David C. Claypoole), 661. See also United States Continental Congress, Congressional Resolution, November 17, 1778, in United States Library of Congress, *Journals of the Continental Congress, 1774-1789*, vol. 12/Sept 2-Dec 31, 1778, ed. Worthington C. Ford (Washington, DC: Government Printing Office, 1908), 1139.

[890] United States Continental Congress, Congressional Resolution, March 20, 1779, in *Journals of the Continental Congress, 1774-1789*, vol. 13/Jan 1-Apr 22, 1779, ed. Worthington C. Ford (Washington, DC: Government Printing Office, 1909), 343-344.

[891] United States Continental Congress, Congressional Resolution, Mar 7, 1778, in United States Library of Congress, *Journals of Congress*, Jan 1778-Jan 1779, vol. 4 (Philadelphia: U. S. Library of Congress, Printed by David C. Claypoole), 138.

[892] United States Continental Congress, Congressional Resolution, Mar 19, 1782, in *Journals of the American Congress, From 1774 to 1788, in Four Volumes*, vol. 3/Aug 1, 1778-Mar 30, 1782 (Washington, DC: Printed and Published by Way and Gideon, 1823), 736.

[893] John Adams to Abigail Adams, 17 June 1775, in *Letters of John Adams Addressed to His Wife*, vol. 1, ed. Charles F. Adams (Boston, MA: Charles C. Little and James Brown, 1841), 46.

[894] United States Continental Congress, Congressional Resolution, March 20, 1781, in *Journals of the Continental Congress, 1774-1789*, vol. 19/Jan 1-Apr 23, 1781, ed. Gaillard Hunt (Washington, DC: Government Printing Office, 1912), 285.

[895] United States Continental Congress, Thanksgiving Day Proclamation, November 1, 1777, in United States Library of Congress, *Journals of the Continental Congress, 1774-1789*, vol. 9/Oct 3-Dec 31, 1777, ed. Worthington C. Ford (Washington, DC: Government Printing Office, 1907), 854-855. See also A [Thanksgiving] Proclamation, November 1, 1777, in Jedidiah Morse, *Annals of the American Revolution* (Hartford, CT: 1824), 296.

[896] United States Continental Congress, Thanksgiving Proclamation, October 20, 1779, in *Journals of the American Congress, From 1774 to 1788, in Four Volumes*, vol. 3/Aug 1, 1778-Mar 30, 1782 (Washington, DC: Printed and Published by Way and Gideon, 1823), 378.

[897] George Washington, Thanksgiving Proclamation, September 25, 1789, in *Proclamations for Thanksgiving*, ed. Franklin B. Hough (Albany, NY: Munsell & Rowland by order of U. S. Continental Congress and Pres. Washington, 1858), 30-32.

[898] Abraham Lincoln, Proclamation for Thanksgiving, 3 October 1863, in *State Papers, 1861-1865*, in *Life and Works of Abraham Lincoln*, vol. 7, ed. Marion M. Miller (New York: Current Literature Publishing Co., 1907), 161; Abraham Lincoln, His Proclamation for a Day of Thanksgiving, 3 October 1863, in *Speeches and Letters of Abraham Lincoln, 1832-1865*, Vol. 14721 of Project Gutenberg (Mundus Publishing, 2007), unpaged.

[899] United States Continental Congress, Articles of War, September 20, 1776, in United States Library of Congress, *Journals of the Continental Congress, 1774-1789*, vol 5./June 5-Oct 8, 1776, ed. Worthington C. Ford (Washington, DC : Government Printing Office, 1906), 788-789.

[900] United States Continental Congress, *Rules for the Regulation of the Navy of the Colonies of North-America*, November 28, 1775 (Philadelphia, PA: William and Thomas Bradford, 1775; repr. Washington, DC: Naval Historical Foundation, 1994), 3.

[901] Hutson, *Religion and the Founding*, 55.

[902] United States Continental Congress, An Address of Congress to the Inhabitants of the United States of America, May 8, 1778, in *Journals of the Continental Congress, 1774-1789*, vol. 11/May 2-Sept 1, 1778, ed. Worthington C. Ford (Washington, DC: Government Printing Office, 1908), 477.

[903] United States Continental Congress, Definitive Treaty of Peace Between the United States of America and his Britannic Majesty, Sept 3, 1783, in United States Continental Congress, *The Public Statutes at Large of the United States of America, From the Organization of Government in 1789 to Mar 3, 1845*, vol. 8, ed. Richard Peters (Boston: Charles C. Little and James Brown, 1848), 80.

[904] Hutson, *Religion and the Founding*, 49.

[905] George Washington, General Order, Orderly Book, July 2, 1776, quoted in *The Writings of George Washington: 1776*, vol. 4, ed Worthington C. Ford (New York: G. P. Putnam's Sons, 1889), 202 (footnote).

[906] George Washington, General Order, Orderly Book, December 17, 1777, quoted in *The Writings of George Washington*, vol. 12, ed. Jared Sparks (New York: Harper & Brothers, 1848), 402.

[907] George Washington to Rev. Israel Evans, Valley Forge, March 13, 1778, in *The Writings of George Washington*, vol. 5, ed. Jared Sparks (Boston: Russell, Odiorne, and Metcalf, and Hilliard, Gray, and Co., 1834), 276.

[908] George Washington to Lund Washington, Headquarters Middlebrook, May 29, 1779, in *Proceedings of the Massachusetts Historical Society, 1871-1873* (Boston: Published by the Massachusetts Historical Society, 1873), 56, 136.

[909] George Washington, General Order, Orderly Book, February 27, 1776, quoted in *The Writings of George Washington*, vol. 3/ 1775-1776, ed Worthington C. Ford (New York: G. P. Putnam's Sons, 1889), 440-441.

[910] See George Washington, General Order, July 9, 1776, Orderly Book, May 26, 1777, Instructions to the Brigadier-Generals, December 17, 1777, Orderly Book, Oct 20, 1781, quoted in *The Writings of George Washington*, vol. 12, ed. Jared Sparks (New York: Harper & Brothers, 1848), 401-2. Washington's July 9 Order stated, "The honorable Continental Congress having been pleased to allow a chaplain to each regiment, with the pay of thirty-three dollars and one third per month, the colonels or commanding officers of each regiment are directed to procure chaplains accordingly, persons of good characters and exemplary lives, and to see that all inferior officers and soldiers pay them a suitable respect."

[911] George Washington, General Order, Orderly Book, July 9, 1776, quoted in *The Writings of George Washington*, vol. 12, ed. Jared Sparks (New York: Harper & Brothers, 1848), 401.

[912] George Washington, General Order, Headquarters, Valley Forge, May 2, 1778, in *Revolutionary Orders of General Washington, Issued During the Years 1778, '80, '81, & '82*, ed. Henry Whiting (New York: Wiley and Putnam, 1844), 75.

[913] George Washington, General Order, Orderly Book, July 4, 1775, quoted in *The Writings of George Washington*, vol. 3, ed. Jared Sparks (Boston: Russell, Odiorne, and Metcalf and Hilliard, Gray, and Co., 1834), 491. See also George Washington, General Order, Orderly Book, July 4, 1775, quoted in *The Writings of George Washington*, vol. 3/1775-1776, ed. Worthington C. Ford (New York: G. P. Putnam's Sons, 1889), 5 (footnote).

[914] George Washington, General Order, Orderly Book, August 3, 1776, quoted in *The Writings of George Washington*, vol. 12, ed. Jared Sparks (New York: Harper & Brothers, 1848), 401.

[915] George Washington, General Order, Headquarters, Valley Forge, May 2, 1778, in *Revolutionary Orders of General Washington Issued During the Years 1778, '80, '81, & '82*, ed. Henry Whiting (New York: Wiley and Putnam, 1844), 75.

[916] George Washington to Brigadier-General Nelson, Camp at White Plains, Virginia, 20 August 1778, in *The Writings of George Washington*, Vol. 6, Part 2 cont, ed. Jared Sparks (Boston, MA: Russell, Odiorne, and Metcalf, 1834), 36.

[917] George Washington, Orderly Book, Oct 20, 1781, quoted in *The Writings of George Washington*, vol. 12, ed. Jared Sparks (New York: Harper & Row, 1848), 402.

[918] George Washington, Orderly Book, April 18, 1783, quoted in *The Writings of George Washington*, vol. 12, ed. Jared Sparks (New York: Harper & Row, 1848), 402.

[919] Amos, *Defending the Declaration*, 150.

[920] Sandoz, *Republicanism*, 109.

[921] Lutz, *Origins*, 120.

[922] Mark A. Noll, *America's God: From Jonathan Edwards to Abraham Lincoln* (New York: Oxford U Press, 2002), 192.

[923] John Adams, *Defence of the Constitution of Government*, 4.

[924] John Adams, Footnote in *Discourses on Davila; A Series of Papers on Political History*, in *The Works of John Adams, Second President of the United States*, vol. 6, ed. Charles F. Adams (Boston: Charles C. Little and James Brown, 1851), 313.

[925] John Adams to Hezekiah Niles, Quincy, 13 February 1818, in *The Works of John Adams, Second President of the United States*, vol. 10, ed. Charles F. Adams (Boston, MA: Little, Brown, & Co., 1856), 282.

[926] Abraham Lincoln, Address in Independence Hall, Philadelphia, Feb 22, 1861, in *Abraham Lincoln: Complete Works, Comprising His Speeches, Letters, State Papers, and Miscellaneous Writings*, vol. 1, ed. John G. Nicolay and John Hay (New York: Century Co., 1907), 691.

[927] John Quincy Adams, *An Oration Delivered Before the Inhabitants of the Town of NewburyPort, 61st Anniversary of the Declaration of Independence*, 4 July 1837 (Newburyport, MA: Printed by Morss & Brewster, 1837), 5-6.

[928] James Madison, Federalist Paper #14, in *The Federalist Papers*, ed. Clinton Rossiter (New York: Mentor/Penguin, 1961), 104-5.

[929] John Adams to Mrs. Adams, Philadelphia, 3 July 1776, in *The Works of John Adams, Second President of the United States*, vol. 9, ed. Charles F. Adams (Boston, MA: Little, Brown, & Co., 1854), 420.

[930] U. S. Continental Congress, Thanksgiving Day Proclamation, 1 November 1777, in U. S. Library of Congress, *Journals of the Continental Congress, 1774-1789*, vol. 9/Oct 3-Dec 31, 1777, ed. Worthington C. Ford (Washington, DC: Government Printing Office, 1907), 854-855. See also A [Thanksgiving] Proclamation, November 1, 1777, in Jedidiah Morse, *Annals of the American Revolution* (Hartford, CT: 1824), 296.

[931] George Washington, Thanksgiving Proclamation, 25 September 1789, in *Proclamations for Thanksgiving*, ed. Franklin B. Hough (Albany, NY: Munsell & Rowland by order of U. S. Continental Congress and Pres. Washington, 1858), 30-32.

[932] Abraham Lincoln, Proclamation for Thanksgiving, 3 October 1863, in *State Papers, 1861-1865*, in *Life and Works of Abraham Lincoln*, vol. 7, ed. Marion M. Miller (New York: Current Literature Publishing Co., 1907), 161; Abraham Lincoln, His Proclamation for a Day of Thanksgiving, 3 October 1863, in *Speeches and Letters of Abraham Lincoln, 1832-1865*, Vol. 14721 of Project Gutenberg (Mundus Publishing, 2007), unpaged.

Chapter 8: The Making of a Nation Under God

[933] Slater, *Teaching and Learning*, 241.

[934] A. James Reichley, *Religion in American Public Life* (Washington, DC: Brookings Institution, 1985), 219.

[935] James Madison, *Memorial and Remonstrance Against Religious Assessments, 1785*, in *The Writings of James Madison: 1783-1787*, vol. 2, ed. Gaillard Hunt (New York: G. P. Putnam's Sons, 1901), 189.

[936] Isaac Backus, *A Declaration of the Rights, of the Inhabitants of the State of Massachusetts-Bay, in New England*, 1779, in *The Sacred Rights of Conscience: Selected Readings on Religious Liberty and Church-State Relations in the American Founding*, eds. Daniel L. Dreisbach and Mark D. Hall (Indianapolis, IN: Liberty Fund, 2009), 276.

[937] Virginia Citizens, *Petition Against The Religious Assessment Bill to the Virginia General Assembly*, 2 November 1784, in *The Sacred Rights of Conscience: Selected Readings on Religious Liberty and Church-State Relations in the American Founding*, eds. Daniel L. Dreisbach and Mark D. Hall (Indianapolis, IN: Liberty Fund, 2009), 308.

[938] Fea, *Was America Founded*, 139.

[939] Madison, *Memorial*, 184-5.

[940] Madison, *Memorial*, 188-90.

[941] Madison, *Memorial*, 186.

[942] Madison, *Memorial*, 188.

[943] Locke, *Letter Concerning Toleration*, 6.

[944] Madison, *Memorial*, 189.

[945] Thomas Jefferson, *Notes on Religion*, October 1776, in *The Works of Thomas Jefferson in Twelve Volumes*, vol. 2, Federal Edition, ed. Paul L. Ford (New York: G. P. Putnam's Sons, 1904), 252-268. Jefferson, who was influenced by Locke's *Letters Concerning Toleration*, was a strong proponent of religious freedom and total separation of church and state. He believed true Christianity supported religious freedom. His views were shared by Madison. In his endorsed 1776 "Notes on Religion," Jefferson—referencing the example of Christ, Christian charity, faith, Romans 14:23, and Locke—expounds on religious tolerance and freedom. He writes, "How far does the duty of toleration extend? ... 2. We have no right to prejudice another in his *civil* enjoiments because he is of another church. In any man err from the right way, it is his own misfortune, no injury to thee; nor therefore art thou to punish him in the things of this life because thou supposeth he will be miserable in that which is to come—on the contrary accdg to the spirit of the gospel, charity, bounty, liberality is due to him. Each church being free, no one can have jurisdn over another one, not even when the civil magistrate joins it. ... Every church is to itself orthodox; to *others* erroneous or heretical. ... The care of every man's soul belongs to himself. ... Laws provide against injury from others; but not from ourselves. God himself will not save men against their wills. ... If the magistrate command me to bring my commodity to the publick store house I bring it because he can indemnify [compensate or insure, brackets mine] me if he erred & I thereby lose it; but what indemnification can he give one for the kdom of heaven? I cannot give up my guidance to the magistrates, bec. he knows no more the way to heaven than I do, & is less concerned to direct me right than I am to go right. If the Jews had followed their Kings, among so many, what number would have led them to idolatry? ... Why persecute for diffce [difference] in relig opinion? ... Our Savior [Jesus Christ] chose not to propagate his religion by temporal punmts or civil incapacitation, if he had, it was in his almighty power. But he chose to extend it by it's influence on reason, there by shewing to others how they should proceed. The commonwealth is 'a Society of men constituted for protecting their civil interests.' *Civil interests* are 'life, health, indolency of body, liberty and property.' That the magistrate's jurisdn extends only to civil rights appears from these considns. ... 1. The magistrate has no power but wt ye people gave. The people hve nt givn hm [have not given him] the care of souls bec. ye cd [because you could] not, he cd [could] not, because no man hs *right* to abandon ye care of his salvation to another. No man has *power* to let another prescribe his faith. Faith is not faith witht believing. No man can conform his faith to the dictates of another. The life & essence of religion consists in the internal persuasion or belief of the mind. External forms of worship, when against our belief are hypocrisy & impiety. Rom. 14. 23 "he that doubteth is damned, if he eat, because he eateth not of faith: for whatsoever is not of faith, is sin?" 2. If it be said the magistrate may make use of arguments & so draw the heterodox to truth, I answer, every man has a commission to admonish, exhort, convince another of error. 12. A church is 'a *voluntary* society of men, joining themselves together of their own accord, in order to the public worshipping of god in such a manner as they judge acceptable to him & effectual to the salvation of their souls.' ... If he find anything wrong with it, he should be as free to go out as he was to come in. ... Truth will do well enough if left to shift for herself. ... She has no need of force to procure entrance into the minds of men. Error indeed has often prevailed by the assistance of power or force. Truth is the proper & sufficient antagonist to error. If anything pass in a religious meeting seditiously and contrary to the public peace, let it be punished in the same manner & no otherwise than as if it had happened in a fair or market. These meetings ought not to be sanctuaries for faction & flagitiousness. Locke denies toleration to those who entertain opns contrary to those moral rules necessary for the preservation of society.... He sais [says] 'neither Pagan nor Mahomedan nor Jew ought to be excluded from the civil rights of the Commonwealth because of his religion.' Shall we suffer a Pagan to deal with us and not suffer him to pray to his god? Why have Xns [Christians] been distinguished above all people who have ever lived, for persecutions? Is it because it is the genius of their religion? No, it's genius is the reverse. It is the refusing *toleration* to those of a different opn which has produced all the bustles and wars on account of religion. It was the misfortune of mankind that during the darker centuries the Xn priests following their ambition and avarice combining with the magistrate to divide the spoils of the people, could establish the notion that schismatics might be ousted of their possessions & destroyed. This notion we have not yet cleared ourselves from. In this case no wonder the oppressed should rebel, & they will continue to rebel & raise disturbance until their civil rights are fully restored to them & all partial distinctions, exclusions & incapacitations removed."

[946] Virginia Citizens, *Petition Against the Bill*, 308.

[947] Virginia Citizens, *Petition Against the Bill*, 307-308.

[948] Madison, *Memorial*, 187.

[949] Jefferson, *Notes on Religion*, 252-268.

[950] Locke, *Letter Concerning Toleration*, 12, 20. Locke saw Christianity as the true religion as indicated in his *Letter*, p. 8, and *Second Letter Concerning Toleration*, 1690, p. 63, of this source.

[951] Locke, *Second Letter Concerning Toleration*, 81-82.

[952] Madison, *Memorial*, 187.

[953] James Madison to Edward Everett, Montpelier, 19 March 1823, in United States Congress, *Letters and Other Writings of James Madison: 1816-1828*, vol. 3 (Philadelphia: J. B. Lippincott & Co., 1865), 307.

[954] Benjamin Franklin to Dr. Richard Price, Passy, 9 October 1780, in *The Life and Writings of Benjamin Franklin in Two Volumes*, vol. 1, eds. William Temple Franklin and William Duane (Philadelphia: M'Carty & Davis, 1834), 367.

[955] Jefferson, *Notes on Religion*, 252-268.

[956] Virginia Citizens, *Petition Against the Bill*, 308.

[957] Thomas Jefferson, *Notes on Virginia*, 1782, excerpted in *The Life and Writings of Thomas Jefferson*, ed. Samuel E. Forman (Indianapolis: Bowen-Merrill Co., 1900), 154.

[958] Madison, *Memorial*, 189.

[959] Williams, *Bloudy Tenent*, 107.

[960] Penn, *Liberty of Conscience*, 21-22. See also pp. v and vii in Penn.

[961] Jefferson, *Notes on Religion*, 252-268.

[962] Virginia Citizens, *Petition Against the Bill*, 308.

[963] Virginia Citizens, *Petition Against the Bill*, 308.

[964] Madison, *Memorial*, 187.

[965] James Madison to Edward Livingston, Montpelier, 10 July 1822, in United States Congress, *Letters and Other Writings of James Madison: 1816-1828*, vol. 3, Congress (Philadelphia: J. B. Lippincott & Co., 1865), 275.

[966] John Carroll to the Editor of *Columbian Magazine*, 1 September 1787, in *Biographical Sketch of the Most Rev. John Carroll: first archbishop of Baltimore*, ed. John Carroll Brent (Baltimore, MD: John Murphy, 1843), 142-3.

[967] Madison, *Memorial*, 186.

[968] Virginia Declaration of Rights, 1776, in *Documents of American Democracy: A Collection of Essential Works*, ed. Roger L. Kemp (Jefferson, NC: McFarland & Co., 2010), 54.

[969] Waldman, *Founding Faith*, 114-5.

[970] Madison, *Memorial*, 189.

[971] Thomas Jefferson, *An Act for Establishing Religious Freedom*, 1786, in Thomas Jefferson, *Notes on the State of Virginia*, 8th ed. (Boston, MA: Printed by David Carlisle, 1801), 326-328.

[972] Fea, *Was America Founded*, 140.

[973] Lambert, *Founding Fathers*, 225, 235.

[974] See Virginia Statute for Religious Freedom, 1786, in *A History of Us: Sourcebook and Index: Documents That Shaped the American Nation*, vol. 11, ed. Steven Mintz (New York: Oxford U Press, 2002), 56-58.

[975] In Massachusetts, Unitarians had gained control of many local parishes, and Congregationalists did not want to subsidize the opposing sect. Thus they disestablished.

[976] *Church of the Holy Trinity v. United States*, 143 U.S. 457 (1892).

[977] Hall, "Vindiciae," 38-39.

[978] Amos and Gardiner, *Never Before in History*, 144.

[979] See Brutus's *Vindiciae*, Althusius's *Politics*, Pufendorf's *Whole Duty of Man*, bk. 2, 293-294; and Locke, *Second Treatise*, Routledge, 241. See also Locke's *Second Treatise*, Routledge, ch. 8, sects. 95-99, 240-242. For scholarship, see Elazar, "Political Theory of Covenant," 5, 8-9, 20; Lutz, "From Covenant to Constitution," 104; McCoy and Baker, *Fountainhead of Federalism*, 46, 50, 53-56; Lessnoff's *Social Contract*; Klosko, *Oxford Handbook*, 578; and Amos and Gardiner, *Never Before in History*, 143-145.

[980] Missouri Bar Association, Proceedings, *Report of the Tenth Annual Meeting of the Missouri Bar Association*, 24-26 June 1890 (Saint Louis, MO: Continental Printing Co., 1891), 48.

[981] Sandoz, *Republicanism*, 68.

[982] Lutz, *Origins*, 112.

[983] Lutz, *Origins*, 69, 112, 114-115, 121, 135.

[984] James Madison, *The Writings of James Madison*, vol. 3/1787: The Journal of the Constitutional Convention, ed. Gaillard Hunt (New York: G. P. Putnam's Sons, 1902), 310-311; Dreisbach, "Bible in the Political Rhetoric," 17-18. Job 12:24-25: "He [God] takes away the understanding of the chiefs of the people of the earth, And makes them wander in a pathless wilderness. They grope in the dark without light, And He makes them stagger like a drunken *man*." James 1:17: "Every good gift and every perfect gift is from above, and comes down from the Father of lights, with whom there is no variation or shadow of turning." Daniel 4:17: "'This decision *is* by the decree of the watchers, And the sentence by the word of the holy ones, In order that the living may know That the Most High rules in the kingdom of men, Gives it to whomever He will, And sets over it the lowest of men.'" Matthew 10:29-31 (Luke 12:6-7): "Are not two sparrows sold for a copper coin? And not one of them falls to the ground apart from your Father's will. But the very hairs of your head are all numbered. Do not fear therefore; you are of more value than many sparrows." Psalm 127:1: "Unless the Lord builds the house, They labor in vain who build it...." Genesis 11:1-9: "Now the whole earth had one language and one speech. ... And they said, 'Come, let us build ourselves a city, and a tower whose top *is* in the heavens; let us make a name for ourselves, lest we be scattered abroad over the face of the whole earth.' But the Lord came down to see the city and the tower which the sons of men had built. And the Lord said, 'Come, let Us go down and there confuse their language, that they may not understand one another's speech.' So the Lord scattered them abroad from there over the face of all the earth, and they ceased building the city. Therefore its name is called Babel, because there the Lord confused the language of all the earth; and from there the Lord scattered them abroad over the face of all the earth." Deuteronomy 28:37: "'And you shall become an astonishment, a proverb, and a byword among all nations where the Lord will drive you.'" 1 Kings 9:7: "then I will cut off Israel from the land which I have given them; and this house which I have consecrated for My name I will cast out of My sight. Israel will be a proverb and a byword among all peoples."

[985] John Adams, *Defense of the Constitutions of Government*, 219.

[986] Lutz, "From Covenant to Constitution," 102.

[987] Tocqueville, *Democracy in America*, ed. Richard Heffner, 45-6.

[988] Lutz, "From Covenant to Constitution," 101.

[989] Kirk, *Roots*, 416-7.

[990] Hall, "Vindiciae," 42-43.

[991] James Madison, Federalist Paper #37, in *The Federalist Papers*, ed. Clinton Rossiter (New York: Mentor Penguin, 1961), 231; James Madison, Federalist Paper #55, in *The Federalist Papers*, ed. Clinton Rossiter (New York: Mentor Penguin, 1961), 346.

[992] Alexander Hamilton, Federalist Paper #78, in *The Federalist Papers*, ed. Clinton Rossiter (New York: Mentor Penguin, 1961), 471.

[993] Alexander Hamilton, Federalist Paper #15, in *The Federalist Papers*, ed. Clinton Rossiter (New York: Mentor Penguin, 1961), 110.

[994] James Madison, Federalist Paper #51, in *The Federalist Papers*, ed. Clinton Rossiter (New York: Mentor Penguin, 1961), 322.

[995] Thomas Jefferson, Resolutions Relative to the Alien and Sedition Laws, 1798, in *The Writings of Thomas Jefferson*, Definitive ed., vol. 17, ed. Albert E. Bergh (Washington, DC: Thomas Jefferson Memorial Association, 1907), 389. Jefferson's resolutions are understood to be the original draft of the Kentucky Resolutions of 1798.

[996] Sandoz, *Republicanism*, 49.

[997] James Madison, "Property," from *The National Gazette*, 29 March 1792, in *The Writings of James Madison*, Vol. 6/1790-1802, ed. Gaillard Hunt (New York: G. P. Putnam's Sons, 1906), 101.

[998] Madison, "Property," 101.

[999] Madison, "Property," 102.

[1000] Madison, "Property," 103.

[1001] John Jay, Federalist Paper #2, *The Federalist Papers*, ed. Clinton Rossiter (New York: Mentor Penguin, 1961), 38-39.

[1002] Madison, Federalist Paper #51, *Federalist Papers*, 322, 324.

[1003] Wilson, *Lectures on Law*, 25.

[1004] Slater, *Teaching and Learning*, 72, 175, 208.

[1005] Felix M. Morley, *The Power in the People* (New York: D. Van Nostrand Co., 1949), 5.

[1006] James M. Beck, *The Constitution of the United States* (1922; repr., Whitefish, MT: Kessinger, 2004), 56; James M. Beck, *The Constitution of the United States* (London: Hodder and Stoughton, 1922), 131. As the theme and basis of his ideas, Beck cited Proverbs 29:18, "Where there is no vision, the people perish; but he that keepeth the Law, happy is he," and Proverbs 22:28, "Remove not the ancient landmark, which thy fathers have set."

[1007] Richard Frothingham, *The Rise of the Republic of the United States* (Boston, MA: Little, Brown, & Co., 1872), 14.

[1008] Charles Pinckney, Speech, Wednesday, 14 May 1788, in South Carolina General Assembly, *Debates Which Arose in the House of Representatives of South Carolina, on the Constitution Framed for the United States, by a Convention of Delegates Assembled at Philadelphia* (Charleston, SC: Printed by A. E. Miller, 1831), 62.

[1009] Sandoz, *Republicanism*, 62; Sir William Holdsworth, *A History of English Law*, 13 vols. (London: Methuen, 1923-66), 5:493; 6:66, 70 (2nd ed.).

[1010] Sandoz, *Republicanism*, 69.

[1011] Locke, *Second Treatise*, Routledge, 262-264.

[1012] Tocqueville, *Democracy in America*, ed. Richard Heffner, 34.

[1013] See James Madison, Federalist Paper #39, in *The Federalist Papers*, ed. Clinton Rossiter (New York: Mentor Penguin, 1961), 241. In Federalist Paper #57, Madison noted the republican practice of electing representatives: "The elective mode of obtaining rulers is the characteristic policy of republican government." See Madison, Federalist Paper #57, *Federalist Papers*, 350-1.

[1014] Madison, Federalist Paper #39, *Federalist Papers*, 240.

[1015] Benjamin Rush to Thomas Jefferson, 22 August 1800, in *Letters of Benjamin Rush, 1793-1813*, vol. 2, Lyman H. Butterfield, ed. (Princeton: Princeton U Press for American Philosophical Society, 1951), 820-21.

[1016] Noah Webster, *History of the United States* (New Haven: Durrie & Peck, 1832), 6, 300.

[1017] Morris, *Christian Life and Character*, 262-3.

[1018] Montesquieu, *Spirit of Laws*, vol. 2, bk. 24, 112.

[1019] Stout, *Soul*, 310.

[1020] Benjamin Franklin to Messrs. Les Abbés Chalut and Arnaud, Philadelphia, 17 April 1787, in *The Works of Benjamin Franklin in Philosophy, Politics, and Morals, 1753-1790*, vol. 6, ed. William T. Franklin (Philadelphia, PA: William Duane, 1817), 199.

[1021] Richard Henry Lee to Colonel Martin Pickett, Chantilly, 5 March 1786, in *Memoir of the Life of Richard Henry Lee and His Correspondence*, vol. 2, ed. grandson Richard H. Lee (Philadelphia, PA: Carey and Lea, 1825), 70.

[1022] George Mason to Patrick Henry, Fairfax County, Gunston Hall, 6 May 1783, in *The Life of George Mason, 1725-1792*, vol. 11, Kate Mason Rowland (New York: G. P. Putnam's Sons, 1892), 44.

[1023] Washington, Farewell Address, ed. Worthington Ford, 308.

[1024] James Madison, Speech on the Power of Judiciary at the Virginia Ratifying Convention, 20 June 1788, in *The Writings of James Madison*, Vol. 5/1787-1790, ed. Gaillard Hunt (New York: G. P. Putnam's Sons, 1904), 223.

[1025] James Madison, Federalist Paper #55, *The Federalist Papers*, ed. Clinton Rossiter (New York: Mentor Penguin, 1961), 346.

[1026] Alexander Hamilton, Federalist Paper #76, *The Federalist Papers*, ed. Clinton Rossiter (New York: Mentor Penguin, 1961), 458.

[1027] John Adams to the Officers of the First Brigade of the Third Division of the Militia of Massachusetts, 11 October 1798, in *The Works of John Adams, Second President of the United States*, vol. 9, ed. Charles F. Adams (Boston: Little, Brown, and Co., 1854), 229.

[1028] Samuel Adams to John Winthrop, Philadelphia, 21 December 1778, in *The Writings of Samuel Adams: 1778-1802*, vol. 4, ed. Harry A. Cushing (New York: G. P. Putnam's Sons, 1908), 104.

[1029] Lutz, *Origins*, 82-83.

[1030] Edward A. Rauchet, *American Vision and Values: A Companion to the Kirkpatrick Signature Series* (Bellevue, NE: Bellevue U Press, 2008), 32, 33; Robert P. George, "Freedom and Its Counterfeit," *Imprimis* 32-34 (August 2003), Center for Constructive Alternatives, Hillsdale College. See also Robert P. George, *In Defense of Natural Law* (New York: Oxford U Press, 1999) and Robert P. George, *The Clash of Orthodoxies: Law, Religion, and Morality in Crisis* (Wilmington, DE: ISI Books, 2001).

[1031] William V. Wells, ed., *The Life and Public Service of Samuel Adams*, vol. 1 (Boston, MA: Little, Brown, & Co., 1865), 22-23. Essay reprinted from *The Independent Advertiser*, a weekly political journal which Adams founded in 1748.

[1032] United States Constitutional Convention, *The Records of the Federal Convention of 1787*, vol. 2, ed. Max Farrand (New Haven, CT: Yale U Press, 1911), 249.

[1033] James Madison, Federalist Paper #57, *The Federalist Papers*, ed. Clinton Rossiter (New York: Mentor Penguin, 1961), 350.

[1034] Noah Webster, *History of the United States*, 336-7.

[1035] Waldman, *Founding Faith*, 61.

[1036] Pufendorf, *Duty of Man*, bk. 1, 69-70.

[1037] Pufendorf, *Duty of Man*, bk. 1, 70-73.

[1038] Benjamin Rush, *Of the Mode of Education Proper in a Republic*, in *Essays, Literary, Moral and Philosophical*, 2nd ed. (Philadelphia, PA: Printed by Thomas and William Bradford, 1806), 8.

[1039] David Ramsay, *History of the United States, From Their First Settlement as English Colonies in 1607 to the Year 1808*, 3 vols., vol. 3. 2nd ed. (Philadelphia, PA: M. Carey and Son, 1818), 64.

[1040] John Adams to Zabdiel Adams, Philadelphia, 21 June 1776, in *The Works of John Adams, Second President of the United States*, vol. 9, ed. Charles F. Adams (Boston: Little, Brown, & CO., 1854), 401.

[1041] George Washington, Farewell Address, 17 September, 1796, in *The Addresses and Messages of the Presidents of the United States, 1789-1846*, vol. 1, comp. Edwin Williams (New York: Edward Walker, 1846), 75.

[1042] See Slater, *Teaching and Learning*, 189, 221-2.

[1043] See Slater, *Teaching and Learning*, 159. Christianity's two commandments of love—to love God and man, affirmed Slater, were the moral laws of inner virtue: "The Gospel brings forth a higher standard of liberty than *external* law—rather that *internal* law of the Two Commandments of our Lord." See also David Barton, *Original Intent: The Courts, the Constitution, & Religion* (Aledo, TX: Wallbuilder Press, 1996), 317-318.

[1044] Matthew 5:21-22 references Exodus 20:13 and Deuteronomy 5:17.

[1045] Calvin, *Institutes*, vol. 1, bk. 2, 434-435.

[1046] Montesquieu, *Spirit of Laws*, vol. 2, bk. 24, 115.

[1047] Thomas Jefferson to Benjamin Rush, Washington, 21 April 1803, in *The Writings of Thomas Jefferson*, vol. 4, ed. Henry A. Washington (New York: Derby & Jackson, 1859), 483.

[1048] John Witherspoon, *Lectures on Divinity*, Lecture 4, in *The Works of John Witherspoon*, Vol. 8 (Edinburgh: Printed for Ogles, Duncan, Cochran, and Johnston, 1815), 38-39.

[1049] John Quincy Adams to his son George Washington Adams, St. Petersburg, 10 January 1813, in *Letters of John Quincy Adams to His Son On the Bible and Its Teachings* (Auburn, NY: Derby, Miller, & Co., 1848), 62; John Quincy Adams to G. W. Adams, St. Petersburg, 10 January 1813, in *Letters of Mrs. Adams, The Wife of John Adams*, ed. Charles F. Adams, 4th ed., (Boston, MA: Wilkins, Carter, & Co., 1848), 449.

[1050] Morris, *Christian Life and Character*, 72.

[1051] John Quincy Adams to his son George Washington Adams, St. Petersburg, 1 and 8 September 1811, in *Writings of John Quincy Adams, 1811-1813*, Vol. 4, ed. Worthington C. Ford (New York: Macmillan Co., 1914), 216; John Quincy Adams to his son G. W. Adams, St. Petersburg, 1 and 8 September 1811, in *Letters of John Quincy Adams to His Son On the Bible and Its Teachings*, (Auburn, NY: Derby, Miller, & Co., 1848), 18.

[1052] Henry Barnard, *History of the School Fund of Connecticut* in *Report of the Commissioner of the School Fund to the Legislature of the State, May 1853*, (Hartford: Printed by Order of the Legislature, 1853), 101.

[1053] Reuben O. Moon, Speech of Hon. Reuben O. Moon on Revision of the Laws—The Judiciary, 7 December 1910, in United States Congress, *Senate Documents*, 62nd United States Congress, April 4-August 22, 1911, vol. 27, n. 23 (Washington, DC: Government Printing Office, 1911), 9.

[1054] John Adams, Inaugural Address, March 4, 1797, in *The Addresses and Messages of the Presidents of the United States*, 4th ed. (New York: Edward Walker, 1843), 70.

[1055] Noah Webster, *History of the United States*, 339.

[1056] Joseph Story, *Commentaries of the Constitution of the United States*, vol. 3 (Boston, MA: Hilliard, Gray, & Co., 1833), 722-723.

[1057] Charles Carroll to James McHenry, Annapolis, 4 November 1800, in *The Life and Correspondence of James McHenry*, Bernard C. Steiner (Cleveland, OH: Burrows Brothers Co., 1907), 475.

[1058] Bernard C. Steiner, *One Hundred and Ten years of Bible Society Work in Maryland, 1810-1920* (Baltimore, MD: Maryland Bible Society, 1921), 14.

[1059] Noah Webster to David McClure, New Haven, 25 October 1836, in Noah Webster, *A Collection of Papers on Political, Literary, and Moral Subjects* (New York: Webster & Clark, 1843), 291.

[1060] Jedidiah Morse, *A Sermon Exhibiting the Present Dangers, and Consequent Duties of the Citizens of the United States of*

America, Charlestown, April 25, 1799 (Charlestown, MA: Published at the Request of the Hearers, 1799), 11.

[1061] Thomas Jefferson to Moses Robinson, Washington, 23 March 1801, in *The Writings of Thomas Jefferson: Correspondence,* vol. 4, ed. Henry A. Washington (New York: Derby & Jackson, 1859), 380.

[1062] Benjamin Rush, *Of The Mode of Education Proper in a Republic,* in *Essays, Literary, Moral and Philosophical,* 2nd ed. (Philadelphia, PA: Printed by Thomas and William Bradford, 1806), 8-9.

[1063] John Hancock, Inaugural Address of John Hancock as Governor of Massachusetts, 1780, in Abram E. Brown, *John Hancock: His book* (Boston: Lee and Shepard, 1898), 269.

[1064] Reichley, *Public Life,* 166.

[1065] Montesquieu was influential in America and Europe for his pro-Christian exposition on moral law, the nature and rule of law, the influence of custom and habit on government and law, federalism, decentralization of government, and separation of powers in government. During the revolution, Americans had cited Montesquieu's assertion of monarchy's risk of despotism as an argument against the acts of King George III. See Russell Kirk's *Roots of American Order,* p. 357, and Donald Lutz's *The Origins of American Constitutionalism,* p. 142-3.

[1066] Charles Louis Secondat Baron de Montesquieu, *The Spirit of Laws, 1748,* Revised ed., vol. 1, trans. Thomas Nugent, ed. Jean Le Rond D'Alembert (London: Colonial Press, 1900), bk. 1, 3.

[1067] Montesquieu, *Spirit of Laws,* vol. 1, bk. 11, 150.

[1068] Montesquieu, *Spirit of Laws,* vol. 1, bk. 11, 151-152.

[1069] Benjamin Rush, *Observations Upon the Present Government in Pennsylvania: In Four Letters to the People of Pennsylvania,* (Philadelphia, PA: Printed by Styner and Cist, 1777), 20.

[1070] Thomas Jefferson to Mr. Thomas Mann Randolph, New York, 30 May 1790, in *The Writings of Thomas Jefferson,* vol. 7, ed. Albert E. Bergh (Washington, DC: Thomas Jefferson Memorial Association, 1907), 31.

[1071] James Madison, Federalist Paper #47, in *The Federalist Papers,* ed. Clinton Rossiter (New York: Mentor Penguin, 1961), 302-3. Madison asserted, "From these facts, by which Montesquieu was guided, it may clearly be inferred that, in saying 'There can be no liberty where the legislative and executive powers are united in the same person, or body of magistrates,' or, 'if the power of judging be not separated from the legislative and executive powers,' he did not mean that these departments ought to have no *partial agency* in, or no *control* over, the acts of each other. His meaning, as his own words import, and still more conclusively as illustrated by the example in his eye, can amount to no more than this, that where the *whole* power of one department is exercised by the same hands which possess the *whole* power of another department, the fundamental principles of a free constitution are subverted." Madison continued, "The reasons on which Montesquieu grounds his maxim are a further demonstration of his meaning. 'When the legislative and executive powers are united in the same person or body,' says he, 'there can be no liberty, because apprehensions may arise lest *the same* monarch or senate should *enact* tyrannical laws to *execute* them in a tyrannical manner.' Again: 'Were the power of judging joined with the legislative, the life and liberty of the subject would be exposed to arbitrary control, for *the judge* would then be *the legislator.* Were it joined to the executive power, *the judge* might behave with all the violence of *an oppressor.*'"

[1072] James Madison, Federalist Paper #47, *Federalist Papers,* 301.

[1073] George Washington, Farewell Address to the People of the United States, 17 September 1796, in *The Writings of George Washington, 1794-1798,* vol. 13, ed. Worthington C. Ford (New York: G. P. Putnam's Sons, 1892), 306.

[1074] See Madison's Federalist Paper #57.

[1075] Slater, *Teaching and Learning,* 208-209.

[1076] Reichley, *Public Life,* 106.

[1077] James Madison, Federalist Paper #10, in *The Federalist Papers,* ed. Clinton Rossiter (New York: Mentor Penguin, 1961), 77-84.

[1078] Madison, Federalist Paper #51, *Federalist Papers,* 324.

[1079] James Madison, Federalist Paper #10, *Federalist Papers,* 83.

[1080] Gordon S. Wood, *The Creation of the American Republic, 1776-1787* (New York: W. W. Norton & Co., 1969), 449.

[1081] James Bryce, *The American Commonwealth: The National Government, The State Governments,* new ed., vol. 1 (New York: Macmillan, 1919), 306.

[1082] Rauchet, *American Vision and Values,* 33.

[1083] Sandoz, *Republicanism,* 49-50.

[1084] Joseph Story, *The Constitutional Class Book: Being A Brief Exposition of the Constitution of the United States* (Boston, MA: Hilliard, Gray, & Co., 1834), 148.

[1085] See *Treaty of Peace and Friendship Between the United States of America and the Bey and Subjects of Tripoli, of Barbary, Concluded November 4, 1796,* in United States Department of State, *Treaties and Conventions Concluded Between the United States of America and Other Powers, Since July 4, 1776* (Washington, DC: Government Printing Office, 1871), 838. The 1797 Treaty of Tripoli negotiated a dispute between the Muslim nation of Tripoli and the United States over freedom of the seas. It stated, "As the Government of the United States of America is not in any sense founded on the Christian religion; as it has in itself no character of enmity against the laws, religion, or tranquility of Mussulmen; and as the said States never entered into any war or act of hostility against any Mehometan nation, it is declared by the parties that no pretext arising from religious opinions shall ever produce an interruption of the harmony existing between the two countries."

[1086] Joseph Story, *Commentaries on the Constitution of the United* States, vol. 3 (Boston, MA: Hilliard, Gray, & Co., 1833), 726.

[1087] Tocqueville, *Democracy in America,* ed. Richard Heffner, 145.

[1088] Kirk, *Roots,* 438-9.

[1089] Hutson, *Religion and the Founding*, 77-8.

[1090] George Washington to Hebrew Congregation in Newport, Rhode Island, 1790, in *Publications of the American Jewish Historical Society*, No. 3 (New York: American Jewish Historical Society, 1895), 91-2.

[1091] Thomas Jefferson to James Smith, Monticello, 8 December 1822, in *Memoir, Correspondence, and Miscellanies From the Papers of Thomas Jefferson*, vol. 4, ed. Thomas J. Randolph (Charlottesville, VA: F. Carr & Co., 1829), 360.

[1092] James Madison, Prayer and Thanksgiving Proclamation, 23 July 1813, in *A Compilation of the Messages and Papers of the Presidents, 1789-1897*, vol. 1, ed. James D. Richardson (Washington, DC: Government Printing Office, 1896), 533.

[1093] Ephesians 4:1-3: "I, therefore, the prisoner of the Lord, beseech you to walk worthy of the calling with which you were called, with all lowliness and gentleness, with longsuffering, bearing with one another in love, endeavoring to keep the unity of the Spirit in the bond of peace." Colossians 3:12-14: "Therefore, as *the* elect of God, holy and beloved, put on tender mercies, kindness, humility, meekness, longsuffering; bearing with one another, and forgiving one another, if anyone has a complaint against another; even as Christ forgave you, so you also *must do.* But above all these things put on love, which is the bond of perfection."

[1094] Alexis de Tocqueville, *Democracy in America*, 2nd American ed., trans. Henry Reeve (New York: George Adlard, 1838), 287.

[1095] Tocqueville, *Democracy in America*, trans. Henry Reeve, 25-26.

[1096] Tocqueville, *Democracy in America*, trans. Henry Reeve, 286-7.

[1097] Reichley, *Public Life*, 165-6.

[1098] Fea, *Was America Founded*, 163.

[1099] Waldman, *Founding Faith*, 156-7.

[1100] Thomas Jefferson to Rev. Mr. Millar, Washington, 23 January 1808, in *Memoirs, Correspondence and Private Papers of Thomas Jefferson, Late President of the United States*, vol. 4, ed. Thomas J. Randolph (London: Henry Colburn and Richard Bentley, 1829), 106; Thomas Jefferson, Second Inaugural Address, 4 March 1805, in *The Addresses and Messages of the Presidents of the United States, 1789-1846*, vol. 1, comp. Edwin Williams (New York: Edward Walker, 1849), 174. In his January 23, 1808, letter to Presbyterian minister Samuel Millar, Thomas Jefferson wrote: "I consider the government of the United States as interdicted by the constitution from intermeddling with religious institutions, their doctrines, discipline, or exercises. This results not only from the provision that no law shall be made respecting the establishment, or free exercise of religion [1st Amendment], but form that also which reserves to the States the powers not delegated to the United States [10th Amendment]. Certainly, no power to prescribe any religious exercise, or to assume authority in any religious discipline, has been delegated to the General Government. It must then rest with the States, as far as it can be in any human authority." In his second Presidential Inaugural Address on March 4, 1805, Jefferson asserted, "In matters of religion, I have considered that its free exercise is placed by the constitution independent of the powers of the general government. I have therefore undertaken, on no occasion, to prescribe the religious exercises suited to it; but have left them, as the constitution found them, under the direction and discipline of state or church authorities acknowledged by the several religious societies."

[1101] Waldman, *Founding Faith*, 131.

[1102] Locke, *Second Treatise*, Routledge, 260-261.

[1103] Alexander Hamilton, Federalist Paper #1, *The Federalist Papers*, ed. Clinton Rossiter (New York: Mentor Penguin, 1961), 33.

[1104] Alexander Hamilton, Federalist Paper #22, *The Federalist Papers*, ed. Clinton Rossiter (New York: Mentor Penguin, 1961), 152.

[1105] James Wilson, Oration at the Procession Formed at Philadelphia to Celebrate the Adoption of the Constitution of the United States, Philadelphia, 4 July 1788, in *The Works of the Honourable James Wilson*, vol. 3, ed. Bird Wilson (Philadelphia, PA: Printed for Bronson and Chauncey, 1804), 299.

[1106] Lutz, "From Covenant to Constitution," 105, 115, 122-123.

[1107] Lutz, "From Covenant to Constitution," 128.

[1108] Elazar, "Political Theory of Covenant," 28.

[1109] See Lutz, "From Covenant to Constitution," 115-118. See Bruce Feiler's *America's Prophet*, 27, 75-6.

[1110] Elazar, "Political Theory of Covenant," 11.

[1111] Lutz, "From Covenant to Constitution," 104.

[1112] Locke, *Second Treatise*, Routledge, 241. See Locke's *Second Treatise*, Routledge, ch. 8, sects. 95-99.

[1113] Lutz, "From Covenant to Constitution," 104.

[1114] John Jay, Federalist Paper #2, *Federalist Papers*, 37.

[1115] Jay, Federalist Paper #2, *Federalist Papers*, 41.

[1116] James Madison, Federalist Paper #37, *The Federalist Papers*, ed. Clinton Rossiter (New York: Mentor Penguin, 1961), 230-31.

[1117] Benjamin Franklin, "A Comparison of the Conduct of the Ancient Jews and of the Anti-Federalists in the United States of America," in *The Works of Benjamin Franklin*, vol. 5, ed. Jared Sparks (New York: Hillard, Gray, and Co., 1837), 162. Franklin alluded to Acts 17:26-28 in which the Apostle Paul stated, "And He has made from one blood every nation of men to dwell on all the face of the earth, and has determined their preappointed times and the boundaries of their dwellings, so that they should seek the Lord, in the hope that they might grope for Him and find Him, though He is not far from each one of us; for in Him we live and move and have our being, as also some of your own poets have said, 'For we are also His offspring.'"

[1118] Benjamin Rush, Observations on the Fourth of July Procession in Philadelphia, in *Documentary History of the Ratification of the Constitution*, vol. 18, eds. John P. Kaminski, Richard Leffler, and Gaspare J. Saladino (Madison, WI: State Historical Society of Wisconsin, 1976), 266; Benjamin Rush, Observations on the Federal Procession of the Fourth of July, 1788, in the City of Philadelphia, in a Letter From a Gentleman in This City to His Friend in a Neighboring State, in Sarah Alcock, *A Brief History of the Revolution* (Philadelphia, PA: Published by Sarah Alcock, 1843), 109-110. See also *Pennsylvania Mercury*, 15 July 1788, reprinted in *American Museum*, July 1788.

[1119] Benjamin Rush, Observations on the Fourth of July Procession in Philadelphia, in *Documentary History of the Ratification of the Constitution*, 265-266; Benjamin Rush, Observations on the Federal Procession of the Fourth of July, 1788, in *Brief History of the Revolution*, 108-109. See also *Pennsylvania Mercury*, 15 July 1788, reprinted in *American Museum*, July 1788.

[1120] Bruce Feiler, *America's Prophet: Moses and the American Story* (New York: William Morrow, 2009), 27-28.

[1121] U. S. Department of State, Bureau of Public Affairs, *The Great Seal of the United States* (Washington, DC: U. S. Department of State, 2003), 2. <http://www.state.gov/documents/organization/27807.pdf>.

[1122] United States Continental Congress, Congressional Resolution, August 20, 1776, Library of Congress, *Journals of the Continental Congress, 1774-1789*, vol. 5/Jun 5-Oct 8, 1776, ed. Worthington C. Ford (Washington, DC: U. S. Government Printing Office, 1906), 690-1.

[1123] John B. McMaster and Frederick D. Stone, eds., *Pennsylvania and the Federal Constitution, 1787-1788* (Philadelphia, PA: Historical Society of Pennsylvania, 1888), 420.

[1124] George Washington to Hebrew Congregation of the City of Savannah, May 1790, in *Publications of the American Jewish Historical Society*, no. 3 (New York: American Jewish Historical Society, 1895), 89-90.

[1125] Thomas Jefferson, Inaugural Speech of President Jefferson, 4 March 1805, in *American State Papers: Documents, Legislative and Executive of the Congress of the United States, 1st-13th Congress, Mar 3 1780-Mar 3 1815*, class 1, vol. 1 (Washington, DC: Gales and Seaton, 1832), 66.

[1126] John Adams, *Dissertation on the Canon and the Feudal Law*, 456.

[1127] John Locke, *Some Thoughts Concerning Education*, 1690, in *The Works of John Locke*, vol. 3 (London: Printed for Arthur Bettesworth, John Pemberton, and Edward Symon, 1727), 26.

[1128] Benjamin Rush to Rev. Jeremy Belknap, "Defense of the Use of the Bible in Schools," in Benjamin Rush, *Essays, Literary, Moral and Philosophical*, 2nd ed. (Philadelphia: Printed by Thomas and William Bradford, 1806), 105; Benjamin Rush to Citizens of Philadelphia, "A Plan For Free Schools," 28 March 1787, in Benjamin Rush, *Letters of Benjamin Rush, 1761-1792*, vol. 1 (Princeton, NJ: Princeton U Press for American Philosophical Society, 1951), 414.

[1129] Benjamin Rush to Rev. Jeremy Belknap, "A Defence of the Use of the Bible in Schools," 112-13.

[1130] George Washington to the Delaware Chiefs, Middle Brook, 12 May 1779, Transcript of Speech, 1H78-80, in *Frontier Advance on the Upper Ohio, 1778-1779*, Draper vol. 4, Collections vol. 23, ed. Louise P. Kellogg (Madison, WI: Wisconsin Historical Society, 1916), 323.

[1131] Gouverneur Morris, Notes on the Form of A Constitution for France, c1791, in Jared Sparks, *The Life of Gouverneur Morris*, vol. 3 (Boston, MA: Gray & Bowen, 1832), 483.

[1132] Samuel Adams to John Adams, Boston, 4 October 1790, in *The Writings of Samuel Adams, 1778-1802*, vol. 4, ed. Harry A. Cushing (New York: G. P. Putnam's Sons, 1908), 343.

[1133] Charles Turner, Speech in the Massachusetts Ratifying Convention, 6 February 1788, in *The Complete Anti-Federalist, An Electronic Version of the Four Volumes*, vol. 4, ed. Herbert J. Storing (Chicago, IL: University of Chicago Press, 1981), 221.

[1134] University of Georgia Charter, 27 January 1785, in Augustus L. Hull, *A Historical Sketch of the University of Georgia* (Atlanta, GA: Foote & Davies Co., 1894), 4; Charles E. Jones, Excerpts From The Bill for the Establishment of the University of Georgia, in *Education in Georgia* (Washington, DC: Government Printing Office, 1889), 42-43.

[1135] Noah Webster to David McClure, New Haven, 25 October 1836, in *A Collection of Papers on Political, Literary, and Moral Subjects*, Noah Webster (New York: Webster & Clark, 1843), 291.

[1136] United States Continental Congress, An Ordinance for the Government of the Territory of the United States North West of the River Ohio, 13 July 1787, in *Journals of the Continental Congress, 1774-1789*, vol. 32, ed. Roscoe R. Hill (Washington, DC: Government Printing Office, 1936), 340. See also Northwest Ordinance, An Ordinance for the Government of the Territory of the United States North-West of the River Ohio, 13 July 1787, in Emlin McClain, *Constitutional Law in the United States* (London: Longmans, Green, & Co., 1907), 402.

[1137] Reichley, *Public Life*, 112.

[1138] Hutson, *Religion and the Founding*, 57-8.

[1139] Reichley, *Public Life*, 135-6, 157.

[1140] Danbury, Connecticut, Baptist Association to Thomas Jefferson, 7 October 1801, in *The Thomas Jefferson Papers*, Series 1, General Correspondence, 1651-1827, American Memory (Washington, DC: Library of Congress), <http://memory.loc.gov/cgi-bin/ampage?collId=mtj1&fileName=mtj1page024.db&recNum=956> (August 2012). A full text of the letter is available in Charles C. Haynes, *Religion in American History: What to Teach and How* (Alexandria, VA: Association for Supervision and Curriculum Development, 1990), 44, or at Digital History <http://www.digitalhistory.uh.edu/disp_textbook.cfm?smtID=3&psid=1276>.

[1141] Thomas Jefferson to the Danbury Baptist Association in Connecticut, 1 January 1802, in *The Writings of Thomas Jefferson*, ed. Henry. A. Washington (New York: Derby & Jackson, 1859), 113.

[1142] Roger Williams, "Mr. Cotton's Letter Examined and Answered," London, 1644, in *The Bloudy Tenent of Persecution For Cause of Conscience Discussed and Mr. Cotton's Letter Examined and Answered*, ed. Edward B. Underhill (London: Printed for Hanserd Knollys Society, 1848), 435. Isaiah 5:3-6 states, "And now, O inhabitants of Jerusalem and men of Judah, Judge, please, between Me and My vineyard. What more could have been done to My vineyard That I have not done in it? Why then, when I expected *it* to bring forth *good* grapes, Did it bring forth wild grapes? And now, please let Me tell you what I will do to My vineyard: I will take away its hedge, and it shall be burned; *And* break down its wall, and it shall be trampled down. I will lay it waste; It shall not be pruned or dug, But there shall come up briers and thorns. I will also command the clouds That they rain no rain on it."

[1143] See *Murdock v Pennsylvania*, 319 U.S. 105 (1943), *Everson v Board of Education*, 330 U.S. 1 (1947), and *Cantwell v Connecticut*, 310 U.S. 296 (1940).

[1144] Reichley, *Public Life*, 135.

[1145] Waldman, *Founding Faith*, 156.

[1146] Tocqueville, *Democracy in America*, ed. Richard Heffner, 145.

[1147] George Washington, Inaugural Address, April 30, 1789, in *The Addresses and Messages of the Presidents of the United States, 1789-1846, in Two Volumes*, vol. 1, comp. Edwin Williams (New York: Edward Walker, 1849), 31-33. Washington writes, "…[I]t would be peculiarly improper to omit, in this first official act, my fervent supplications to that Almighty Being who rules over the universe, who presides in the councils of nations, and whose providential aids can supply every human defect, that his benediction may consecrate to the liberties and happiness of the people of the United States a government instituted by themselves for these essential purposes, and may enable every instrument employed in its administration to execute with success the functions allotted to his charge. … No people can be bound to acknowledge and adore the invisible Hand which conducts the affairs of men, more than the people of the United States. Every step by which they have advanced to the character of an independent nation seems to have been distinguished by some token of providential agency; and in the important revolution just accomplished in the system of their united government, the tranquil deliberations and voluntary consent of so many distinct communities from which the event has resulted, can not be compared with the means by which most governments have been established, without some return of pious gratitude, along with an humble anticipation of the future blessings which the past seem to presage. …

…[T]he foundation of our national policy will be laid in the pure and immutable principles of private morality… …[T]here is no truth more thoroughly established than that there exists in the economy and course of nature an indissoluble union between virtue and happiness, between duty and advantage, between the genuine maxims of an honest and magnanimous policy and the solid rewards of public prosperity and felicity; since we ought to be no less persuaded that the propitious smiles of Heaven can never be expected on a nation that disregards the eternal rules of order and right which Heaven has ordained… …

…Having thus imparted to you my sentiments…I shall take my present leave; but not without resorting once more to the benign Parent of the human race in humble supplication that, since he has been pleased to favor the American people with opportunities for deliberating in perfect tranquility, and dispositions for deciding with unparalleled unanimity on a form of government for the security of their union and the advancement of their happiness, so his divine blessing may be equally conspicuous in the enlarged views, the temperate consultations, and the wise measures, on which the success of this government must depend."

[1148] John Adams to Thomas Jefferson, Quincy, 28 June 1813, in *The Works of John Adams, Second President of the United States*, vol. 10, ed. Charles F. Adams (Boston, MA: Little, Brown, & Co., 1856), 45-46.

[1149] John Quincy Adams to George W. Adams, St. Petersburg, 1 and 8 September 1811, in *Writings of John Quincy Adams, 1811-1813*, vol. 4, ed. Worthingon C. Ford (New York: Macmillan Co., 1914), 216-17.

[1150] Daniel Webster, "The Dignity and Importance of History: An Address Delivered Before the New York Historical Society," New York, 23 February 1852, in *The Writings and Speeches of Daniel Webster*, vol. 1/vol.13, ed. Edward Everett (Boston: Little, Brown & Co., 1903), 492-3.

[1151] George Washington, Unused Notes for the First Inaugural Address, April 1789, in Michael Novak and Jana Novak, *Washington's God: Religion, Liberty, and the Father of Our Country* (New York: Basic Books, 2006), 236; George Washington, "Fragments of the Discarded First Inaugural Address," [April 1789] in *George Washington: A Collection*, ed. W. B. Allen (Indianapolis, IN: Liberty Fund, 1988), 456.

[1152] Abraham Lincoln, Address at Gettysburg, 19 November 1863, in *The Writings of Abraham Lincoln*, vol 7: 1863-1865, ed. Arthur B. Lapsley (New York: G. P. Putnam's Sons, 1906), 20-21.

[1153] Thomas Sternhold and John Hopkins, *Four Score and Seven Psalmes of David in English Metre* (Geneva, Switzerland, 1561). See also Samuel J. Rogal, *A General Introduction to Hymnody and Congregational Song* (Metuchen, NJ: Scarecrow Press, 1991), 39.

[1154] Will and Ariel Durant, *The Lessons of History* (New York: Simon and Schuster, 1968), 101.

A true life is one which has been worked out through difficulties, dangers, struggles, and suffering. Self-indulgence leads to degeneracy and decay. Self-denial is the pathway of usefulness, nobility, and happiness.

The men [and women] who have enriched the world have been those who fought and struggled and braved hardship and danger. Men and women who have lived in ease and luxury have seldom made any valuable contribution to the progress and happiness of their fellow man.

Struggle and hardship build character. The ore must pass under the hammer and through the fire before the pure gold is extracted from it. God's aim is not merely to make us comfortable. He is trying to make...real men [and women] of us.

The people who are struggling and enduring for the sake of others are truly happy people. There is no real joy in living in ease and self-indulgence. The dissatisfied, pessimistic, cynical people today are the ones who are living in ease and indolence. The downward way is broad and easy; the upward way is narrow and difficult.

He who did most for this world *suffered* most. He walked the way of loneliness, hardship, abuse, self-denial, suffering, and—the cross.

–Norman E. Nygaard, ed., *Strength for Service to God and Country: Daily Devotional Messages for Those in the Services* (New York: Abingdon-Cokesbury Press, 1942), Aug 27.

One of the really great heritages of the American people is the heritage of noble ancestry. It is with a spirit of just pride that we point to their achievements in the growth and development of our democracy. They blazed a new trail in a wilderness. This was done, not only with their axes as they carved roadways across the continent from the eastern seaboard to the Pacific Ocean, but also with their freedom-loving minds. They blazed a new trail with mind and heart as they laid the firm foundation for our "land of the free and home of the brave."

We must never lose sight of the fact that these men [and women] whom we honor were enabled to do great deeds because they had great faith. Their faith was in God. Belief in a God of justice and righteousness, a God of mercy and love, moved them to heroic deeds in the cause of freedom and liberty.

If we would preserve, extend, and perpetuate the ideals for which our fathers [and mothers] gave their all, then we too must be inspired by faith in their God. If the day should ever come when we should lose our fathers' God, if enough of the people of our land should definitely turn aside from His teaching, then would we also lose our own and our children's freedom. May the God of our fathers inspire our lives to loyal service in protecting their ideals for those who shall come after us.

–Norman E. Nygaard, ed., *Strength for Service to God and Country: Daily Devotional Messages for Those in the Services* (New York: Abingdon-Cokesbury Press, 1942), Feb 3.